X Window System
User's Guide

Volume Three

X Window System
User's Guide

OSF/Motif 1.2 Edition

by Valerie Quercia and Tim O'Reilly

O'Reilly & Associates, Inc.

X Window System User's Guide

by Valerie Quercia and Tim O'Reilly

Editor: Tim O'Reilly

Printing History:

September 1988:	Athena First Edition.
July 1989:	Athena Second Edition. Revised to reflect Release 3.
October 1989:	Athena Edition. Minor corrections.
May 1990:	Athena Third Edition. Revised to reflect Release 4.
January 1991:	Motif First Edition.
March 1992:	Motif Edition. Minor corrections.
January 1993:	Motif Second Edition. Revised to reflect Release 5 and Motif 1.2.
May 1993:	Motif Edition. Minor corrections.
August 1993:	Motif Edition. Minor corrections.

Motif Edition ISBN 1-56592-015-5

Table of Contents

Chapter 12 Specifying Color 343

Chapter 13 Customizing mwm 365

Appendix G Widget Resources 827

Figures

Examples

Tables

Preface

The preface provides a map through the most important topics covered in this guide. It also describes the book's conventions.

In the Preface:

Preface

The X Window System is a network-based graphics windowing system. It was developed by MIT and has been adopted as an industry standard. X provides the bare bones of a window system upon which almost any style of graphical user interface (GUI) can be built. One of the most popular user interfaces available in the market today is OSF/Motif developed by the Open Software Foundation.

The *X Window System User's Guide, Motif Edition* describes window system concepts, the application programs (clients) commonly distributed with Version 11, Release 5 of X, and how you can expect programs to operate with OSF/Motif. (The *Motif Edition* is intended for those using X with the OSF/Motif interface. Another edition of the *X Window System User's Guide* is available for those using X without Motif.)

Do I Have To Read This WHOLE Book?

Let's end the suspense: the answer is no. Though the sheer weight of this guide implies that learning X is a difficult task, this is not strictly true. You can quickly learn enough about the X Window System to begin working productively.

A Quick Start Approach to X

Much of this guide (all of Part Three, for instance) is reference material, which we think you'll want to have after working a while, but which you certainly don't have to digest to get going.

The current section outlines what you probably need to know to begin working productively and gives suggestions on shortcuts through some of the other material. Throughout the guide, we've also tried to let you know how to get to the most basic material. (Pay attention to the introductory section of each chapter.)

Once you know your way around the X environment, you may want to take advantage of additional clients and customization features. The remainder of the guide should help you.

For starters, we think you should read the following sections:

Chapter 1, *An Introduction to the X Window System*

Read all of "Anatomy of an X Display" and "Standard X Clients versus Motif Clients." Browse the subsequent sections about "System Architecture" and get an idea what the basic "Clients" (i.e., programs) are. The sections "Other Standard X Clients" and "Customizing Clients" will help you figure out what other system features you might eventually want to take advantage of.

Chapter 2, *Getting Started*

The already short Chapter 2 is written to direct you through it in the briefest possible time. Follow the pointers in the chapter. The information you need will become apparent.

Chapter 3, *Working in the X Environment*

If you read *anything* in this guide, make it Chapter 3. It's a little on the long side, but it covers virtually everything you need to begin working productively. If you get bogged down, think about the chapter covering roughly three topics: window management, setting up your display, and some rudimentary client customization.

Chapter 5, *The xterm Terminal Emulator*

A terminal emulator is probably the most important program you will use. Read the following sections (and any subsections): "Running xterm with a Scrollbar," "Copying and Pasting Text Selections," and the "VT Fonts Menu."

That's it! About 70 pages—many of which have illustrations. : -) The remaining chapters deal with the range of available clients and how to customize them. Now, you may wonder, if it's really so easy, why do you need so much information? In other words, why is the *X Window System User's Guide* so long? The answer is also simple: because we think you'll soon outgrow the basic skills and want to know more.

The most basic X session requires only two programs (called *clients* in X parlance): a terminal emulator, a window which provides all the functionality of a standard terminal; and a window manager, which allows you to move, resize, and otherwise control the windows on your screen. You should have a working knowledge of these programs after getting through the "Quick Start Approach" we've outlined. Running even just these two applications should help you appreciate the benefits of a windowing system such as X.

However, even the most basic incarnation of the X Window System includes dozens of other useful utilities. We provide tutorials for many of these clients in Part One (and a few in Part Two) of this guide. Read "Other Standard X Clients" at the end of Chapter 1 and browse through the following chapters to get a better idea of what sorts of programs are available: Chapter 7, *Graphics Utilities*, Chapter 8, *Other Clients*, and Chapter 14, *Setup Clients*.

In addition, as you'll soon see, you can customize virtually every feature of X to better suit your own needs. For instance, once you get used to moving the pointer around and see how the cursor symbol follows it on the screen, you might want to specify a different cursor. You can do that using the *xsetroot* client described in Chapter 14. Appendix D, *Standard Cursors* lists some of the alternative symbols you can use. If you're really ambitious, you can even create your own symbol using the *bitmap* client, described in Chapter 7, *Graphics Utilities*. (Changing a cursor symbol is just one of the thousands of customizations you can make within the X environment.)

Even the most experienced user will probably need to verify command-line options and so-called resource variables that can be used to customize client appearance and behavior. Part Two of the *X Window System User's Guide, Motif Edition* describes how to customize X, and the reference pages in Part Three detail the valid command-line options and resource variables for each of the standard clients.

Additional reference information appears in Part Four, the Appendices. This information includes the names and pictures of some of the fonts, bitmaps, and cursor symbols available with X. These graphic aids should be helpful in designing your user environment. Other appendices present more "technical" information, including some rudimentary X system management.

Before we let you get started, here are some additional maps through the material. The following sections deal with some potentially important topics:

Chapter 4, *More about the mwm Window Manager*
> The window management skills taught in Chapter 3 will probably be enough to get you started. If you run up against a problem you can't solve, the sections "Using the Window Menu" and "The Root Menu" might provide the answer.

Chapter 6, *Font Specification*
> The section "If You Just Want to Pick a Font" simplifies choosing and specifying a readable X font.

Chapter 10, *Command-line Options*
> A short chapter outlining some powerful "standard" options that can be used with most clients.

Chapter 11, *Setting Resources*
> You can get a basic idea of how to customize clients using resource variables by reading the following sections of Chapter 11: "Resource Naming Syntax" and "How to Set Resources."

Chapter 12, *Specifying Color*
> The section "Available RGB Colors" (and its subsections) survey the color names that you should be able to specify on any X system.

Appendix A, *Managing Your Environment*
> "A Startup Shell Script" can automatically bring up the environment you want.

You can learn more about the Motif window manager and Motif Toolkit applications by reading Chapter 13, *Customizing mwm*, and Chapter 9, *Working with Motif Applications*, respectively.

We hope these guidelines will help you get working quickly—and maybe experimenting with the flexible X Window System. There are many more pointers throughout the text. Best of luck!

Assumptions

This book assumes that X is already installed on your system and that all standard MIT clients are available. In addition, although X runs on many different systems, this book assumes that you are running it on a UNIX system and that you have basic familiarity with UNIX. If you are not using UNIX, you will still find this book useful—UNIX dependencies are not that widespread—but you may occasionally need to translate a command example into its equivalent on your system. This book also assumes that you are using a three-button pointer (e.g., a mouse) and that the operation of the *mwm* window manager is controlled by the *system.mwmrc* file provided with OSF/Motif 1.2. (If this is not the case, the book provides information that will allow you to understand how *mwm* is configured on your system.)

This book is written for both first-time and experienced users of the X Window System. First-time users should use the preceding section, "A Quick Start Approach to X," as a guide to getting started.

Experienced users can use this book as a reference for the client programs detailed here. Since there is great flexibility with X, even frequent users need to check on the syntax and availability of options. Reference pages for each client detail command-line options, customization database (resource database) variables, and other detailed information.

What's New in Release 5?

This guide describes Release 5 of X from MIT as it runs with the OSF/Motif graphical user interface. Throughout the guide, we've tried to highlight what's new. (Look for pointers in the text.) The current section gives an overview of the Release 5 innovations that may be relevant to users and also directs you to further information.

New Client Programs

The following programs (*clients* in X parlance) have been added to X at R5:

bdftopcf   Converts a font file from bitmap distribution format to portable compiled format.

fs   A font server program. (See Chapter 6, *Font Specification*, for more information.)

fsinfo   Provides information about a font available from a font server. (See Chapter 6.)

fstobdf   Converts a font file from font server format to bitmap distribution format.

fslsfonts   Lists fonts available from a font server. (See Chapter 6.)

showfont   Displays data about a font available from a font server. See Chapter 6 and Chapter 7.

editres	Helps you set resource variables that control how programs look and operate. (See Chapter 11, *Setting Resources*.)
viewres	Displays a tree showing the organization of a program's component parts (known as widgets).
xcmsdb	Helps you manage color screen data.
xconsole	Intercepts system console messages that would otherwise obscure your screen. (See Appendix A, *Managing Your Environment*.)

Each of these programs is also described in a reference page in Part Three of this guide.

Defunct Programs

The following clients have been removed from the standard distribution in Release 5:

bdftosnf	Converts a font file from bitmap distribution format to server natural format. *bdftosnf* has in effect been replaced by the *bdftopcf* program.
xlswins	Shows how windows on the display are related to one another. *xlswins* has been replaced by the -tree and -children options to *xwininfo*.

Clients that Work Differently in Release 4 and Release 5

Most clients vary slightly from one release to the next, though in many cases the differences are superficial (e.g., the names of menu items might change) or not immediately obvious (e.g., new options may be available). The following clients look or function significantly differently in Release 4 and Release 5.

bitmap	The *bitmap* editor has been radically redesigned in Release 5. Notable improvements include copy and paste capabilties and dynamic file loading. Chapter 7, *Graphics Utilities*, provides an overview of what's new and also extensive tutorials.
xmag	The *xmag* magnification program has been redesigned to work in concert with *bitmap*. You can now copy and paste between the two applications. See Chapter 7.

R5 changes for other clients are detailed in the tutorials throughout the guide and should also be noted on the reference pages in Part Three.

Available Fonts

Release 5 adds several miscellaneous fonts, including two Hangul fonts, two Hebrew fonts, an additional Kanji font. R5 also sees the addition of *font scaling* and includes some new *outline fonts*, which are suitable for scaling.

The new font server program (*fs*) provides access to fonts resident on other machines in the network.

Chapter 6, *Font Specification*, describes X's latest font capabilities.

Available Colors

Predefined colors and their text names appear in the file *rgb.txt*, which is generally located in */usr/lib/X11*. These so-called RGB colors are not portable—that is, they look different on different monitors.

In Release 5, X also provides *device-independent* color capabilities. Now you can specify colors that will look the same, regardless of the type of screen. See Chapter 12 for details.

Screen-specific Resources

R5 allows you to specify different application defaults for color and monochrome screens. Use the mechanisms described in Chapter 11 to specify program characteristics that will be automatically implemented depending on the type of monitor you're using.

Bulk Sales Information

This guide is being resold by many workstation manufacturers as their official X Window System documentation. For information on volume discounts for bulk purchases, call O'Reilly & Associates, Inc., at 617-354-5800, or send email to linda@ora.com (uunet!ora!linda). For companies requiring extensive customization of the guide, source-licensing terms are also available.

Acknowledgements

The current edition of this guide was written by Valerie Quercia, with the invaluable editorial assistance of Tim O'Reilly. Special thanks to Linda Mui and Eric Pearce (the co-authors of Volume Eight, *X Window System Administrator's Guide*) for their expert technical and editorial support. Thanks also to Paula Ferguson for updating Appendix G, *Widget Resources*.

Previous editions of this guide were written by Valerie Quercia and Tim O'Reilly, with the exception of the first edition, which was written by Tim O'Reilly, Valerie Quercia, and Linda Lamb. The first edition was based in part on three previous X Window System user's guides: one from Masscomp, which was written by Jeff Graber; one from Sequent Computer Systems, Inc., and one from Graphic Software Systems, Inc.; both of which were written by Candis Condo (supported by the UNIX development group). Some of Jeff's and Candis's material in turn was based on material developed under the auspices of Project Athena at MIT.

Most of the reference pages in Part Three of this guide have been adapted from reference pages copyright © 1991 the Massachusetts Institute of Technology, or from reference pages produced by Graphic Software Systems. Refer to the "Authors" section at the end of each reference page for details. Other copyrights are listed on the relevant reference pages.

Permission to use this material is gratefully acknowledged.

This guide was primarily developed using the MIT sample server on a Sun-3 Workstation and a Sun SPARCstation™ SLC, with additional testing done on a Sony NEWS workstation running Sony's X implementation, a Visual 640 X Display Station, and NCD16™ and NCD19 Network Display Stations.

We'd also like to thank the Open Software Foundation for permission to reprint the *system.mwmrc* file in Chapter 13, *Customizing mwm*. Special thanks to Elizabeth Connelly of OSF for arranging this.

Of course, the authors would also like to thank those who worked on the production of the book: Donna Woonteiler and Leslie Chalmers for copy editing, Chris Reilly and Jeff Robbins for creating the illustrations, Ellie Cutler for indexing, and Leslie Chalmers, Kismet McDonough, Laura Parker, and Mike Sierra for helping to produce the final copy. Thanks also to Lenny Muellner for his expert tools assistance.

Despite the efforts of these people, the standard authors' disclaimer applies: any errors that remain are our own.

Font and Character Conventions

These typographic conventions are used in this book:

Italics	are used for:
	• new terms where they are defined.
	• file and directory names, and command and client names when they appear in the body of a paragraph.
`Courier`	is used within the body of the text to show:
	• command lines or options that should be typed verbatim on the screen.
	is used within examples to show:
	• computer-generated output.
	• the contents of files.
`Courier bold`	is used within examples to show command lines and options that should be typed verbatim on the screen.
`Courier italics`	are used within examples or explanations of command syntax to show a parameter to a command that requires context-dependent substitution (such as a variable). For example, *`filename`* means to use some appropriate filename; *`option(s)`* means to use some appropriate option(s) to the command.
Helvetica	is used to show menu titles and options.

These symbols are used within the *X Window System User's Guide*:

[ ]	surround an optional field in a command line or file entry.
$	is the standard prompt from the Bourne shell, *sh*(1).
%	is the standard prompt from the C shell, *csh*(1).
name(1)	is a reference to a command called *name* in Section 1 of the *UNIX Reference Manual* (which may have a different name depending on the version of UNIX you use).

Part One:

Using X

Part One provides an overview of the X Window System and concepts, and describes how to use the most important programs available in the X environment.

An Introduction to the X Window System
Getting Started
Working in the X Environment
More about the mwm Window Manager
The xterm Terminal Emulator
Font Specification
Graphics Utilities
Other Clients
Working with Motif Applications

1

An Introduction to the X Window System

This chapter describes the features of a typical X display, while introducing some basic window system concepts. It also provides an overview of the X Window System's client-server architecture and briefly describes the most commonly used clients.

In This Chapter:

1
An Introduction
to the X Window System

Introduction to X

The X Window System, called X for short, is a network-based graphics window system that was developed at MIT in 1984. Several versions of X have been developed, the most recent of which is X Version 11 (X11), first released in 1987.*

X11 has been adopted as an industry standard windowing system. X is supported by a consortium of industry leaders such as DEC, Hewlett-Packard, Sun, IBM, and AT&T that have united to direct, contribute to, and fund its continuing development. In addition to the system software development directed by the X Consortium, many independent developers are producing application software specifically for use with X, including spreadsheets, database programs, and publishing applications.

Before you plunge into Chapter 1, we suggest you read "A Quick Start Approach to X" in the Preface. This section will explain how to slice your way through the guide to some of the most basic and pertinent information.

Then we'll take a look at a typical X display and consider some general system features. We'll also briefly compare a standard X application (written with the X Toolkit) to a Motif application (written with the Motif Toolkit). Then we'll discuss what distinguishes the X Window System from other window systems. We'll also introduce some of the more important programs included in the standard distribution of X, and the *mwm* window manager shipped with OSF/Motif.

---

*There have been several revisions to X since then. This guide describes the latest release, X11 R5.

Anatomy of an X Display

X is typically run on a workstation with a large screen or on a special graphics terminal known as an X terminal. (It also runs on PCs and on many larger systems.) X allows you to work with multiple programs simultaneously, each in a separate *window*. The display in Figure 1-1 includes five windows.

The operations performed within a window can vary greatly, depending on the type of program running it. Certain windows accept input from the user: they may function as terminals, allow you to create graphics, control a database, etc. Other windows simply display information, such as the time of day or a picture of the characters in a particular font, etc.

The windows you will probably use most frequently are *terminal emulators*, windows that function as standard terminals. The terminal emulator included with the standard release of X is called *xterm*. Figure 1-1 depicts three *xterm* windows. In an *xterm* window, you can do anything you might do in a regular terminal: enter commands, run editing sessions, compile programs, etc.

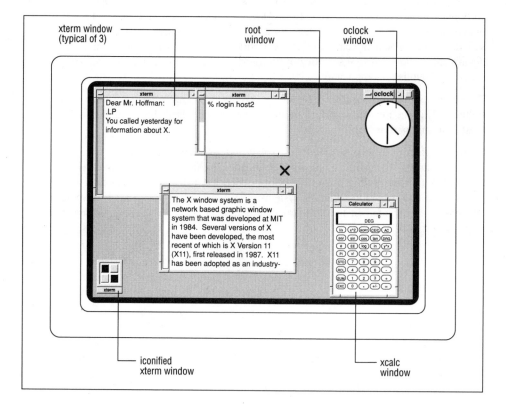

Figure 1-1. X display with five windows and an icon

The display in Figure 1-1 also includes two other application windows: a clock (called *oclock*) and a calculator (*xcalc*). X provides many such small utility programs—analogous to the so-called "desk accessories" of the Macintosh environment—intended to make your work easier.

The shaded area that fills the entire screen is called the *root* (or *background*) window. Application windows are displayed on top of this root window. X considers windows to be related to one another in a hierarchy, similar to a family tree. The root window is the root or origin within this hierarchy and is considered to be the *parent* of application windows displayed on it. Conversely, these application windows are called *children* of the root window. In Figure 1-1, the *xterm*, *oclock*, and *xcalc* windows are children of the root window.

As we'll see later, the window hierarchy is actually much more complicated than this "two generation" model suggests. Various *parts* of application windows are windows in their own right. For example, many applications provide menus to assist the user. Technically speaking, these menus are separate windows. Knowledge of the complexity of the window hierarchy (and the composite parts of an application) will become important when we discuss how to tailor an application to better suit your needs.

One of the strengths of a window system such as X is that you can have several processes going on simultaneously in several different windows. For example, in Figure 1-1, the user is logging in to a remote system in one *xterm* window and editing a text file in each of the two other *xterm* windows. (As we'll see in Chapter 5, *The xterm Terminal Emulator*, you can also cut and paste text between two windows.) Be aware, however, that you can only input to one window at a time.

Another strength of X is that it allows you to run programs on machines connected by a network. You can run a process on a remote machine while displaying the results on your own screen. You might want to access a remote machine for any number of reasons: to use a program or access information not available on your local system, to distribute the work load, etc. We'll discuss X's networking capabilities in more detail in the section "X Architecture Overview," later in this chapter.

Now let's take another look at our sample display in Figure 1-1. Notice that the *xterm* windows overlap each other. Windows often overlap much like sheets of paper on your desk or a stack of cards. This overlapping does not interfere with the process run in each window. However, in order to really take advantage of windowing, you need to be able to move and modify the windows on your display. For example, if you want to work in a window that is partially covered by another window, you need to be able to raise the obscured window to the top of the window stack.

Window management functions are provided by a type of program called a *window manager*. The window manager controls the general operation of the window system, allowing you to change the size and position of windows on the display. You can reshuffle windows in a window stack, make windows larger or smaller, move them to other locations on the screen, etc. The window manager provides part of the user interface—to a large extent it controls the "look and feel" of the X Window System.

The window manager provided with OSF/Motif is called *mwm*, the *Motif window manager*. The most distinguishing feature of *mwm* is the "frame" it places around all windows on the display. Notice that most top-level application windows on our typical display are surrounded by this frame. (The *oclock* window is an exception. With non-rectangular windows such as this, a titlebar appears to "float" above the window.) As we'll see, by clicking a mouse or other pointing device on various parts of the window frame (or titlebar, if that's what's available), you can perform management functions on the window.

The *mwm* window frame is a composite of several parts, the most prominent of which are shown in Figure 1-2.

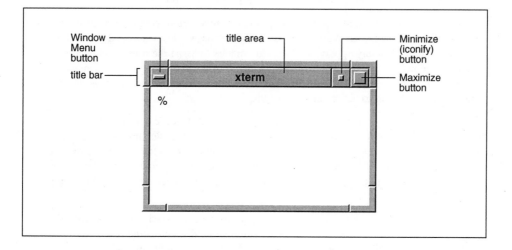

Figure 1-2. mwm frames each window on the display

The top edge of the frame is wider than the other three edges and features most of the window management tools. This wide horizontal bar spanning the top of the window is known as a *titlebar*. The large central portion of this top edge is called the *title area* mainly because it contains a text description of the window. (Generally, this is the application name, but as we'll see later, you can often specify an alternate title.) The titlebar also features three command buttons whose functionality we'll discuss in Chapter 3 and Chapter 4. We'll also see how to use the sides and bottom of the frame to resize a window and to raise it to the top of the window stack.

mwm attempts to create a three-dimensional appearance, which is somewhat more aesthetic than the look provided by many other window managers. You'll probably notice that window frames, various command buttons, icons, etc., appear to be raised to varying heights above screen level. This illusion is created by subtle shading and gives many display features a "beveled" look, similar to the beveled style of some mirrors.

mwm is intended to be used with the OSF/Motif graphical user interface. For those not using Motif, there are several other window managers available in the market today. In the standard distribution of X from MIT, the official window manager is called *twm*. (*twm* originally stood for "Tom's window manager," in honor of its developer, Tom LaStrange. However, it has since been renamed the "tab window manager.") The *twm* window manager provides a different "look and feel" than *mwm*. Rather than framing application windows, *twm* simply provides each window with a titlebar, different from the *mwm* titlebar in style, but offering similar window management functions. The user-contributed part of the MIT X distribution includes several other window managers and still others are available commercially.

Aesthetics notwithstanding, one of the primary advantages *mwm* has over other window managers is inherent in the nature of a frame: it provides window management tools on four sides of the window. *twm*'s titlebar is a useful window management tool, but a titlebar is often covered by other windows in the stack. In most cases at least a part of a window's frame should be visible—and thus accessible to the user.

Also pictured in Figure 1-1 is an *icon*. An icon is a small symbol that represents a window in an inactive state. The window manager allows you to convert windows to icons and icons back to windows. You may want to convert a window to an icon to save space on the display or to prevent input to that window. Each icon has a label, generally the name of the program that created the window. The icon in Figure 1-1 represents a fourth *xterm* window on the display. Icons can be moved around on the display, just like active windows.

The contents of a window are not visible when the window has been converted to an icon but they are not lost. In fact, a client continues to run when its window has been iconified; if you iconify a terminal emulator client such as *xterm*, any programs running in the shell will also continue.

If you've used other window managers, you may notice that icon symbols generated by *mwm* are somewhat larger and more decorated. The detail on icons is another aesthetic advantage of *mwm*.

All X displays require you to have some sort of pointer, often a three-button mouse, with which you communicate information to the system. As you slide the pointer around on your desktop, a cursor symbol on the display follows the pointer's movement. For our purposes, we will refer to both the pointing device (e.g., a mouse) and the symbol that represents its location on the screen as pointers. Depending on where the pointer is on the screen (in an *xterm* window, in another application window, on the root window, etc.), it is represented by a variety of cursor symbols. If the pointer is positioned on the root window, it is generally represented by an X-shaped cursor, as in Figure 1-1. If the pointer is in an *xterm* window, it looks like an uppercase I and is commonly called an *I-beam cursor*.*

A complete list of standard X cursors is shown in Appendix D. OSF/Motif provides some additional cursors. Some of the most common standard cursor shapes, as well as two Motif-specific cursors, are shown in Figure 1-3. As we'll see later, some applications allow you to select the cursor to use.

---

*Even though the actual image on the screen is called a cursor, throughout this guide we refer to "moving the pointer" to avoid confusion with the standard text cursor that can appear in an *xterm* window.

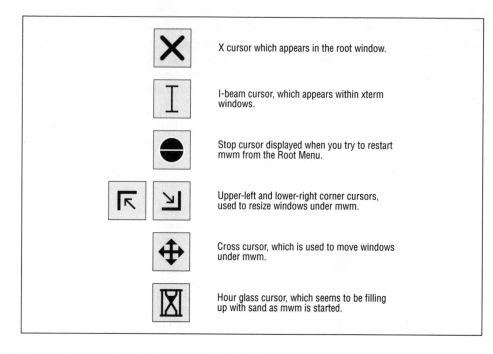

X cursor which appears in the root window.

I-beam cursor, which appears within xterm windows.

Stop cursor displayed when you try to restart mwm from the Root Menu.

Upper-left and lower-right corner cursors, used to resize windows under mwm.

Cross cursor, which is used to move windows under mwm.

Hour glass cursor, which seems to be filling up with sand as mwm is started.

Figure 1-3. Some standard cursors and two Motif-specific cursors

You use the pointer to manage windows and icons, to make selections in menus, and to select the window in which you want to input. You can't type in an *xterm* window until you select that window using the pointer. Directing input to a particular window is called *focusing*. When an *xterm* window has the input focus, the window frame and the text cursor are highlighted, as in Figure 1-4. (The highlighted cursor is a characteristic of *xterm*; other applications may not have a cursor, or may not highlight it to indicate focus.) The window to which input is directed is often called the *active* window.

Be aware that the frame may be highlighted in different ways, depending on the version of *mwm* you are running and the color resources specified for your system. The frame may change from black to white, from grey to white, etc. In any case, the active window's frame will be a different color than the frames of all other windows on the display.

Most window managers require you to select the active window in one of two ways: either by moving the pointer so that it rests within the desired window or by clicking the pointer on the window. By default, the Motif window manager requires you to click the pointer on the window to which you want to direct input. This focusing style is commonly referred to as "click-to-type" or ("explicit focus"). However, as we'll see in Chapter 13, *mwm* can be customized to allow you to direct input focus simply by moving the pointer. This focusing style is commonly referred to as "real-estate-driven" (or "pointer focus").

X Window System User's Guide, Motif Edition

Figure 1-4. Focus on an xterm window

In the real-estate-driven style, you direct input focus by moving the pointer into the desired window and leaving it there. As long as the pointer remains within the window's borders, the keystrokes you type will appear in that window (when the application accepts text input) or will somehow affect its operation (perhaps serve as commands). If you accidentally knock the pointer outside the window's borders, the keystrokes you type will not appear in that window or affect its operation. If you inadvertently move the pointer into another window, that window becomes the focus window. If you move the pointer onto the root window, the keystrokes are in effect lost—no application will interpret them.*

As previously mentioned, by default the Motif window manager uses the click-to-type focusing style: you must click the pointer on a window to focus input on that window. When you begin using X with *mwm*, you'll need to select the window to receive input by placing the pointer anywhere within the window and clicking the first (generally the leftmost) button. Once you select the focus window in this way, all input is directed to that window until you move the pointer and deliberately click on another window.

---

*In a few cases, the window manager may interpret these keystrokes. For example, you can customize *mwm* to display a menu when you type certain keystrokes while the pointer rests on the root window. See Chapter 13, *Customizing mwm*, for more information about mapping window manager functions to certain keys and pointer actions.

One of Motif's greatest strengths is that it allows you to choose the focus policy. This flexibility makes *mwm* a desirable choice for users with a variety of needs and work habits. As you might imagine, both focusing policies have their advantages. Click-to-type focus requires a little more work than pointer focus. (It's simpler to move the pointer than to move and click.) On the other hand, click-to-type focus is more precise—you can't inadvertently change the focus by moving the pointer.

We find click-to-type focus somewhat laborious. However, a touch typist, who is not inclined to look at the screen, might consider pointer focus too risky. It's possible to knock the pointer out of a window and lose a large amount of text before noticing. Another disadvantage of pointer focus is that it sometimes takes a moment for the input focus to catch up with the pointer, especially on slower machines. If you type right away, some keystrokes may end up in the window you left rather than in the new window. This is actually a bug that happens because of the additional overhead involved in complex window managers such as *mwm* or *twm*. Since you can change the focus policy rather simply, you might want to experiment with both methods. For now, we'll assume you're using the default click-to-type focus.

The most important thing to recognize is that focusing on the proper window is integral to working with an application running with a window system. If something doesn't work the way you expect, make sure that the focus is directed to the correct window. After you use X for a while, awareness of input focus will come naturally.

The pointer is also often used to display menus. Some X programs, notably *mwm* and *xterm*, have menus that are displayed (or *posted*) by keystrokes and/or pointer button motions. More versatile than many other window managers, *mwm* provides two default menus, each representing a different menu "style."

The Window Menu is a "pull-down" menu that can be displayed on any window by placing the pointer on the square button in the upper-left corner of the frame (decorated by a short horizontal bar in its center) and either clicking or pressing and holding down the first pointer button. Roughly defined, a pull-down menu is accessed from a graphical element that is always displayed, such as a command button or a menu bar. Figure 1-5 shows an *xterm* window with the Window Menu displayed by clicking the first pointer button in the menu button on the frame.

As you might infer from some of the menu items, you can use the Window Menu to move, resize, and otherwise manage the window on which it is displayed. When you display the Window Menu by clicking the first pointer button (as opposed to pressing and holding it down), the first item available for selection is surrounded by a box. In this case, the first available selection is Move. The first item on the menu, Restore, is used to change an icon back into a window; therefore, it is not useful at this time. The fact that Restore is not selectable is indicated by the fact that it appears in a lighter typeface. The Window Menu is discussed in detail in Chapter 4, *More about the mwm Window Manager*.

mwm also supports "pop-up" menus, which are displayed at the current pointer position. (Many X clients also use pop-up menus.) In addition to keyboard keys and pointer button motions, the location of the pointer plays a role in displaying menus. For example, *xterm* menus can only be displayed when the pointer is within an *xterm* window. Figure 1-6 shows the *mwm* Root Menu, which is generally displayed by placing the pointer on the root window and pressing and holding down the third pointer button.*

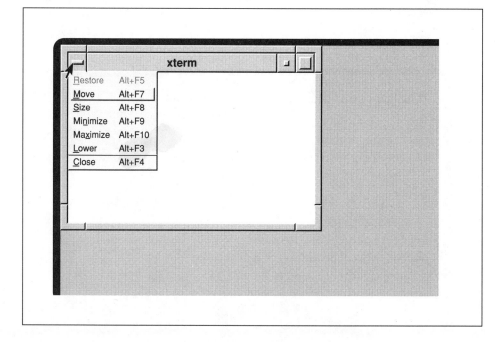

Figure 1-5. A pull-down menu: mwm's Window Menu

In Figure 1-6, the arrow next to the menu title represents the pointer. As you drag the pointer down the menu, each of the menu selections is highlighted. Regardless of the program, you generally select a menu item by dragging the pointer down the menu, highlighting the item you want, and releasing (or sometimes clicking) the pointer button. (*mwm* generally highlights an item by placing a rectangular box around it.) The Root Menu provides commands that can be thought of as affecting the entire display (as opposed to a single window). For example, the first menu item, New Window, creates a new *xterm* window on the local machine and display.

Though *mwm*'s menus can be useful, you'll probably find that you perform most window management functions simply by using the pointer on the window frame. In Chapter 3, *Working in the X Environment*, we'll describe several of these functions. Keep in mind, however, that both of the menus can be useful in certain circumstances. For instance, the Window Menu may be useful when parts of the window frame are obscured by another window. The Root Menu can be customized to execute system commands, such as the *xterm*

---

*With Motif applications, you generally use pointer button 3 to display pop-up menus. Standard X clients many require another button (often the first). (See "Standard X Clients Versus Motif Clients" later in this chapter.) Chapter 9, *Working with Motif Applications* explains Motif pointer button conventions. Pointer commands for the standard X clients appear in the relevant tutorials throughout this guide.

command initialized by the New Window menu item. It's fairly simple to add items to the Root Menu; you might want to add menu items to start some of the applications you use regularly. Chapter 13, *Customizing mwm*, describes how to add menu items and to perform a variety of modifications.

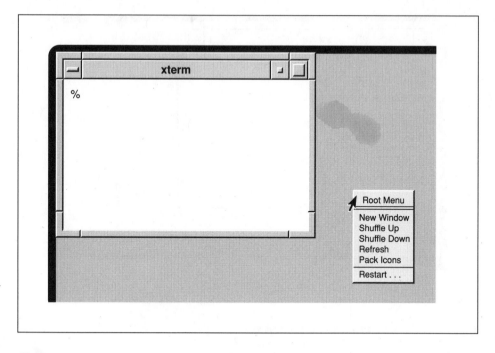

Figure 1-6. A pop-up menu: mwm's Root Menu

As we'll see in Chapter 8, *Other Clients*, some programs provide menus that you can display simply by placing the pointer on a particular part of the window, e.g., a horizontal menu bar across the top.

Some Motif applications offer a variation of a pull-down or pop-up menu that you can display and *leave displayed* while you continue to work. Such a menu is called a "tear-off" menu because it appears to be perforated at the top. Chapter 9, *Working with Motif Applications*, discusses how to tear off one of these menus, select options, and also remove the menu.

A final note about the X display: in X, the terms *display* and *screen* are not equivalent. A display may consist of more than one screen. (However, each display has only one keyboard and pointer.) A multiple screen display might be implemented in several ways. There might be two physical monitors, linked to form a single display, as shown in Figure 1-7. Alternatively, two screens might be defined as different ways of using the same physical monitor. For example, on the Sun-3/60 color workstation, screen 0 is color, and screen 1 is black and white. Each screen is the size of the monitor; you can only view one screen at a time. In practice, the two screens seem to be side by side: you can "scroll" between them by moving the pointer off either horizontal edge of the screen. By default, windows are always placed on screen 0 but you can place a client window on screen 1 by specifying the screen number in the `-display` option when starting the client. (See Chapter 3 for instructions on using the `-display` option.)

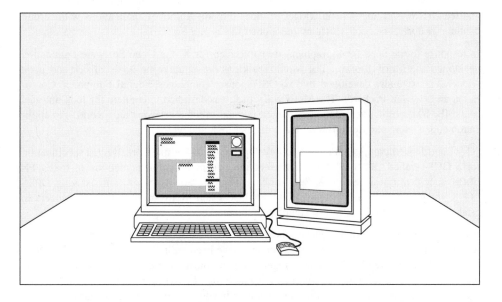

Figure 1-7. A display made up of two physical screens

Standard X Clients versus Motif Clients

The window manager running on a display helps determine the "look and feel" of an application. The *mwm* window manager frames each window on the display and allows you to manage a variety of application windows using the same mechanisms.

However, the look and feel of an application is not wholly determined by the window manager. In addition, the programming routines used to create the application also distinguish it. With the exception of *mwm*, all of the applications we've looked at so far have been written (or rewritten) using what is known as the X Toolkit, developed at MIT.

The X Toolkit is a collective name for two subroutine libraries designed to simplify the development of X Window System applications: the X Toolkit (Xt) Intrinsics and the Athena widget set (Xaw). The Xt library consists of low-level C programming routines for building and using widgets, which are predefined user interface components or objects. Typical widgets create graphical features such as menus, command buttons, dialog boxes, and scrollbars. Widgets make it easier to create complex applications. A common widget set also ensures a consistent user interface between applications.

Remember that X does not provide a distinct graphical user interface (GUI). X is a basic window system upon which almost any style of GUI can be built. The X Toolkit provides a simplified approach to creating graphical user interface components—guidelines for writing and implementing widgets—rather than offering a set of components with a predefined look and feel. (However, the Athena widget set does provide X Toolkit applications with certain common features, many of which are mentioned in Chapter 8.)

In response to the need for a graphical user interface for X, the Open Software Foundation developed the Motif Toolkit. The Motif Toolkit is based upon the Xt Intrinsics and upon widget sets originally developed by two OSF sponsor companies, Digital Equipment Corporation and Hewlett-Packard. The Motif widget set was designed to emulate the look and feel of the IBM/Microsoft Presentation Manager, popular in the microcomputer world. An application coded using the Motif Toolkit has a distinct look and feel.

AT&T and Sun Microsystems have also developed a GUI—or more precisely, a specification for a GUI—called OPEN LOOK. At present the two major implementations of the OPEN LOOK specification are Sun's XView toolkit (which is not Xt based) and AT&T's OPEN LOOK widget set (which is Xt based). OPEN LOOK and Motif are the prime contenders to establish a graphical user interface standard in the market.

With a few exceptions (notably *mwm*), most of the clients discussed in this guide are standard X clients shipped by MIT. Most of these clients have been built with the X Toolkit and illustrate the use of many of the Athena widgets. When you run these standard clients with the *mwm* window manager, your environment is something of a hybrid—neither a vanilla X nor a pure Motif environment (with Motif applications in addition to the window manager).

A standard X client running with *mwm* is different from a true Motif application, one coded using the Motif Toolkit. At first look, they may seem very similar—when *mwm* is running all clients on the display are framed in the same way. In addition, certain graphical features provided by the Motif widgets are also provided, albeit with slight variations, by the Athena widgets. However, other features are unique to Motif.

Without dissecting every component or closely examining how it functions, let's briefly compare a standard X application to a Motif application, highlighting some of the major differences (primarily in appearance). Many features of Motif and standard X applications also *operate* differently. We'll examine the functionality of various Motif and Athena widgets in more detail in Chapter 8, *Other Clients*, and Chapter 9, *Working with Motif Applications*.

For the comparison, we'll use a now defunct Motif demo program called *mre*, the Motif resource editor. Developed at OSF by Mitch Trachtenberg, *mre* can be used to edit a resource specification file. The editing help *mre* provides is minimal, but the program clearly demonstrates many of the Motif widgets—as it was intended to do. (*mre* has been eliminated from the Motif distribution in version 1.2, but it is appropriate for our purposes—it illustrates several features of a Motif application within a very compact window.)

The standard X client we're using is *xclipboard*, which you use in concert with *xterm*'s "cut and paste" facility, described in Chapter 5. The *xclipboard* client provides a window in which you can paste multiple text selections and from which you can copy text selections to other windows. Similar to the clipboard feature of the Macintosh operating system, *xclipboard* is basically a storehouse for text you may want to paste into other windows, perhaps multiple times.

The *mre* window in Figure 1-8 contains a resource file to be edited. (Resources are a mechanism that allow you to customize the operation of X clients.) The *xclipboard* window in Figure 1-9 contains a long text selection "cut" from an *xterm* window. Some prominent features of each application are labeled. Both clients are illustrated without the *mwm* frame. (When the window manager is running, the frame creates a superficial resemblance among all clients on the display.)

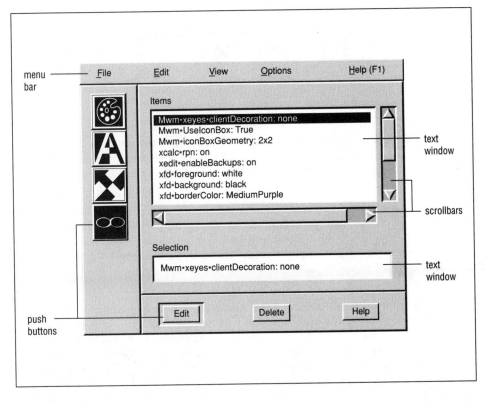

Figure 1-8. A Motif application: mre

The most striking difference between the two clients is simply the amount of detail. Like the Motif window manager, the individual Motif widgets create a three-dimensional appearance. The subwindows labeled Items and Selection seem to be set in to the application window. The push buttons (and drawn buttons) are shaded to suggest that they are raised above the level of the application window. (The drawn buttons also feature bitmapped images, three of them rather elaborate.) The menu bar is shaded to appear raised. The scrollbars have clearly distinguishable components, all of which are shaded and contoured to maintain the 3-D impression.

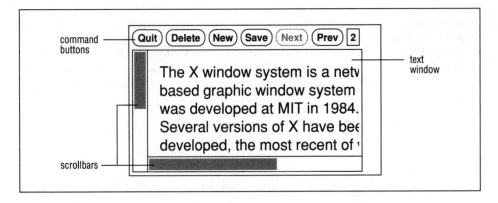

Figure 1-9. A standard X application: xclipboard

By contrast, the *xclipboard* window seems almost like a preliminary sketch of an application. It is basically flat. The text window, command buttons, and scrollbars are rendered in simple lines, without contouring, and with virtually no shading (though a portion of each scrollbar is shaded).

Another difference is that the *mre* window has a menu bar. Each word on the menu bar is the title of a pull-down menu that you can access by placing the pointer on it and clicking (or pressing and holding down) the first pointer button. The *xclipboard* application doesn't provide any menus—it's a fairly simple program. However, some standard X clients (notably *xman* discussed in Chapter 8) provide pull-down menus accessed by pressing and holding down a pointer button.

Motif pull-down menus generally have a few advantages over pull-down menus provided by standard X clients. While you must press and hold down a pointer button to dislay a menu provided by a standard X client, you can display a Motif menu simply by clicking a pointer button—and the menu stays displayed until you click again. Motif menu items can also be invoked in multiple ways (including pointer actions and keystrokes); the only way to invoke an item from a standard X menu is by dragging the pointer down the menu and releasing the button. The various ways you can work with a Motif pull-down menu are described for *mwm*'s Window Menu in Chapter 4.

Despite differences in general appearance and complexity, *mre* and *xclipboard* have many analogous components. Both applications feature a subwindow containing text that can be edited. (*mre* actually has two such windows, labeled Items and Selection.)

Both applications feature buttons: push buttons in the *mre* window; command buttons in the *xclipboard* window. From a user's viewpoint, push buttons and command buttons are functionally equivalent (though you can invoke a push button's function in more ways). The Motif and Athena widget sets simply identify them by different names. The four push buttons on the left side of the *mre* window are actually called drawn buttons. Drawn buttons are just push buttons decorated with a bitmap image rather than a text label.

Both the *mre* and *xclipboard* windows have a horizontal and a vertical scrollbar, which are used to look at text that is currently outside the viewing window. (These scrollbars are only displayed when the text read into the window extends beyond the bounds of the viewing area. If the text only exceeds the viewing area in one direction—either horizontally or vertically—only one scrollbar will be displayed.) The Athena scrollbar is basically rectangular (actually one rectangle within another). The Motif scrollbar is somewhat more elaborate. Notice the arrows on either end, for instance. These arrows are the hallmark of a Motif scrollbar and can help you readily identify a Motif application. The arrows also provide functionality not duplicated by the Athena scrollbar.

Most of this guide will help you master the basics of working with the MIT client programs running under the *mwm* window manager. Chapter 9, *Working with Motif Applications*, describes how to use some of the additional features provided by commercial applications built with the Motif widget set.

X Architecture Overview

Most window systems are *kernel-based*: that is, they are closely tied to the operating system itself and can only run on a discrete system, such as a single workstation. The X Window System is not part of any operating system but instead is composed entirely of user-level programs.

X is based on what is known as a *client-server* model. The system is divided into two distinct parts: *display servers* that provide display capabilities and keep track of user input and *clients*, application programs that perform specific tasks.

In a sense, the server acts as intermediary between client application programs, and the local display hardware (one or perhaps multiple screens) and input devices (generally a keyboard and pointer). When you enter input using the keyboard or a pointing device, the server conveys the input to the relevant client application. Likewise, the client programs make requests (for information, processes, etc.) that are communicated to the hardware display by the server. For example, a client may request that a window be moved or that text be displayed in the window.

This division within the X architecture allows the clients and the display server either to work together on the same machine or to reside on different machines (possibly of different types, with different operating systems, etc.) that are connected by a network. For example, you might use a relatively low-powered PC or workstation as a display server to interact with clients that are running on a more powerful remote system. Even though the client program is actually running on the more powerful system, all user input and displayed output occur on the PC or workstation server and are communicated across the network using the X protocol. Figure 1-10 shows a diagram of such a network.

You might choose to run a client on a remote machine for any number of reasons. Generally, however, the remote machine offers some feature unavailable on your local machine: a more efficient or powerful processor; a completely different architecture better suited to a particular task; different application software; file server capabilities (and perhaps large data files you'd rather not transfer over the network). X allows you to take advantage of these remote features and to see the results on your local terminal.

The distinction between clients and the server also allows somewhat complicated display situations. For instance, you can access several machines simultaneously. (This can greatly simplify the work of a system administrator.) X also allows you to output to several displays simultaneously. This capability can be very helpful in educational situations. Hypothetically, a teacher could display instructional material to a group of students each using a graphics workstation or terminal hooked up to a network.

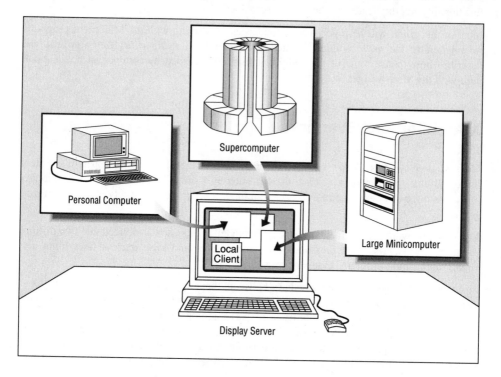

Figure 1-10. A sample X Window System configuration

There is another less obvious advantage to the client-server model: since the server is entirely responsible for interacting with the hardware, only the server program must be machine-specific. X client applications can easily be ported from system to system.

The X Display Server

The X display server is a program that keeps track of all input from input devices, such as the keyboard and pointer, and conveys that input to the relevant client applications; the server also keeps track of output from any clients that are running and updates the display to reflect that output. Each physical display (which may be multiple screens) has only one server program.

User input and several other types of information pass from the server to a client in the form of *events*. An event is a packet of information that tells the client something it needs to act on, such as keyboard input. Moving the pointer or pressing a key, etc., causes *input* events to occur.

When a client program receives a meaningful event, it responds with a *request* to the server for some sort of action affecting the display. For instance, the client may request that a window be resized to particular dimensions. The server responds to requests by a client program by updating the appropriate window(s) on your display.

Servers are available for many types of systems, including PCs, workstations, and X terminals, which may have the server downloaded from another machine or stored in ROM.

Clients

As previously mentioned, a client is an application program. The standard release of X from MIT includes more than 50 client programs that perform a wide variety of tasks. X allows you to run many clients simultaneously: each client displays in a separate window. For example, you could be editing a text file in one window, compiling a program source file in a second window, reading your mail in a third, all the while displaying the system load average in a fourth window.

While X clients generally display their results and take input from a single display server, they may each be running on a different computer on the network. It is important to note that the same programs may not look and act the same on different servers since X has no standard user interface, since users can customize X clients differently on each server, and since the display hardware on each server may be different.

Remember that the server conveys input from the various input devices to the appropriate client application; likewise, the client issues output in the form of requests to the server for certain actions affecting the display.

In addition to communicating with the server, a client sometimes needs to communicate with other clients. For example, a client may need to tell the window manager where to place its icon. Interclient communication is facilitated by the use of *properties*. A property is a piece of information associated with a window or a font and stored in the server. Properties are used by clients to store information that other clients might need to know, such as the name of the application associated with a particular window. Storing properties in the server makes the information they contain accessible to all clients.

A typical use of properties in interclient communication involves how a client tells the window manager the name of the application associated with its window. By default, the application name corresponds to the client's name, but many clients allow you to specify an alternative name when you run the program. A window manager that provides a titlebar needs to know the application name to display in that area. The client's application name is stored in the server in the property called WM_NAME and is accessed by the window manager.

See the *xprop* reference page in Part Three of this guide, and Volume One, *Xlib Programming Manual*, for more information about properties and the *xprop* client.

Several of the more frequently used client programs are discussed in the following sections.

The Window Manager

The way a kernel-based window system operates is inherent in the window system itself. By contrast, the X Window System concentrates control in a special kind of client application called a window manager. The window manager you use largely determines the look and feel of X on a particular system.

The window manager shipped with OSF/Motif is called *mwm*. As we've discussed, *mwm* allows you to move and resize windows, rearrange the order of windows in the window stack, create additional windows, and convert windows into icons, etc. These functions are discussed more fully in Chapter 3 and Chapter 4.

mwm is compliant with the X Consortium's *Inter-Client Communication Conventions Manual* (ICCCM), introduced at Release 3. The ICCCM contains standards for interaction with window managers and other clients. It defines basic policy intentionally omitted from X itself, such as the rules for transferring data between applications, for transferring keyboard focus, for installing colormaps, and so on. If window managers and other applications follow the conventions outlined in the ICCCM, they should be able to coexist and work together on the same server—even if they have been written using different toolkits.

In this guide, we assume you are using *mwm*. Other popular window managers, such as *twm* (the tab window manager), *olwm* (the OPEN LOOK™ window manager), *awm* (Ardent™ window manager), and *rtl* (tiled window manager, developed at Siemens Research and Technology Laboratories, RTL), are also widely used.

If the *mwm* window manager has been customized at your site or you are using a different window manager, many of the concepts should remain the same. However, the actual procedures shown may differ. See Chapter 13, *Customizing mwm*, for a discussion of how to tailor *mwm* to your particular needs.

The xterm Terminal Emulator

X11 itself is designed to support only bitmapped graphics displays. For this reason, one of the most important clients is a terminal emulator. The terminal emulator brings up a window that allows you to log in to a multiuser system and to run applications designed for use on a standard alphanumeric terminal. Anything you can do on a terminal, you can do in this window.

xterm is the most widely available terminal emulator. *xterm* emulates a DEC® VT102 terminal or a Tektronix® 4014 terminal. For each *xterm* process, you can display both types of windows at the same time but only one is active (i.e., responding to input) at a time.

Running multiple *xterm* processes is like working with multiple terminals. Since you can bring up more than one *xterm* window at a time, you can run several programs simultaneously. For example, you can have the system transfer files or process information in one window while you focus your attention on a text-editing session in another window. As you might imagine, having what are in effect multiple terminals can increase your productivity remarkably. See Chapter 3, *Working in the X Environment*, and Chapter 5, *The xterm Terminal Emulator*, for more information about *xterm*.

The Display Manager

The display manager, *xdm*, is a client that is designed to start the X server automatically (from the UNIX */etc/rc* system startup file) and to keep it running. (X can also be started manually, as described in Chapter 2, *Getting Started*.) In its most basic implementation, the display manager emulates the *getty* and *login* programs, which put up the login prompt on a standard terminal, keeping the server running, prompting for a user's name and password, and managing a standard login session.

However, *xdm* has far more powerful and versatile capabilities. From a user's perspective, you can design your own session, automatically running several clients and setting personal resources (such as keyboard, pointer, and display characteristics). Resources are introduced in Chapter 3, *Working in the X Environment*, and discussed fully in Chapter 11, *Setting Resources*.

The system administrator can customize special *xdm* files to manage several connected displays (both local and remote) and to set system-wide X resources (for example, client default features). See Volume Eight, *X Window System Administrator's Guide*, for a discussion of how to set up and customize the *xdm* display manager. Keep in mind that many commercial vendors provide alternative display/session managers. If you are using a display manager other than *xdm*, many of the concepts should remain the same. However, the actual setup procedures may differ.

Other Standard X Clients

The standard distribution of X from MIT includes more than 50 client applications. The client you will probably use most frequently is *xterm*. We've grouped some of the other more useful applications as follows:

Desk accessories

xbiff	Mail notification program
xclock, *oclock*	Clock applications
xcalc	Desktop calculator
xload	System load monitor
xman	Manual page browser

Display and keyboard preferences

xset	Allows you to set various display and keyboard preferences, such as bell volume, cursor acceleration, and screen saver operation.
xsetroot	Allows you to set the appearance of the root window. You might specify a particular color, bitmap graphic image, etc.
xmodmap	Allows you to map keyboard keys and pointer buttons to particular functions.

Font utilities

fs	The font server, a Release 5 innovation, allow you to access fonts over the network. (Fonts no longer need to be resident on your local machine.)
xlsfonts	Lists fonts available on the local machine.
fslsfonts	Lists fonts available via the font server.
xfd	Displays the characters in a single font.
xfontsel	Allows you to display multiple fonts sequentially and select a font to be used by another application.
showfont	Displays the contents of a compiled font file in an (readable) ASCII form. Can be used to convert a font character to a bitmap image using *atobm*.

Graphics utilities

bitmap	Bitmap editor.
xmag	Magnification utility.
atobm, *bmtoa*	Programs to convert ASCII characters to bitmaps and bitmaps to ASCII characters.

Printing applications

xwd	Dumps the image of a window to a file.
xpr	Translates an image file produced by *xwd* to PostScript® or another format, suitable for printing on a variety of printers.
xwud	Redisplays a window dump file created using *xwd*.

Removing a window

xkill	Terminates a client application.

Resource management

xrdb	The X resource database manager allows you to load customized client preferences into the server.
appres	Lists the resources that might be applied to a particular client.
editres	Tests and edits resource specifications.

Window and display information utilities

xlsclients	Lists the clients running on the display.
xdpyinfo	Lists general characteristics of the display.
xwininfo	Lists general characteristics of a selected window.
xprop	Lists the properties associated with a window.

These and other client applications are described in Chapters 5 through 8, and in Chapter 14. In addition, a reference page describing each client and listing its options appears in Part Three of this guide. As more commercial and user-contributed software is developed, many more specialized programs will become available.

Customizing Clients

Most X clients are designed to be customized by the user. A multitude of command-line options can be used to affect the appearance and operation of a single client process. A few of the more useful command-line options are introduced in Chapter 3. Chapter 10 discusses some additional standard options. Part Three of this guide includes a reference page for each client that details all valid options.

X also provides a somewhat more convenient way to customize the appearance and operation of client programs. Rather than specifying all characteristics using command-line options, default values for most options can be stored in a file (generally called *.Xresources* or *.Xdefaults*) in your home directory. Each default value is set using a variable called a *resource*; you can change the behavior or appearance of a program by changing the *value* associated with a resource variable.

Generally, these resource values are loaded into the server using a program called *xrdb* (*X resource database* manager). Then the values are accessed automatically when you run a client. Storing your preferences in the server with *xrdb* also allows you to run clients on multiple machines without maintaining an *.Xresources* file on each machine.

There is a separate customization file for the *mwm* window manager called *.mwmrc*, which is also kept in your home directory. By editing the *.mwmrc* file, you can modify several aspects of the window manager's operation, such as the contents of menus, and the key and pointer button sequences used to invoke actions. See Chapter 13, *Customizing mwm*, for more information.

Client customization is introduced in Chapter 3, *Working in the X Environment*, and described fully in Part Two of this guide.

2

Getting Started

This chapter helps you start the X server, the first xterm *(terminal emulator) window, and the* mwm *window manager. These processes may be started automatically when you log in, or you may have to start them manually.*

In This Chapter:

2
Getting Started

Before you can begin using the X Window System, you must do three things:

- Start the X server.

- Start at least one *xterm* terminal emulator.

- Start a window manager. (Although you *can* run X without a window manager, this is fairly limiting.)

Depending on how X is configured on your system, some or all of these steps may be performed for you automatically. This chapter explains how you can tell if the X server, an *xterm* window, and the *mwm* window manager are being started automatically. This chapter also describes how to start these processes manually on a stand-alone system such as a UNIX workstation.

After you've started these preliminary processes, skip to the section "Typing In a Window Once mwm is Running," later in this chapter.

Starting X

Depending on how X is being run on your system, the initial screens you see and the way you log in will be slightly different.

On many systems (and on most X terminals) the display manager, *xdm*, starts X and keeps it running. If your system is set up to use *xdm*, you log on in a special window provided for that purpose. If *xdm* is running, you should never have to start X manually.

On other systems (often UNIX workstations), you may be required to log in at a prompt displayed on the full screen. In these situations, X may or may not be started automatically when you log in. If X is not started automatically, you must start it yourself from the command line, as we'll describe later in this chapter.

Be aware that X is very easy to customize. There are countless command options as well as startup files that control the way the screen looks or even what menus a program displays. If X has been customized on your system, or you are trying out X using someone else's system or login account, things may not work exactly as described here. Customizing the X environment is introduced in Chapter 3, *Working in the X Environment*, and described in detail in Chapters 10 through 14.

Logging On in the Special xdm Window

If the display manager, *xdm*, is running X on your system, you'll probably see a window simi-lar to Figure 2-1 when you turn on your terminal.

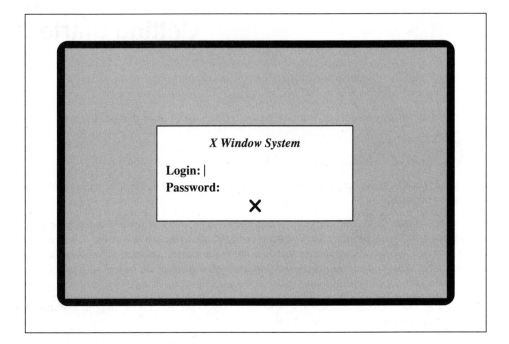

Figure 2-1. xdm login window

Log in just as if you were using a standard alphanumeric terminal. Without any user custom-ization, the display manager executes a standard login "session," providing the first *xterm* window and starting the window manager. The *xterm* window will be displayed in the upper-left corner of the screen. If the Motif window manager is running, you will see the character-istic frame around the *xterm* window, as in Figure 2-2. The name of the application ("xterm") appears in the frame's title area.

The frame provides a quick and easy way to move, iconify, resize, and otherwise manage windows on the screen. Some of the basic window manager functions are introduced in the section "Managing Windows Using the mwm Frame" in Chapter 3.

If the *mwm* window manager is running, skip to the section "Typing In a Window Once mwm is Running," later in this chapter. If the window manager is not running, skip to the section "Bringing Up the Window Manager," for instructions on how to start it.

Be aware that, in addition to *xdm*, other display/session managers are commercially avail-able. For example, Digital Equipment Corporation provides a display manager called *dxses-sion*, which functions similarly to *xdm*. If your system is using a display manager other than *xdm*, the login procedure may be slightly different. (See Volume Eight, *X Window System*

Administrator's Guide, for instructions on setting up the xdm *display manager to run X in a variety of environments.)*

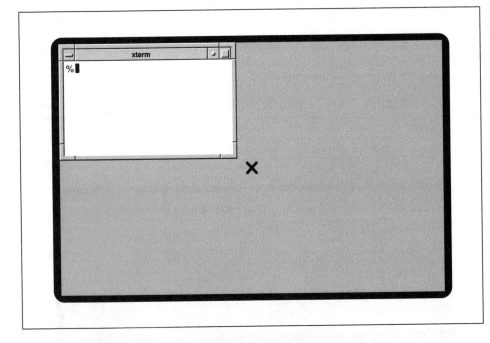

Figure 2-2. Window frame indicates that mwm is running

If you have an *xterm*, but the window manager is not running, skip to the section "Starting the mwm Window Manager" for instructions on how to start it.

As mentioned previously, most X terminals are configured to run X via a display manager, such as *xdm*. When you turn on your X terminal, a login window similar to the one in Figure 2-1 should be displayed to allow you to log in to a local host. If no such login window is provided, there may be a problem with the display manager or the terminal may be configured to connect to the host in another way (commonly via *telnet*). If there's no obvious way to log in on your X terminal, see your system administrator or Volume Eight, *X Window System Administrator's Guide*.

If you are trying to run X on a stand-alone system, such as a workstation, or in a more complex network environment, see Volume Eight for instructions on configuring *xdm*.

Logging In at a Full Screen Prompt

If you log in at a prompt displayed on the full screen, your system is probably set up to work in one of three ways. First, some workstations may be set up to start the server, open up the first *xterm* window, and possibly even start the window manager automatically. If all of these processes are running when you log in, the initial *xterm* window will be framed, as in Figure 2-2. Once the server, initial *xterm*, and the *mwm* window manager are running, you can skip to the section "Typing In a Window Once mwm is Running."

Some systems are set up to start the server and initial *xterm* window when you log in, but not the window manager. If this is the case, your screen should then look something like the one in Figure 2-3.

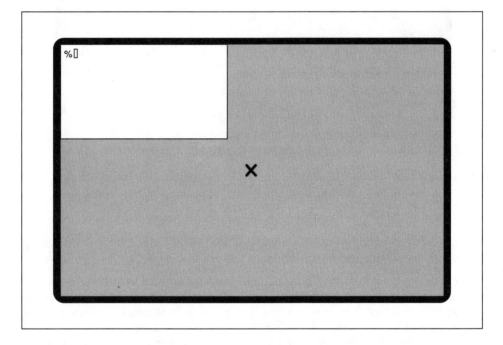

Figure 2-3. Workstation with login xterm window on the root window

If you have an *xterm* window without a frame, you must start *mwm* yourself. Skip to the section "Starting the mwm Window Manager" later in this chapter.

Be aware, however, that on some systems, X is not started automatically. When you log in at the prompt displayed on the full screen, no windows are opened; instead the entire screen functions as a single terminal, as shown in Figure 2-4.

Figure 2-4. *Workstation functioning as a single terminal: X isn't running*

If no windows are displayed when you log on at a full screen prompt, you must start the X Window System manually.

Starting X Manually

To start X manually, first make sure that the X11 directory containing executable programs is in your search path.* If not, add the pathname */usr/bin/X11* to the path set in your *.profile* or *.login* file.

If another windowing system (such as SunView™) is running, you must first kill it.

Then at the system prompt, enter:

```
% xinit
```

---

*For more information on how to set your search path, see Appendix A, *Managing Your Environment.* Note that the appropriate pathname to add may be different in vendor distributions.

The *xinit* program starts the X server and creates the first *xterm* window in the upper-left corner of your display.* The *xterm* window indicates that X is running on your display. (In Appendix A, *Managing Your Environment*, we'll show you a simple way to run *xinit* automatically when you log in. For more information on automating X, see Volume Eight, *X Window System Administrator's Guide*.)

Starting the mwm Window Manager

To bring up the *mwm* window manager, you must enter the *mwm* command in the login *xterm* window. As described in Chapter 1, *An Introduction to the X Window System*, you can only provide input to one window at a time. X does not automatically know which window you want to type in, even if only one window appears on the display, as in Figure 2-3. In order to type in the *xterm* window on the display, you must first focus input to that window. The window to which input is focused is often referred to as the active window.

When no window manager is running, you focus input simply by moving the pointer so that the cursor symbol on the screen rests within the window. Depending on where the pointer rests, the cursor symbol representing it on the screen differs. When the pointer rests on the root window, it appears as a large X (another indication that X is running). When you move the pointer into the *xterm* window, it should change to what is known as the I-beam cursor symbol, which looks like a very thin letter "I".

When you move the pointer into the *xterm* window, input is focused there. Notice that the rectangular text cursor changes from an outline to a solid color. The change in the text cursor is another indication that input is focused on the window. Once you've selected the *xterm* window as the active window, the characters you type will appear on the window's command line.

Start the *mwm* window manager by typing:

```
% mwm &
```

The screen will momentarily go blank. Then while *mwm* is starting up, the root window pointer changes to an hour glass that appears to be filling up with sand. When the hour glass is full, the *xterm* window will be redisplayed, this time with the characteristic frame, indicating that *mwm* is running.

---

*If *xinit* produces a blank background with no terminal window, software installation was not completed correctly. Reboot your workstation and try again. Before invoking *xinit*, look in the directory */usr/bin/X11* for a file whose name begins with a capital X but otherwise has a similar name to your workstation (e.g., Xsun). When you find one that seems a likely possibility, try this command:

```
% xinit -- Xname
```

If that works, link X*name* to X, and *xinit* will work correctly thereafter. For example:

```
% cd /usr/bin/X11
% ln Xsun X
```

Note that it is important to run *mwm* in the background by typing an ampersand (&) at the end of the command line so you can continue to enter additional commands in the *xterm* window. If you neglected to do this on a system that supports job control, type Control-Z to suspend *mwm*, then use the *bg* command (see *csh*(1)) to place it in the background.

If the system you're on does not support job control, interrupt the process using the appropriate key sequence (Control-C on many systems) and start over.

Typing In a Window Once mwm is Running

Now that you've started the X server, the first *xterm* window, and the *mwm* window manager, you'll want to proceed by entering commands in the *xterm* window. However, if you type some characters, you'll find that the keystrokes do not appear in the *xterm*—or anywhere else on the display!

In order to type in a window when *mwm* is running, you must first move the pointer into the window and click the first button. As described in Chapter 1, this focus policy is commonly referred to as click-to-type or explicit focus. (When *mwm* is not running, you select the window to receive input—the active or focus window—simply by moving the pointer into that window.) Until you select the *xterm* window as the window to receive input, any keystrokes are lost.

This feature of *mwm* can be even more confusing if *mwm* is not started automatically when you log in. Before you start the window manager, you can focus input on a window simply by moving the pointer. As described in the preceding section, you must move the pointer into the first *xterm* window in order to enter the *mwm* command. However, once you run *mwm*, the focus policy changes to click-to-type. If you try to type additional characters without clicking on the window, the keystrokes will be lost.

To select the focus window when *mwm* is running:

1. Move the pointer into the *xterm* or other client window.

2. Click the first pointer button. (To click a pointer button, you press it down and release it without pausing. Pointer actions are explained in the section "Using the Pointer" in Chapter 3.)

You can tell which window has the input focus by several changes in the appearance of the display, illustrated in Figure 2-5 and described below. (Once you are running several windows simultaneously, it's important to be able to identify the focus window easily.)

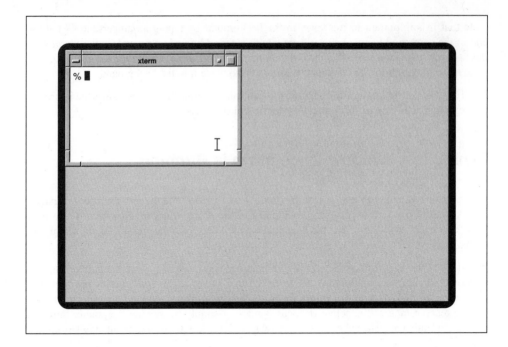

Figure 2-5. Changes in appearance indicate a window has the input focus

First, the color of the window frame will change in some way. As described in Chapter 1, *An Introduction to the X Window System*, the active window's frame may be highlighted in different ways, depending on the version of *mwm* you are running and the color resources specified for your system. The frame may change from black to white, from gray to white, etc. In any case, the active window's frame will be a different color than the frames of all other windows on the display.

The cursor symbol that represents the pointer will also change. Depending on where the pointer rests, the cursor symbol representing it on the screen differs. When the pointer rests on the root window, it generally appears as a large X (another indication that X is running). When you move the pointer into the *xterm* window, it should change to what is known as the I-beam cursor symbol, which looks like a very thin letter "I".

In the *xterm* application window itself, the rectangular text cursor changes from an outline to a solid color, and the window border is highlighted.

Once you've selected the *xterm* window as the active window, the characters you type will appear on the window's command line.

When you are using explicit (click-to-type) focus and the other default *mwm* resources, selecting a window to receive input also raises that window to the top of the window stack. As we'll see in Chapter 13, *Customizing mwm*, this behavior is controlled by an *mwm* resource variable called focusAutoRaise, which is true by default when explicit focus is in effect.

If you are working with a stack of windows that overlap, selecting a focus window automatically raises that window to the top of the stack (in effect the front of the display).

Keep in mind that *mwm* is highly customizable. You can specify dozens of features, including the color of the active window's frame, the options available on menus, and how certain window management functions are invoked. As we've discussed, one of the most significant modifications you can make to *mwm* is to change the focus policy from click-to-type (or explicit focus) to real-estate-driven (or pointer focus).

3

Working in the X Environment

This chapter shows you how to begin working productively in the X environment. It describes how to:

- Open a second xterm window.

- Move windows; raise windows to the front of the display; convert windows to icons.

- Close an xterm window.

- Start other clients in convenient places on the display.

- Run clients on remote machines.

- Customize a single client process using command-line options.

- Specify alternate default characteristics for a client using resource variables.

In This Chapter:

3
Working in the X Environment

At the end of the last chapter, you should've had the X server, the first *xterm* window, and the *mwm* window manager running. The current chapter illustrates some of the system's basic capabilities so you can begin working more productively. This chapter shows you how to:

* Open a second *xterm* window.

* Use the pointer to affect windows on the display.

* Iconify, deiconify, maximize, raise, move, resize, and close windows using the pointer on the *mwm* frame.

* Close an *xterm* window from the command line.

* Start additional client programs, on both local and remote machines.

* Organize the display.

This chapter also introduces some basic ways to customize X clients to better suit your needs.

Creating Other Windows

Once you focus input on the first *xterm* window, as described in Chapter 2, you can enter commands to open other client windows. For example, you can open a second *xterm* window by typing this command at the prompt in the first *xterm* window:

```
% xterm &
```

After a few moments, a second *xterm* window will be displayed on the screen. As we'll see later in this chapter, you can specify the location for a new window using a command-line option (or in many cases using a resource variable stored in a file in your home directory). If you don't specify position on the command line (or in a resource file), by default *mwm* automatically places new windows offset from the upper-left corner of the screen, as shown in Figure 3-1.*

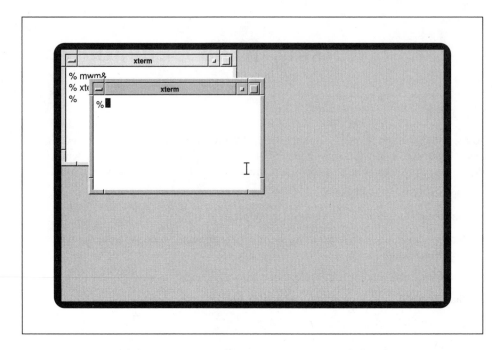

Figure 3-1. mwm automatically places the second xterm window

The new *xterm* window displays a prompt from whatever shell you are using. In this case, the new window is running the UNIX C shell.

Notice that the second window's frame is a dark gray, indicating that input is focused on it. The first window's frame has changed from dark to light gray; it no longer has the input focus. It's important to be aware that when you start a new window (and click-to-type focus is being used), the new window automatically takes over the input focus. (Note that the colors may vary according to system defaults.)

In the default *mwm* configuration, to switch back and forth between windows you must move the pointer from one window to the other and click the first button. Notice that if you are working with a stack of windows that overlap, selecting a window as the active window automatically raises that window to the top of the stack (in effect, the front of the display).

---

*If you start multiple processes in a row, the windows will be placed progressively further from the upper-left corner (towards the opposite corner), so that no window completely overlaps another.

You can customize *mwm* to allow you to place new windows interactively using the pointer. This modification is performed by setting a resource variable called `interactivePlacement` to a value of true. See Chapter 13 for instructions on modifying *mwm*. See the *mwm* reference page in Part Three of this guide for more information about `interactivePlacement`.

Whatever you type will appear in the window with the highlighted frame. Try starting a command in both windows. For example, start up *vi* or another text editor in the second *xterm* window. Notice how you can switch back to the first window to type a new command, by moving the pointer and clicking—even if you leave *vi* in insert mode or some other command in the process of sending output to the screen. Whatever process was running in the window you left will continue to run. If it needs input from you to continue, it will wait.

You must always switch focus to work with multiple windows. However, *mwm* has complicated matters by placing the second *xterm* window in Figure 3-1 in a very inconvenient place. The second window overlies the first window and almost completely obscures it.

Windows commonly overlap on the display. The window manager allows you to change the position and size of windows so that you can work effectively in such situations.

The primary window management tool *mwm* provides is the window frame. The section "Managing Windows Using the mwm Frame," later in this chapter, shows you how to perform these functions simply by using the pointer on various parts of the frame. But before we can learn to perform these window management functions, we need to learn more about pointer actions.

Using the Pointer

As explained in Chapter 1, the cursor on the screen follows the pointer's movement on the desktop. Move your pointer around on the desk to get used to this. Keep in mind that different pointers respond differently. If you move to another display, the screen cursor may move more quickly or slowly than the one you're used to. The *xset* client (described in Chapter 14, *Setup Clients*) lets you modify pointer behavior.

You use the pointer to indicate a graphical element on the screen, such as a window, icon, or command button. Most pointers have three buttons. For our purposes, we'll refer to these buttons as first, second, and third, where the first button is the leftmost on the pointer, the second is in the middle, and third is the rightmost.* By placing the pointer on a particular element and then performing some button action (and possibly a pointer motion), you can invoke a variety of commands. The types of button actions and pointer motions you can perform are:

Click   To click a button, you press the pointer button down and release it. A click is a rapid action; there is no pause between the press and release. A double click is two full clicks in succession, with no pause between clicks. A triple click is three clicks in succession.

Press   To press a button, you push the button down and hold it down.

---

*Keep in mind that "first" is a logical distinction made by X, not a physical one. The first logical pointer button generally corresponds to the leftmost button on the pointer. (Thus, in some contexts you may find the buttons referred to as left, middle, and right.) However, X allows you to change the correspondence of logical and physical buttons. For example, you can reassign the first logical button to be the rightmost button on the pointer. A lefthanded person might opt to reverse the order of the buttons. You remap pointer buttons using a client called *xmodmap*, which is described in detail in Chapter 14, *Setup Clients*.

Release   After pressing a button down, you release it by letting up on the button.

Drag   To drag a graphical object (such as a window or icon) from one location on the screen to another: place the pointer on the object; press one or more pointer buttons; move the pointer to another location (dragging the object); and release the button(s).

Keep in mind that some commands or actions are invoked by a simple click on a particular graphic element, as illustrated by *mwm*'s click-to-type focus. Alternatively, some actions require a button press and pointer motion (i.e., dragging).

When dragging is used to move an object, the actual object does not appear in the new location until you complete the movement and release the pointer button. Instead, you appear to drag an outline representing the object. When you release the pointer button, the actual object appears in the new location. This effect is illustrated in the section "Moving a Window," later in this chapter.

Dragging is also commonly used to change the size of a window. Again, an outline indicates that the window's size is changing. When the outline approximates the size you want, you release the pointer button and the actual window is redrawn using the selected dimensions.

The following sections describe how to perform the most basic window management functions, which require you to use the pointer in the ways we've discussed.

Managing Windows Using the mwm Frame

Figure 3-2 shows an *xterm* window "framed" by *mwm*. The window frame itself and several features of it are tools that allow you to manage the window using the pointer.

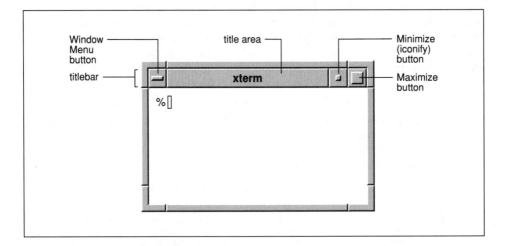

Figure 3-2. An xterm window framed by mwm

The wider top edge of the frame is the titlebar. The titlebar is composed of several parts including a title area (displaying the name of the application) and three command buttons (Minimize, Maximize, and Window Menu). Notice that whenever you move the pointer into the titlebar, the pointer changes to the arrow cursor.

Though it's not apparent from Figure 3-2, you can perform most window management functions by using the pointer on various parts of the frame. The following sections explain how to iconify, maximize, move, raise, resize, and close windows using the frame. Chapter 4 describes menu items and keyboard shortcuts that can be used as alternatives to the frame. These are important when a window's frame is obscured by other features of the display. Chapter 4 also describes additional functions provided by *mwm* menus.

Converting a Window to an Icon

As discussed in Chapter 1, an icon is a symbol that represents a window in an inactive state. There are many circumstances in which it might be desirable to iconify a window:

- To prevent yourself from inadvertently terminating a window, as in the case of the login *xterm*.

- While running a program whose progress you don't need to monitor; if a window is tied up running a process and you don't have to see it, the window is just taking up space.

- If you are only using an application occasionally. For example, you might be running the *xcalc* calculator program, but only using it every so often.

- If you want to use several application windows, but only display a few at a time; this arrangement can be somewhat less confusing than a display crowded with windows. Having some windows iconified also frees you from constantly shuffling the stacking order.

The Minimize command button on the *mwm* frame allows you to convert a window to an icon (iconify it). The Minimize button appears immediately to the right of the title area and is identified by a tiny square in its center. To iconify a window, use the following steps:

1. Place the pointer within the Minimize command button. The pointer simply has to rest within the button's outer border, not within the tiny square identifying it.

2. Click the first pointer button. The window is iconified. Figure 3-3 shows a window being converted to an icon in this way.

By default, icons are displayed in the bottom left corner of the root window. *mwm* can also be set up to place icons in another location, to allow you to place them interactively using the pointer, or to organize icons within a window known as an *icon box*. In Chapter 13, *Customizing mwm*, we'll discuss the specifications necessary to set up an icon box.

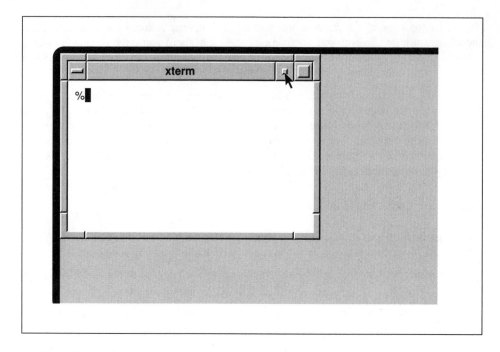

Figure 3-3. Converting a window to an icon with the Minimize button

Converting an Icon to a Window

To convert an icon back to a window (deiconify it), place the pointer on the icon and double click, using the first pointer button. The window is redisplayed in the position it appeared before it was iconfied (and is also raised to the top of the stack).

Between the first and second clicks, you'll probably notice that another small window is displayed for an instant above the icon. This window is actually a menu, called the Window Menu. (This menu can be displayed from a window or from an icon and can be used to invoke several window management functions on the window or icon. We'll discuss the Window Menu in more detail in Chapter 4, *More about the mwm Window Manager*.)

Be aware, however, that if you pause too long between the two clicks in deiconifying a window, the second click will not be interpreted and the icon will not be converted back to a window. Instead the Window Menu will remain on the screen, as in Figure 3-4.

Notice that in addition to displaying the menu, clicking has caused the icon image to change in appearance. The icon label is wider and the label and the frame surrounding the icon are highlighted. These changes indicate that the icon has the input focus; thus the icon will interpret subsequent keystrokes as window manager commands.

Notice also that the first item on the menu, Restore, is surrounded by a box, indicating that it is available for selection. Restore means to restore an icon to a window (or, as we'll see, a maximum size window to its original size). When the Window Menu is displayed above an icon, you can convert the icon to a window by placing the pointer on the Restore menu item and clicking the first pointer button. (Whenever a Window Menu item is boxed, you can also select it by pressing either the Return key or the space bar.)

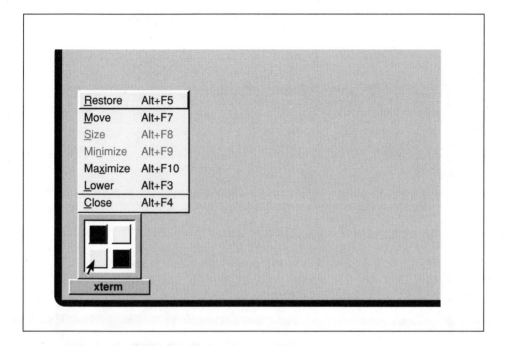

Figure 3-4. Window Menu being displayed over an icon

If you want to remove the menu without invoking a command, simply move the pointer off the icon and menu and click the first pointer button. The menu will be removed; however, the icon will retain the input focus—the label and border will remain highlighted—until you focus input on another window or icon.

Maximizing a Window

Maximizing a window generally means enlarging it to the size of the root window. (In some cases, a client application may specify its own maximum window size and maximizing will produce a window of this size.) This action can be performed using the Maximize command button, which is located to the right of the Minimize command button (in the upper-right corner of the window).

The Maximize command button is identified by a larger square in its center. It allows you both to enlarge the window to the size of the root window (or to the maximum size the client allows), and once it has been enlarged, to convert it back to its original size.

To maximize a window, use the following steps:

1. Place the pointer within the Maximize command button. The pointer simply has to rest within the button's outer border, not within the square identifying it.

2. Click the first pointer button. The window is maximized, as illustrated in Figure 3-5.

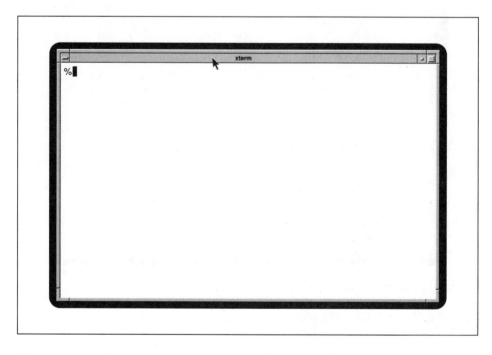

Figure 3-5. A maximized window

The large window should function in the same way it did before it was maximized. Theoretically, you can maximize an *xterm* window to have a single, very large terminal screen. However, be aware that certain programs you may run within an *xterm*, such as the *vi* text editor, do not always work properly within a window of this size (even if you've used the *resize* client, as described in Chapter 5, *The xterm Terminal Emulator*). The Maximize function is more safely used with an application that displays a graphic image or performs a simple function, such as *xclock*.

Also, some client programs that do not support resizing, such as the Release 3 version of *xcalc*, cannot be maximized correctly. In the case of *xcalc*, the frame surrounding the calculator application is maximized, but the actual calculator remains the same size.

The Maximize button is a toggle. To convert a maximized window back to its original size, click on the Maximize button again with the first pointer button. The Restore item on the Window Menu will also perform this function.

Raising a Window or Icon

We've already seen the necessity for raising windows on the display: frequently windows overlap. In order to work with a window that is all or partially covered by another window, you'll want to raise it to the top of the window stack. Using the default *mwm*, you raise a window with the following steps:

1. Place the pointer on any part of the window frame, except the three command buttons (Minimize, Maximize, and Window Menu).

2. Click the first pointer button. The window is raised to the top of the stack.

When you are using explicit (click-to-type) focus, this click also selects the window to receive input, i.e., makes the window the active window. Once you have raised a window to the top of the stack, you should be able to enter input and read output easily.

Windows may obscure icons on the display. (*mwm* does not allow one icon to obscure another.) If an icon is partially visible under a window, you can raise it using the following steps:

1. Place the pointer on the obscured icon.

2. Click the first pointer button.

The icon is raised to the top of the stack.

Figure 3-6 illustrates an icon being raised in front of a window.

Notice that in addition to being raised to the top of the window stack, a menu (called the Window Menu) is displayed over the icon. (This menu can be displayed from a window or from an icon and can be used to invoke several management functions on the window or icon. We'll discuss the Window Menu in more detail in Chapter 4.) To remove the menu, move the pointer off of the icon and menu and click the first button.

Notice also that the icon image changes in appearance when you raise the icon to the top of the stack (as it did when we paused between the double click to deiconify). The wider label and the highlighted label and frame indicate that the icon has the input focus. (Remember, when an icon has the input focus, it will interpret subsequent keystrokes as window manager commands.) Even when you remove the Window Menu, the icon will retain the focus (and remain highlighted). When you direct focus to another window (or icon), the icon label will become normal again.

Working in X

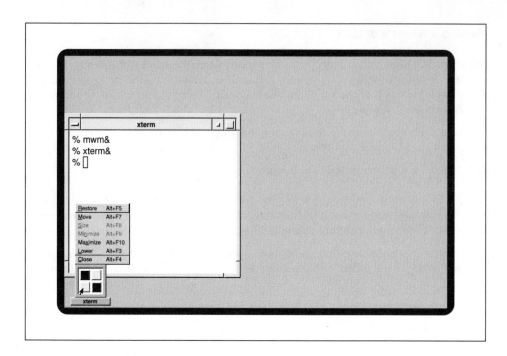

Figure 3-6. Raising an icon

Moving a Window

In many cases you'll want to move a window from one location on the display to another. The largest part of the titlebar is known as the *title area*, primarily because it displays the name of the application. The title area allows you to move the window, using the following steps:

1. Place the pointer within the title area. The pointer changes to the arrow cursor.

2. Press and hold down the first pointer button.

3. Move the window by dragging the pointer. Figure 3-7 shows a window being moved in this way. When you begin to move the window, the pointer changes to a cross arrow pointer and a window outline appears. This outline tracks the pointer's movement. In the center of the screen, a small, rectangular box also appears, displaying the x and y coordinates of the window as you move it.

4. Drag the cross arrow pointer with the window outline to the desired location on your screen.

5. Release the first pointer button. The window will move to the selected location.

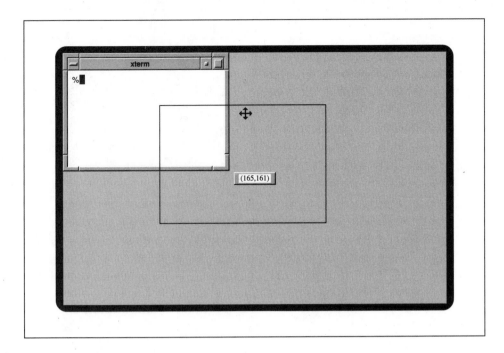

Figure 3-7. Moving a window by dragging the title area

With the default configuration of *mwm*, moving a window also selects that window as the active or focus window.

Moving an Icon

Moving an icon is similar to moving a window. To move an icon:

1. Place the pointer on the icon.

2. Press the first pointer button.

3. Move the icon by dragging the pointer. Figure 3-8 shows an icon being moved in this way. When you begin to move the icon, the pointer changes to a cross arrow pointer and an icon outline appears. This outline tracks the pointer's movement.

4. Drag the cross arrow pointer with the icon outline to the desired location on your screen.

5. Release the first pointer button. The icon will move to the selected location.

With the default configuration of *mwm*, moving an icon also selects that icon to receive the input focus.

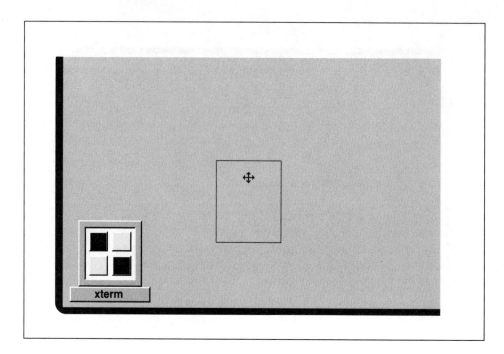

Figure 3-8. Dragging an icon to a new location

Resizing a Window

One of the most distinctive and useful features of the *mwm* window frame is not at all obvious. The entire frame (other than the titlebar—i.e., the title area and command buttons) is designed to allow you to resize the window using the pointer. Notice that the frame is divided by small lines into eight sections: four long borders (two horizontal and two vertical) and four corners. Figure 3-9 shows these sections of the window frame.

You can resize a window horizontally, vertically, or simultaneously in both directions. Resizing is a bit trickier than any of the other window management functions we've tried, since the way you move the pointer determines the size of the window. It will probably take some practice.

If you place the pointer within a window and then move it into one of the long horizontal or vertical borders, you'll notice the pointer changes to a new shape: an arrow (pointing toward the window border), with a short line perpendicular to it. This short line represents the window border. Try moving the pointer in this fashion in one of the windows on your display to get a better idea of what the pointer looks like. If you move the pointer from within a window into the outer border at one of the corners, the pointer will become an arrow pointing diagonally at a small corner symbol, as pictured in Figure 3-10. Figure 3-11 shows all of the possible resize pointers.

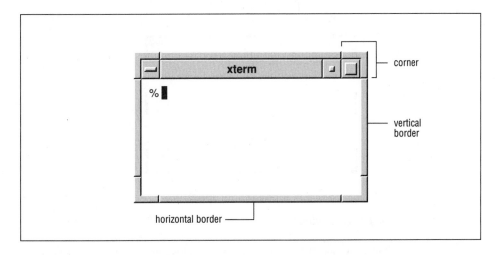

Figure 3-9. The outer frame is divided into four long borders and four corners

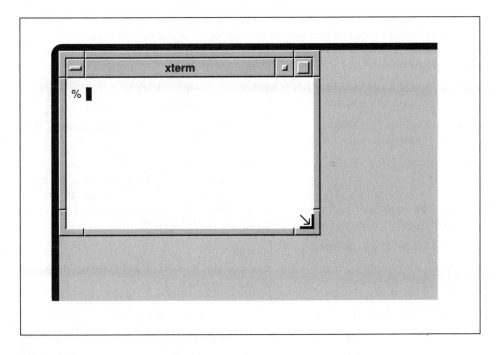

Figure 3-10. Window with resizing pointer

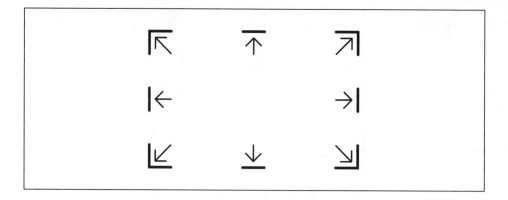

Figure 3-11. Resizing pointer symbols

Once the pointer changes to one of these shapes, you can move the border (or corner) of the window. Resizing from one of the long borders only allows you to change one dimension of the window: a horizontal border can only be moved up or down, changing the height; a vertical border can only be moved left or right, changing the width.

Resizing from a corner offers the most flexibility. You can move a corner in any direction you choose, changing both dimensions of the window if you want. For example, you can drag the lower-right corner of a window down and to the right to enlarge the window in both dimensions.

You determine the size and shape of the window by choosing the border or corner you want to extend (or contract) and moving it the desired amount using the following steps:

1. Move the pointer from within the window to the border or corner you want to move. The pointer changes to one of the symbols pictured in Figure 3-11.

2. Press and hold down the first pointer button and drag the window border or corner in the direction you want. As you resize the window, an image of the moving border(s) tracks the pointer movement. Also, in the center of the display, a small rectangular window shows the dimensions of the window as they change (in characters and lines for *xterm* windows, in pixels for most other clients).

3. Resize the window as desired.

4. Release the first pointer button. The window is redisplayed in the new shape. (The border image and window geometry tracking box disappear.)

Figure 3-12 shows a window being "stretched" from the lower-right corner.

Note that resizing an *xterm* window will not change the dimensions of the text currently in the window. If you make the window smaller, for instance, some of the text may be obscured. On most operating systems, this should not be a problem. As you continue to work, perhaps starting a text editor, the text will be adjusted to display in the newly sized window. Problems are more likely to occur if you resize a window *during* a text editing session. It's likely that the text editing program will not know about the window's new size and will operate incorrectly. To solve this problem, simply quit out of the editor and start another session.

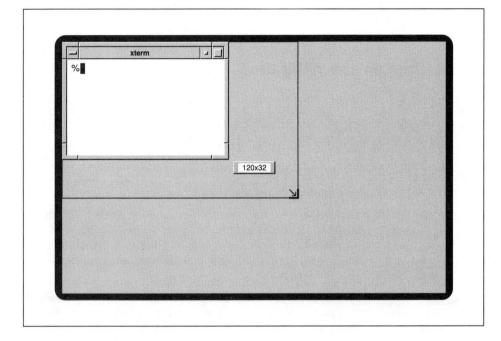

Figure 3-12. Dragging the corner to make a window larger

If your resized *xterm* window does not seem to know its new size, you may be working with an operating system that does not support terminal resizing capabilities. Refer to the discussion of the *resize* client in Chapter 5, *The xterm Terminal Emulator*, and to the *resize* reference page in Part Three of this guide for alternative solutions.

Closing a Window: The Window Menu Button

The command button on the left side of the titlebar is used to bring up the Window Menu, which provides seven items that can be used to manage the window and its icon. Chapter 4, *More about the mwm Window Manager*, describes how to bring up the Window Menu and invoke its various functions.

This command button also has another function. Double-clicking the first pointer button on the Window Menu command button kills the client program and closes the window. Be aware, however, that like other methods of "killing" a program (such as the *xkill* client), double-clicking on the Window Menu button can adversely affect underlying processes.

Refer to the section on *xkill* in Chapter 8, *Other Clients*, for a more complete discussion of the hazards of killing a client and a summary of alternatives.

You can customize *mwm* so that double clicking performs no function by setting a resource variable, wMenuButtonClick2, to false. See the sections "Setting mwm Resources" and "mwm-Specific Appearance and Behavior Resources" in Chapter 13, and the *mwm* reference page in Part Three of this guide for details.

Exiting from an xterm Window

When you are finished using an *xterm* window, you can remove it by typing whatever command you usually use to log off your system. Typically, this might be exit or Control-D. We'll close the second *xterm* window in Figure 3-13 by typing exit.

Notice that when we terminate the second *xterm* window, the first *xterm* window takes over the input focus. When explicit focus is being used and a window is terminated, the input focus reverts to the window that previously had the focus.

Be aware that terminating the login *xterm* window (the first *xterm* to appear) kills the X server and all associated clients. (If *xdm* is running X, the server will be reset but only after all client processes have been killed.) Be sure to terminate all other *xterm* windows before terminating the *xterm* login window. Also, if you are in an editor such as *vi*, be sure to save your data before you terminate the window.

In fact, it may be wise to iconify the login window and use other *xterm* windows instead, so that you don't inadvertently terminate it. Remember: you iconify a window by placing the pointer on the Minimize command button on the frame and clicking the first pointer button.

If you are worried about typing Control-D (end-of-file) accidentally and you normally use the C shell (*csh*), you can enter:

```
% set ignoreeof
```

in the login window. Then typing exit becomes the only way you can terminate the window.

Note that some C shell implementations have an autologout variable, which will automatically terminate the shell if there is no activity for a given period of time. If your C shell supports this feature, be sure to disable it in the login *xterm* window using this command:

```
% unset autologout
```

As an alternative to entering the command used to log off the system, you can also terminate an *xterm* window by selecting Send HUP Signal, Send TERM Signal, Send KILL Signal, or Quit from the *xterm* Main Options menu. (These menu options send different signals to the *xterm* process. Depending on what signals your operating system recognizes, some of the options may not work as intended. See Chapter 5 for more information.)

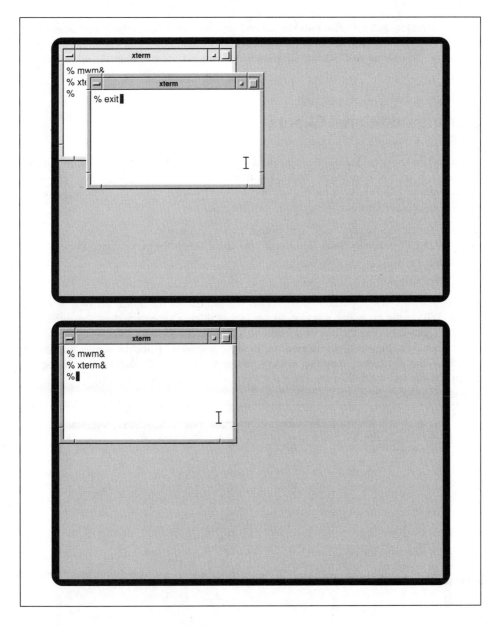

Figure 3-13. Closing an xterm window

The *mwm* window manager also provides several ways to remove an *xterm* or any other client window, among them double-clicking on the Window Menu command button, as described previously. Additional methods are described in Chapter 4, *More about the mwm Window Manager*.

Starting Additional Clients

Now that you know the basics of managing windows, you can start other X clients just like you can start another instance of *xterm*. The following sections describe how to open more client windows, place them on the display in convenient positions, and take advantage of X's networking capabilities by running clients on other machines.

To start a client, at the command-line prompt in any *xterm* window, type the name of the client followed by an ampersand (&) to make the client run in the background. For example, by typing:

```
% oclock &
```

you can start a clock application. The clock will appear in the upper-left quarter of the screen. With non-rectangular windows like *oclock*, a titlebar appears to float above the window. You can then drag the *oclock* window to a more convenient location—say the upper-right corner, as in Figure 3-14. (Remember, to move a window, place the pointer on the title area, press the first button, drag the window outline to the desired location, and release the button. Notice that the outline is rectangular, even if the *oclock* window isn't!)

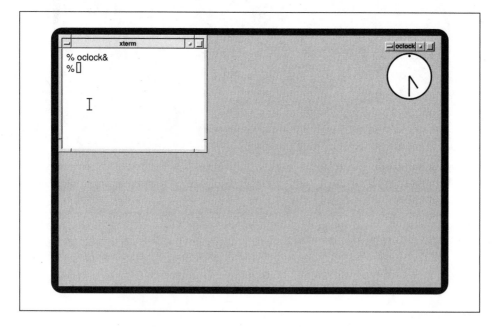

Figure 3-14. The oclock window

Though moving windows on the display is fairly simple, manually positioning every window is not particularly convenient. For most clients, X provides a way to specify a window's location (and also its size) automatically—using an option when you run the command. A window's size and position is referred to as its *geometry* and you set these attributes using the -geometry option. The use of this option is discussed in the section "Window Geometry: Specifying Size and Location," later in this chapter.

Unfortunately the developers of *oclock* neglected to provide an easy way to remove it. For instructions on removing an *oclock* window, see Chapter 8, *Other Clients*.

Command-line Options

Most X clients accept two powerful and extremely useful options: the -geometry option, which allows you to specify the size and location of a window on the screen; and the -display option, which allows you to specify on which screen a window should be created. (Most commonly, you'd use the -display option to run a client on a remote machine and display the window locally, that is, on your display.)

The next few sections illustrate some typical uses of these important options. In explaining how to use them, we introduce some new, perhaps somewhat involved concepts (such as the way distances can be measured on your screen). Bear with us. We feel that you need to master the -geometry and -display options in order to begin to take advantage of the powers of X.

After explaining these options in detail, we'll briefly consider some of the characteristics you can specify using other common options.

Window Geometry: Specifying Size and Location

The command-line option to specify a window's size and location has the form:

    -geometry *geometry*

The -geometry option can be (and often is) abbreviated as -g, unless the client accepts another option that begins with "g."

The parameter to the geometry option (*geometry*), referred to as the "standard geometry string," has four numerical components, two specifying the window's dimensions and two specifying its location. The standard geometry string has the syntax:

    *width*x*height*±*xoff*±*yoff*

Obviously, the first half of the string provides the *width* and *height* of the window. Many application windows are measured in pixels. However, application developers are encouraged to use units that are meaningful in terms of the application. For example, *xterm*'s dimensions are measured in columns and rows of font characters. More precisely, an *xterm* window is some number of characters wide by some number of lines high (80 characters wide by 24 lines high by default).

The second half of the geometry string gives the location of the window relative to the horizontal and vertical edges of the screen. Imagining the screen to be a grid (where the upper-left corner is 0,0), *xoff* (x offset) and *yoff* (y offset) represent the x and y coordinates at which the window should be displayed. The x and y offsets are measured in pixels.

Many users may not be accustomed to thinking in terms of pixels. What exactly is a pixel? A pixel is the smallest element of a display surface that can be addressed by a program. You can think of a pixel as one of the tiny dots that make up a graphic image, such as that displayed by a terminal or a television. The number of dots (or pixels) per inch of screen determines the screen's *resolution*.* The more dots per inch, the higher the resolution (and, hypothetically, the sharper the picture).†

Since a pixel is a tiny unit of measurement, gauging sizes and distances in pixels will take some practice. For instance, what are the dimensions of your screen in pixels (its resolution)? The *xdpyinfo* client, described in Chapter 8, will tell you this; your workstation or X terminal documentation may also provide this information. *xdpyinfo* also tells you the screen's resolution in dots per inch.

Keep in mind that monitors can vary substantially. The Sun 19-inch monitor has dimensions of 1152×900 pixels and a resolution of 90×90 dots per inch (commonly abbreviated to dpi). The NCD 16-inch X terminal has dimensions of 1024×1024 pixels and a resolution of 106×106 dpi.

What are the implications of such hardware differences in specifying client geometry? The size and location of client windows is related to the size and resolution of your screen. For example, if you specify a window with dimensions of 125×125 pixels, it will appear somewhat larger on the Sun monitor than on the NCD X terminal.

So how do we use the geometry option to specify a window's size and location? First, be aware that you can specify any or all elements of the geometry string. Incomplete geometry specifications are compared to the application's default settings and missing elements are supplied by these values. All client windows have a default size. For example, if you run an *xterm* window with the geometry option and specify a location but no dimensions, the application default size of 80 characters by 24 lines is used.

If you don't specify the x and y coordinates at which to place a client window, the client may provide a default location; if the application doesn't provide a default and *mwm* is running, the window manager will automatically position the window in the upper-left quarter of the screen.

For now, let's just specify a window's location and let the size be the application default. The x and y offsets can be either positive or negative. If you specify positive offsets, you're positioning the left side and top side of the window. Negative offsets are interpreted differently. The possible values for the x and y offsets and their effects are shown in Table 3-1.

---

*Hardware manufacturers generally equate resolution with the screen's overall dimensions in pixels. Thus, you also need to know the actual physical size of the monitor (in inches) to determine the dots per inch. We find the dpi figure more useful.

†There are other factors that determine the "picture quality" of a monitor, including "depth," or the number of bits per pixel. Depth relates to how many colors a monitor can display. See "How Many Colors are Available on My Screen?" in Chapter 12, *Specifying Color*, for more information.

Table 3-1. Geometry Specification x and y Offsets

Offset Variables	Description
+*xoff*	A positive x offset specifies the distance by which the left edge of the window is offset from the left side of the display.
+*yoff*	A positive y offset specifies the distance by which the top edge of the window is offset from the top of the display.
-*xoff*	A negative x offset specifies the distance by which the right edge of the window is offset from the right side of the display.
-*yoff*	A negative y offset specifies the distance by which the bottom edge of the window is offset from the bottom of the display.

For example, the command line:

```
% xclock -geometry -10+10 &
```

places a clock of the default size in the upper-right corner of the display, 10 pixels from the right and top edges of the screen.

To place a window in any of the four corners of the screen, flush against its boundaries, use the following x and y offsets.

Offset Specification	Window Location
+0+0	Upper-left corner of the display.
+0-0	Lower-left corner of the display.
-0+0	Upper-right corner of the display.
-0-0	Lower-right corner of the display.

If you want a window placed away from one or both edges of the screen, the guesswork starts. How many pixels away from the left side of the screen? How many pixels down from the top? You'll have to experiment with placing some clients on your screen to get a better idea of x and y offsets.

It's actually a good idea to start some windows and move them around on your screen using the pointer. While you're dragging a window, check the x and y offsets displayed in the small box *mwm* places in the center of the screen. These coordinates are the positive x and y offsets of the window (i.e., the offsets relative to the upper-left corner of the screen). This method for gauging location is fairly reliable.*

---

*There seems to be a very slight delay between pointer motion and update to the *mwm* coordinate box. When you finish dragging the window, the last coordinates visible in the box may differ from the true coordinates by a pixel in either or both directions. But this variance is so trivial that you can supply the coordinates as part of the geometry string and come very close.

You can also place some windows in different places by dragging and then determine their geometry specifications using the *xwininfo* client, described in Chapter 8, *Other Clients*.

Now what about the size of a window? For *xterm*, the size of the window is measured in characters and lines (by default 80 characters by 24 lines). If you want to use a large VT100 window, say 100 characters wide by 30 lines long, you could use this geometry specification:

```
% xterm -geometry 100x30-0-0 &
```

This command creates a large *xterm* window in the lower-right corner of the screen, as illustrated by Figure 3-15.

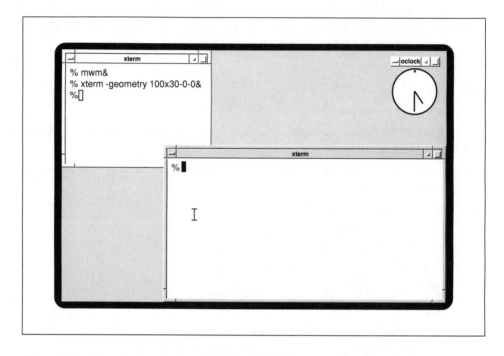

Figure 3-15. xterm window sized and positioned with the -geometry option

As stated previously, most of the standard clients (other than *xterm*) are measured in pixels. For example, *xclock* is 164 pixels square by default (exclusive of the *mwm* frame). A client's default dimensions may appear on its reference page in Part Three of this guide. However, you'll probably need to experiment with specifying sizes (as well as locations) on your display. (See Chapter 8, *Other Clients*, and the client reference page, for more about *xclock*.)

Be aware that the geometry option is not necessarily the only means available to specify window size and location. Several clients, including *xterm*, allow you to set the size and location of a window (and often its icon or an alternate window) using resource variables (in an *.Xresources* or other defaults file). We'll introduce some of the basics of specifying resources later in this chapter. See Chapter 11, *Setting Resources*, for more detailed instructions. See the appropriate client reference pages in Part Three of this guide for a complete list of available resources.

You should be aware that, as with all user preferences, you may not always get exactly what you ask for. Clients are designed to work with a window manager, which may have its own rules for window or icon size and placement. However, priority is always given to specific user requests, so you won't often be surprised.

Running a Client on Another Machine: Specifying the Display

We have yet to take advantage of X's networking capabilities. Remember that X allows you to run a client on a remote machine across a network. Generally, the results of a client program are displayed on a screen connected to the system where the client is running. However, if you are running a client on a remote system, you probably want to see the results on your own display (connected to a local server).

Running a client on a remote machine may give you access to different software, it may increase the efficiency of certain processes, or benefit you in a number of other ways. We discussed some of the advantages of running a client on a remote machine in Chapter 1, *An Introduction to the X Window System*. See the section "X Architecture Overview" for details.

But how does running a client on a remote system affect how you work with the X display? Once a client is running, it doesn't. You can display the application window on your own screen, enter input using your own keyboard and pointer, and read the client's output in the window on your screen—all while the actual client process occurs on another machine.

In order to run a client remotely and display its results locally, you must tell the client process where to display its window. For this purpose, X provides a command-line option: -display. Think of -display as a pointer to the physical display on which you want the window to appear. Like -geometry, the -display option is recognized by most X clients. The display option tells the client on which server to display results (i.e., create its window). The option has the syntax:

```
-display [host]:server[.screen]
```

The -display option can be abbreviated as -d, unless the client accepts another option that begins with "d."

The argument to the -display option is a three-component *display name*. The *host* specifies the machine on which to create the window, the *server* specifies the server number, and the *screen* specifies the screen number.

In this context, "host" refers to the Internet address name of the display hardware. It might be the name of a single-user workstation, an X terminal, a PC running an X server, or another hardware device.

"Server" refers to an instance of the X server program, which controls a single physical display. An X display may be composed of multiple screens, but the screens share one keyboard and pointer. Most workstations have only one keyboard and pointer and thus are classified as having only one display. Multiuser systems may have multiple independent displays, each running a server program. If one display exists, as in the case of most workstations and X terminals, it is numbered 0; if a machine has several displays, each is assigned a number (beginning with 0) when the X server for that display is started.

Similarly, if a single display is composed of multiple screens (sharing one keyboard and pointer), each screen is assigned a number (beginning with 0) when the server for that display is started. Multiple screen displays may be composed of two or more physical monitors. Alternatively, two screens might be defined as different ways of using the same physical monitor. For example, on our Sun-3/60 color workstation, screen 0 is color, and screen 1 is monochrome.* Each screen is the size of the monitor; you can only view one screen at a time. In practice, the two screens seem to be side by side: you can "scroll" between them by moving the pointer off either horizontal edge of the screen.

Note that the *server* parameter of the display option always begins with a colon (a double colon after a DECnet node†), and that the *screen* parameter always begins with a period. If the host is omitted or is specified as unix, the local machine is assumed. If the screen is omitted, screen 0 is assumed.

Although much of the current X Window System documentation suggests that any of the parameters to the -display option can be omitted and will default to the local node, server and screen 0, respectively, we have not found this to be true. In our experience, only the *host* and *screen* parameters (and the period preceding *screen*) can be omitted. The colon and *server* are necessary in all circumstances.

The DISPLAY Environment Variable

Technically speaking, the -display option allows you to override the contents of the DISPLAY environment variable, which stores the display name on UNIX systems. On UNIX systems, the display name is stored in the DISPLAY environment variable. Clients running on the local system access this variable to determine which physical display to connect to (for most clients, "connecting" is equivalent to opening a window). The DISPLAY variable is set automatically by *xinit* or *xdm* when you log in and the *xterm* terminal emulator inherits it. Thus it is set when you start X and conveyed to the first *xterm* window.

For most single-user systems, such as workstations, the X startup program sets the server and screen numbers to 0 and omits a hostname (the local host is assumed). (Prior to Release 5, in some cases the startup program sets the hostname to "unix," a generic name, which also defaults to the local host.) If you are working on a single-user system and run all processes on it, you don't have to deal with setting the display. Clients running locally access the DISPLAY variable and open windows on a display connected to the local host.

If you are using an X terminal, it should already be configured so that the DISPLAY variable is set properly when you log on to the local host. Again, if you run all process on the local machine (to which your terminal is connected), you don't have to deal with specifying the display. Clients will access the DISPLAY variable and open windows on your X terminal screen.

---

*See Volume Eight, *X Window System Administrator's Guide*, to learn how to configure your Sun workstation to use dual frame buffers.

†By convention, DECnet node names end with a colon.

Complications arise when you want to run a process on a remote machine and display the results locally. A client running on a remote machine does not have access to the DISPLAY variable, which is stored in the local shell. You can use the -display option to specify which display the client should access.

Using –display

Suppose you're using a single display workstation and the display also has only one screen. The hostname of the workstation is *kansas*. In order to tell a client to connect to a display, you must identify it by its unique name on the network. (You cannot identify your display by the shorthand setting given to it by the X startup program—unix:0.0, :0.0 or some variation.) Let's assume that the complete display name for the workstation *kansas* is:

    kansas:0.0

Now let's say you want to run an *xterm* window on a faster system—let's call it *oz*—on your network. In order to run an *xterm* on *oz* but display the window on your screen connected to *kansas* (the local server), you would run the *xterm* command using a remote shell* (*rsh*):

    % rsh oz xterm -display kansas:0.0 &

The *xterm* process runs on *oz*, but you've directed the client to use the display and screen numbered 0 on *kansas*, your local system. Notice that kansas:0.0 is the complete display name. Hypothetically, if the workstation (*kansas*) has only one screen or it has multiple screens but you want to specify screen 0, you can omit the screen number and the preceding period (.0).

Keep in mind that for this process to succeed, the remote client (running on *oz*) must have permission to "open" the local display (on *kansas*). (See "Server Access Control" in Appendix A, *Managing Your Environment*, and the *xhost* reference page in Part Three of this guide, for more information.) If *oz* has not been granted access to the server running on *kansas*, the window will not be opened, and you may also get an error message similar to:

    Error: Can't Open display

If your command fails, try entering the command:

    % xhost +

in an *xterm* window running on your display. Then run the remote shell (*rsh*) again. If that works, consult your system administrator or Volume Eight, *X Window System Administrator's Guide*, to learn how to set up access control properly.

The following command illustrates a common mistake:

    % rsh oz xterm &

---

*The command to run the remote process might be different depending on the available networking software. Ask your system administrator for the proper command.

If you try to run a client using a remote shell and forget to direct the client to create its window on your own display, the window will not be displayed and you'll get an error message stating that the display cannot be opened.

If you're using an X terminal, it will have a name unique to the terminal (e.g., ncd8), which should be used as the *host* component of the -display argument. You should not use the name of the system to which the terminal is connected.

Suppose we have a terminal with the full display name:

    ncd8:0.0

(connected to *kansas*) and we want to run an *xterm* on *oz*. The command:

    % rsh oz xterm -display ncd8:0.0 &

will open the window on our X terminal.

In addition to specifying a local display, if permissions allow you can also use the display option to open a window on someone else's display. You might want to display a window on another user's screen for instructional purposes. Multiuser systems can even be set up to allow teachers to display educational material simultaneously to several students, each using an X display of some sort. And, of course, you might want to display a window on a friend's screen, just for the fun of it. (The security problems that allow both innocent pranks like this, as well as more serious breaches, are described in Volume Eight, *X Window System Administrator's Guide*.)

If you're working on *kansas* and you want to open an *xterm* window on the first display connected to *oz*, you could use the command:

    % xterm -display oz:0.0 &

Note that you can only open a window on another display if the server running that display permits the client program access. (Access must be granted from the remote server, perhaps using *xhost*.) If *oz* does not allow *kansas* access, this command will fail and an error message will indicate that the display cannot be opened.

Once You Run a Remote xterm Using –display

A less than obvious repercussion of using -display to run a remote *xterm* is that the option sets the DISPLAY variable for the new *xterm* window—and that DISPLAY setting is passed on to all child processes of the client. Therefore, once you run an *xterm* on a remote system and correctly specify your own display, you can run any number of clients from that *xterm* and they will all be displayed on your screen automatically (no -display option is necessary).

In one of the examples in the preceding section, we ran an *xterm* on the remote system *oz*, specifying the local display kansas:0.0 with the -display option. To query the contents of the DISPLAY variable in the resulting *xterm* (under the C shell), use the command:

    % echo $DISPLAY

The system should echo:

```
kansas:0.0
```

verifying that the display name has been passed to the DISPLAY variable in the new *xterm* window. You can then run any client you want on *oz* by entering the command in this *xterm* window and the window will automatically be displayed on `kansas:0.0`. The DISPLAY setting will also be passed to any children of *this* process as well, and will be propagated for any number of "generations."

Logging In to a Remote System

If you log in to a remote UNIX system using *rlogin* (or *telnet*) in an *xterm* window, it's a good idea to set the DISPLAY variable in the new shell to reflect your local display. Then if you run a client process from this window, the new window will be placed on your local display and the DISPLAY setting will be passed on to all child processes.

When you set the DISPLAY variable from the command line, the syntax varies depending on the UNIX shell running. The following command sets the variable under the C shell.

```
% setenv DISPLAY kansas:0.0
```

To set the DISPLAY variable under the Bourne shell, use:

```
$ DISPLAY=kansas:0.0; export DISPLAY
```

Monitoring the Load on a Remote System

A client you may wish to run on another machine is *xload*, which is used to keep track of the system load average. By default, *xload* polls the system for the load average at ten-second intervals and displays the results in a simple histogram.

If you are running processes on more than one machine, it's useful to gauge the level of activity on the systems in question. This information should help you judge when to start processes and monitor how your processes are impacting system resources.

Suppose you're running clients both on the local machine *kansas* and on the remote machine *oz*. On the local display, you can have two *xload* windows, one showing activity on *kansas* and another showing activity on *oz*.

To create an *xload* window monitoring activity on *kansas*, use the command:

```
% xload &
```

Once the *xload* window is created, move it to a convenient location on the screen.

Then run an *xload* process on *oz* using a remote shell and display the results in a window on *kansas*:

```
% rsh oz xload -display kansas:0.0 &
```

The display option tells *xload* to create its window on the local display (*kansas*). Again, move the window using the pointer.

Figure 3-16 shows the resulting *kansas* display: two *xload* windows—the top window monitoring activity on the local system and the bottom one monitoring activity on the remote system.

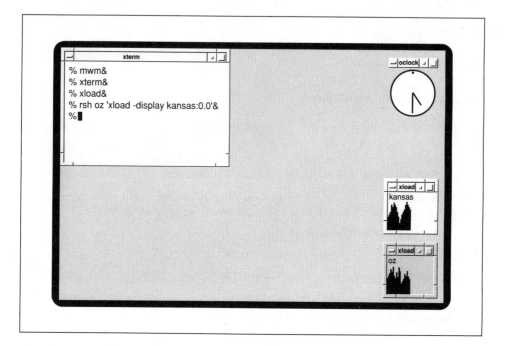

Figure 3-16. Monitoring activity on two systems with xload

Putting It All Together

Now that we've learned something about the tools of the display, how to size and position windows, and run remote processes, let's try to set up a useful working display.

Suppose we're using a Sun 3/60 workstation with the hostname *jersey*. The workstation has a single display with two screens: screen 0 is color and screen 1 is black and white. Once X and the window manager* are running, we might set up the display using the following commands.

---

*Note that you should run *mwm* with the -multiscreens option to have the program manage all screens on the display. If you start *mwm* without this option, it only manages screen 0. In this case, you can either kill and restart it with -multiscreens or run another instance of it on screen 1.

First, run an *xterm* on a more powerful remote system called *manhattan* and place it on screen 0 of *jersey*.

```
% rsh manhattan xterm -geometry +0-0 -display jersey:0.0 &
```

Run *xload* windows on both *jersey* and *manhattan* to monitor loads on these systems. Again, place the windows on *jersey*'s color screen in convenient locations.

```
% xload -geometry -10-200 &
```

```
% rsh manhattan xload -geometry -10-20 -display jersey:0.0 &
```

Run another *xterm* window on *jersey*.

```
% xterm -geometry +50-0 &
```

Then iconify the login *xterm* window so that you don't inadvertently kill it (and shut down X in the bargain). Remember: to iconify a window place the pointer on the Minimize command button on the window's frame and click the first button. (See "Converting a Window to an Icon" earlier in this chapter.)

Run an *oclock*.

```
% oclock -geometry +5+5 &
```

Figure 3-17 shows the *jersey* display, screen 0: a fairly useful layout.

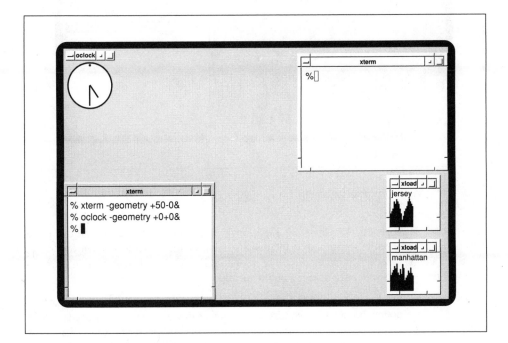

Figure 3-17. A working display, screen 0

You might also place client windows on the workstation's alternate screen, the black and white screen numbered 1. By default, windows are always placed on screen 0 but you can place a client window on screen 1 by specifying the screen number in the -display option when starting the client. For instance, each of the following commands places an *xterm* window on screen 1.

```
% xterm -display jersey:0.1 &
```

```
% rsh manhattan xterm -geometry -0-0 -display jersey:0.1 &
```

Figure 3-18 illustrates screen 1.

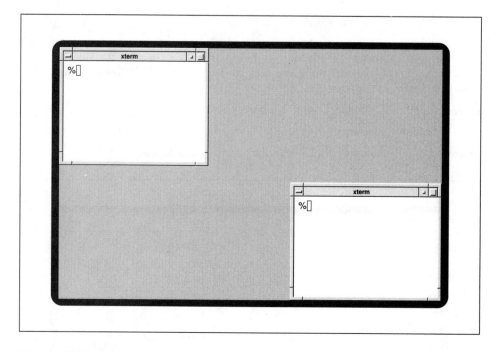

Figure 3-18. A working display, screen 1

As we'll see in Appendix A, *Managing Your Environment*, on most systems you can place the commands you run to set up your display in a special file that is invoked when you log in. Once this file (usually called either *.xinitrc* or *.xsession*) is in place, when you log in your display will be set up to your specifications automatically.

Notice that the commands we used to set up *jersey* illustrate the power of the -geometry and -display options to create a working environment that suits individual needs. However, these options barely hint at the number of features you can specify for each client. The following section introduces some principles of client customization. Part Two of this guide examines customization in depth.

Customizing a Program

In a sense, command-line options allow you to customize one program. We've already seen how to use the -geometry and -display options, which are accepted by most clients. Chapter 10, *Command-line Options*, describes some of the other options accepted by most of the standard clients. These options set window features such as:

- The font in which text is displayed.

- The background color.

- The foreground color (such as the color of text).

- The text displayed in the title area.

- The text of an icon label.

Many clients also accept a large number of application-specific options (listed on the reference page for each client in Part Three of this guide). Using a combination of standard and application-specific options, you can tailor a client to look and behave in ways that better suit your needs.

Like most clients, *xclock* accepts a variety of options. Some of *xclock*'s options are intended to enhance the clock display aesthetically and some to affect its operation. Taking a look at a few of *xclock*'s options should give you a better idea of the flexibility of X.

The following command line runs a custom *xclock* display:

```
% xclock -hd green -hl royalblue -bg lightblue -fg royalblue -update 1 -chime &
```

As you can see, these specifications are intended for a color monitor. (X is highly flexible in the use of color. See Chapter 12, *Specifying Color*, for more information.) The -hd option sets the color of the clock's hands to green. The -hl option provides even more detail, specifying the color of the outline of the hands as royal blue. -bg and -fg are two of the options accepted by most clients; they set the window's background and foreground color, in this case to light blue and royal blue, respectively.

The -update option takes as its argument the frequency in seconds at which the time on the clock should be updated. We've specified that the time be updated at one second intervals. Thus a second hand (also green) will be added to the *xclock* display. (The *xclock* reference page in Part Three of this guide specifies that a second hand is added if -update is given an argument of less than 30 seconds.)

The -chime option specifies that the keyboard bell will ring once on the half hour and twice on the hour.

These options create a somewhat fancy *xclock* display. You might or might not want to use so many options, but these and several more are available.

By default, *xclock* displays a traditional clock face (an analog clock). You can create a digital *xclock* using the following option:

```
% xclock -digital &
```

The digital *xclock* is pictured in Figure 3-19.

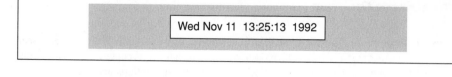

Wed Nov 11 13:25:13 1992

Figure 3-19. Digital xclock display

Logically, the −hd and −hl options, which set the color of the clock hands, are only valid with the analog (default) *xclock*. For a complete list of options, see the *xclock* reference page in Part Three of this guide.

Command-line options override the default characteristics of a client for the *single client process*. Traditional UNIX applications rely on command-line options to allow users to customize the way they work. X also offers many command-line options, but these options have some limitations and liabilities.

First, the number of client features that can be controlled by command line options is limited. Most applications have many more customizable features than their command-line options indicate. Actually, a client can have so many customizable features that typing a command line to set them all would be impractical. And if you generally use the same options with a client, it is tedious (and a waste of time) to type the options each time you run the program.

X offers an alternative to customizing a single client process on the command line. You can specify default characteristics for a client using variables called *resources*.

Customizing the X Environment

Command-line options allow you to customize one instance of a client program. In addition, X provides a mechanism that allows you to specify characteristics that take effect *every* time you run a client. Almost every feature of a client program can be controlled using a variable called a *resource*. You can change the behavior or appearance of a program by changing the *value* associated with a resource variable. (In some cases, a resource variable controls the same characteristic as a command-line option. However, while the option specifies a characteristic for the single client process being invoked, a resource variable makes the characteristic the program default.)

You generally place resource specifications in a file in your home directory. (The file can have any name, but is often called *.Xresources* or *.Xdefaults*.) The resources you specify are one of several factors that affect the appearance and behavior of a client.

By default, the way a client looks and behaves is determined by the program code, and in some cases, by a system-wide file of *application defaults*. Several clients have application defaults files that determine certain client features.* Within an application defaults file, defaults are set using resources. The resources specified in a client's application defaults files are usually just a subset of a greater number of resources that can be set.

If the characteristics you set in your own resources file already have system-wide application defaults, your own settings take precedence. Keep in mind, however, that command-line options override both your own defaults and any system-wide defaults for the single client process.

To make your resource specifications available to all clients, X provides a program called *xrdb*, the X resource database manager. *xrdb* stores resources directly in the server where they are accessible to all clients, regardless of the machine the clients are running on.

The basic syntax of a resource specification is fairly simple. Each client recognizes certain resource variables that can be assigned a value. The variables for each client are listed on its reference page in Part Three of this guide.

A resource definition file is basically a two-column list, where each line specifies a different resource. The simplest resource definition line has the name of the client, followed by an asterisk, and the name of the variable, followed by a colon, in the left column. The right column (separated from the left by a tab or whitespace) contains the value of the resource variable.

```
client*variable:    value
```

The following example shows five simple resource specifications for the *xclock* client. These particular resources specify the same characteristics as the command-line options we used to create the green and blue *xclock* in the preceding section.

Example 3-1. Resources to create a custom xclock

```
xclock*hands:  green
xclock*highlight:  royalblue
xclock*background:  lightblue
xclock*foreground:  royalblue
xclock*update:  1
xclock*chime:  true
```

To set up your environment so that these characteristics apply each time you run *xclock*, you would perform the following steps:

1. In your home directory, create a file containing the resources listed in Example 3-1. Name the file *.Xresources*. (A resource file can actually have any name, but is often called *.Xresources* or *.Xdefaults*.)

---

*For *xterm*, the application defaults specify such things as the labels for menu items, the fonts used to display menu items, and the shape of the pointer when it's in an *xterm* window.

Application defaults files generally reside in the directory */usr/lib/X11/app-defaults* and are named for the client application. In describing the appearance and behavior of clients in this guide, we assume all of the standard application defaults files are present on your system and accessible by the client programs. If, by some chance, a client's application defaults file has been edited or removed from your system, the client may not look or behave exactly as we describe it. If a client application appears substantially different than depicted in this guide, you may be using a different version of the program or the application defaults may be different. Consult your system administrator.

2. Load the resources into the server by entering the following command in an *xterm* window:

```
% xrdb -load .Xresources
```

Then each time you run *xclock* without options (for the remainder of that login session), the window will reflect the new defaults.

You should load resources using *xrdb* every time you log in. In Appendix A, *Managing Your Environment*, we'll describe how to automate this process using a special startup script, which also opens the client windows you want on your display.

If you want to run an application with different characteristics (colors, update frequency, etc.) from the defaults, use the appropriate command line options to override the resource specifications.

Resource specifications can be much more complicated than our samples suggest. For applications written with a toolkit (such as the X Toolkit or the Open Software Foundation's Motif Toolkit), X allows you to specify different characteristics for individual components, or *widgets*, within the application. Typical widgets create graphical features such as menus, command buttons, dialog boxes, and scrollbars. Within most toolkit applications is a fairly complex widget hierarchy—widgets exist within widgets (e.g., a command button within a dialog box).

Resource naming syntax can parallel the widget hierarchy within an application. For instance, you might set different background colors for different command buttons and specify still another background color for the dialog box that encloses them. In such cases, the actual widget names are used within the resource specification. Chapter 11, *Setting Resources*, explains the resource naming syntax in greater detail and outlines the rules governing the precedence of resources. It also explains how to use the *editres* program to examine a (standard) client's widget hierarchy and set resources accordingly.

Where to Go from Here

There are many useful client programs supplied with the X Window System. Details of how to use one of the most important clients, the *xterm* terminal emulator, are provided in Chapter 5. Clients to list and display fonts are described in Chapter 6, *Font Specification*. Chapter 6 also describes the X font naming conventions and various ways to specify fonts on the command line (and in resource files). Chapter 7 describes several *Graphics Utilities* available with X. An overview and tutorial for other standard clients and instructions on using certain public domain clients are provided in Chapter 8, *Other Clients*. Chapter 9, *Working with Motif Applications*, gives instructions on using Motif applications. All clients are described in detail in a reference page format in Part Three of this guide.

We've introduced some basic operations you can perform using the *mwm* window manager. For instructions on performing additional window manager operations, such as lowering a window, read Chapter 4, *More about the mwm Window Manager*. You can then go on to read more about *xterm* in Chapter 5 and about some of the other standard clients in Chapters 6 through 8.

4

More About the mwm
Window Manager

This chapter describes additional functions you can perform using the Motif window manager, mwm.

In This Chapter:

4
More About the mwm Window Manager

Chapter 2, *Getting Started*, describes how to tell if *mwm* is running on your display and how to start it if you need to. Chapter 3, *Working in the X Environment*, describes some of *mwm*'s most basic and useful capabilities, which you can perform using the pointer on a window's frame. It explains how to iconify, maximize, raise, move, resize, and close windows, how to move icons, and how to convert icons back to windows.

The current chapter describes how to perform some of these window management functions in alternative ways and also describes some additional functions, including:

* Creating additional *xterm* windows.

* Lowering windows (moving them to the back of others).

* Shuffling windows on the display.

* Refreshing your screen.

* Restarting the window manager.

The Motif window manager allows you to invoke window management functions in a variety of ways:

* Using the window "frame" and various features available on it: the Minimize (iconify) button, Maximize button, title area, Window Menu, etc.

* Using the Root Menu.

* Using keyboard keys, pointer buttons, and key and button combinations.

In this chapter, we'll review some basics about focusing input to a window or icon and consider how window management functions rely on focus being directed properly. Then we'll take a closer look at the Window Menu and Root Menu.

As we'll see, some window management functions can be performed using keyboard shortcuts. These shortcuts involve using special keys, commonly called modifier keys. Before considering window management functions, we'll take a brief look at the special keys significant to X.

Keep in mind that *mwm* is very flexible. In Chapter 13, we'll consider how to customize various features of the window manager. Perhaps the most useful customization that can be performed involves selecting a keyboard focus policy, either pointer focus or click-to-type (also

mwm Manager

referred to as *explicit*) focus. By default, *mwm* uses click-to-type focus. Keyboard focus is described in Chapter 1.

The current chapter is intended primarily for those using Version 1.2 of *mwm*. (Unlike the 1.1 version, *mwm* 1.2 is compatible with Release 5 of X.) If *mwm* has been customized at your site or you are running a different version, the principles should be basically the same, but the window management functions may be invoked in different ways. From time to time, we'll mention how commands or functionality might vary, depending on the version of *mwm*.

Using Special Keys

Undoubtedly you know the basics of using a keyboard. However, X interprets certain keys somewhat differently than the labels on the keys would indicate.

Most workstations have a number of "modifier" keys, so-called because they modify the action of other keys. Generally these keys are used to invoke commands of some sort, such as window manager functions.

Three of these modifier keys should be familiar to any user of a standard ASCII terminal or a personal computer—Shift, Caps Lock, and Control. However, many workstations have additional modifier keys as well. A PC has an "Alt" key, a Macintosh™ has a "fan" key, a Sony workstation has keys named "Nfer" and "Xfer," and certain model Sun workstations have three additional modifier keys, labeled "Left," "Right," and "Alternate."

Because X clients are designed to run on many different workstations, with different keyboards, it is difficult to assign functions to special keys on the keyboard. A developer can't count on the same key always being present!

For this reason, many X clients make use of "logical" modifier keynames, which can be mapped by the user to any actual key on the keyboard.

Up to eight separate modifier keys can be defined. The most commonly used (after Shift, Caps Lock, and Control) has the logical keyname "Meta."

We'll talk at length about this subject in Chapter 14, *Setup Clients*, but we wanted to warn you here. When we talk later in this chapter about pressing the "Meta" key, you should be aware that there is not likely to be a physical key on the keyboard with that name. For example, on one workstation, the Meta key might be labeled "Alt" and, on another, "Funct." And as we'll show in Chapter 14, you can choose any key you want to act as the Meta key.

Unfortunately, X provides no easy way to find out which key on your keyboard has been assigned to be the Meta key. When you need to know, please turn to the discussion of key mapping in Chapter 14, for information on how you can find out.

Input Focus and the Window Manager

As explained in Chapter 3, the default operation of *mwm* is that you select the window to receive input (the active window) by clicking the first pointer button anywhere within the window. This focus policy is called click-to-type, or explicit. Whether *mwm* is started automatically or you started it by typing in an *xterm* window, you must then click in a window in order to enter text.

Once you focus input to a window, all text typed is interpreted by that client, regardless of where you move the pointer. In the case of *xterm* and similar clients, the text appears in the window. Other clients might simply interpret the keystrokes as possible commands. Some clients, such as *xclock*, do not recognize keyboard input at all. Regardless of the client, certain keystrokes might also be interpreted as commands to the window manager to effect changes on the focus window. In order to type in or issue commands to affect another window, you must transfer focus to that window by clicking the first pointer button within it. In Chapter 13, *Customizing mwm*, we'll describe how to make the keyboard focus follow pointer movement.

Also keep in mind that in order to manage a window using the various methods provided by *mwm*, the window must have the input focus. Since most actions you'll perform involve placing the pointer somewhere on the frame and performing some kind of pointer action (such as clicking, pressing, releasing, etc.), controlling a window using the frame selects that window to receive the input focus at the same time.

However, before invoking certain window management functions, you must first select a focus window (or icon). For example, each Window Menu item has a keyboard shortcut. If you want to affect a window using a keyboard shortcut, you must *first* select it as the focus window by clicking on it with the pointer—otherwise the keyboard shortcut will affect the current focus window. This is probably the only circumstance in which you would select a window that doesn't accept keyboard input (such as *xclock*) as the focus window. Keyboard shortcuts for Window Menu functions are described in "Using the Window Menu."

As we've seen, when you focus input on a window, the window frame changes color. The color of the active window's frame depends on the version of *mwm* you are running and the color resources for your system. In some versions, be aware that the black window frame of non-active windows obscures the titlebar text, which also appears in black. Only the title of the active window is visible in these cases.

If you are working with a stack of windows that overlap, selecting a window as the active window automatically raises that window to the top of the stack. This behavior is controlled by an *mwm* resource variable called `focusAutoRaise`, which is true by default when click-to-type focus is in effect. (This resource is described in Chapter 13, *Customizing mwm*.) If the focus window is killed or converted to an icon, the focus switches back to the window that previously had it.

Focusing Input on an Icon

Though it may not be immediately obvious, you can select an iconified window to receive the input focus. You direct input to an icon by placing the pointer on it and clicking the first button. As illustrated in Chapter 3, *Working in the X Environment*, this action displays an *mwm* menu (the Window Menu) over the icon. (See Figure 3-4.)

The icon label also becomes wider and the label and the frame surrounding the icon are highlighted. These changes indicate that the icon has the input focus. Even after the menu is removed, the label will remain wider and the border highlighted (that is, the icon will retain the focus), until you direct focus to another window or icon.

When an icon has the input focus, the application window the icon represents will not interpret keystrokes. However, the window manager will interpret relevant keystrokes as commands. For instance, you need to focus input to an icon in order to invoke a Window Menu item on it using the item's keyboard shortcut. Keyboard shortcuts for Window Menu functions are described in "Using the Window Menu on Icons" later in this chapter.

Changing the Stacking Order with Keystrokes

Regardless of the focus policy in effect (either pointer focus or the default click-to-type), you can shuffle windows on the display using the following key combinations.

Table 4-1. Key Combinations to Change the Stacking Order

Key Combination	Action
Meta-Escape	Move top window to bottom of stack.
Meta-Shift-Escape	Move bottom window to top of stack.

The only difference between these keystroke combinations is the direction in which they reorder the windows.

The key combination Meta-Escape moves the window currently at the top of the stack to the bottom. (The second highest window becomes the top window.)

The key combination Meta-Shift-Escape moves the window currently at the top and given the input focus. (The second lowest window becomes the bottom window.)

As explained previously, there is probably no key labeled "Meta" on your keyboard. Meta is a logical keyname recognized by X which is mapped to a physical key. Also be aware that, in most cases, *mwm* considers the Meta key and the Alt key interchangeable. (Alt is another logical keyname that may be mapped to a key with another label.) Thus, the actions in Table 4-1 should also work if you substitute Alt for Meta. For help in locating the Meta and Alt keys on your keyboard, see the discussion of *xmodmap* in Chapter 14, *Setup Clients*.

Note that changing the stacking order in this way does not affect which window has the input focus. If you're using click-to-type (i.e., explicit) focus, you can also transfer focus using keystrokes, as we'll see in the next section.

Perhaps somewhat less relevant to the average user is a client's "local" stacking order. Since many client applications provide transient subwindows (dialog boxes, help windows, etc.), a client itself can be thought to have a stacking order. By default, when you raise or lower a window, all associated subwindows are moved with the primary application window and remain on top of it. However, version 1.2 of *mwm* provides mechanisms to affect how the local stacking order is affected when the main window is shuffled. For more information, see the "Actions" f.lower, f.raise, and f.raise_lower on the *mwm* reference page in Part Three of this guide.

Transferring (Explicit) Focus with Keystrokes

If you are running the default version of *mwm* (which assumes click-to-type focus and focusAutoRaise), you can cause the focus to circulate from window to window (including iconified windows) within the stack using any of the key combinations that appear in Table 4-2.

Table 4-2. Key Combinations to Change Focus Window

Key Combination	Action
Meta-Tab	Move focus to next window in stack.
Meta-Shift-Tab	Move focus to previous window in stack.

The key combination Meta-Tab circulates the focus from the current top of the stack to the bottom. What this means is that the top window in the stack is moved to the bottom; the second highest window becomes the top window and gets the input focus.

The key combination Meta-Shift-Tab circulates the focus from the current bottom of the stack to the top. In other words, the lowest window in the stack is moved to the top and given the input focus.

Again, note that the key that performs the "Meta" function varies from keyboard to keyboard. Remember also that in most cases, *mwm* considers the Meta key and the Alt key interchangeable. Thus, the actions in Table 4-2 should also work if you substitute Alt for Meta. For help in locating the Meta and Alt keys on your keyboard, see the discussion of *xmodmap* in Chapter 14, *Setup Clients*.

mwm's ability to transfer focus from window to window according to keystrokes is important to some Motif applications. The Motif Toolkit supports the building of applications that use several subwindows, each with a different, albeit related, purpose. (Such applications can be described as *form-based*.) A form-based Motif application can be built that allows users to move among the subwindows using keystrokes.

mwm Manager

Some of the more common elements of Motif applications are described in Chapter 9, *Working with Motif Applications*.

What To Do if mwm Dies and the Focus Is Lost

If the *mwm* process dies, the focus policy should revert to pointer focus. To restart the window manager, you should simply be able to move the pointer into an *xterm* window and enter the *mwm* command. However, *mwm* has a bug that makes it possible to lose the focus entirely when the window manager dies. Obviously, restarting the window manager in such a situation is problematic. If *mwm* dies and no window retains the focus, you can restore focus to an *xterm* window using the Secure Keyboard item of the client's Main Options menu. See Chapter 5, *The xterm Terminal Emulator*, for details.

A Quick Review of Frame Features

If you're comfortable with managing windows using the frame, skip this section and go on to "Using the Window Menu."

When *mwm* starts up, it places a frame around every window on the screen. The frame has several components: a titlebar, featuring the name of the application (in the *title area*) and three command buttons (Maximize, Minimize, and Window Menu); and an outer border that permits resizing of the window.

In Chapter 3, *Working in the X Environment*, we demonstrated the window management functions you can perform using the pointer on the *mwm* frame, which appears surrounding an *xterm* window in Figure 4-1.

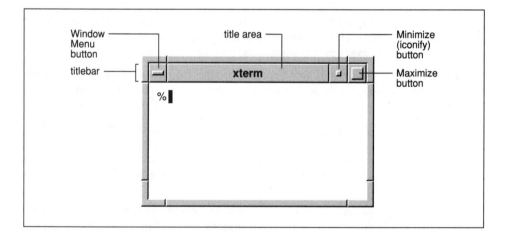

Figure 4-1. An xterm window running with the Motif window manager

Using the pointer on various parts of the frame, you can:

- Iconify the window, by clicking the first pointer button on the Minimize command button, the lefthand button in the upper-right corner of the frame (decorated with the smaller square). To convert an icon back to a window, double-click on the icon with the first pointer button.

- Maximize the window (convert it to the maximum size allowed by the client, often root window size), by clicking the first pointer button on the Maximize command button. The Maximize button is to the right of the Minimize button and is decorated with the larger square. To convert the window back to its original size, click on the Maximize button again.

- Raise a window, by clicking the first pointer button on any part of the window frame, except the three command buttons (Minimize, Maximize, and Window Menu). To raise an icon, click the first pointer button on it. This action also posts the Window Menu over the icon. (Remove the menu by clicking somewhere off the menu.) When you are using explicit (click-to-type) focus, raising also focuses input.

- Move the window, by pressing and holding down the first pointer button on any part of the title area (except the command buttons), dragging the window outline to a new location, and releasing the pointer button. (A small box in the center of the screen displays the changing coordinates.) To move an icon, place the pointer on the icon, press and hold down the first pointer button, drag the icon outline to a new location, and release the pointer button.

- Resize the window, by moving the pointer into one of the resize borders or corners, pressing and holding the first pointer button, and dragging the border or corner in the direction you want. A window outline tracks the resize operation. Release the pointer button to redraw the window in the selected dimensions.

- Close the window, by double-clicking the first pointer button on the Window Menu command button (in the upper-left corner of the frame). See the section on *xkill* in Chapter 8, *Other Clients*, for a discussion of the liabilities of "killing" a client.

All of these items can also be invoked using Window Menu items or keyboard shortcuts for these items. The Window Menu also provides an additional item to Lower a window or icon. Let's take a look at the Window Menu, see how to display it, and consider the various ways to invoke its functions. Then we'll look at pointer commands and menu items to manage icons. Finally, we'll consider those functions available on *mwm*'s Root Menu.

Using the Window Menu

The command button on the left side of the titlebar is used to bring up the Window Menu, which provides seven items that can be used to manage the window and its icon. The next few sections describe how to bring up the Window Menu and invoke its various functions.

As we saw in Chapter 3, this command button also has another function. Double-clicking the first pointer button on the Window Menu command button kills the client program and closes the window. See *xkill* in Chapter 8, *Other Clients*, for a discussion of the hazards of this action.

Though it is not readily apparent, the Window Menu can actually be displayed from either a window or an icon. As we'll see, certain menu functions apply only to one or the other. This section describes using the Window Menu to perform various management functions on a window. (The sections "Pointer Commands to Manage Icons" and "Using the Windown Menu on Icons," later in this chapter, describe the use of Window Menu items, pointer commands, and other shortcuts on icons.)

The Window Menu command button is in the upper-left corner of the window frame and is identified by a short horizontal bar in its center. You can display the Window Menu from a window by moving the pointer to the command button and either:

- Clicking the first pointer button.

- Pressing and holding down the first pointer button.

If you've clicked the first pointer button to display the menu (the easier method), the first item that is available for selection is highlighted by a box. Figure 4-2 shows the default Window Menu, which has been displayed by clicking the first pointer button in the menu command button.

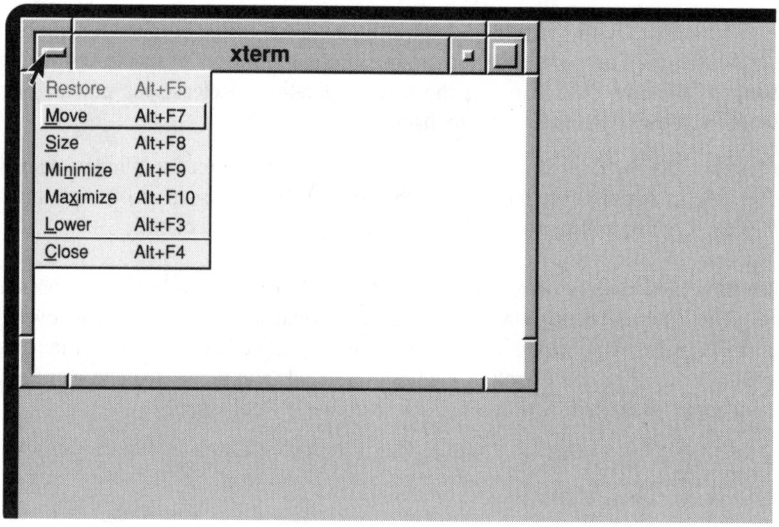

Figure 4-2. The Window Menu

You can also display the Window Menu by placing the pointer anywhere on the frame (other than the command buttons) and pressing and holding down the third button. The following keyboard shortcuts display the menu on the focus window: Shift-Escape or Meta-space.*

The function performed by each of the Window Menu items is fairly obvious. Six of the seven menu items (all but Lower) allow you to perform functions that can also be performed by simple pointer actions on the *mwm* window frame. Since effecting changes on a window using the frame is very simple and accessible, you will probably not use the Window Menu often.

You may want to use the menu to Lower a window (to the bottom of the stack), since this function cannot be performed by a simple pointer action on the frame. (If you learn the keyboard shortcut for this menu item, explained later in this section, you may not need the Window Menu to manage windows at all. You might also customize the *.mwmrc* file to include a key/button combination to lower a window. See Chapter 13 for details.) You may find the menu more helpful in managing icons, as described later in this chapter.

In any case, learning how to invoke the Window Menu items is helpful in orienting yourself within the Motif environment.

Note that if your keyboard does not have an F10 function key, the Maximize item will not appear on the Window Menu without some customization. A possible workaround is to edit the line defining the Maximize menu item in your *.mwmrc* file. Changing F10 to F2 will suffice in most cases. See Chapter 13, *Customizing mwm*, for information about the *.mwmrc* file.

Invoking Window Menu Items

Let's take another look at the Window Menu in Figure 4-2. Notice that the first item available for selection (indicated by the surrounding box) is Move. The first item on the menu, Restore, is used to change an icon back into a window or a maximized window back to its normal size; therefore, it is not useful at this time. The fact that Restore is not selectable is indicated by the fact that it appears in a lighter typeface.

Notice also that one letter of each menu item is underlined. This letter represents a unique abbreviation for the menu item, called a *mnemonic*, which can be used to select the item (when the menu is posted).

A keyboard shortcut follows each command. These shortcuts are known as *accelerators* because they facilitate the action. The keyboard accelerators allow you to perform all of the functions without having to display the menu (though they also work while the menu is displayed). To invoke an action using an accelerator, the window must have the input focus.

All of the keyboard accelerators for the menu items involve the Alt key and a function key. Remember that *mwm* considers the Alt and Meta keys to be equivalent. What this boils down to is that, for any of the shortcuts, you can substitute Meta for Alt.

---

*When a menu is displayed using a key or key combination, the same keystroke(s) can be used to remove it. Thus, Shift-Escape and Meta-space will also toggle the Window Menu off.

Once the Window Menu is displayed, you can select an item in the following ways:

- If you displayed the menu by pressing and holding down the first pointer button, drag the pointer down the menu to the desired item and release the first button.

- If you displayed the menu by clicking the first pointer button, either:

  — Move the pointer onto the item and click the first button.

  — Type the unique abbreviation or mnemonic (the underlined letter). (Though several of the abbreviations are capital letters, you should type the lowercase equivalent.)

  — Type the accelerator key combination. (Though these are intended to save you the trouble of displaying the menu, they also work when it is displayed.)

  — To select the boxed item (the first available for selection), you can alternatively press either the Return key or the space bar.

To remove the menu without making a selection, move the pointer off of the menu and release or click the first pointer button, as appropriate.

Most items work similarly to the comparable functions performed using the pointer on the frame. The primary difference relates to moving or resizing a window. Using the frame, you press and hold down a pointer button, move the pointer, and release the button to complete the action. Once you invoke the Move or Size item from the Window Menu (by any of the methods described previously), you simply move the pointer (without holding a button down); then click the first pointer button to complete the action.

If you test the various items, you'll find that each item works in a fairly predictable way. When you select Move, for instance, the pointer changes to the cross-arrow cursor, which appears in the center of the window; as you move the pointer, a window outline follows; you place the window in its new location by clicking the first pointer button. When you select Size, the pointer again changes to the cross-arrow cursor in the center of the window; move the pointer into any part of the resize border and the pointer symbol becomes one of the resize cursors; as you drag the border or corner, a window outline follows the pointer; then complete the resizing by clicking the first pointer button.

Pointer Commands to Manage Icons

In addition to managing windows, *mwm* provides several easy methods for managing icons. The following functions can be invoked using simple pointer button actions on an icon:

Move   Hold down the first pointer button and drag the icon to the desired position. Then release the button.

Raise   Click on the obscured icon with the first pointer button. The icon is raised to the top of the stack. (*mwm* does not allow icons to overlap one another; you'll need to raise an icon only when it's obscured by a window.) Note that this action also posts the Window Menu.

Restore (Deiconify)

> To convert an icon back to a window, double click on the icon with the first pointer button. The window is displayed in the state it was in before it was iconified. (Thus, if the window was previously maximized, double clicking will convert the icon to the maximum size window.)

Each of these icon management function using the pointer is described in greater detail in the section "Managing Windows Using the mwm Frame" in Chapter 3, *Working in the X Environment*.

Using the Window Menu on Icons

You can also display the Window Menu from an icon and invoke menu items that affect it. To display the menu, just place the pointer on the icon and click the first button.* (You can also press and hold down the third button; or you can use either of these keyboard shortcuts: Shift-Escape or Meta-space.)

The Window Menu displayed from an icon is virtually identical to the menu displayed from a window; it contains all of the same items, but only five of the seven are selectable. (When displayed from a window, six of the seven items are selectable.) The five selectable items are: Restore, Move, Maximize, Lower, and Close. These items perform actions on an icon analogous to those performed on a window (see "Using the Window Menu" earlier in this chapter).

Two menu items, Size and Minimize, appear in a lighter typeface, indicating they are not available for selection. Size cannot be selected because, unlike a window, an icon cannot be resized. Obviously, Minimize cannot be used to iconify an icon.

Table 4-3 summarizes the Window Menu functions when invoked from an icon. For instructions on selecting an item and performing the various functions, read "Using the Window Menu" earlier in this chapter. Note that the keyboard shortcuts (accelerators) for the commands are also the same as those described for windows.

Table 4-3. Window Menu Actions on an Icon

Menu Item	Function	Shortcut
Restore	Converts the icon back to a window (in its previous state).	Alt+F5
Move	Moves the icon on the display.	Alt+F7
Size	Not available for selection.	n/a
Minimize	Not available for selection.	n/a

---

*This behavior is controlled by an *mwm* resource variable called iconClick, which is true by default. If the menu is not posted when you click the first button, check the setting for this variable. See Chapter 13, *Customizing mwm*, and the *mwm* reference page in Part Three of this guide. See Chapter 11, *Setting Resources*, for more information about resource file syntax.

mwm Manager

Table 4-3. Window Menu Actions on an Icon (continued)

Menu Item	Function	Shortcut
Maximize	Converts an icon to a window the size of the root window.	Alt+F10
Lower	Sends an icon to the bottom of the window/icon stack.	Alt+F3
Close	Exits the client, removing the icon.	Alt+F4

To invoke a Window Menu action on an icon using the keyboard accelerator, the icon must have the input focus. As explained earlier in this chapter, you can direct focus to an icon by placing the pointer on it and clicking the first button (which also displays the Window Menu). The icon label becomes wider and the border is highlighted.

An icon also retains the input focus when you display the Window Menu and then remove it without selecting an item (by clicking anywhere outside the menu). The icon label will remain wide and the border highlighted until you direct focus to another window or icon. As long as an icon remains highlighted, you can invoke Window Menu commands using their keyboard accelerators.

In Chapter 13, we'll discuss using *mwm* resources to set up an icon box, a window for organizing icons on the display. Using an icon box changes the way you work with the Window Menu from an icon and introduces another menu item, Pack Icons, which reorganizes icons in the icon box. As we'll see in the next section, the 1.2 Root Menu offers the same function.

The Root Menu

The Root Menu is *mwm*'s main menu. Most of the commands it provides can be thought of as affecting the entire display. To display the Root Menu, move the pointer to the root window and press and hold down the third pointer button. The default Root Menu appears in Figure 4-3.

When you display the Root Menu, the pointer changes to the arrow pointer. As you can see, the default Root Menu offers only six items. To select an item, use the following steps:

1. As you continue to hold down the third pointer button, move the pointer onto the desired item name. (If you accidentally move the pointer off the menu, it will still remain displayed, as long as you continue to hold the third button down.) As you move the pointer onto an item, notice that a rectangular box is displayed around the item to highlight it.

2. Once the pointer is positioned on the item you want, release pointer button three. The action is performed.

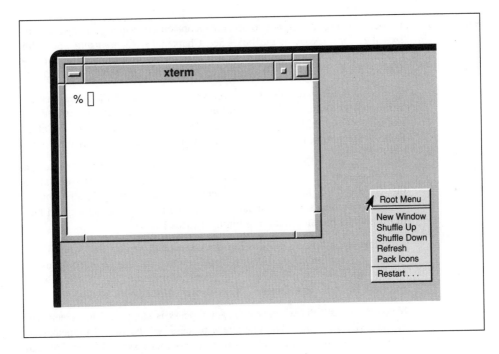

Figure 4-3. The mwm Root Menu

The functions performed by the default Root Menu are described below.

New Window   By default, this command runs an *xterm* window on the display specified by the DISPLAY environment variable, generally the local display. When you create a new window (by using the menu or typing the command in an *xterm*), the new window automatically becomes the active window.

Shuffle Up   If windows and/or icons are stacked on your display, this command moves the bottom window or icon in the stack to the top (raises it). (It's generally simpler to raise a window or icon by placing the pointer on it and clicking the first button, but this item is useful when an object is entirely obscured.)

Shuffle Down   If windows and/or icons are stacked on your display, this command moves the top window or icon in the stack to the bottom (lowers it).

Refresh   This command is used to *refresh* the display screen, that is, redraw its contents. Refresh is useful if system messages appear on the screen, overlaying its contents. (The *xrefresh* client can be used to perform the same function. Simply type xrefresh at the system prompt in an *xterm* window. If you own the "console," you can avoid many such problems by running the *xconsole* client, described in Appendix A, *Managing Your Environment*.)

Pack Icons   If you are using an icon box to organize icons on the display, this item optimizes the icons layout in the box. See Chapter 13, *Customizing mwm*, for instructions on setting up *mwm* to use an icon box. Note that the Window Menu provides the same item when displayed on the icon box window.

Restart...   Stops and restarts *mwm*. This is useful when you've edited the *.mwmrc* configuration file, which specifies certain *mwm* features, and want to activate the changes. Since this function is potentially more dangerous than the other Root Menu options, it is separated from the other options by a horizontal line.

When you select Restart, a dialog box appears in the center of the screen with command buttons asking you to either OK the restart process or Cancel the request. Click on the appropriate command button using the first pointer button. (In most cases, you should also be able to select the highlighted button simply by pressing Return or hitting a space.)

Note that the ellipse (...) following the menu item signals that you will be queried for confirmation. (Dialog boxes commonly appear in applications written using the Motif Toolkit. For more information, see "Dialog Boxes and Push Buttons" in Chapter 9, *Working with Motif Applications*.)

If you select OK, the window manager process is stopped. The screen will momentarily go blank. The new *mwm* process will be started immediately. While the new *mwm* process is starting, an hourglass symbol is displayed in the center of the otherwise blank screen. The hourglass appears to be filling up with sand until the window manager is running and the windows again are displayed on the screen.

Keep in mind that you can add, change, or remove menu items using the *mwm* configuration file, *.mwmrc*, in your home directory. We'll discuss customizing the Root Menu in Chapter 13.

5

The xterm Terminal Emulator

This chapter describes how to use xterm, *the terminal emulator. You use this client to create multiple terminal windows, each of which can run any programs available on the underlying operating system.*

In This Chapter:

The xterm Terminal Emulator

As we've seen, *xterm* provides you with a terminal within a window. Anything you can do using a standard terminal, you can do in an *xterm* window. Once you have an *xterm* window on your screen, you should be able to work productively immediately. From the *xterm* window, you can also run other clients.

To take advantage of X's windowing and networking capabilities, you'll probably want to run more than one *xterm* at a time (as well as other clients), perhaps on different systems in your network. (See Chapter 3, *Working in the X Environment*, for instructions on running clients on different systems using the `-display` option.)

Running multiple *xterm*s allows you to perform multiple tasks simultaneously—and to coordinate those tasks—neither of which you can do very successfully on a standard terminal. For instance, you can display the contents of a directory in one window while you edit a file in another window. Or you can have a program compiling in one window while you read mail in a second window. Note that, although you can display output simultaneously in several windows, you can type in only one window at a time.

Some important (and not so obvious) features of *xterm*: When you start an *xterm* process on the command line in one *xterm* window, the second *xterm* inherits the environment variables of the first (including the DISPLAY setting); the second shell also starts in the working directory of the first shell.

But *xterm* provides much more than basic terminal capabilities. Two of *xterm*'s most useful features are a scrollbar, which allows you to review text in the window, and a "copy and paste" facility, which allows you to select text from one window using the pointer and paste it into another (or even the same) window.

As we'll see, you can create an *xterm* window with a scrollbar using the `-sb` command-line option or specify a scrollbar as a default characteristic of *xterm* using the `scrollbar` resource variable. You can also add a scrollbar to (or remove one from) an *xterm* window already running on the display by using one of the client's four menus. Without customizing the client in any way, you can cut and paste text between *xterm* windows.

Among the less obvious features of *xterm* is a dual functionality. By default, *xterm* emulates a DEC VT102 terminal, a common alphanumeric terminal type. However, *xterm* can also emulate a Tektronix 4014 terminal, which is used to display graphics. For each *xterm* process, you can switch between these two types of terminal windows. You can display both a VT102 and a Tektronix window at the same time but only one of them can be the "active" window, i.e., the window receiving input and output. Hypothetically, you could be editing in the VT102 window while looking at graphics in the Tektronix window.

You switch between the VT102 window and the Tektronix window using items from certain *xterm* menus. *xterm* has four menus that can be used to control the VT102 and Tek windows, to select many terminal settings, and to run other commands that affect the *xterm* process.

Perhaps the most useful menu is the VT Fonts menu, you can change the font used to display text in the VT102 window. You may want to change the font for a number of reasons. Perhaps you need a larger font to read text more easily; or maybe you want to use a smaller font to reduce the size of a window while a program is running and you don't need to monitor its progress. Prior to this innovation (at Release 4), if you didn't like the display font, you had to start a new *xterm* process, specifying an alternative. The VT Fonts menu makes *xterm* much more flexible.

We'll take a look at some of the more useful items on each menu as well as some alternatives to menu items later in this chapter. For more complete information about menus, see the *xterm* reference page in Part Three of this guide.

We'll also consider how to run a program in a temporary *xterm* window, which goes away when the program finishes.

But first, let's consider some preliminary issues: which terminal type to specify for *xterm* and what to do when resizing an *xterm* window causes problems with its terminal emulation.

Then we'll look at the *xterm* features you'll probably use most frequently: the scrollbar and the text selection mechanism.

Terminal Emulation and the xterm Terminal Type

Anyone who has used a variety of terminals knows that they don't all work the same way. Each time you run *xterm*, it looks for a terminal type, which tells the system how the window should operate (i.e., the terminal type determines what sort of terminal *xterm* emulates). When *xterm* is assigned an inappropriate terminal type, the window does not always display properly, particularly when using a text editor such as *vi*. If your *xterm* windows seem to be displaying properly, chances are *xterm* is finding a valid terminal type and you can skip to the next section. If *xterm* is having emulation problems, read on.

When you're working with *xterm*, there are two ways the terminal type can be assigned. First, as in any UNIX environment, the terminal type can be specified in one of your shell startup scripts (e.g., *.login*, *.profile*, etc.). If you've recently switched from a standard UNIX environment to UNIX with X, one of your scripts probably does set a terminal type (maybe by setting the TERM environment variable, maybe by specifying multiple characteristics using *tset*(1), etc.). Second, if none of the startup files contains a terminal assignment, *xterm* automatically searches the database of terminal entries for the first suitable entry and sets the TERM environment variable accordingly.

xterm can emulate a variety of terminal types, which are listed on the client reference page in Part Three of this guide. An *xterm* window most successfully emulates a terminal when it has been assigned the terminal type "xterm."

If one of your shell startup scripts currently specifies a default terminal type, you (or your system administrator) will need to replace this with an appropriate type (preferably "xterm")—or remove the terminal type altogether. Deleting the terminal type assignment from all login files may actually be preferable. The only liability in deleting the terminal type line from a login file is that you might mistakenly delete other important settings. If necessary, consult your system administrator.

Note that for the "xterm" terminal type to be recognized on your system, the system administrator will have had to add it to the file containing valid *termcap* or *terminfo* entries. (The "xterm" entries are supplied with the standard release of X.) If this has not been done and you specify "xterm" in a startup file, *xterm* will assume a terminal type of "unknown" and you will have emulation problems. (This is another argument for deleting any terminal type assignment from a startup file.)

Regardless of whether you specify a terminal type or let *xterm* find its own entry, your system administrator should add "xterm" to the terminal database. See the *xterm* reference page in Part Three of this guide, and Volume Eight, *X Window System Administrator's Guide*, for more information. The Nutshell Handbook *termcap and terminfo* describes how to work with the terminal entry databases.

Resizing and Terminal Emulation

When you run *xterm*, the client sets the appropriate environment variables to reflect the dimensions of the window. Many programs use this information to determine the physical dimensions of output to the window.

If you resize an *xterm* window, the shell must be notified so that programs that rely on this information can work with the correct dimensions. If the underlying operating system supports terminal resizing capabilities (for example, the SIGWINCH signal in systems derived from BSD 4.3), *xterm* will use these facilities to notify programs running in the window whenever it is resized. However, if your operating system does not support terminal resizing capabilities, you may need to request explicitly that the environment variables be updated to reflect the resized window.

The *resize* client sends a special escape sequence to the *xterm* window and *xterm* sends back the current size of the window. The results of *resize* can be redirected to a file that can then be sourced to update TERMCAP (on *termcap* systems) or LINES and COLUMNS (on *terminfo* systems).

To update the appropriate variables to match a window's changed dimensions using the Bourne shell, enter:

```
$ resize > filename
```

and then execute the resulting shell command file:

```
$ . filename                        Bourne shell syntax
```

The variable(s) will be updated and the dimensions of the text within the window will be adjusted accordingly.

If your version of UNIX includes the C shell, you *source* the shell command file:

    % source filename   C shell syntax

However, in the C shell, it's preferable to define this alias for *resize*:

    alias rs 'set noglob; eval `resize`; unset noglob'

Then use rs to update the variable(s) to reflect a window's new dimensions.

Note that even if your operating system supports terminal resizing capabilities, *xterm* may have trouble notifying programs running in the window that the window has been resized. On some older systems (based on BSD 4.2 or earlier), certain programs, notably the *vi* editor, cannot interpret this information. If you resize a window during a *vi* editing session, *vi* will not know the new size of the window. If you quit out of the editing session and start another one, the editor should know the new window size and operate properly. On newer systems (e.g., BSD 4.3 and later), these problems should not occur.

Running a Program in a Temporary xterm Window

Normally, when you start up an *xterm* window, it automatically runs another instance of the UNIX Bourne or C shell (depending on which is set in your *Xresources* file or the SHELL environment variable). If you want to create an *xterm* window that runs some other program and goes away when that program terminates, you can do so with the *xterm* -e option:

    % xterm -e command [arguments]

For example, if you want to look at the file *temp* in a window that will disappear when you quit out of the file, you can use the UNIX *more* program as follows:

    % xterm -e more temp

When you are using other options to *xterm* on the command line, the -e option must appear last because everything after the -e option is read as a command.

Note that the titlebar of the *xterm* window will display the name of the command following -e (unless you've specified an alternative string using -title—see Chapter 10).

Running xterm with a Scrollbar

When using *xterm*, you are not limited to viewing the 24 lines displayed in the window at one time. By default, *xterm* actually remembers the last 64 lines that have appeared in the window. If the window has a scrollbar, you can scroll up and down through the saved text.

To create a single *xterm* window with a scrollbar, use the -sb command-line option:

    % xterm -sb &

Figure 5-1 shows an *xterm* window with a scrollbar.

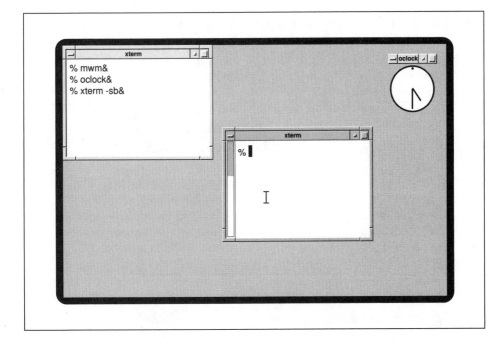

Figure 5-1. An xterm window with a scrollbar

To display all *xterm* windows with a scrollbar by default, set `scrollBar` in your *.Xresources* file, as described in Chapter 11. The appropriate resource setting is illustrated below:

```
XTerm*scrollBar: true
```

If an *xterm* window was not created with a scrollbar, you can add one using the Enable Scrollbar item on the VT Options menu. See the section "VT Options Menu" later in this chapter for instructions on selecting a menu item.

The Athena Scrollbar

Many applications provide horizontal and/or vertical scrollbars that allow you to look at a window's contents that extend beyond the viewing area. You move text (or images in graphics applications) in the window by placing the pointer on the scrollbar and performing some sort of action.

xterm's scrollbar is created by the Athena Scrollbar widget. (As we'll see in subsequent chapters, several of the standard X clients use Athena scrollbars.) An Athena scrollbar looks and operates differently than a scrollbar provided by a Motif application (that is, one created using the Motif widget set), as described in Chapter 9. If you're accustomed to using a Motif (or even a Macintosh) scrollbar, the Athena scrollbar may take some getting used to. While

Motif and Mac scrollbars have separate parts to invoke different types of scrolling, the Athena scrollbar moves text according to which pointer button you use and how you use it.

The Athena scrollbar has two parts: a *thumb* (the highlighted area within the scrollbar) which moves within the *scroll region*, as indicated in Figure 5-2.

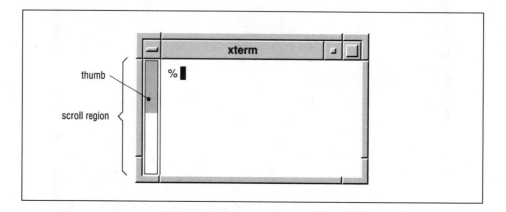

Figure 5-2. The parts of the Athena scrollbar

The thumb displays the position and amount of text currently showing in the window relative to the amount saved. When an *xterm* window with a scrollbar is first created, the thumb fills the entire scrollbar. As more text is saved, the size of the thumb decreases. The number of lines saved is 64 by default but an alternative can be specified with either the -sl command-line option or the saveLines value in an *.Xresources* file.

How to Use the Scrollbar

You scroll through the saved text using various pointer commands. When the pointer is positioned in the scrollbar, the cursor changes to a two-headed arrow. You can then scroll the text in various ways by clicking or dragging with certain pointer buttons.

Table 5-1 summarizes all of the scrollbar commands. However, the first command may be all you need to know. You can drag the text either up or down using the second pointer button. This command is the simplest and offers the most control over how much scrolling takes place. To drag the text in this manner:

1. Place the pointer on the scrollbar.

2. Press and hold down the second pointer button.

3. Then drag the thumb up and down.

Notice that text moves as you move the thumb. If you drag up, the window scrolls back toward the beginning of information saved in the window. If you drag down, the window scrolls forward toward the end of information in the window. When you release the button, the window displays the text at that location. This makes it easy to get to the top of the data by pressing the second button, dragging the thumb to the top of the scroll region, and releasing the pointer button.

To get back to the current cursor position, press any key. Either the space bar or Return is a good choice.

Note that there are three additional scrollbar commands, listed in Table 5-1 and explained subsequently. If you're satisfied to drag the scrollbar using the second pointer button, feel free to skip ahead and learn something about copying and pasting text.

Table 5-1. Athena Scrollbar Commands

To move text in this direction:	Place pointer on scrollbar and:	Notes:
Either up or down	Hold down second pointer button and drag thumb.	Text follows pointer movement.
Down	Click first pointer button.	Scrolls towards latest saved text (towards bottom of window).
Up	Click third pointer button.	Scrolls towards earliest saved text (towards top of window).
Either up or down	Click second pointer button.	Scrolls to a position in saved text that corresponds to the pointer's position in scroll region.

The next three pointer commands in Table 5-1 involve a click that causes the text to scroll However, if you test them, you'll find that it's difficult to judge how much text you're going to scroll with a single click.

Clicking the first pointer button in the scrollbar causes the window to scroll toward the end of information in the window.

Clicking the third pointer button in the scrollbar causes the window to scroll toward the beginning of information in the window.

Clicking the second pointer button moves the display to a position in the saved text that corresponds to the pointer's position in the scroll region. For example, if you move the pointer to the very top of the scroll region and click the second button, the window scrolls to a position very near the beginning of the saved text. As you might imagine, it's very difficult to guess how much scrolling will take place when you use the scrollbar in this way.

Copying and Pasting Text Selections

Once your *xterm* window is created, you can select text to copy and paste within the same or other *xterm* windows using the pointer. You don't need to be in a text editor to copy and paste. You can also copy or paste text to and from the command line.

Text copied into memory using the pointer is saved in a global cut buffer and also becomes what is known as the PRIMARY text "selection."* Both the contents of the cut buffer and the contents of the PRIMARY text selection are globally available to all clients. When you paste text into an *xterm* window, by default the contents of the PRIMARY selection are pasted. If no text is in the PRIMARY selection, the contents of the cut buffer (called CUT_BUFFER0), are pasted. In most cases, these will be the same and you don't have to think about it. As we'll see later, this background to the text selection mechanism becomes important when you want to perform certain customizations, particularly those involving the *xclipboard* client.

For now, however, let's just consider the standard methods for copying and pasting text between *xterm* windows.

Selecting Text to Copy

There are several ways to select (copy) text, all using the pointer. You can select a passage of text, or you can select text by individual words or lines. Table 5-2 summarizes all of the text selection methods. Hypothetically, the passage can be of any length. However, the size of the window limits the amount of text you can copy at one time; also keep in mind that there can be problems pasting long selections.

In order to copy text from a window, the window must have the input focus. The click to focus input is not interpreted as an attempt to start a text selection.

There are two methods for selecting a passage of text. The simpler way is to:

1. Click the first pointer button at the beginning of the text you want to select.

2. Move the pointer to the end of the text selection and click the third pointer button.

The text between the marks is highlighted and copied into memory. (Technically speaking, the text is copied into CUT_BUFFER0—a global cut buffer—and is also made the PRIMARY text selection.)

As an alternative, you can make the selection by dragging the pointer:

1. Place the pointer at the beginning of the text you want to select.

2. Hold down the first button.

---

*The PRIMARY selection and the cut buffer are stored as *properties* of the root window. A property is a piece of information associated with a window (or font) and stored in the server, where it can be accessed by any client. The property mechanism permits "cut" text to be stored and later "pasted" into the windows of other clients. See Chapter 1 and Chapter 11 for more about properties and interclient communication.

3. Drag the pointer to the end of the desired text.

4. Release the button.

The text is highlighted and copied into memory (i.e., copied into the global cut buffer and also made the PRIMARY selection, as in Figure 5-3).

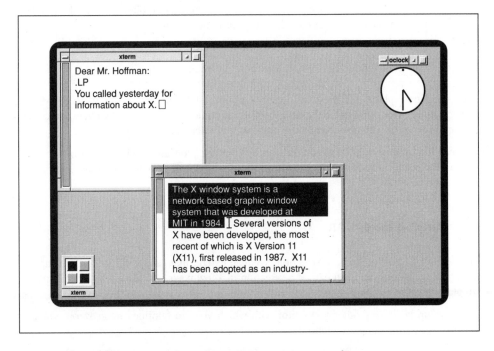

Figure 5-3. Highlighted text saved as the PRIMARY selection

You can select a single word or line simply by clicking. To select a single word, place the pointer on the word and double-click the first button.* To select a single line, place the pointer on the line and triple-click the first button.

Table 5-2 lists the possible pointer actions and the selections they make. You always begin by placing the pointer on the text you want to select.

---

*To be more precise, double-clicking selects all characters of the same class (e.g., alphanumeric characters). By default, punctuation characters and whitespace are in a different class from letters or digits—hence, the observed behavior. However, character classes can be changed. For example, if you wanted to double-click to select email addresses, you'd want to include the punctuation characters !, %, @, and . in the same class as letters and digits. However, redefining the character classes is not something you'd do every day. See the *xterm* reference page in Part Three of this guide for details.

Table 5-2. Button Combinations to Select Text for Copying

To select	Do this
Passage	Click the first button at the start of the selection and the third button at the end of the selection. Or:
	At the beginning of the selection, hold down the first button; move the pointer to the end of the desired text; and release the button.
Word	Double-click the first button anywhere on the word.
Line	Triple-click the first button anywhere on the line.

Each selection replaces the previous contents of CUT_BUFFER0 and the previous PRIMARY text selection. You can make only one selection at a time. (The *xclipboard* client, described later in this chapter, can be used to store multiple text selections.)

To clear the highlighting, move the pointer off the selection and click the first button anywhere else in the window. Note, however, that the text still remains in memory until you make another selection.*

Extending a Selection

Regardless of how you make a selection, you can extend that selection, generally using the third pointer button. You can extend a selection in a few ways. To learn what is perhaps the simplest way, follow these steps:

1. Bring up *vi* (or any other text editor with which you are familiar) in an *xterm* window, and type in this sample sentence:

   ```
   The X Window System is a network-based graphics window system that
   was developed at MIT in 1984.
   ```

2. Place the pointer at the beginning of the word *network-based* and click the first button.

3. Then move the pointer to the end of *graphics* and click the third button. The words *network-based graphics* are selected:

   ```
   The X Window System is a network-based graphics window system that
   was developed at MIT in 1984.
   ```

4. Then move the pointer away from the selected words to the left or right to encompass additional text. For the purposes of our example, let's move the pointer to the beginning of the sentence. Then click the third pointer button. A new selection now extends from

---

*Technically speaking, this action clears the PRIMARY selection, but the text remains in CUT_BUFFER0. When you subsequently try to paste the text, *xterm* finds the PRIMARY selection empty, so (according to its defaults) it pastes the contents of the cut buffer instead. See Chapter 11, *Setting Resources*, for more information about these so-called *xterm translations*.

the previous selection (*network-based graphics*) to the pointer's location and looks something like this:

```
The X Window System is a network-based graphics window system that
was developed at MIT in 1984.
```

Alternatively, you can press and hold down the third pointer button and drag the pointer to extend the selection. Then release the pointer button.

Remember that an extension always begins from the previous selection. By moving the pointer up or down, or to the right or left of the last selection, you can select part of one line or add or subtract several lines of text.

If the previous selection was by word or line (by double- or triple-clicking), when you extend it, the extension is automatically by word(s) or line(s). There are a few ways of extending a selection made by word or line.

First, if you hold the button down after double- or triple-clicking (rather than releasing it) and move the pointer, you will select additional text by words or lines at a time. Then release the button to end the selection.

More commonly you will probably decide to extend the selection after making it (and releasing the first pointer button). Under these circumstances, you can extend it as in the following example:

1. Starting again with our sample sentence, place the pointer on the word *graphics* and select it by double-clicking the first pointer button.

   ```
   The X Window System is a network-based graphics window system that
   was developed at MIT in 1984.
   ```

2. Then move the pointer to the right, onto any part of the word *window*, and click the third button. The new selection encompasses *graphics* and the entire word *window*.

   ```
   The X Window System is a network-based graphics window system that
   was developed at MIT in 1984.
   ```

3. You can also click to extend the selection by multiple words. Try moving the pointer to the left this time, to the middle of the word *System*, and click the third button. The new selection encompasses every word between *System* and *window*, inclusive:

   ```
   The X Window System is a network-based graphics window system that
   was developed at MIT in 1984.
   ```

If you originally selected an entire line by triple-clicking the first pointer button, moving the pointer to another line and clicking the third button extends the selection to encompass that new line and all lines in between.

As an alternative, you can also extend a word or line selection by pressing and holding down the third pointer button, dragging the pointer, and releasing the third button. The extension still increments by word or line as appropriate.

Table 5-3. Button Combinations to Extend a Text Selection

To select	Do this
By passage	Move the pointer to the place in the text to which you want the selection to extend; click the third button. Or:
	Hold down the third button; move the pointer to the end of the text you want to include; and release the button.
By word	Move the pointer to the word to which you want the selection to extend (either to the left or right of the previous selection); click the third button anywhere on the word. Or:
	Hold down the third button; drag the pointer onto the last word you want to include (either to the left or right of the previous selection); release the button. Or:
	After double-clicking the first button anywhere on the word to select it, continue to hold the button down and drag the pointer to the left or right. The selection will be extended by word. When you've included the words you want, release the button.
By line	Move the pointer to the line to which you want the selection to extend (either above or below the previously selected line); click the third button anywhere on the line. Or:
	Hold down the third button; drag the pointer onto the last line you want to include (either above or below the previously selected line); release the button. Or:
	After triple-clicking the first button anywhere on the line to select it, continue to hold the button down and drag the pointer up or down. The selection will be extended by line. When you've included the lines you want, release the button.

To select text that fills more than one screen, select the first screenful. Use the scrollbar to view the additional text. Then use the third pointer button to extend the selection. The original selection does not need to be in view; clicking the third button will extend it to the point you choose.

To clear the highlighting, move the pointer off the selection and click the first button anywhere else in the window. Note, however, that the text still remains in memory until you make another selection.

Complications can arise if you're copying text that includes tabs. With the current implementation of the copy and paste feature, tabs are saved as spaces. If you're copying a large amount of text with many tabs from one text file to another, having tabs converted to spaces can create problems. A possible workaround is to change all tabs in the first file to some unique character or string (using a global command provided by your text editor); copy and paste the text into the second file; convert the unique strings back to tabs in both files using your text editor.

Pasting Text Selections

Clicking the second button inserts the text from the PRIMARY selection (or CUT_BUFFER0, if the selection is empty) as if it were keyboard input. You can move data from one *xterm* window to another by selecting the data in one window with the first button (or extending the selection with the third button), moving the pointer to another window, and clicking the second button.

You can paste text either into an open file or at a command-line prompt. To paste text into an open file, as illustrated in Figure 5-4, click the second button within the window containing the file. The text from the memory area will be inserted at the text editor cursor. (Of course, the file must be in a mode where it is expecting text input, such as the insert mode of an editor.) You can paste the same text as often as you like. The contents of the PRIMARY selection remain until you make another selection.

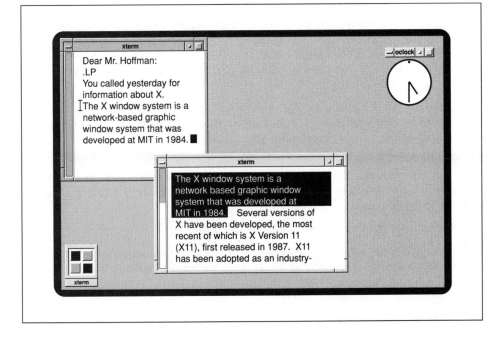

Figure 5-4. Pasting text into an open file

To paste text at a command-line prompt, you must first close any open file within the window. Then click the second button anywhere within the window to place the text on the command line at the end of text in the window. (Note that the window will scroll to the bottom on input.) You can make multiple insertions by repeatedly clicking the second button.

Note that you can paste text into a window when click-to-type focus is in effect, even if the window does not have the input focus. The act of pasting does not transfer focus either.

(Similarly, if you click on a window to focus input, the click is not interpreted as an attempt to start a text selection.)

Keep in mind that you can paste *over* existing text in a file with the *vi* change text commands (such as cw, for change word). For example, you can paste over five words by specifying the *vi* command 5cw, and then pasting text by clicking the second pointer button. Note that you can paste over existing text in any editor that has an overwrite mode.

The Text Selection Mechanism and xclipboard

Prior to Release 3, many clients exchanged information solely by means of global cut buffers, which are, in effect, owned by the server, and available to all clients. Cut buffers are useful only for copying and pasting information that does not need to be translated to another format, such as ASCII text between two *xterm* windows.

In accordance with the newer interclient communication conventions developed since Release 2, most clients, notably *xterm*, primarily exchange information via selections. The advantage of the selection mechanism is that it allows data from one client to be converted to a different format to be used by another client. Cut buffers do not perform this type of translation.

A selection is globally available but not owned by the server. A selection is owned by a client—initially by the client from which you copy it. Then when the text selection is pasted in another window, that window becomes the owner of the selection.

The selection mechanism has a couple of limitations you should be aware of, although it's likely only one of them will present a problem. Because of the rules of precedence governing cut buffers and selections and the nature of selections (particularly the issue of ownership), the following problems can arise in transferring data:

1. By default, you can save only one selection at a time.

2. For a selection to be transferred to a client, the selection must be owned by a client. If the client that owns the selection no longer exists, the transfer cannot be made.

The *xclipboard* client can address both of these problems.

In the next section, we'll show you how to use *xclipboard*. To work properly with *xclipboard*, you need to do some customization, which is explained in Chapter 11, *Setting Resources*. The short story is that the *xclipboard* window is a storehouse for text that is copied to what is known as the CLIPBOARD selection. Like the PRIMARY selection, the CLIPBOARD selection is another *property* of the root window—a piece of information stored in the server where it is available to any client.

Most users will probably not encounter the second problem. You are probably doing all of your copying and pasting between *xterm* windows. If you've made a selection from an *xterm* window and the window is killed, the *selection* contents are lost. However, the cut buffer contents remain intact and are pasted instead. (Since all *xterm* windows interpret ASCII text, the translation capabilities of the selection mechanism are not needed.)

Problems involving the loss of selections are more likely to happen if you are transferring information between clients that require information to be in different formats. Although *xclipboard* is primarily intended to allow you to store multiple text selections, it can also avert problems of selection ownership by providing centralized ownership (via the CLIP-BOARD selection). Once the CLIPBOARD owns a selection, the selection can be transferred (and translated to another format), even if the client that previously owned the selection goes away.

You can customize a client to send data to the CLIPBOARD selection by using *event transla-tions*, which are discussed in Chapter 11. The client you'll probably want to use in conjunc-tion with *xclipboard* is *xterm*; Chapter 11 suggests appropriate translations to do this. To use another client with *xclipboard*, see the client reference page in Part Three of this guide for information on the appropriate translations. For more information on selections and transla-tions, see Volume One, *Xlib Programming Manual*.

Saving Multiple Selections with xclipboard

The *xclipboard* client provides a window in which you can paste multiple text selections and from which you can copy text selections to other windows. Similar to the clipboard feature of the Macintosh operating system, the *xclipboard* is basically a storehouse for text you may want to paste into other windows, perhaps multiple times. The *xclipboard* window is shown in Figure 5-5.

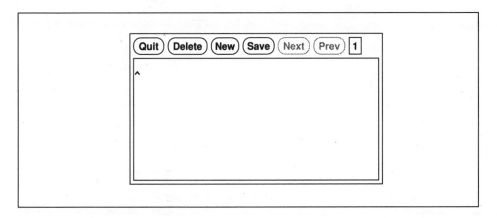

Figure 5-5. The xclipboard window

To open an *xclipboard*, type:

```
% xclipboard &
```

You can paste text into the *xclipboard* window using the pointer in the manner described pre-viously and then copy and paste it elsewhere but this is not its intended use. To use the *xclip-board* most effectively, you must do some customization involving a resource file, such as *.Xresources*. The necessary steps are described in detail in Chapter 11. For now, suffice it to say that you want to set up the *xclipboard* so that you can select text to be made the CLIP-BOARD selection and have that text *automatically pasted* in the *xclipboard* window, as illustrated in Figure 5-5.

Since the *xclipboard* client is intended to be coordinated with the CLIPBOARD selection, the X server allows you to run only one *xclipboard* at a time.

In order to illustrate how the clipboard works, let's presume it has been set up according to the guidelines in Chapter 11. According to those guidelines, you make text the CLIPBOARD selection by:

1. Holding down the first pointer button and dragging the pointer to highlight the text (one of the usual selection methods); and then,

2. while continuing to hold the first button, clicking the third button. (Then you can release button 1.)

(You could specify another button combination or a button and key combination but we've found this one works pretty well.) The first pointer action makes the text the PRIMARY selection (and it is available to be pasted in another window using the pointer); the second pointer action additionally makes the text the CLIPBOARD selection (and it is automatically sent to the *xclipboard* window, as in Figure 5-6).

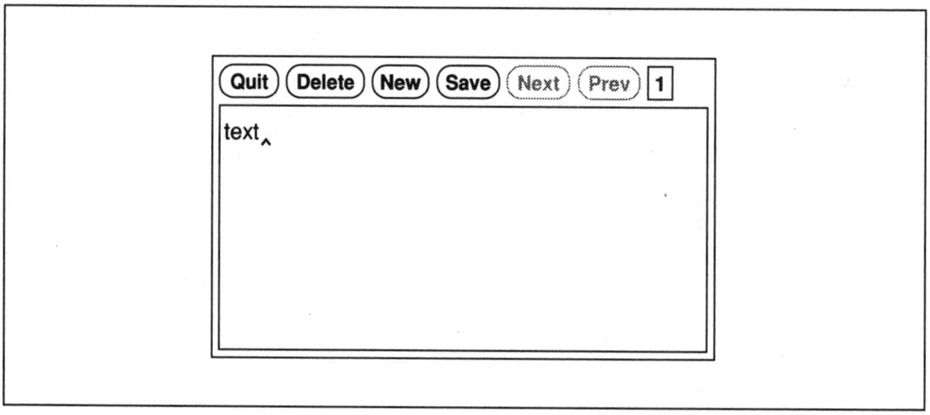

Figure 5-6. Selected text appears automatically in the xclipboard window

These guidelines still allow you to select text with the first pointer button alone and that text will be made the PRIMARY selection; however, the text will not automatically be sent to the *xclipboard*. This enables you to make many selections but to direct to the *xclipboard* only those selections you consider important (perhaps those you might want to paste several times). (The guidelines in Chapter 11 give you different ways to paste the PRIMARY and CLIPBOARD selections, as we'll see later in this section.)

In order to allow you to store multiple text selections, the seemingly tiny *xclipboard* actually provides multiple screens, each of which can be thought of as a separate buffer. (However, as we'll see, a single text selection can span more than one screen.) Each time you use the pointer to make text the CLIPBOARD selection, the *xclipboard* advances to a new screen in which it displays and stores the text. Several command buttons allow you to manage the *xclipboard* window and its selections.

To the right of the command buttons is a tiny box which displays a number corresponding to the current CLIPBOARD selection. This handy box has been added in Release 5. When the client is first run, the box displays the number "1;" the number is automatically incremented for each additional selection (or reduced by 1 if you select the Delete command button).

Once you have saved multiple selections, the client's Next and Previous command buttons allow you to move forward and backward among these screens of text. (The box to the right of the command buttons displays the number of the selection currently in the window to help you keep track.)

Pasting the CLIPBOARD selection has different ramifications than pasting the PRIMARY selection. When you paste the PRIMARY selection (by clicking the second pointer button), you always get the last PRIMARY selection you made (by any of several acceptable methods—see "Selecting Text to Copy" earlier in this chapter).

When you paste the CLIPBOARD selection, you get the selection that's currently being displayed in the *xclipboard* window (which is not necessarily the last one you sent there). For example, you might send four selections to the CLIPBOARD, then use the Prev button to go back to selection #2. If you then paste the CLIPBOARD selection, selection #2 is pasted.

If you've coordinated *xterm* with *xclipboard* using the guidelines outlined in Chapter 11, you paste the CLIPBOARD selection in an *xterm* window by:

1. Holding down the Shift key.

2. Clicking the second pointer button.

Remember that you generally paste a text selection by clicking the second pointer button; we've added the Shift key to distinguish the CLIPBOARD selection from the PRIMARY selection.

The functionality of the client's command buttons is summarized in Table 5-4. They are all selected by clicking the first pointer button.

Table 5-4. xclipboard Command Buttons and Functions

Button	Function
Quit	Causes the application to exit.
Delete	Deletes the current *xclipboard* buffer; the current screenful of text is cleared from the window and the next screenful (or previous, if there is no next) is displayed.

Table 5-4. xclipboard Command Buttons and Functions (continued)

Button	Function
New	Opens a new buffer into which you can insert text; the window is cleared.
Save	Allows you to save the currently displayed text selection to a file. Pops up a dialog box with a text window displaying a default filename (*clipboard*) and two command buttons: Accept and Cancel. Clicking on Accept or pressing Return saves the current selection as the file *clipboard* (in the directory from which you ran the program). Or you can change the filename using the same commands used with *xedit* (see Chapter 8) before hitting Accept.

You can only Save one selection at a time (subsequent saves overwrite the filename); so if you want to save multiple selections, you'll need to change the filename each time.

To bail out without saving, click on Cancel. |
| Next and Previous | Once you have sent multiple selections to the *xclipboard*, Next and Previous allow you to move from one to another (e.g., display them sequentially). Before two or more CLIPBOARD selections are made, these buttons are not available for use. (Their labels will appear in a lighter typeface to indicate this.) |

The command buttons you will probably use most frequently are Delete, Next, and Previous.

When you select text using the first and third pointer buttons, the text will automatically be displayed in the *xclipboard* window and will, in effect, be the first screenful of text (or first buffer) saved in the *xclipboard*. Subsequent CLIPBOARD selections will be displayed and saved in subsequent screens.

You can remove a screenful of text from the *xclipboard* by displaying that screenful and then clicking on the Delete command button. When you delete a screenful of text using this command button, the next screenful (if any) will be displayed in the window. If there is no next screenful, the previous screenful will be displayed.

Certain features of *xclipboard* become apparent only when you make a very large CLIP-BOARD selection. Say you select a full *xterm* window of text with the first and third pointer buttons, as described above. The text extends both horizontally and vertically beyond the bounds of a single *xclipboard* screen. (As we suggested earlier, a CLIPBOARD selection can actually span more than one *xclipboard* screen. Pressing Delete will remove all screensful the selection comprises.) When you make a selection that extends beyond the bounds of the *xclipboard* screen (either horizontally, vertically, or both), scrollbars will be activated in the window to allow you to view the entire selection.

If the text extends both horizontally and vertically beyond the bounds of the *xclipboard* screen, as it does in Figure 5-7, the window will display both horizontal and vertical scrollbars. If the text extends beyond the screen in only one of these two ways, the window will display either a horizontal or vertical scrollbar, as needed.* These scrollbars are selection-specific: they are only displayed as long as the current selection cannot be viewed in its entirety without them. If you move to a previous or subsequent selection that *can* be viewed without them, the scrollbars will be deactivated.

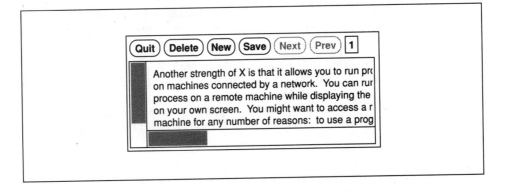

Figure 5-7. xclipboard with scrollbars to view large text selection

Problems with Large Selections

If you experiment making large selections with *xclipboard*, you may discover what seems to be a bug in the program. Though in most circumstances, making a new selection causes the screen to advance and display the new text, this does not happen reliably after a selection vertically spanning more than one screenful. In these cases, the new selection *is* saved in the *xclipboard* (and the number in the small box is incremented to indicated this); however, the *xclipboard* window does not automatically advance to show you the new current selection. Instead, the previous long selection is still displayed. (For example, though the box says "5," indicating that a fifth selection has been saved, the window is still displaying selection #4.) This is a bit of *xclipboard* sleight-of-hand. The new selection has been successfully made but the appearance of the window belies this fact. (The Next button will probably add to your confusion; it will not be available for selection, suggesting that the text in the window is the last selection saved. This is not the case.)

In order to get around this problem and display the actual current selection, press the Previous button. The same long selection (which is, in actuality, the Previous selection) will again be displayed. (The small box will flip back to display the preceding number as well.) Then the Next button will be enabled, and you can click on it to display the actual current selection. (The selection displayed in the window and the number in the small box will correspond.)

---

*An application created using the X Toolkit, which provides horizontal and vertical scrollbars, is described as a *viewport*. See Chapter 8 for more information about viewports and other X Toolkit features.

Editing Text Saved in the xclipboard

You can edit text you send to the *xclipboard* using the same commands recognized by *xedit*. These commands are described in the section "The xedit Text Editor" in Chapter 8. A small caret cursor will be visible in each screenful of text. You can move this cursor by clicking the pointer where you'd like it to appear. Then you can backspace to delete letters or type to insert them. When you edit a screenful of text, the *xclipboard* continues to store the edited version, until you delete it or exit the program.

Be aware that, without performing customization, you can still use *xclipboard* on a very simple level. You can paste text into and copy text from the *xclipboard* window just as you would any other, using the pointer movements described earlier in this chapter. You can also type in the *xclipboard* window and then copy and paste what you've typed. Just move the pointer into the window and try typing. However, keep in mind that this is not the intended use of the *xclipboard*.

If you do choose to use the clipboard in a limited way, it can still be a helpful editing tool. For example, say you wanted to create a paragraph composed of a few lines of text from each of two files. You could copy the text from each file using the pointer and paste it into the *xclipboard* window. (Each time you paste text into the *xclipboard* window, the text is appended to whatever text was already pasted there.) Again using the pointer, you could copy the newly formed paragraph from the *xclipboard* window and paste it into a file in another window.

The xterm Menus

xterm has four different menus, each providing items that serve different purposes. You display a menu by placing the pointer on the window and simultaneously pressing the Control (keyboard) key and a pointer button. (The exact key and button combinations are described in subsequent sections with each menu.) When you're using a window manager, such as *mwm*, that provides a titlebar or frame, the pointer must rest within the window proper—not on any window decoration. (Note that the pointer must be within the window, even if click-to-type focus is enabled. See Chapter 1 for a discussion of focus policy.)

The following menus are available:

- Main Options menu

- VT Options menu

- VT Fonts menu

- Tek Options menu

As shown in Figure 5-8, three of the four *xterm* menus are divided into sections separated by horizontal lines. The top portion of each divided menu contains various modes that can be toggled. (The one exception is the Redraw Window item on the Main Options menu, which is a command.) A check mark appears next to a mode that is currently active. Selecting one of these modes toggles its state.

The items on the VT Fonts menu change the font in which text is displayed in the *xterm* window. Only one of these fonts can be active at a time. To toggle one off, you must activate another.

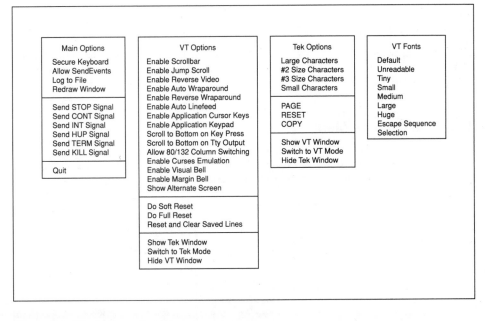

Figure 5-8. The Release 5 xterm menus

Most mode entries can also be set by command-line options when invoking *xterm*, or by entries in a resource startup file (such as *.Xdefaults* or *.Xresources*) as described in Chapter 11. (See the *xterm* reference page in Part Three of this guide for a complete list of command options and resource variables.) The various modes on the menus are very helpful if you've set (or failed to set) a particular mode on the command line and then decide you want the opposite characteristic.

The sections below the modes portion of each menu contain various commands. Selecting one of these commands performs the indicated function. Many of these functions can only be invoked from the *xterm* menus. However, some functions can be invoked in other ways: for example, from an *mwm* menu, on the command line, by a sequence of keystrokes (such as Control-C). This chapter includes alternatives to some of the menu items which, in certain cases, may be more convenient. Of course, the *xterm* menus can be very helpful when other methods to invoke a function fail.

When you display an *xterm* menu, the pointer becomes the arrow pointer and initially appears in the menu's title. Once the menu appears, you can release any keyboard key. The menu will remain visible as long as you continue to hold down the appropriate pointer button. (You can move the pointer off the menu without it disappearing.)

If you decide not to select a menu item after the menu has appeared, move the pointer off the menu and release the button. The menu disappears and no action is taken.

We think users will be most interested in the mode toggles on the VT Options menu (that allow you to turn features like the scrollbar on and off) and the items on the VT Fonts menu (that allow you to change the display font once the client is running). For the short story on *xterm* menus, just take a look at these sections.

The remaining sections of this chapter survey additional menu items and also discuss some alternatives to using the menus. For a brief description of all menu items, see the *xterm* reference page in Part Three.

The Main Options Menu

The Main Options menu, shown in Figure 5-9, allows you to set certain modes and to send signals (such as SIGHUP) that affect the *xterm* process.

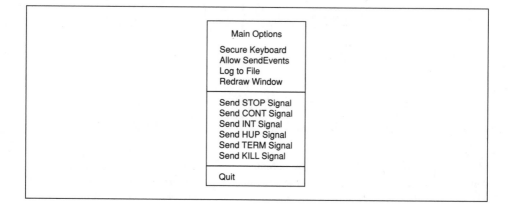

Figure 5-9. The Main Options menu

To bring up the Main Options menu, move the pointer to the *xterm* window you want to change, hold down the Control key, and press the first (usually the left) pointer button.* The pointer changes to the menu pointer, and this menu of three modes and eight commands appears. (You can release the Control key but must continue to press the first pointer button to hold the Main Options menu in the window.) Note that Main Options menu items apply only to the *xterm* window the pointer is in when you display the menu. To effect changes in another *xterm*, you must move the pointer to that window, display the menu, and specify the items you want.

---

*The right button can be made to function as the "first" button. This is especially useful if you are left-handed. See Chapter 14, *Setup Clients*, for instructions on how to customize the pointer with *xmodmap*.

To select a menu item, move the menu pointer to that item and release the first button. After you have selected a mode (Secure Keyboard, Allow SendEvents, or Log to File), a check mark appears before the item to remind you that it is active. The Log to File mode on the Main Options menu can also be set by a command-line option when invoking *xterm*. In addition, both Log to File and Allow SendEvents can be set by entries in a resource startup file such as *.Xresources*. The menu selections enable you to change your mind once *xterm* is running. (See the *xterm* reference page in Part Three for more information on these modes.)

The Secure Keyboard mode toggle is intended to help counteract one of the security weaknesses of X. You may want to activate it before you type a password or other important text in an *xterm* window. Generally, when you press a keyboard key or move the pointer, the X server generates a packet of information that is available for other clients to interpret. These packets of information are known as *events*. Moving the pointer or pressing a keyboard key causes input events to occur.

There is an inherent security problem in the client-server model. Because events such as the keys you type in an *xterm* window are made available via the server to other clients, hypothetically an adept system hacker could access this information. (Naturally, this is not an issue in every environment.) A fairly serious breach of security could easily occur, for instance, if someone were able to find out a user's password or the *root* password. Enabling Secure Keyboard mode causes all user input to be directed *only* to the *xterm* window itself.

Of course, in many environments, precaution is probably not necessary: if the nature of the work is in no way sensitive, if the system administrator has taken pains to secure the system in other ways, etc. If your environment might be vulnerable, you can enable Secure Keyboard mode before typing passwords and other important information and then disable it again using the menu.

When you enable Secure Keyboard mode, the foreground and background colors of the *xterm* window will be exchanged (as if you had enabled the Reverse Video mode from the VT Options menu), as shown in Figure 5-10. When you disable Secure Keyboard mode, the colors will be switched back.

Be aware that only one X client at a time can secure the keyboard. Thus, if you have enabled Secure Keyboard mode in one *xterm*, you will not be allowed to enable it in another *xterm* until you disable it in the first. If Secure Keyboard mode is not available when you request it, the colors will not be switched and a bell will sound.

If you request Secure Keyboard mode and are not refused but the colors are *not* exchanged, be careful: you are not in Secure Keyboard mode. If this happens, there's a good chance that someone has tampered with the system. If the application you're running displays a prompt before asking for a password, it's a good idea to enable Secure Keyboard mode before the prompt is displayed and then verify that the prompt is displayed in the proper colors. Before entering the password, you can also display the Main Options menu again and verify that a check mark appears next to Secure Keyboard mode.

Be aware that Secure Keyboard will be disabled automatically if you iconify the *xterm* window, or start *mwm* or another window manager that provides a titlebar or other window decoration. (You can enable Secure Keyboard mode once *mwm* is running, though.) This limitation is due to the X protocol. When the mode is disabled, the colors will be switched back and the bell will sound to warn you.

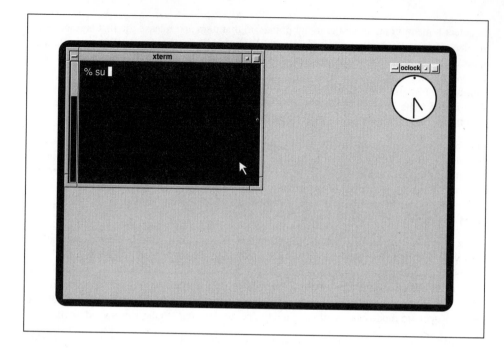

Figure 5-10. Reverse video is enabled when the keyboard is secure

Though intended to counteract a security weakness, the Secure Keyboard mode toggle can also be used to get around a weakness of *mwm*. As described in Chapter 4, if *mwm* dies, it's possible that the focus can be lost—i.e., the focus is no longer directed to any application window. Selecting Secure Keyboard mode for any *xterm* should cause that window to grab the focus again.

In addition to modes that can be toggled, the Main Options menu includes several commands. All of the commands (except for Redraw Window) send a signal that is intended to affect the *xterm* process: suspend it (Send STOP Signal), terminate it (Send TERM Signal), etc. Given that your operating system may recognize only certain signals, every menu item may not produce the intended function.

Note that most of these commands are equivalent to common keystroke commands, which are generally simpler to invoke. For example, in most terminal setups Control-C can be used to interrupt a process. This is generally simpler than using the Send INT Signal menu command, which performs the same function.

Similarly, if your system supports job control, you can probably suspend a process by typing Control-Z and start the process again by typing Control-Y, rather than using the Send STOP Signal and Send CONT Signal menu commands. If your system does not support job control, neither the menu commands nor the keystrokes will work.

Four of the commands (Send HUP Signal, Send TERM Signal, Send KILL Signal, and Quit) send signals that are intended to terminate the *xterm* window. Depending on the signals your system recognizes, these commands may or may not work as intended. Be aware that in most cases you can probably end an *xterm* process simply by typing some sequence (such as Control-D or `exit`) in the window. Of course the menu items may be very helpful if the more conventional ways of killing the window fail. Also be aware that, in addition to being recognized only by certain systems, some signals are more gentle to systems than others. See the *xterm* reference page in Part Three of this guide for information on the signal sent by each of the menu commands and the *signal*(3C) reference page in the *UNIX Programmer's Manual* for more information on what each signal does.

The Quit command sends a SIGHUP to the process group of the process running under *xterm*, usually the shell. (The Send HUP Signal command sends the same signal.) This ends up killing the *xterm* process, and the window disappears from the screen.

Quit is separated from the earlier commands by a horizontal line so it's easier to point at. Sending a SIGHUP with Quit is slightly more gentle to the system than sending a SIGKILL with Send KILL Signal.

The Redraw Window command redraws the contents of the window. As an alternative, you can redraw the entire screen using the *xrefresh* client. See the *xrefresh* reference page in Part Three of this guide for more information about this client.

VT Options Menu

The VT Options menu provides many VT102 setup functions, which can be used to specify certain characteristics of the *xterm* window. Some of these mode settings are analogous to those available in a real VT102's setup mode; others, such as *scrollbar*, are *xterm*-only modes.

The VT Options menu items allow you to reset several characteristics/modes at once, select the Tektronix window to accept input, hide the VT window, etc.

To bring up the VT Options menu, move the pointer to the *xterm* window, hold down the Control key, and then press and hold down the second pointer button. (You can release the Control key but must continue to press the second button to keep the VT Options menu in the window.) The menu shown in Figure 5-11 appears.

Check marks indicate the active modes. For example, Jump Scroll, Auto Wraparound, and Scroll to Bottom on Tty Output* are active in the VT Options menu displayed in Figure 5-11.

These are the only modes active by default. To turn off one of these modes, move the menu pointer to that mode and release the second button.

---

*This mode indicates that if you are using the scrollbar and the window receives output (or a key is pressed, if `stty echo` is enabled), the window scrolls forward so that the cursor is at the current line. (You can use the menu to toggle off this mode but it is generally desirable to have.)

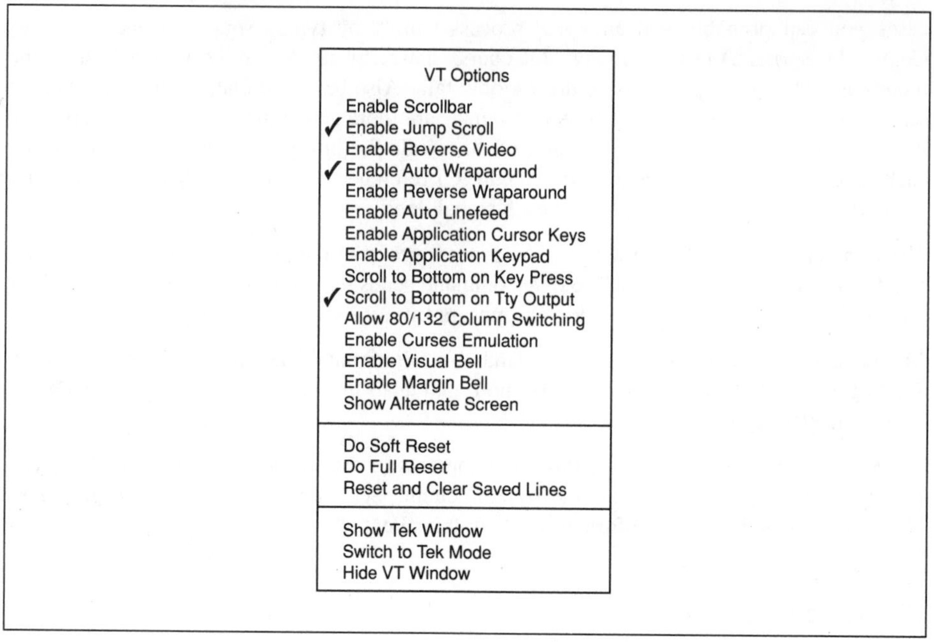

```
                    VT Options
            Enable Scrollbar
          ✓ Enable Jump Scroll
            Enable Reverse Video
          ✓ Enable Auto Wraparound
            Enable Reverse Wraparound
            Enable Auto Linefeed
            Enable Application Cursor Keys
            Enable Application Keypad
            Scroll to Bottom on Key Press
          ✓ Scroll to Bottom on Tty Output
            Allow 80/132 Column Switching
            Enable Curses Emulation
            Enable Visual Bell
            Enable Margin Bell
            Show Alternate Screen

            Do Soft Reset
            Do Full Reset
            Reset and Clear Saved Lines

            Show Tek Window
            Switch to Tek Mode
            Hide VT Window
```

Figure 5-11. The VT Options menu

Most of these modes can also be set by command-line options when invoking *xterm* or by
entries in a resource startup file like *.Xresources* (see Chapter 11). The menu selections
allow you to change your mind once *xterm* is running.

The toggle Allow 80/132 Column Switching warrants a little more explanation. This mode
allows *xterm* to recognize the DECCOLM escape sequence, which switches the terminal
between 80- and 132-column mode. The DECCOLM escape sequence can be included in a
program (such as a spreadsheet) to allow the program to display in 132-column format. See
Appendix E, *xterm Control Sequences*, for more information. This mode is off by default.

The VT Options menu commands (in the second and third partitions of the menu) perform two
sets of functions, neither of which can be performed from the command line or a resource
definition file. The commands Soft Reset and Full Reset reset some of the modes on the
menu to their initial states. See the *xterm* reference page in Part Three of this guide for more
information.

The Show Tek Window, Switch to Tek Mode, and Hide VT Window menu items allow you to
manipulate the Tektronix and VT102 windows.

The Show Tek Window command displays the Tek window and its contents without making it
the active window (you can't input to it). Use the Switch to Tek Mode command to display a
Tektronix window and make it the active window. When you select Switch to Tek Mode, the
Show Tek Window command is automatically enabled, since the Tek window is displayed.
(Note that a Tektronix window is not commonly used for general purpose terminal emulation
but for displaying the output of graphics or typesetting programs.)

Both of these commands are toggles. If Show Tek Window is active and you toggle it off, the Tek window becomes hidden. (As we'll see, you can also do this with the Hide Tek Window item on the Tek Options menu.) If both Switch to Tek Mode and Show Tek Window are active (remember, enabling the former automatically enables the latter), toggling off either one of them switches the *xterm* back to VT mode. (This can also be done from the Tek Options menu with the Switch to VT Mode item.)

The Hide VT Window command hides the VT102 window but does not destroy it or its contents. It can be restored (and made the active window) by choosing Select VT Mode from the Tek Options menu.

VT Fonts Menu

The VT Fonts menu allows you to change the display font of an *xterm* window while the window is running, a powerful and very useful capability. To bring up the VT Fonts menu, move the pointer inside the *xterm* window. Press and hold down the Control key on the keyboard and press the third (usually the right) pointer button. The VT Fonts menu* is shown in Figure 5-12.

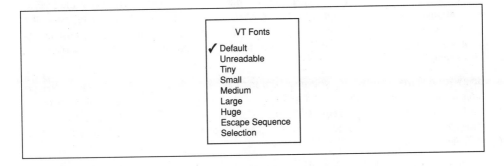

Figure 5-12. VT Fonts menu

If you have not toggled any items on this menu, a check mark will appear before the Default mode setting. The Default is the font specified when the *xterm* window was run. This font could have been specified on the *xterm* command line or in a resource file such as .Xresources. Whatever the case, this font remains the Default for the duration of the current *xterm* process.

The items Default, Unreadable, Tiny, Small, Medium, Large, and Huge can be toggled to set the font displayed in the *xterm* window. The font can be changed any number of times to accommodate a variety of uses. You might choose to use a large font for editing a file (chances are you've chosen a large enough default font, though). You could then change to a

---

*This menu has changed slightly in Release 5. The Huge item is entirely new. The Unreadable label is new in R5, but it toggles the same font the Tiny label did in R4. (If you've selected it, you know it has been aptly renamed.) The R5 Tiny item toggles a newly included, somewhat more legible choice.

smaller font while a process is running since you don't need to be reading or typing in that *xterm*. Changing the font also changes the size of the window.

There are also default settings for the Unreadable, Tiny, Small, Medium, Large, and Huge fonts. They are all constant-width fonts from the directory */usr/lib/X11/fonts/misc* and are listed in Table 5-5.

Table 5-5. VT Fonts Menu Defaults

Menu Item	Default Font
Unreadable	nil2
Tiny	5x7
Small	6x10
Medium	7x13
Large	9x15
Huge	10x20

Bring up the VT Fonts menu and toggle some of these fonts to see what they look like. If you select the Unreadable font (*nil2*), your *xterm* window becomes very tiny, almost the size of some application icons. Though you cannot read the actual text in a window this size, the window is still active and you *can* observe if additional output, albeit minuscule, is displayed. An *xterm* window displaying text in such a small font can, in effect, serve as an *active icon*.

Be aware that you can specify your own Unreadable, Tiny, Small, Medium, Large, and Huge fonts using entries in a resource startup file such as *Xresources*. The corresponding resource names are `font1`, `font2`, `font3`, `font4`, `font5`, and `font6`. See Chapter 6 for more information about available fonts. See Chapter 11 for instructions on how to set resource variables.

In addition to the menu selections we've discussed, the VT Fonts menu offers two other possible selections: Escape Sequence and Selection. When you first run an *xterm* window, these selections appear on the VT Fonts menu but they are not functional. (They will appear in a lighter typeface than the other selections, indicating that they are not available.) In order to enable these selections for use, you must perform certain actions which are outlined in Chapter 6.

Tek Options Menu

The Tek Options menu controls certain modes and functions of the Tektronix window. The menu can only be displayed from within the Tektronix window. As previously described, you can display the Tek window and make it the active window by using the Switch to Tek Mode command on the VT Options menu.

To display the Tek Options menu, move the pointer inside the Tektronix window. Press and hold down the Control key on the keyboard and press the second pointer button. The Tek

Options menu appears. With this menu you set the size of the text in the Tektronix window and select some commands.

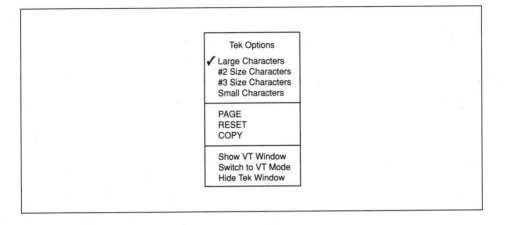

Figure 5-13. The Tek Options menu

Note that these modes (above the first line) can only be set from the Tek Options menu. All of these modes set the point size of the text displayed in the Tektronix window. (Only one of these four modes can be enabled at any time.)

The most important command on the Tek Options menu, shown in Figure 5-13, is Switch to VT Mode. If the Tek window has been made the active window (using the Switch to Tek Mode command from the VT Options menu), you can choose Switch to VT Mode to make the VT window the active window again. (If both windows are showing, you can also toggle Switch to Tek Mode on the VT Options menu to *deactivate* it; that is, switch *from* Tek mode and back to VT mode.) Switch to VT Mode is also a toggle; if you deactivate it, *xterm* will switch back to Tek mode.

Selecting Show VT Window displays the VT window if it has been hidden (using the Hide VT Window command from the VT Options menu) or hides it if it is being displayed. (Again, the command is a toggle.) Remember that you cannot input to the VT window until you make it the active window by using Switch to VT Mode.

6

Font Specification

This chapter describes what you need to know in order to select display fonts for the various client applications. After acquainting you with some of the basic characteristics of a font, this chapter describes the rather complex font naming conventions and how to simplify font specification. This chapter also describes how to use the xlsfonts, xfd, *and* xfontsel *clients to list, display, and select available screen fonts. Finally, this chapter explains the basics of using the font server (a Release 5 innovation) to access fonts resident on other machines on the network.*

In This Chapter:

☞

6
Font Specification

Many clients allow you to specify the font used to display text in the window, in menus and labels, or in any other text fields. For example, you can choose the font used for the text in *mwm* menus or in *xterm* windows.

Unfortunately, for the most part, there are no simple "font menus" like there are on systems such as the Macintosh.* Instead, X has a fairly complex font naming system (which, like most things about X, is designed for maximum flexibility rather than for simplicity or ease of use). Of course, there will no doubt soon be many applications, such as word processors and publishing packages, that provide a simple interface for selecting fonts. However, for the clients in the X distribution, you are generally limited to selecting fonts via command-line options or resource specifications.

This wouldn't be so bad if a typical font name weren't mind-bending at first glance. Imagine typing this command line to create an *xterm* window whose text is to be displayed in a 20-point constant width font:

```
% xterm -fn -misc-fixed-medium-r-normal--20-200-75-75-c-100-iso8859-1
```

Fortunately, you can use asterisks as wildcards to simplify this name to a somewhat more reasonable one:

```
% xterm -fn '*fixed-medium-r-*-200-*'
```

and you can define even simpler aliases, so that you could end up typing a command line similar to this:

```
% xterm -fn 20p
```

In this chapter, we're going to try to make sense out of the sometimes perplexing and arcane information about fonts under X. First, we'll explain the font naming convention in detail. Along the way, we'll acquaint you with the appearance of some of the basic font families (groups of related fonts), and the various permutations (such as weight, slant, and point size) within each family.

Then, we'll talk about how to use font name wildcards to simplify font specification. We'll also talk about the font search path (the directories where the font files are stored), and how to define aliases for font names.

---

*An exception is *xterm*'s VT Fonts menu. But even in this case, you need to know a lot about font naming to change the fonts available on the menu.

X also provides several utilities for dealing with fonts on the local machine:

- *xlsfonts*, which lists the names of the fonts available on your server, as well as any aliases.

- *xfd* (font displayer), which allows you to display the character set for any individual font you specify on the command line.

- *xfontsel* (font selector), which allows you to preview fonts and select the name of the one you want. (This name can then be pasted onto a command line, into a resource file, etc.)

Once we have an understanding of font naming conventions, we'll consider how to use these clients.

In addition, we'll see how to use two options available on *xterm*'s VT Fonts menu.

Note that the current chapter also covers two Release 5 additions, scalable fonts and a font server, which are introduced in the following section.

If you don't want to venture too far into the somewhat bewildering jungle of font names and directories, skip to the section "If You Just Want to Pick a Font," which should cut through the underbrush.

What's New in Release 5?

Prior to Release 5, all of the standard fonts provided with X were *bitmap fonts*. Bitmap fonts require a separate font file for each size of the font. There are several liabilities to this arrangement, not the least of which is that having multiple files for basically the same typeface makes managing fonts more difficult and wastes disk space. Also, because of the different resolution of computer monitors, a font intended to be a particular point size might actually appear larger or smaller on various screens.

Release 5 sees the addition of *font scaling* and includes some new *outline fonts*, which are suitable for scaling. An outline font stored in a single file can be scaled to any point size you request (though the scaling requires some system overhead). Although bitmap fonts *can* be scaled, the resulting scaled font is usually jagged and somewhat illegible. The *Speedo* font directory in the standard distribution contains Charter and Courier outline fonts donated by Bitstream, Inc. For more information about the standard font directories and outline fonts, see "The Font Search Path" and "Specifying Scalable Fonts," respectively.

The standard Release 5 bitmap fonts should be available on your system in *portable compiled font* format. The font files have an extension of *.pcf* to indicate this format. The currently available outline fonts in the *Speedo* directory deviate somewhat from the norm—they have the extension *.spd*.

Also prior to Release 5, fonts needed to be available on the local machine or had to be provided over the network via certain protocols. In Release 5, the X Window System provides a *font server* (*fs*) from which you can request fonts resident on other machines in the network. Later in this chapter, we'll show you how to run the font server with a very simple configuration and how to add the font server to your font search path.

Release 5 also includes a few clients intended to be run when the font server is in use, among them:

- *fslsfonts*, which is analogous to *xlsfonts*, lists the names of the fonts available on the specified font server.

- *fsinfo* gives information about the font server, including the alternate servers that are available.

- *showfont** lists some of the more esoteric characteristics of a font and provides ASCII representations of the individual characters. You can use the output of *showfont* to convert a font character into a bitmap image using the *atobm* client, described in Chapter 7, *Graphics Utilities*.

After considering the font server, we'll take a closer look at these clients.

If You Just Want to Pick a Font

X font names can be so complicated that you might prefer not to deal with them at all. If you want to experiment with fonts or access fonts on remote machines, you'll have to spend some time familiarizing yourself with the conventions anyway. But if you just want to locate some fonts to use with *xterm* and other clients, you can use the predefined aliases for some of the constant width fonts that should be available on most systems. (Later in this chapter we'll discuss how to define your own aliases.)

Figure 6-1 lists the aliases for some constant width fonts that should be appropriate for most of the standard clients, including *xterm*. To give you an idea of the range of sizes, each alias is written in the font it identifies.

In these cases, the aliases refer to the dimensions in pixels of each character in the font. (For example, *10x20* is the alias for a font with characters 10 pixels wide by 20 pixels high.) Note, however, that an alias can be virtually any character string.

The default font for many applications, including *xterm*, is a 6 × 13 pixel font that has *two* aliases: "fixed" and "6x13." Many users consider this font to be too small. If you have enough screen space, you might want to use the 10 × 20 font for *xterm* windows:

```
% xterm -fn 10x20 &
```

You can make this font the default for *xterm* by specifying it as the value for the font resource variable (in an *.Xresources* or other resource file):

```
XTerm*font:  10x20
```

See Chapter 11, *Setting Resources*, for instructions on specifying and loading resources.

---

*Don't confuse the MIT client *showfont* with our public domain client *xshowfonts*, which was used to create the pictures in Appendix B, *Release 5 Standard Fonts*.

See "Font Name Aliasing" later in this chapter for instructions on surveying the predefined aliases (and creating aliases of your own).

The section "Changing Fonts in xterm Windows" (later in this chapter) describes how to use two of the items on the *xterm* VT Fonts menu. Keep in mind, however, that you may need to know a bit more about font naming conventions, wildcards and aliasing to take full advantage of these options.

Font Naming Conventions

The X Window System font naming conventions are intended to allow for complete specification of all of the characteristics of each font. Unfortunately, this completeness makes the font names somewhat difficult to work with—at least until you learn what all the parts of the names mean, and get a handle on which parts you need to remember and which you can safely ignore. (By the end of this chapter, you should have that knowledge.)

The *xlsfonts* client can be used to display the names of all the fonts available locally to your server. When you run *xlsfonts*, you'll get an intimidating list of names similar to the name in Figure 6-1. Upon close examination, this rather verbose name contains a great deal of useful information: the font's developer, or foundry (b&h, Bigelow & Holmes); the font family (Lucida); weight (medium); slant (roman); set width (normal); additional style (sans serif); size of the font in pixels (18); size of the font in tenths of a point (180 tenths of a point, thus 18 points); horizontal resolution (75 dpi); vertical resolution (75 dpi); spacing (p, for proportional); average width (106—measured in tenths of a pixel, thus 10.6 pixels); and character set (iso8859-1).

As mentioned earlier, font name wildcarding can eliminate lots of unnecessary detail. If you are already familiar with font characteristics, skip ahead to the section "Font Name Wildcarding," later in this chapter, for some tips and tricks. If you need a refresher on fonts, read on as we illustrate and explain each of the elements that make up the font name.

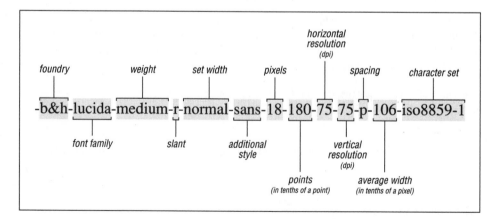

Figure 6-1. Font name components

Font Families

It has been several years since the advent of desktop publishing and, by now, it is unlikely that anyone in the computer industry is unaware that text can be displayed on the screen and printed on the page using different fonts.

However, the term *font* is used somewhat ambiguously. Does it refer to a family of typefaces (such as Times® Roman or Helvetica®), which comes in different sizes, weights, and orientations? Or should each distinct set of character glyphs be considered a separate font?

For the most part, X takes the latter approach. When the documentation says that Release 5 includes more than 500 fonts, this sounds either intimidating or impressive, depending on your mood. But, in fact, the R5 X distribution includes only eight font families (Charter, Courier, Helvetica, Lucida®, New Century Schoolbook®, Symbol, Times, and the Clean family of fixed-width fonts), plus several miscellaneous fonts that are found only in individual sizes and orientations,* and many more special purpose fonts. (R5 also includes a few outline fonts that can be scaled to any size you specify. These represent exceptions—different sizes are not considered different fonts. For further discussion, see "The Size of Bitmap and Outline Fonts" later in this chapter.)

When you think of the X fonts as comprising several large font families rather than as hundreds of individual (unique) fonts, you can quickly reduce the clutter. Figure 6-2 shows the major families of commercial fonts that are available under X. To illustrate the fonts, we've used the simple expedient of printing each font name in the font itself. Font names are truncated to fit on the page.† (For those of you who don't read the Greek alphabet, the fourth line down reads "-adobe-symbol-medium-r-normal--18 ... " This font is used for mathematical equations and so forth, rather than for normal display purposes.) You'll notice that with the exception of Courier and Lucidatypewriter, all of the fonts in the figure are *proportionally spaced*. That is, each character has a different width. This makes them look good on a printed page but makes them less appropriate for screen display in terminal windows (especially for program editing), since text will not line up properly unless all characters are the same width.

You will most likely use these proportional fonts for labels or menu items, rather than for running text. (Word processing or publishing programs will, of course, use them to represent proportional type destined for the printed page.)

Courier and Lucidatypewriter are *monospaced*, which means that every character has the same width. Although monospaced fonts *can* be used for the text font in *xterm* windows, if you do so, you may notice that some "garbage" pixels will occasionally be left on the screen. This effect happens because the characters are not clearly contained or divided from one another.

---

*By contrast, the Macintosh supports dozens of font families; commercial typesetters support hundreds and, in some cases, even thousands of families. Many of these fonts will doubtless be made commercially available for X.

†To generate the figures in this section and in Appendix B, *Release 5 Standard Fonts*, we wrote a short program called *xshowfonts*, which displays a series of fonts in a scrollable window. Source code for *xshowfonts* is listed in Appendix B, *Release 5 Standard Fonts*. In each case, we used wildcards (discussed later in this chapter) to select the fonts we wanted and then did screendumps of the resulting images. Note that the fonts look better on the screen than they do in the illustration, since the scaling factor used to make the screen dumps exacerbates the "jagged edges" endemic to bitmap fonts.

```
 -adobe-courier-medium-r-normal--18-180-75-75
-adobe-helvetica-medium-r-normal--18-180-75-75-p-ﾟ
-adobe-new century schoolbook-medium-r-normal--18-
-αδοβε-σψμβολ-μεδιυμ-ρ-νορμαλ--18-180-75-75-π-107-o
-adobe-times-medium-r-normal--18-180-75-75-p-94-iso8
-b&h-lucida-medium-r-normal-sans-18-180-75-
-b&h-lucidabright-medium-r-normal--18-180-75-7!
-b&h-lucidatypewriter-medium-r-normal-sans-1ﾟ
-bitstream-charter-medium-r-normal--19-180-75-75-p-106-isﾟ
```

Figure 6-2. The major commercial font families available in the standard X distribution

For *xterm* and other terminal emulators, you're better off using *character cell fonts*. These fonts are special monospaced fonts originally designed for computer displays. Each character in a monospaced font has the same width. Character cell fonts go a bit further in that an invisible cell contains every character. The spacing relates to the size of the cell that contains each character, rather than to the character itself.

As you may recall, these character cell fonts have simple aliases that correspond to their dimensions in pixels. For example, in the font named 8x13, each character occupies a box 8 pixels wide by 13 pixels high. (To fit the logical font naming conventions, these fonts have been given a foundry name of "misc" and a font family of "fixed.") There are also one or two larger fixed fonts donated by Sony for use with their extra-high resolution monitor, with a foundry name of "sony." Figure 6-3 shows some of the character cell fonts, using their aliases in R5.

Table 6-1 shows the correspondence between these aliases and full font names. Note that the 6x13 font also has an additional alias called "fixed" defined for it. The "fixed" alias is used as the default font for *xterm* windows. (Twelve-point Helvetica bold roman has the alias "variable," which several applications use as the default font for labels. *mwm* uses this font for the application name that appears in the title area of the window frame.)

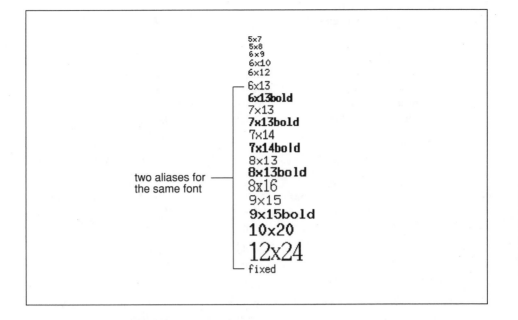

two aliases for the same font

Figure 6-3. Miscellaneous fonts for xterm text

Table 6-1. Fixed Font Aliases and Font Names

Alias	Filename
fixed	-misc-fixed-medium-r-semicondensed--13-120-75-75-c-60-iso8859-1
5x7	-misc-fixed-medium-r-normal--7-70-75-75-c-50-iso8859-1
5x8	-misc-fixed-medium-r-normal--8-80-75-75-c-50-iso8859-1
6x9	-misc-fixed-medium-r-normal--9-90-75-75-c-60-iso8859-1
6x10	-misc-fixed-medium-r-normal--10-100-75-75-c-60-iso8859-1
6x12	-misc-fixed-medium-r-semicondensed--12-110-75-75-c-60-iso8859-1
6x13	-misc-fixed-medium-r-semicondensed--13-120-75-75-c-60-iso8859-1
6x13bold	-misc-fixed-bold-r-semicondensed--13-120-75-75-c-60-iso8859-1
7x13	-misc-fixed-medium-r-normal--13-120-75-75-c-70-iso8859-1
7x13bold	-misc-fixed-bold-r-normal--13-120-75-75-c-70-iso8859-1
7x14	-misc-fixed-medium-r-normal--14-130-75-75-c-70-iso8859-1
7x14bold	-misc-fixed-bold-r-normal--14-130-75-75-c-70-iso8859-1
8x13	-misc-fixed-medium-r-normal--13-120-75-75-c-80-iso8859-1
8x13bold	-misc-fixed-bold-r-normal--13-120-75-75-c-80-iso8859-1
8x16	-sony-fixed-medium-r-normal--16-120-100-100-c-80-iso8859-1

Table 6-1. Fixed Font Aliases and Font Names (continued)

Alias	Filename
9x15	-misc-fixed-medium-r-normal--15-140-75-75-c-90-iso8859-1
9x15bold	-misc-fixed-bold-r-normal--15-140-75-75-c-90-iso8859-1
10x20	-misc-fixed-medium-r-normal--20-200-75-75-c-100-iso8859-1
12x24	-sony-fixed-medium-r-normal--24-170-100-100-c-120-iso8859-1

R5 also includes the Clean family of fixed-width fonts from Schumacher, and DEC's terminal fonts, both of which are illustrated in Appendix B, *Release 5 Standard Fonts*.

There are also many other special purpose fonts, such as the Greek Symbol font that we already saw, the cursor font, the OPEN LOOK™ cursor and glyph fonts, Hangul fonts, Hebrew fonts, and Kana and JIS Kanji Japanese fonts.

As mentioned previously, Bitstream, Inc. has donated a few Charter and Courier outline fonts. For more information, see "The Size of Bitmap and Outline Fonts" and "Specifying Scalable Fonts" later in this chapter.

See Appendix B, *Release 5 Standard Fonts*, for comprehensive lists of all standard fonts, as well as pictures of the complete character set in some representative fonts.

Stroke Weight and Slant

The characters in a given font family can be given a radically different appearance by changing the *stroke weight* or the *slant*, or both.

The most common weights are medium and bold. The most common slants are roman (upright), italic, or oblique. (Both italic and oblique are slanted; however, italic versions of a font generally have had the character shape changed to make a more pleasing effect when slanted, while oblique fonts are simply a slanted version of the upright font. In general, *serif* fonts (those with little decorations on the ends and corners of the characters) are slanted via italics, while *sans-serif* fonts are made oblique.) (Whether a font is sans serif comes under the category of additional style; see "Other Information in the Font Name.")

Figure 6-4 compares the medium and bold weights, and the roman and italic or oblique slants in the Charter® and Helvetica font families.

```
-adobe-helvetica-medium-o-normal--18-180-75-75-p-98-
-adobe-helvetica-medium-r-normal--18-180-75-75-p-98-
-adobe-helvetica-bold-o-normal--18-180-75-75-p-104-
-adobe-helvetica-bold-r-normal--18-180-75-75-p-103·
-bitstream-charter-medium-i-normal--19-180-75-75-p-103-iso885
-bitstream-charter-medium-r-normal--19-180-75-75-p-106-iso88
-bitstream-charter-bold-i-normal--19-180-75-75-p-117
-bitstream-charter-bold-r-normal--19-180-75-75-p-119
```

Figure 6-4. The same fonts in different weights and slants

Release 5 also includes one font that has an in-between weight called *demibold*. Weight names are somewhat arbitrary, since a demibold weight in one family may be almost as dark as a bold weight in another.

The font naming convention also defines two counter-clockwise slants called *reverse italic* (ri) and *reverse oblique* (ro), as well as a catch-all called *other* (ot).

The Size of Bitmap and Outline Fonts

Font sizes are often given in a traditional printer's measure known as a *point*. A point is approximately one seventy-second of an inch. You'll probably need to look at some fonts to get a better idea of point sizes, but most typewriters produce characters in either 10 or 12 point type. The characters in X fonts are measured both in points and in *pixels*, which can also be thought of as *dots*, or the individual picture elements that make up an image.

As mentioned previously (in "What's New in Release 5?"), the standard distribution of X includes two types of fonts: *bitmap fonts* and *outline fonts*. Outline, or scalable, fonts are intended to be scaled to any size you request. Thus, outline font names have zeros in the columns for point and pixel size. You normally request a particular size by filling in a point size. The most important thing to remember about these scalable outline fonts is that they are device-independent and, thus, true-to-size regardless of the screen. The section "Specifying Scalable Fonts" later in this chapter explains how to get the size font you want.

Most of the fonts provided with X are bitmap fonts. Though bitmap fonts *can* be scaled, they are not intended to be and scaled versions of bitmap fonts may have a jagged appearance. Each size and orientation of a bitmap font must be stored in a separate file. Most of the bitmap font families are provided in the six point sizes shown in Figure 6-5.

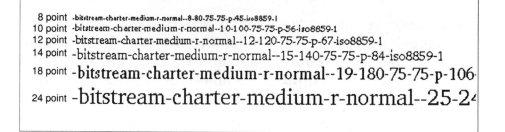

Figure 6-5. The same font in six different point sizes

Font size is not much of an issue when you're dealing with outline fonts. However, because of the different resolution of computer monitors, a bitmap font with a given point size might actually appear larger or smaller, depending on the particular screen. In the remainder of this section, we'll discuss the various factors that determine how large a font appears on your screen. This information might seem somewhat arcane, but it will be relevant to those dealing extensively with fonts. Everyone else should skip ahead.

Resolution is often spoken about in terms of the screen's dimensions in pixels. The *xdpyinfo* client, described in Chapter 8, *Other Clients*, will tell you this information; your workstation or X terminal documentation may also provide it. *xdpyinfo* also tells you the screen's resolution in dots per inch. Most monitors on the market today have a resolution between 75 dots per inch (dpi) and 100 dots per inch.

Accordingly, there are both 75-dpi and 100-dpi versions of most of the bitmap fonts in the standard distribution. These separate versions of each font are stored in different directories. By setting the font search path so that the appropriate directory comes first, you can arrange to get the correct versions without having to specify them in the font name.* Keep in mind that monitors can vary substantially. The Sun 19-inch monitor has a resolution of 1152 x 900 pixels (approximately 90 dpi). The NCD 16-inch X terminal has a resolution of 1024 x 1024 pixels (approximately 106 dpi).

What happens if you select the wrong resolution for your monitor? Given the difference in the pixel size, the same size font will appear larger or smaller than the nominal point size.

For example, consider the 75- and 100-dpi versions of the 24-point charter medium italic font:

```
-bitstream-charter-medium-i-normal--25-240-75-75-p-136-iso8859-1
-bitstream-charter-medium-i-normal--33-240-100-100-p-179-iso8859-1
```

If you look at the pixel size field, you will notice that the height of the 75-dpi version is 25 pixels, while the height of the 100-dpi version is 33 pixels. If you use the 75-dpi version on the Sun, you actually get something closer to 20 points (75/90*24); on a 100-dpi monitor, you will actually get something closer to 18 points (75/100*24). We noticed this right away when we first began using the NCD X terminal. Because of the NCD's higher resolution, the font size we had been using on the Sun appeared smaller.

---

*We'll talk about how to set the font search path later in this chapter.

If you are working on a lower-resolution monitor, you can take advantage of this artifact to display type as large as 32 points (the size that a 24-point 100-dpi font will appear on a 75-dpi monitor.) Figure 6-6 shows the 75- and 100-dpi versions of the same 24-point font, as displayed on a Sun workstation with a 19-inch monochrome monitor. As shown, neither is actually 24 points. The 75-dpi version is actually 20 points, as discussed above; the 100-dpi version is about 26.4 points.*

Note that the logical font-naming convention allows for different horizontal and vertical resolution values. This would allow server manufacturers to support fonts that were "tuned" for their precise screen resolution. However, the bitmap fonts shipped with the generic X11 distribution all use the same horizontal and vertical resolution.

-adobe-new century schoolbook-medium-r-
-adobe-new century schoolbook-n

Figure 6-6. The 100-dpi version of a 24-point font appears larger on a 75-dpi monitor

As suggested above, this resolution may not exactly match the actual resolution of any particular screen, resulting in characters that are not true to their nominal point size. On the Sun monitor, neither the 75- nor 100-dpi fonts will be right. (Of course, if you are using scalable outline fonts, this isn't a problem.)

Other Information in the Font Name

What we've already shown summarizes the most important information in the font name. The remaining fields are explained below:

Foundry
: Font manufacturers are still referred to as foundries, from the days when type was cast from lead. The X font naming convention specifies the foundry as the company that digitized or last modified the font, rather than its original creator.

  For the fonts contained in the standard X distribution, the foundry is not terribly significant since there are no cases where the same font family is available from different foundries. However, there are numerous commercial font families available from more than one foundry. In general, the appearance of the fonts should be quite similar since the font family defines the design of the typeface. However, there may be some small differences

---

*Note that the differences are exaggerated further in printing the screen dump of this display. *xpr* lets you select a scale factor such that each pixel on the screen appears as *scale* pixels in the printout. Since the laser printer has a 300-dpi resolution, a scale factor of 4 would produce a true scale screen dump if the resolution on the Sun monitor were truly 75 dpi by 75 dpi. Since it is actually 90 by 90, the printed image is enlarged by about 16 percent.

in the quality of some of the characters, and there may be more significant differences in the font metrics (the vertical or horizontal measurements of the characters). This might be significant for a publishing application that was using the bitmapped font for a *wysiwyg** screen display that needed to match the fonts in a particular laser printer or typesetter.

Set width   A value describing a font's proportionate width, according to the foundry. Typical set widths include: normal, condensed, semicondensed, narrow, double width. Most of the Release 5 fonts have the set width *normal*. A few fonts have the set width *semicondensed*.

Additional Style Not represented in most R5 font names. However, according to the logical font convention, the style of a font may be specified in the field between set width and pixels. Some of the possible styles are *i* (informal), *r* (roman), *serif* and *sans* (serif). Currently all of the standard fonts have *sans* or an empty field. Note that the *r* for roman may also be used in the slant field.

Spacing   All standard Release 5 fonts are either: *p* (proportional, i.e., variable-width); *m* (monospace, i.e., fixed-width); or *c* (character cell, a fixed-width font based on the traditional typewriter model, in which each character can be thought to take up the space of a "box" of the same height and width).

Average width Mean width of all characters in the font, measured in tenths of a pixel. You'll notice, if you look back at Figure 6-2, that two fonts with the same point size (such as New Century Schoolbook and Times) can have a very different average character width. This field can sometimes be useful if you are looking for a font that is especially wide or especially narrow.

             The Schumacher Clean family of fonts offers several fonts in the same point size but with different average widths.†

Character set In the initial illustration of the font naming convention, Figure 6-1, we identified the character set as a single field. If you look more closely, you'll realize it is actually two fields, the first of which identifies the organization or standard registering the character set, the second of which identifies the actual character set.

             Most fonts in the standard X distribution contain the string "iso8859-1" in their names, which represents the ISO Latin-1 character set. The ISO Latin-1 character set is a superset of the standard ASCII character set, which includes various special characters used in European languages other than English. See Appendix H of Volume Two, *Xlib Reference Manual*, for a complete listing of the characters in the ISO Latin-1 character set.

---

*This is an acronym for "what you see is what you get" and describes a type of text editor or word processor that purports to display the page exactly as it would appear in print. There is some approximation due to the differences between screen fonts and printer fonts. MacWrite® is a *wysiwyg* program in the MacIntosh world; FrameMaker, Interleaf and others offer wysiwyg programs in the X world.

†These fonts all (incorrectly to our minds) have a set width of "normal." They should be distinguished by set widths such as condensed, semi-condensed, etc. Since they do not, they can be distinguished by the difference in their average width.

Note, however, that the symbol font contains the strings "adobe-fontspecific" in this position. This means that Adobe Systems defined the character set in this font, and that it is font-specific. You can see from this example that the use of these fields is somewhat arbitrary.

For a complete technical description of font naming conventions, see the X Consortium Standard, *X Logical Font Description Conventions*. This document is available as part of the standard MIT X distribution, and is reprinted as Appendix M in the second edition of Volume 0, *X Protocol Reference Manual*.

Font Name Wildcarding

To simplify font specification, X supports the use of wildcards within font names. An asterisk (*) can be used to represent any part of the font name string; a question mark (?) can be used to represent any single character. You can usually get the font you want by specifying only the font family, the weight, the slant, and the point size, and wildcarding the rest. For example, to get Courier bold at 14 points, you could use the command-line option:

```
-fn '*courier-bold-r*140*'
```

That's starting to seem a little more intuitive!

However, there are a number of "gotchas."

- First, since the UNIX C shell also has a special meaning for the * and ? wildcard characters, wildcarded font names must be quoted. This can be done by enclosing the entire font name in quotes (as in the previous example), or by "quoting" each wildcard character by typing a backslash before it. (If you don't do this, the shell will try to expand the * to match any filenames in the current directory, and will give the message "No match.") Wildcards need not be quoted in resource files.

- Second, if the wildcarded font name matches more than one font, the server will use the first one that matches. And unfortunately, because the names are sorted in simple alphabetical order, the bold weight comes before medium, and italic and oblique slants before roman. As a result, the specification:

```
-fn '*courier*'
```

will give you Courier bold oblique, rather than the Courier medium roman you might intuitively expect.

If you aren't sure whether your wildcarded name is specific enough, try using it as an argument to *xlsfonts*. If you get more than one font name as output, you may not get what you want. Try again with a more specific name string.

The exception to this rule has to do with the *75dpi* and *100dpi* directories. If a wildcard matches otherwise identical fonts in these two directories, the server will actually use the one in the directory that comes first in the font path. This means that you should put the appropriate directory first in the font path. (We'll tell you how to do this in the next section.) Thereafter, you can generally wildcard the resolution fields (unless you specifically want a font from the directory later in the path).*

• Third, the asterisk (*) wildcard expansion is resolved by a simple string comparison. So, for example, if you type:

```
-fn '*courier-bold*r*140*'
```

instead of:

```
-fn '*courier-bold-r*140*'
```

(the difference being the asterisk instead of the hyphen before the "r" in the slant field), the "r" would also match the "r" in the string "normal" in the set width field. The result is that you would select all slants. Since o (oblique) comes before r (roman), and you always get the first font that matches, you'd end up with Courier oblique.

The trick is to be sure to include at least one of the hyphens to set the -r- off as a separate field rather than as part of another string.

Even though a wildcarded name such as:

```
*cour*b*r-*140*
```

should get you 14-point Courier bold roman, we think it is good practice to spell out the font family and weight and use hyphens between adjacent fields. As usual there are exceptions: the Lucida family really has three subfamilies; you can get all three by specifying the family as "Lucida*" rather than "Lucida-"; and you might certainly want to abbreviate "New Century Schoolbook" to "New Century*" or "*Schoolbook."

• Font names are case-insensitive. "Courier" is the same as "courier."

Table 6-2 summarizes the values you should use to specify a font name (assuming only the standard fonts are loaded). Choose one element from each column. Don't forget to include the leading and trailing asterisks and the hyphen before the slant.

---

*Unlike *xfontsel*, which displays fonts in the order of wildcard matches, *xlsfonts* will always list fonts in straight-sort order, with the sort done character by character across the line. Since size in pixels comes before point size in the name, and the size in pixels of the 100-dpi fonts is larger than that of the equivalent 75-dpi font, the 75-dpi font will always be listed first for a given point size. But when listing more than one point size, the fonts will be jumbled. For example, the size in pixels of the 8-point Charter font at 100-dpi is 11, so it will come after the 10-point Charter font at 75 dpi, with a size in pixels of 10. The 8-point Charter font at 75 dpi gets sorted to the very end of the list, since to a character-by-character sort, its size in pixels (8) looks larger to the size in pixels of even the largest 100-dpi font (the 24 point, with a height of 33 pixels).

X Window System User's Guide, Motif Edition

Table 6-2. Essential Elements of a Font Name

*	Family	–	Weight	–	Slant	*	Point Size	*
	charter		medium		r (roman)		80 (8 pt.)	
	clean		bold		i (italic)		100 (10 pt.)	
	courier		demibold		o (oblique)		120 (12 pt.)	
	fixed				ri (reverse italic)		140 (14 pt.)	
	gothic				ro (reverse oblique)		180 (18 pt.)	
	helvetica				ot (other)		240 (24 pt.)	
	lucida							
	lucidabright							
	lucidatypwriter							
	mincho							
	new century schoolbook							
	nil							
	open look cursor							
	open look glyph							
	symbol							
	terminal							
	times							

Note that the point sizes listed in the table correspond to the point sizes of the standard bitmap fonts in the *75dpi* and *100dpi* directories. If you are specifying one of the scalable outline fonts, you do not have to limit yourself to these sizes. You can also specify alternative sizes for the bitmap fonts, but the results may not be very legible. See "Previewing and Selecting Fonts: xfontsel" for information about previewing fonts.

Note also that if you specify either Charter or Courier in a medium or bold weight, with either a roman or italic slant, you will get one of the scalable outline fonts in the *Speedo* directory before an analogous bitmap font in the *75dpi* directory. (This assumes that the default font search path is in effect.) You can avoid this issue with Courier fonts by additionally providing the foundry name ("adobe" for the bitmap version, "bitstream" for the outline version). Bitstream provides analogous Charter fonts in the *Speedo*, *75dpi*, and *100dpi* directories, so the font path is critical. See "The Font Search Path" and "Specifying Scalable Fonts" for more information.

Another way to avoid these issues is to provide unique aliases for all bitmap fonts. See "Font Name Aliasing" later in this chapter for more information.

Specifying Scalable Fonts

The *Speedo* directory in the standard distribution provides eight scalable outline fonts, whose names are listed below:

```
-bitstream-charter-medium-r-normal--0-0-0-0-p-0-iso8859-1
-bitstream-charter-medium-i-normal--0-0-0-0-p-0-iso8859-1
-bitstream-charter-bold-r-normal--0-0-0-0-p-0-iso8859-1
-bitstream-charter-bold-i-normal--0-0-0-0-p-0-iso8859-1
-bitstream-courier-medium-r-normal--0-0-0-0-m-0-iso8859-1
-bitstream-courier-medium-i-normal--0-0-0-0-m-0-iso8859-1
-bitstream-courier-bold-r-normal--0-0-0-0-m-0-iso8859-1
-bitstream-courier-bold-i-normal--0-0-0-0-m-0-iso8859-1
```

Notice that the three fields relating to size (pixels, points, and average width), plus the two resolution fields, have zeroes in them. You can specify any one of these scalable outline fonts simply by adding a point size. The following name scales the Courier bold italic font to 24 points (on most screens, a huge font):

```
-bitstream-courier-bold-i-normal--0-240-0-0-m-0-iso8859-1
```

Note that you can also scale any of the bitmap fonts (to a different size than those offered) by taking the font name and:

1. Changing the pixel and average width fields to zero;

2. Specifying the point size you want (in tenths of a point).

Note that every field must have something in it (even if you use an asterisk wildcard). Don't use an asterisk to replace multiple adjacent fields. The following name scales the Adobe Courier bold font (roman slant) to 15 points (a size not usually available).

```
-adobe-courier-bold-r-normal--0-150-75-75-m-0-iso8859-1
```

Remember, however, that scaling bitmap fonts may produce "jagged" results.

The Font Search Path

In Release 5, fonts are stored in four directories, as shown in Table 6-3.

Table 6-3. Standard Font Directories, Release 5

Directory	Contents
/usr/lib/X11/fonts/misc	Fixed-width fonts suitable for terminal emulation, the standard cursor font, several Clean family fonts provided by Schumacher, two JIS Kanji fonts, several Kana fonts from Sony Corporation, two Hangul fonts from Daewoo Electronics, two Hebrew fonts from Joseph Friedman, two cursor fonts from Digital Equipment Corporation, and OPEN LOOK cursor and glyph fonts from Sun Microsystems, Inc.
/usr/lib/X11/fonts/Speedo	Charter and Courier (scalable) outline fonts donated by Bitstream, Inc. (New in Release 5.)
/usr/lib/X11/fonts/75dpi	Fixed- and variable-width fonts, 75 dpi, contributed by Adobe Systems, Inc., Digital Equipment Corporation, Bitstream, Inc., Bigelow and Holmes, and Sun Microsystems, Inc.
/usr/lib/X11/fonts/100dpi	Fixed- and variable-width fonts, 100 dpi, many the 100 dpi versions of the fonts in the *75dpi* directory.

These four directories (in this order) constitute X's default font path.

Modifying the Font Search Path

You can change the font path using the *xset* client with the fp (font path) option. *xset* allows you to:

- Rearrange the order of the directories in the font search path;
- Add directories to or substract directories from the font path;
- Completely replace the font path.

For example, say you add fonts to a directory called *newfonts*, a subdirectory of your home directory.* To access these fonts, you add the directory to the font path (in effect, inform the X server about the directory).

---

*Whenever you add fonts to a directory (according to the guidelines in Volume Eight), before running *xset* you must first run the command:

```
% mkfontdir directory_name
```

Volume Eight, *X Window System Administrator's Guide*, explains how to convert, compile, and install fonts.

Use *xset* with the fp+ option to add a directory or list of directories to the end of the font path. The following command appends the ~/*newfonts* directory* to the path:

```
% xset fp+ ~/newfonts
```

We can verify that the new path is in effect by running *xset* with the q option (which "queries" the settings):

```
% xset q
    .
    .
    .
```

```
Font Path:
/usr/lib/X11/fonts/misc/,/usr/lib/X11/fonts/Speedo/,/usr/lib/X11/fonts/75dpi/,\
/usr/lib/X11/fonts/100dpi/,~/newfonts
```

(The preceding output is broken onto two lines escaped with a backslash (\) only so that it can be printed within the page margins.)

Notice that in adding directories to the font search path, the location of the plus sign is significant. The command:

```
% xset +fp ~/newfonts
```

adds ~/*newfonts* to the beginning of the existing path.

You can remove a directory from the font path using either the -fp or fp- option. The location of the minus sign is not significant. To remove ~/*newfonts* from the font path, enter:

```
% xset -fp ~/newfonts
```

or:

```
% xset fp- ~/newfonts
```

Note that you can add or subtract multiple directories from the font path with a single invocation of *xset*. After the relevant fp option, the argument should be a comma-separated list of directories, as in the command:

```
% xset fp+ ~/newfonts,/usr/lib/X11/fonts/new
```

This command adds the directories ~/*newfonts* and */usr/lib/X11/fonts/new* to the end of the current font path.

To completely replace the font path (rather than append to or subtract from the current path), use fp= followed by a comma-separated list of directories:

```
% xset fp= fontdir1,fontdir2,fontdir3,...
```

Note that a space must follow the equal sign (=).

You would also use xset fp= to change the order of directories in the current path. For example, to put the *100dpi* directory before the *75dpi* directory, you would enter:

```
% xset fp= /usr/lib/X11/fonts/misc,/usr/lib/X11/fonts/Speedo,\
           /usr/lib/X11/fonts/100dpi,/usr/lib/X11/fonts/75dpi
```

You can restore the default font path at any time by entering:

```
% xset fp default
```

Note that if you want to access fonts via a remote (or even a local) font server (*fs*) program, you must add the font server to the path. See "Using the Font Server" later in this chapter for more information.

The fonts.dir Files

In addition to font files, each font directory contains a file called *fonts.dir*. The *fonts.dir* files serve, in effect, as databases for the X server. When the X server searches the directories in the default font path, it uses the *fonts.dir* files to locate the font(s) it needs.

Each *fonts.dir* file contains a list of all the font files in the directory with their associated font names in two-column form. (The first column lists the font file name and the second column lists the actual font name associated with the file.) The first line in *fonts.dir* lists the number of entries in the file (i.e., the number of fonts in the directory).

Example 6-1 shows a portion of the *fonts.dir* file from the Release 5 */usr/lib/X11/fonts/100dpi* directory. As the first line indicates, the directory contains 200 fonts. The first group of fonts listed below (up to the second ellipse) are all Courier family fonts. The second group of fonts shown in the list below are a few sizes from the Charter family.

Example 6-1. Subsection of the Release 5 fonts.dir file in /usr/lib/X11/fonts/100dpi

```
200
  .
  .
  .
courBO08.snf -adobe-courier-bold-o-normal--11-80-100-100-m-60-iso8859-1
courBO10.snf -adobe-courier-bold-o-normal--14-100-100-100-m-90-iso8859-1
courBO12.snf -adobe-courier-bold-o-normal--17-120-100-100-m-100-iso8859-1
courBO14.snf -adobe-courier-bold-o-normal--20-140-100-100-m-110-iso8859-1
courBO18.snf -adobe-courier-bold-o-normal--25-180-100-100-m-150-iso8859-1
courBO24.snf -adobe-courier-bold-o-normal--34-240-100-100-m-200-iso8859-1
courB08.snf -adobe-courier-bold-r-normal--11-80-100-100-m-60-iso8859-1
courB10.snf -adobe-courier-bold-r-normal--14-100-100-100-m-90-iso8859-1
courB12.snf -adobe-courier-bold-r-normal--17-120-100-100-m-100-iso8859-1
courB14.snf -adobe-courier-bold-r-normal--20-140-100-100-m-110-iso8859-1
courB18.snf -adobe-courier-bold-r-normal--25-180-100-100-m-150-iso8859-1
courB24.snf -adobe-courier-bold-r-normal--34-240-100-100-m-200-iso8859-1
courO08.snf -adobe-courier-medium-o-normal--11-80-100-100-m-60-iso8859-1
courO10.snf -adobe-courier-medium-o-normal--14-100-100-100-m-90-iso8859-1
courO12.snf -adobe-courier-medium-o-normal--17-120-100-100-m-100-iso8859-1
courO14.snf -adobe-courier-medium-o-normal--20-140-100-100-m-110-iso8859-1
courO18.snf -adobe-courier-medium-o-normal--25-180-100-100-m-150-iso8859-1
courO24.snf -adobe-courier-medium-o-normal--34-240-100-100-m-200-iso8859-1
courR08.snf -adobe-courier-medium-r-normal--11-80-100-100-m-60-iso8859-1
courR10.snf -adobe-courier-medium-r-normal--14-100-100-100-m-90-iso8859-1
courR12.snf -adobe-courier-medium-r-normal--17-120-100-100-m-100-iso8859-1
courR14.snf -adobe-courier-medium-r-normal--20-140-100-100-m-110-iso8859-1
courR18.snf -adobe-courier-medium-r-normal--25-180-100-100-m-150-iso8859-1
courR24.snf -adobe-courier-medium-r-normal--34-240-100-100-m-200-iso8859-1
  .
  .
  .
```

```
charBI08.snf -bitstream-charter-bold-i-normal--11-80-100-100-p-68-iso8859-1
charBI10.snf -bitstream-charter-bold-i-normal--14-100-100-100-p-86-iso8859-1
charBI12.snf -bitstream-charter-bold-i-normal--17-120-100-100-p-105-iso8859-1
charBI14.snf -bitstream-charter-bold-i-normal--19-140-100-100-p-117-iso8859-1
charBI18.snf -bitstream-charter-bold-i-normal--25-180-100-100-p-154-iso8859-1
charBI24.snf -bitstream-charter-bold-i-normal--33-240-100-100-p-203-iso8859-1
   .
   .
   .
```

The *fonts.dir* files are created by the *mkfontdir* client when X is installed. In the case of bit-map fonts, *mkfontdir* reads the font files in the relevant directories in the path, extracts the font names, and creates a *fonts.dir* file in each directory. Scalable outline fonts (in the *Speedo* directory) require an intermediary file called *fonts.scale*, which *mkfontdir* converts to a *fonts.dir* file. The standard distribution includes a *fonts.scale* file in the *Speedo* directory.

If *fonts.dir* files are present on your system, you probably won't have to deal with them or with *mkfontdir* at all. If the files are not present, or if you have to load new fonts or remove existing ones, you will have to create files with *mkfontdir*. Refer to the *mkfontdir* reference page in Part Three of this guide and Volume Eight, *X Window System Administrator's Guide*, for more information.

Font Name Aliasing

Another way to abbreviate font names is by aliasing (that is, by associating fonts with alternative names of your own choosing). You can edit or create a file called *fonts.alias*, in any directory (or multiple directories) in the font search path, to set aliases for existing fonts. The X server uses both *fonts.dir* files and *fonts.alias* files to locate fonts in the font path.

Release 5 provides a default *fonts.alias* file for each of the three bitmap font directories (*misc*, *75dpi*, and *100dpi*). (The scalable outline fonts in the *Speedo* directory cannot be aliased because you must provide a point size!) Take the time to look at the contents of each of these files, since many of the existing aliases may be easier to type than even wildcarded font names. If you have write permission for the directory, you can also add aliases to the file, change existing aliases, or even replace the entire file. However, this should be done with caution. To play it safe, it's probably a good idea merely to *add* to existing *fonts.alias* files. If you're working in a multiuser environment, the system administrator should definitely be consulted before aliases are added or changed. Note that when you create or edit a *fonts.alias* file, the server does not *automatically* recognize the aliases in question. You must make the server aware of newly created or edited alias files by resetting the font path with *xset*.

The *fonts.alias* file has a two-column format similar to the *fonts.dir* file: the first column contains aliases, the second column contains the actual font names. If you want to specify an alias that contains spaces, enclose the alias in double quotes. If you want to include double quotes (") or other special characters as part of an alias, precede each special symbol with a backslash (\).

When you use an alias to specify a font in a command line, the server searches for the font associated with that alias in every directory in the font path. Therefore, a *fonts.alias* file in one directory can set aliases for fonts in other directories as well. You might choose to create a single aliases file in one directory of the font path to set aliases for the most commonly used fonts in all the directories. Example 6-2 shows three sample entries that could be added to an existing *fonts.alias* file (or constitute a new one).

Example 6-2. Sample fonts.alias file entries

```
cour12    -adobe-courier-medium-r-normal--12-120-75-75-m-70-iso8859-1
cour14    -adobe-courier-medium-r-normal--14-140-75-75-m-90-iso8859-1
cour18    -adobe-courier-medium-r-normal--18-180-75-75-m-110-iso8859-1
```

As the names of the aliases suggest, these sample entries provide aliases for three Courier fonts of different point sizes. You can also use wildcards within the font names in the right column of an alias file. For instance, the alias file entries above might also be written as follows:

```
cour12    *courier-medium-r-*-120*
cour14    *courier-medium-r-*-140*
cour18    *courier-medium-r-*-180*
```

If you would like to be able to use font filenames as aliases, you must explicitly assign every font name an alias corresponding to the name of the file in which it is stored. (It's a good idea to use the filename without the *.pcf* extension.) This could actually be done rather easily by editing a copy of each *fonts.dir* file and appending the copy to the *fonts.alias* file in the same directory. (These aliases could also be appended to the *fonts.alias* file in the *misc* directory, since the server searches all directories in the font path.)

Once the server is made aware of aliases, you can specify an alias on the command line. For example, you can use a font name alias as an argument to *xfd*. If you've used an alias file or files to specify font names (minus extensions) as aliases, you can display the font stored in the file *courR12.pcf* using the command:

```
% xfd -fn courR12 &
```

A special note about the *misc* directory: when X was configured for your system, a *fonts.alias* file should have been created in this directory. The first two entries in this file are shown below:

```
fixed    -misc-fixed-medium-r-semicondensed--13-120-75-75-c-60-iso8859-1
variable -*-helvetica-bold-r-normal-*-*-120-*-*-*-*-iso8859-1
```

The default file contains an additional 64 entries but the entries pictured above are particularly important. The aliases called "fixed" and "variable" are invoked as the default fonts for many clients. The "fixed" font can be thought of as a system-wide default. The "variable" font, described in the right column as a 12-point bold Helvetica font, is used as the default font by *bitmap*, as well as by other clients. If this file is removed or replaced, when you run *bitmap*, you'll get an error message that the server cannot open the variable font, and text in the *bitmap* window will display in the smaller, somewhat less readable "fixed" font.

If you do choose to edit the *fonts.alias* file in the *misc* directory, it is important to preserve at least these two aliases. As we've said, it's probably a better idea to keep all the default entries and merely append any new ones.* Regardless of what edits you make to the file, the line specifying the variable alias must not be changed.

Making the Server Aware of Aliases

After you create (or update) an alias file, the server does not automatically recognize the aliases in question. You must make the server aware of newly created or edited alias files by "rehashing" the font path with *xset*. Enter:

```
% xset fp rehash
```

on the command line. The *xset* option fp (font path) with the rehash argument causes the server to reread the *fonts.dir* and *fonts.alias* files in the current font path. You need to do this every time you edit an alias file. (You also need to use *xset* if you want to change the font path. See "Modifying the Font Search Path" earlier in this chapter for details.)

Utilities for Displaying Information about Fonts

We've already mentioned *xlsfonts*, which simply displays the names and aliases of available fonts. In addition, *xfd* can be used to display the full character set of a particular font, and *xfontsel* can be used interactively to preview and select a font for use in another window.

The Font Displayer: xfd

If you're unfamiliar with the general appearance of a particular font, we've included pictures of some representative fonts in Appendix B, *Release 5 Standard Fonts*.

You can also display the characters in a font using the *xfd* (font displayer) client. Note that *xfd* takes the -fn option before the font name. For example, to display the default system font, a 6×13 pixel fixed-width font known by the alias *fixed*, enter:

```
% xfd -fn fixed &
```

The *xfd* window will display the specified font as shown in Figure 6-7.

---

*If you don't have the necessary permissions to edit the *fonts.alias* files, simply create a new file in a directory of your choosing. Then use *xset* to add the directory to the server's font search path and to direct the server to reread all *fonts.dir* and *fonts.alias* files, as described in "Modifying the Font Search Path" earlier in this chapter.

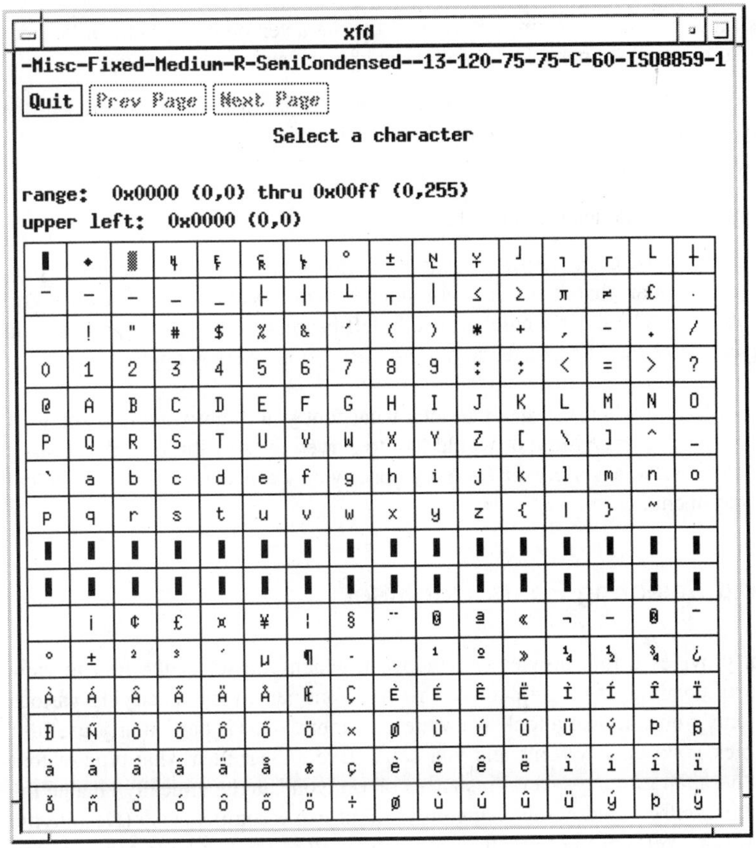

Figure 6-7. Fixed font, 6 × 13 pixels

The font name is displayed across the top of the window. (This is the actual font name, which we specified on the command line by the alias *fixed*.) Three command buttons appear in the upper-left corner of the window below the font name. If the font being displayed doesn't fit within a single *xfd* screen, Prev Page and Next Page allow you to scroll through multiple screens. (The horizontal and vertical window dimensions can vary slightly to accommodate different fonts but certain fonts will still require multiple screens.) The Quit button causes the application to exit, though this can also be done by typing q or Q while input is focused on the *xfd* window.

In addition to displaying a font, *xfd* also allows you to display certain information about the individual characters. But before we examine these capabilities, let's take a closer look at the way the characters in a font are identified and how the *xfd* window makes use of this information.

Within a font, each character is considered to be numbered. The *xfd* client displays a font's characters in a grid. By default, the first character of the font appears in the upper-left position; this is character number 0. The two text lines above the grid identify the upper-left character and the range of characters in the window by character numbers both in hexadecimal and in decimal notation (in parentheses following the hex character number).

You can specify a character other than character number 0 to be in the first position in the window using the -start option. For example, if you enter this command line:

```
% xfd -start 15 -fn fixed &
```

the *xfd* window begins with character number 15.

Notice the instruction Select a character below the command buttons. To display information about a particular character, click any pointer button within the character's grid square. Statistics about the character's number, width, left bearing, right bearing, ascent, and descent are displayed where the line Select a character previously appeared.

The *xfd* client is most useful when you have an idea what font you might want to display. If you don't have a particular font in mind or would like to survey the possibilities, the *xfontsel* client allows you to preview a variety of fonts by specifying each component of the font name using a different menu.

Previewing and Selecting Fonts: xfontsel

The *xfontsel* client provides a font previewer window in which you select the font to view using 14 menus corresponding to the 14 components of a font name. By specifying various font name components, you can take a look at a variety of fonts. This is particularly useful if you are trying to pick good display fonts and you don't have a clear idea what type of font would be best. Rather than running several instances of *xfd*, you can dynamically change the font displayed in the *xfontsel* window by changing the font name components. (Despite the flexibility of *xfontsel*, it's certainly not practical to preview *all* of the available fonts. If you have no idea what a particular font family looks like, see the discussion earlier in this chapter, or refer to Appendix B, *Release 5 Standard Fonts*, for pictures of some representative fonts.)*

Once you've displayed the desired font using the menus, you can make the name of that font the PRIMARY text selection by clicking on the window's **select** button. You can then paste the font name into another window using the pointer: onto a command line, into a resource file, etc. Making a font name the PRIMARY selection also enables you to choose that font from the *xterm* VT Fonts menu. (Selecting text and using *xterm* menus are described in Chapter 5, *The xterm Terminal Emulator*.)

---

*To our minds, the major drawback of *xfontsel* is that it shows you only the first font that matches a given wildcarded font name. A far better interface would list all of the matching fonts so that you could compare and choose the one that best suited your needs. There is no way in the standard X distribution to display the appearance of a group of fonts. To produce the figures in this book, we had to write such a program, which we called *xshowfonts*. The program has since been posted to *comp.sources.x*, and a listing appears in Appendix B, *Release 5 Standard Fonts*.

Previewing Fonts with the xfontsel Menus

To run *xfontsel*, enter this command in an *xterm* window:

```
% xfontsel &
```

If your system is using the standard Release 5 fonts, the *xfontsel* window initially displays a 12 point, character cell Hangul font (the Korean alphabet) from the *misc* font directory, the complete name of which is:

```
-daewoo-gothic-medium-r-normal--16-120-100-100-c-160-ksc5601.1987-0
```

This is the first font in the default font search path. (The foundry "daewoo" comes first alphabetically in the *misc* directory, the first directory in the default font path.) Figure 6-8 shows the initial *xfontsel* window.

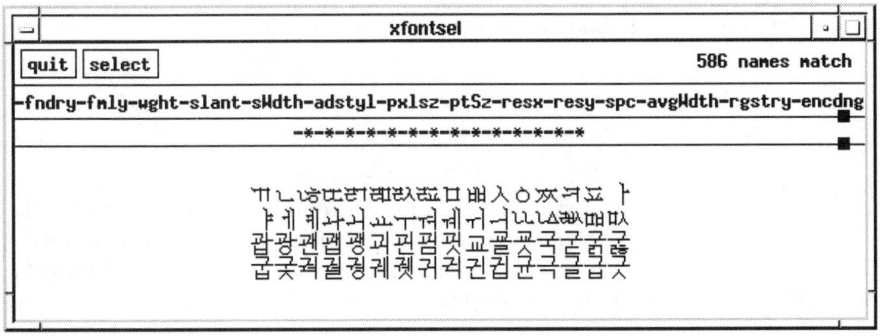

Figure 6-8. xfontsel window displaying Hangul font

The upper-left corner of the *xfontsel* window features two command buttons: quit and select. As we've explained, clicking on select with the first pointer button makes the font displayed in the window the PRIMARY text selection; obviously, quit causes the application to exit.

Below the command buttons is, in effect, a generic font name or font name template. It is divided into 14 fields corresponding to the 14 parts of a standard font name. Each field is an abbreviation for one part of a font name. Take a look again at the sample font name in Figure 6-1 to refresh your memory as to the components. Each of the fields in the *xfontsel* window is actually the handle to a menu which lets you specify this part of the font name.

To get a clearer idea of how this works, move the pointer onto the generic font name—specifically onto the first field, fndry. (This is an abbreviation for the first part of a font name, the foundry.) When you place the pointer on fndry, the field title should be highlighted by a box. You can then display a menu of foundry names by pressing and holding down the first pointer button, as in Figure 6-9.

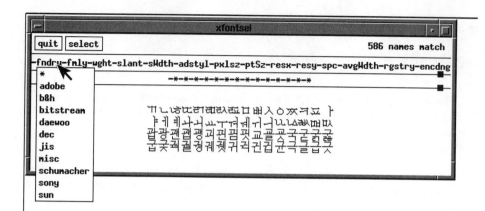

Figure 6-9. xfontsel window with foundry menu displayed

Notice that the first choice is the asterisk (*) wildcard character. This is the first choice on all of the menus, allowing you to include wildcards in the font name you specify rather than explicitly selecting something from all 14 menus.

To specify a font name component (i.e., make a selection from the menu), first display the menu by pressing and holding down the first pointer button. Then move the pointer down the menu. As the pointer rests on each menu item, it is highlighted by reverse video. To select a highlighted menu item, release the first pointer button.

The line below the font name menus represents the actual font name. When you first run *xfontsel*, all of these fields contain wildcard characters because no menu selections have been made. The number of fonts matched by the font name is displayed in the upper-right corner of the window. The number of fonts initially matched depends on the number of fonts with this naming convention available on your system. In this example, 586 fonts match. (Since this line of wildcards can match *any* 14-part font name, the server chooses the first font in the font path that reflects this naming convention.)

When you select a font name component from one of the 14 menus, the component appears in the actual font name, and the *xfontsel* window displays the first font that matches this name. For example, say we select **adobe** from the **fndry** menu, the *xfontsel* window would look like Figure 6-10. The font name is now:

```
-adobe-*-*-*-*-*-*-*-*-*-*-*-*-*
```

and the window displays the first font in the font path that matches this wildcarded name. In this case, the first font to match is a 12-point bold Oblique Courier font, which is stored in the file *courBO12.pcf* and has the actual font name:

```
-adobe-courier-bold-o-normal--12-120-75-75-m-70-iso8859-1
```

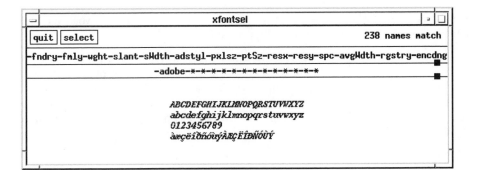

Figure 6-10. xfontsel after choosing adobe from the foundry menu

Once you make a selection from one menu, the number of possible fonts matched by the name changes. (Notice the line 238 fonts match in the upper-right corner of the window.) Choosing one font name component also eliminates certain choices on other menus. For example, after you select Adobe as the foundry, the possible choices for font family (the second menu, fmly) are narrowed from 17 to 5 (not counting the asterisk). Again display the fmly menu using the first pointer button. The available choices for font family appear in a regular typeface; the items that are unavailable (i.e., cannot be selected) appear in a lighter typeface. Families such as Clean, Lucida, and Charter are in a lighter typeface because none of the standard X fonts provided by Adobe is from these families. Adobe fonts in the standard X distribution are limited to the five families Courier, Helvetica, New Century Schoolbook, Symbol, and Times; these are the items available on the fmly menu.

In order to display a particular font, you'll probably have to make selections from several of the menus. As described earlier in the section "Font Name Wildcarding," we suggest you explicitly select at least these parts of the font name:

- Font family
- Weight
- Slant
- Point size

Thus, you would make selections from the fmly, wght, slant, and ptSz menus.

You can also use the -pattern option with a wildcarded font name to start out with a more limited range of options. For example, if you typed:

```
% xfontsel -pattern '*courier-bold-o-*'
```

you'd start out with the pattern you specified in the filename template part of the *xfontsel* display. You could then simply select from the ptSz menu to compare the various point sizes of Courier bold oblique until you found the one you wanted.

Note that if the pattern you specify to *xfontsel* matches more than one font, the one that is displayed (the first match found) is the one that the server will use. This is in contrast to *xlsfonts*, which sorts the font names. You can always rely on *xfontsel* to show you the actual font that will be chosen, given any wildcard specification.

As of Release 5, you can use *xfontsel* to preview (and select) a scaled version of any standard font (both bitmap and outline fonts). (As you might remember, though outline fonts are *intended* to be scaled, X supports scaling of bitmap fonts as well.) This capacity of X to scale fonts is reflected in a new **ptSz** menu. If you display the menu, you'll notice that it offers a wider range of sizes than the actual font files do. To view any of the standard fonts scaled to one of these new sizes:

1. Run *xfontsel* without the -fn option.

2. Narrow your selections using the menus, choosing 0 for both pixel size and average width.

3. The point size menu will offer several sizes not generally available in the standard font files. Choose the point size to which you want the font scaled.

If you like the font, you can select it from the *xfontsel* window for use elsewhere, as described in the next section.

Selecting a Font Name

Once you make selections from the menus to compose the name of the font you want, the corresponding font is displayed in the *xfontsel* window. Then you can select that font name by clicking on the **select** command button with the first pointer button. The font name becomes the PRIMARY text selection and thus can be pasted in another window using the second pointer button, as described in Chapter 5, *The xterm Terminal Emulator*.

You might paste the font name on a client command line in an *xterm* window in order to specify it as the client's display font. (See Chapter 10, *Command-line Options*.) You might paste it into a resource file such as *.Xresources* to specify it as the default font for a client or some feature of a client (such as a menu). (See Chapter 11, *Setting Resources*, for more information.)

Less obviously, once a font name is made the PRIMARY text selection, it can be toggled as the *xterm* display font using the **Selection** item of the *xterm* VT Fonts menu. The **Selection** menu item can only be chosen from the VT Fonts menu when there is a PRIMARY text selection. (Otherwise, the menu item appears in a lighter typeface, indicating that it is not available.) If the PRIMARY text selection is a valid font name (as it is when you've pressed the **select** button in the *xfontsel* window), the *xterm* window displays in that font. (In cases where the PRIMARY selection is not a valid font name, the *xterm* display font does not change.)

By default, *xfontsel* displays the alphabetic characters (and the digits 0 through 9, if the character set includes them). You can specify alternative sample text using the `-sample` option. For more information about this and other options, see the *xfontsel* reference page in Part Three of this guide.

Changing Fonts in xterm Windows

xterm includes a VT Fonts menu that allows you to change fonts on the fly. We discussed most of the menu entries in Chapter 5. However, two of the many items require a greater understanding of font naming than we'd covered by that point. So we've saved them until now.

The Great Escape

Though it is by no means obvious, *xterm* allows you to change the display font by sending an escape sequence, along with the new font name, to the terminal window. Once you change the font in this way, the Escape Sequence item on the *xterm* VT Fonts menu becomes available and choosing it toggles the font you first specified with the escape sequence. (In effect, whatever font you specify using the escape sequence is stored in memory as the menu's Escape Sequence font selection.)

You send an escape sequence to the terminal window by using the UNIX *echo*(1) command. The escape sequence to change the *xterm* display font comprises these keystrokes:

```
Esc ] 50 ; fontname Control-G
```

To clarify, these keystrokes are: the Escape key, the right bracket (]), the number 50, a semicolon (;), a *fontname*, and the Control-G key combination. We've shown the keystrokes with spaces between them for readability, but when you type the sequence on the command line, there should be no spaces. Note also that to supply this sequence as an argument to *echo*, you must enclose it in quotes:

```
% echo "Esc]50;fontnameControl-G"
```

These are the literal keys you type. However, be aware that when you type these keys as specified, the command line will not look exactly like this. Certain keys, such as Escape, and key combinations, such as Control-G, are represented by other symbols on the command line. When you type the previous key sequence, the command line will actually look like this:

```
% echo "^[]50;fontname^G"
```

Pressing the Escape key generates the ^[symbol; typing the Control-G key combination generates ^G. You can use a full fontname, an alias, or a wildcarded font specification as the font name. You should be aware that if the wildcarded specification matches more than one font, you will get the first font in the search path that matches. For example:

```
% echo "^[]50;*courier*^G"
```

will get you a 10-point courier bold oblique. The advantage of being able to change the display font with an escape sequence is that it allows you to add another font to your choices on the fly.*

Changing the fonts associated with the Unreadable, Tiny, Small, Medium, Large, and Huge menu items is a more laborious process. It involves specifying other fonts in a resource file, making those resources available to the server, and then running another *xterm* process. (See Chapter 11, *Setting Resources*, for more information.) However, you can change the font specified by the Escape Sequence menu item as often as you want during the current *xterm* process, simply by typing the escape sequence described previously.

Now that we've looked at the mechanics of the escape sequence, let's consider its practical use. Say you want to run a program in an *xterm* window and you want to be able to read the output easily, but you would like the window to be moderately small. You discover that toggling the Medium font, the 7x13 font by default, makes the window a good size, but the typeface is too light to be read· easily. (We presume you are using the default menu fonts and have not customized them using a resource file.) You could dynamically change the display font to a bold font of the same size by entering the following command line:

```
% echo "Esc]50;7x13boldControl-G"
```

The *xterm* font becomes the desired 7x13bold, a good choice; in addition, the Escape Sequence item of the VT Fonts menu becomes available for selection. This menu item allows you to toggle the 7x13bold font at any time during the *xterm* process. Thus, you could switch back to any of the other fonts available on the menu (Small, Large, etc.) and then use Escape Sequence to again select 7x13bold.

This font will remain the Escape Sequence font for the duration of the *xterm* process, unless you again change the display font with an escape sequence. If you enter another font name using the escape sequence described above, the window will display in that new font and the Escape Sequence menu item will toggle it.

The Selection Menu Item

The Selection menu item allows you to toggle a font whose name you've previously "selected." For example, you could select the font name with the pointer from *xlsfonts* output, using the "cut-and-paste" techniques described in Chapter 5, *The xterm Terminal Emulator*. It is far more likely, though, that you would use this menu item after selecting a font with *xfontsel*. This menu item was clearly designed with *xfontsel* in mind. (If no text is currently selected, the Selection menu item appears in a lighter typeface, indicating that it is unavailable.)

---

*Specifying a font with an escape sequence affects only the current *xterm* window and enables only that window's Escape Sequence menu selection.

The main limitation of this menu item is that it uses the *last text selected* as the font name, regardless of what that text is. If you select a font name, that name is only available through Selection until you use the pointer to select other text. Since cutting and pasting text is one of the most useful features of *xterm*, you will probably be making frequent selections. If the last selected text was not a valid font name, toggling Selection will not change the display font, and a beep will inform you that the toggle failed.

Using the Font Server

The font server (*fs*) program acts as intermediary between your X server and the fonts resident on the system where the font server is running. If the font server is running on one or more remote machines, you can add those servers to your font path on the local host and then access the remote fonts.* Once a font server is added to your path, you can request a font in the normal manner (e.g., on the command line, in a resource file, etc.) and both the local and remote directories will be searched. The access is invisible.

You can also add a font server running on the local system to your font path, though the advantages of this are more subtle. Primarily, having the local font server in your path enables you to use certain "Font Server Clients" (described later in this chapter) with local fonts.

The operation of the font server program is controlled by a special configuration file called *config*, which is commonly located in the directory */usr/lib/X11/fs*. The sample configuration file provided in the MIT distribution should be sufficient in many environments.

In the following section, we'll take a quick look at the sample configuration file. Then we'll see how to run the font server program and how to add servers to the font path. (Keep in mind, however, that the system administrator for the machine in question will generally be the one to run *fs*.) Finally, we'll consider some of the clients you can run to find out information about the font server and the available fonts.

Be aware that environment- and vendor-specific issues may necessitate customizing the *config* file. Volume Eight, *X Window System Administrator's Guide*, provides instructions on customizing the *config* file and explains how to run the font server in a variety of environments.

---

*Technically, if the font server is not running on a host whose fonts you want to use, you can run it yourself—presuming you have access. We'll show you a rudimentary way to do this; however, in most cases, running *fs* will be up to the system administrator. See Volume Eight, *X Window System Administrator's Guide*, for more information.

The Font Server config File

The font server *config* file has a fairly simple syntax, though some of the variables it sets may be unfamiliar. (They deal with functionality that is generally the province of the system administrator.) Here's the sample file provided with the standard distribution:

```
# font server configuration file
# $XConsortium: config.cpp,v 1.7 91/08/22 11:39:59 rws Exp $

clone-self = on
use-syslog = off
catalogue =
/usr/lib/X11/fonts/misc/,,/usr/lib/X11/fonts/Speedo/,,/usr/lib/X11/fonts/75
dpi/,,/usr/lib/X11/fonts/100dpi/
error-file = /usr/lib/X11/fs/fs-errors
# in decipoints
default-point-size = 120
default-resolutions = 75,75,100,100
```

This file sets six variables:

clone-self
: The default value of on specifies that the font server should spawn another copy of itself to handle more than 10 client connections (the default maximum).

use-syslog
: The default value of off specifies that error messages will not be logged (using *syslog*).

catalogue
: A list of the font directories available from the server. (By default, this is the standard font path.)

error-file
: An error log file (an alternative to *syslog*).

default-point-size
: In decipoints (or tenths of a point); thus, the default is 12 points.

default-resolutions
: Typical horizontal and vertical resolutions.

The defaults the file provides should be reasonable for most environments. You would need to change the catalogue to match an alternative font path.

Running the Font Server

There's a reasonable chance that the font server will already be running on the hosts you want to access. (The system administrator may keep the font server running all the time by placing it in a system startup file, such as */etc/rc.local*.) You can verify that the font server is running either by asking the system administrator or by logging in to the system in question and searching for the relevant process number:

```
% ps -aux | grep fs
```

(Depending on the system, you may need to use an analogous command.) If the font server is running, you'll see output containing a line similar to the one in bold:

```
·
·
·
root      103  0.0  0.0    40     0 ?  S    Sep 30  0:02  (nfsd)
root      104  0.0  0.0    40     0 ?  S    Sep 30  0:02  (nfsd)
root      366  0.0  0.0  4496     0 p3 IW   Oct  3  4:40  /usr/bin/X11/fs
val      1069  0.0  3.0    40   224 p3 S    19:20   0:00  grep fs
```

which corresponds to the *fs* process. If the font server is running, you can skip ahead to the next section, "Adding a Server to the Font Path."

If *fs* is not running on a host you want to use as a font server, ask the system administrator to start it or to give you permission to start it from the command line. If you need to start the font server yourself, log in to the machine you want and enter:

```
% fs &
```

An error message such as:

```
Error: Can't open error file "/usr/lib/X11/fs/fs-errors"
```

means that the font server probably doesn't have write permission for the error file. Any errors will be sent to the controlling *xterm* or the console. You can specify an another file with the `error-file` keyword in the font server *config* file; or ask the system administrator to add write permission to *fs-errors*.

If for some reason you can't run *fs* or if you want to configure the font server in a particular way, speak to the system administrator. Volume Eight, *X Window System Administrator's Guide*, describes several possible font server configurations.

Adding a Server to the Font Path

When the *fs* (font server) program is running on a remote host, you can identify the host as a font server to access from your local machine. To specify that a remote font server should be searched along with the current (local) font path, you use the *xset* client.

The format of a font server name is:

```
transport/hostname:port
```

`transport` refers to the protocol used by the font server. For UNIX environments, the protocol is `tcp`. The default `port` is `7000`. Here is a typical font server name:

```
tcp/ruby:7000
```

Say you're working on a machine called *harry*, but you want to access fonts available on another machine called *ruby*. Assuming that the *fs* program is running on *ruby* (a reasonable assumption), you simply have to add the the font server *ruby* to your font path on *harry*. (We'll use a "harry%" prompt to make things clearer.)

```
harry% xset fp+ tcp/ruby:7000
```

If you get no error message, query the font path setting using *xset* to verify that the server *ruby* has been added.

```
harry% xset q
```
.
.
.
```
Font Path:
 /usr/lib/X11/fonts/misc/,/usr/lib/X11/fonts/Speedo/,/usr/lib/X11/fonts/75dpi/,
/usr/lib/X11/fonts/100dpi/,tcp/ruby:7000
```

If *fs* is not running on *ruby* or if you've supplied an incorrect server name, when you try to add a font server to the path you will get the error message:

```
X Error of failed request:  BadValue (integer parameter out of range
   for operation)
   Major opcode of failed request:  51 (X_SetFontPath)
   Value in failed request:  0x5
   Serial number of failed request:  5
   Current serial number in output stream:  8
```

If *fs* isn't running on *ruby*, you can speak to the system administrator or try to run it on the command line yourself.

Note that you can also add an instance of the font server running on the local machine to your path. The following command prepends the font server running on *harry* to your font path on *harry*:

```
harry% xset +fp tcp/harry:7000
```

We can verify this by checking the path:

```
harry% xset q
```
.
.
.
```
Font Path:
 tcp/harry:7000,/usr/lib/X11/fonts/misc/,/usr/lib/X11/fonts/Speedo/,\
/usr/lib/X11/fonts/75dpi/,/usr/lib/X11/fonts/100dpi/,tcp/ruby:7000
```

If you have access to a local font server, you can use the following clients with local fonts.

Font Server Clients

Once you've added a font server to your path, you can specify a font from that host on the command line or in a resource file. You can also use a few clients that are intended to be run with the font server.

fslsfonts is analogous to *lsfonts* in that it list the names of all fonts available from a specified font server, as in the following example:

```
harry% fslsfonts -server tcp/ruby:7000
```

Since this output is sizeable, it's a good idea to pipe it to a paging program like *more*:

```
harry% fslsfonts -server tcp/ruby:7000 | more
```

You can also limit your search to a particular font (an alias is acceptable) or a group of fonts (a wildcarded name in quotes) by using the additional command-line option, -fn:

```
harry% fslsfonts -server tcp/ruby:7000 -fn fixed
fixed
```

Notice that the program echoes back the alias "fixed," indicating that the font is available from the server *ruby*.

If you get an error such as:

```
fslsfonts: pattern "huh" unmatched
```

you may have specified an invalid font name, or the font server *config* file may have an error in one of the path names.

The *fsinfo* client simply verifies that a server is running and lists alternative servers (in this case, none):

```
harry% fsinfo -server tcp/ruby:7000
name of server: tcp/ruby:7000
version number: 1
vendor string:  MIT X Consortium
vendor release number:  5000
maximum request size:   16384 longwords (65536 bytes)
number of catalogues:   1
        all
Number of alternate servers: 0
number of extensions:    0
```

The *showfont* client provides some rather arcane information about a font (much of which is provided without a font server by *xfd*). *showfont* also provides an ASCII representation of each character in a font. (You can convert a character into a bitmap image using the *atobm* program. See Chapter 7, *Graphics Utilities*, for instructions.)

To gather data about a font from a server, you'd use a command line similar to:

```
harry% showfont -server tcp/ruby:7000 -fn fixed > fixed.info
```

In our example, we've redirected the information to a file. You might instead pipe it to a paging program, as in the *fslsfonts* example.

In Chapter 7, *Graphics Utilities*, we grab the Gumby character from the cursor font and convert it into a bitmap image. If you're working on *harry* and the local font server is in your path, you can save the cursor font to a file by entering:

```
% showfont -server tcp/harry:7000 cursor > /tmp/cursor.array
```

Notice that we've used the alias for the cursor font.

See Chapter 7, *Graphics Utilities*, for instructions on converting a font character to a bitmap using *atobm*.

For more information on *fslsfonts*, *fsinfo*, and *showfont*, see the client reference pages in Part Three of this guide.

7

Graphics Utilities

This chapter describes how to use the major graphics clients included with X, notably the bitmap *editor.*

In This Chapter:

☞

7
Graphics Utilities

A *bitmap* is an image composed of individual pixels, or picture elements (you might think of them as dots), each of which is white, black, or, in the case of color displays, a color. Most of the images on an X display are actually bitmaps. For example, the various cursor symbols representing the pointer on the screen, such as the arrow, crosshair, and I-beam, are bitmap images (in this case, incorporated into the cursor font).

The standard release of X includes four utilities to help you create bitmap images: *bitmap*, *xmag*, *bmtoa*, and *atobm*. The most powerful and useful of these clients is *bitmap*, a program that lets you create and edit bitmap files. This chapter provides detailed instructions for using the *bitmap* client. You can use *bitmap* to create images to use as backgrounds, icons, and pointer symbols.

In a sense, the *xmag* client is a desk accessory for graphics programs. This client is used to magnify a portion of the screen, to assist you in creating images with a graphics editor, such as *bitmap*, or in capturing screen images with the *xwd* window dump utility, described in Chapter 8, *Other Clients*. As of Release 5, *xmag* is designed to work in concert with *bitmap*. You can copy and paste bitmap images between these clients. This chapter provides all the information you need to get started with *xmag*.

The *bmtoa* and *atobm* clients are programs that convert bitmaps to arrays (of ASCII characters) and arrays to bitmaps. They are used to facilitate printing and file manipulation and can help you convert a font character to a bitmap, as we'll demonstrate.

In addition to these standard clients, the user-contributed part of the X distribution includes a very useful library of graphic utilities: the Portable Bitmap Toolkit, developed by Jef Poskanzer. The PBM Toolkit is made up of dozens of programs that convert graphic images to and from portable formats. Some of the conversions you can perform are described later in this chapter.

Overview of the bitmap Editor

The *bitmap* program allows you to create and edit small bitmaps. At this point in X Window System development, *bitmap* is primarily a tool for application developers. However, several clients allow you to specify a bitmap as an icon, cursor symbol, or background pattern. Thus, you can create a bitmap image using *bitmap*, save it in a file, and specify that filename on the command line.* For example, *xsetroot* (described in Chapter 14, *Setup Clients*) allows you to specify a bitmap that will be used as the background pattern for the root window or as the root window pointer.

To bring up an empty *bitmap* window in which to edit, type:

```
% bitmap &
```

Note that no filename argument is necessary. (The Release 4 *bitmap* requires one.) The default *bitmap* window is shown in Figure 7-1.

The window that *bitmap* creates has three sections: a menu bar, a column of editing command buttons, and the actual editing area.

Menu Bar

The menu bar across the top of the application window provides two menus, File and Edit. You display a menu by placing the pointer on the appropriate command button and pressing and holding down any pointer button. More about the available menu options later. The menu bar also displays the name of the bitmap file. When you run a new instance of the program, this name will be *none*.

Editing Command Buttons

Below the menu bar, on the left side of the window, is a list of editing commands in buttons. Place the pointer on a command button and click the first pointer button to invoke the command. These commands help you draw the bitmap image. The section "Bitmap Command Buttons" later in this chapter provides an overview of these functions.

---

*There are many bitmaps included in the X distribution. These can generally be found in the directory */usr/include/X11/bitmaps*. Samples are shown in Appendix C, *Standard Bitmaps*.

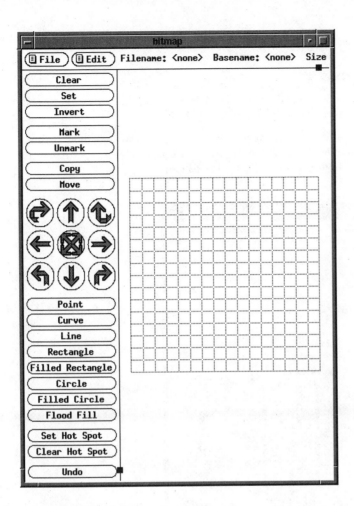

Figure 7-1. Release 5 Bitmap window

Editing Area

To the right of the command buttons is a grid in which you create/edit the bitmap. Each square in the grid represents a single pixel on the screen. The default size of the grid is 16 × 16 squares, representing an area of the screen 16 × 16 pixels—a fairly tiny spot. The grid affords a close-up look at this area and allows you to edit an image that would otherwise be too small to work with.

Once you begin playing with *bitmap*, you may find the 16 × 16 space too restricting. You can specify another grid size using the -size command-line option, which has the syntax:

    -size *widthxheight*

The following command line opens a *bitmap* window with a 32 × 32 grid, a more workable space:

```
% bitmap -size 32x32 &
```

The -size option is new in Release 5. In prior releases, you could supply the dimensions simply as a command-line argument, without a preceding option.

Figure 7-2 shows a 40 × 40 grid with a bitmap we created of Gumby. We think it makes a fun root window pattern. (See the discussion of *xsetroot* in Chapter 14, *Setup Clients*, for instructions on specifying a bitmap as your root window pattern.)

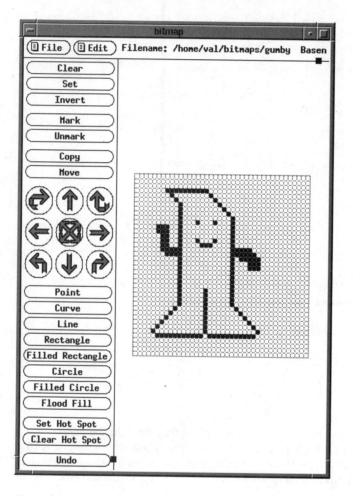

Figure 7-2. Gumby bitmap

The standard cursor font also contains a Gumby character. (You can specify the Gumby cursor as the *xterm* window pointer, as described in Chapter 11, *Setting Resources*, or as the root window pointer using the *xsetroot* client, as described in Chapter 14, *Setup Clients*.) Later in this chapter, we'll show you how to convert the Gumby character of the cursor font to a bitmap file using the *atobm* client.

Image Size Versus Window Size

Keep in mind that there is an interaction between the size of the bitmap image being edited and the size of the *bitmap* window. By default, each cell in the *bitmap* editing area is 13 pixels square. If you specify grid dimensions of 40 × 40, the editing area alone will be 520 pixels square. Specifying a very large editing area may even result in an application window larger than the screen. (Since *bitmap* does not provide a scrollbar, a large window makes it very difficult to edit!)

You can change the size of the editing area (not the number of squares) by: specifying an explicit size for the overall application using the -geometry option; or resizing the application window using the window manager. In either case, *bitmap* will automatically adjust the size of each square in the grid to fit the overall window size. (If the bitmap image is very large and *bitmap* window cannot incorporate it, the image will appear truncated. If you resize the window to be larger, more of the image should be revealed.)

A mild caution about using the -geometry option: when you specify a size for the overall application window, it may be difficult to estimate what size the editing squares will be. So if you use -geometry, there's a reasonable chance you'll have to resize anyway.

You can control the size of the editing grid even more precisely by using the -sw and -sh command-line options, which set the width and height of each square in pixels. We find that we need at least 10 × 10 pixel grid squares to edit comfortably, but this is clearly an individual preference.

As you're probably realizing, the number of factors that can determine the size of the application window and the editing grid make specifying the size on the command line rather complicated. Your best bet may be to confine yourself to the -size option for a while and make any necessary adjustments using the window manager. (You may never need to use -geometry, -sw, or -sh.)

Once you run *bitmap*, you can adjust either the size of the squares in the grid, or the actual number of squares. You change the size of squares in the grid by resizing the *bitmap* window using the window manager. For example, if the cells in the grid aren't large enough for comfortable editing, make the window larger. Each square on the grid will be enlarged proportionally. Alternatively, you might have a grid with large dimensions and make the window smaller so it takes up less space. The squares will be made smaller proportionally. (Note, however, when the squares are made very small, the grid lines are suppressed. Though editing is still possible in such circumstances, it is difficult.)

You can change the number of squares in the editing grid using the Resize option on the File menu. (See "The File Menu" later in this chapter.) Of course, if you want, you can also change the dimensions of each square using the window manager!

You can open an existing bitmap file to edit by supplying the filename on the *bitmap* command line. Keep in mind that if no size is specified and the image you display is larger than 16 × 16, *bitmap* will try to fit the image into an editing area the same overall size as the default. However, to accomplish this, each pixel in the image will be scaled down and the grid lines will be suppressed. In this case, you can still use all the editing commands, but chances are the image will be too small to work with precisely. If the image is large enough, one pixel in the image may actually be represented by a single pixel in the editing area! Some images may even be too large to fit under this circumstance, in which case the image will appear truncated. If you resize to make the window larger, more of the image should be revealed. As a general rule, if you know the dimensions of the image in pixels, it's a good idea to give them with `-size`.

What's New in Release 5

The Release 5 *bitmap* is actually much more powerful and versatile than the Release 4 version, but is unfortunately somewhat less intuitive. If you're using *bitmap* for the first time, you can skip this section altogether. If you're trying to switch from R4 to R5, you might want to at least glance through this section.

As mentioned previously, a filename argument is no longer required on the command line. The `-size` option, which allows you to specify the dimensions of the editing grid, is also new in Release 5. See the section "Editing Area" earlier in this chapter for some syntax examples and the *bitmap* reference page in Part Three of this guide for a list of valid options.

Release 5 sees the addition of a menu bar, which provides two menus, File and Edit, each offering many useful new functions. There are also keyboard shortcuts for all menu commands (as well as for some of the command buttons). Among the new functions provided on the menus are those that allow you to:

- Dynamically load another bitmap file into the editing window.

- Insert another bitmap image into the current bitmap file.

- Save one image and start editing a new one.

- Change the current filename.

- Change the dimensions of the grid.

- Copy/cut and paste between *bitmap* windows (or between *bitmap* and *xmag*).

In addition to the new functionality provided by the menus, there are additional editing command buttons (on the left side of the window). You can now draw a Rectangle or Filled Rectangle. Don't miss the Undo command, a long overdue improvement. Also helpful (if somewhat less than intuitive) are "arrow" command buttons (halfway down in the window) to flip or move the image (or part of it).

There is perhaps one obvious negative change to *bitmap*: by default the Release 4 *bitmap* shows you an actual size picture of the bitmap—in a tiny box below the command buttons (also an inverted version of the same bitmap). Each time the grid changes, the same change occurs in the actual size bitmap and its inverse. In Release 5, you must select the Image item of the Edit menu to bring up these two tiny images, which then appear in a small window on top of the *bitmap* window, above and to the left of the editing grid.

Note also that the command buttons to Clear Area, Set Area, and Invert Area have been removed. You can perform the equivalent of Clear Area by marking an area (Mark command button) and using the Cut command (on the Edit menu). Flood Fill can do in place of Set Area in some cases. There is no replacement for Invert Area.

bitmap Editing Commands

You can create and edit a bitmap using a combination of pointer commands and command buttons (on the left side of the window), and certain File and Edit menu items. The pointer commands work on one grid square at a time, while the relevant Edit menu items and many of the command buttons can work on the entire grid or on a specified area.

Pointer Commands to Draw

If you want, you can draw an image pixel by pixel simply by using the pointer (though the command buttons and menu items can make things easier). When you first open a *bitmap* window, before you select any commands, the following pointer actions are in effect. The same actions also apply whenever you've selected any of the drawing command buttons (Point, Curve, Line, Rectangle, Filled Rectangle, Circle, and Filled Circle).

Note that each pointer button has a different effect on the single square under the pointer.

First button   Changes a grid square to the foreground color and sets the corresponding bitmap bit to 1. (On most displays, the default foreground color is black.)

Second button   Inverts a grid square, changing its color and inverting its bitmap bit.

Third button   Changes a grid square to the background color (often white) and sets the corresponding bitmap bit to 0.

If you click the pointer, you change one square at a time (regardless of which drawing command is in effect). You can hold down a pointer button and drag the pointer to change several squares in a row. Depending on which drawing command is in effect, the shape you can draw in this way is limited. See "Drawing: Point, Curve, Line, Rectangle, Circle."

Pointer actions in the whitespace surrounding the grid affect the outermost row on that side of the grid.

Note that if any of the drawing commands is in effect and you click in the editing area to raise the window, you will change the pixel closest to the pointer.

Bitmap Command Buttons

The command buttons on the left side of the window are intended to make drawing and editing easier. To invoke a *bitmap* editing command, move the pointer to the appropriate command button and click the first pointer button. When you select a command button, the button is inverted (i.e., it displays in reverse video). Most choices are mutually exclusive. For example, you can't draw a Curve and a Line at the same time. Thus, only one of those command buttons can be active at a time.

Most of the commands have keyboard *accelerators*, or shortcuts. To use a shortcut, the pointer must rest inside the editing grid or the surrounding whitespace (not in the menu bar or the command button column).

Note that, as of Release 5, *bitmap* provides an Undo command (and a keyboard accelerator for it, u).

When you start *bitmap*, the Point command is in effect (though there is no indication—the button is not inverted). Point means that you can use the "Pointer Commands to Draw" described previously.

The following sections describe the various command buttons in what we consider to be a logical order, rather than the order in which they appear in the window.

Undo

Last in the *bitmap* window but perhaps first in importance is the Undo command button, which negates the effect of the last action you performed. Typing u while the pointer rests in the editing area has the same effect.

Drawing: Point, Curve, Line, Rectangle, Circle

Though you can draw pixel by pixel by clicking the pointer (as described in "Pointer Commands to Draw" earlier in this chapter), *bitmap* provides several command buttons that can make drawing easier. If you use the first pointer button to draw, the drawing is done in the foreground color. If you use the third pointer button, the drawing is done in the background color. (The second button inverts each square in the area drawn.)

Point   As we've said, Point is in effect when you start *bitmap*. It allows you to draw using the pointer on individual pixels. If you click the pointer, you change one pixel. If you hold down a pointer button and drag the pointer, you change the pixels over which the pointer travels.

Curve   Curve (new in R5) is intended to let you draw continuous curved lines—a good idea. Note, however, that drawing the curve you want is not necessarily easy. Curve merely insures that when you hold a pointer button down and drag (as you can with Point, Line, etc.), you'll get a *continuous* line. The way you move the pointer determines the arc (if any). (Curve allows you to draw a straight line as well.) To draw a curve:

1. Click the first pointer button over the Curve command button. The button displays in reverse video.

2. Move the pointer to the editing grid. The pointer becomes the crosshair symbol.

3. Hold a pointer button and drag the pointer to draw a curve. The button you use determines whether the curve will be drawn using the foreground or background color. (See "Pointer Commands to Draw" earlier in this chapter.)

Figure 7-3 shows a curve drawn in the foreground color (by holding the first pointer button and dragging).

Line   If you select Line and then hold down and drag the pointer in the grid, *bitmap* will draw a continuous line that is *as straight as possible*. Again, the pointer button you hold determines the color in which the line is drawn. Note that this command works differently than in previous releases in which you chose the beginning and ending points of the line and *bitmap* connected them. To draw a line:

1. Click the first pointer button on the Line command button. The button displays in reverse video.

2. Move the pointer into the editing area. It changes to a cross symbol.

3. Place the cross pointer on the square you want to be one end of the line. (The left end is easier for a righthanded person, right end for someone left-handed.) Press and hold down the first pointer button to draw in the foreground color. A gray shading covers the square the pointer is on.

4. Drag the pointer away from that square. The line you trace with the pointer will be highlighted in gray.

5. When you've traced the line you want (still in gray shading), release the pointer button. The line will be drawn (in this case in the foreground color).

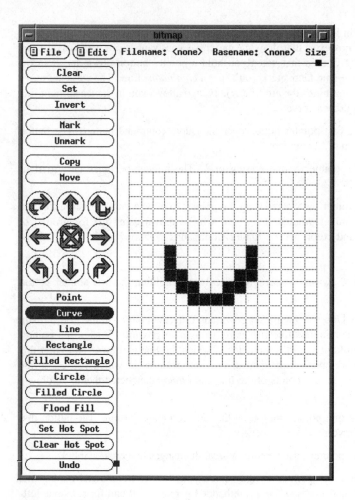

Figure 7-3. Drawing a curve

In Figure 7-4 we've drawn a diagonal line from the bottom left corner to the top right corner of the editing area.

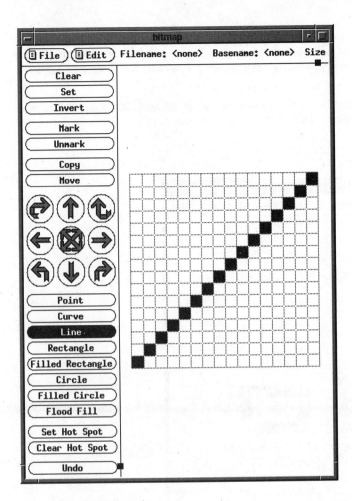

Figure 7-4. Drawing a line

Rectangle and Filled Rectangle   Rectangle and Filled Rectangle are new in R5. They allow you to draw an outline of a rectangle and a solid rectangle, respectively. Here's how to draw a rectangle:

1. Click the first pointer button on the Rectangle (or Filled Rectangle) command button. The button displays in reverse video.

2. Move the pointer into the editing area. It changes to a cross symbol.

3. Place the cross pointer on the square you want to be the upper-left corner of the rectangle. (Upper-left is easy for a righthanded person, but you can actually drag from any corner.) Press and hold down any pointer button. A gray shading covers the square the pointer is on.

4. Drag the pointer away from that square. The area you cover with the pointer will be outlined in gray. In our example, we drag the pointer diagonally to the right, highlighting an area 6 squares wide by 4 squares high.

5. When you've specified the outline of the rectangle you want, release the pointer button. The rectangle will be drawn.

In Figure 7-5 we've drawn a plain rectangle.

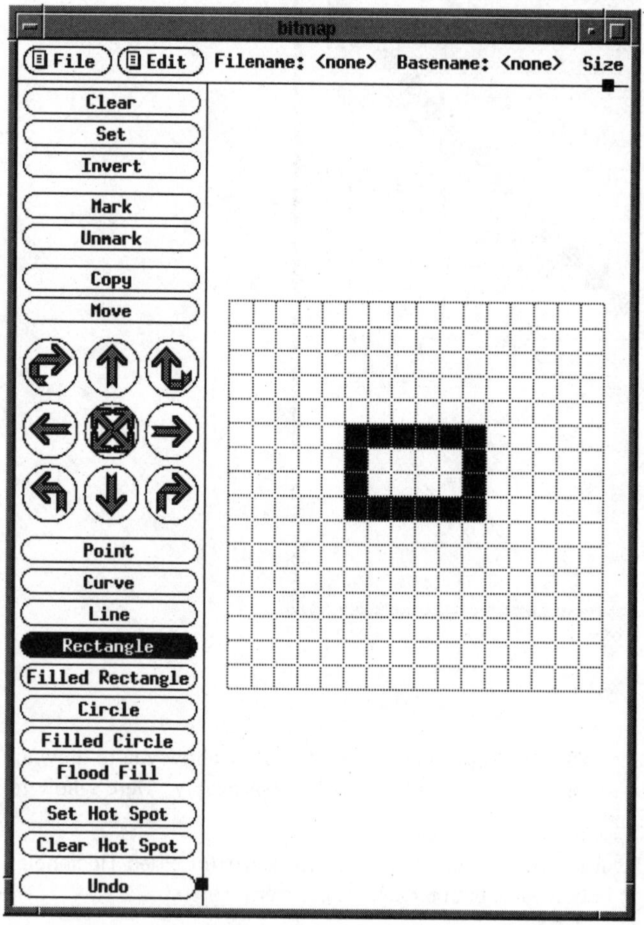

Figure 7-5. Drawing a rectangle

| Circle and | Circle and Filled Circle are carried over from Release 4, but (like Line) work |
| Filled Circle | differently in Release 5. In R4, you click twice, to mark the center of the circle |

Circle and Filled Circle are carried over from Release 4, but (like Line) work differently in Release 5. In R4, you click twice, to mark the center of the circle and a point on the perimeter, and bitmap draws the circle accordingly. To draw a circle in R5:

1. Click the first pointer button on the Circle (or Filled Circle) command button. The button displays in reverse video.

2. Move the pointer to the grid square you want to be the center of the circle.

3. Press and hold the first pointer button (to draw in the foreground color). The selected square is grayed out.

4. Now drag the pointer out toward the perimeter you want. Gray shading tracks the circle as you draw it.

5. When the circle is the size you want, release the pointer button. The circle is drawn.

In Figure 7-6 we've drawn a filled circle.

Filling in a Shape: Flood Fill

Flood Fill changes all squares in a closed shape. Most people probably think of filling a hollow shape with the foreground color. (You can do this by selecting Flood Fill and then clicking on the shape with the first pointer button.) But you can click with the third pointer button to change the squares to the background color. (The second pointer button will invert, but is not particularly useful in this case; if you experiment a bit, you'll see buttons one and three cover all possible situations.) To "fill" an area:

1. Click the first pointer button on the Flood Fill command button. The button displays in reverse video.

2. Move the pointer to the area of the grid you want to fill.

3. Click the first pointer button to change the squares to the foreground color.

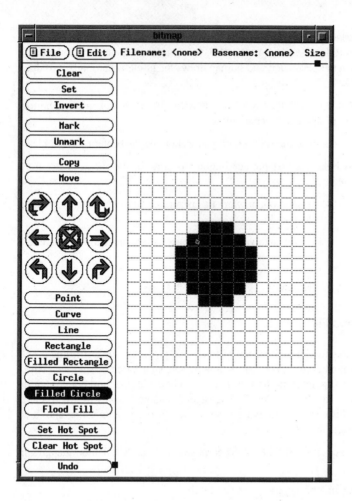

Figure 7-6. Drawing a filled circle

Figure 7-7 shows three concentric circles and then the result of filling the second circle.

Note that you could create the same bitmap just by using the circle drawing commands creatively. For instance, draw the second circle as a Filled Circle before the drawing the innermost one. Then you draw the inner Circle holding the third pointer button—and thus getting a white one inside the black. Finally draw the outer Circle using the first pointer button (you could actually draw the outer circle at any point). There are many ways to create most pictures.

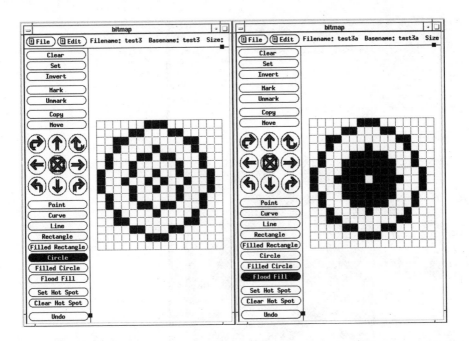

Figure 7-7. Flood Fill

Clear, Set, and Invert

Clear, Set, and Invert work on the entire grid. Note that each command has a keyboard shortcut, or accelerator (the first letter of the command). To use a shortcut, the pointer must rest in the grid or the whitespace surrounding it on the same side of the *bitmap* window.

Clear   Changes all the grid squares to the background color (often white) and sets all bitmap bits to 0. You can perform the same function by typing c while the pointer rests inside the grid or the surrounding whitespace.

Set   Changes all the grid squares to the foreground color (often black) and sets all bitmap bits to 1. You can perform the same function by typing s while the pointer rests inside the grid or the surrounding whitespace.

Invert   Inverts all the grid squares and bitmap bits, as if you had clicked the second pointer button over each square. You can perform the same function by typing i while the pointer rests inside the grid or the surrounding whitespace. In Figure 7-8 we've inverted the concentric circles from the Flood Fill example.

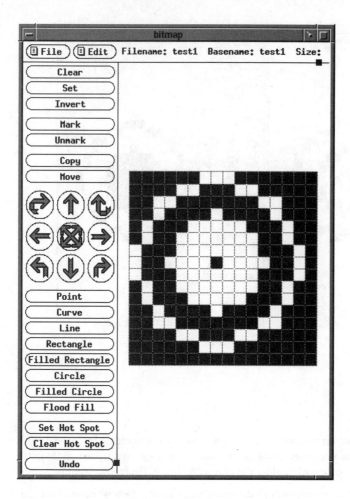

Figure 7-8. Inverting all squares in the grid

Marking an Area for Editing or Pasting

The Mark and Unmark commands are not particularly intuitive, but they are extremely important. When you Mark a part of the grid, many subsequent editing commands apply to that
area only. For instance, you might mark a portion of a bitmap and then delete (cut) it. If you
mark a part of a bitmap, you can then use the arrow buttons to move that part within the editing area one square at a time.

Note that Mark requires you to select a rectangular area (a line counts); no irregular areas can
be marked. The smallest area you can mark is a line composed of two squares.

The most important aspect of marking is that any marked area is available to be pasted from a global buffer. Specifically, the image is copied to the PRIMARY selection, where it is globally available to be pasted via the server. Chapter 5, *The xterm Terminal Emulator*, describes the selection mechanism as it applies to *xterm*, which interprets only "text" selections. However, a selection can be in a variety of formats. The main limitation in the selection mechanism is that copying and pasting must be performed between clients that interpret data in the same format. For our purposes, this means that you can paste part of a bitmap image to a *bitmap* or *xmag* window; you can't paste a bitmap image into an *xterm* window, or paste text into *bitmap*.*

Since there can only be one PRIMARY selection on a display at any time, any area you mark in a *bitmap* window supercedes the previous selection—whether the previous selection is text or graphics. (*Only one area on the display can be marked at any time.*)

To mark part of a bitmap image:

1. Click the first pointer button on the Mark command button. The button displays in reverse video.

2. Move the pointer into the editing area. It changes to a crosshair symbol.

3. Place the crosshair pointer on the upper-left square of the area you want to mark. (Upper left is easy for a righthanded person, but you can actually drag from any corner.) Press and hold down any pointer button. A gray shading covers the square the pointer is on.

4. Drag the pointer away from that square. The area you cover with the pointer will be outlined in gray. In Figure 7-9, we drag the pointer diagonally to the right, highlighting an area 9 squares wide by 11 squares high.

5. When you've marked the area you want, release the pointer button. The entire area will be highlighted in gray.

An area remains marked until you explicitly Unmark it or until you mark another area (or make a selection in any application).

Having a marked area does not interfere with any drawing you do in the window (using the pointer, command buttons such as (Point, Line, etc.). However, if an area is marked, the following commands will act only on that area:

• Copy command button.

• Move command button.

• Cut item on Edit menu (and its keyboard shortcut, Meta-C).

• Copy item on Edit menu (and its keyboard shortcut, Meta-W).

• The arrow command buttons to flip, move, etc., and the corresponding keyboard shortcuts. The center arrow button, which performs the Fold function, is the exception. It acts on the entire bitmap image.

---

*If you try to paste a text selection into a *bitmap* window, you may cause the client to hang.

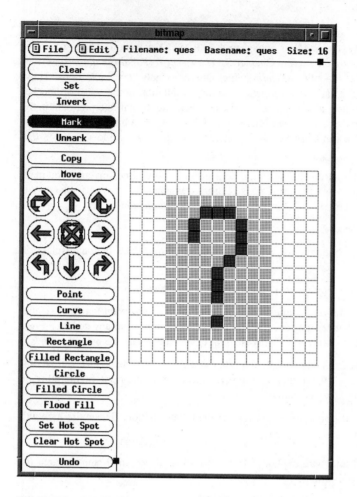

Figure 7-9. Marking an area

Keep in mind that if you select a copy or move and an area is already marked, you will be copying or moving that area. Note, however, that you don't have to select Mark before selecting the Copy or Move command buttons. These functions have "marking" built into them. See "Copying or Moving an Area Within the Bitmap Window" for details. If you want to move part of a bitmap using the arrow command buttons, on the other hand, you *must* Mark it first.

Copying or Moving an Area Within the Bitmap Window

The Copy and Move command buttons allow you to copy or move a rectangular area you select to another position within the current *bitmap* window. (Note, however, that the area you select for the copy or move can be pasted into another *bitmap* window, or into an *xmag* window, using other mechanisms. See "Transferring Bitmap Images Using the Edit Menu" later in this chapter for information about transferring images from window to window.) The Copy and Move command buttons are very useful, if slightly confusing. You perform both functions the same way, but the result is slightly different:

Copy   Makes a copy of a rectangular area and allows you to place it on another part of the grid. (You end up with two copies of that part of the image.)

Move   Moves a rectangular area from one part of the grid to another. (You end up with one copy of that part of the image.)

The first step in either function involves marking the area to be copied or moved. Marking is built into both functions. To Copy or Move part of an image, perform the following steps. (If you've previously marked an area using the Mark command button, you can skip steps 2-5.)

1. Click the first pointer button on the Copy or Move command button, as appropriate. The button displays in reverse video.

2. Move the pointer into the editing area. It changes to a crosshair symbol.

3. Mark the area you want to copy or move. To do so, place the crosshair pointer on the upper-left square of the area in question. (Upper-left is easy for a righthanded person, but you can actually drag from any corner.) Press and hold down any pointer button. A gray shading covers the square the pointer is on.

4. Drag the pointer away from that square. A gray rectangle will surround the area you indicate with the pointer.

5. When you've surrounded the area you want, release the pointer button. The entire area will be highlighted in gray.

6. Then you can move the area or a copy of it, depending on which command you selected initially. To do so, place the pointer on the gray rectangle and hold down any pointer button.

7. Then move the pointer to position the copy/original. An outline of the rectangle follows the pointer's movement. When the outline is positioned where you want it, release the pointer button. The image is redrawn in the place you indicated.

Notice that the area remains highlighted until you select another command. You can continue to move/copy the highlighted area by following steps 6 and 7 above. Note that if you copy an area and place the copy overlapping the original, the next copy will incorporate that image. In other words, when you perform steps 6 and 7, you're copying or moving what you see at the moment (not necessarily the same image you originally marked).

Graphics Utilities

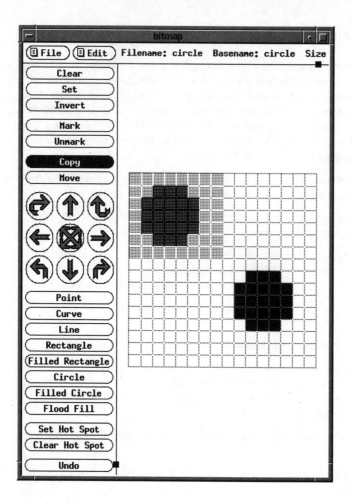

Figure 7-10. Copying an image

Figure 7-11 shows a circle being copied. Remember: if you previously highlighted an area using the Mark command, you can move or copy that area by selecting either Move or Copy (step 1) and then performing steps 6 and 7.

X Window System User's Guide, Motif Edition

Rotating or Moving with Arrow Buttons

Halfway down in the column of command buttons are 9 circular buttons each marked with some sort of arrow. These buttons correspond to functions that flip or move the bitmap image in various ways. The developer of the *bitmap* client associates each of these buttons with a text name (though obviously the name does not appear on the button). Figure 7-11 shows the button images on the left and their corresponding "names" on the right.

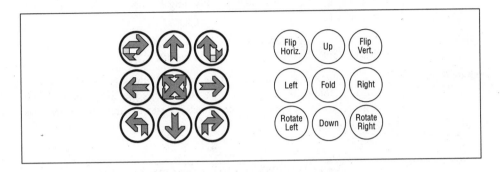

Figure 7-11. Arrow command buttons and their functions

Note that all of the buttons (except Fold) will act on a part of the bitmap, if it has been marked. (See "Marking an Area for Editing or Pasting" earlier in this chapter.)

When you mark an area, the commands to move (Left, Right, Up, Down) do so *only within that area*. Thus, if you have a square 3 × 3 pixels and you want to move it 5 pixels to the right, you must mark an area larger than the square itself.

Note also that to use a keyboard shortcut, the pointer must rest inside the editing grid or the surrounding whitespace (not in the menu bar or the command button column).

Flip Horizontally	Flips the image with respect to the horizontal axis. Pressing h inside the editing area has the same effect.
Up	Moves the image up one pixel (grid square) at a time. Pressing the up arrow on your keypad has the same effect.
Flip Vertically	Flips the image with respect to the vertical axis. Pressing v inside the editing area has the same effect.
Left	Moves the image to the left one pixel (grid square) at a time. Pressing the left arrow on your keypad has the same effect.
Fold	A confusing command. Technically, it "folds" the image so that opposite corners become adjacent, but this explanation is just about as topsy-turvey as the reality. To get a better idea, imagine that the bitmap image is divided into four parts (along the vertical and horizontal axes of the editing area); then the diagonally opposite quadrants are swapped. Since it's much easier to see this for yourself, we provide an

Graphics Utilities

example in Figure 7-12. Note that pressing f inside the editing area has the same effect.

Right	Moves the image to the right one pixel (grid square) at a time. Pressing the right arrow on your keypad has the same effect.
Rotate Left	Rotates the image 90 degrees to the left (i.e., counterclockwise). Thus, selecting this command four times in a row brings the image around 360 degrees, to its original position. Pressing l inside the editing area has the same effect.
Down	Moves the image down one pixel (grid square) at a time. Pressing the down arrow on your keypad has the same effect.
Rotate Right	Rotates the image 90 degrees to the right (i.e., clockwise). Thus, selecting this command four times in a row brings the image around 360 degrees, to its original position. Pressing r inside the editing area has the same effect.

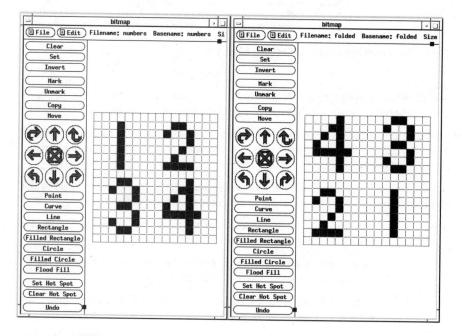

Figure 7-12. Folding an image: before and after

Setting and Clearing a Hot Spot

A *hot spot* is significant if you create a bitmap you want to use as a pointer symbol. If a program is using your bitmap as a pointer, the hot spot indicates which point on the bitmap will track the actual location of the pointer. For instance, if your pointer is an arrow, the hot spot should be the tip of the arrow; if your pointer is a cross, the hot spot should be the intersection point of the perpendicular lines. There can only be one hot spot on a bitmap.

Set Hot Spot   Designates a point on the bitmap as the hot spot.

Clear Hot Spot   Removes a hot spot defined on this bitmap.

To set a hot spot:

1. Click the first pointer button on Set Hot Spot. The button displays in reverse video.

2. Move the pointer to the location of the hot spot. Click the first or second pointer button. When a hot spot is active a diamond (◊) appears in the square.

In Figure 7-13, we set the hot spot of our arrow bitmap to be the tip. Note that the Set Hot Spot button remains active (in reverse video) until you select a mutually exclusive option (any of the drawing commands, Mark, Copy, or Move).

To clear a hot spot:

- Click pointer button one on Clear Hot Spot. The button flashes and the diamond symbol is removed from the bitmap image. Or:

- Click the second or third pointer button on the hot spot.

While Set Hot Spot is selected, the second pointer button toggles the hot spot on and off.

Note that if you use the Move command button to move a bitmap image with a hot spot, the hot spot remains stationary (i.e., it does not move with the image). If you use the arrow buttons to move an image with a hot spot, however, the hot spot will move with the image.

Using the Menus

As mentioned previously, the Release 5 *bitmap* provides two menus that can assist you in creating bitmap images. File menu items help you manage bitmap files, while Edit menu items assist with editing tasks such as cutting and pasting. Both are accessed from the menu bar that spans the top of the application window. To select an item from either menu:

1. Place the pointer on the appropriate menu command button (labeled either File or Edit).

2. Press and hold down the first pointer button. The menu is displayed.

3. Drag the pointer down the menu. A highlight bar tracks the pointer's movement. When you highlight the item you want, select it by releasing the pointer button; then menu is removed.

Each of the menu items has a keyboard shortcut (or accelerator), which appears on the menu following the text label for the item. If you familiarize yourself with these shortcuts, you can invoke any function from the menus without actually having to display them.

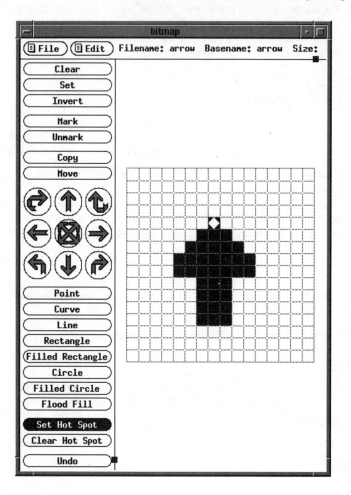

Figure 7-13. Setting a hot spot

Dialog Boxes and Command Buttons

Certain menu selections require you to supply additional information, such as the name of a file, new dimensions for the editing area, etc. In such cases, *bitmap* provides a *dialog box* in which you can enter the information. A dialog box is a small window some applications provide to request information from a user or to notify the user of something. (Figure 7-14 shows the dialog box *bitmap* displays when you try to quit the application without first saving changes.) The dialog box provided by *bitmap* is an X Toolkit feature. It differs somewhat from a dialog box created with the Motif Toolkit. See "Dialog Boxes and Push Buttons" in Chapter 9, *Working with Motif Applications*, for information about Motif dialogs.

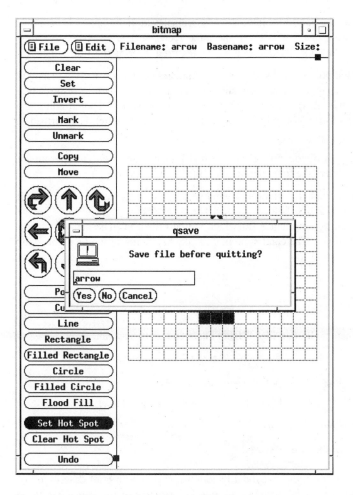

Figure 7-14. Bitmap window with quit dialog box

A dialog box created using the X Toolkit typically has three elements: it always has the first element, and may or may not have the second and/or third elements in this list:

• A prompt that identifies the purpose of the widget. For example, if you try to quit *bitmap* without having saved changes to the current file, the dialog prompts: "Save file before quitting?" If you want to Load another file, *bitmap* prompts: "Load file:" and you respond with the filename. Some prompts merely provide information to the user.

- An area in which you can type your response (if required).

- Command buttons that allow you either to acknowledge the prompt's message, or to confirm or cancel the dialog input, as appropriate.

When a dialog box pops up, the pointer is automatically redisplayed in the box (this is known as "warping the pointer"), and the box is given the input focus, so you can type. A dialog box is usually a pop-up window that disappears after the required information is provided.

Each command button in the box is itself a widget. A command button is usually a rectangle or oval that contains a text label. When you click a on a command button, some action (presumably indicated by the label) is performed by the program. The X Toolkit command button is analogous to the push button provided by the Motif Toolkit, which is described in Chapter 9.

To respond to the *bitmap* quit dialog box, click the first pointer button on the appropriate command button. You can select the first command (Yes) simply by pressing Return.

Notice that the dialog box contains a small text window displaying the name of the file. If you like, you can edit this filename before saving. The text window is an instance of the Athena Text widget, the editing commands for which are described in "The xedit Text Editor" in Chapter 8, *Other Clients*. The caret symbol (^) at the beginning of the filename is the text cursor.

The File Menu

The File menu helps you manage bitmap files. Using File menu items you can:

- Dynamically load another bitmap file into the editing window (Load).

- Insert another bitmap image into the current bitmap file (Insert).

- Save the current file (Save or Save As) and start editing a new one (New).

- Change the current filename (Filename).

- Change the dimensions of the grid (Resize).

Table 7-1 lists the File menu items, their keyboard shortcuts, and gives a brief description of what each item does. You can probably figure out how to use most of the items simply by trying them. Following the table is a tutorial that should help you use the somewhat less intuitive Insert command, which lets you insert another bitmap image into the current file.

Table 7-1. File menu items

Menu Item	Keyboard Shortcut(s)	What Item Does
New	Control-N	Clears the window so you can create a new image; prompts for a name for the new file. If you haven't saved the current file, the changes will be lost.
Load	Control-F	Dynamically loads another bitmap file into the editing window; if you haven't saved the current file, prompts you as to whether to save before loading the next file.
Insert	Control-I	Inserts a bitmap file into the image currently being edited. See the next section, "Inserting a File," for instructions.
Save	Control-S	Saves the current image using the filename in the menu bar.
Save As	Control-W	Saves the current image but prompts for the filename. That name is subsequently displayed in the menu bar.
Resize	Control-R	Changes the dimensions of the editing grid to match dimensions you supply (*widthxheight*), without changing the size of the image. Thus, specifying a larger grid gives you more room to edit. Specifying a smaller grid may cause part of the current image to be truncated.
Rescale	Control-X	Changes the dimensions of the grid to match dimensions you supply (*widthxheight*) and changes the image so that the proportions (the ratio of the image to the grid) remain the same. Thus, if you specify a grid twice the size of the current one, the grid and the image will both be doubled. Specifying a smaller grid may cause part of the current image to be truncated.
Filename	Control-E	Lets you change the filename of the current file without changing the basename (which appears in the header lines of the file) or saving the file.
Basename	Control-B	Lets you change the basename (if you want one different from the filename). The basename appears in the bitmap file, as part of the C code.
Quit	Control-C, q, Q	Exits the application. If changes have been made and not saved, a dialog box will ask whether to save before quitting.

Graphics Utilities

Inserting a File

To insert a bitmap file into the image you're editing, select Insert from the File menu. A dialog box will prompt you for a filename, as in Figure 7-15.

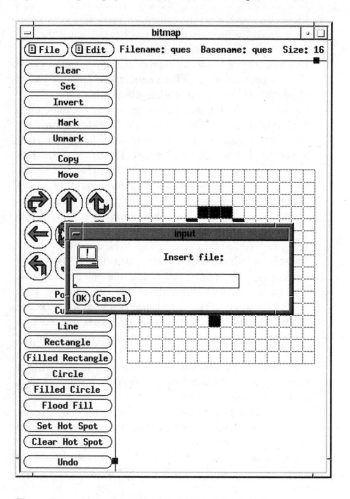

Figure 7-15. Dialog box requests name of file to insert

The pointer will be warped to the dialog box, enabling you to enter the path of the file you want. Use the editing commands for the Athena Text widget (described in the section "The xedit Text Editor" in Chapter 8, *Other Clients*). Once you type the filename, click on OK or press Return to request the file.

If the file exists, the pointer will change to the crosshair symbol. Move the pointer onto the grid and press and hold down the first pointer button. You should see a gray outline that represents the image to be inserted. Drag the image to the position you want and release the pointer button. The image is inserted into the current file. In Figure 7-16, we've inserted a large circle into the arrow file.

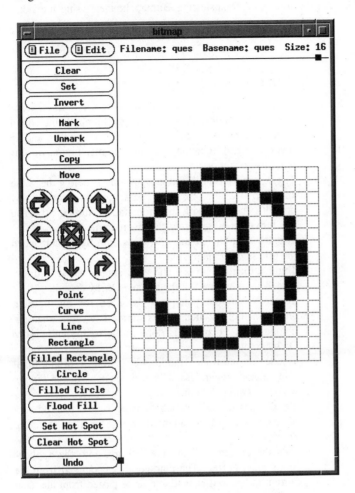

Figure 7-16. Image is inserted into open file

The Edit Menu

The Edit menu is divided into two sections by a horizontal line. The top portion contains items that determine characteristics of the editing area, such as its dimensions, whether or not grid lines are used, etc. Most of these items turn a characteristic on and off (i.e., the items are toggles). The bottom portion contains commands to Copy, Cut, and Paste images within the same *bitmap* window, between *bitmap* windows, or between *bitmap* and *xmag*.

Table 7-2 lists the Edit menu items, their keyboard shortcuts, gives a brief description of what each item does. You can probably figure out how to use most of the items simply by trying them. Following the table is a discussion of "Transferring Bitmap Images Using the Edit Menu."

Table 7-2. Edit Menu Items

Menu Item	Keyboard Shortcut(s)	What Item Does
Image	Meta-I	Displays a window showing what the bitmap being edited looks like at its actual size (both as it appears and in reverse video). Clicking the first pointer button on this window pops it down.
Grid	Meta-G	Toggles grid lines. If the grid spacing is below the value specified by the gridTolerance resource (8 by default), the grid will be automatically turned off. You can turn it on by selecting this menu item.
Dashed	Meta-D	Toggles stippling in the grid lines. On by default when the grid lines are activated.
Axes	Meta-A	Toggles diagonal axes. The axes simply assist in drawing; they are not part of the image. Off by default.
Stippled	Meta-S	Toggles a stipple pattern to be used for highlighting within the editing area. (This stipple is a subtle shading; if toggled off, marking is done in the foreground color.) On by default.
Proportional	Meta-P	Toggles proportional mode which forces proportional grid squares, regardless of the dimensions of the *bitmap* window. On by default.
Zoom	Meta-Z	Toggles zoom mode, which focuses in on a marked area of the image. (You can mark before or after selecting Zoom.)
Cut	Meta-C	Cuts the contents of any marked area into the application's local buffer. The marked area is deleted from the current image, but is available to be pasted from the local buffer. (If this was the last area marked, it is also available to be pasted into other applications via a global buffer.)
Copy	Meta-W	Copies the contents of any marked area into the applications's local buffer. The marked area remains a part of the current image and is also available to be pasted from the local buffer. (If this was the last area marked, it is also available to be pasted into other applications via a global buffer.)

Table 7-2. Edit Menu Items (continued)

Menu Item	Keyboard Shortcut(s)	What Item Does
Paste	Meta-Y, Control key and mouse button click	Pastes the contents of the global buffer (the marked area in any *bitmap* or *xmag* application), or if the global buffer is empty, the contents of the local buffer, into the current image. To place the copied image, press and hold the first pointer button in the editing area, drag the outlined image to the position you want, and then release the button.

Transferring Bitmap Images Using the Edit Menu

Though it is hardly obvious, the Copy and Cut items on the Edit menu provide more powerful image transferring capabilities than the Copy and Move command buttons. As we've seen, the Copy and Move command buttons allow you to transfer images within the current *bitmap* window. These buttons copy the part of the image you select into a *local* buffer (available only within the particular window).

However, in addition to this local buffer, *bitmap* works with a *global* buffer. Specifically, a "marked" part of an image becomes the PRIMARY selection—and is available to be pasted to any *bitmap* or *xmag* window. Moreover, when you mark an area and then Copy or Cut it using the Edit menu (or the keyboard shortcuts for those items), the image is also available to be pasted globally.* Admittedly, this business of transferring images can seem confusing, but it's fairly easy in practice. Let's consider an example and then try to clarify the precedence rules for pasting from the global and local buffers.

First, let's run two *bitmap* windows, one with a question mark image and the other an exclamation point, as in Figure 7-17.

---

*You *can* use these items to copy or cut images within the current window—but this is not their primary intent.

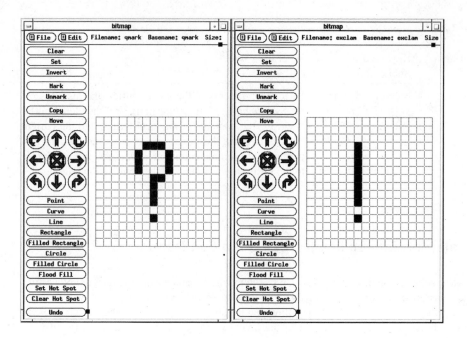

Figure 7-17. Two bitmap windows

Say we want to copy the exclamation mark from the right *bitmap* window into the left window, so that it appears after the question mark. There are a few ways to do this. We could:

1. Mark the exclamation using the procedure outlined for the Mark command button. While the exclamation is highlighted in this way, it is available to be pasted via the global buffer. In Figure 7-18, we've marked an area encompassing the exclamation and one additional pixel on all sides. (The entire area will be pasted.)

2. To paste the marked area into the question mark window, select Paste from the Edit menu in that window. Then move the pointer into the editing area. The crosshair pointer represents the upper-left pixel of the image to be pasted. Place the image where you want and click the first pointer button. The image is pasted, as in Figure 7-18.

Rather than selecting the Paste menu item, you could instead direct the focus to the question mark window and use either of the two keyboard/pointer shortcuts for the item: Meta-Y or Control and any mouse button click. Note that in the latter case, the click places the image. Until you mark another image, invoking the paste function in any *bitmap* or *xmag* window will paste the exclamation.

There are other ways to place the exclamation image in the question mark window. You could also highlight the exclamation image, then select either Copy or Cut from the Edit menu in the same window. (These items are only available for selection when a image is marked in the window.) Obviously, the former menu item makes a copy of the marked image, while the latter makes a copy but deletes the original from the window. In both cases, the image is available globally. Once you've selected Copy or Cut from the Edit menu, you can transfer the exclamation by invoking the paste function in any *bitmap* or *xmag* window.

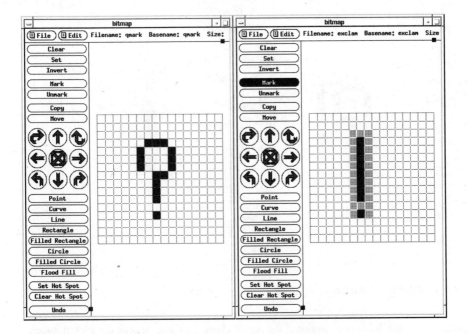

Figure 7-18. Marking the exclamation so that it can be pasted

If you run multiple *bitmap* windows and cut and paste frequently, the contents of the global and local buffers will often be different. In trying to determine what image you'll be pasting, the following rules of precedence apply:

1. If an image is currently marked (highlighted) in any *bitmap* window, that image will be copied to any *bitmap* or *xmag* window in which you invoke a paste command.

2. If no image is currently marked, the image that is pasted will be: the last image cut, copied, or pasted in any currently running *bitmap* window (using the analogous Edit menu options or their keyboard accelerators); or the last image selected in a currently running *xmag* window.

3. Whatever image you Copy or Move using the command buttons can only be pasted within the same *bitmap* window, *unless it remains highlighted*. In this case, the image is available via the global buffer and will be pasted according to rule 1 above.

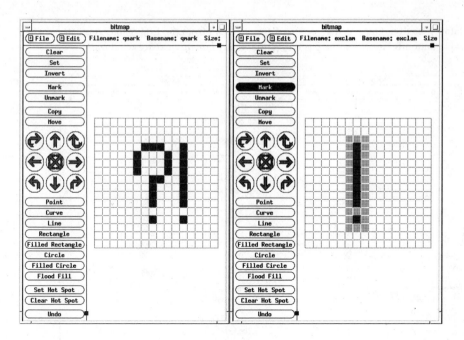

Figure 7-19. Pasting the exclamation next to the question mark

As we'll see in the following sections, the *xmag* client can also access the global image buffer.

Magnifying Portions of the Screen: xmag

The *xmag* client enables you to magnify a portion of the screen. The close-up look *xmag* affords can assist you in creating and editing bitmaps and other graphic images. You can also copy and paste images between *xmag* windows or between *xmag* and the *bitmap* editor.

One instance of the *xmag* program lets you magnify several different areas of the screen and display the images either sequentially (in the same window) or concurrently (in multiple windows). In addition to giving you a look at a magnified bitmap image, *xmag* also provides certain information about the individual pixels in the image.

The Release 5 version *xmag* is clearly intended to be used in concert with the *bitmap* editor. (Previous incarnations of the program were not integrated with *bitmap*.) Of course, application developers may also find it useful when working with more sophisticated graphics programs.

When might you use *xmag*? Say you're running a program that creates a special image on the root window and you'd like to create a *bitmap* file of a part of that image. You can display a magnification of the image you want with *xmag*. Then you can either try to recreate the image by editing in an open *bitmap* window or copy the *xmag* image and paste it into the *bitmap* editor.

xmag is also useful for capturing a screen image that can then be saved as a window dump file with the *xwd* client (described in Chapter 8, *Other Clients*). *xwd* makes a dump file of a single window at a time (though that window may be the root). In some cases, however, you might want to make a dump file of a portion of a window or of multiple windows. *xmag* allows you to magnify any portion of the screen; thus the *xmag* window can capture portions of several windows at once. You can then use *xwd* to make a dump file of the *xmag* window. (Since *xmag* is intended to magnify, if you want the window image to be the actual size, you must specify that no magnification is performed. To do this, run *xmag* with the option -mag 1. See the *xmag* reference page in Part Three of this guide for more information.)

Selecting an Area to Magnify

If you invoke *xmag* without options, you can interactively choose the area to be magnified (the *source* area). At the command line, type:

```
% xmag &
```

The pointer changes to an upper-left corner symbol from which extends a small, hollow square with a wavering border. (By default, the square is 64 pixels on each side.) Move the corner cursor, placing the square over the area you want to magnify, and click the first pointer button.

The image inside the hollow square is magnified and displayed in the *xmag* window. Unless you specify a location using -geometry, *mwm* places the *xmag* window in the upper-left quadrant of the display. An *xmag* window, containing a magnified bitmap image, is shown in Figure 7-20.

The default size *xmag* window shows an area 64 pixels square, magnified five times; thus, the image itself is 320 pixels on each side. This magnification enables you to see the individual pixels, which are represented by squares of the same color as the corresponding pixels in the source image.

Rather than use the default source area and magnification, you can specify other values on the command line. See the *xmag* reference page in Part Three of this guide for a complete list of options.

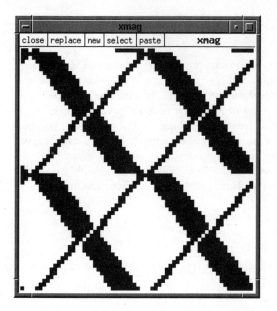

Figure 7-20. xmag window displaying magnified screen area

xmag Command Buttons

The Release 5 version of *xmag* offers many improvements over previous versions, the most obvious being the five command buttons that appear above the magnified image (to the right of the string "xmag"). Once you understand what the command buttons do, you should have you a fairly good idea of *xmag*'s capabilities. You invoke a command button by placing the pointer on it and clicking the first pointer button. When you place the pointer on a command button, the button will be highlighted by a black border; when you select it, the button will flash in reverse video.

Magnifying A Different Source Area: replace or new

If you want to magnify another portion of the screen using the same source area size and magnification factor, you do not have to start *xmag* again. You can choose another source area and either display it in the same *xmag* window or open an additional window in which to display it, using the replace and new command buttons, respectively.

To replace the image in the current window with another magnified image:

1. Place the pointer on the replace command button and click the first pointer button (the replace command button will flash in reverse video). Once again, the pointer becomes an upper-left corner bordering a hollow square.

2. Choose a source area in the manner described in the section "Selecting an Area to Magnify."

3. The *xmag* window is redrawn to display the new magnified image.

As an alternative, you might want to keep the first *xmag* image, but also magnify another area of the screen. In order to display a second *xmag* window:

1. Place the pointer on the new command button and click the first pointer button. The pointer becomes an upper-left corner bordering a hollow square.

2. Choose a source area in the manner described earlier.

3. The source area is magnified and displayed in a second *xmag* window.

You can select any number of source areas during a single *xmag* session.

Copying and Pasting Images: select and paste

You can copy the image displayed in an *xmag* window and paste it in another *xmag* window—or in a *bitmap* window. (As we've seen, you can paste images between *bitmap* windows; but you can also paste an image from *bitmap* into *xmag*.)

To copy the contents of *xmag*, click on the select command button. The *xmag* select function is analogous to "marking" an image in a *bitmap* window. The image is copied to the PRIMARY selection where it is globally available via the server.

There will be no indication that the image has been copied into memory, although the select button will flash in reverse video when you click on it. However, if you then move the pointer to *another xmag* window and click on paste, the image from the first window will be displayed in it.

Think of the select and paste buttons as accessing the same invisible graphics clipboard—which has room for only one image. The *bitmap* copy and paste mechanism accesses the same space in memory. Thus, you can select images from any *xmag* or *bitmap* window (by the mechanism appropriate to the particular client), but only the last image you copy remains in memory to be pasted elsewhere.

A note about pasting an *xmag* image into a *bitmap* window: the default *xmag* image represents a 64×64 pixel square while the default *bitmap* image is 16×16 pixels. If you intend to transfer images between these clients, it's a good idea to specify comparable dimensions. If you have the screen space, you might run:

```
% bitmap -size 64x64 &
```

However, this is a very large window. You can make the *bitmap* window smaller by specifying dimensions for the individual editing squares (using the -sw and -sh options), or you can specify another size for the *xmag* source area:

```
% xmag -source 16x16 &
```

Regardless of the area you want to work with, the important thing to remember is to keep the dimensions comparable.

What xmag Shows You

xmag enables you to determine the x and y coordinates, bitmap bit setting, and RGB color value of every pixel in the *xmag* window. (See Chapter 12, *Specifying Color*, for a discussion of the RGB color model.) If you move the pointer into the *xmag* window, the cursor becomes an arrow. Point the arrow at one of the magnified pixels and press and hold down the first pointer button. A banner across the top edge of the window displays information about the pixel, as shown in Figure 7-21.

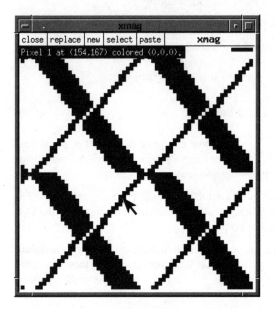

Figure 7-21. Displaying pixel statistics with pointer in xmag window

The banner displays the following information about the specified pixel:

- The positive x and y coordinates relative to the root window. These are the coordinates of the original image—not of the *xmag* window.

- The bitmap bit setting. This is either 0 if the pixel is in the background color or 1 if the pixel is in the foreground color.

- The RGB value. This is a 16-bit value. The RGB specification is in three parts (of four hexadecimal digits each), corresponding to the three primaries in the RGB color model.

If you are trying to create a graphic image on a grid (such as the *bitmap* client provides), the x and y coordinates of each pixel can be especially useful. Also, the 16-bit RGB value specifies the color of each pixel with incredible precision. Depending on the number of colors available on your display, you can learn to use RGB values to specify an enormous range of colors. (Keep in mind, however, that RGB colors are not portable. See Chapter 12, *Specifying Color*, for more information.)

xmag provides these pixel statistics dynamically. If you continue to hold down the first pointer button and drag the pointer across the window, the banner will display values for each pixel as the pointer indicates it.

Note that if you select a pixel near the top edge of the window, the banner will appear across the bottom edge. Otherwise, the banner would obscure the pixel you are pointing at.

Removing an xmag Window: close

To remove a magnification window, either:

- Place the pointer on the close command button and click the first pointer button; or

- Type q, Q, or Control-C while the pointer rests in the window. Note that the window must have the input focus.

These are "kind" methods for removing a window, which allow all relevant processes to finish.

If *mwm* is running, you could also remove a single window by double-clicking on the Window Menu button on the *mwm* frame; or by selecting the Close item from the Window Menu. You can remove *all xmag* windows (started under the same instance of the program) using the *xkill* client. These three methods all involve "killing" a program, which can adversely affect underlying processes. Refer to the section on *xkill* in Chapter 8, *Other Clients*, for a more complete discussion of the hazards of killing a client.

Creating a Bitmap from a Cursor

The *atobm* and *bmtoa* clients allow you to convert *a*rrays (of ASCII characters) *to b*itmap files and to convert *b*itmap files *to a*rrays. These clients are commonly used to facilitate printing: a bitmap file that is converted to ASCII text can be printed more readily and can also be included in standard ASCII text files. Once converted to ASCII, bitmap files can also be more quickly copied or mailed to other directories or systems, where they can be used in ASCII format or converted back to bitmap format.

Among their uses, the *bmtoa* and *atobm* utilities make it possible to convert a character from a font, such as the cursor font, to the *bitmap* file format. Once converted, the file can be edited using the *bitmap* client and used as you would any other bitmap file: specified as the root window pattern (with *xsetroot*), etc.

When a bitmap file is converted to ASCII text, it is in the form of an array consisting of two types of characters. (An array is a number of elements arranged in rows and columns; it is sometimes called a matrix.) One character represents set or filled squares of the bitmap (bitmap bit 1) and the other character represents empty squares (bitmap bit 0). By default, the number sign character (#) represents filled squares and the hyphen (–) represents empty squares. Figure 7-22 shows the British pound sign character of the 9 × 15 font (in the *misc* directory) as an array of these ASCII symbols.

```
---###-
--#---#
--#----
#####--
--#----
-###--
#-#--##
-#-----
```

Figure 7-22. ASCII array representing the British pound sign

As you can see, the array is a rectangle. In a sense, the array is similar to the *bitmap* grid. (You can edit or create the array using an ASCII text editor, as long as you use the standard two characters and keep the array rectangular.)

To convert the Gumby character of the cursor font to a bitmap, the first thing you must do is display the cursor font as ASCII text. This can be done with the *showfont* client, which allows you to display the contents of a font file (with a *.pcf* extension), if the file is accessed via a font server. (See "Using the Font Server" in Chapter 6, *Font Specification*, for a discussion of the font server and the *showfont* client.)

To display the cursor font with each character represented as an array, use *showfont* (giving the required `-server` option to identify the server and the font name as an argument) and redirect output to a file called */tmp/cursor.array*:

```
% showfont -server server_name cursor > /tmp/cursor.array
```

In this case, we've used the alias for the cursor font, rather than the actual (lengthy) font name.

The *cursor.array* file contains information about the font and an array for each character. Using your ASCII text editing program, edit the file, writing the Gumby array to another file called */tmp/gumby.array*. (Appendix D, *Standard Cursors*, saves us some scanning by telling us that Gumby is character number 56, so we search *cursor.array* for 56.) The Gumby array is pictured in Figure 7-23.

```
--######--------
---#----#-------
##--#----#------
###-#-#-#-#-----
##--#-----#-----
##--#-###-#-----
####-----###--
--###-----######
----#-----#--###
----#-----#--###
----#--#--#-####
----#--#--#--###
----#--#--#-----
---#---#---#----
--#----#----#---
--####-####---
```

Figure 7-23. /tmp/gumby.array

X Window System User's Guide, Motif Edition

You can then use the *atobm* client to convert this array to a bitmap. Use the *gumby.array* file as an argument and redirect the output to a bitmap file:

```
% atobm /tmp/gumby.array > /tmp/gumby.bitmap
```

Figure 7-24 shows the Gumby bitmap. As you can see from the bitmap, the Gumby character of the cursor font is considerably smaller than the Gumby we created (Figure 7-14) with *bitmap*.

If you want, you can then edit the *gumby.bitmap* file using the *bitmap* client.

If you specify the unedited bitmap as the root window pattern, you'll notice that there is virtually no space between the Gumby figures. This is because the array file had no extra hyphens (representing empty *bitmap* squares) padding it. If you want, you can add some hyphens to the *gumby.array* file (keeping the image symmetrical) and then use *atobm* to create a more padded version of the bitmap. Figure 7-25 shows the *gumby.array* file after it was padded with hyphens.

See the *bitmap* reference page in Part Three of this guide for more information on the *atobm* and *bmtoa* conversion clients.

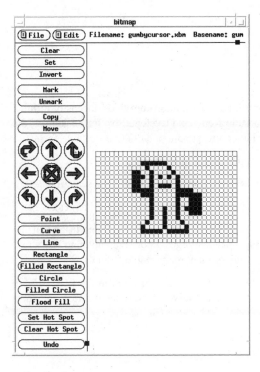

Figure 7-24. Bitmap of the Gumby cursor

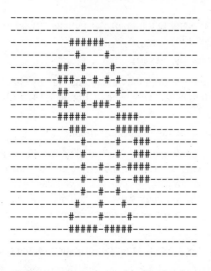

Figure 7-25. gumby.array padded by hyphens

The Portable Bitmap Toolkit

The Portable Bitmap Toolkit (in the user-contributed distribution) provides dozens of utilities for converting graphics files to and from portable formats. Developed by Jef Poskanzer, the Toolkit is composed of four parts, three of which correspond to a particular portable format:

- PBM: utilities to convert files to and from portable bitmap format.

- PGM: utilities to convert files to and from portable graymap format (grayscale images).

- PPM: utilities to convert files to and from portable pixmap format (color images).

The fourth part of the toolkit, PNM, provides utilities to manipulate images in any of the three formats. For example, the program *pnmenlarge* enlarges a portable "anymap" by a factor you supply. *pnminvert* inverts an image in any of the three portable formats.

The available utilities and the conversions they perform are summarized in the *README* file in the source directory. Table 7-1 lists some representative conversion utilities and their functions.

Table 7-3. Some PBM Toolkit Conversion Utilities

Utility	Converts
giftoppm	GIF to portable pixmap
ppmtogif	Portable pixmap to GIF
ppmtopgm	Portable pixmap to portable graymap
fstopgm	Usenix FaceSaver file to portable graymap
pnmtops	Portable anymap to Encapsulated PostScript
pgmtopbm	Portable graymap to portable bitmap
pbmtomacp	Portable bitmap to MacPaint
macptopbm	MacPaint to portable bitmap
pbmtoxbm	Portable bitmap to X11 bitmap
pbmtox10bm	Portable bitmap to X10 bitmap
xbmtopbm	X10 or X11 bitmap to portable bitmap
pnmtoxwd	Portable anymap to X11 window dump
xwdtopnm	X10 or X11 window dump to portable anymap

As the table indicates, some of the available utilities come in pairs—they can be used to convert a file to a portable format and back to its original format again. (The table also includes a group of three related utilities to convert X10 and X11 bitmaps to portable bitmaps and back again.)

Certain conversions can only be performed in one direction. For example, you can convert a portable graymap to a portable bitmap (using *pgmtopbm*), but you can't convert a bitmap to a graymap. The one-way conversions generally involve changing a file to a simpler format.

You'll probably be most interested in converting graphics files to formats suitable for use with X, namely X bitmaps or window dump files. Keep in mind that a portable bitmap has a different format than an X bitmap. The program *pbmtoxbm* converts a portable bitmap to a bitmap compatible with X11.

The conversions you may want to perform can be simple (directly from one format to another) or complex (through several intermediate formats). An example of a simple conversion is changing a portable pixmap to a portable graymap using *ppmtopgm*:

```
% ppmtopgm pixmap > graymap
```

The PBM Toolkit source directory includes a file called *TIPS* that provides helpful hints on using the utilities. Based on these suggestions, we performed a fairly complex conversion: a Usenix FaceSaver image to a bitmap suitable for use with X. The following command performed the conversion on the file *myface* to create *myface.bitmap*:

```
fstopgm myface | pnmenlarge 3 | pnmscale -yscale 1.125 | pgmnorm |\
     pgmtopbm | pbmtoxbm > myface.bitmap
```

Notice that this particular conversion requires six utilities! This procedure is by no means intuitive. We relied heavily on the *TIPS* provided.

The six conversions performed are:

- Convert FaceSaver image to portable graymap (`fstopgm`).

- Enlarge a portable anymap three times (`pnmenlarge 3`).

- Scale pixels in y dimension; x dimension is adjusted accordingly (`pnmscale -yscale 1.125`).

- Normalize contrast of portable graymap (`pgmnorm`).

- Convert portable graymap to portable bitmap (`pgmtopbm`).

- Convert portable bitmap to X11 bitmap (`pbmtoxbm`).

Be aware that the command:

```
pnmscale -yscale 1.125
```

may not be necessary on all systems or the necessary arguments may vary. If you omit *pnmscale* and the command is necessary, the system should return a message to that effect and also tell you what arguments to use.

The possible uses of the PBM Toolkit programs and the ways in which they can be combined are extremely varied. You'll have to do some experimenting. To orient yourself, read the files *README*, *TIPS*, and *FORMATS* in the source directory. The source directory also includes reference pages for each utility.

8

Other Clients

This chapter gives an overview of other clients available with X, including window and display information clients, printing utilities, the xkill *program, and several "desk accessories." It also describes how to use three public-domain clients that can assist you in creating and specifying colors for your display:* xcol, xcoloredit, *and* xtici.

In This Chapter:

8
Other Clients

In addition to *xterm*, the MIT distribution includes many other clients. This chapter discusses some of the more useful clients, grouped according to basic functionality:

- Program to redraw the screen: *xrefresh*.

- Desk accessories: *xclock*, *oclock*, *xcalc*, *xbiff*, *xload*, and *xman*.

- Text editor: *xedit*.

- Printing utilities: *xwd*, *xpr*, and *xdpr*.

- Program to remove a client window: *xkill*.

- Window and display information programs: *xwininfo*, *xlsclients*, and *xdpyinfo*.

- Alternative window managers and other user-contributed clients, including: a program to display available colors and change color preferences: *xcol*; two programs to create or "mix" your own colors, *xcoloredit* and *xtici*.

Most sections in this chapter are intended to acquaint you with the major features of some of the available clients. Additional detailed information is provided on the reference pages for each client in Part Three of this guide.

Many of the standard clients have been written (or rewritten) with a programming library called the X Toolkit. As explained in Chapter 1, the X Toolkit includes a set of predefined components (or widgets), known as the Athena widget set. Widgets make it easier to create complex applications; they also ensure a consistent user interface between applications.

Although most of the standard clients described in this guide were originally written before the X Toolkit was fully developed, many have since been rewritten to use the Toolkit. In discussing various clients in this chapter, we'll point out some of the features attributable to the X Toolkit. (For a comprehensive treatment of the X Toolkit, see Volume Four, *X Toolkit Intrinsics Programming Manual*, and Volume Five, *X Toolkit Intrinsics Reference Manual*.)

In Chapter 9, we'll take a look at some of the features common to applications written with the Motif Toolkit.

Redrawing the Screen: xrefresh

Depending on your environment, system messages may sometimes be displayed over the windows on your screen, obscuring them and making it difficult, if not impossible, for you to work. As described in Chapter 4, *More about the mwm Window Manager*, you can clear messages from the screen using the Refresh item on *mwm*'s Root Menu. The Refresh menu item actually runs a client called *xrefresh*, which redraws the screen as it was before the messages covered it.

When your screen is obscured, it's probably easiest to use the Refresh menu item, but you could also run *xrefresh* directly. Just focus input on an *xterm* window whose command line isn't obscured and enter:

```
% xrefresh
```

Then press Return. (You can run *xrefresh* in the foreground because it does its work and exits immediately.)

If the Refresh menu item is not available and you don't have a clear *xterm* to type in, you still may have a somewhat less desirable (but not entirely obvious) alternative: enter *xrefresh* in one of the obscured windows. Although it isn't readily apparent, you can actually enter text in any *xterm*, regardless of whether the window is obscured, if the window has the input focus. Thus, you can probably manage to click on (or place the pointer on) a window and peck out the *xrefresh* command on the keyboard, even if you're working blind.

You can avoid the problem of an obscured screen by running the *xconsole* client. *xconsole* provides a window to which system console messages are directed. For more information, see Appendix A, *Managing Your Environment*.

Desk Accessories

The clients *xclock*, *oclock*, *xcalc*, *xload*, *xbiff*, and *xman* can be thought of as *desk accessories*. (Desk accessories is a term we've borrowed from the Macintosh environment, meaning small applications that are available—and useful—at any time.)

You can start these clients from the command line in any *xterm* window or, if you like, you can add them to an *mwm* menu. (See Chapter 13, *Customizing mwm*.)

Clock Programs: xclock and oclock

The standard release of X includes two clients that display the time: *xclock* and *oclock*. The time displayed by both *xclock* and *oclock* is the system time set and displayed with the UNIX *date*(1) command (the MS-DOS *date* and *time* commands, etc.)—in other words, the operating system's notion of the correct time.

xclock continuously displays the time, either in analog or digital form, in a standard window. The analog *xclock* shows a round 12-hour clock face with tick marks representing the minutes. The digital *xclock* shows the 24-hour time (2:30 PM would be represented as 14:30) as well as the day, month, and year. You can run more than one clock at a time. The analog clock is the default. Figure 8-1 shows two *xclock* applications being run: an analog clock above a digital clock.

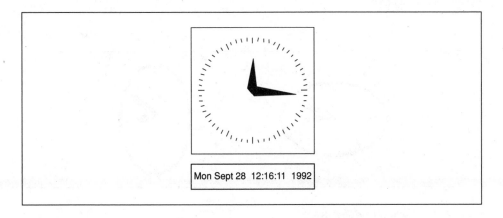

Figure 8-1. Two xclock displays: analog clock above digital clock

The *oclock* client displays the time in analog form on a round 12-hour clock face without tick marks. The only features of an *oclock* display are the round clock outline, hour and minute hands, and the "jewel" marking 12 o'clock.

oclock also makes use of the X Shape Extension, which supports non-rectangular windows. If you try to resize the round *oclock*, you'll discover that it's possible to "stretch" it into various oblong shapes, as shown in Figure 8-2.

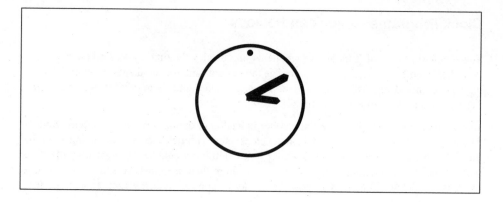

Figure 8-2. oclock display

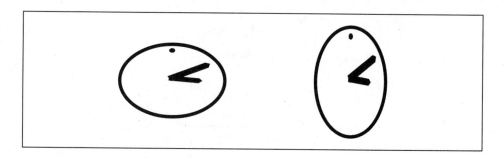

Figure 8-3. Oblong oclock displays

Note, however, that resizing is a little more complicated with *oclock* than with most other clients. When you run an application that creates a non-rectangular window with the 1.2 version of the *mwm* window manager, only a titlebar is displayed. The rest of the frame is suppressed, as shown in Figure 8-4.

Obviously, having only a titlebar limits how you can perform certain window manager functions. You can pull down the Window Menu and use the Minimize and Maximize buttons. Since you can't resize using the pointer on the frame, you either have to choose Size from the Window Menu or use the keyboard accelerator for the command (Alt+F8). Resizing from the rounded borders might also take some practice.

Having a titlebar with *oclock* has its advantages in window management, but you may not find it very aesthetic. See Chapter 13 for instructions on suppressing parts of the *mwm* window decoration.

If you don't suppress the window decoration, be aware that the titlebar may appear to blink on the minute when the clock is updated (redrawn).

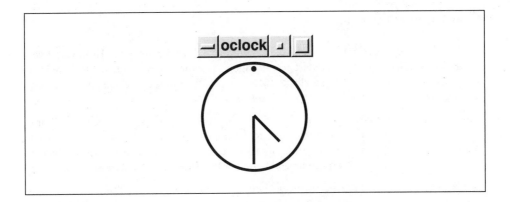

Figure 8-4. oclock with mwm titlebar

Running *oclock* with the -transparent option creates a transparent clock display, which can be fun, particularly on a root window with an interesting pattern. (You use the *xsetroot* client to specify root window characteristics. See Chapter 14 for details.)

Running a transparent *oclock* has a minor and not immediately obvious implication for window management. If you need to place the pointer on the transparent *oclock* "window," you must place it directly on the hands, border, or jewel—or on the titlebar, if it's displayed. When you place the pointer on the clock face, you're really pointing at whatever the background is—perhaps the root window, perhaps another application window. Since the *oclock* is transparent, it actually has no face!

This fact becomes important if you want to manage the *oclock* window using *mwm*. For instance, in many environments you can raise a window by clicking on any part of it. In this case, you'd be limited to the clock outline and the titlebar, if any.

You can also specify a color *oclock*. Though the default colors for *oclock* are black and white, it was designed to be run in color. The minute hand, hour hand, jewel, clock border, and background can all be set to a color. As of Release 5, the standard distribution of X includes a file of suggested color defaults for *oclock*. See Chapter 11, *Setting Resources*, and the *oclock* reference page in Part Three of this guide for instructions on using the suggested colors.

You can set your own color preferences (independent of the defaults) using either command-line options or by specifying client resources. See the *oclock* reference page in Part Three of this guide for the specific command-line options and resource variables.

Other Clients

Removing an xclock or oclock

Usually when you invoke *xclock* or *oclock* you will leave the clock running. However, if you experiment with these programs to test size, location, or color, you will notice that there is no obvious way to delete an unwanted clock. (Moving the cursor to the clock and pressing Control-C, Control-D, q, or Q doesn't work with *xclock* or *oclock*.)

You can remove an *xclock* or *oclock* window by using the *xkill* client, described later in this chapter. (Note that if you want to remove a transparent *oclock* with *xkill*, you have to click on the border, hands, jewel, or titlebar, if any.) You can also remove either clock by double-clicking on *mwm*'s Window Menu command button or by using the menu's Close item.

Another way to remove an *xclock* or *oclock* window is to identify and kill the process using the standard UNIX control mechanisms. First, find the process identification (PID) number for the client. For example, to determine the process ID number for *xclock*, go to an *xterm* window and type:

```
% ps -aux | grep xclock
```

at a system prompt. Under System V, type:

```
% ps -e | grep xclock
```

at a system prompt. The resulting display should look something like this:

```
128  p0  0:00  xclock
142  p0  0:00  grep xclock
```

The number in the first column is the process ID. Type:

```
% kill process_ID
```

The *xclock* display will be removed, and you will get the message:

```
Terminated     xclock
```

The same sequence of commands can be used to remove an *oclock* window.

Be aware, however, that these and other methods of "killing" a client have certain liabilities. See "Problems with Killing a Client" later in this chapter.

A Scientific Calculator: xcalc

xcalc is a scientific calculator that can emulate a Texas Instruments TI-30 or a Hewlett Packard HP-10C. Once you place the pointer within the *xcalc* window, the calculator can be operated in two ways:

- With the pointer, by clicking the first pointer button on the buttons in the calculator window.

- With the keyboard, by typing the same numbers and symbols that are displayed in the calculator window. (Most of the calculator keys have keyboard equivalents. The not-so-obvious equivalents are described on the *xcalc* reference page in Part Three of this guide.)

When using the first method, notice that the pointer appears as a small hand, enabling you to "press" the buttons. The values punched on the calculator and the results of the calculations are displayed in the long horizontal window along the top of the *xcalc*. Figure 8-5 shows *xcalc* on the screen.

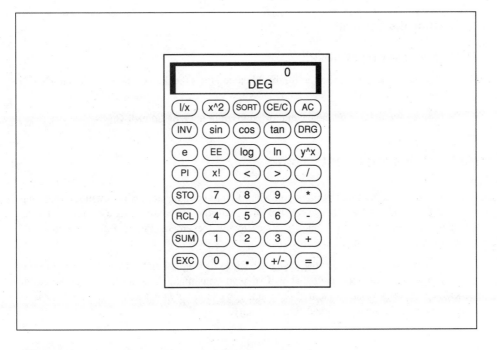

Figure 8-5. The default xcalc (TI-30 mode) on the screen

Figure 8-5 depicts the version of the calculator provided with Release 5 of X. As you can see, it features oval buttons. If you are running an earlier release, the calculator will have rectangular buttons and may also have a darker background color. These differences do not affect functionality. For additional information, see the *xcalc* reference page in Part Three of this guide.

By default, *xcalc* works like a TI-30 calculator. To run *xcalc* in this mode, enter:

```
% xcalc &
```

You can also operate the calculator in Reverse Polish Notation (as an HP-10C calculator operates), by entering:

```
% xcalc -rpn &
```

In Reverse Polish Notation the operands are entered first, then the operator. For example, 5 * 4 = would be entered as 5 Enter 4 *. This entry sequence is designed to minimize keystrokes for complex calculations.

xcalc allows you to select the number in the calculator display. You select the number using the first pointer button and paste it in another window using the second button. See Chapter 5, *The xterm Terminal Emulator*, for information about copying and pasting text selections. For more information on the function of each of the calculator keys, see the *xcalc* reference page in Part Three of this guide.

Terminating the Calculator

Terminate the calculator by either:

* Clicking the third pointer button on the TI calculator's AC key or the HP calculator's ON key, or:

* Positioning the pointer on the calculator and typing q, Q, or Control-C.

Mail Notification Client: xbiff

xbiff is a simple program that notifies you when you have mail. It puts up a window showing a picture of a mailbox. When you receive new mail, the keyboard emits a beep, the flag on the mailbox goes up, and the image changes to reverse video. Figure 8-6 shows the *xbiff* mailbox before and after mail is received.

After you read your mail, the image changes back to its original state. (You only need to run a mail program to convince *xbiff* that you've read your mail. You don't have to delete all messages.) Or, rather than run a mail program, you can simply click on the full mailbox icon with any pointer button to change it back to empty.

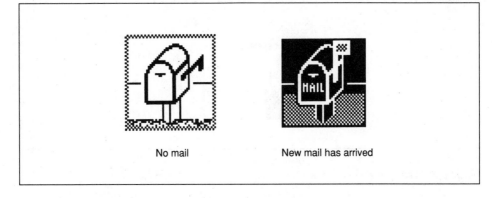

No mail   New mail has arrived

Figure 8-6. xbiff before and after mail is received

Regardless of whether you reset the mailbox to empty, *xbiff* causes the keyboard to beep each time more mail arrives.

The Release 5 version of *xbiff* is noticeably smarter than the R4 version which notified you of *any* change in the size of the mail file. (Thus, you were notified when you deleted messages and the file became smaller!)

While *xbiff* is intended to monitor a mail file, it can actually be set up to watch any file whose size changes using the -file option (followed by the name of the file to be monitored). For instance, if you're running a program that produces output intermittently, you can start *xbiff* with -file followed by the name of the output file; then *xbiff* will notify you when output is returned. (You can even specify an image other than the mailbox using resource variables—even for a single *xbiff* process.) See the *xbiff* reference page in Part Three of this guide for a list of options and resources. See Chapter 11, *Setting Resources*, for the syntax of resource specifications.

Monitoring System Load Average: xload

xload periodically polls the system for the load average and graphically displays that load using a simple histogram. By default, *xload* polls the system every ten seconds. You can change this frequency with the -update option. For example, if you enter this command in an *xterm* window:

```
% xload -update 3 &
```

the resulting *xload* window will poll the system every three seconds, as in Figure 8-7.

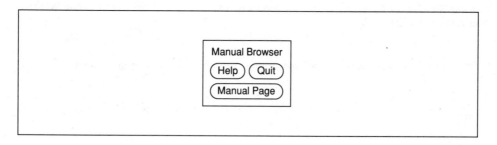

Figure 8-7. A sample xload window

If you are using both the local machine and remote machines, you can display loads for all systems and do your processing on the system that is fastest at the time.

Like *xclock* and *oclock*, *xload* provides no exit command. To remove an *xload* window, you need to kill the client process. See "Removing an xclock or oclock" earlier in this chapter.

Browsing Reference Pages: xman

The *xman* client allows you to display and browse through formatted versions of reference pages. By default, *xman* searches for manpages found in the directories specified by the MANPATH environment variable. (If you set the MANPATH, individual directory names should be separated by colons.) If MANPATH is not defined, *xman* searches the subdirectories of the directory */usr/man*. In a typical UNIX environment, there are 10 subdirectories: *man1* through *man8*, corresponding to the eight sections of reference pages in the UNIX documentation set; *manl* (man local) and *mann* (man new).

You run *xman* by typing:

```
% xman &
```

in an *xterm* window.

The initial *xman* window, shown in Figure 8-8, is a small window containing only a few commands.

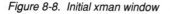

Figure 8-8. Initial xman window

This window is small enough to be displayed for prolonged periods during which you might have need to examine UNIX manual pages. You select a command by clicking on it with the first pointer button.

The Manual Page command brings up a larger window in which you can display a formatted version of any manual page in the MANPATH. By default, the first page displayed contains general help information about *xman*. Use this information to acquaint yourself with the client's features.* (The actual *xman* reference page in Part Three of this guide primarily describes how to customize the client.)

Once you've opened this larger window, you can display formatted manual pages in it. Notice the horizontal bar spanning the top edge of the window. (If you're running *mwm* or a similar window manager, this bar appears beneath the titlebar provided by the window manager.) The bar is divided into three parts labeled Options, Sections, and Xman Help. The part currently labeled Xman Help is merely informational and the text displayed in it will change depending on the contents of the window. The parts labeled Options and Sections are actually handles to two *xman* menus.

If you place the pointer on the Options box and press and hold down the first button, a menu called Xman Options will be displayed below. The menu is pictured in Figure 8-9.

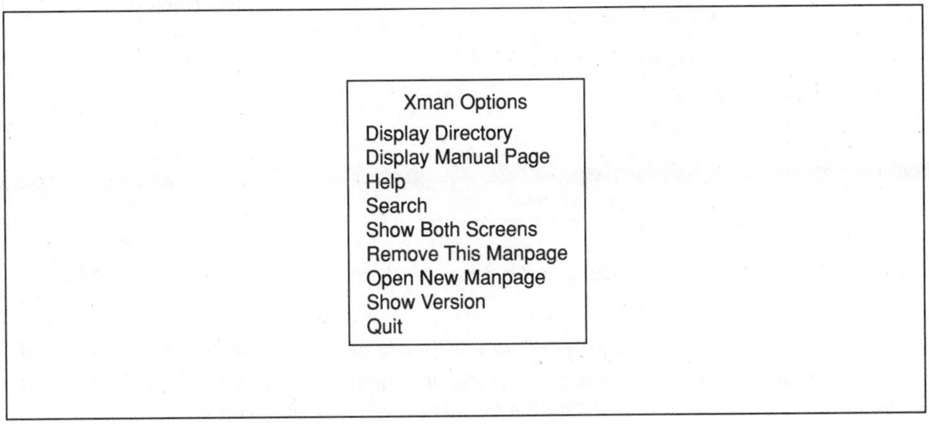

Figure 8-9. Xman Options menu

The functionality of these options is described in the online *xman* help page. To select an option, move the pointer down the menu and release the first button on the option you want. The option you will probably use most frequently is the first one, Display Directory.

Display Directory lists the reference pages in the current reference page directory (also called a *section*). By default, this is *man1*, the user commands. When you list the contents of *man1* in this way, the informational section of the horizontal bar reads Directory of: (1) User Commands.

---

*Selecting the Help command also opens a large window in which the same help information is displayed. The Help command is something of a dead end, however; you cannot display any other text in this window.

Once you've listed a reference page directory in the *xman* window, you can display a formatted version of any page in the list simply by clicking on the name with the first pointer button. Figure 8-10 shows the formatted reference page for the UNIX *cd*(1) command.

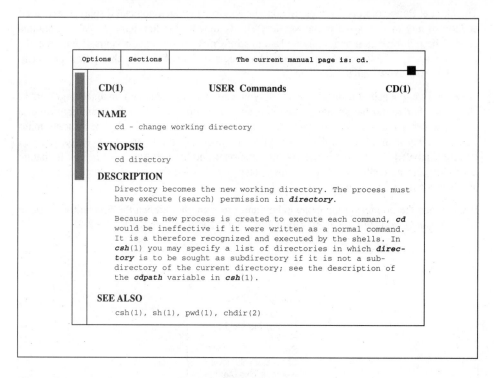

Figure 8-10. cd reference page displayed in xman window

As we'll see later in this section, if you know the name of the page you want to display, you can skip displaying the relevant section listing and simply search for the name. For now, let's assume you need to glance at the directory listings to find what you want.

To display another manual page from the same directory, display the Xman Options menu again. Select Display Directory and the directory listing is again displayed in the window. Then click on another command name to display its manual page in the window. (If you decide not to display another reference page, you can remove the directory listing and go back to the reference page previously displayed by using the second item on the Xman Options menu, Display Manual Page. Display Directory and Display Manual Page are toggles of one another.)

To display a manual page from another directory in the MANPATH, you can change to that directory using the Xman Sections menu. Bring up the menu by placing the pointer in the Sections box in the application's titlebar and holding down the first button. The Xman Sections menu lists the directories of UNIX manual pages under the MANPATH, as shown in Figure 8-11.

X Window System User's Guide, Motif Edition

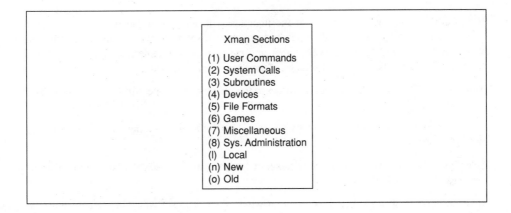

Figure 8-11. Xman Sections menu

Keep in mind that the available sections may vary from system to system. Figure 8-11 shows the manual page sections typical to a UNIX environment.

Click on the first pointer button to select another directory of reference pages from which to choose. Once you select a directory, the files in that directory are listed in the window. Again, you display a page by clicking on its name with the first pointer button.

You can display more than one "browsing" window simultaneously by selecting the Open New Manpage option from the Xman Options menu. An additional reference page window will be opened again starting with the help information.

If you know the name of the page you want to display (regardless of the section), you don't need to use either of *xman*'s menus. While the *xman* window has the input focus, typing Control-S pops up a dialog box prompting for a specific manual page to display, as in Figure 8-12.

```
┌─────────────────────────────────────┐
│ Type string to search for:          │
│ ┌─────────────────────────────────┐ │
│ │                                 │ │
│ └─────────────────────────────────┘ │
│ ( Manual Page ) (   Apropos   )      │
│ (          Cancel           )        │
└─────────────────────────────────────┘
```

Figure 8-12. xman's search dialog prompts for a manpage to display

Note that the dialog box takes over the input focus. If you know the exact name of the page you want, type it and either press Return or click on the Manual Page button in the search window. The specific page will be displayed in a browsing window. (If you requested the search from an existing Manual Page window, the new page will be displayed there. If you requested the search from the initial *xman* window, the page will be displayed in a new browsing window.)

Other Clients

If you don't know the exact name of the manpage you want, you can type a guess in the search window and click on the Apropos button, which displays a list of pages containing the string you've entered. Note, however, that you cannot select a name from the Apropos list. Instead, type Control-S again and search for the exact name you want.

You can iconify any of the various windows *xman* creates; each one will be represented by a separate icon symbol.

You can remove a browsing window by selecting the Remove This Manpage option from the Xman Options menu.

Selecting Quit from the Xman Options menu or from the initial *xman* window causes the client to exit.

xman displays each manpage directory in a window known as a *viewport*, created with the Athena Viewport widget from the X Toolkit. A viewport is a composite widget that provides a main window and horizontal and/or vertical scrollbars. The Athena Viewport widget is analogous to the Motif Toolkit's ScrolledWindow, described in Chapter 9, *Working with Motif Applications*.

xman's scrollbar is also an Athena widget. (See Chapter 5, *The xterm Terminal Emulator*, for instructions on using an Athena scrollbar.) The Motif Toolkit also provides a scrollbar widget, described in Chapter 9, which looks and operates somewhat differently than the Athena scrollbar.

The xedit Text Editor

The *xedit* client provides a window in which you can create and edit text files. The editing commands *xedit* recognizes are provided by the Athena Text widget. Many other standard and user-contributed clients also include areas in which you can enter text. Several of these clients, including *xclipboard* and *xmh*, also use the Text widget, and thus recognize the same editing commands as *xedit*.

The *xedit* client is valuable to illustrate the use of the Athena Text widget. (*xedit* can also be used to illustrate several other widgets.) However, we do not recommend using *xedit* as your primary text editor. The program is somewhat buggy and its behavior can be erratic. For example, it's fairly easy to overwrite files inadvertently, as explained in the discussion of the Load button later in this section. The redraw command (Control-l) causes text in the window to scroll so as to reposition the cursor in the center of the editing window—not a welcome surprise. Some of the commands to create a new paragraph may also inadvertently copy preceding text. These are just a few of *xedit*'s inconvenient features.

Still, it is necessary to know something about the Athena Text widget in order to be able to enter and edit text in windows provided by many clients.

xedit recognizes various Control and Meta keystroke combinations that are bound to a set of commands similar to those provided by the *emacs* text editor.* In addition, you can use the

---

*The commands may be bound to keys different from the defaults described below through the standard X Toolkit key translation mechanisms. See Chapter 11, *Setting Resources*, for more information.

pointer to move the cursor in the text or to select a portion of text. The *xedit* cursor is a caret symbol (^). A caret cursor appears in each of the three areas that accept text entry. (These areas are described later in this section.) Pressing the first pointer button causes the insertion point (cursor) to move to the location of the pointer. Notice that the cursor always appears between characters, rather than on a character as the *xterm* cursor does. Double-clicking the first pointer button selects a word, triple-clicking selects a paragraph, and quadruple-clicking selects everything. After you select text, the selection may be extended in either direction by using the third pointer button.

You can invoke *xedit* by entering:

```
% xedit &
```

Since no filename has been specified, the main section of the *xedit* window is empty, as illustrated by Figure 8-13.

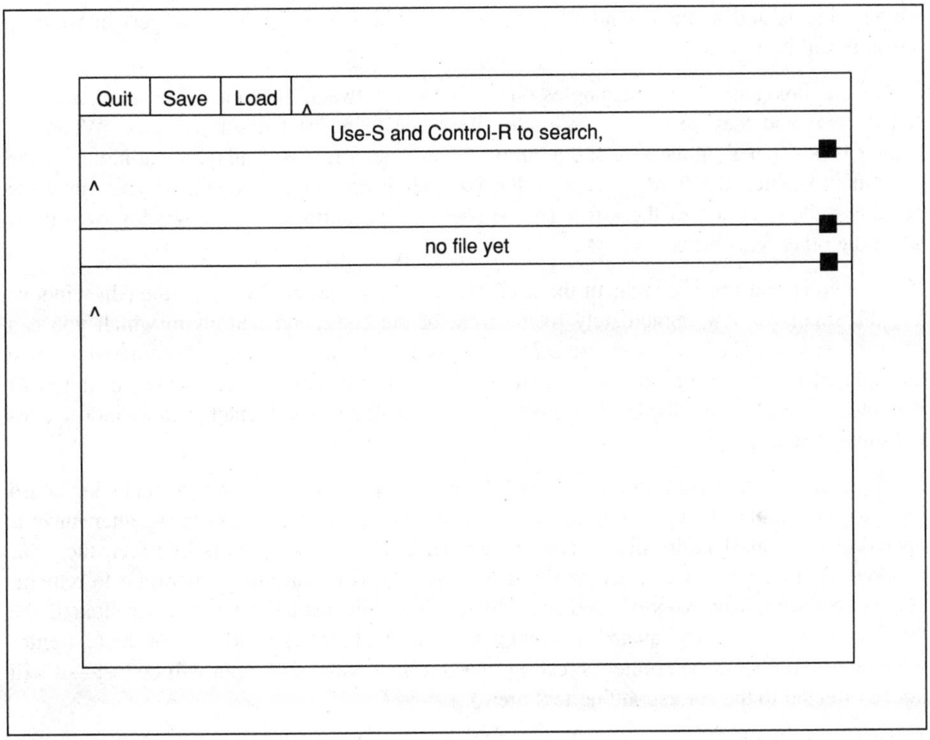

Figure 8-13. xedit window before text file is read in

Notice that the *xedit* window is divided into four parts:

- A commands section, which features three command push buttons (Quit, Save, and Load) and an area to their right in which a filename can be entered.

- A message window, which displays messages from the client and can also be used as a scratch pad.

- The filename display, which shows the name of the file being edited and the read/write permissions for the file.

- The edit window, in which the text of the file is displayed and in which you issue the editing commands.

The *xedit* application uses the Athena VPaned widget (of the X Toolkit), which arranges subwindows one above the other without overlapping. The subwindows are also known as *vertical panes* and the non-overlapping, top-to-bottom arrangement is commonly described as *vertical tiling*.

The individual panes organized by a VPaned widget can be any other type of widget. In the case of *xedit*, for example, the commands section is one pane that contains three command button widgets and a small window to the right of the buttons (a Text widget) in which a filename can be entered.

Notice the three small black rectangles on the borders between the panes. These features are called *grips* and they serve as handles to allow you to resize the subwindows. When the pointer is positioned on the grip and a button pressed, an arrow is displayed that indicates the direction in which the border between the two windows can be moved. If you move the pointer in the direction of the arrow (while pressing the button), one subwindow will grow while the other will shrink.

You can enter text in three areas of the *xedit* window: the message window, the edit window, and the small window immediately to the right of the command buttons in which you can enter a filename. (Thus all three use a Text widget.) Note that the small filename window to the right of the command buttons is different from the filename display (lower in the *xedit* window). The filename display is simply that—a display of the filename; the window does not support editing.

All three areas that permit editing display the caret text cursor. In order to focus keyboard input to a particular area, the pointer must rest in that area—regardless of whether *mwm* is operating with the default click-to-type focus. (If click-to-type focus is in effect, the *xedit* window must also be selected as the focus window.) This is extremely important to remember. Both the message window and the edit window will display a vertical scrollbar if the text is too large to fit. (Be aware also that a scrollbar technically is not part of the text entry window it borders. If the pointer is resting in a scrollbar, keyboard input will be lost—it will not be directed to the corresponding text area!)

The three push buttons in the commands section have the following functions:

Quit   Exits the current editing session and closes the window. If changes have not been saved, *xedit* displays a warning in the message window, and does not exit, thus allowing the user to save the file.

Save	Writes the file. If file backups are enabled (using the `enableBackups` resource), *xedit* first stores a copy of the unedited file as *filename.BAK* and then overwrites *filename* with the contents of the edit window. The *filename* used is the text that appears in the area immediately to the right of the Load button.
Load	Loads the file displayed immediately to the right of the button into the edit window. If a file is currently being displayed and has been modified, a warning message will ask the user to save the changes, or to press Load again.

This interface has at least two serious pitfalls. First, if you're working on a file that has unsaved changes and you try to load a second file, it's possible to overwrite the second file. This is how it happens. In order to load a second file, you must enter the name of the file in the area next to the Load button; then press Load. If you try to load a second file while editing a file with unsaved changes, *xedit* warns you to save or press Load again. If you press Save the current file will be saved—but as the name to the right, the second file you intended to load.

If backups are not enabled, this action will overwrite the file you wanted to load. If backups are enabled, the first file will be saved under the name of the second file with a *.BAK* extension and the second file will not be overwritten. Because of this potential problem, we recommend that you set the resource `enable-Backups` to on (and load the resources using *xrdb*) before using *xedit*.

A second problem can occur after you've loaded a file by entering the name in the window next to the Load button. Say you've been editing the file for some time, but haven't saved the changes. If you go to save the changes and accidentally double-click on Load (not that difficult to do), you'll reload the version of the file before you made the edits. The changes are lost!

Now, after considering some of the possible pitfalls, let's load a file into the empty *xedit* window as shown in Figure 8-13. (Obviously, in this case, there's no danger of overwriting an existing file.) To load a file called *test*:

1. Place the pointer in the area to the right of the Load button.

2. Type *test*. Notice that the caret cursor moves as you type.

3. Place the pointer on the Load command button and press the first pointer button.

The file called *test* is displayed in the edit window, as shown in Figure 8-14.

The simpler commands to edit or append text are intuitive. A backspace deletes the character to the left of the cursor. Typing enters characters immediately before the cursor point, causing the cursor to advance to the right. When you first load a file, the cursor appears at the beginning of the text in the edit window. If you want to append text to the end of the file, move the pointer to the end of the text and click the first button. The caret cursor appears where the pointer is and any text you type is added to the end of the file, moving the cursor to the right.

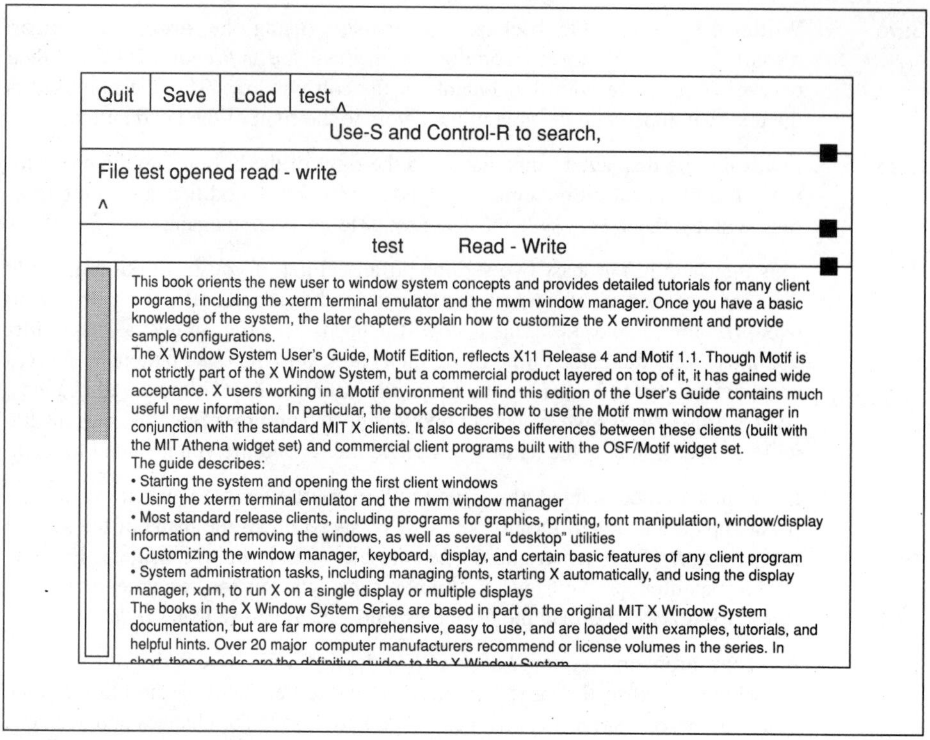

Figure 8-14. test file displayed in edit window

The list at the end of this section summarizes all of the editing command recognized by *xedit*. In this list of commands, a *line* refers to one row of characters displayed in the window. A *paragraph* refers to the text between manually inserted carriage returns or blank lines. Text within a paragraph is automatically broken into lines based on the current width of the window.

The keystroke combinations are defined as indicated. (Note that "Control" and "Meta" are two of the "soft" keynames X recognizes. They are mapped to particular physical keys which may vary from keyboard to keyboard. See the "xmodmap" section in Chapter 14, *Setup Clients*, for a discussion of modifier key mapping.) If you are using an earlier release of X, a few of these keystroke combinations may produce slightly different results.

Keep in mind that you can redefine any of these key combinations using what are known as *translations*. Translations allow you to assign actions recognized by a client to particular key combinations, or key and pointer button combinations. For example, *xedit* recognizes actions to delete text, to copy text, to move the cursor, etc. *xedit* defines key combinations to invoke these actions. (The key/action mappings appear in the list at the end of this section.) For information on specifying alternate mappings, see "Event Translations" in Chapter 11, *Setting Resources*.

Note that the function assigned to the Return key in the following list applies only to the edit window and message window. In the filename window (next to the command buttons), Return simply moves the cursor to the end of the line.

Control-a   Move to the beginning of the current line.

Control-b   Move backward one character.

Control-d   Delete the next character.

Control-e   Move to the end of the current line.

Control-f   Move forward one character.

Control-h or Backspace   Delete the previous character.

Control-j, Control-m, Return, LineFeed   New line.

Control-k   Kill the rest of this line. (Does not kill the carriage return at the end of the line. To do so, use Control-K twice. However, be aware that the second kill overwrites the text line in the kill buffer.)

Control-l   Redraw the window. (Also scrolls text so that cursor is positioned in the middle of the window.)

Control-n   Move down to the next line

Control-o   Divide this line into two lines at this point and move the cursor back up.

Control-p   Move up to the previous line.

Control-r   Search and replace backward.

Control-s   Search and replace forward.

Control-t   Transpose characters. (Swap the characters immediately before and after the cursor.)

Control-u   Control-u, Control-n moves the cursor down four lines.

Control-v   Move down to the next screenful of text.

Control-w   Kill the selected text.

Control-y   Insert the last killed text. (If the last killed text is a carriage return—see Control-k above—a blank line is inserted.)

Control-z   Scroll up the text one line.

Meta-<	Move to the beginning of the file.
Meta->	Move to the end of the file.
Meta-[	Move backward one paragraph.
Meta-]	Move forward one paragraph.
Meta-b	Move backward one word.
Meta-d	Delete the next word.
Meta-D	Kill the next word.
Meta-f	Move forward one word.
Meta-h, Meta-Backspace, Meta-Delete	Delete the previous word.
Meta-H, Meta-Shift-Backspace, Meta-Shift-Delete	Kill the previous word.
Meta-i	Insert a file. A dialog box will appear in which you can type the desired filename.
Meta-k	Kill to the end of the paragraph.
Meta-q	Join lines to form a paragraph.
Meta-v	Move up to the previous screenful of text.
Meta-y	Insert the last selected text here. This command is the equivalent of clicking the second pointer button. See Chapter 5, *The xterm Terminal Emulator*, for more information about text selections.
Meta-z	Scroll down the text one line.
Delete	Delete the previous character.

Printing Utilities: xwd, xpr, xdpr

xwd stores window images in a formatted window dump file. This file can be read by various other X utilities for redisplay, printing, editing, formatting, archiving, image processing, etc.

To create a window dump file, type:

```
% xwd > file
```

The pointer will change to a small crosshair symbol. Move the crosshair pointer to the desired window and click any button. The keyboard bell rings once when the dump starts and twice in rapid succession when the dump is finished.*

To make a dump of the entire root window (and all windows on it), use the `-root` option:

```
% xwd -root > file
```

When you select a single window, by default *xwd* takes an image of the window proper. To include a window manager frame or titlebar, use the `-frame` option.

xwd allows you to capture a single window or the entire root window. But what if you want an image that includes more than one window or parts of multiple windows? You can use *xmag* (described in Chapter 7) to capture an image of multiple windows and then use *xwd* on the *xmag* window! Since *xmag* is intended to magnify, if you want the window image to be the actual size, you must specify that no magnification is performed. To do this, you run *xmag* with the option `-mag 1`. See Chapter 7, *Graphics Utilities*, and the *xmag* reference page in Part Three of this guide for more information.

To redisplay a file created with *xwd* in a window on the screen, use the *xwud* client, an undumping utility. Specify the dump file to display as an argument to the `-in` option:

```
% xwud -in file
```

Then remove the image by typing Control-C in the *xterm* from which you started *xwud*.

xpr takes as input an X Window System dump file produced by *xwd* and converts it to a printer-specific format that can be printed on a PostScript printer (such as the Apple Laser-Writer), the Digital LN03 or LA100 printer, the IBM PP3812 page printer, the HP LaserJet (or other PCL printers) or the HP PaintJet. By default, output is formatted for PostScript. Use the `-device` option to format for another printer. For example, to format a window dump file for the DEC LN03 printer, type:

```
% xpr -device ln03 file > file.ps
```

Other options allow you to change the size, add headers or footers, and so on. See the *xpr* reference page in Part Three of this guide for details.

You can use *xwd* and *xpr* together, using the standard UNIX pipe mechanism. For example:

```
% xwd | xpr -device ln03 | lp
```

---

*If the keyboard bell is turned off, you won't hear the double beep that signals the dump is finished. You control bell volume with the *xset* client, described in Chapter 14, *Setup Clients*.

The *xdpr* command combines these three separate commands into one. (On System V, *lp* is used; on BSD-based systems, *xdpr* uses *lpr*.) *xdpr* accepts most of the options accepted by *xwd*, *xpr*, and *lp*(1) or *lpr*(1). Thus, you could use the command:

```
% xdpr
```

to take a window dump (xwd), convert that file to PostScript (xpr converts to PostScript by default), and print the output (*lpr* or *lp*). See the *xdpr* reference page in Part Three of this guide for more information.

Note that when you start piping together the output of X clients, you run into some ambiguities. For example, if you pipe the output of *xwd* to *xpr* and for some reason the *xpr* command fails, *xwd* will still be there waiting for pointer input. The original UNIX pipe mechanism doesn't have the concept of data dependent on pointer input! The integration of the UNIX model of computing (in which standard input and output are always recognized) and the window model is not always complete, sometimes leading to unexpected behavior.

As an even more flagrant example, you can create a pipe between two programs, the first of which doesn't produce standard output and the second of which doesn't recognize standard input. The shell doesn't know any better and the programs themselves go on their merry way with pointer and windows.

However, it is nice to know that you can pipe together program output, even when some of those programs may not produce output until you intervene with the pointer.

Even without pipes, you should start thinking about how these programs could work together. For example, you could create and print a picture of a font using the following steps:

1. Display a font with *xfd*. (See Chapter 6, *Font Specification*, for instructions on how to use *xfd*.)

2. Resize the window to improve readability, using the *mwm* resize handles or the **Resize** item of the **Window Menu**.

3. Create a window dump file with the command xwd > *file*.

4. Create a PostScript file from the dump with the command:

```
xpr file> file.ps
```

5. Print the PostScript file the appropriate print command (*lp* or *lpr*).

Even though the UNIX shell will accept a pipe between *xfd*, *xwd*, and *xpr*, what actually happens is that *xwd* starts up faster than *xfd* and is ready to dump a window before the *xfd* window appears.

Killing a Client Window with xkill

The *xkill* program allows you to kill a client window or, more specifically, to force the server to end the connection to the client. The process exits and the associated window is removed.

xkill is a fairly drastic method of terminating a client and should *not* be used as the method of choice. In most cases, clients can be terminated in other ways. The possible repercussions of using *xkill* and some of the alternatives are discussed in the next section.

xkill is intended primarily to be used in cases where more conventional methods of removing a client window do not work. It is especially useful when programs have displayed undesired windows on the screen. To remove a stubborn client window, type:

    % xkill

on the command line of an *xterm* window. The pointer changes to a "draped box" pointer and you are instructed to:

Select the window whose client you wish to kill with button 1 . . .

Move the draped box pointer to the window you want to remove, as shown in Figure 8-15, and click the first pointer button. The window is removed. (*xkill* does not allow you to select the root window.)

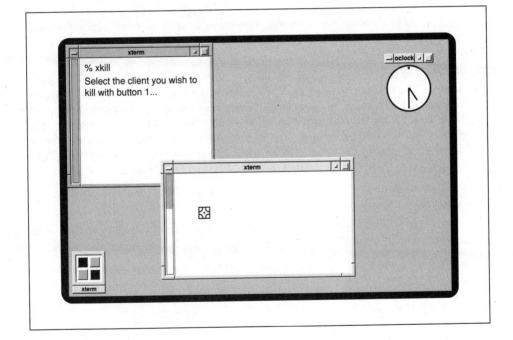

Figure 8-15. Selecting the window to be removed

You can also specify the window to be killed by its *window ID* (also called the *resource ID*). Every window has an identification number associated with it. The *xwininfo* client can be used to display a window's window/resource ID (see the section "Window and Display Information" later in this chapter).

To remove a window using its ID number, type:

```
% xkill -id number
```

The window with the ID *number* is removed. Killing a window by its ID number is more cumbersome but it's somewhat safer than choosing the window to be killed with the pointer. It's too easy to click in the wrong place. (Of course, it's less treacherous to use the pointer on an isolated window than a window in a stack.)

Problems with Killing a Client

The most obvious problem with *xkill* is that it's possible to kill the wrong window inadvertently. Perhaps less obvious is a problem inherent in "killing" a program. As a general rule, a command that "kills" a program does not give the program time to save or complete processes that are still running—in effect, to clean up after itself. The processes that can be adversely affected may be visible to the user, such as an editing session, or they may be underlying system processes, such as writing to or reading from a socket.

Most clients can be terminated in ways that allow them to finish all relevant processes and then exit cleanly. These methods should be attempted *before* you use *xkill* or some other method that kills the client.

For example, you can generally remove an *xterm* window by typing in the window the same command you use to log off the system. You should also be able to remove an *xterm* window with various Main Options menu commands, depending on the signals that can be interpreted by your system. (Some of these signals, such as SIGHUP and SIGTERM, are more gentle to the system. See the *xterm* reference page in Part Three of this guide for a list of menu commands and the signals they send.) Both *xcalc* and *bitmap* can be removed by typing q, Q, or Control-C in the window. The *bitmap* File menu also has a Quit item.

A few clients, such as *oclock*, cannot be removed *except* by killing. You must use *xkill* or a similar method to remove an *oclock* window.

Generally, however, you should exhaust the safer alternatives before you use *xkill* and other commands that kill a client.

When you want to remove a window, depending on the client and what commands it recognizes, try these methods (roughly) in the following order.

1. Methods that cause the client to exit after finishing relevant processes:

   a. Special commands (e.g., `exit`) or key sequences (e.g., Control-D, Control-C, q, Q) recommended to stop a client.

   b. Certain application-specific menu items (e.g., for *xterm*, the Main Options menu commands Send HUP Signal, Send TERM Signal, and Quit; the Quit item on the *bitmap* File menu).

2. When these methods don't work or don't apply (as in the case of *oclock*), *then* use commands or menu items that kill the client:

   a. The Close item on the *mwm* Window Menu; or a double click on the Window Menu command button.

   b. The *xkill* client.

   c. The UNIX *kill* command with the client's process ID number, which is determined using *ps*. (This method of removing a window is described for *xclock* and *oclock* earlier in this chapter.*)

   d. For removing *xterm* windows only: the Send KILL Signal item on the client's Main Options menu.

Window and Display Information Clients

The standard release of X includes three clients that provide information about windows on the display and about the display itself. Much of the information is probably more relevant to a programmer than to the typical user. However, these clients also provide certain pieces of information, such as window geometry, window ID numbers, and the number and nature of screens on the display, that can assist you in using other clients.

Displaying Information About a Window: xwininfo

The *xwininfo* client can display information about a particular window or about how windows are related to one another on the display. (We'll discuss this latter capability in the next section.) Among the most useful information the client provides is the size and location of the window—in the form of a geometry string that can be specified on the command line. (Chapter 3 describes how to specify a window's size and location using the `-geometry` option.)

---

*This method is powerful but in practice has limitations. Many versions of UNIX only allow you to kill a process if you are the owner of the process or if you are root. Thus, if a client has been started on your display from a remote system and you don't know the root password, you may not be in a position to use the UNIX *kill* command.

xwininfo also provides you with the *window ID* (also called the resource ID). Each window has a unique identification number associated with it. This number can be used as a command-line argument with several clients. Most notably, the window ID can be supplied to the *xkill* client to specify the window be killed.

You can also use the window ID as an argument to the *xprop* client, which displays various window properties. As described in Chapter 1, a property is a piece of information associated with a window or a font and stored in the server. Properties facilitate interclient communication; they are used by clients to store information that other clients might need to know. Storing properties in the server makes the information they contain accessible to all clients.

To display information about a window, type this command in an *xterm* window:

```
% xwininfo
```

The pointer changes to the crosshair pointer and you are directed to select the window about which you want information:

```
xwininfo: Please select the window about which you
          would like information by clicking the
          mouse in that window.
```

You can select any window on the display, including the window in which you've typed the command and the root window. (Rather than using the pointer, you can specify a window on the command line by supplying its title, or name if it has no title, as an argument to *xwininfo*'s own -name option. See Chapter 10 for information about setting a client's title and name. See the *xwininfo* reference page in Part Three of this guide for a list of its options.)

Example 8-1 shows the statistics *xwininfo* supplies, with some typical readings.

Example 8-1. Window information displayed by xwininfo

```
xwininfo: Window id: 0x280000f "xterm"

  Absolute upper-left X:  8
  Absolute upper-left Y:  25
  Relative upper-left X:  0
  Relative upper-left Y:  0
  Width: 819
  Height: 484
  Depth: 8
  Visual Class: PseudoColor
  Border width: 0
  Class: InputOutput
  Colormap: 0x27 (installed)
  Bit Gravity State: NorthWestGravity
  Window Gravity State: NorthWestGravity
  Backing Store State: NotUseful
  Save Under State: no
  Map State: IsViewable
  Override Redirect State: no
  Corners:  +8+25   -325+25   -325-391   +8-391
  -geometry 80x24+0+0
```

These readings are for a login *xterm* window displayed using a 10×20 pixel fixed-width font. The *mwm* window manager is also running. Most of the numerical information is in pixels. Depth is in bits per pixel. The colormap is represented by a hexadecimal number. Since we've selected an *xterm* window, the width and height components of the geometry string are in characters and lines (80×24).

For the average user, the first and last lines from Example 8-1 are most significant:

```
xwininfo: Window id: 0x280000f "xterm"
                  .
                  .
                  .
   -geometry 80x24+0+0
```

The first line provides the window ID, which can be used as an argument to *xkill*. Specifying the window to be killed by its ID number is somewhat less risky than choosing it with the pointer.

Probably most important is the final line, which provides the appropriate `-geometry` option to create this client window. (As described in Chapter 3, `-geometry` allows you to specify a window's size and position.)

The other statistics provided by *xwininfo* are listed below:

```
Absolute upper-left X:  8
Absolute upper-left Y:  25
Relative upper-left X:  0
Relative upper-left Y:  0
Width: 819
Height: 484
Depth: 8
Visual Class: PseudoColor
Border width: 0
Class: InputOutput
Colormap: 0x27 (installed)
Bit Gravity State: NorthWestGravity
Window Gravity State: NorthWestGravity
Backing Store State: NotUseful
Save Under State: no
Map State: IsViewable
Override Redirect State: no
Corners:  +8+25  -325+25  -325-391  +8-391
```

Generally, the absolute upper-left X and Y correspond to the positive x and y offsets (the third and fourth components of the geometry string). However, the *mwm* frame complicates matters. When *mwm* is running, the absolute upper-left X and Y correspond to the x and y coordinates of the application window—but not the framed window!

Let's take another look at the sample *xwininfo* output. The absolute upper-left X and Y suggest that the window is located at coordinates 8,25. However, the output is actually for an *xterm* located at coordinates 0,0! The 8,25 are the coordinates of the *xterm* window itself; the coordinates represent the distance of the window from 0,0 *including the dimensions of the frame*. The default frame is actually 8 pixels in the x dimension and 25 pixels in the y dimension (because of the titlebar).

Other Clients

The relative upper-left X and Y are not meaningful if you're running *mwm*. Regardless of a window's location, the relative upper-left X and Y are 0 and 0.

The four corners (again, including the frame) are listed with the upper-left corner first and the other three clockwise around the window (i.e., upper-right, lower-right, lower-left). The coordinates of the upper-left corner are, of course, the absolute upper-left X and Y. The width and height in pixels are somewhat less useful, since the geometry option to *xterm* requires that these figures be specified in characters and lines.

The values for window depth and colormap relate to how color is specified. See Chapter 12, *Specifying Color*, for more information.

The remaining statistics have to do with the underlying mechanics of how a window is resized, moved, obscured, unobscured, and otherwise manipulated. They are inherent in the client program and you cannot specify alternatives. For more information on these and other window attributes, see Chapter 4 in Volume One, *Xlib Programming Manual*.

Examining the Window Hierarchy

Windows are arranged in a hierarchy, much like a family tree, with the root window at the top. Prior to Release 5, you could display the window tree (starting with the root window) using the *xlswins* client. In Release 5, *xlswins* is no longer available. Instead, you can perform the same functions using *xwininfo* with the -children and -tree options.

The -children and -tree options give information about how windows on the display are related to one another. Remember that most application windows are actually composed of several subwindows. These options also allow you to see a client's internal window hierarchy.

Naturally, the information returned using these options largely depends on the window you choose with the pointer. If you choose an application window (such as an *xterm*), you get information about that client's internal hierarchy. If you choose the root window, you get information about all of the application windows on the display—which are the children of the root window.

The command:

```
% xwininfo -children
```

gives information about the immediate children of the window you select (a single generation). Example 8-2 shows the results of this command for an *xterm* window at coordinates 0,0 on the root window. (No window manager is running.)

Example 8-2. Window tree displayed by xwininfo –children

```
xwininfo: Window id: 0x2c0000f "xterm"

  Root window id: 0x2d (the root window) (has no name)
  Parent window id: 0x2d (the root window) (has no name)
     1 child:
     0x2c00016 (has no name): ()   819x484+0+0   +1+1
```

Any client that displays an application window, such as *xterm*, *xclock*, *xfd*, *bitmap*, etc., will be listed by name (in quotes) following the window ID number.* The remaining lines show how the selected window fits in the hierarchy. First the root window is listed, with its ID number. (Obviously, this line will be the same, regardless of the window you select.) Client windows displayed on the root window are called *children* of the root window, in keeping with the family tree analogy; thus, the root window is also the parent of the *xterm* window. The "1 child" of the *xterm* application window is the *xterm* VT102 window. (The first line lists the application shell window, which can be displayed both as a VT102 and a Tektronix window.) In the *xwininfo* listing, a child window is indented once under its parent.

Notice the geometry information at the end of the final line. The first geometry string gives the dimensions of the VT102 window in pixels and its coordinates relative to the *root* window. Since *mwm* is not running, frames are not an issue. Thus, a window at coordinates 0,0 has the position +0+0 relative to the root. The second geometry string gives the window's coordinates relative to its *parent* window. The VT102 window is +1,+1 pixels from the application window because of a single pixel border.

The -children option displays a single "generation" below the selected window. If you run *xwininfo* with this option and select the root window, you'll get the resource ID numbers for all client windows on the display. As you might recall, you can supply this number to *xkill* to specify the window to kill. You can also supply a resource ID to *xwininfo* to specify the window you want information about, or to *xprop* to get the window's properties. Being able to display the ID numbers of all client windows on the screen simultaneously is especially helpful if one or more windows is obscured in the stack. Running *xwininfo* -children and selecting the root can help you determine by process of elimination which window is hidden—without having to circulate all the windows on your screen. You can then use the resource ID number of that window in the ways we've discussed.

To list additional generations of windows, run *xwininfo* with the -tree option. In Example 8-3, we've used -tree and then selected the root window.

Example 8-3. Run xwininfo –tree and select the root to see the complete window hierarchy

```
xwininfo: Window id: 0x2d (the root window) (has no name)

  Root window id: 0x2d (the root window) (has no name)
  Parent window id: 0x0 (none)
     2 children:
     0x300000a "xclock": ("xclock" "XClock")  164x164+986+0  +986+0
        1 child:
        0x300000b (has no name): ()  164x164+0+0  +987+1
     0x2c0000f "xterm": ("xterm" "XTerm")  819x484+0+0  +0+0
        1 child:
        0x2c00016 (has no name): ()  819x484+0+0  +1+1
           1 child:
           0x2c00017 (has no name): ()  14x484+-1+-1  +0+0
```

---

*Most likely, you will not have to deal with the ID numbers for windows other than the explicitly named client windows. You can use the IDs of the client windows in all of the ways we've discussed: with *xkill*, *xwininfo*, *xprop*, etc.

You'll probably notice the application windows "xclock" and "xterm" right away. These are listed as the "2 children" of the "Parent window," which in this case is the root window. But what are the other windows listed in Example 8-3? A superficial examination of these other windows provides a brief introduction to the inner workings of X. An underlying feature of X is that menus, boxes, icons, and even *features* of client windows, such as scrollbars, are actually windows in their own right. What's more, these windows (and client window icons) may still exist, even when they are not displayed.

The three remaining windows are unnamed. From the relative indents of the windows, we can tell certain information. The first unnamed window is a child of the *xclock*. From our prior examples, it seems clear that this is the client window running under the application shell. The second unnamed window is a child of the *xterm*. (As we've seen, this is the VT102 window) The third unnamed window is a child of the child (or the *grandchild* of the *xterm*). The geometry information can help us identify this window. It is the window's scrollbar.

An additional note about the -tree listing. On the line introducing each application window are what are known as the instance and class resource names for the client (for example, xterm, XTerm). You use the instance and class resource names to specify default window characteristics, generally by placing them in a file in your home directory. This is described in detail in Chapter 11, *Setting Resources*.

The listing in Example 8-3 was generated when the *mwm* window manager was not running. If *mwm* is running, the output is considerably more complicated. Many of the features provided by *mwm*, such as the window frame and its command buttons, and the Root Menu and Window Menu, are actually all windows. This *greatly* complicates the window hierarchy. If you run *xwininfo –tree* while *mwm* is running and select the root, even if the display has only a single application window, the output will be dozens of lines long; you can assume that most of the mysterious windows in the hierarchy are features provided by the window manager.

You may also notice that application windows, such as *xterm*, are now at level 3 in the hierarchy. This is because *mwm reparents* all client windows; that is, the window manager creates another window that is the parent window of the application window and is itself the child of the root window. (The frame is actually a window in its own right; think of the window manager as creating a window that contains the application window.)

The geometry strings for application windows will also be different when *mwm* is running because of this reparenting and because of the presence of the frame. The first geometry string, which gives the position relative to the parent window, will always end with the x,y coordinates +0+0, since the parent is the window manager. The second geometry string, which gives the position relative to the root window, will include the dimensions of the frame. A window located at coordinates 0,0 will have the string +12,+29 because the x and y dimensions of the default frame are 12 and 29 pixels, respectively.

Listing the Currently Running Clients: xlsclients

You can get a listing of the client applications running on a particular display by using *xlsclients*. Without any options, *xlsclients* displays a two-column list, similar to:

```
harry   xterm -geometry 80x24+10+10 -ls
harry   xclock -geometry -0+0
ruby    xterm -geometry 80x24-0-0 -display harry:0.0
```

The first column shows the name of the host and the second column shows the client running on it. The client is represented by the command line used to initiate the process.

This sample listing indicates that there is one *xterm* window and one *xclock* window running on the machine `harry`. (The option `-ls` following the *xterm* command reveals that the shell running in this window is a login shell.) A second *xterm* is running on the machine `ruby`.

You can use *xlsclients* to help create an *.xsession* or *.xinitrc* file, which specifies the clients you want to be run automatically when you log in. In order to do this, you must have set up client windows in an arrangement you like using command-line options alone (that is, without having moved or resized windows via the window manager). You can then run *xlsclients* to print a summary of the command lines you used to set up the display and include those command lines in your *.xsession* or *.xinitrc* file.

Note, however, that the *xlsclients* listing has limitations. Our sample output above, for instance, does not explain how the remote process (on ruby) was started. From this information, it's impossible to tell if the user logged on to ruby (perhaps using *rlogin* or *telnet*) and started an *xterm* or simply ran a remote shell (*rsh*) from the machine harry. In such cases, you have to edit *xlsclients* output in order to incorporate it into a login script. From the previous output, we might come up with the script:

```
xclock -geometry -0+0 &
rsh ruby xterm -geometry 80x24-0-0 -display harry:0.0 &
xterm -geometry 80x24+10+10 -ls
```

(Because of the way X works, the final process must remain in the foreground. See Appendix A, *Managing Your Environment*, for an explanation.)

Keep in mind, also, that *xlsclients* only lists clients that are window-based (*xterm*, *xclock*, *xbiff*, etc.). It will not list the window manager or clients you want to run to set keyboard and display preferences, such as the pattern of the root window. (Chapter 14, *Setup Clients* explains how to set such preferences using the *xset*, *xsetroot*, and *xmodmap* clients.)

By default, *xlsclients* lists the clients running on the current screen of the display corresponding to the DISPLAY environment variable (almost always the local display). If your display is composed of multiple screens, you can list the clients running on all of them by using the `-a` command-line option. Note, however, that the output will not distinguish between the screens (though the command lines may contain a `-display` option revealing this information). If you have multiple screens, you're probably better off running *xlsclients* on each screen sequentially.

You can list the clients running on another physical display by using the `-display` option. See Chapter 3, *Working in the X Environment*, for more information about `-display`.

The bottom line is that you can use *xlsclient*'s output as the *foundation* for your session file, but you will need to add to it. See Appendix A for more detailed instructions on setting up a user session.

With the `-1` option (indicating long), *xlsclients* generates a more detailed listing. Example 8-4 shows the long version of the listing on the previous page.

Example 8-4. Long xlsclients listing

```
Window 0x30000e:
  Machine:  harry
  Name:  xterm
  Icon Name:  xterm
  Command:  xterm -geometry 80x24+10+10 -ls
  Instance/Class:  xterm/XTerm
Window 0x40000b:
  Machine:  harry
  Name:  xclock
  Icon Name:  xclock
  Command:  xclock -geometry -0-0
  Instance/Class:  xclock/XClock
```

For each client, *xlsclients* displays six items of information: the window ID number, display name, client name, icon name, command line used to run the client, and the instance and class resource names associated with the client.

As we'll see in Chapter 10, many clients, including *xterm*, allow you to specify an alternate name for a client and a title for the client's window. If you've specified a title, it will appear in the *xlsclients* Name field. If you haven't specified a title but have specified a name for the application, the name will appear in this field. Neither of the clients in the sample display has been given an alternate name or title.

You use the instance and class resource names to specify default window characteristics, generally by placing them in a file in your home directory. This is described in detail in Chapter 11, *Setting Resources*.

Generating Information About the Display: xdpyinfo

The *xdpyinfo* client gives information about the X display, including the name of the display (contents of the DISPLAY variable), version and release of X, number of screens, current screen, and statistics relating to the color, resolution, input, and storage capabilities of each screen. The *xdpyinfo* reference page in Part Three of this guide shows a listing for a display that supports both a color and monochrome screen.

Much of the information provided by *xdpyinfo* has to do with how clients communicate information to one another and is more relevant to a programmer than to the typical user. However, the basic statistics about the name of the display, the version and release of X, and the number and nature of screens might be very helpful to a user, particularly one who is using a display for the first time.

In addition, the detailed information about each screen's color capabilities can also be very valuable in learning how to use color more effectively. This information includes the default number of colormap cells: the number of colors you can use on the display at any one time. See Chapter 12, *Specifying Color*, for more information on the use of color and how to specify colors for many clients.

See Volume One, *Xlib Programming Manual*, for insights into some of the other information provided by *xdpyinfo*.

User-contributed Clients

In addition to the clients in the standard MIT X distribution, there are many user-contributed clients available in the X source tree, distributed over Usenet and perhaps included with various commercial distributions. If you have access to Usenet, the newsgroup *comp.windows.x* contains voluminous discussions of X programming and the newsgroup *comp.sources.x* contains sources.

For example, several window managers are available. Some of the more popular window managers are:

twm   The tab window manager, which is the standard window manager shipped with MIT's X distribution.

awm   The Ardent window manager (written by Jordan Hubbard of Ardent Computer Corporation).

rtl   The tiled window manager (written by Ellis Cohen at Siemens Research & Technology Laboratories, RTL).

olwm   OPEN LOOK window manager (developed by AT&T).

A version of the OPEN LOOK window manager is available as a user-contributed client.

Commercial products (such as spreadsheets, word processors, and graphics or publishing applications) based on the X Window System are also becoming available.

In the next sections, we describe how to use three public domain programs that can assist you in using color on your display. *xcol* allows you to see how X's standard colors will look on your monitor. *xcoloredit* and *xtici* allow you to create shades of your own, which you can then use for backgrounds, borders, etc. See Chapter 10 for a discussion of the color options accepted by most clients and Chapter 12, *Specifying Color*, for an overview of X's color capabilities and the standard colors provided.

Previewing Colors for Your Monitor: xcol

Among the more useful user-contributed clients is *xcol*, developed by Helmut Hoenig.* The standard colors the X server recognizes are listed in a file called *rgb.txt*, which is generally

---

*Although this application has not been rewritten for Release 5, we've found that the latest version of the client does work with an R5 server.

stored in */usr/lib/X11*. These standard colors are not portable. A color can look different on different monitors, perhaps much different than the color name suggests. Hypothetically, you could spend a lot of time testing the various colors provided. The *xcol* client allows you to see how the standard colors look on your display before you specify the colors for a client. Once you've selected certain colors, *xcol* can also assist you in editing the color specifications in your *Xresources* file.

To run the *xcol* program, simply enter:

```
% xcol &
```

A window titled ColorView will be placed on your screen. The ColorView window displays the outline of a cube containing scattered pixels of the available colors, almost like a universe of colored stars. The position of each of the colored pixels in the cube represents its RGB value (see Chapter 12, *Specifying Color*).

In many cases, a primary shade is associated with several subshades, which are distinguished from the primary shade by a number appended to its name. For example, you can specify the color dark sea green, and also DarkSeaGreen1 through DarkSeaGreen4. Within *xcol*'s ColorView window, colors with the same name but different RGB values (signaling different intensities) are represented by a single pixel.

The pixels are not labeled but you should be able to distinguish basic colors on a good quality color monitor. If you place the pointer on any of the pixels, a small box containing the color name will be displayed. The color name appears in white and the border of the box appears in the color specified. If the pixel represents several associated colors of differing intensities, the box will also contain a spectrum of those colors (though the individual shades are lumped under the primary name). By moving the pointer onto various pixels, you should be able to get an idea of how certain colors look on your display.

Some areas of the window are more cluttered with pixels than others. In these areas, you may not be able to distinguish individual pixels. However, if you move the pointer slowly over these "bunches," the individual color names will be displayed, outlined in the color.

While the pointer focus is directed to the ColorView window, you may notice the rest of the display becomes slightly darkened. This darkening happens because *xcol* provides its own colormap, different from the default. It is a normal effect and will stop when you switch the focus to another window.

In addition to letting you preview colors, *xcol* can also be used to edit color resource specifications. If you want to edit the color specifications in your *Xresources* file, start the client using the command line:

```
% xcol ~/.Xresources &
```

This time two windows will be displayed: the ColorView window and a second window titled TextView, which contains the specifications pertaining to color from the *Xresources* file, as in Figure 8-16.

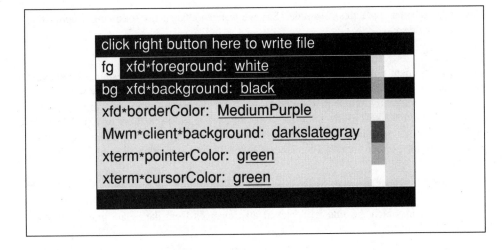

Figure 8-16. xcol's TextView window

The size of the TextView window depends on the number of color specifications in the *.Xresources* file. Though you can't tell from our black and white illustration, each specification in the TextView window appears in the color it names (the color is the foreground color of the text line). If you click the second pointer button on a specification line, a reverse video effect takes place: the named color becomes the background and the previous background color (gray by default) becomes the foreground (text) color. An "R" appears to the left of the text line, indicating that reverse video is enabled. Although reverse video is not necessary, it sometimes provides a better look at a color than the default display—and also a better look than the boxes surrounding color names in the ColorView window. Reverse video display is a toggle: if you want to return to the default display, click the second pointer button on the text line again.

By using the pointer on both the TextView and ColorView windows, you can change the colors specified in the *.Xresources* file. To select the resource to change, place the pointer on the corresponding line in the TextView window and click the first button. The selected line will be outlined in the current foreground color.

Once you've selected a resource, you can change the corresponding color value:

1. Place the pointer on a pixel in the ColorView window; wait until the color name box is displayed.

2. While the pointer rests on the pixel, click the first button.

The color value of the resource in the TextView window is changed to the color you select. The named color is also displayed as either the foreground or background color of the text line—background if reverse video was active. You can change the color any number of times without saving changes to the text file—just to take a look at some colors.

Other Clients

Now let's consider a practical example. Say we want to change the following specification in our sample resource file:

```
Mwm*client*background: darkslategray
```

which makes client window frames dark slate gray. First we select the resource by clicking on it with the first pointer button. Then we move the pointer to the ColorView window and search for an alternative color that would be good for the *mwm* frame. Moving the pointer among the colored pixels in the ColorView window, we settle on medium orchid. While the pointer rests on the medium orchid pixel and the box enclosing the color name is displayed, we click the first pointer button. The resource in the TextView window changes to reflect our choice:

```
Mwm*client*background: mediumorchid
```

and the color in which the line is displayed also changes from dark slate gray to medium orchid.

If the file displayed in the TextView window includes background and foreground specifications for the same resource, those resources are grouped together, and the letters "fg" and "bg" appear to the left of the foreground and background resources, respectively. These associated resources are displayed using the foreground and background color specifications they name. In our sample TextView window, the following resources are grouped:

```
xfd*foreground: white
xfd*background: black
```

These resources set the foreground and background colors for the *xfd* font displayed, described in Chapter 6, to white and black respectively. Thus, in the TextView window these specification lines appear in white with a black background.

To switch the colors specified by a foreground/background pair, place the pointer on either resource line and click the second button. Our sample resources would be changed to:

```
xfd*foreground: black
xfd*background: white
```

and the resources in the TextView window would also switch to black on white.

Keep in mind that you can change only one of the associated resources if you want, by using the method described previously.

Once you've selected colors you like, you can save the changes to the text file by placing the pointer in the horizontal bar at the top of the TextView window right below the frame and clicking the third button. The bar contains the message:

```
click right button here to write file.
```

When you click the third pointer button on this bar, *xcol* beeps and asks you to confirm the choice by displaying:

```
confirm writing with right button!
```

To write the file, click the third button on the bar again. The *.Xresources* file is saved and the following message is displayed in the horizontal bar:

```
file written with backup.
```

The previous version of the *.Xresources* file is saved as a backup and given the filename *.Xresources˜*. To restore the old settings, simply rename the backup file *.Xresources*.

If you want to cancel writing the file, click any button other than the third on the horizontal bar and you will get the message:

```
writing aborted.
```

To quit the application, focus input on either the TextView or ColorView window and type q. Be aware that *xcol* will allow you to quit without saving changes and will not inform you.

Creating Colors of Your Own: xcoloredit and xtici

Several public-domain clients are available to help you create your own colors. In the following sections, we'll consider two of them: *xcoloredit* and *xtici* (also known as the Tek-Color™ Editor).

Of the two, *xcoloredit* is simpler to use. It works on the principle that you can "mix" red, green, and blue to create a color. (See Chapter 12, *Specifying Color*, for an explanation of the RGB color model.) The primary limitation: *xcoloredit* outputs only RGB color values, which are not portable. (They look different on different monitors.)

xtici is more complicated; to use it effectively, it's helpful to understand some of the more "scientific" terms used to describe color, namely *hue*, *value*, and *chroma*. The average person uses "blue," "light," "dark," "bright," etc. However, you can also describe (and specify) a color in terms of the following characteristics:

Hue   Generally speaking, the shade (e.g., red).

Value   A range of the hue from light to dark. The lightest possible shade of any hue is white; the darkest is black.

Chroma   Also called *saturation*. The amount of the hue present (roughly speaking, the hue's intensity).

As we'll see, when using *xtici*, you create a color by manipulating these three factors. However, these characteristics don't just apply to colors created using *xtici*—they can be used to describe any color. Though you'll undoubtedly think in terms of red, green, and blue when mixing colors with *xcoloredit*, the program does allow you to adjust the color based on hue, value, and chroma as well.

But before you can really understand what all this means, you'll need to run the color editors and play with them a bit. If you want more background information before this hands-on session, see Chapter 12, *Specifying Color*.

xcoloredit

The *xcoloredit* program is a public-domain client that can assist you in "mixing" your own RGB color specifications.* You can copy and paste a value *xcoloredit* supplies to specify a color on the command line or in a resource file. You might also pair this value with a name and place it in the RGB or Xcms color database, as described in Chapter 12, *Specifying Color*. Then you can specify the color by its name on the command line or in a resource file. But for now, let's just see how to mix some colors. *xcoloredit* is a simple and highly useful program with a fairly intuitive interface. You should quickly be able to use it effectively. To start the program, simply enter:

```
% xcoloredit &
```

Figure 8-17 shows the initial state of the *xcoloredit* window. The various parts of the application are labeled.

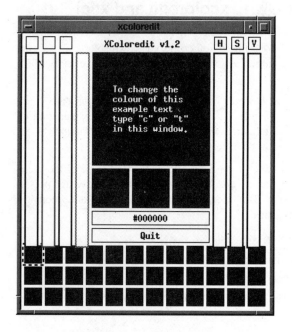

Figure 8-17. Initial xcoloredit window

Don't be deceived by this blank looking window. *xcoloredit* lets you mix colors as easily as a kid mixes finger paints—but a little more neatly.

---

*xcoloredit is available via anonymous *ftp* from *export.lcs.mit.edu* as */contrib/xcoloredit.tar.Z*. See Appendix H, *Obtaining Example Programs*, for instructions on retrieving files using *ftp*. For instructions on compiling public-domain programs, see Volume Eight, *X Window System Administrator's Guide*.

The idea behind *xcoloredit* is that you can mix parts of red, green, and blue to make a color that is displayed in the large central square—we'll call this the mixing area. Initially, the mixing area is black and displays the following text in white:

```
To change the
colour of this
example text
type "c" or "t"
in this window.
```

Below the mixing area are three smaller squares, which will show you how much red, green, and blue you have added. The red square is on the left, green in the middle, and blue on the right. To begin with, these three squares are also black.

Below the mixing area and the three component squares are 36 much smaller squares called "color cells." The color cells allow you to save up to 36 colors (and their hex values). More about this later. When you begin, all of the cells are black and the first cell (the upper-left one) is surrounded by a red dotted line.

To mix a new color in the large square (mixing area), you can use the three vertical bars on the left side of the window, which are outlined in red, green, and blue, respectively. These color sliders or scrollbars operate exactly like the Athena scrollbar (explained in Chapter 5, *The xterm Terminal Emulator*). Though you cannot tell immediately, each scrollbar has a "thumb" which can be dragged up from the base of the bar to add more of the color it represents. (Initially, no colors are present, so the mixing area is black.)

To get an idea how this works, place the pointer at the base of the red scrollbar (the leftmost one). When the thumb is accessible, the pointer changes to a vertical double-sided arrow. Press and hold down the second pointer button. The pointer again changes, this time to an arrow pointing right. Now drag the (pinkish) thumb toward the top of the scrollbar. As you drag up, you're in effect adding more and more red. As the thumb moves, notice that five other parts of the display are being constantly updated:

1. The mixing area is changing to reflect the amount of red you're selecting.

2. The red square (the leftmost square beneath the mixing area) also displays the amount of red you're selecting.

3. The hexadecimal window beneath the three color squares is being updated to show the numeric color value.

4. The dotted line surrounding the first color cell becomes a solid line. The color cell displays what is in the mixing area.

5. On the right side of the window, three additional sliders (labeled H, S, and V) move concurrent with the red slider.

To mix a color, you'll probably want to play with the green and blue sliders as well. Note that if you also select green and/or blue, the mixing area and the first color cell display the new combination, while the smaller squares below the mixing area display the component colors—to show you the amount of each color you're adding.

Using a Color Within an Application

If you click the first pointer button in the hexadecimal window, the text becomes the PRIMARY selection (the hex window becomes reverse video to signal this); you can then paste the hex value into an *xterm* window by clicking the second pointer button. This is handy for transferring the text to the command line or to a resource file.

For example, in Figure 8-18 we've mixed a color like pea soup; it has the hex value #a8bc49.* (Since these illustrations are black and white, I'm afraid this will take some imagination!)

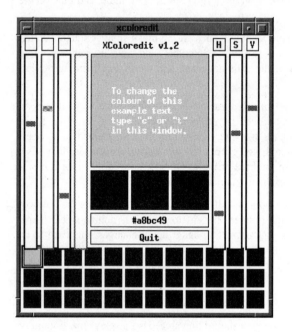

Figure 8-18. Mixing pea soup with xcoloredit

In Figure 8-19, we click the first pointer button in the hex window, which becomes reverse video as the value is made the PRIMARY text selection.

Then we can paste the hex value on the command line or in a resource file. For instance, we can type:

```
% xload -fg
```

---

*This RGB color value may produce a different shade depending on the display hardware and the X server. See Chapter 12, *Specifying Color*, for more information.

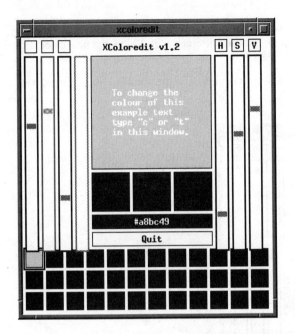

Figure 8-19. Copying the hex value into memory for pasting

Then click the second pointer button to paste the hex value for our new pea soup color (and add an ampersand to run the process in the background):

```
% xbiff -fg #a8bc49 &
```

This command line should create an *xbiff* window with a pea soup colored mailbox.

We could also paste the hex value into a resource file like *.Xresources*. The following line specifies that all *xbiff* windows use the pea soup color as the foreground color.

```
XBiff*Foreground:  #a8bc49
```

See Chapter 11, *Setting Resources*, for more information.

Saving Multiple Colors Using the Color Cells

Once you've mixed one color, you can retain the image of that color in the first color cell and mix a second color which appears in the second cell. The hex values will also be saved so you can copy and paste them.

To begin, place the pointer on the second color cell (the one immediately to the right of the first) and click the first pointer button. The second cell becomes surrounded by a dotted outline; it also changes from displaying black to displaying the color in the first cell (and the mixing area).

Now you can begin mixing a second color, just as you did the first, by dragging the color sliders. As you move the sliders, the five parts of the window described previously are updated. Most significantly, the mixing area and the second color cell will display the new color, and the hex window will display its numeric value.

For our second color we've come up with a very bright blue (remember: imagination) with the hex value #09e5fb, as in Figure 8-20.

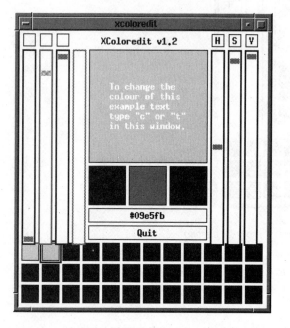

Figure 8-20. Mixing a second color

You can go back to the first color (display it in the mixing area) by placing the pointer on the first color cell and clicking the first button. All parts of the window go back to the state associated with the first color: the mixing area displays that color, the first color cell is outlined, the hex window displays its value (so you can copy and paste it), the sliders indicate the red, green, and blue components, etc.

To switch back to the second color, click on the second color cell. The display now reflects the second color.

If you want to use all of the color cells, you can actually mix and save 36 colors! Then you can "browse" through them by clicking on associated color cell. In effect, *xcoloredit* serves as a sort of color clipboard.

Moving on to the next color cell doesn't mean the previous one is frozen as it is. You can select any color cell and continue to edit it at any time. Or you can consider a cell to be static and move on to edit within another cell.

X Window System User's Guide, Motif Edition

What Are the H, S, and V Sliders For?

Anyone who's mixed finger paints can get used to the red, green, and blue sliders fairly easily. Most people can conceive of color as this sort of mixture. When you move any one of the red, green, and blue sliders, on the right side of the window, three additional sliders (labeled H, S, and V) move concurrently. While the red, green, and blue sliders (obviously) represent the amount of each of those colors, the H, S, and V sliders represent other characteristics used to "measure" color: hue, saturation, and value (also sometimes called chroma).

These characteristics are described in the introduction to this section. If you want to, you can mix a color in the *xcoloredit* window using the H, S, and V sliders (the red, green, and blue sliders will move concurrently), but the program is not actually intended to be used in this way. Hue, saturation (or chroma), and value probably won't be very meaningful (or relevant)—unless you experiment with the TekColor editor, *xtici*.

Quitting xcoloredit

To quit the application, click the first pointer button on the Quit button, which is located just below the hex window.

xtici (The TekColor Editor)

For many users, *xtici* will be somewhat unintuitive, but it offers a significant advantage over *xcoloredit*—namely, that it can provide color values in two portable formats (as well as the non-portable RGB format). Playing with *xtici* for a while should help you relate the characteristics hue, chroma, and value to the typical terms with which people describe color: "red," "green," "light," "bright," etc.

Note that *xtici* is useful because of the X Consortium's adoption (in Release 5) of the X Color Management System (Xcms), developed by Tektronix. Xcms is intended to overcome the limitations of the (still available) RGB model by providing *device-independent* color. A device-independent color looks the same on any monitor.

Xcms accepts color values in several different formats, called *color spaces*. Most of these color spaces describe color in a device-independent manner, using scientific terms and values commonly applied to color (like hue, value, and chroma). Xcms also recognizes the non-portable RGB color format. (For more information, see "The Xcms Color Spaces" in Chapter 12.) *xtici* interprets and also outputs color values in two of the Xcms portable color spaces and in RGB format.

xtici has an elaborate interface, complete with several menus. We'll just take a look at a few of the features you'll need to create your own colors. For more information, see the *TekColor Editor Reference Manual*, distributed in PostScript form with *xtici*.

To run the program, simply enter:

```
% xtici &
```

Figure 8-21 shows a typical *xtici* window with some of the more significant features labeled.

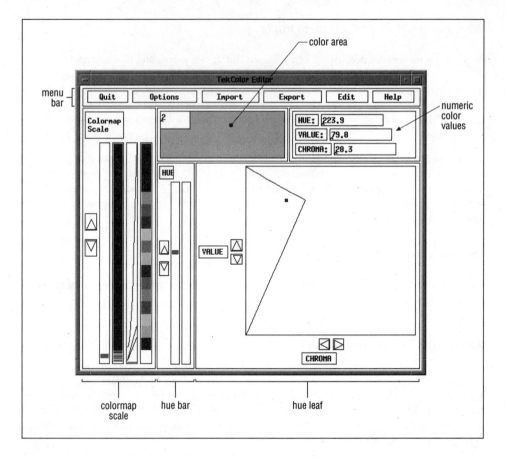

Figure 8-21. Initial xtici window

For our purposes, the most important parts of the window are:

- The Quit, Options, and Edit menus on the menu bar.

- The color area, in which the current shade is displayed.

- The numeric color values, which can be used to specify the current shade. (The Edit menu allows you to select these values to paste on the command line, in a resource file, in an Xcms color database, etc.)

- The Colormap Scale, from which you can change the hue to be edited.

- The Hue Bar provides a sampling of a wider range of hues than is initially visible in Colormap Scale. The Hue Bar also allows you to change the hue to be edited.

- The Hue Leaf, which shows the value and chroma range for the selected hue. You can adjust the value (lightness) and chroma (intensity) from this area.

The color area shows an initial color, the numeric values for which appear in the boxes immediately to the right. *xtici* allows you to change or edit this color in a variety of ways. Some of the editing methods involve dragging or clicking on graphical elements in the window, but you can also change the color in the color area by entering other numeric values in the boxes to the right. If you edit using the former style, the numeric values will change concurrently.

Because *xtici* provides many different ways to change the color in the color area, editing can be complicated. We'll show you some of the basic editing strategies in the next few sections, but regardless of the method you choose, you'll probably want to perform the following tasks:

1. Select a hue.

2. Adjust the value and chroma of the selected hue, if desired.

3. Select the numeric value of the color (using the Edit menu) in order to specify it on the command line, etc.

Choosing a Hue to Edit

When you first run *xtici*, the color in the color area will probably be a color that is currently being used elsewhere on the display. You can work from this initial hue—adjust its value (or lightness) and chroma (or intensity)—or select another hue and edit that.

In Figure 8-20 our initial hue is the standard RGB color named sky blue. (See Chapter 12 for a discussion of the RGB color model and the RGB color database.) The box to the right of the color area contains numeric values that correspond to this color. By default, the color is expressed as three numbers corresponding to hue, value, and chroma. This so-called Tek-HVC format (or color space) is portable. *xtici* also recognizes and can return values in another portable format, introduced by the prefix CIEuvY, as well as in the non-portable RGB format.

Notice that the hue in the color area also appears in the so-called Colormap Scale area of the *xtici* window. Within the Colormap Scale area are four parallel vertical bars. The first bar is a slider. (You can use the slider or the up and down arrows to its left to adjust the hue in the color area.) The second bar shows a spectrum of some of the possible colors. (When you first run *xtici*, this second bar shows the colormap of the current screen—thus, the colors will be those the clients are using.) The fourth vertical bar shows a magnification of part of the second bar—specifically, the shade that also appears in the color area and the shades that surround it in the colormap. (The third bar simply contains lines indicating what part of the second bar is being magnified in the fourth.)

If you want to work from the hue in the color area (adjust its value and chroma), skip ahead to the section "Adjusting the Color with the Hue Leaf."

If you want to change the initial hue, there are several ways to do it:

• Click the first pointer button on the color you want from either the second or fourth vertical bars in the Colormap Scale area.

- Click the first pointer button on either the up or down arrow (the slider in the first vertical bar echoes this motion). This action causes the color area to display the next shade above or below the current shade in the colormap. (If you press and hold down the pointer button, the motion is continuous—you can browse several adjacent shades in the colormap this way.)

- Instead of using the arrow keys, use the slider in the first vertical bar to browse adjacent shades. The slider operates in the same way the *xterm* scrollbar's "thumb" does. (If you're not familiar with the scrollbar's operation, see Chapter 5.)

- Use the Hue Bar. See the next section for instructions.

- Enter alternate numeric values in the three small text windows to the right of the color area. (These Text widgets operate as described under "The xedit Text Editor" earlier in this chapter.) To enter meaningful values that approximate what you want, you may need to understand the science of color a bit more. Chapter 12 should be helpful in this regard. The section "Working with the Numeric Color Values" (later in this chapter) also provides some insights.

The first method is the simplest, but it is also the least precise. It's particularly difficult to click on the hue you want in the second vertical bar, which represents the adjacent hues using very narrow bands of color. It's much easier to click on the shade you want in the fourth vertical bar (with the liability that the spectrum is more limited).

In our example, the current color (sky blue) is represented by the second shade from the bottom on the fourth vertical bar. The lines in the third bar—as well as the number 2 in the color area—indicate this fact. (Though it appears that the current color is the third block from the bottom of the fourth vertical bar, the first block is actually blank—not a part of the colormap.) Let's select another color for the color area by clicking the first pointer button seven shades higher on the fourth vertical bar (a darker blue). Figure 8-22 shows the resulting *xtici* window.

Notice that the number in the color area has been changed to 9, to indicate the ninth shade in the colormap. The slider in the first vertical bar has also moved. The numbers for hue, value, and chroma reflect the new shade. The other major change in the *xtici* window is the appearance of the Hue Leaf, the meaning and use of which we'll discuss later on.

Changing the Hue with the Hue Bar

The Hue Bar allows you to view the hues the Colormap Scale offers in a wider spectrum of lightness and intensity—and to choose one of these shades to edit. The Hue Bar area contains arrow keys, a vertical bar with a slider, and the actual Hue Bar itself. When you first run *xtici*, the Hue Bar is blank. To fill the bar:

1. Display the Options menu by clicking the first pointer button on the menu command box.

2. Click on the Fill Hue Bar item.

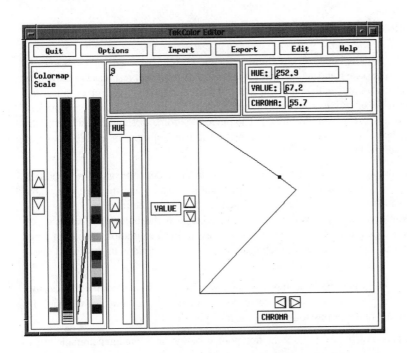

Figure 8-22. Changing the hue by clicking in the Colormap Scale area

The Hue Bar will display a range of hues. (A shorter representation of the same spectrum will also be added to the second vertical bar in the Colormap Scale area.) You can select one of the hues in the bar to edit in the color area in several ways:

- Click the first pointer button on the color you want in the Hue Bar.

- Click the first pointer button on either the up or down arrow (the slider echoes this motion). This action causes the color area to display the next shade above or below the current shade in the bar. (Press and hold down the pointer button to browse several shades.)

- Use the slider in the vertical bar to the right of the arrows to select a hue. See the instructions for using the *xterm* scrollbar's "thumb" in Chapter 5.

Note that you don't have to fill the Hue Bar in order to adjust the hue using any of these methods. (You can even click on the blank Hue Bar, though this "blind" method is not particularly desirable.) The color area and the numeric values will be updated to match the shade you choose regardless.

If you select a hue by any of the mechanisms in the Hue Bar, you can then adjust the color using the Hue Leaf or by the less intuitive method of changing the numeric values.

If you fill the Hue Bar and then try to select a hue from the Colormap Area, there may occasionally be minor problems allocating color cells for the *xtici* application. In such cases, a dialog box will request your input. See "Problems Allocating Color Cells" for more information.

Other Clients

Adjusting the Color with the Hue Leaf

The Hue Leaf represents a range of possibilities for the current hue. The hue can vary in value (lightness to darkness) and in chroma (the amount of the hue present; also known as saturation or intensity)—and within the Hue Leaf, it varies dramatically. For instance, the lightest possible shade of *any hue* is white; the darkest is black. (That is, the spectrum of possible values always spans white to black.) The range of chroma or saturation is more reliant on the actual hue. For example, in most cases, a red hue can exist in a wider range of intensities than a yellow hue.

The Hue Leaf is always triangular, but the shape of the triangle depends on the possibilities of varying the hue. The triangular Hue Leaf is turned on its side, so that the base is actually vertical—flush against the left side of the box containing the leaf. The range of value is represented along this vertical edge (white is at the top; black at the bottom). The range of chroma (saturation) is represented horizontally, with least to most saturation appearing from left to right. The Hue Leaf is intended to represent all possible variations of the hue in question.

When you first run *xtici*, the Hue Leaf appears blank and contains a small square dot cursor. This cursor marks the place in the leaf that corresponds to the current version of the hue. To get a better idea of the range of possibilities for the hue, you can fill the leaf:

1. Display the Options menu by clicking the first pointer button on the menu command box.

2. Click on the Fill Leaf item.

The Hue Leaf will display the range of possibilities for the current hue. Variations between shades create a sort of striped or checkerboard pattern.

The Hue Leaf allows you to fine tune the hue in question. Notice the arrow keys beside the Value and Chroma labels bordering the leaf. You can adjust the value and chroma by clicking on these arrows. For example, you would click on the up arrow next to Value to make the hue lighter (white is at the top of the value range). The dot cursor will move up within the leaf and the color area and numeric values will be updated to reflect the changes.

Click on the right arrow next to Chroma to get a more intense hue. The dot cursor will move to the right within the leaf and the color area and numeric values will be updated to reflect the changes.

As an alternative to using the arrow keys, you can use the pointer to move the square dot within the leaf. Either click on the shade you want within the leaf or hold down the pointer on the dot and drag it within the leaf.

As is the case with the Hue Bar, you don't have to fill the Hue Leaf to adjust the color using any of these methods. The color area and the numeric values will be updated regardless.

If you fill the Hue Leaf and then try to select a hue from the Colormap Area, *xtici* may have trouble allocating color cells and a dialog box with be displayed. See "Problems Allocating Color Cells" for more information.

Selecting and Pasting the Numeric Color Value

Once you have the color you want in the color area, you can select the numeric description of that color to paste on the command line, in a resource file, in a color database file, etc. To make the color value the PRIMARY text selection:

1. Display the Edit menu by clicking the first pointer button on the menu command box.

2. Click on the Copy Color –> item. A submenu is displayed.

3. Click on the format (color space) you want. The TekHVC and CIE u'v'Y items select portable color values; the RGB item selects the non-portable RGB color format.

TekHVC is a good choice. You can then paste the color value by clicking the second pointer button. For example, you might enter:

```
% xbiff -fg
```

and then click the second button to specify the color (and run the process in the background):

```
% xbiff -fg TekHVC:223.93036/72.45283/29.67013 &
```

On our display, this color value produces a deeper version of the sky blue from our original example. If you intend to use a color multiple times, it's a good idea to pair the numeric value with a name in an Xcms database.

Note that *xtici* handles RGB values in an unusual way. The window displays RGB values in decimal notation; however, if you select RGB from the Edit menu, the output is in hexadecimal notation! This can be a bit confusing, particularly if you want to place RGB values in an RGB or Xcms database. An RGB database requires decimal values; an Xcms database recognizes RGB values (among others), but they must be in hexadecimal notation. If you have the decimal numbers to input to *xtici*, the editor can in effect perform the conversion to hex; or you can use the UNIX *bc*(1) utility to convert numbers from one notation to another. See Chapter 12 for instructions on using *bc* and on creating color databases.

Working with the Numeric Color Values

We've seen several ways to edit color specifications using *xtici*'s graphic elements: bars, sliders, arrow buttons, etc. When you change a color using one of these methods, the numeric values corresponding to the color are updated dynamically. However, you can also interact with *xtici* by entering numeric values yourself.

Thus far we've only seen the default Hue, Value, and Chroma number displays. (These provide a number in the portable TekHVC color space.) But remember that *xtici* can interpret and output two additional color spaces: the portable CIE u'v'Y format and the non-portable RGB format. You can display the specification for the current color in any of these formats by using the Options menu.

1. Display the menu by clicking the first pointer button on the Options command button.

2. Click on the Coordinates –> item. A submenu is displayed revealing two options: RGB and CIE u'v'Y.

3. These menu items are toggles between the color space named and the default TekHVC color space. Thus, selecting RGB once toggles the decimal values for RED, GREEN, and BLUE. Selecting RGB a second time recalls the TekHVC values. Click on the format (color space) you want.

Let's consider a couple of ways you might work with *xtici* using numbers. Keep in mind that all of the numeric values are contained in small text windows. Use the editing commands described under "The xedit Text Editor" (earlier in this chapter) to change the values.

Suppose you want to edit a color from the standard RGB database. To place that color in the *xtici* color area:

1. Check the RGB decimal values in *rgb.txt*. (See Chapter 12.)

2. Using the Coordinates submenu of the Options menu, toggle the RGB numeric values.

3. Place the values from *rgb.txt* in the RED, GREEN, and BLUE text windows to the right of the color area.

As soon as you move the pointer out of the text window area, a dialog box will prompt:

```
Apply last keyboard input?
```

If you've entered the correct figures, select OK and the color area will be updated; otherwise, Cancel and continue editing.

As another example, say you've created a color using another editor, such as *xcoloredit*, that outputs values in the non-portable RGB format. If you enter the decimal versions of these values in the *xtici* window (as described in the previous example), *xtici* provides the portable color space equivalents.

Problems Allocating Color Cells

Because of the nature of colormaps and the way color cells are allocated, certain problems may arise in working with *xtici*. One is a simple, albeit confusing "technicolor" effect. Depending on where the input focus is, applications may appear to swap colors and the shade in the *xtici* color area may not appear accurate. You're liable to get a more precise picture when the *xtici* window has the input focus, however.

Another potential problem: you may not be able to select a color in one area of the *xtici* window if it is being used in another area. If such a conflict arises, a dialog box will inform you. For example, say you select a color in the Colormap Area that is also being used in the Hue Bar, you may get a dialog to the effect that:

```
This color cell is used to fill the Hue Bar.
Hues will be removed to edit this cell.
```

The box provides the possible responses OK and Cancel. The safest course of action is to click on Cancel and then try to select the hue by another method. Clicking on the shade you want in the Hue Bar should work; or you might turn the Hue Bar off (the menu item is a toggle) and try to select the color by dragging the Hue Bar slider; or you could enter the appropriate numeric values, etc.

If you click on OK, the Hue Bar (and possibly the leaf and part of the Colormap Scale area) will be blanked out and the colors *xtici* is displaying will be changed. In such a case, try clicking on any visible color in the Colormap Scale area to begin editing again.

A similar conflict can arise if you select a hue in the Colormap Scale area that is also being used in the Hue Leaf:

```
This color cell is used to fill the leaf.
Fill will be removed to edit this cell.
```

Again, it's a good idea to click on Cancel and then try to select the hue by another method. Clicking on the shade you want on the Hue Bar or Leaf should work; or you might turn either or both the bar and leaf off (the menu items are toggles) and try to select the color by another method.

Selecting OK will blank out the leaf (and possibly the bar and part of the Colormap Scale area) and change the colors the *xtici* window is displaying. Again, try clicking on any visible color in the Colormap Scale area.

Various other colormap conflicts can arise. Use the dialog boxes—and your own experience—for guidance.

Quitting xtici

To quit the application, click the first pointer button on the Quit command button—the leftmost one on the menu bar.

Part Two:

Customizing X

X has been designed to put the user in the driver's seat. Everything from the colors and sizes of windows to the contents of mwm *menus can be customized by the user. This part of the book tells you how to reshape X to your liking.*

Command-line Options
Setting Resources
Specifying Color
Customizing mwm
Setup Clients

9

Working with Motif Applications

This chapter examines some of the features common to applications written with the Motif Toolkit.

In This Chapter:

Working with Motif Applications

The Athena widget set provides X Toolkit applications with certain common features, many of which have been described in Chapter 8. An application coded using the Motif widget set has a slightly different look and feel.

In the remainder of this chapter, we'll look at some of the features you're liable to encounter in a Motif application and learn how to use them. Some of these features are provided in a slightly different flavor by the Athena widget set; others are unique to Motif.

Many of the sample components we're using are taken from the Motif *periodic* demo program, which is a "periodic table" of the Motif widgets. You can play with *periodic* to begin learning to use many common features of Motif applications. However, since the program simply demonstrates the various widgets without actually performing any practical action, you'll probably need to use some real applications as well. If you've been running *mwm*, you already know how to use several Motif features.

The following sections mention the comparable Athena widgets where appropriate. Some of the Athena widgets are illustrated using the standard MIT clients in Chapters 5, 7, and 8.

Before examining the various Motif features, however, let's consider some basics of using the pointer with a Motif application.

Pointer Button Usage

When you're working with an application coded using the Motif toolkit, you can generally rely on the pointer buttons to work as follows:

Button one: Referred to in program internals as "BSelect" (for "Button Select"), the first button enables you to "select" or activate graphical components. For example, you would use the first button to direct focus, to select text, to respond to a dialog box, etc.

Button two: Referred to as "BTransfer" (for "Button Transfer"), the second button is used to "drag" text, graphic images, etc., from one widget and "drop" them into another widget. As we'll see later, this "drag and drop" capability is one of the major improvements of Motif 1.2.

Button three: Referred to as "BMenu" (for "Button Menu"), the third button is used to post pop-up menus. For example, you post the *mwm* Root Menu by pressing and holding the third pointer button on the root window.

Now that you understand the basics of pointer actions, let's consider the various application components you're liable to encounter.

The Periodic Table of Motif Widgets

The *periodic* demo program (pictured in Figure 9-1) provides a compact and comprehensive survey of the Motif 1.2 widget set.

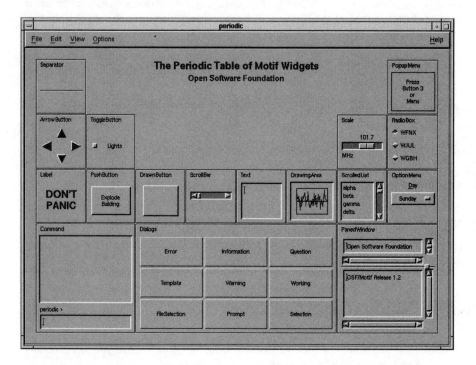

Figure 9-1. The periodic table of Motif widgets

Widgets are the building blocks of applications coded using Xt-based toolkits, such as the Motif toolkit. From a user's perspective, this definition of "widget" is not particularly significant. What is significant is that widgets create graphical elements like scrollbars, text windows, and push buttons, which you use to work with an application.

Keep in mind that some widgets don't help you do anything. For instance, the Separator widget (in the upper-left corner of the periodic table) is simply a divider line, often used below menu titles. Other widgets represented in the table are *composites*: several simpler widgets combined for a particular purpose. For example, the FileSelectionBox widget contains two text input fields, two scrollable lists (each also a composite!), and four or more push buttons, the sum total of which help you select a file from a directory hierarchy. The file selection box is a particularly complicated example. However, in most cases, when you know how to use the various components, you can deal with them in any combination.

We mention the names of the various widgets discussed in this chapter, but unless you're interested in programming, this sort of classification is probably superfluous. (If you want to set resources at the widget level, the names will be more relevant. See Appendix G, *Widget Resources*, for more information.) When you're running an application, it doesn't matter what a feature is called—only how it's used. Now let's learn how to use some of the most important Motif features. After reading this chapter and playing with a client or two, these skills will become intuitive.

Menus

Motif applications may feature three types of menus, the first two of which you have already encountered:

- Pull-down menus, such as *mwm*'s Window Menu.

- Pop-up menus, such as *mwm*'s Root Menu.

- Option menus.

The following sections describe these three types of menus. Keep in mind that each of these menus can also be what is known as a "tear-off" menu: that is, you can choose to post the menu and "tear off" an image of it that remains posted (in its own window) until you remove it. We'll take a closer look at tear-off menus after considering the three basic menu types.

Pull-down Menus

You display a pull-down menu from a graphical element on an application window. The *mwm* Window Menu is a pull-down, which is displayed from a button in the upper-left corner of the frame. More often, though, a pull-down is displayed from a horizontal bar known as a *menu bar*. Figure 9-2 illustrates the menu bar on the *periodic* window.

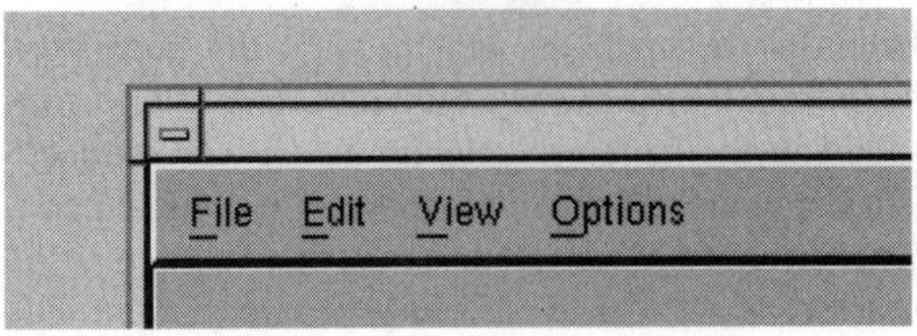

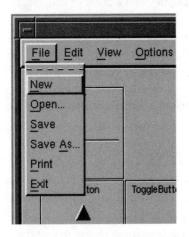

Figure 9-2. Periodic menu bar

Each word on the bar is a menu title; you display the menu by placing the pointer on its title and clicking the first pointer button. The title becomes raised and highlighted by a box, the menu is displayed and the first selectable item is also raised and boxed. Figure 9-3 shows *periodic*'s File pull-down menu.

Figure 9-3. Periodic File menu

Notice that one letter of each menu item is underlined. As explained in Chapter 4, that letter represents a unique abbreviation, or mnemonic, for the menu item, which can be used to select the item.

Some menus (such as *mwm*'s **Window Menu**) may also provide a keyboard shortcut, or *accelerator*, for each item. These shortcuts generally appear in a right-hand column, opposite the item labels. An accelerator can be used to invoke the action without displaying the menu at all (though they also work while the menu is displayed).

When you've displayed a menu by placing the pointer on the title and clicking the first button, you can select an item by:

• Placing the pointer on the item and clicking the first button.

• Typing the mnemonic abbreviation for the menu item.

- Typing the accelerator key combination, if available. (Though these are intended to save you the trouble of displaying the menu, they also work when it is displayed.)

- To select the boxed item (the first available for selection), you can alternatively press either the Return key or the space bar.

You can also display a menu from a menu bar by placing the pointer on the title and pressing the first pointer button. The menu is displayed as long as you continue to hold the pointer button down. To select an item, drag the pointer down the menu (each item is highlighted by a box in turn), and release the button on the item you want.

Notice the apparant "perforation" below the File menu title. This dotted line indicates that the menu has "tear-off" functionality—that is, you can keep the menu displayed in its own window and access it whenever you like. We'll discuss tear-off menus a bit later.

Pop-up Menus

The *mwm* Root Menu is a typical pop-up menu. Depending on the application, you pop up a menu by placing the pointer in a particular context (that is, on a particular graphical element) and either:

- Pressing and holding the third pointer button. (This is how *mwm*'s Root Menu is displayed.)

- Clicking the third pointer button.

When you display a menu by the former method, you make a selection by dragging the pointer down the menu and releasing the button on the item you want.

When you display a menu by the latter method, you select an item by clicking on it with either the first or third pointer button. You can pop the menu down by clicking either of these buttons off the menu.

Keep in mind that pop-up menus generally provide shortcuts for functions that can be performed in other ways. Since there are no labels to indicate that a pop-up menu exists, you'll have to rely on the individual program documentation.

Option Menus

You display an option menu from a button that shows the last item chosen—rather than from the menu title. You can display an option menu by either:

- Clicking the first pointer button on the option menu button.

- Pressing and holding the first pointer button down on the option menu button.

The *periodic* demo provides a dummy "Days of the Week" option menu. Figure 9-4 shows the option menu button and the menu itself. (You can always tell an option menu button by the small rectangle that decorates it.)

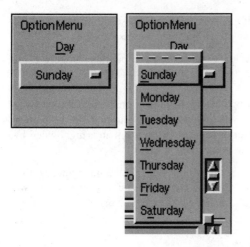

Figure 9-4. Sample option button and option menu

If you display an option menu by the former method, you can select an item by clicking on it with the first pointer button. If you display the menu using the latter method, drag the pointer down the menu and release on the item you want or type the mnemonic abbreviation (the underlined letter).

When you select an item, the menu disappears and the option menu button then displays your selection. To remove an option menu without making a selection, click elsewhere or release the pointer off of the menu, as appropriate.

Tear-off Menus

Pull-down, pop-up, and option menus may also be "tear-off" menus, which you can post in subwindows that remain on the display until you remove them. This feature is very handy if you use a menu frequently. If a menu is not torn off, it disappears after you select an item.

If a menu can be torn off, it will have a "perforated" line as the first item on the menu. Regardless of the menu type, you tear off a menu by clicking or releasing the pointer on this dotted line. For example, to tear off a pull-down menu, you could:

1. Post the menu by clicking the first pointer button. In Figure 9-5, we've again posted *periodic*'s File menu. The perforation below the title indicates that the menu can be torn off.

2. To tear the menu off, click the first pointer button on the perforation. Figure 9-6 shows the torn off File menu.

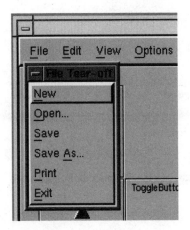

Figure 9-5. Perforation means you can tear off menu

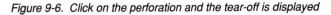

Figure 9-6. Click on the perforation and the tear-off is displayed

To tear off a pop-up menu:

1. Display the pop-up menu. In many cases, you do this by pressing and holding down the third pointer button.

2. Drag the pointer down the menu, highlighting the perforated line.

3. Release the pointer button. The menu is torn off.

Once you tear off a menu, you can work with it much as you would with any application window, with a few limitations. These limitations are borne out by the File tear-off menu's modified *mwm* frame. It has no Minimize or Maximize buttons and no resize handles. The frame does offer a Window Menu button. However, if you display the Window Menu from the

Motif Applications

tear-off window, you'll see that it offers only three items: Move, Lower, and Close. Basically, you can move the tear-off window, lower it in the stack, and remove it—and that's all. In Figure 9-7, we've moved the menu out of the way of the *periodic* application window.

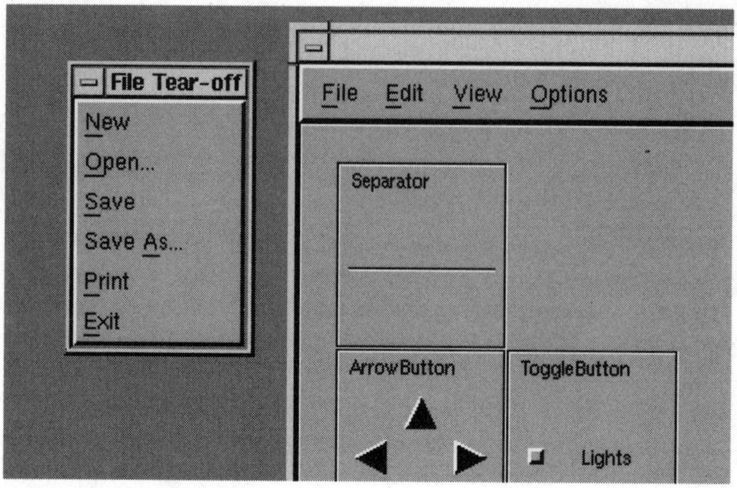

Figure 9-7. Moving a tear-off to a convenient place

There are several ways to remove a tear-off menu. First, direct the input focus to the menu and then perform any one of the following actions:

- Press the key that performs the Cancel function (often Escape).

- Double-click the first pointer button on the menu's own Window Menu button.

- Display the menu's Window Menu and select the Close or type its mnemonic abbreviation, c.

- Use the keyboard accelerator for the Close item, Alt-F4.

Push Buttons

Many Motif applications feature *push buttons* (PushButton widgets). Commonly, a push button has a text label corresponding to some function. You invoke the function by clicking the first pointer button on the push button widget. Figure 9-8 shows the sample push button from the *periodic* demo.

Figure 9-8. Click on a push button to invoke the function

In a real application, clicking on the push button causes some action to occur. Unless James Bond has been working on the *periodic* demo, we can safely assume this button is a dummy! However, you *can* click on it to get an idea what a push button looks like when pressed.

A dialog box always contains one or more push buttons that allow you to respond to the message in the box, but push buttons are also used in other applications. Regardless of the application, in many cases one push button will be highlighted, generally by outlining. If click-to-type focus is in effect, you can push the highlighted push button simply by pressing the Return key on your keyboard. To push another button, you must place the pointer on it and click the first pointer button. (With pointer focus, you need to click on any choice.)

Note that if you press the first pointer button on a push button and then change your mind about invoking the function, there is an escape hatch. Simply move the pointer off the push button before you release the pointer button. (The action of releasing the pointer is actually what invokes the push button.)

An Athena widget set provides a command button with virtually the same functionality as a Motif push button. The most obvious difference is that you must click on an Athena command button to invoke it. The Return key shortcut only works with a Motif push button (click-to-type focus must also be in effect). See "Dialog Boxes and Command Buttons" in Chapter 7, *Graphics Utilities*.

We'll come back to Motif push buttons later, in the discussion of dialog boxes. But before moving on, let's take a quick look at another type of button, called a *drawn button* (Drawn-Button widget). From a user's perspective, a drawn button is a push button decorated with a pixmap rather than a text label. You invoke a drawn button just as you do a push button—by clicking the first pointer button on it.* Figure 9-9 shows a drawn button from the *periodic* window. (Note that you can toggle the image on this button on and off using the sample ToggleButton widget in the *periodic* window, which is illustrated in the next section.)

---

*Push buttons and drawn buttons actually differ from a programming perspective, but a user can expect to interact with them in the same way.

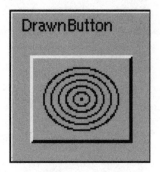

Figure 9-9. A drawn button

The drawn button from the *periodic* demo is simply illustrative—it does nothing. Generally, however, the image on a drawn button will signal its function. If an application uses drawn buttons effectively, they can transcend language barriers, as well as enhance the program's aesthetics. For example, a button decorated with the image of a paint brush might invoke graphics capabilities, a button decorated with the image of a keyboard might open a text editor, etc.

Note that some applications may dynamically change the image on a drawn button to signal some change in the state of the program.

Radio Boxes and Toggle Buttons

A *radio box* is made up of a column of mutually exclusive choices, each represented by a *toggle button* (ToggleButton widget). Figure 9-10 shows a radio box from the *periodic* demo program.

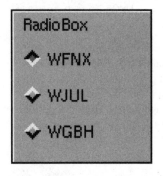

Figure 9-10. A radio box

The column is a single radio box. Several radio boxes may appear side by side in an application. Typically, a radio box contains several diamond-shaped toggle buttons. The radio box from the *periodic* demo features three buttons, in this case corresponding to—what else—three radio stations. You push a toggle button by placing the pointer on the diamond symbol (or the corresponding text label) and clicking the first pointer button. The toggle button becomes darker (appearing as if it's been pressed). Actually, if you examine the button closely, the highlighting has just switched from the bottom edge to the top edge of the button. In our example, the button next to WFNX is currently selected.

When you first make a selection, the button and the accompanying text label are highlighted by a box. When you make another selection in the same or another column (radio box), the highlighting box appears around that item (and disappears from the previous one).

Toggles in the same radio box are mutually exclusive. If you select one and then select another from the same column, the first one is toggled off. (The button appears to pop up—i.e., the highlighting switches back to the bottom edge of the button; also the highlighting box appears around the latest selection.)

In addition to appearing in radio boxes, toggle buttons may also appear in columns known as *check boxes*. In a check box, toggle buttons *are not* mutually exclusive. You can "check" multiple items in the same column by toggling the corresponding buttons (or labels). The toggle buttons in a check box appear square-shaped to distinguish a check box from a radio box (in which the toggles appear diamond-shaped).

Figure 9-11 shows one such toggle button, the sample from *periodic*, as it appears both off and on. Notice that toggling the button on switches the highlighting from the lower-right corner (it appears to be raised) to the upper-left corner (it appears to have been pushed).

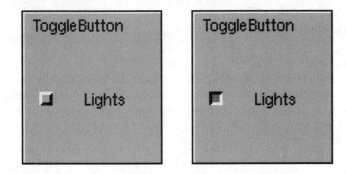

Figure 9-11. Lights off, lights on

Note also that toggle buttons are sometimes labeled with graphic images rather than text. One image represents "on" and another represents "off."

The Motif Scrollbar

Each of the list boxes in the file selection box features both a horizontal and a vertical scrollbar. A vertical scrollbar is commonly used to review text that has scrolled off the top of a window or extends past the bottom. In the case of the Files box in *periodic*'s file selection dialog, the vertical scrollbar is used to scan a list of files too long to fit in the window at one time. A horizontal scrollbar is commonly used to view text or graphics that are too wide to fit in the viewing area. You'll probably encounter vertical scrollbars most often.

Both the Motif and Athena widget sets provide scrollbar widgets. A Motif scrollbar differs in both appearance and operation from an Athena scrollbar, such as the one used by *xterm*. As you know, an Athena scrollbar is simple in design—just a rectangular thumb within a rectangular scroll region. Both parts are flat; the thumb is distinguished from the scroll region only by its (generally) darker color. While a Motif scrollbar has separate parts to invoke different types of scrolling, the Athena scrollbar moves text according to which pointer button you use and how you use it. (See Chapter 5, *The xterm Terminal Emulator*, for instructions on how to use *xterm*'s scrollbar.)

Take another look at the Files box from *periodic*'s file selection box, which is bordered by two scrollbars. A Motif scrollbar is comprised of four parts: two *arrows* (one at either end of the bar), the *scroll region* between the arrows, and the *slider* (analogous to the Athena scrollbar's "thumb"), the raised area that moves within the scroll region. The slider displays the position and amount of text currently showing in the window relative to the amount saved. If text does not extend beyond the window, the slider fills the entire scroll region. In Figure 9-17, the sliders in both scrollbars indicate that text extends beyond the bounds of the window.

Let's consider the pointer commands used to operate a vertical scrollbar. (You'll probably use a vertical scrollbar most often.) To scroll the text forward one window, place the pointer below the slider and click the first button. To scroll the text back one window, place the pointer above the slider and click the first button. In text-based applications, clicking on one of the arrows scrolls the text one line at a time: each click on a down arrow lets you view one more line of text at the bottom of the window; each click on an up arrow lets you view one more line of text at the top of the window.

A horizontal scrollbar lets you view the remaining part of lines that are too wide to fit in a single window. You use the same pointer commands to use a horizontal scrollbar as you do a vertical scrollbar; obviously the orientation of text and directions of movement are different. Clicking to the right of the slider scrolls the text horizontally to the right. Clicking to the left of the slider scrolls the text horizontally to the left. In Figure 9-17, the Files box is displaying filenames only—the earlier parts of the pathnames are not in view. Notice that the horizontal scrollbar's slider is all the way to the right of the scroll region. If you place the pointer to the left of the slider and click the first button, the text is scrolled to the left to reveal the earlier parts of the pathname. In text-based applications, clicking on either arrow of the horizontal scrollbar moves the text one character to the left or right, depending on the direction of the arrow.

Regardless of the orientation of the scrollbar, you can drag the slider by placing the pointer on it and holding down the second pointer button. The text in the window follows the motion of the slider. Release the pointer button when the window displays the text you want.

A final note: the unit scrolled when you click on an arrow varies by application. For instance, scrollbars are sometimes featured on application windows that contain graphic elements rather than text. Obviously, such a window cannot be scrolled by text characters or lines. For example, clicking the pointer on a scrollbar arrow in the *mwm* icon box (described in Chapter 13), scrolls the box the height or width of one icon.

Text Windows

We've already seen several instances of the Athena Text widget, which allows you to enter text in standard X clients like *xedit*, *xman*, *bitmap*, etc. Many Motif applications also provide areas in which you can enter text. A text window may be as small as a single line (many dialog boxes provide one-line text windows) or it may accommodate a file of any length. Regardless of the size of a Motif text window, there are various commands you can use to enter text. This section explains some of the more useful commands.

As you may recall, in most standard X applications, the text cursor is a caret. In Motif text windows, the text cursor is the I-beam symbol. (We've encountered the I-beam cursor before, in a different context: the root window pointer becomes an I-beam when it rests in an *xterm* window.)

Figure 9-12 shows the sample text window from the *periodic* demo. (This is a simple window; in many cases, text windows will also have scrollbars.)

Figure 9-12. Sample text window

The I-beam cursor in the text window marks the point at which text can be inserted. When the window has the input focus, you can begin to enter text simply by typing. Backspace over characters to erase them. To erase multiple characters at once, do the following steps:

1. Select the text by holding the first pointer button and dragging (as you would in any *xterm* window). If the text you want to highlight extends beyond the bounds of the text window, move the pointer outside the window; the window will scroll and additional text will be highlighted. Once you've selected the text you want, release the pointer button.

2. Press the Delete key to erase the selected text.

You can move the I-beam cursor to another insertion point in the text by moving the root window pointer (often represented by an arrow) and clicking the first pointer button. You can also move the cursor within the text using various keyboard commands, summarized in Table 9-1.

Table 9-1. Keyboard Commands to Move the Text Cursor

Keystrokes	Cursor movement
Left arrow	Back one character
Right arrow	Forward one character
Up arrow	Back one line
Down arrow	Forward one line
Control-Left arrow	Back one word
Control-Right arrow	Forward one word
Control-Up arrow	Back one paragraph
Control-Down arrow	Forward one paragraph
PageUp	Back one window
PageDown	Forward one window

The location of the PageUp and PageDown keys may vary per site. In some cases, these keys may be clearly marked. If not, these functions may or may not be assigned to keys and you'll have to perform a little detective work if you want to use them. First, find out if your system administrator has copied a file called *.motifbind* to your home directory. This file maps functions commonly used in Motif applications to convenient keys on your keyboard. If you have a *.motifbind* file, you can use it (along with the *xev* client, described in Chapter 14) to determine the location of keys like PageUp and PageDown. Note, however, that in most cases, you can either fall back on the less powerful Control key combinations—or use scrollbars, if they are provided.

You can copy (or cut) and paste text within a Motif text window or between windows using a few different methods. We'll describe two of them here. See the section "Drag and Drop" for instructions on transferring text using a more graphic interface.

The first method is virtually the same as one of the *xterm* copy and paste methods. We've already explained the selection method under number 1 in the instructions to delete a passage.

1. Select text by pressing and holding down the first pointer button, dragging, and releasing.

2. Move the pointer to the place at which you want to insert the selected text.

3. Click the second pointer button to insert a copy of the text. Press Shift and click the second button to move the text to this position (i.e., the text is cut from the initial selection and copied to this place).

If you've copied the text, so long as it remains highlighted in the first position, it will be pasted when you click the second pointer button. To remove the highlighting, move the pointer outside the highlighted area (but keep it within the same text window) and click the first button again. This action will also move the text cursor. If you want to move the cursor without removing the highlighting, press Control and click the first button in the position you want.

A second copy (or cut) and paste method works in the opposite manner. First you select the destination, then the text to be placed there.

1. Move the pointer to the place you want the text to be inserted and click the first button. (The I-beam moves there.)

2. Select the text you want to copy by pressing the Alt (or Meta) key, holding down the second pointer button, and dragging. Text selected in this manner is underlined rather than highlighted in reverse video. (If you begin by pressing and holding the Shift key in addition, the text will be cut rather than copied.)

3. Release the second pointer button and the selected text appears at the insertion point.

Motif provides many ways to perform most functions. See "Drag and Drop" for a discussion of still another text transfer method.

Dialog Boxes

If you've tried to restart *mwm* from the window manager's Root Menu, you've already encountered a Motif dialog box. When you select the Restart menu item, the dialog box pictured in Figure 9-13 is displayed.

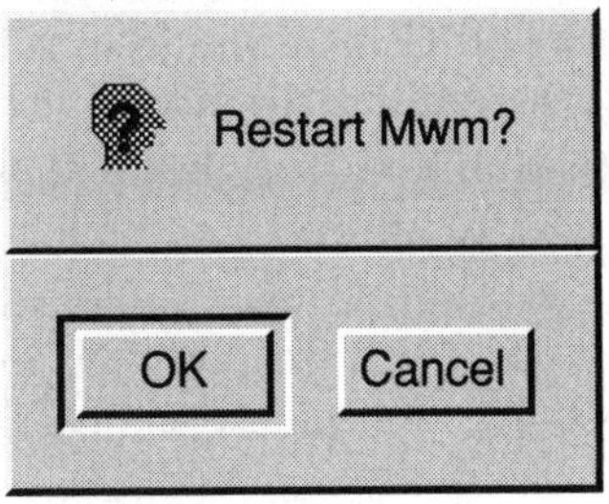

Figure 9-13. Typical Motif dialog box with two push buttons

This sample is a "message" dialog: it displays a message relevant to the application and requires a response from the user. In this case, the dialog box queries whether you really want to `Restart mwm?`.

The *periodic* demo program provides nine sample dialog boxes, which you can display by clicking on one of the buttons in Figure 9-14.

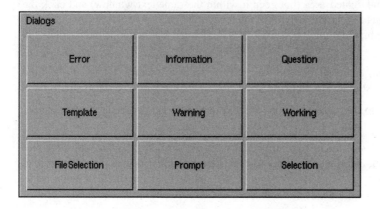

Figure 9-14. Nine push buttons to display periodic's sample dialogs

The first six dialog boxes listed (if you're reading left to right) are all message dialogs, each with a slightly different purpose. The dialog in Figure 9-13 fits into the category of "Question" dialogs. The appropriate response to any message dialog should be obvious. We don't have to consider all six samples here, but browse through them if you like. To display any of the sample dialogs, simply click the first pointer button on the box corresponding to its name.

Regardless of the purpose of a Motif dialog box, it always contains one or more push buttons that allow you to respond to the message. When a dialog is displayed and the default click-to-type focus is in effect, the input focus is usually switched to the dialog window. Until you respond to the dialog box, the application cannot continue. Once you respond to the dialog, the focus should switch back to the main application window.

Whether the dialog box contains one push button or multiple buttons, one button is always highlighted, generally by outlining. If click-to-type focus is in effect, you can activate the highlighted push button simply by pressing the Return key on your keyboard. To push another button, you must place the pointer on it and click the first pointer button. (With pointer focus, you need to click on any choice.)

A response might be a simple acknowledgment that you've seen the message: some dialogs feature only one button that reads OK. For instance, say you invoke a text editor on a particular file and that file does not exist. The program may display a dialog with a message similar to the following:

```
Couldn't open /home/val/vacation.
```

with an OK button. When a dialog has only one button, the button is always highlighted. Pressing Return or clicking the first pointer button on the OK button informs the client that you've seen the message and removes the dialog window.

Some responses request an action, such as proceeding with a previously invoked process, cancelling the process, or even exiting the program. The dialog box in Figure 9-13 contains two push buttons labeled OK and Cancel. Pushing the OK button tells *mwm* to proceed with the restart process. The Cancel button gives you a chance to avert the restart process in case you invoked the command by mistake or have changed your mind. Since Cancel is highlighted, you can push it either by pressing Return or by using the pointer.

Whatever the message or potential responses, you react to a dialog box either by pressing Return (to push the highlighted push button) or by placing the pointer on one of the push buttons and clicking the first pointer button. Action will be taken if requested and the dialog box will be removed.

The Athena widget set provides comparable widgets to the Motif dialog box and push button. An Athena dialog box provides virtually the same functionality as a Motif dialog. The most obvious difference is that, in an Athena dialog, you must click on a command button to invoke it. The Return key shortcut only works with a Motif push button (click-to-type focus must also be in effect). See "Dialog Boxes and Command Buttons" in Chapter 7, *Graphics Utilities*, for more information about Athena dialogs.

In the next few sections, we'll consider some more specialized Motif dialog boxes.

Prompt Dialog

Typically, a prompt dialog box asks the user to supply some small item of information, such as a filename. Figure 9-15 shows the sample prompt dialog provided by *periodic*.

Figure 9-15. A prompt dialog box

In this mock prompt dialog, you enter the "name" you want in the one-line text window. To confirm your entry, you can either press Return or click on OK push button. Click on Cancel to pop down the dialog box without specifying a name.

Selection Dialog

A *selection box* (SelectionBox widget) is a composite dialog that provides a list of items from which you can make a selection. Figure 9-16 shows *periodic*'s sample selection box.

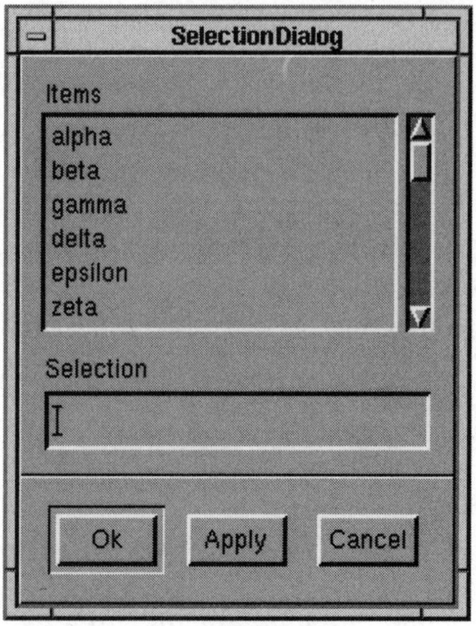

Figure 9-16. A selection dialog box

Using a selection box is fairly simple. (Things become slightly more complicated with a file selection box, described in the next section.) A selection box is generally composed of a *list box* (in this case labeled Items), a one-line text window labeled Selection, and a few push buttons.

Notice that the list box has a vertical scrollbar, which allows you to view text that is currently outside the box. A list box and its accompanying scrollbar(s) form what is known as a ScrolledWindow. (This composite widget is contained in the even more complicated SelectionBox widget!) The Motif ScrolledWindow is comparable to the Athena Viewport widget, discussed in the section "Browsing Reference Pages: xman" in Chapter 8.

You want to place the name of your selection in the one-line Selection window. To do this, you can:

1. Place the pointer on the item you want in the Items list box. (You can use the scrollbar to view additional possibilities.)

2. Click the first pointer button. The item is highlighted and appears in the Selection window.

(Of course, since the Selection window is a text window, you might instead choose to type the name yourself.) Then you can confirm your selection by pressing Return or clicking on the appropriate push button (in this case, OK); or pop down the box without making a selection by clicking on the Cancel push button.

File Selection Dialog

Several Motif applications feature a rather complicated type of dialog called a *file selection box* (FileSelectionBox widget), which allows you to browse a directory structure and select a file. A file selection box is similar to a selection box, but is a bit more complicated.

Using a file selection box is not exactly difficult, but it's not particularly obvious either. Let's consider the file selection box that is displayed when you click on *periodic*'s File-SelectionDialog button. The box appears in Figure 9-17.

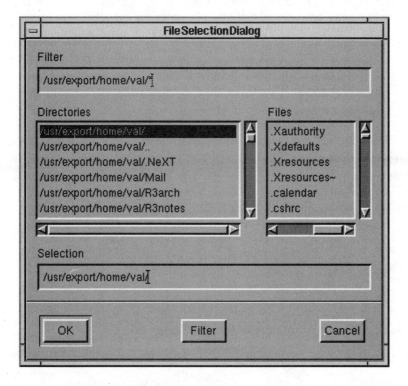

Figure 9-17. A file selection dialog box

Motif Applications

As in the selection box, the file selection features a window labeled Selection near the bottom of the box. You want to place the name of the file to select in this window. Initially this window contains an incomplete pathname—a directory is specified but no file. You can specify a file in a variety of ways.

Notice the two areas labeled Directories and Files. These are list boxes that are contained within the larger window. The Directories box lists the directories from which you can choose a file; the first directory is usually highlighted. The Files box lists the files within the highlighted directory. (In your version of *periodic*, this box may be labeled List, but this is anomolous; virtually all applications have a Files box instead.)

Notice that the list boxes are bordered by both horizontal and vertical scrollbars, which allow you to view text that is currently outside the box. These list boxes are ScrolledWindow widgets contained in the more complicated FileSelectionBox widget.

The file selection box allows you to select a file from any directory on the system, using various procedures. You can select a file from the list currently in the Files box; you can list the files in another directory currently displayed in the the Directories box and select one of those files; or you can list the contents of an entirely different directory and select a file from that directory.

Selecting a File from the Files Box

To select a file currently in the Files box:

1. Place the pointer on the filename.

2. Click the first pointer button. The filename is highlighted by a dark bar; the letters appear in reverse video.

   The Selection window will be updated to reflect the filename; and the push button to confirm the selection (OK in many applications) will be highlighted, indicating that you can select the file by pressing Return.

3. Select the filename either by pressing Return or by placing the pointer on the OK or other appropriate push button and clicking the first pointer button.

When you select a file, the file selection box disappears.

Choosing a File from Another Directory in the Directories Box

To list the files in another directory in the Directories box and select one of those files:

1. Place the pointer on the directory name and click the first button. The directory name is highlighted. Notice that the box labeled Filter is updated to reflect the new pathname and the Filter push button at the bottom of the box is highlighted for selection.

2. Then, to display the contents of the highlighted directory in the Files box either:

   • Press Return; or

   • Click on the Filter push button.

3. To select a file from the updated Files box, follow the steps outlined previously in "Selecting a File from the Files Box."

Choosing a File from Another Directory on the System

You can specify an alternative directory from which a file can be selected by changing the filter, that is, the path in the Filter window (near the top of the file selection box). Initially the Filter window reflects the current working directory. In Figure 9-17, the filter is */usr/export/home/val/** and the Directories box lists several directories:

```
/usr/export/home/val/.         \"the current directory
/usr/export/home/val/..        \"previous directory in the tree
/usr/export/home/val/.NeXT     \"subdirectories
/usr/export/home/val/Mail      \"
/usr/export/home/val/R3arch    \"
/usr/export/home/val/R3notes   \"
                .
                .
                .
```

The vertical scrollbar indicates that there are several more directories in the list (which you can browse using the Motif scrollbar commands). To specify another filter, place the pointer within the Filter window and double click the first pointer button. The window becomes highlighted with a black bar (the text is visible in reverse video); now whatever you type will replace the current text.

When you type a pathname and hit Return (or click on the Filter push button at the bottom of the file selection box), the Directories box will be updated to reflect the filter you've specified. For example, if you enter the following pathname in the Filter window:

```
/usr/export/home/paula/*
```

and hit Return or click on the Filter push button, the Directories box will be updated to reflect the directory */usr/export/home/paula*, its subdirectories, and the directory above it in the tree. The first directory in the Directories box, */usr/export/home/paula/.*, will be highlighted and the files in that directory will appear in the Files box.

You can then choose any of the files in the Files box using the steps outlined previously in "Selecting a File from the Files Box."

Command Box

A *command box* (Command widget) is a composite widget that operates something like a selection box—only in the reverse. You enter a command (presumably to be invoked) in a one-line text field at the bottom of the box; that command is then echoed in a larger text window above the command field. (The larger text window maintains a history of the commands you enter. You cannot edit this history.) Figure 9-18 illustrates *periodic*'s sample command box. Although *periodic* uses a command box in the main application window, they are often used in dialog boxes. (The Command widget could legitimately appear as a tenth sample dialog; thus, we've included it here.)

Motif Applications

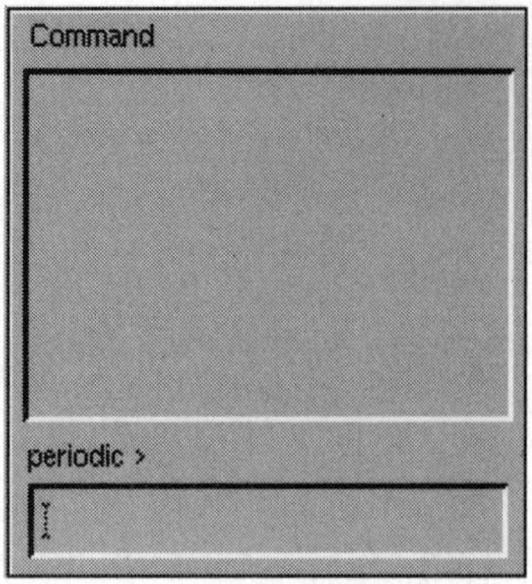

Figure 9-18. A command box

The command entry window is at the bottom of the box; it is generally introduced by a prompt, in this case:

```
periodic >
```

Direct the input focus to the small text window, type the name of a command, and press Return. The command window is cleared and the command name appears in the history window above, as in Figure 9-19. (In a functioning application, the command would also be executed.)

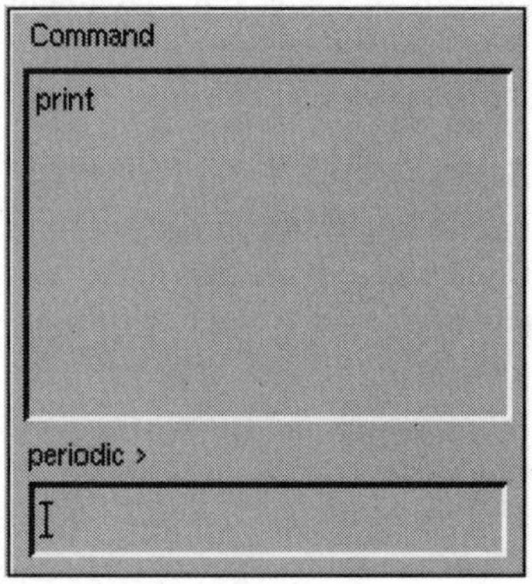

Figure 9-19. Command entered in small text window appears in history window

When you enter subsequent commands, they appear on subsequent lines in the history window. Figure 9-20 illustrates entering a second command.

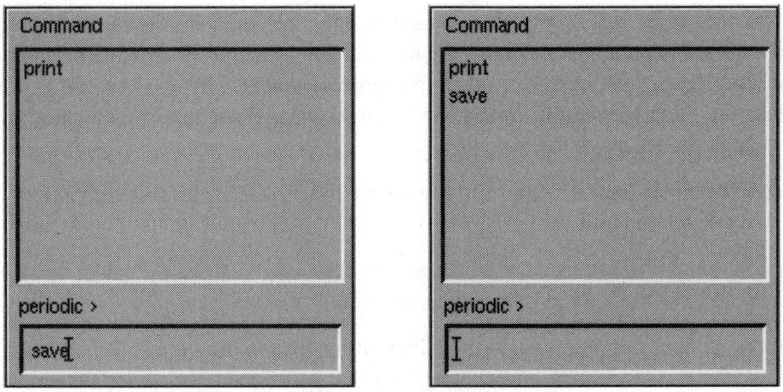

Command	Command
print	print
	save
periodic >	periodic >
save	I

Figure 9-20. Entering another command: before and after

If you click on any item in the history window, it will be highlighted and the text will appear in the smaller command window. This provides a way to repeat commands without retyping. You can then edit the command in the small command window, if you want. Remember, however, that you cannot edit text in the history window.

Scale

A *scale* (Scale widget) displays a numeric value within a range of values. A scale consists of a narrow, rectangular trough that contains a slider. The slider's position marks the current value within the range. Typically, the slider is bordered by labels that indicate the unit of measure (which remains static) and the current value (which is updated dynamically). Figure 9-21 shows the scale provided by the *periodic* demo, which represents a range of radio bandwidth in megahertz.

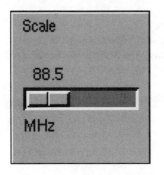

Figure 9-21. Scale widget

In the sample, the unit of measure is mHZ (megahertz); the current value is 88.5. In some implementations, the user can adjust the value by moving the slider. In other cases, the scale simply registers changes to the numeric value (presumably tracked by the program)—the user cannot modify it. The *periodic* sample allows you to change the value. You can move the slider (and change the value) in the following ways:

- Clicking the first pointer button within the trough on either side of the slider increases or decreases the value by one unit.

- Clicking the second pointer button anywhere within the trough causes the slider to move to that position and the value to be changed accordingly.

- Holding the first pointer button down on the slider allows you to drag the slider within the trough. (You release the pointer button when you've positioned the slider where you want it.)

Try dragging the slider by holding down the first pointer button. As you move the slider, notice that the value changes. In Figure 9-22 we've dragged the slider to the right and the value has increased to 100.1.

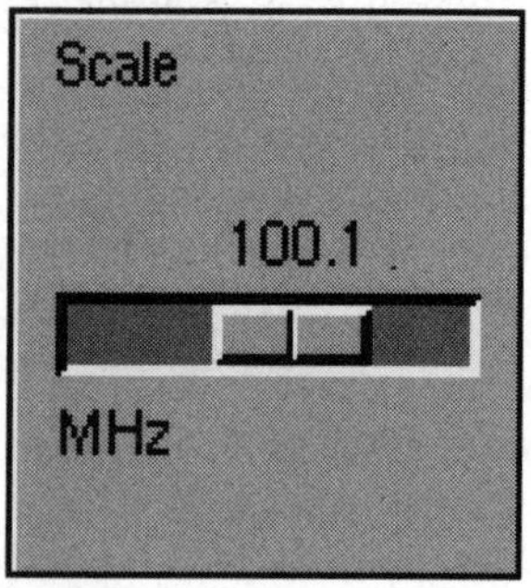

Figure 9-22. When you move the slider, the value changes

In our example, the scale is horizontal, but a scale may also be vertical. Some scales have "tick marks"—labels that indicate values within the range. In some cases, a scale will also have arrow buttons at either end (similar to the scrollbar). Clicking the first pointer button on either arrow increases or decreases the value by one unit.

Drag and Drop

Motif 1.2 provides an additional way to transfer information within an application and between applications: "drag and drop." Basically, you select an element (text, graphics, etc.) from one place, drag a copy of it (or sometimes the original) to another place, and drop it in. In many applications, drag and drop simply transfers information, but in some cases, you might drag an image and drop it to invoke an action.

When used to transfer information, drag and drop presumes that the two windows interpret data in the same format. You can't drag a graphic image and drop it in a text window, for instance. Keep in mind that drag and drop greatly depends on application-specific factors. Some elements in an application may be available for selection (and transfer), but others won't. Without considering application-specific enhancements, you can assume that the following data can be dragged:

- Text within text windows

- Labels (on push buttons, toggle buttons, etc.)

- One or more items within a list

The only default "drop site" for this data is a Motif text field.

As of the publication of this guide, commercial applications had not yet taken advantage of drag and drop functionality, so our discussion is necessarily limited. This section gives an overview and some examples from the *periodic* program. These guidelines should help when you begin using commercial applications that support drag and drop, but also consult the individual program documentation.

In our discussion of the Text widget, we considered two methods of transferring text. Drag and drop represents a third method. To drag text from one place to another:

1. Select (highlight) the text using the first pointer button (as described in the "Text Windows" section).

2. Place the pointer on the selected text and press and hold the second pointer button. An icon representing the information being dragged is displayed. (If you additionally press the Shift key, the text will be moved, rather than copied. If you press Control or no key, the text will be copied.)

3. Drag the icon to the position you want to place the text (within the same or another text window). Note that the text cursor in that window should be at the proper insertion point.

4. Release the second pointer button. (If you're holding any modifier keys, continue to hold them until the button is released.) If you've selected a valid drop site, the icon disappears and the text is inserted. If the drop site is not valid, the icon appears to spring back to its source.

The so-called "drag icon" varies depending on the application and the type of information being dragged. It may also change dynamically to indicate whether the pointer is over a valid drop site.

You can also drag items from a list and drop them in a Text widget, using virtually the same steps. If you want to drag a single item, there's no need to select it first; just follow steps two through four above. To drag multiple list items:

1. Select the items you want. (Press and hold the first pointer button and drag to select multiple items in a row.)

2. Complete the drag and drop using steps two through four from the procedure to transfer text.

Finally, you can drag a label and drop it in a Text widget. There's no need to select it first. Simply follow steps two through four from the procedure to transfer text.

To cancel a drag operation, while you continue to hold the second pointer button, press the key that invokes the Cancel function (often the Escape key). The drag icon appears to spring back to its source.

As we've said, application developers will undoubtedly implement drag and drop in additional ways. Motif 1.2 includes a program called *DNDDemo* that allows you to drag one of six colors into a rectangle. If you have a color monitor, playing with this demo might give you a better idea of the possibilities of drag and drop.

Once you run the program, you must first draw the rectangle within a white space in the application window. To do so, press and hold the first pointer button, drag, and release (much as you would draw a rectangle using the standard *bitmap* client). Initially, the rectangle is black. To color it, move the pointer into one of six colored squares arranged along the bottom of the window. Then press and hold the second pointer button to drag the color. The drag icon is an artist's palette in the chosen color.

When you drag the icon over an invalid drop source (anywhere except the rectangle), a red international negation symbol is superimposed over the palette, indicating that you cannot make the transfer. When the icon is over the rectangle, the palette appears normal. Release the pointer over the rectangle and the shape is redrawn in the selected color. You can change the color as many times as you like. Of course, this is only mildly diverting, but it will give you an idea how drag and drop might be implemented in the future—in more graphically-oriented applications.

10

Command-line Options

*This chapter describes command-line options that are common to most cli-
ents. Some arguments to command-line options can also be specified as the
values of resource variables, described in Chapter 11, Setting Resources.
For example, the format of a geometry string or a color specification is the
same whether it is specified as an argument to an option or as the value of a
resource definition.*

In This Chapter:

10
Command-line Options

As explained in Chapter 3, *Working in the X Environment*, X allows the user to specify numerous (very numerous!) command-line options when starting most clients. The command-line options for each client are detailed on the reference pages in Part Three of this guide.

As a general rule, all options can be shortened to the shortest unique abbreviation. For example, -display can be shortened to -d if there is no other option beginning with "d." (Note that while this is true for all the standard MIT clients, it may not be true of any random client taken off the net.)

In addition to certain client-specific options, all applications built with the X Toolkit (or a toolkit based on the Xt Intrinsics, such as the Motif Toolkit) accept certain standard options, which are listed in Table 10-1. (Some non-Toolkit applications may also recognize these options.) The first column contains the name of the option, the second the name of the resource to which it corresponds (see Chapter 11, *Setting Resources*), and the third a brief description of what the option does.

This chapter discusses some of the more commonly used Toolkit options and demonstrates how to use them. (For the syntax of the other Toolkit options, see the *X* reference page in Part Three of this guide.)

Table 10-1. Standard Options

Option	Resource	Description
-bg	background	Background color of window.
-background	background	Background color of window.
-bd	borderColor	Color of window border.
-bordercolor	borderColor	Color of window border.
-bw	borderWidth	Border width of window in pixels.
-borderwidth	borderWidth	Border width of window in pixels.
-display	display	Display on which client is run.
-fn	font	Font for text display.
-font	font	Font for text display.

Table 10-1. Standard Options (continued)

Option	Resource	Description
-fg	foreground	Foreground (drawing or text) color of window.
-foreground	foreground	Foreground (drawing or text) color of window.
-geometry	geometry	Geometry string for window size and placement.
-iconic		Start the application in iconified form.
-name	name	Specify a name for the application being run.
-rv	reverseVideo	Reverse foreground and background colors.
-reverse	reverseVideo	Reverse foreground and background colors.
+rv	reverseVideo	Don't reverse foreground and background.
-selectionTimeout	selectionTimeout	Timeout in milliseconds within which two communicating applications must respond to one another for a selection request.
-synchronous	synchronous	Enable synchronous debug mode.
+synchronous	synchronous	Disable synchronous debug mode.
-title	title	Specify a window title (e.g., to be displayed in a titlebar).
-xnllanguage	xnlLanguage	The language, territory, and codeset for National Language Support; this information helps resolve resource and other filenames.
-xrm	value of next arg	Next argument is a quoted string containing a resource manager specification, as described in Chapter 11, *Setting Resources*.

Though all Toolkit options are preceded by a minus sign, client-specific options may or may not require it. See the reference page for each client in Part Three of this guide for the syntax of all options.

Display and Geometry

Perhaps the most useful of the Toolkit options are -display and -geometry, which allow you to specify the display on which a client window should appear, and the size and position of that window, respectively. See Chapter 3, *Working in the X Environment*, for detailed instructions on using these options. In the remainder of this chapter we'll discuss some of the other useful Toolkit options.

Window Title and Application Name

You can specify the title of a window (as it appears in the titlebar) and the name of the program (as known to the server) using the -title and -name options, respectively.

The -title option allows you to specify a text string as the title of the application's window. If your application has a titlebar or if the window manager you are using puts titlebars on windows, this string will appear in the titlebar. (Note that most applications use the name of the program as the default title.)

Window titles can be useful in distinguishing multiple instances of the same application. For example, say you're running three *xterm* windows, each on a different system in the network. You can give each of the windows a title that matches the system on which the client is running:

```
% xterm -title jersey -geometry +0+0 &
% rsh manhattan xterm -title manhattan -display jersey:0.0 -geometry -0+0 &
% rsh bronx xterm -title bronx -display jersey:0.0 -geometry -0-0 &
```

In this case, the user is working on a workstation named *jersey*. She is running an *xterm* on the local machine and giving it a title to match (-title jersey). She is also running *xterm* windows on the remote systems *manhattan* and *bronx*, displaying the windows on *jersey* (using -display), and titling each window to match its system. (The -geometry option allows her to provide convenient placement for all three windows. See Chapter 3, *Working in the X Environment*, for a complete discussion of the -display and -geometry options.) The resulting three windows appear in the display in Figure 10-1.

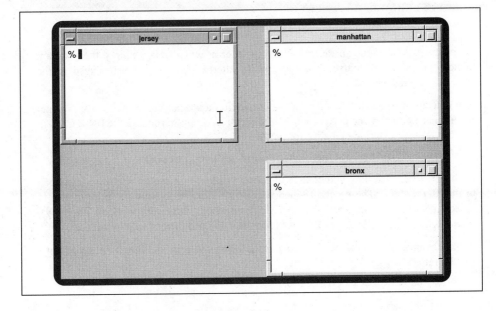

Figure 10-1. Window titles showing client's host system

Specifying the machine name as the title string is just one use of -title. You might choose to title a window based on any number of factors, perhaps even its intended function. For instance, you might have windows titled *editing*, *mail*, *sales*, *book project*, etc. If you want to specify a title that is composed of multiple words, enclose the title in quotation marks:

```
% xterm -title "X Window System User's Guide, Motif Edition" &
```

The -name option actually changes the name by which the server identifies the program. If a name string is defined for an application, that string will appear as the application name in its icon. More significantly, using -name to change the name of the application itself affects the way the resource definitions are applied. By renaming one instance of a client, you can specify resources that apply only to that renamed version. Because the new name can be used in resource definitions, it should be limited to a single word. The -name option is discussed further in Chapter 11, *Setting Resources*.

If you display information about a currently running window using the *xwininfo* client (without options), title strings will appear in parentheses after the associated window ID numbers. If there is no title string but there is a name string, the name string will be displayed. If you use the -tree option (to list information about the window tree), both title and name strings are returned.

You can also use the *xwininfo* client to request information about a particular window by title, or name, if no title string is defined, using that application's own -name option. See the *xwininfo* reference page in Part Three of this guide and the section "Window and Display Information Clients" in Chapter 8, *Other Clients*, to learn more about this client.

Displaying the Current Directory in an xterm Titlebar

Without customization, an *xterm* window's titlebar will display simply the program name ("xterm"). Of course, you can specify alternative text to be displayed in the titlebar using the -title option.

You can use a somewhat fancier trick—employing a special escape sequence—to get the titlebar to display the current working directory. If you're running the UNIX C shell, you can do this by writing an alias for *cd*(1):

```
alias cd 'chdir \!*;echo -n "Escape]2;$cwdControl-G"'
```

With this alias, each time you change directory (with *cd*), an escape sequence is echoed to the *xterm* shell. The escape sequence tells the *xterm* to update the titlebar text to reflect the *cwd* environment variable (which contains the current working directory). (See Appendix E, *xterm Control Sequences*, for a complete list of valid sequences.)

In the example above, the escape sequence is represented by the literal keys you type, which are:

```
Escape ] 2 ; $cwd Control-G
```

(continued on next page)

Displaying the Current Directory in an xterm Titlebar (continued)

Be aware, however, that when you type these keys as specified, the command line will not look exactly like this. Certain keys, such as Escape, and key combinations, such as Control-G, are represented by other symbols on the command line. When you type the previous key sequence (without spaces), the command line will actually look like this:

```
alias cd 'chdir \!*;echo -n "^[]2;$cwd^G"'
```

Pressing the Escape key generates the ^[symbol; typing the Control-G key combination generates ^G.

You can specify this alias on the command line or add it to your *.cshrc* file. We recommend entering it in your *.cshrc* file. If you enter it in the file, you'll probably need to preface the special keys Escape and Control-G with other keys to get them to appear. If you're using the *vi* text editor, type Control-V before a special key or key combination. If you're using *emacs*, type Control-Q first. If you're using another text editor, see your documentation or your system administrator for details.

If you're using another UNIX shell or are working in an entirely different environment, consult your system administrator for the proper way to supply the escape sequence to the *xterm* window.

Starting a Client Window as an Icon

The -iconic command-line option starts the client window in iconified form. To start an *xterm* window as an icon, type:

```
% xterm -iconic &
```

This can be especially useful for starting the login *xterm* window. As described in Chapter 3, *Working in the X Environment*, terminating the login *xterm* window kills the X server and all other clients that are running. It's always possible to terminate a window inadvertently by selecting the wrong menu option or typing the wrong key sequence. If your login *xterm* window is automatically iconified at startup, you are far less likely to terminate the window inadvertently and end your X session.

Normally, *mwm* handles icon placement, so you shouldn't have to worry about it. By default, icons are displayed in the bottom left corner of the root window. *mwm* can also be set up to place icons in another location, to allow you to place them interactively using the pointer, or to organize icons within an *icon box*. Chapter 13, *Customizing mwm*, describes the specifications necessary to set up an icon box. See the *mwm* reference page in Part Three of this guide for additional information on icon placement.

Specifying Fonts on the Command Line

Many clients allow you to specify the font to be used when displaying text in the window. (These are known as *screen fonts* and are not to be confused with *printer fonts*.) For clients written with the X Toolkit, the option to set the display font is -fn. For example, the command line:

```
% xterm -fn fontname &
```

creates an *xterm* window in which text will be displayed with the font named `fontname`.

Chapter 6, *Font Specification*, describes the available screen fonts and font naming conventions.

Reverse Video

There are three options to control whether the application will display in reverse video—that is, with the foreground and background colors reversed. The -rv or -reverse option is used to request reverse video.

The +rv option is used to override any reverse video request that might be specified in a resource file. (See Chapter 11, *Setting Resources*.) This is important, because not all clients handle reverse video correctly, and even those that do usually do so only on black and white displays.

Border Width

Many clients accept a -bw option that is intended to specify the width of the window border in pixels. However, if you're using the *mwm* window manager, this customization is generally useless because the *mwm* frame effectively replaces most window borders.

As an alternative, you *can* change the width of the frame by specifying resources for *mwm* in a *.Xresources* or *.Xdefaults* file in your home directory. For more information, see Chapter 11, *Setting Resources*, and the `frameBorderWidth` and `resizeBorderWidth` resources on the *mwm* reference page in Part Three of this guide.

Specifying Color

Many clients accept standard options that allow you to specify the color of the window background, foreground (the color in which text or graphic elements will be displayed), and border. These options generally have the form:

−bg *color*   Sets the background color.

−fg *color*   Sets the foreground color.

−bd *color*   Sets the border color.

By default, the background of an application window is usually white and the foreground black, even on color workstations. The −bg and −fg options allow you to specify alternatives.

Many clients accept the −bd option that is intended to specify the color of the window border. However, as in the case of the −bw (border width) option, if you're using the *mwm* window manager, this customization is generally useless: the *mwm* frame effectively replaces most window borders. As an alternative, you can change the color of the frame by specifying resources for *mwm* in a *.Xresources* or *.Xdefaults* file in your home directory. For more information, see Chapter 11, *Setting Resources*, and the *mwm* reference page in Part Three of this guide.

You can name another *color* on the command line in a variety of ways, which are described in Chapter 12, *Specifying Color*. Some color specifications are simply names (blue, green, hot pink); others are symbolic "names"—actually numeric values that signify a particular shade. (As you're probably guessing, this can get complicated.) For now, suffice it to say that you can keep color specification as simple as you want—and most color names you can think of are probably valid.

Let's consider the syntax of a command line specifying an *xterm* to be displayed in two colors:

```
% xterm -bg lightblue -fg darkslategray &
```

This command creates an *xterm* window with a background of light blue and foreground of dark slate gray.

At the command line, you should either type a color name as a single word (for example, darkslategray) or enclose the separate words in quotes, as in the command line:

```
% xterm -bg "light blue" -fg "dark slate gray" &
```

As we'll see in Chapter 12, if you specify colors using these "standard" names X allows for a range of spelling, spacing, and capitalization.

Some clients allow additional options to specify color for other elements, such as the cursor, highlighting, and so on. See the appropriate client reference pages in Part Three of this guide for details.

See Chapter 12, *Specifying Color*, for more about the standard color names and customized color values.

11

Setting Resources

This chapter describes how to set resource variables that determine application features such as color, geometry, fonts, and so on. It describes the syntax of resource definition files such as .Xresources, as well as the operation of xrdb, *a client that can be used to change resource definitions dynamically, and make resources available to clients running on other machines.*

In This Chapter:

11
Setting Resources

Virtually all X clients are customizable. You can specify how a client looks on the screen—
its size and placement, its border and background color or pattern, whether the window has a
scrollbar, and so on. Some applications even allow you to redefine the keystrokes or pointer
actions used to control the application.

Traditional UNIX applications rely on command-line options to allow users to customize the
way they work. As we've already discussed in Chapter 10, *Command-line Options*, X applications support command-line options too, but often not for all features. Also, there can be
so many customizable features in an application that entering a command line to set them all
would be completely impractical. (Imagine the aggravation of misspelling an option in a
command that was three lines long!)

X offers an alternative to customizing an application on the command line. Almost every
feature of a program can be controlled by a variable called a *resource*; you can change the
behavior or appearance of a program by changing the *value* associated with a resource variable. (All of the standard X Toolkit *Command-line Options* described in Chapter 10 have
corresponding resource variable names. See Table 9-1 for more information.)

Resource variables may be Boolean (such as `scrollBar: True`) or take a numeric or
string value (`borderWidth: 2` or `foreground: blue`). What's more, in applications
written with the X Toolkit (or an Xt-based toolkit such as the Motif toolkit), resources may
be associated with separate *objects* (or "widgets") within an application. There is a syntax
that allows for separate control over both a *class* of objects in the application and an individual *instance* of an object. This is illustrated by these resource specifications for a hypothetical application called *xclient*:

```
xclient*Buttons.foreground:      blue
xclient*help.foreground:         red
```

The first resource specification makes the foreground color of all buttons in the *xclient* application (in the class `Buttons`) blue; the second resource specification makes the foreground
color of the `help` button in this application (an instance of the class `Buttons`) red.
Resource settings can be simpler than this. If you want to set very simple resources, read the
next section, "Resource Naming Syntax." You can delve more deeply into a client's widget
hierarchy to set more complicated and precise resources. The *editres* client (described later
in this chapter) helps you determine a client's hierarchy and set the resources you want.

The values of resources can be set as application defaults using a number of different mechanisms, including resource files in your home directory and a program called *xrdb* (X resource database manager). As we'll see, the *xrdb* program stores resources directly in the server, making them available to all clients, regardless of the machine the clients are running on.

Placing resources in files allows you to set many resources at once, without the restrictions encountered when using command-line options. In addition to a primary resource file (often called *.Xdefaults, .Xresources, xrdb*) in your home directory, which determines defaults for the clients you yourself run, the system administrator can create system-wide resource files to set defaults for all instances of the application run on this machine. It is also possible to create resource files to set some resources only for the local machine, some for all machines in a network, and some for one or more specific machines.

The various resource files are automatically read in and processed in a certain order within an application by a set of routines called the *resource manager*. The syntax for resource specifications and the rules of precedence by which the resource manager processes them are intended to give you the maximum flexibility in setting resources with the minimum amount of text. You can specify a resource that controls only one feature of a single application, such as the red help button in the hypothetical *xclient* settings above. You can also specify a resource that controls one feature of multiple objects within multiple applications with a single line.

As of Release 5, the resource manager also allows you to specify different resources for color and monochrome screens. In addition, you can invoke predefined color defaults for an application by using the new customization resource variable.

It is important to note that command-line options normally take precedence over any prior resource settings; so you can set up the files to control the way you *normally* want your application to work and then use command-line options to specify changes you need for only one or two instances of the application.

In this chapter, we'll first look at the syntax of resource specifications. Then we'll consider some methods of setting resources, primarily some special command-line options and the *xrdb* program. Finally, we'll take a brief look at other sources of resource definition, additional files that can be created or edited to set application resources.

Resource Naming Syntax

The basic syntax of a resource definition file is fairly simple. Each client recognizes certain resource variables that can be assigned a value. The variables for each client are documented on its reference page in Part Three of this guide.

Most of the common clients are written to use the X Toolkit. As described in Chapter 1, *An Introduction to the X Window System*, toolkits are a mechanism for simplifying the design and coding of applications and making them operate in a consistent way. Toolkits provide a standard set of objects, or widgets, such as menus, command buttons, dialog boxes, scrollbars, and so on. As we'll see, the naming syntax for certain resources parallels the object hierarchy that is built into X Toolkit programs.*

The most basic line you can have in a resource definition file consists of the name of a client, followed by a period or an asterisk, and the name of a variable. A colon and whitespace separate the client and variable names from the actual value of the resource variable. The following line specifies that all instances of the *xterm* application have a scrollbar:

```
xterm*scrollBar:     True
```

If the name of the client is omitted, the variable applies to all instances of all clients (in this case, all clients that can have a scrollbar). If the same variable is specified as a global variable and a client-specific variable, the value of the client-specific variable takes precedence for that client. Note, however, that if the name of the client is omitted, the line should generally begin with an asterisk.

Be sure not to inadvertently omit the colon at the end of a resource specification. This is an easy mistake to make and the resource manager provides no error messages. If there is an error in a resource specification (including a syntax error such as the omission of the colon or a misspelling), the specification is ignored. The value you set will simply not take effect. To include a comment in a resource file or comment out one of the resource specifications, begin the line in question with an exclamation point (!). If the last character on a line is a backslash (\), the resource definition on that line is assumed to continue on the next line.

Syntax of Toolkit Client Resources

As mentioned above, X Toolkit applications (and Xt-based toolkit applications) are made up of predefined components called widgets. There can be widgets within widgets (e.g., a command button within a dialog box). The syntax of resource specifications for Toolkit clients parallels the levels of the widget hierarchy. Accordingly, you should think of a resource specification as having this format:

```
object.subobject[.subobject...].attribute: value
```

where:

object   is the client program or a specific instance of the program. (See "The –name Option" later in this chapter.)

*subobject*s   correspond to levels of the widget hierarchy (usually the major structures within an application, such as windows, menus, scrollbars, etc.).

---

*If a client was built with the X Toolkit, this should be noted on the reference page. In addition to certain application-specific resource variables, most clients that use the X Toolkit recognize a common set of resource variables, listed in Table 10-1.

In addition, X Toolkit clients recognize a set of Core resource variables, listed in Table G-1. However, though all Toolkit applications recognize these variables, not all applications make use of them. This fine distinction is addressed in Appendix G, *Widget Resources*, which gives a more technical discussion of how widgets use resources, and how applications use widgets. Appendix G also gives a detailed listing of the resources defined by each of the Athena widgets.

`attribute`	is a feature of the last *subobject* (perhaps a command button), such as background color or a label that appears on it.
`value`	is the actual setting of the resource `attribute`, i.e., the label text, color, or other feature.

The type of `value` to supply is often evident from the name of the resource or from the description of the resource variable on the reference page. Most of these values are similar to those used with the command-line options described in Chapter 10.

For example, various resources, such as `borderColor` or `background`, take color specifications; `geometry` takes a geometry string, `font` takes a font name, and so on. Logical values, such as the values taken by `scrollBar`, can generally be specified as: on or off; yes or no; or `True` or `False`.

Tight Bindings and Loose Bindings

Binding refers to the way in which components of a resource specification are linked together. Resource components can be linked in two ways:

- By a *tight* binding, represented by a dot (.).

- By a *loose* binding, represented by an asterisk (*).

A tight binding means that the components on either side of the dot must be next to one another in the widget hierarchy. A loose binding is signaled by an asterisk, a wildcard character which means there can be any number of levels in the hierarchy between the two surrounding components (including none).

If you want to specify tight bindings, you must be very familiar with the widget hierarchy: it's easy to use tight bindings incorrectly.

For example, this resource specification to request that *xterm* windows be created with a scrollbar doesn't work:

```
xterm.scrollBar:    True
```

The previous specification ignores the widget hierarchy of *xterm*, in which the VT102 window is considered to be one widget, the Tektronix window another, and the menus a third. This means that if you want to use tight bindings to request that *xterm* windows be created with a scrollbar, you should specify:

```
xterm.vt100.scrollBar:    True
```

Of course rather than decipher the widget hierarchy (which may even change with subsequent versions of an application), it is far simpler just to use the asterisk connector in the first place:

```
xterm*scrollBar:    True
```

Note that the asterisk is interpreted very differently in resource syntax than in the UNIX C shell. In the shell, the asterisk is a wildcard that can represent zero or more *characters*. In a resource file, the asterisk represents zero or more *complete components* in the resource name.

(Zero refers to the case in which the asterisk simply connects the previous and subsequent components.) Don't make the mistake of trying to use the asterisk to match *partial* component names. If you want to set the same specification for clients with similar names, you cannot use a common abbreviation. For example, if you would like *xcalc*, *xclock*, and *xclipboard* to display in reverse video, you can't write:

```
xc*reverseVideo:   True
```

In an application that supports multiple levels of widgets, you can mix asterisks and periods. In general, though, the developers of X recommend always using the asterisk rather than the dot as the connector even with simple applications, since this gives application developers the freedom to insert new levels in the hierarchy as they produce new releases of an application.

Instances and Classes

Each component of a resource specification has an associated *class*. Several different widgets, or widget attributes, may have the same class. For example, in the case of *xterm*, the color of text (`foreground`), the pointer color, and the text cursor color are all defined as *instances* of the class `Foreground`. This makes it possible to set the value of all three with a single resource specification. That is, if you wanted to make the text, the pointer, and the cursor dark blue, you could specify either:

```
xterm*foreground:      darkblue
xterm*cursorColor:     darkblue
xterm*pointerColor:    darkblue
```

or:

```
xterm*Foreground:      darkblue
```

Initial capitalization is used to distinguish class names from instance names. By convention, class names always begin with an uppercase letter, while instance names always begin with a lowercase letter. Note, however, that if an instance name is a compound word (such as `cursorColor`), the second word is usually capitalized.

The real power of class and instance naming is not apparent in applications such as *xterm* that have a simple widget hierarchy. In complex applications written with the X Toolkit or the Motif Toolkit, class and instance naming allows you to do such things as specify that all buttons in dialog box be blue but that one particular button be red. For example, in the hypothetical *xclient* application, you might have a resource file that reads:

```
xclient*buttonbox*Buttons*foreground:      blue
xclient*buttonbox*delete*foreground:       red
```

where `Buttons` is a class name and the `delete` button is an instance of the `Buttons` class. This type of specification works because an instance name always overrides the corresponding class name for that instance. Class names thus allow default values to be specified for all instances of a given type of object. Instance names can be used to specify exceptions to the rules outlined by the class names. Note that a class name can be used with a loose binding to specify a resource for all clients. For example, this specification would say that the foreground colors for all clients should be blue:

```
*Foreground:     blue
```

The reference page for a given program should always give you both instance and class names for every resource variable you can set. You'll notice that in many cases the class name is identical to the instance name, with the exception of the initial capital letter. Often (but not always) this means that there is only one instance of that class. In other cases, the instance with the same name is simply the primary or most obvious instance of the class.

Wildcarding a Component Name with ?

As of Release 5, you can use a question mark (?) to represent *any single component* in a resource specification. (Naturally, you can't use a question mark as the final component, the resource variable itself.) The use of the question mark wildcard is a bit confusing and is best learned by example.

```
xclient.?.?.Background:     whitesmoke
```

The preceding line sets the background color for all widgets that are two subobjects below the application level. (You can also think of these subojects/widgets as the *grandchildren* of the top level window in the client's own window hierarchy. Typical "grandchildren" might be dialog boxes, menus, etc.)

Note also that the specification sets the background color for *only* those widgets. (The tight bindings ensure this.) A loose binding between the second question mark wildcard and the resource variable (Background) expands the coverage to include the second subobject level and also all further subobects:

```
xclient.?.?*Background:     whitesmoke
```

The use of the question mark requires a bit of finesse, but it simplifies specifications that have previously been very involved. Prior to Release 5, if you wanted to set the background color for grandchildren of the top level application window, you would have to provide a resource line for each one. Our first example line:

```
xclient.?.?.Background:     whitesmoke
```

does the same thing.

The use of the question mark and the asterisk wildcards together may confuse you, but there is an important distinction between them. The question mark always represents a single component. Thus, unless it is the first component, it must always be bracketed by connectors. (You'll generally use periods as the connectors between question mark wildcards to indicate a tight binding, but as we saw in the second example, sometimes an asterisk is the appropriate connector.) The most important thing to remember is that the presence of a question mark specifies that a component exists (though it does not specify the name of the component).

The asterisk specifies that zero or more (adjacent) components have been omitted from the resource. In effect, it is both a wildcard (that may represent adjacent components) and a connector.

The following section explains how the question mark wildcard is interpreted in determining the precedence of resource specifications. The section "Other Ways to Specify the Same Resource" (at the end of the *editres* tutorial) gives additional examples of how to use the question mark wildcard.

Precedence Rules for Resource Specification

Even within a single resource file, such as *.Xresources*, resource specifications often conflict. For instance, recall the example from the first page of the chapter involving the hypothetical *xclient* application:

```
xclient*Buttons.foreground:        blue
xclient*help.foreground:           red
```

The first resource specification makes the foreground color of all buttons (in the class `But-tons`) blue. The second resource specification overrides the first in one instance: it makes the foreground color of the `help` button (an instance of the class `Buttons`) red. In the event of conflicting specifications, there are a number of rules that the resource manager follows in deciding which resource specification should take effect.

We've already seen two of these rules, which are observable in the way the resource manager interprets definitions in a user-created resource file. (The first rule applies in the previous *xclient* example.)

- Instance names take precedence over class names.

- Tight bindings take precedence over loose bindings.

From just these two rules, we can deduce a general principle: the more specific a resource definition is, the more likely it is to be honored in the case of a conflict.

However, for cases in which you want to set things up very carefully, you should know a bit more about how programs interpret resource specifications.

For each resource, the program has both a complete, fully specified, tightly bound instance name and class name. In evaluating ambiguous specifications, the program compares the specification against both the full instance name and the full class name. If a component in the resource specification matches either name, it is accepted. If it matches more than one element in either name, it is evaluated according to these precedence rules:

1. The levels in the hierarchy specified by the user must match the program's expectations or the entry will be ignored. For example, if the program expects either:

    ```
    xterm.vt100.scrollBar:        value          instance name
    ```

    or:

    ```
    XTerm.VT100.ScrollBar:        value          class name
    ```

    the resource specification:

    ```
    xterm.scrollBar:     True
    ```

won't work, because the tight binding is incorrect. The objects xterm and scroll-Bar are not adjacent in the widget hierarchy: there is another widget, vt100, between them. The specification would work if you used a loose binding, however:

```
xterm*scrollBar:    True
```

(Note that the class name of *xterm* is XTerm, not Xterm as you might expect.) You might instead use the question mark wildcard to represent vt100 in the widget hierarchy:

```
xterm.?.scrollBar:   True
```

This specification is perfectly valid. Note also that this line is more specific than (and thus takes precedence over) xterm*scrollBar: True.

2. Tight bindings take precedence over loose bindings. That is, entries with instance or class names prefixed by a dot are more specific than entries with names prefixed by an asterisk, and more specific entries take precedence. For example, the entry xterm.vt100.geometry will take precedence over the entry xterm*geometry.

3. Similarly, instances take precedence over classes. For example, the entry *scroll-Bar will take precedence over the entry *Scrollbar.

4. Left components carry more weight than right components. For example, the entry xterm*background will take precedence over *background.

5. An instance or class name that is explicitly stated takes precedence over one represented by the question mark wildcard, which in turn takes precedence over an omitted component. Thus, the specification xterm*scrollbar is more specific than ?*scrollBar, which is still more specific than *scrollBar.

To illustrate these rules, let's consider the following resource specifications (shown in Example 11-1) for the hypothetical Toolkit application *xclient*.

Example 11-1. Sample resources

```
xclient.toc*Command.activeForeground:       black
*Command.Foreground:      green
```

Each of these lines specifies a foreground color. Both specifications are valid. Now, applying the rules of precedence, let's try to figure out what foreground color would be used for the *xclient* application's include command button. To determine how conflicting specifications are applied, the program tries to match these specifications against the complete tightly bound instance and class specifications. In this case, say the complete specifications are:

```
xclient.toc.messageFunctions.include.foreground        instance name
Xclient.Box.SubBox.Command.Foreground                  class name
```

Note that these specifications are the instance and class names for the same resource—which determines the foreground color of the include button. Each component of the instance name belongs to the class in the corresponding component of the class name. Thus, the instance toc occurs in the class Box, the messageFunctions instance name is from the class SubBox, etc. The include button is an instance of the Command class.

Both resource specification in Example 11-2 matches these instance and class names. However, with its tight bindings and instance names, `xclient.toc*Command.foreground` matches more explicitly (i.e., with higher precedence). The resource is set: the `foreground` color of the `include` button is `black`.

The specification `*Command.Foreground` also matches the instance and class names but is composed entirely of class names which are less specific; thus, it takes lower precedence than the first line in Example 11-2 (which sets the `include` button to `black`).

However, since the second line is also an acceptable specification, hypothetically it would set the foreground color of other objects in the `Command` class. Thus, if there were other *xclient* command buttons comparable to the `include` button in the hierarchy, this second line would set the foreground color of these buttons to `green`. Note that, since the line begins with the asterisk wildcard, the resource would be set for *xclient*, as well as any other application with a `Command` class.

Now let's consider some actual conflicting resource specifications and apply the rules of precedence. All three of the resources in Example 11-2 are valid specifications for the font of all instances of the class `Command` (without the jargon, the font for the labels on command buttons).

Example 11-2. What takes precedence?

```
*Command*Font:   -*-helvetica-bold-r-normal--*-120-*-*-*-*-iso8859-1
?*Command*Font:  7x14
XClipboard*Command*Font:  6x10
```

We've listed the resources in Example 11-2 in increasing order of specificity. Because of the initial loose binding, the first specification applies to any client with a command widget. The second specification also applies to any client with a command widget, but the introductory question mark (representing all clients) makes it more specific. Thus, the second line overrides the first and specifies that the font for command buttons for all applications is `7x14`.

The third line is even more specific because it begins with an actual class name (`XClipboard`) rather than the question mark wildcard. The third line specifies that the font for *xclipboard* command buttons is `6x10`. Note, however, that the second line still applies to all other clients—they will use the font `7x14` for command buttons. The third line simply introduces an exception.

If you want a more detailed description of how resource precedence works, see Chapter 9 of Volume Four, *X Toolkit Intrinsics Programming Manual*.

Some Common Resources

Each Toolkit command-line option (listed in Table 9-1) has a corresponding resource variable. Most X Toolkit (and Motif Toolkit) applications recognize some subset of these resources.

Table 11-1 lists the resource variables recognized by most Toolkit clients.

Table 11-1. Common Toolkit Resources

Instance Name	Class Name	Default	Description
background	Background	White	Background color
foreground	Foreground	Black	Foreground color
borderColor	BorderColor	Black	Border color
borderWidth	BorderWidth	1 pixel	Border width

Note that in a complex Toolkit application these values can occur at every level in a widget hierarchy. For example, our hypothetical *xclient* application might support these complete instance names:

```
xclient.background
xclient.buttonBox.background
xclient.buttonBox.commandButton.background
xclient.buttonBox.quit.background
```

These resources would specify the background color for the application window, the button-box area, any command buttons, and the quit command button, respectively.

Of course, the specification:

```
xclient*background
```

would match any and all of them.

Appendix G lists resources for each of the Athena widgets.

Event Translations

We've discussed the basics of resource naming syntax. From the sample resource settings, it appears that what many resource variables do is self-evident or nearly so. Among the less obvious resource variables, there is one type of specification, an event translation, that can be used with many clients and warrants somewhat closer examination.

User input and several other types of information pass from the server to a client in the form of *events*. An event is a packet of information that tells the client something it needs to act on, such as keyboard input. As mentioned in Chapter 1, *An Introduction to the X Window System*, moving the pointer or pressing a key, etc., causes *input* events to occur. When a program receives a meaningful event, it responds with some sort of action.

For many clients, the resource manager recognizes mappings between certain input events (such as a pointer button click) and some sort of action by the client program (such as selecting text). A mapping between one or more events and an action is called a *translation*. A resource containing a list of translations is called a *translation table*.

Many event translations are programmed into an application and are invisible to the user.* For our purposes we are only concerned with very visible translations of certain input events, primarily the translation of keystrokes and pointer button clicks to particular actions by a client program.

The Syntax of Event Translations

The operation of many clients, notably *xterm*, is partly determined by default input event translations. For example, as explained in Chapter 5, *The xterm Terminal Emulator*, selecting text with the first pointer button (an event) saves that text into memory (an action).

In this case, the input "event" is actually three separate X events:

1. Pressing the first pointer button.

2. Moving the pointer while holding down the first button.

3. Releasing the button.

Each of these input events performs a part of the action of selecting text:

1. Unselects any previously selected text and begins selecting new text.

2. Extends the selection.

3. Ends the selection, saving the text into memory (both as the PRIMARY selection and CUT_BUFFER0).

The event and action mappings would be expressed in a translation table as:

```
<Btn1Down>: select-start()\n\
<Btn1Motion>: select-extend()\n\
<Btn1Up>: select-end(PRIMARY,CUT_BUFFER0)
```

where each event is enclosed in angle brackets (<>) and produces the action that follows the colon (:). A space or tab generally precedes the action, though this is not mandatory:

```
<event>: action
```

A translation table must be a continuous string. In order to link multiple mappings as a continuous string, each event-action line should be terminated by a newline character (\n), which is in turn followed by a backslash (\) to escape the actual newline.

These are default translations for *xterm*.† All of the events are simple, comprised of a single button motion. As we'll see, events can also have modifiers: i.e., additional button motions or keystrokes (often Control or Meta) that must be performed with the primary event to pro-

---

*For more information on events and translations, see Volume Four, *X Toolkit Intrinsics Programming Manual*.
†They are actually slightly simplified versions of default translations. Before you can understand the actual translations listed on the *xterm* reference page in Part Three of this guide, you must learn more about the syntax of translations. In addition to the current chapter, read Appendix F, *Translation Table Syntax*.

duce the action. (Events can also have modifiers that *must not* accompany the primary event if the action is to take place.)

As you can see, the default actions listed in the table are hardly intuitive. The event-action mappings that can be modified using translation resources are usually described on the reference page for the particular client.

You can specify non-default translations using a translation table (a resource containing a list of translations). Since actions are part of the client application and cannot be modified, what you are actually doing is specifying alternative events to perform an action.* Keep in mind that only applications written with the X Toolkit (or an Xt-based toolkit such as the Motif Toolkit) recognize translation table syntax.

The basic syntax for specifying a translation table as a resource is:

```
[object*[subobject...]]*translations:    #override\
     [modifier]<event>:    action
```

The first line is basically like any other resource specification with a few exceptions. First, the final `argument` is always `translations`, indicating that one (or more) of the event-action bindings associated with the `[object*[subobject . . .]]` are being modified.

Second, note that `#override` is not the `value` of the resource; it is literal and indicates that what follows should override any default translations. In effect, `#override` is no more than a pointer to the true `value` of the resource: a new event-action mapping (on the following line), where the event may take a modifier.†

A not-so-obvious principle behind overriding translations is that you only literally "override" a default translation when the event(s) of the new translation match the event(s) of a default translation *exactly*. If the new translation does not conflict with any existing translation, it is merely appended to the defaults.

In order to be specified as a resource, a translation table must be a single string. The `#override` is followed by a backslash (\) to indicate that the subsequent line should be a continuation of the first.

In the previous basic syntax example, the `value` is a single event-action mapping. The `value` could also be a list of several mappings, linked by the characters "\n\" to make the resource a continuous string.

The following *xterm* translation table shows multiple event-action mappings linked in this manner:

```
*VT100.Translations:    #override\
     <Btn1Down>:      select-start()\n\
     <Btn1Motion>:    select-extend()\n\
     <Btn1Up>:        select-end(PRIMARY,CUT_BUFFER0)
```

---

*As we'll see, in certain cases you may be able to supply an alternative *argument* (such as a selection name) to an action. These changes *are* interpreted by the resource manager.
†The use of modifiers can actually become quite complicated, sometimes involving multiple modifiers. For our purposes, we'll deal only with simple modifiers. For more information on modifiers, see Appendix F in this guide and Volume Four, *X Toolkit Intrinsics Programming Manual.*

xterm Translations to Use xclipboard

As explained in Chapter 5, the *xclipboard* client provides a window in which you can store text selected from other windows. You can also paste text from the *xclipboard* window into other windows. See the discussion of *xclipboard* in Chapter 5 before proceeding.

You can specify translations for *xterm* so that text you copy with the pointer is made the CLIPBOARD selection. The CLIPBOARD selection is the property of the *xclipboard* client. If you are running *xclipboard* and you copy text to be made the CLIPBOARD selection, this text automatically appears in the *xclipboard* window.

Some sample translations that would allow you to use the *xclipboard* in this way are:

```
*VT100.Translations: #override\
    Button1 <Btn3Down>: select-end(PRIMARY,CUT_BUFFER0,CLIPBOARD)\n\
    !Shift <Btn2Up>:        insert-selection(CLIPBOARD)\n\
    ~Shift ~Ctrl ~Meta <Btn2Up>:  insert-selection(PRIMARY,CUT_BUFFER0)
```

According to this translation table, while selecting text with Button1 (the modifier), the event of pressing the third pointer button (Btn3Down), while continuing to hold down the first button, produces the action of making the text the CLIPBOARD selection (as well as making it the PRIMARY selection and saving it to CUT_BUFFER0). Basically, we've taken the default select-end translation—which uses the first pointer button and the arguments PRIMARY, CUT_BUFFER0—and added the Btn3Down action and the CLIPBOARD argument.

The second line specifies a way to paste the CLIPBOARD selection: by holding the Shift key and clicking the second pointer button.

The third line modifies the way the contents of the PRIMARY selection or CUT_BUFFER0 are pasted into a window. As described in Chapter 5, by default pressing the second pointer button pastes the contents of the PRIMARY selection. If there is no PRIMARY selection, the contents of the cut buffer are pasted. The default translation that sets this behavior is the following:

```
    ~Ctrl ~Meta <Btn2Up>:   insert-selection(PRIMARY,CUT_BUFFER0)
```

This translation specifies that clicking (actually releasing) pointer button 2 (while pressing any modifier button or key *other than Control or Meta*) performs the insert-selection action. The arguments to insert-selection indicate that this action inserts text from the PRIMARY selection or, if the selection is empty, from cut buffer 0. Excluding the Control and Meta keys is intended to prevent conflict with other action mappings.* We've added ~Shift to prevent a conflict with the action that pastes the CLIPBOARD selection.

Thus, according to the translations in the example, if you select text as usual with the first pointer button, and then additionally press the third button (while continuing to hold down the first button), the text becomes the CLIPBOARD selection and appears automatically in the *xclipboard* window, as shown in Figure 11-1.

---

*~Ctrl is specified to keep this translation from conflicting with the translations that invoke the *xterm* menus; ~Meta prevents a conflict with *twm* functions. (As you may recall, *twm* is the window manager MIT ships with the standard version of X.)

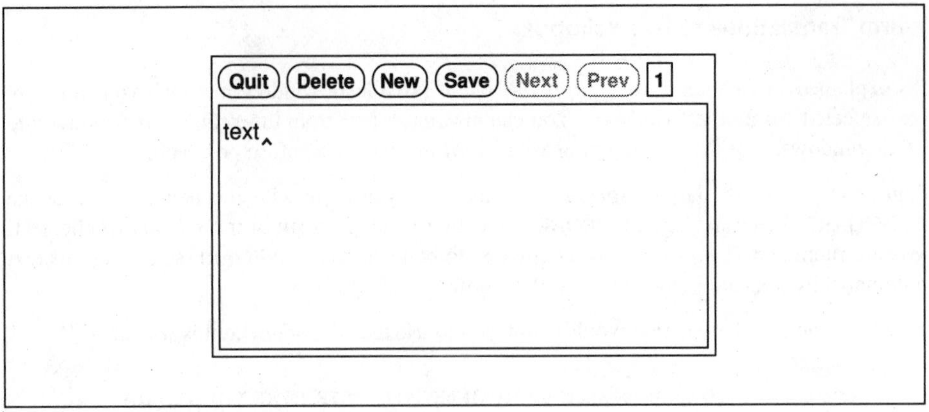

Figure 11-1. Selected text appears automatically in the xclipboard window

Since our first translation specifies a different event/action mapping than the default translation for selecting text (discussed in the previous section), the default translation still applies. If you select text with the first pointer button alone, that text is still made the PRIMARY selection and fills CUT_BUFFER0. To send text to the *xclipboard*, you would need to press the third pointer button as well; thus, not all selected text needs to be made the CLIPBOARD selection (and sent automatically to the *xclipboard*).

There are advantages to making only certain selections CLIPBOARD selections. You can keep *xclipboard* running and make many text selections by the default method (first pointer button), without filling up the *xclipboard* window. And chances are you don't want to save every piece of text you copy for an extended period of time, anyway.

The CLIPBOARD selection and the *xclipboard* client also get around the potential problems of selection ownership discussed in Chapter 5. Once text becomes the CLIPBOARD selection, it is owned by the *xclipboard* client. Thus, if the client from which text was copied (the original owner) goes away, the selection is still available, owned by the *xclipboard*, and can be transferred to another window (and translated to another format if necessary).

Entering Frequently Used Commands with Function Keys

The sample *xterm* translations to use the *xclipboard* client involve just a few of the actions *xterm* recognizes. Among the more useful translations you can specify for *xterm* are function key mappings that allow you to enter frequently used commands with a single keystroke. This sort of mapping involves an action called string, which passes a text string to the shell running in the *xterm* window.

The translation table syntax for such a function key mapping is fairly simple. The following line maps the text string "lpq –Pprinter1" (the BSD 4.3 command to check the queue for the printer named printer1) to the F1 function key:

```
<Key>F1:        string("lpq -Pprinter1")
```

Notice the quotes surrounding the text string. If the argument to string includes spaces or non-alphanumeric characters, the whole argument must be enclosed in one pair of double quotes. (Don't make the mistake of quoting individual words.)

The translation table would be:

```
*VT100.Translations: #override\
        <Key>F1:        string("lpq -Pprinter1")
```

This sample translation causes lpq -Pprinter1 to be passed to the command line in the active *xterm* window when you press the F1 function key, as in Figure 11-2.

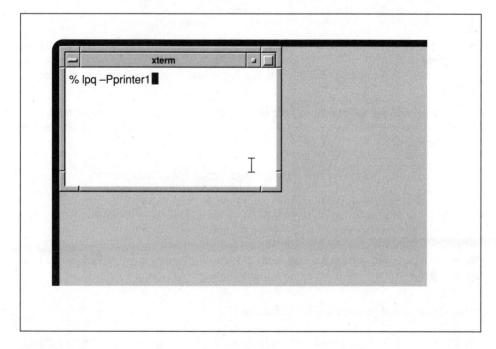

Figure 11-2. Pushing F1 passes command text to xterm shell

Notice, however, that the command is not invoked because there has been no carriage return. The sample translation does not specify a return. You can add a return as the argument to another string action within the same translation.

To specify the Return (or any) key, use the hexadecimal code for that key as the argument to string. Keycodes and the procedure for determining them are explained in Chapter 14, *Setup Clients*. The letters "0x" signal a hexadecimal key code. If you want to enter a key as an argument to `string`, use "0x" followed by the specific code. The code for the Return key is "d" or "0d."* The following translation table specifies that pressing F1 passes the line `lpq -Pprinter1` followed by a carriage return to an *xterm* window:

```
*VT100.Translations: #override\
        <Key>F1:        string("lpq -Pprinter1") string(0x0d)
```

Remember, you can list several translations in a single table. The following table maps function keys F1 through F3:

```
*VT100.Translations: #override\
        <Key>F1:        string("lpq -Pprinter1") string(0x0d)\n\
        <Key>F2:        string("cd ~/bitmap;ls") string(0x0d)\n\
        <Key>F3:        string("cd /usr/lib/X11") string(0x0d)
```

According to these translations, pressing F2 inserts the command string cd ~/bitmap;ls, which changes directory to *~/bitmap* and then lists the contents of that directory. Notice that you can issue multiple commands (*cd*, *ls*) with a single key. Pressing F3 changes directory to */usr/lib/X11*.

Keep in mind that all the translations for an application can appear in the same table. For example, we can combine the *xterm* translations to use the *xclipboard* with the translations to map function keys.

```
*VT100.Translations: #override\
        Button1 <Btn3Down>: select-end(PRIMARY,CUT_BUFFER0,CLIPBOARD)\n\
        !Shift <Btn2Up>:        insert-selection(CLIPBOARD)\n\
        ~Shift ~Ctrl ~Meta <Btn2Up>:   insert-selection(PRIMARY,CUT_BUFFER0)
        <Key>F1:        string("lpq -Pprinter1") string(0x0d)\n\
        <Key>F2:        string("cd ~/bitmap;ls") string(0x0d)\n\
        <Key>F3:        string("cd /usr/lib/X11") string(0x0d)
```

The order of the translations is not important. However, it is necessary to end all but the final line with the sequence "\n\" to make the resource a continuous string.

Other Clients that Recognize Translations

xterm is not the only client whose operation can be modified by specifying event translations as resources (though it is probably the client you'll be most interested in modifying). Among the standard clients, *xbiff*, *xcalc*, *xdm*, *xman*, and *xmh* all recognize certain actions that can be mapped to particular keys or key combinations using the translation mechanism. See the relevant client reference pages in Part Three of this guide for complete lists of actions.

You can also modify the operation of the Text widget used by *xedit*, *xmh*, and other X Toolkit applications. See the *xedit* reference page in Part Three for a list of actions recognized by the Text widget. Keep in mind, however, that the default Text widget recognizes dozens of com-

---

*As explained in Chapter 14, *Setup Clients*, the command xmodmap -pk returns a long listing of all keycodes. The codes have the either of the following forms:

    0xff*ab*
    0x00*ab*

where *ab* represents two alphanumeric characters. To specify a key as an argument to string, you can omit the "ff" or "00" in the *xmodmap* listing.

mands, which are summarized in the discussion of *xedit* in Chapter 8, *Other Clients*. It may not be practical or desirable to modify them all.

If you choose to modify the Text widget, you can do so for all relevant clients by introducing the translations with the line:

```
*Text*Translations: #override\
```

You can also specify different translations for different clients that use the widget by prepending the client's name. To affect the operation of the Text widget only under *xedit*, introduce the translation table with the line:

```
Xedit*Text*Translations: #override\
```

In modifying the operation of the Text widget, keep in mind that insert mode is the default. In other words, like *emacs*, most of the individual keystrokes you type are added to the text file; an exception is Backspace, which predictably deletes the preceding character. The commands to move around in a file, copy and delete text, etc., involve a combination of keys, one of which is generally a modifier key. If you want to modify a command, you should use an alternative key combination, rather than a single key.

For example, the following table offers two suitable translations:

```
*Text*Translations: #override\
        Meta<Key>f:     next-page()\n\
        Meta<Key>b:     previous-page()
```

The first translation specifies that pressing the key combination Meta-f moves the cursor ahead one page in the file (scrolls the file forward one window); the second translation specifies that Meta-b moves the cursor back one page. The actions performed are fairly obvious from their names. For a complete list of actions recognized by the Text widget, see the *xedit* reference page.

For more information about events, actions, and translation table syntax, see Appendix F, *Translation Table Syntax*, and Volume Four, *X Toolkit Programming Manual*.

Though *mwm* does not provide actions that can be modified using a translation table, you can change the key and pointer button events used to invoke window manager functions by editing a special file called *.mwmrc* in your home directory. See Chapter 13, *Customizing mwm*, for details.

How to Set Resources

Learning to write resource specifications is a fairly manageable task, once you understand the basic rules of syntax and precedence. In contrast, the multiple ways you can set resources—for a single system, for multiple systems, for a single user, for all users—can be confusing. For our purposes, we are primarily concerned with specifying resources for a single user running applications both on the local system and on remote systems in a network.

As we've said, resources are generally specified in files. A resource file can have any name you like. Resources are generally "loaded" into the X server by the *xrdb* client, which is normally run from your startup file or run automatically by *xdm* when you log in. (See Appendix A, *Managing Your Environment*, for information about startup files and *xdm*.) Prior to Release 2 of X, there was only one resource file called *.Xdefaults*, placed in the user's home directory. If no resource file is loaded into the server by *xrdb*, the *.Xdefaults* file will still be read.

Remember that X allows clients to run on different machines across a network, not just on the machine that supports the X server. The problem with the older *.Xdefaults* mechanism was that users who were running clients on multiple machines had to maintain multiple *.Xdefaults* files, one on each machine. By contrast, *xrdb* stores the application resources directly in the server, thus making them available to all clients, regardless of the machine on which the clients are running. As we'll see, *xrdb* also allows you to change resources without editing files.

Of course, you may want certain resources to be set on all machines and others to be set only on particular machines. See the section "Other Sources of Resource Definition" later in this chapter for information on setting machine-specific resources. This section gives an overview of additional ways to specify resources using a variety of system files.

In addition to loading resource files, you can specify defaults for a particular instance of an application from the command line using two options: `-xrm` and `-name`.

First we'll consider a sample resources file. Then we'll take a look at the use of the `-xrm` and `-name` command-line options. Finally, we'll discuss various ways you can load resources using the *xrdb* program and consider other sources of resource definition, later in this chapter.

A Sample Resources File

Figure 11-3 shows a sample resources file. This file sets the border width for all clients to a default value of two pixels, and sets other specific variables for *xclock* and *xterm*. The meaning of each variable is obvious from its name (for example, `xterm*scrollBar:    True` means that *xterm* windows should be created with a scrollbar.

Note that comments are preceded by an exclamation point (!).

For a detailed description of each possible variable, see the appropriate client reference pages in Part Three of this guide.

```
*borderWidth:           2
!
! xclock resources
!
xclock*borderWidth:     5
xclock*geometry:        64x64
!
! xterm resources
!
xterm*curses:           on
xterm*cursorColor:      skyblue
xterm*pointerShape:     pirate
xterm*jumpScroll:       on
xterm*saveLines:        300
xterm*scrollBar:        True
xterm*scrollKey:        on
xterm*background:       black
xterm*borderColor:      blue
xterm*borderWidth:      3
xterm*foreground:       white
xterm*font:             8x13
```

Figure 11-3. A sample resources file

Specifying Resources from the Command Line

Two command-line options supported by all clients written with the X Toolkit can be useful in specifying resources.

The –xrm Option

The -xrm option allows you to set on the command line any specification that you would otherwise put into a resources file. For example:

```
% xterm -xrm 'xterm*Foreground: blue' &
```

Note that a resource specification on the command line must be quoted using the single quotes in the line above.

The -xrm option only specifies the resource(s) for the current instance of the application. Resources specified in this way do not become part of the resource database.

The -xrm option is most useful for setting classes, since most clients have command-line options that correspond to instance variable names. For example, the -fg command-line option sets the foreground attribute of a window, but -xrm must be used to set Foreground.

Note also that a resource specified with the -xrm option will not take effect if a resource that takes precedence has already been loaded with *xrdb*. For example, say you've loaded a resource file that includes the specification:

```
xterm*pointerShape:  pirate
```

The command-line specification of another cursor will fail:

```
% xterm -xrm '*pointerShape:  gumby' &
```

because the resource xterm*pointerShape is more specific than the resource *pointerShape. Instead, you'll get an *xterm* with the previously specified pirate cursor.

To override the resource database (and get the Gumby cursor), you'd need to use a resource equally (or more) specific, such as the following:

```
% xterm -xrm 'xterm*pointerShape:  gumby' &
```

How —name Affects Resources

The -name option lets you name one instance of an application; the server identifies the single instance of the application by this name. The name of an application affects how resources are interpreted.

For example, the following command sets the *xterm* instance name to bigxterm:

```
% xterm -name bigxterm &
```

When this command is run, the client uses any resources specified for bigxterm rather than for xterm.

The -name option allows you to create different instances of the same application, each using different resources. For example, you could put the following entries into a resource file such as *.Xresources*:

```
XTerm*Font:          8x13
smallxterm*Font:     6x10
smallxterm*Geometry: 80x10
bigxterm*Font:       9x15
bigxterm*Geometry:   80x55
```

You could then use these commands to create *xterm*s of different specifications:

```
% xterm &
```

would create an *xterm* with the default specifications, while:

```
% xterm -name bigxterm &
```

would create a big *xterm*, 80 characters across by 55 lines down, displaying in the font 9x15. The command:

```
% xterm -name smallxterm &
```

would create a small *xterm*, 80 characters across by 10 lines down, displaying in the font 6x10.

Setting Resources with xrdb

The *xrdb* program saves you from the difficulty of maintaining multiple resource files if you run clients on multiple machines. It stores resources in the X server, where they are accessible to all clients using that server. (Technically speaking, the values of variables are stored in a data structure referred to as the RESOURCE_MANAGER property of the root window of screen 0 for that server. From time to time, we may refer to this property simply as the resource database.)

The appropriate *xrdb* command line should normally be placed in your *.xinitrc* file or *.xsession* file to initialize resources at login, although it can also be invoked interactively. It has the following syntax:

xrdb [*options*] [*filename*]

The *xrdb* client takes several options, all of which are documented on the reference page in Part Three of this guide. Several of the most useful options are discussed in subsequent sections. (Those that are not discussed here have to do with *xrdb*'s ability to interpret C preprocessor-style defined symbols; this is an advanced topic. For more information, see the *xrdb* reference page in Part Three of this guide, and the *cpp*(1) reference page in your *UNIX Reference Manual*.)

The optional *filename* argument specifies the name of a file from which the values of client variables (resources) will be read. If no filename is specified, *xrdb* will expect to read its data from standard input. That is, the program will appear to hang, until you type some data, followed by an end-of-file (Control-D on many UNIX systems). Note that whatever you type will override the previous contents of the RESOURCE_MANAGER property, so if you inadvertently type *xrdb* without a filename argument, and then quit with Control-D, you will delete any previous values. (You can append new settings to current ones using the −merge option discussed later in this chapter.)

The resource *filename* can be anything you want. Two commonly used names are *.Xresources* and *.Xdefaults*.

You should load a resource file with the *xrdb* −load option. For example, to load the contents of your *.Xresources* file into the RESOURCE_MANAGER, you would type:

```
% xrdb -load .Xresources
```

Querying the Resource Database

You can find out what options are currently set by using the −query option. For example:

```
% xrdb -query
XTerm*ScrollBar:      True
bigxterm*font:        9x15
bigxterm*Geometry:    80x55
smallxterm*Font:      6x10
smallxterm*Geometry:  80x10
xterm*borderWidth:    3
```

If *xrdb* has not been run, this command will produce no output.

Loading New Values into the Resource Database

By default, *xrdb* reads its input (either a file or standard input) and stores the results into the resource database, replacing the previous values. If you simply want to merge new values with the currently active ones (perhaps by specifying a single value from standard input), you can use the -merge option. Only the new values will be changed; variables that were already set will be preserved rather than overwritten with empty values.

For example, let's say you wanted to add new resources listed in the file *new.values*. You could say:

```
% xrdb -merge new.values
```

As another example, if you wanted all subsequently run *xterm* windows to have scrollbars, you could use standard input, and enter:

```
% xrdb -merge
xterm*scrollBar:    True
```

and then press Control-D to end the standard input. Note that because of precedence rules for resource naming, you may not automatically get what you want. For example, if you specify:

```
xterm*scrollBar:    True
```

and the more specific value:

```
xterm*vt100.scrollBar:    False
```

has already been set, your new, less specific setting will be ignored. The problem isn't that you used the -merge option incorrectly—you just got caught by the rules of precedence.

If your specifications don't seem to work, use the -query option to list the values in the RESOURCE_MANAGER property and look for conflicting specifications.

Note also that when you add new specifications, they won't affect any programs already running, but only programs started after the new resource specifications are in effect. (This is also true even if you overwrite the existing specifications by loading a new resource file. Only programs run after this point will reflect the new specifications.)

Saving Active Resource Definitions in a File

Assume that you've loaded the RESOURCE_MANAGER property from an *.Xresources* or other file. However, you've dynamically loaded a different value using the -merge option and you'd like to make the new value your default.

You don't need to edit the file manually (although you certainly could.) The -edit option allows you to write the current value of the RESOURCE_MANAGER property to a file. If the file already exists, it is overwritten with the new values. However, *xrdb* is smart enough to preserve any comments and preprocessor declarations in the file being overwritten, replacing only the resource definitions.

For example:

```
% xrdb -edit ~/.Xresources
```

will save the current contents of the RESOURCE_MANAGER property in the file *.Xresources* in your home directory.

If you want to save a backup copy of an existing file, use the -backup option:

```
% xrdb -edit .mydefaults -backup old
```

The string following the -backup option is used as an extension to be appended to the old filename. In the prior example, the previous copy of *.mydefaults* would be saved as *.mydefaults.old*.

Removing Resource Definitions

You can delete the definition of the RESOURCE_MANAGER property from the server by calling *xrdb* with the -remove option.

There is no way to delete a single resource definition other than to read the current *xrdb* values into a file. For example:

```
% xrdb -query > filename
```

Use an editor to edit the file, deleting the resource definitions you no longer want and save the file:

```
% vi filename
```

Then read the edited values back into the RESOURCE_MANAGER with *xrdb*:

```
% xrdb -load filename
```

Listing the Current Resources for a Client: appres

The *appres* (*app*lication *res*ource) program lists the resources that currently might apply to a client. These resources may be derived from several sources, including the user's *.Xresources* file and a system-wide application defaults file. The directory */usr/lib/X11/app-defaults* contains application default files for several clients. The function of these files is discussed in the next section. For now, be aware that all of the resources contained in these files begin with the class name of the application.

Also be aware that *appres* has one serious limitation: it cannot distinguish between valid and invalid resource specifications. It lists all resources that might apply to a client, whether or not the resources are correctly specified.

appres lists the resources that apply to a client having the `class_name` and/or `instance_name` you specify. Typically, you would use *appres* before running a client program to find out what resources the client program will access.

For example, say you want to run *xterm* but you can't remember the latest resources you've specified for it, whether you've loaded them, or perhaps what some of the application defaults are, etc. You can use the *appres* client to check the current *xterm* resources. If you specify only a class name, as in this command line:

```
% appres XTerm
```

appres lists the resources that any *xterm* would load. In the case of *xterm*, this is an extensive list, encompassing all of the system-wide application defaults as well as any other defaults you have specified in a resource file.

You can additionally specify an instance name to list the resources applying to a particular instance of the client, as in:

```
% appres XTerm bigxterm
```

If you omit the class name, *xappres* assumes the class -NoSuchClass-, which has no defaults, and returns only the resources that would be loaded by the particular instance of the client.

Note that the instance can simply be the client name, for example, `xterm`. In that case none of the system-wide application defaults would be listed, since all begin with the class name XTerm. For example, the command:

```
% appres xterm
```

might return resources settings similar to these:

```
xterm.vt100.scrollBar:     True
xterm*PhonyResource:       youbet
xterm*pointerShape:        gumby
xterm*iconGeometry:        +50+50
*VT100.Translations:       #override\
     Button1 <Btn3Down>:    select-end(CLIPBOARD) \n\
     ~Ctrl ~Meta <Btn2Up>: insert-selection(PRIMARY,CLIPBOARD)
```

Most of these resources set obvious features of *xterm*. The translation table sets up *xterm* to use the *xclipboard*. Notice also that *appres* has returned an invalid resource called Phony-Resource that we created for demonstration purposes. You can't rely on *appres* to tell you what resources a client will actually load because the *appres* program cannot distinguish a valid resource specification from an invalid one. Still, it can be fairly useful to jog your memory as to the defaults you've specified in your *.Xresources* file, as well as the system-wide application defaults.

Other Sources of Resource Definition

If *xrdb* has not been run, the RESOURCE_MANAGER property will not be set. Instead, the resource manager looks for a file called *.Xdefaults* in the user's home directory. As we discussed earlier, resources found in this way are only available to clients running on the local machine.

Whether or not resources have been loaded with *xrdb*, when a client is run these sources of resource definition are consulted in this order:

1. The client's application defaults file(s) (if any), which usually reside in the directory */usr/lib/X11/app-defaults*, will be loaded into the resource manager. (Note that the path can be reset with the XFILESEARCHPATH environment variable.) Application-specific resource files generally have the name *Class*, where *Class* is the class name of the client program.

   Any other application-specific resource files: a resource file named by the variable XUSERFILESEARCHPATH; or if this variable is not set, a file in the directory named by the environment variable XAPPLRESDIR.

2. Resources loaded into the RESOURCE_MANAGER property of the root window with *xrdb*; these resources are accessible regardless of the machine on which the client is running.

   If no resources are loaded in this way, the resource manager looks for an *.Xdefaults* file in the user's home directory; these resources are only available on the local machine.

3. Screen-specific resources loaded into the SCREEN_RESOURCES property of the root window with *xrdb*. The resource manager will sort and place the resources in RESOURCE_MANAGER (where they will apply to all screens) or in SCREEN_RESOURCES (where they will apply to the appropriate screen).

4. Next, the contents of any file specified by the shell environment variable XENVIRONMENT will be loaded.

   If this variable is not defined, the resource manager looks for a file named *.Xdefaults-**hostname*** in the user's home directory, where **hostname** is the name of the host where the client is running.

   These methods are used to set user- and machine-specific resources.

5. Any values specified on the command line with the `-xrm` option will be loaded for that instance of the program.

The resource specifications from these various sources will be loaded and merged according to the precedence rules described earlier in the section "Precedence Rules for Resource Specification."

The client will then merge these various defaults specified by the user with its own internal defaults, if any.

Finally, if the user has specified any options on the command line (other than with the -xrm option), these values will override those specified by resource defaults, regardless of their source.

Setting Resources for Color
Versus Monochrome Screens

Chances are you would specify different resources for a client running on a color screen than for a client running on a monochrome screen. Prior to Release 5, the resource manager could not apply different sets of color resources for different screen types. Release 5 offers two innovations to help users specify resources for both color and monochrome displays:

1. A resource variable called customization (class Customization), which can be used to invoke a special set of application defaults for color or monochrome screens.

2. Screen-specific resource databases. The *xrdb* program has been updated to sort resources according to screen specifics, making certain resources available on a per screen basis and other available globally.

The first innovation relies on the existence of customized application defaults files. A few of the standard Release 5 clients come with additional defaults files suitable for color screens; the system administrator would have to create them for other clients.

You can apply these customized application defaults files—or specify your own special defaults—on a per screen basis (number 2 above) using a particular syntax in your *.Xresources* file.

The following two sections explain how to access the available customized app-defaults files and how to set your own resource file so that custom defaults (the system's or your own) are applied in the appropriate circumstances.

Loading Custom Application Defaults Files

As introduced in Chapter 3, *Working in the X Environment*, several clients have so-called *application defaults files* that provide resource definitions for certain client features. The defaults used on a particular system combine with other factors (program internals, user-supplied resources, and command-line options, etc.) to determine how the client looks and behaves.

Application defaults files are generally kept in the directory */usr/lib/X11/app-defaults*. (This path can be reset using the XFILESEARCHPATH environment variable, but setting up and maintaining the app-defaults directory is usually the system administrator's responsibility.) App-defaults files are often named *Class* to match the class name of the client, but there are exceptions.

In order to deal with the limitations of having a single app-defaults file when clients might be displayed on either a color or monochrome screen, X developers have added the `customization` resource in R5. You can use this resource to specify an alternative application defaults file. Commonly this alternative file will be a list of color resources. The naming convention for a color app-defaults file is the name of the standard app-defaults file (generally the class name) followed by a hyphen and the word "color" (i.e., *Class-color*). A few standard R5 clients come with both a standard app-defaults file and also an alternative color file:

- bitmap

- editres

- xcalc

- xlogo

The *oclock* client comes with only one app-defaults file—called *Clock-color*. Note that this is an exception to the naming convention. *Clock* is the class name of the widget around which the *oclock* client is built.

With the exception of *oclock*, all of the app-defaults filenames follow the conventions outlined previously. Thus, the standard app-defaults file for *bitmap* is called *Bitmap* and the color file is called *Bitmap-color*. *xcalc* is shipped with two files called *XCalc* and *XCalc-color*, etc.

You invoke the color defaults for a single instance of a client program by using the `-customization` resource with the `-xrm` option and supplying the resource value `-color`, as in the following example:

```
bitmap -xrm "*customization:  -color" &
```

This command creates a *bitmap* window that uses the color defaults in *Bitmap-color*. This file provides the most vivid defaults of all the files currently included in the standard distribution.

The "color" defaults for *xcalc* are particularly uninteresting—all black, white and gray! Run the following command if you want to see for yourself.

```
xcalc -xrm "*customization:  -color" &
```

Depending on the particular defaults, if you run a "colorized" version of a client on a monochrome (or grayscale) screen, you may not be able to see all of the window's features. *xcalc* seems to be an exception. Even with color defaults, it should work fine on most screens.

When a client has both a standard and a custom defaults file, they usually do not have any conflicting specifications. In many cases, the custom file will begin with a line that invokes the standard file, which contains the more "global" defaults that can be applied regardless of the screen. The following line appears as the first specification in *Bitmap-color*, invoking the standard app-defaults:

```
#include "Bitmap"
```

It is possible for the system administrator to create files with defaults intended for monochrome screens. These files should generally be called *Class-mono*. You can then supply

-mono as the value to the customization resource:

```
bitmap -xrm "*customization:  -mono" &
```

A monochrome defaults file might be simply a symbolic link to the regular app-defaults file or it might provide other specifications. Note, however, that Release 5 of X provides no such "–mono" files.

Thus far, we've shown you how to access the customized resource files on your system from the command line. The next section describes how to make certain resources apply depending on the kind of screen you're using.

Setting Screen-specific Resources

If you would like certain color (or mono) defaults to be used whenever you're working on a color (or mono) screen, you can edit your *.Xresources* file so this happens. These screen-specific resources may be accessed from custom defaults files or may be settings you write yourself.

The following lines specify that *bitmap* should be run using the color app-defaults file *when the screen is color*. (The line #ifdef COLOR establishes this condition; #endif marks the end of the conditional.)

```
#ifdef COLOR
bitmap*customization:  -color
#endif
```

Remember that the file *Bitmap-color* begins by "including" the standard defaults file (*Bitmap*). When you use *xrdb* to load a resource file that conditionally calls *Bitmap-color*, the resource manager sorts those resources that rely on a color monitor from those that can be applied regardless of the monitor (i.e., globally). When you subsequently run the client, you get the defaults appropriate for the monitor you are using!

If you want all existing "–color" app-defaults files to be used, omit the client name:

```
#ifdef COLOR
*customization:  -color
#endif
```

Note that you're not limited to using the customized files in the app-defaults directory. You can also use #ifdef conditionals with your own resource specifications. The following example introduces another level of the conditional (using #else) that allows you to specify resources that only apply on a monochrome screen.

```
#ifdef COLOR
! Place your own color resource specifications here
*Background:    whitesmoke
*Foreground:    darkorchid
xclock*background:  lightseagreen
xclock*foreground:  navy
#else
! Place your own monochrome settings here
xclock*reverseVideo:  True
#endif
```

Note that you can include your own specifications *and* custom color files in the same conditional:

```
#ifdef COLOR
! Use any customized color app-defaults files
*customization:  -color
! And your own definitions
*Background:    whitesmoke
*Foreground:    darkorchid
xclock*background:  lightseagreen
xclock*foreground:  navy
#endif
```

Or you can have multiple conditionals in the same *.Xresources* file:

```
! You might place your own settings in one conditional
#ifdef COLOR
*Background:    whitesmoke
*Foreground:    darkorchid
xclock*background:  lightseagreen
xclock*foreground:  navy
#endif

! And place any customized app-defaults files in another conditional
#ifdef COLOR
*customization:  -color
#else
*customization:  -mono
#endif
```

Note that the preceding example invokes app-defaults files ending in "–mono" when the screen is not color. Unless these files exist, the color defaults will be applied regardless of the screen and you may not be able to see all of the window's features.

Testing and Editing Resources with editres

The *editres* (*resource editor*) client is another welcome Release 5 innovation. By now you have an idea of the potential complexities surrounding resource settings and how they are intrepreted. *editres* is most useful in helping you to examine the often complicated hierarchy of a client's widgets and to devise correct resource specifications. Using *editres* you can:

- Display and scan through the client's widget hierarchy.

- Display what resources may be set for a particular widget.

- Create resource specifications.

- Dynamically apply the new specifications to a client already running on the display!

- Write the new definitions to your own resource file.

editres can be incredibly helpful, but it is not simple to use. In the following sections, we provide a tutorial that gives you an idea of what *editres* can do, but we will not cover every feature.

Note that the usefulness of the program will be limited somewhat by your understanding of widgets and the resources that can be applied to them. *editres* will show you *all* the resources that can be set for a widget, but it will not differentiate between those you can set at the user level and those that must be set by programming routines. Use the client reference pages in Part Three and Appendix G, *Widget Resources*, to get a better idea of what resources you can set yourself.

Note also that *editres* can only work with certain clients—those that understand the so-called *editres protocol*. Most clients built using the Athena widget set will work with *editres*. A Motif Toolkit client may not be compatible. If you try to use *editres* with an incompatible client, the following message will be displayed in the *editres* window:

```
It appears that this client does not understand
the Editres Protocol.
```

What Widget Is That, Anyway?

Let's consider a scenario in which *editres* would be helpful to a user. This case happens to be actual and we won't even change the names. One of my co-workers, Jerry, was trying to make screen dumps of the *xmh* client,* but he found that the default font being used for the menus was too small. He wanted to change the font for menu text only, leaving the default font for command buttons, etc. The specification:

```
xmh*font:  bigger_font
```

would change the font in *every* widget for which a font could be set. We used *editres* to determine the particular widgets for which to set the font.

In order for *editres* to examine a client's widget hierarchy, the client must be running, so we ran both *xmh* and *editres*:

```
% xmh &
% editres &
```

Figure 11-4 shows the clients.

---

xmh is the X version of the *mh* mail handler. Part Three of this guide includes a reference page for *xmh*. For further information, see the Nutshell Handbook *Using mh and xmh*, written by Jerry Peek and also published by O'Reilly & Associates, Inc.

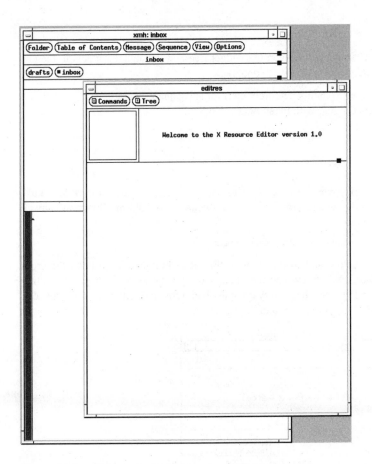

Figure 11-4. editres and xmh

editres Menus

editres provides two menus: Commands and Tree. To display a menu, place the pointer on the appropriate command button and press and hold down the first pointer button. Select an item by dragging the pointer down the menu and releasing on the item you want.

The most important things the Commands menu allows you to do are:

- Display a client's widget tree (Get Widget Tree);

- Access a subwindow (called the *resource box*) from which you can test, set, and save resource specifications (Show Resource Box);

- Quit *editres*.

The Tree menu helps you:

- Determine the correspondence between the widget tree and the actual widgets in the client (Select Active Widget; Flash Active Widgets).

- Select groups of widgets (parents, children, etc.) for subsequent operations (e.g., showing the widget in the actual client with Flash Active Widgets).

Displaying the Widget Tree

Now, how do we figure out what resource line to use to specify the font for *xmh* menus? First, we must display *xmh*'s widget tree. Select Get Widget Tree from the Commands menu and you will be prompted to

```
Click the mouse pointer on any Xaw client.
```

in the message window below and to the right of the menu buttons. Then click the cross pointer anywhere on the *xmh* window and the client's widget hierarchy is displayed in tree format in the *editres* window. *xmh* has a very complex hierarchy and only part of the tree can be viewed in the *editres* window, as shown in Figure 11-5.

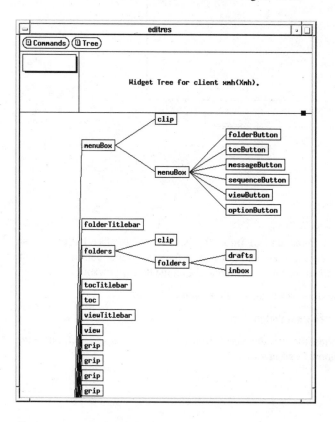

Figure 11-5. editres displays xmh's widget tree

Notice that the box beneath the menu command buttons has become smaller. This box is called the *panner* and it is actually a tool that allows you to scan the entire tree. The size and location of the panner in the larger square surrounding it suggests the portion of the widget tree that is visible—in this case, approximately the top third of the tree. To view the rest of the tree, place the pointer on the panner, hold the first pointer button and drag. The *editres* window scrolls to reveal the remaining widgets.

Tracking Down the Widgets

We're trying to set the font for *xmh* menu items like Open Folder on the Folder menu. Figure 11-5 displays a few widgets that sound as if they might be part of the menus. The menuBox widget and its children (to the right of it and connected to it by lines) seem promising. We can determine where the menuBox widget appears in the *xmh* application by performing the following actions:

1. Place the pointer on the menuBox square in the *editres* tree and click the first button. This action highlights the widget (which appears in reverse video); certain menu actions will affect only the highlighted widget(s).

2. Then select Flash Active Widgets from the Tree menu. The widget highlighed in the *editres* window will be "flashed" in the *xmh* window.

This action shows that the menuBox is the entire top portion of the *xmh* window—not even an individual menu. A look at the names of the widget's children, all of which end in Button, suggests that these are merely the menu command buttons and we have to examine the tree further to find the actual menu definitions.

Before scrolling, it's important to deselect the menuBox widget by clicking on it again. *editres* allows you to select multiple objects in order to perform certain operations, but we're only interested in one right now.

Figure 11-6 shows the *editres* window after we pan down to the more promising widget name folderMenu, the children of which seem to approximate this menu's choices.

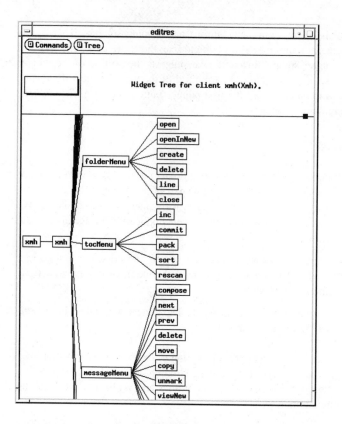

Figure 11-6. Middle portion of xmh's widget tree reveals menu items

Using the Resource Box to Create a Specification

Now we can try to write a resource to specify the font. First, select the folderMenu widget in the tree. Then select Show Resource Box from the Commands menu. The resource box subwindow appears on top of the main *editres* application window, as in Figure 11-7.

The resource box is fairly complicated, but we can determine one disappointing fact quickly. Neither list of resources it provides (Normal Resources and Constraint Resources) includes a font resource! Seems we're on the wrong track.

Click on the Popdown Resource Box button that appears in the lower righthand corner of the resource box. The box goes away. Now let's deselect folderMenu on the widget tree and instead try selecting one of its children, open, the widget of the first Folder menu item. Then select Show Resource Box from the Commands menu again. This time the resource box includes font under the list of Normal Resources (there are no constraint resources).

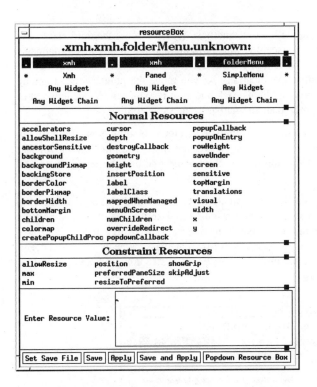

Figure 11-7. The editres resource box

Across the top of the resource box is a template resource specification for the selected widget, which at this stage shows the tightly bound instance name ending with an unknown resource variable. You can select the resource you want from the list in the box by highlighting it in the same way you did a widget in the tree—simply click the pointer on it. When we click on font, the unknown variable in the template is changed to font.

We still have to supply a value (a readable font), but first let's look at the specification more closely.

```
.xmh.xmh.folderMenu.open.font:
```

(Don't be confused by the two instances of xmh beginning the specification; the first represents the client and the second represents the next level widget in the client, which in this case has the same name! This is fairly unusual.) The folderMenu and open widgets suggest that this line would set the font for the Open Window item on the Folder Menu. But we need to specify a resource that will cover *all* menu items. At this point, you might be tempted to highlight the other menu item widgets in the tree, but if you do so and try to display the resource box again, you'll discover that the box can only be used when a single widget is highlighted.

Instead, *editres* provides a way for you to edit the template resource specification. Notice that below the template are four lines of text, the first one of which matches the full instance name in the template, with each component (including connectors) highlighted. The next line down shows the full class name with loose bindings. (We'll discuss the third and fourth lines in the next section.) As you can see, the four lines are spaced so that the components and connectors fall into columns. These lines provide four sets of alternatives for each of the components in the template resource specification. As you move the pointer around among the various choices, notice that a box highlights each one in turn. You can change any part of the template specification by clicking on an alternative in the same column.

For instance, to switch any tight binding in the template to a loose binding, you would simply click on the corresponding loose binding on the class name line. The highlighting for that column will be switched to loose binding on the class name line and the template will be redrawn to include the asterisk.

You can also replace any component in the template by clicking on the alternative component you want. Since we want to specify a font resource that applies to all menus, perhaps we should select the class name that corresponds to the folderMenu widget, Simple-Menu. When we click the pointer on SimpleMenu, that class name is highlighted and replaces folderMenu in the template line (folderMenu is also unhighlighted), as in Figure 11-8.

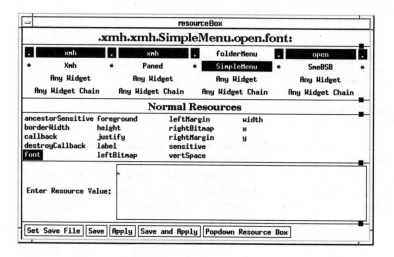

Figure 11-8. Edit the template resource by clicking on another component

Now we're close to the solution, but the open widget is still too specific. We then click on the corresponding class name, SmeBSB to produce the template line:

    .xmh.xmh.SimpleMenu.SmeBSB.font:

If we move the resource box away from the main *editres* window, we'll see that all of the widgets covered by this specification (i.e., those corresponding to the menu items) are now highlighted.

Now we must enter a value for this resource (a font name) in the text window near the lower right corner of the *editres* window. The phrase "Enter Resource Value:" appears to the left of the text window. To enter a value, place the pointer in the text window and type. (The text window is an instance of the Athena Text widget. To learn the valid editing commands, see "The xedit Text Editor" in Chapter 8, *Other Clients*.) We enter a fixed width font with the alias *7x14*.

Here's where *editres* comes in very handy. We can test our specification on the currently running *xmh* client. Just click on Apply, the third of five command buttons that appear along the bottom of the resource box. If the template resource can be applied successfully to the client in question, the message area to the right of the panner will display:

```
SetValues was Successful.
```

We verify that our new font resource has been incorporated into the running client by displaying one of the *xmh* menus and *7x14* seems large enough to reproduce well in the screen dump Jerry wants to make. Figure 11-9 shows one of the resulting screen dumps, borrowed from Jerry's book, *Using mh and xmh*.

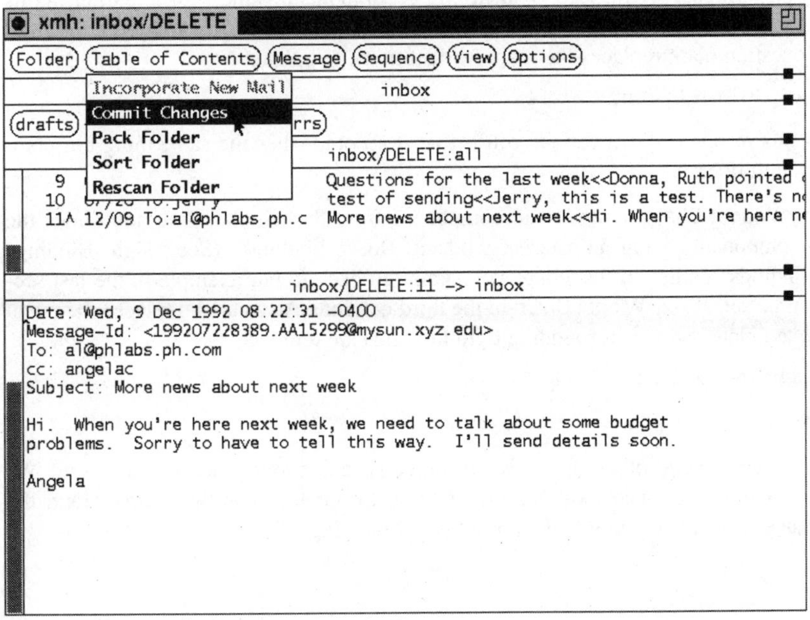

Figure 11-9. Custom font makes xmh menus readable in screen dump

All of the command buttons at the bottom of the resource box help you either "Apply" the custom resource specification to the running client or "Save" the specification in a resource file. Set Save File prompts you to specify the resource filename:

```
Enter file to dump resources into:
```

If you select any command with "Save" in it and haven't previously provided the filename, you will be prompted in the same way before the command proceeds.

Other Ways to Specify the Same Resource

Our sample resource line:

```
.xmh.xmh.SimpleMenu.SmeBSB.font:  7x14
```

will do for our purposes, but the following resources would accomplish the same result:

```
.xmh.xmh.?.SmeBSB.font:  7x14
.xmh.xmh*SmeBSB.font:  7x14
```

These resource specifications illustrate the use of the alternative components in the third and fourth lines below the template in the resource box. If you look back at Figure 10-5, you'll see that these lines offer the phrases Any Widget and Any Widget Chain as alternatives at every level in the resource specification.

Selecting Any Widget replaces the component with the question mark wildcard, which represents exactly one widget level. (See "Wildcarding a Component Name with ?" earlier in this chapter.) If you go back to our example in the last section and select Any Widget in the third column, the question mark replaces the menu widget in the template:

```
.xmh.xmh.?.SmeBSB.font:  7x14
```

If you apply this resource specification, you'll find it accomplishes the same thing our complete specification does.

Selecting Any Widget Chain removes the component from the template line and elides the surrounding components using an asterisk wildcard (loose binding). (See "Tight Bindings and Loose Bindings" earlier in this chapter.) Again, go back to our example in the last section and this time select Any Widget Chain in the third column. An asterisk replaces the menu widget in the template and the surrounding tight bindings are removed.

```
.xmh.xmh*SmeBSB.font:  7x14
```

Again, this resource accomplishes the same thing.

Of course, there are several other alternative resource specifications you could also use. We won't get into them here. The most important thing to remember is that *editres* (and the resource manager itself) allow you to do a bit of experimenting.

12

Specifying Color

This chapter gives an overview of the color names you can use in virtually any X environment. These names specify so-called RGB colors, which look different on different monitors. Release 5 introduces support for device-independent color. This chapter explains the principles behind these two "color models" and describes how to specify colors according to each model. It also explains how to create your own color database.

In This Chapter:

12
Specifying Color

What Color Names Can I Use?

As mentioned in Chapter 10, *Command-line Options*, specifying colors can become rather complicated, but you can also keep it simple. The next section ("Available RGB Colors") gives an overview of the basic color names you should be able to use in virtually any environment—without any system customization. If you think the set of predefined colors will be sufficient for your needs, you shouldn't have to read more than that section (and its subsections).

If you want to know more about color (including how to create a private database of your own colors), you'll need a little more background. X actually recognizes two "color models": a server-side (non-portable) RGB color model (primarily a database) and a client-side (device-independent) X Color Management System (Xcms). Keep in mind that you can use take advantage of both color models. (See "A Mixed Bag: Using both RGB and Xcms" for an explanation of precedence.) Xcms has been introduced in Release 5; if you are satisfied with the older RGB functionality, you can ignore Xcms. However, it does have many interesting and powerful capabilities. In the remainder of this section, we'll give you an overview of both of these models.

The RGB color model includes a database of color names which can be accessed by the server. This database exists in a readable form in a system file called *rgb.txt*, which generally lives in the directory */usr/lib/X11*. (Most of the color names you can think of—plus many esoteric names—are included in this database.) Within the *rgb.txt* file, each color name is associated with three numeric values, corresponding to the amount of red, green, and blue in the shade. The display hardware uses these values to produce a color. (For a more technical discussion of this color model, see "Beyond the Rainbow: Inside the Color Models" later in this chapter.)

The RGB model accepts color values in two different formats: color names from the database (which pairs names with decimal values for red, green, and blue); numeric color values in hexadecimal notation. (You can use either of these on command lines, in resource files, etc.) As we'll see later in this chapter, the hex values allow you to specify a wider spectrum of colors than is covered by the database.

From a user's standpoint, the advantages of the RGB database are:

- It provides a wide range of colors whose names you can simply plug in to command lines and resource specifications;

- It requires no customization, but allows customization if you're ambitious enough to want to come up with your own colors or tune existing ones. (Note, however, that since it is available on a system-wide basis, the RGB database is generally the private preserve of the system administrator.)

The primary disadvantage of the RGB database (and the model itself) is that the colors it defines can look very different on different types of display hardware. This is because the server accesses the database (or the numeric hex specifications) and simply applies the color values, without any tuning for the type of monitor, the platform, etc. Certain intensities of red, green, and blue might produce orange on one display and pink on another. In other words, RGB colors are hardware-specific and thus, non-portable.

We speculate that most users won't care too much if their "pink" is too "orangy" and will just experiment with other colors in the *rgb.txt* file to find shades they like. (The public domain *xcol* program, described in Chapter 8, will help you preview the *rgb.txt* colors for your monitor.)

If you are interested in coming up with your own colors, there are several public-domain "color editors" available. See Chapter 8, *Other Clients*, for instructions on using two of these clients, *xcoloredit* and *xtici*. Once you come up with your own shade, the RGB model allows you to either add the color name/value pair to the database (see "Changing the RGB Color Name Database" later in this chapter); or to specify the alternative color on the command line (or in a resource file) by providing its value in hexadecimal notation (see "Specifying RGB Colors as Hexadecimal Numbers"). Keep in mind, however, that a color in RGB format is *not* portable. If you use a variety of monitors, an RGB color (even one you create with a color editor) will look different on each of them.

If you're not entirely satisfied with the hardware-specific RGB model, an additional, more precise color model has been made available in Release 5. The X Color Management System (Xcms), developed by Tektronix (and now adopted by the X Consortium), is intended to overcome the limitations of the (still available) RGB model by providing *device-independent* color. Under Xcms, colors are based upon internationally recognized standards. The idea behind Xcms is that color relies upon human vision. Simply put, red should look basically the same on any monitor, under any platform.

Xcms accepts color values in several different formats, called *color spaces* (outlined later in this chapter). Most of these color spaces describe color in a device-independent manner, using scientific terms and values commonly applied to color. (For more information, see "The Xcms Color Spaces" later in this chapter.) Note, however, that Xcms will recognize an RGB color space—only the values are not portable.

From a user's standpoint, the primary advantages of Xcms are:

- It recognizes several types of color specification (color spaces), which can be supplied on the command line or in resource files.

- It enables you to make a database of colors you "mix" yourself, using a color editor. (While the server-side RGB model allows for a single system-wide database, Xcms allows any user to have a private database.) In the Xcms database, you pair a name with a value in any of the accepted color spaces (formats). The Xcms database can then serve as an alternative to the default RGB database (you can specify colors from either).

- Xcms can "tune" colors to display more accurately on specific hardware. (Some X terminals are configured to do this automatically; on most other displays, you need to install a special file to perform this tuning. For more information, see "The X Color Management System" later in this chapter.)

- Xcms allows users to take advantage of sophisticated color printer technology.

If you're at all interested in coming up with your own colors, it's worth reading more about Xcms (later in this chapter) and learning how to create your own database. Your system administrator might also want to create a system-wide Xcms database. (See "Creating an Xcms Color Database" later in this chapter for details.)

But before we go any deeper into the technology of color, let's take a look at the simplest source of color specifications: the RGB database. Then we'll consider the Xcms color spaces (formats), which have been made available in Release 5. Finally, we'll take a more technical look behind the color models and learn how to make additional color names available under either model. If you want to customize the RGB database or possibly create an Xcms database of your own, read the relevant sections.

Available RGB Colors

As previously mentioned, the server-side RGB color model allows you to specify colors using either:

- Text names from the standard database (*rgb.txt* file);

- Numeric color values in hexadecimal notation.

The simplest way to specify colors for your display is to look over the *rgb.txt* file and pick some names. The many colors defined in this file are probably more than most users will need.

Specifying a color as a hexadecimal number comes in handy when you've used a color editor, such as *xcoloredit*, to create a new shade and the program gives its output in hex. Chapter 8, *Other Clients*, describes how to use *xcoloredit*. The section "Changing the RGB Color Name Database" later in this chapter describes how to add one of these new colors to the *rgb.txt* file so that you can access it by a name.

The following sections give you an idea what colors are available in the RGB database. Then we'll take a look at specifying a color as a hex value.

Surveying the RGB Database: rgb.txt

The *rgb.txt* file, usually located in */usr/lib/X11*, is supplied with the standard distribution of X and consists of predefined color values (in decimal notation) assigned to specific text names. Corresponding compiled files called *rgb.dir* and *rgb.pag* contain the definitions used by the server; these machine-readable files serves as a color name database. The *rgb.txt* file is the human-readable equivalent.

The default *rgb.txt* file shipped with Release 5 of X contains 738 color name definitions. This number is slightly deceptive, since a number of the color names are merely variants of another color name (differing only in spelling, spacing, and capitalization). Still others are shades of the same color:

```
light sea green
sea green
medium sea green
dark sea green
SeaGreen1
SeaGreen2
SeaGreen3
SeaGreen4
DarkSeaGreen1
DarkSeaGreen2
DarkSeaGreen3
DarkSeaGreen4
```

Each of these names corresponds to a color definition (of three RGB values). (This list does not include the variant syntax names SeaGreen, LightSeaGreen, MediumSeaGreen, and DarkSeaGreen, which also appear in the file.) As you can see, some of these shades are distinguished in the fairly traditional way of being called "light," "medium," and "dark." The light, medium, and dark shades of a color can probably be distinguished from one another on virtually any monitor.

Beyond this distinction, there are what might be termed "sub-shades": gradations of a particular shade identified by number (SeaGreen1, SeaGreen2, etc.). Numerically adjacent sub-shades of a color may not be clearly distinguishable on all monitors. For example, Sea-Green1 and 2 may look very much the same. (You certainly would not choose to create a window with a SeaGreen1 background and SeaGreen2 foreground! On the other hand, sub-shades a couple of numbers apart are probably sufficiently different to be used on the same window.)

By supplying many different shades of a single, already fairly precise color like sea green, X developers have tried to provide definitions that work well on a variety of commonly used monitors.* You may have to experiment to determine which colors (or shades) display best on your monitor. (For *device-independent* color, use the Xcms color model.)

---

*The color database shipped with prior releases of X was originally designed to display optimally on the vt240 series terminals manufactured by Digital Equipment Corporation.

The color names in the *rgb.txt* file are too numerous to list here. Although there are no literal dividers within the file, it can roughly be considered to fall into three sections:

Section 1: A standard spectrum of colors (red, yellow, sea green, powder blue, hot pink, etc.), which seem to be ordered roughly as: off-whites and other pale colors, grays, blues, greens, yellows, browns, oranges, pinks, reds, and purples.

Section 2: Sub-shades of Section 1 colors (such as SeaGreen 1 through 4). These sub-shades make up the largest part of the file.

Section 3: One hundred and one additional shades of gray, numbered 0 through 100. This large number of precisely graduated grays provides a wide variety of shading for grayscale displays.

Rather than list every color in the *rgb.txt* file, we've compiled this table of representative colors. We've chosen some of the more esoteric color names. Naturally all of the primary and secondary colors are also available.

Section 1:

ghost white	peach puff	lavender blush	lemon chiffon
slate gray	midnight blue	cornflower blue	medium slate blue
dodger blue	powder blue	turquoise	pale green
lawn green	chartreuse	olive drab	lime green
khaki	light yellow	goldenrod	peru
sienna	sandy brown	salmon	coral
tomato	hot pink	maroon	violet red
magenta	medium orchid	blue violet	purple

Section 2:

snow1 - 4	bisque1 - 4	cornsilk1 - 4	honeydew1 -4
azure1 - 4	SteelBlue1 - 4	DeepSkyBlue1 - 4	LightCyan1 - 4
PaleTurquoise1 - 4	aquamarine1 - 4	PaleGreen1 - 4	DarkOliveGreen1 - 4
SpringGreen1 -4	gold1 - 4	RosyBrown1 - 4	burlywood1 - 4
chocolate1 - 4	firebrick1 - 4	DarkOrange1 - 4	OrangeRed1 - 4
DeepPink1 - 4	PaleVioletRed1 - 4	plum1 - 4	DarkOrchid1 - 4

Section 3:

gray0 (grey0) through gray100 (grey100)

If you want to look more closely at the *rgb.txt* file, you can open it with any text editor. As an alternative, you can display the contents of the file using the *showrgb* client. *showrgb* seems to do nothing more than *cat*(1) the file to your terminal window. In fact, it consults the database (*dbm*) version of the file. Given the size of the database, it's necessary to pipe the command's output to a paging program, such as *pg*(1) or *more*(1), as shown below:

```
% showrgb | more
```

Be aware that *showrgb* will display the color names in a different order than they appear in *rgb.txt*. See "Changing the RGB Color Name Database" for information on customizing the RGB color name definitions.

Keep in mind that RGB colors look different on different monitors. (Later in this chapter, we'll take a closer look at the Xcms Color Management System, which provides device-independent color capabilities.) The *xcol* client, from the user-contributed distribution, allows you to display the colors defined in the *rgb.txt* file. *xcol* can also be used to edit the color specifications in a resource file. See Chapter 8, *Other Clients*, and the *xcol* client reference page in Part Three of this guide.

Alternative Release 5 RGB Color Databases

In addition to the standard color database described previously, Release 5 also includes three other databases your system administrator can compile. These files can be found in the general release in the directory *mit/rgb/others*.

raveling.txt   Designed by Paul Raveling, this database rivals the default database in size and scope but was tuned to display optimally on Hewlett-Packard monitors.

thomas.txt   Based on the Release 3 database, this file has been modified by John Thomas of Tektronix to approximate the colors in a box of Crayola Crayons.

old-rgb.txt   This is nothing more than the Release 3 database.

Specifying RGB Colors as Hexadecimal Numbers

Each RGB color has a numeric value associated with it. In the *rgb.txt* file, these values are in decimal notation—the base 10 numbering system with which most of us are familiar—and they are paired with a color name. But the RGB model also allows you to specify a color using *only* a number—in an alternative format known as hexadecimal notation. Hex is a base 16 numbering system used in many scientific disciplines. We'll discuss the system in more depth in "The RGB Color Model" later in this chapter.

Being able to specify a color by a numeric value means that you can be very precise. It also means that you can define virtually an infinite number of shades—certainly far more than is practical to define in a database like *rgb.txt*. Of course, it's also only practical to *use* a certain number of colors and hardware provides its own limitations. (See "How Many Colors Are Available?" for a clearer idea.)

Being able to supply hex values comes in very handy if you're using a color editor, such as *xcoloredit* (described in Chapter 8). When you "mix" your own color using *xcoloredit*, the program outputs the numeric color value in hexadecimal notation. For example, in Chapter 8 we came up with a bright shade of blue with the hex value:

```
09e5fb
```

We can then supply this number on the command line or in a resource file, prefixed with a pound sign (#), as in the following example:

```
xbiff -fg #09e5fb &
```

On our Sun monitor (remember, RGB values are hardware-specific), this command line produces an *xbiff* window with a bright blue mailbox. The following line from a resource file would have the same effect.

```
xbiff*foreground: #09e5fb
```

See "Changing the RGB Color Name Database" for instructions on converting hex to decimal and pairing these values with names in the *rgb.txt* file. For more about the RGB model and how hex numbering works, see "The RGB Color Model" later in this chapter.

The Xcms Color Spaces

As of Release 5, you are not limited to supplying colors from the *rgb.txt* file or providing hex equivalents of RGB colors. The X Color Management System recognizes color specifications in many different formats called *color spaces*. Most of these formats reflect international standards. (Xcms also recognizes RGB decimal values, though these remain device-specific). This section gives an overview of the valid color spaces.

As with the server-side RGB model, you can supply the Xcms color spaces on the command line and in resource files. You can also create a custom color database. (Note that the standard colors from *rgb.txt* will still be available.) See "Creating an Xcms Color Database" for instructions.

Under Xcms, each color specification has a prefix (some shorthand for the color space) and a numeric value. Table 12-1 summarizes the valid color spaces and their prefixes.

Table 12-1. Xcms Color Spaces

Name	Prefix
Tektronix HVC	TekHVC
various CIE formats	CIEXYZ, CIEuvY, CIExyY, CIELab, CIELuv
RGB	RGB
RGB Intensity	RGBi

Tektronix is the developer of the X Color Management System. The initials HVC refer to hue, value, and chroma, scientific characteristics of color. (See "Creating Your Own Colors: xcoloredit and xtici" in Chapter 8, *Other Clients*, for more information.) CIE stands for *Commission Internationale de l'Eclairage* or *International Commission on Illumination*, an international standards organization.

Of the valid color spaces, the Tektronix HVC and the various CIE formats specify color in a device-independent manner. The RGB color spaces specify color that is hardware-specific. To take advantage of the portability of the X Color Management System, you will want to use TekHVC or any of the CIE formats. Xcms recognizes RGB specifications for compatibility with the older RGB color model.

When you create a shade with a color editor, such as *xcoloredit* or *xtici*, the program supplies you with a numeric color value in one or sometimes multiple formats. To specify the color under Xcms, you combine the numeric value with the appropriate prefix for the color space/format. The syntax is:

```
prefix:value1/value2/value3
```

The following are sample Xcms color specifications:

```
CIEuvY:0.15259/0.40507/0.44336
TekHVC:223.93036/72.45283/29.67013
RGB:6a/bb/d8
```

These three sample values were derived from *xtici* (being run on a Sun 3/60 workstation); the values all define the deeper version of sky blue from the tutorial in Chapter 8, each using a different notation.* Keep in mind that the RGB value is specific to the monitor used, while the TekHVC and CIEuvY values are portable. We can supply *any* of these color spaces on our Sun 3/60 and get the same color. Thus, the following command lines should produce identical *xbiff* windows:

```
xbiff -fg CIEuvY:0.15259/0.40507/0.44336 &
xbiff -fg TekHVC:223.93036/72.45283/29.67013 &
xbiff -fg RGB:6a/bb/d8 &
```

(Note that the Xcms color spaces are case insensitive. Thus, `rgb:6a/bb/d8` and `RGB:6A/BB/D8` are equivalent.) If we want to display this shade of blue on another monitor, we would have to use either of the portable specifications:

```
CIEuvY:0.15259/0.40507/0.44336 &
TekHVC:223.93036/72.45283/29.67013 &
```

You can also use any valid color space as the value of a resource variable:

```
xbiff*foreground: TekHVC:223.93036/72.45283/29.67013
```

It's handy to be able to plug these numbers into a command line or resource specification, but if you want to use your own colors on a regular basis, it's a good idea to pair them with names in your own Xcms database. First read a bit more about Xcms later in this chapter. Then see "Creating an Xcms Color Database" for instructions.

---

xtici outputs each of the three color spaces (CIEuvY, TekHVC, and RGB) in a format Xcms understands, but handles RGB values in a somewhat confusing manner. It accepts input (and displays the RGB values) in decimal notation, but outputs RGB hex values (when you request the RGB values via the Edit menu). You can use decimal numbers in the RGB server-side color database (*rgb.txt* file; see "Changing the RGB Color Name Database"); however, you should use hexadecimal notation for Xcms to recognize the values on the command line, in a resource file, or in an Xcms database (described in "Creating an Xcms Color Database"). "Finding the Color Values" provides instructions on performing this conversion exclusive of the color editor—using the UNIX *bc*(1) utility.

A Mixed Bag: Using Both RGB and Xcms

All this talk of color models can get pretty confusing. But take heart. Even if you use both, in practice you shouldn't have to think too much about it. You can supply color specifications in any form acceptable to either color model and X will resolve any possible conflicts.

X searches to match a color specification in this order:

1. If it begins with the pound sign (#), the subsequent number is interpreted as a hexadecimal RGB value.

2. If it contains a colon (:), the prefix is checked to see if it matches a valid color space; if it does, the subsequent number is interpreted as a value in that color space. All currently valid color spaces recognize the forward slash (/) as the delimiter between numeric values. (Each color space defines its own delimeter, so hypothetically new formats may recognize other delimeters.)

3. If the color specification contains neither a pound sign or a colon, it is assumed to be a color name that should appear in either an Xcms database or the RGB server database. (The Xcms database is checked first, so if a color name appears in both databases, the Xcms color value is applied.)

Beyond the Rainbow: Inside the Color Models

The following sections take a more technical look at the two color models. If you want to edit the RGB database or create an Xcms database of your own, this information might be helpful. Keep in mind, however, that the X Color Management System is far beyond the scope of this guide. For some additional information, see Volume Eight, *X Window System Administrator's Guide*.

The RGB Color Model

Most color displays on the market today are based on the RGB color model. Each pixel on the screen is actually made up of three phosphors: one red, one green, and one blue. Each of these three phosphors is illuminated by a separate electron beam, called a *color gun*. These color guns can be lit to different intensities to produce different colors on the screen.

When all three phosphors are fully illuminated, the pixel appears white to the human eye. When all three are dark, the pixel appears black. When the illumination of each primary color varies, the three phosphors generate a subtractive color. For example, equal portions of red and green, with no admixture of blue, makes yellow.

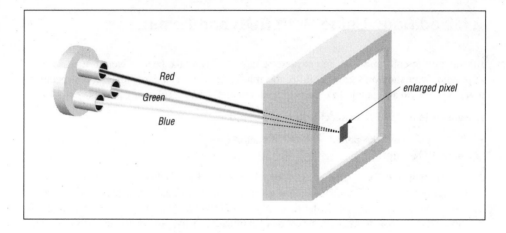

Figure 12-1. Red, green, and blue color guns

As you might guess, the intensity of each primary color is controlled by a numeric value. In the *rgb.txt* file, each color is associated with a decimal number between 0 and 255. Consider the following line from the *rgb.txt* file:

```
173 216 230          light blue
```

The three numbers make up what is known as an *RGB triplet*. As we've seen, the *rgb.txt* file contains 738 mappings of RGB triplets to color names. Inherent in this system is a limitation: a color name is associated with hard-coded intensities of red, green, and blue; these intensities may look different on different displays and under different implementations of the X server. (The X Color Management System transcends these limitations.)

An RGB triplet can also be supplied in hexadecimal notation, which can afford greater precision than the decimal values in *rgb.txt*. Depending on the underlying hardware, different servers may use a larger or smaller number of bits (from 4 to 16) to describe the intensity of each primary. To insulate you from this variation, most clients are designed to take color values containing anywhere from 4 to 16 bits (1 to 4 hex digits), and the server then scales them to the hardware. As a result, you can specify hexadecimal values in any one of these formats:

```
#RGB
#RRGGBB
#RRRGGGBBB
#RRRRGGGGBBBB
```

where R, G, and B represent single hexadecimal digits and determine the intensity of the red, green, and blue primaries that make up each color.

When fewer than four digits are used, they represent the most significant bits of the value. For example, #3a6 is the same as #3000a0006000.*

---

*If you are unfamiliar with hexadecimal numbering, see the Glossary for a brief explanation or a basic computer text-book for a more extended discussion.

What this means concretely is perhaps best illustrated by looking at the values that correspond to some colors in the color name database. We'll use 8-bit values—two hexadecimal digits for each primary. These definitions are the hexadecimal equivalents of the decimal values for some of the colors found in the *rgb.txt* file:

#000000	black
#FFFFFF	white
#FF0000	red
#00FF00	green
#0000FF	blue
#FFFF00	yellow
#00FFFF	cyan
#FF00FF	magenta
#5F9EA0	cadet blue
#6495ED	cornflower blue
#ADD8E6	light blue
#B0C4DE	light steel blue
#0000CD	medium blue
#000080	navy blue
#87CEED	sky blue
#6A5ACE	slate blue
#4682B4	steel blue

As you can see from the colors previously given, pure red, green, and blue result from the corresponding bits being turned on fully. Turning all primaries off yields black, while turning all nearly full on produces white. Yellow, cyan, and magenta can be created by pairing two of the other primaries at full intensity. The various shades of blue shown previously are created by varying the intensity of each primary—sometimes in unexpected ways.

Of course, fiddling with the numbers is fairly unintuitive. If you want to play with color, use a color editor. *xcoloredit* supplies its output in hex. See Chapter 8, *Other Clients*, for instructions.

The X Color Management System

As previously described, the X Color Management System is intended to provide device-independent color. There are actually two components to the system:

- The color spaces or formats (which should look the same on any system);

- *Device Color Characterization* (DCC) data that "tunes" color specifications for a particular hardware display.

We've already taken a look at some of the valid color spaces. If you specify a color using one of the portable Xcms color spaces, you should get the same color regardless of the monitor, server, etc.

Application developers may choose to fine tune Xcms colors for a particular hardware display by additionally installing a *Device Color Characterization* (*DCC*) file (also called a *Device Profile*). This tuning is an optional part of the system. You would probably need two adjacent monitors to see the difference between a system accessing DCC data and one not. The color spaces alone should be sufficient for most users. If you are interested in installing

DCC data, the section "Device-Specific tuning" offers some tips. See Volume Eight, *X Window System Administrator's Guide*, for more information.

How Many Colors Are Available on My Screen?

Regardless of the "model" you use to specify colors, the number of distinct colors available on the screen at any one time depends on the amount of memory available for color specification. (The *xdpyinfo* client provides information about a display, including the number of colors available at one time. See Chapter 8, *Other Clients*, and the *xdpyinfo* reference page in Part Three of this guide for details.)

A color display uses multiple bits per pixel (also referred to as multiple planes or the *depth* of the display) to select colors. Programs that draw in color use the value of these bits as a pointer to a lookup table called a *colormap*, in which each entry (or *colorcell*) contains the RGB values for a particular color.* (Xcms translates its device-independent values into the equivalent RGB values appropriate for the particular monitor.) As shown in Figure 12-2, any given pixel value is used as an index into this table—for example, a pixel value of 16 will select the 16th colorcell.

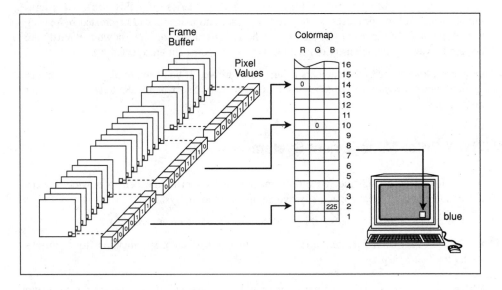

Figure 12-2. Multiple planes used to index a colormap

Why is this technical detail important? Because it explains several issues that you might encounter in working with color displays.

---

*There is a type of high-end display in which pixel values are used directly to control the illumination of the red, green, and blue phosphors. But far more commonly the bits per pixel are used indirectly with the actual color values specified independently.

First, the range of colors possible on the display is a function of the number of bits available in the colormap for RGB specification. If 8 bits are available for each primary, then the range of possible colors is 256^3 (more than 16 million colors). This means that you can create incredibly precise differences between colors.

However, the number of different colors that can be displayed on the screen at any one time is a function of the number of planes. A four-plane system can index 2^4 colorcells (16 distinct colors); an 8-plane system can index 2^8 colorcells (256 distinct colors); and a 24-plane system can index 2^{24} colorcells (more than 16 million distinct colors).

If you are using a 4-plane workstation, the fact that you can precisely define hundreds of different shades of blue is far less significant than the fact that you can't use them all at the same time. There isn't space for all of them to be stored in the colormap at one time or any mechanism for them to be selected even if they could be stored.

This limitation is made more significant by the fact that X is a multi-client environment. When X starts up, usually no colors are loaded into the colormap. As clients are invoked, certain of these cells are allocated. But when all of the free colorcells are used up, it is no longer possible to request new colors. When this happens, you will usually be given the closest possible color from those already allocated. However, you may instead be given an error message and told that there are no free colorcells.

In order to minimize the chance of running out of colorcells, many programs use *shared* colorcells. Shared colorcells can be used by any number of applications but they can't be changed by any of them. They can only be deallocated by each application that uses them, and when all applications have deallocated the cell, it is available for setting one again. Shared cells are most often used for background, border, and cursor colors.

Alternately, some clients have to be able to change the color of graphics they have already drawn. This requires another kind of cell, called *private*, which can't be shared. A typical use of a private cell would be for the palette of a color-mixing application, such as *xcoloredit*. This program has three bars of each primary color and a box that shows the mixed color. The primary bars use shared cells, while the mixed color box uses a private cell.

In summary, some programs define colorcells to be read-only and sharable, while others define colorcells to be read/write and private.

To top it off, there are even clients that may temporarily swap in a private colormap of their own. If this happens, all other applications will be displayed in unexpected colors because of the way color is implemented.

In order to minimize such conflicts, you should request unique numerical colors only when necessary. By preference, use color names or numerical specifications that you've given for other applications.

Adding New Color Names

Both the server-side RGB color model and the X Color Management System allow you to specify a color as a numeric value. Since it's much simpler to use a color name, both models also allow for a database in which numeric values are paired with names.

We've already considered the advantages and limitations of the RGB and Xcms color models. Most importantly, Xcms offers the advantage of portability: the color specifications are intended to be device-independent (i.e., they should look the same on any display hardware).

When you come up with your own color using a color editing program, such as *xtici* or *xcoloredit*, you'll know how that shade is going to look on your screen. If the value you come up with is a one of the portable Xcms color spaces, the color should look the same on any screen. If you intend to use that color multiple times, you'll probably want to pair it with a name in a database. The following sections describe how to edit the default RGB database or to create an Xcms database.

Although creating a color database can be very useful, keep in mind one less than obvious limitation: no color database can be accessed across the network. In other words, if you create an Xcms color database on your own workstation, you can't use any of those color definitions in a remote process. This limitation has nothing to do with whether a particular color specification is portable. A portable color should look the same on any system—but you have to specify the color on that system or have access to the color definition in a database local to the client.

Changing the RGB Color Name Database

The X Window System comes with a predefined set of colors, listed in the file */usr/lib/X11/rgb.txt*. As we've seen, you can use these color names to specify colors either on the command line or in a resource file. If you have access to a color editing program, such as *xtici* or *xcoloredit*, you can also come up with your own colors and add them to the RGB database.

Finding the Color Values

Each color in the RGB database has a name and a three-component numeric value, in decimal form. The fact that *xtici* displays the RGB values in the necessary decimal form is at least one advantage to using this program to come up with your own color(s). (See Chapter 8, *Other Clients*, for instructions on using *xtici*.) If you have a color value consisting of three decimal numbers, you can skip to the next section "Editing and Compiling the RGB Database."

xcoloredit outputs the color value in hexadecimal numbers. If you use *xcoloredit* (or a similar program), you must convert the numbers to decimal before adding the color to the *rgb.txt* file. An easy way to perform this conversion is with the UNIX *bc*(1) program, as in the following example.

Say we have a bright shade of blue with the hex value #09E5FB.

- Enter *bc* and press Return.

  ```
  % bc
  ```

- You can now enter the commands to do the conversion. Set the base of input to 16 (hexadecimal notation has base 16; *bc*'s output defaults to base 10, i.e., decimal).

  ```
  ibase=16
  ```

- Then enter the hex numbers you want to convert, separated by semicolons; the letters in the hex notations must be in uppercase.

  ```
  09;E5;FB
  ```

  When you press Return, *bc* gives the decimal values for the three color components (RGB):

  ```
  9
  229
  251
  ```

- Type Control-D to quit *bc*.

Note that to convert decimal to hexadecimal, you would skip the `ibase` line; instead specify output as base 16 (`obase=16`); enter the decimal numbers (as you did the hex above); and press Return.

Perhaps a more roundabout way to convert decimal to hex involves the *xtici* client. *xtici* accepts RGB input in decimal notation, but outputs RGB values in hex. See Chapter 8 for details.

Editing and Compiling the Database

Once you have the decimal values for red, green, and blue, you pair them with a color name—we'll call our color tropical blue—and add the color definition to the *rgb.txt* source file. This file is located in the directory *mit/rgb* in the X11 source tree. (Note that you must have write permission for the source files. If you're working on a multi-user system, you'll probably need to speak to the system administrator. If you don't have the source files, consult Volume Eight, *X Window System Administrator's Guide*, for instructions on obtaining them.)

The format of a line in the *rgb.txt* file is:

```
red green blue    color_name
```

where *red*, *green*, and *blue* are integers in the range 0 to 255; the *color_name* is case insensitive but must not include any special characters or symbols. There must be a tab separating the values from the name.

If the color name is composed of two or more words, the color should have two entries, one as multiple words and one as a single word. For example:

```
124 252  0     lawn green
124 252  0     LawnGreen
```

These entries allow you to use either a one- or two-word color name on the command line or in a resource file. (When you use multiple words, they must be surrounded by double quotes. See Chapter 10, *Setting Resources*, for more information about color specifications.)

To update the RGB database, use the following steps:

1. Edit the *rgb.txt* source file (from *mit/rgb*) to add the new color specification(s) (or change existing ones). The new line(s) can go anywhere in the file. Our new color requires the entries:

   ```
   9 229 251      tropical blue
   9 229 251      TropicalBlue
   ```

   If we used a one-word name, a single line would do:

   ```
   9 229 251      caribbean
   ```

2. Run the *rgb* program using the makefile also located in the *mit/rgb* directory. This program converts the text file (*rgb.txt*) to the UNIX *dbm*(1) format files (*rgb.dir* and *rgb.pag*), which are the files actually used as the color database. Just type:

   ```
   % make
   rm -f rgb.pag rgb.dir
   ./rgb rgb < rgb.txt
   ```

3. Then install the new files in */usr/lib/X11* by typing:

   ```
   % make install
   install -c -m 0644 rgb.txt /usr/lib/X11
   install -c -m 0644 rgb.dir /usr/lib/X11
   install -c -m 0644 rgb.pag /usr/lib/X11
   install -c -s showrgb /usr/lib/X11
   install in ./rgb done
   ```

Any colors you've added (or edited) should now be available.

Three alternative color databases are available in the X11 source in the subdirectory *mit/rgb/others*. See "Alternative Release 5 RGB Color Databases" earlier in this chapter and the README file in the source directory for details.

Fixing a Corrupted RGB Database

If the color name database gets corrupted in some way (e.g., written to accidentally), the server may not be able to find any colors with which to display. On a monochrome display, you may get error messages similar to the following:

```
X Toolkit Warning:  Cannot allocate colormap entry for White
X Toolkit Warning:  Cannot allocate colormap entry for Black
```

```
X Toolkit Warning:   Cannot allocate colormap entry for white
X Toolkit Warning:   Cannot allocate colormap entry for black
```

If you get errors of this sort, perform steps 2 and 3 in the procedure described above. This will overwrite the corrupted *rgb* database files.

Creating an Xcms Color Database

Once you have some valid color spaces, creating a Xcms color database is easy—much simpler than editing the RGB database. See Chapter 8, *Other Clients*, for instructions on using the *xtici* color editor, and "The Xcms Color Spaces" earlier in this chapter.

The format of the Xcms database file is:

```
XCMS_COLORDB_START 0.1
color_name<tab>color_space
                .
                .
                .
XCMS_COLORDB_END
```

The first and last lines are literal. Don't forget the 0.1 at the end of the first line; it's important. Between the first and last lines you can put any number of color definitions. The text name goes in the first column, followed by a tab (this is also important), and then a valid color space. Note that the arrangement of the columns is the opposite of that in the *rgb.txt* file, in which the numeric values come first and the text name second.

A system administrator might choose to create an Xcms database that all users can access in the directory */usr/lib/X11* (where *rgb.txt* also generally lives). In this case, the database file should be named *Xcms.txt*. (As we'll see, a user's own Xcms database can have any name.)

Here is a sample database file:

```
XCMS_COLORDB_START 0.1
orchid              TekHVC:315.8/83.8/24.5
cobalt              TekHVC:238.3/68.3/30.6
tropical blue       CIEuvY:0.140/0.412/0.615
beach glass         TekHVC:158.2/86.0/15.6
mustard             CIEuvY:0.227/0.538/0.608
XCMS_COLORDB_END
```

The color names are case-insensitive (for example, "orchid," "Orchid," "ORCHID," and "ORchId" are equivalent).

In our sample database, we've used all portable color specifications, but you can include RGB color spaces as well. (Of course, the RGB specifications will be subject to hardware differences.)

Once *Xcms.txt* is set up, you can specify any of the color names it contains. (Unlike the *rgb.txt* file, no compilation is necessary.) Thus, you can immediately enter the command line:

```
% xsetroot -solid beachglass &
```

Multiple word color names must be specified as a single word or be surrounded by quotes.

By default, Xcms looks for */usr/lib/X11/Xcms.txt*. You can specify an alternative database file by setting the XCMSDB environment variable. This enables every user to have a private color database. Note, however, that Xcms will check only *one* database. If you set XCMSDB to another file, Xcms will not check */usr/lib/X11/Xcms.txt*. (In other words, you cannot specify your own private colors and also take advantage of system-wide Xcms definitions.)

You can call your private Xcms database any name you like; then set the XCMSDB environment variable to the full pathname of the file. For example, say you create some colors you like to use in your normal X session (for the root window, window frames, etc.). You might put these into an Xcms file called *.xcolors*. Then specify:

```
% setenv XCMSDB ~/.xcolors
```

If you're going to be logging on to the same machine consistently, you can put this line in your session file (generally *.xsession* or *.xinitrc*). Of course, you can set XCMSDB to another file any time you like.

Device-Specific Tuning

The X Color Management System provides for display-specific fine tuning in the form of a *Device Color Characterization* (*DCC*) file (also known as a *Device Profile*). The data provided in this file should be specific to the manufacturer, model, size, and screen type of your color monitor. For most users, this fine tuning will be unnecessary. You would probably need two adjacent monitors to perceive the fine adjustments DCC can provide. However, an application developer might choose to install a DCC file.

The DCC data is stored in properties on the screen's root window. Some servers are able to automatically load the properties with data appropriate to the attached display(s). For servers that are built from MIT source, you will probably have to load the DCC data by hand. The *xcmsdb* client that comes with the MIT source distribution will load the DCC data from a text file you specify.

There are two sample DCC files in the directory *mit/clients/xcmsdb/datafiles*, for two types of Tektronix monitors. If you have the MIT X11R5 user-contributed source code available, the directory *contrib/clients/xcrtca/monitors* contains additional DCC files for many commercially available displays:

```
Apollo19.dcc    NWP-513.dcc     Sparc2-19.dcc   VR290.dcc       VR299.dcc
Apple13.dcc     SGI-PI19.dcc    Sun3-60.dcc     VR297-0.dcc
HP98782A.dcc    Sparc1-19.dcc   Trini19.dcc     VR297-1.dcc
```

In addition to these DCC files, the directory contains files with *.ca100* extensions. These files represent an intermediary step between raw color data and the actual DCC files. See Volume Eight, *X Window System Administrator's Guide*, for more information.

The top portion of a DCC file (following some comments) gives a description of the monitor. The following lines appear in the file *Sparc1-19.dcc*:

```
SCREENDATA_BEGIN        0.3

    NAME                Sun SPARCstation 1 19" color monitor
    PART_NUMBER         3
    MODEL               Hitachi HM-4119-S-AA-0, July 1989
```

```
SCREEN_CLASS        VIDEO_RGB
REVISION            2.0
        .
        .
        .
```

The remainder of the file provides data about the monitor's color capabilities. This data is loaded into the root window properties and then plugged into Xcms functions, allowing each device-independent color value to be converted into a device-specific value. You load a DCC file using the program *xcmsdb*. For example, if you have a Hitachi 19" color monitor on your Sun SparcStation 1, you would use the command:

```
% xcmsdb Sparc1-19.dcc
```

You would typically want to load the DCC file in your startup script (commonly *.xinitrc* or *.xsession*). See Appendix A, *System Management*, for guidelines on writing a startup script.

Keep in mind that this type of color correction may be completely unnecessary for you. For more information, see Volume Eight, *X Window System Administrator's Guide*.

13

Customizing mwm

This chapter describes the syntax of the .mwmrc *startup file that can be used to customize the operation of the* mwm *window manager. It describes how to bind functions to keys and how to define your own* mwm *menus. This chapter also explains how to set up* mwm *to use an icon box, a window in which icons on the display can be organized.*

In This Chapter:

13
Customizing mwm

The Motif window manager is one of the more flexible window managers available in the X market today. As we saw in Chapter 3 and Chapter 4, *mwm* provides a wide variety of methods for managing windows (i.e., moving, resizing, iconifying, etc.). In addition, virtually every feature of *mwm* can be customized. You can change the appearance of window frames, icons, and menus, the functions available on the Root Menu and the Window Menu, the keyboard focus policy, how icons are arranged on the display, as well as the appearance of client applications running with *mwm*. As we'll see, you can also create additional menus, displayed from the root window, to perform actions on the display as a whole.

Customization of *mwm* is controlled in two ways:

- Through a special file, called *.mwmrc*, in your home directory.

- Through *mwm* resources you can enter in your *.Xresources* file (or other sources of resource specification).

The default operation of *mwm* is largely controlled by a system-wide file, called *system.mwmrc*, which establishes the contents of the Root Menu and Window Menu, how menu functions are invoked, and what key and button combinations can be used to manage windows. To modify the behavior of *mwm*, you can edit a copy of this file in your home directory. The version of this file in your home directory should be called *.mwmrc*. We'll take a look at the *system.mwmrc* and ways to edit your own *.mwmrc* file to make the window manager work more effectively for you.

In addition to the flexibility provided by the *.mwmrc* file, *mwm* provides dozens of application resources that you can set! It's neither practical nor necessary to discuss all of those resources here. (You could spend quite a long time customizing *mwm*, if you had the time and inclination.) We'll just consider some basic categories into which *mwm* resources can be divided and also look at some of the more useful resources. See Chapter 11 for syntax rules and information about loading resources into the server so that they will be accessible to client programs. See the *mwm* reference page in Part Three of this guide for descriptions of all available resources.

In the remainder of this chapter, we're going to demonstrate the *basics* of customizing *mwm* and suggest what we think are helpful modifications. (This is still quite a lot to absorb.) To illustrate, we'll discuss how to customize the following features of *mwm*:

- The menus and how menu functions are invoked.

- The keyboard focus policy.

- How icons are organized (namely, how to set up a window known as an *icon box*, in which icons on the display can be organized).

Before we can customize the *mwm* menus or the ways in which their functions are invoked, we need to take a closer look at the *system.mwmrc* file. First, however, let's consider an important topic: how to make the window manager aware of customizations.

Activating Changes to the Window Manager

Be aware that if you edit your *.mwmrc* or *.Xresources* file to change the way *mwm* works, the changes will not take effect automatically. Whether you change resource settings, edit your *.mwmrc* file, or both, you must restart *mwm* for the changes to take effect.

If you edit your resources file, you must first make the server aware of the new resource specifications by using the *xrdb* client. Generally, you will enter the following command at the prompt in an *xterm* window:

```
% xrdb -load .Xresources
```

The settings in the current version of your *.Xresources* file will replace the resource settings previously stored in the resource database. You can merely append new settings to the old ones using the *xrdb* -merge option. See Chapter 11, *Setting Resources*, for more information.

Once you've loaded the new resource settings, you can restart *mwm*. This can be done using the Restart item of the Root Menu, as described in Chapter 4. When *mwm* has been restarted, it should reflect any changes made to the *.mwmrc* and *.Xresources* files.

Switching Between Custom Version and System Defaults

If you customize any feature of *mwm* and decide you don't like the result, you can restart the window manager with the default settings for your system by typing the keystroke combination:

```
Shift-Control-Meta-!
```

This somewhat involved combination invokes a predefined *mwm* function called f.set_behavior, which is a toggle, or switch, between your customized version of *mwm* and the standard system version. If you've customized *mwm*, f.set_behavior restarts the window manager using the system defaults. If you then invoke f.set_behavior again, the window manager is restarted using your previous customizations.

In either case, a dialog box will ask you to OK or Cancel the process. Click on the appropriate choice with the first pointer button or press Return to select the highlighted button (OK). Figure 13-1 shows the two possible dialog boxes.

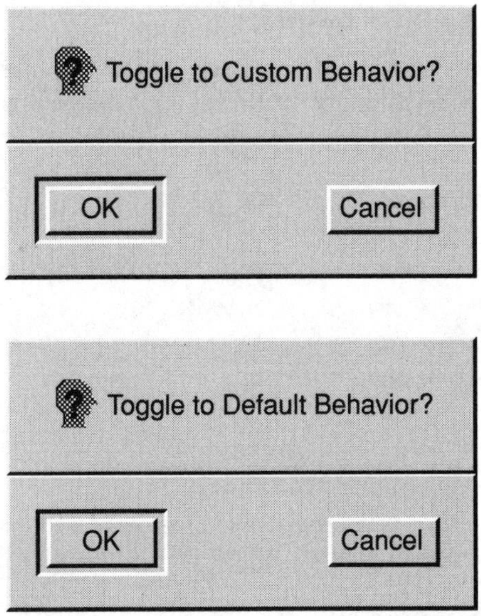

Figure 13-1. Dialog boxes to toggle custom and default mwm environments

The section "mwm Functions" later in this chapter gives an overview of how predefined functions such as f.set_behavior work. All of the available functions are described on the *mwm* reference page in Part Three.

The default Root Menu definition (in the standard *.mwmrc* file) includes an item called Toggle Behavior, which invokes f.set_behavior. This item is commented out in the standard specification. If you want this item to be available on the Root Menu, it's a simple matter of removing the comment mark from your *.mwmrc* file and restarting the window manager (as described in the preceding section). See the sections "Menu Specifications" and "Customizing the Root Menu" for more information.

A final note: To be truly useful, the Toggle Behavior menu item must be added both to your own *.mwmrc* file *and* to the *system.mwmrc* file. If it only appears in your own *.mwmrc* file, when you select it your environment will be changed to reflect the standard Root Menu—which doesn't offer Toggle Behavior! Then the only way to toggle back is to use the Shift-Control-Meta-! keystroke combination.

The system.mwmrc File

Example 13-1 shows the *system.mwmrc* file shipped with OSF/Motif Release 1.2. If you've used other window managers, this file may seem a bit more complicated than other configuration files, but the complexity is deceptive. A line beginning with an exclamation mark (!) or a number sign (#) is treated as a comment. If a line ends with a backslash (\), the subsequent line is considered a continuation of that line.

If you wish to change the operation of *mwm*, you shouldn't change the *system.mwmrc* file. Instead, copy it to your home directory, under the name *.mwmrc*, and make changes to that copy.

Example 13-1. The system.mwmrc file, Release 1.2

```
!
! (c) Copyright 1989, 1990, 1991, 1992 OPEN SOFTWARE FOUNDATION, INC.
! ALL RIGHTS RESERVED
!
!
! Motif Release 1.2
!

!!
!!   DEFAULT Mwm 1.2 RESOURCE DESCRIPTION FILE (system.mwmrc)
!!
!!   NOTE: To personalize this file, copy this file before editing it.
!!         Personalize copies of the Mwm resource file typically
!!         reside as:
!!
!!                       $HOME/.mwmrc
!!

!!
!! Root Menu Description (this menu must be explicitly posted via f.menu)
!!

Menu DefaultRootMenu
{
        "Root Menu"              f.title
        "New Window"             f.exec "xterm &"
        "Shuffle Up"             f.circle_up
        "Shuffle Down"           f.circle_down
        "Refresh"                f.refresh
        "Pack Icons"             f.pack_icons
!       "Toggle Behavior..."     f.set_behavior
         no-label                f.separator
        "Restart..."             f.restart
!       "Quit..."                f.quit_mwm

}

Menu RootMenu_1.1
{
        "Root Menu"              f.title
        "New Window"             f.exec "xterm &"
        "Shuffle Up"             f.circle_up
        "Shuffle Down"           f.circle_down
        "Refresh"                f.refresh
```

Example 13-1. The system.mwmrc file, Release 1.2 (continued)

```
!         "Pack Icons"                f.pack_icons
!         "Toggle Behavior"           f.set_behavior
          no-label                    f.separator
          "Restart..."                f.restart
}

!!
!! Default Window Menu Description
!!

Menu DefaultWindowMenu
{
          Restore        _R           Alt<Key>F5        f.restore
          Move           _M           Alt<Key>F7        f.move
          Size           _S           Alt<Key>F8        f.resize
          Minimize       _n           Alt<Key>F9        f.minimize
          Maximize       _x           Alt<Key>F10       f.maximize
          Lower          _L           Alt<Key>F3        f.lower
          no-label                                      f.separator
          Close          _C           Alt<Key>F4        f.kill
}


!!
!! Key Binding Description
!!

Keys DefaultKeyBindings
{
          Shift<Key>Escape              window|icon         f.post_wmenu
          Alt<Key>space                 window|icon         f.post_wmenu
          Alt<Key>Tab                   root|icon|window    f.next_key
          Alt Shift<Key>Tab             root|icon|window    f.prev_key
          Alt<Key>Escape                root|icon|window    f.circle_down
          Alt Shift<Key>Escape          root|icon|window    f.circle_up
          Alt Shift Ctrl<Key>exclam     root|icon|window    f.set_behavior
          Alt<Key>F6                    window              f.next_key transient
          Alt Shift<Key>F6              window              f.prev_key transient
          Shift<Key>F10                 icon                f.post_wmenu
!         Alt Shift<Key>Delete          root|icon|window    f.restart
}

!!
!! Button Binding Description(s)
!!

Buttons DefaultButtonBindings
{
          <Btn1Down>              icon|frame         f.raise
          <Btn3Down>              icon|frame         f.post_wmenu
          <Btn3Down>              root               f.menu        DefaultRootMenu
}


Buttons ExplicitButtonBindings
{
          <Btn1Down>              frame|icon         f.raise
          <Btn3Down>              frame|icon         f.post_wmenu
          <Btn3Down>              root               f.menu        DefaultRootMenu
!         <Btn1Up>                icon               f.restore
}
```

Example 13-1. The system.mwmrc file, Release 1.2 (continued)

```
            Alt<Btn1Down>           window|icon         f.lower
!           Alt<Btn2Down>           window|icon         f.resize
!           Alt<Btn3Down>           window|icon         f.move

}

Buttons PointerButtonBindings
{
            <Btn1Down>              frame|icon          f.raise
            <Btn3Down>              frame|icon          f.post_wmenu
            <Btn3Down>              root                f.menu      DefaultRootMenu
            <Btn1Down>              window              f.raise
!           <Btn1Up>               icon                f.restore
            Alt<Btn1Down>          window|icon         f.lower
!           Alt<Btn2Down>          window|icon         f.resize
!           Alt<Btn3Down>          window|icon         f.move
}

!!
!!   END OF mwm RESOURCE DESCRIPTION FILE
!!
```

The *system.mwmrc* file can be divided into three sections:

- Menu specifications.

- Key bindings.

- Button bindings.

The menu section of the *system.mwmrc* file defines the contents of the Root Menu and the Window Menu. Menu item labels are paired with predefined *mwm* functions.

A *binding* is a mapping between a user action (such as a keystroke) and a function, in this case a window manager function. The key bindings section specifies keyboard keys that can be used to invoke some of the predefined window manager functions. The button bindings section specifies pointer buttons or key/button combinations that can be used to invoke various functions.

Each section of the *system.mwmrc* file matches the following basic template:

```
Section_Type    Section_Title
{
definitions
}
```

For example, the basic syntax of a menu specification is as follows:

```
Menu menu_name . . .
{
menu items defined
}
```

Menu is the *Section_Type*. The other possible section types are Keys and Buttons. The *Section_Title* is somewhat arbitrary. In this case, it corresponds to the title of a menu. In the key and button sections, it is simply a title assigned to a group of bindings.

However, the *Section_Title* can be very significant. As we'll see, a section title can be used as the value of a resource variable in your *.Xresources* file. Menu titles are often referenced elsewhere in the *.mwmrc* file. The *menu_name* is generally paired with a pointer button action (in the button bindings section of the *.mwmrc* file) to allow you to use a particular button to display the menu.

The syntax of the actual menu items, key bindings, and button bindings requires further explanation. But first, let's take a look at some of the predefined window manager functions.

mwm Functions

mwm has a number of predefined functions. Each of these functions has a name beginning with "f.". Several functions appear in the *system.mwmrc* file, paired with the method by which the function can be invoked: by menu item, pointer button action, keystroke(s), or key and pointer button combinations.

The meaning of most of these functions should be fairly obvious to you from the name, if not from your experience using the window manager. For example, f.resize is used to resize a window, f.move to move a window, and f.minimize to change a window to an icon.

Others are less obvious. The function f.post_wmenu is used to display (or post) the Window Menu. Notice the function f.separator, which appears in the menu definition coupled with the instruction no-label rather than with a menu item. This line in the *.mwmrc* creates a divider line on a menu. For example, such a divider line is used to isolate the Restart item from the other items on the Root Menu.

As we'll see, the function f.menu is used to associate a menu with the key or button binding that is used to display it. The f.menu function takes a required argument: the menu name. This function can also be used to define a submenu.

Each of the functions is described in detail on the reference page for *mwm* in Part Three of this guide.

Menu Specifications

The first section of the *system.mwmrc* file contains specifications for the Root Menu and Window Menu. As we've said, the basic syntax of a menu specification is as follows:

```
Menu menu_name . . .
{
menu items defined
}
```

As you may notice, the *system.mwmrc* file defines two different "Root Menus." The first version has the *menu_name* DefaultRootMenu and the second has the name Root-Menu_1.1. The DefaultRootMenu is just that—the Root Menu you get by default and the one described in Chapter 4, *More about the mwm Window Manager*. As we'll see, the `menu_name` is paired with either a pointer button action or a keystroke combination—in the button or key bindings section of the *.mwmrc* file—to allow you to use the button or key to display the menu. As described in Chapter 4, the `DefaultRootMenu` is displayed by placing the pointer on the root window and holding down the third pointer button.

The `RootMenu_1.1` reiterates the Root Menu definition provided with *mwm* 1.1. The *system.mwmrc* file does not bind this menu to a key or button, so there is no way to display it without customization. Hypothetically, you could edit your *.mwmrc* to be able to display the `RootMenu_1.1` using a different key than the one bound to the `DefaultRoot-Menu`—and thus, have access to *both* versions. However, since the default version provides all of the functionality of the earlier one, there isn't much point. For the purposes of our discussion, we'll just consider the default Root Menu.

Menu items are defined in slightly different ways for the Root Menu and the Window Menu. The following text in the *system.mwmrc* file creates the default Root Menu:

```
# Root Menu Description
Menu DefaultRootMenu
{
        "Root Menu"                   f.title
        "New Window"                  f.exec "xterm &"
        "Shuffle Up"                  f.circle_up
        "Shuffle Down"                f.circle_down
        "Refresh"                     f.refresh
        "Pack Icons"                  f.pack_icons
!       "Toggle Behavior..."          f.set_behavior
        no-label                      f.separator
        "Restart..."                  f.restart
!       "Quit..."                     f.quit_mwm
}
```

The syntax for defining Root Menu items is very simple. Each item is defined by a line of this format:

"label" function

When you pair a label with a menu function, that label appears as a menu item. You can invoke the function by selecting the item from the menu using the pointer. For example, the line:

```
"Refresh"        f.refresh
```

sets up the Refresh menu item, which can be selected from the Root Menu as discussed in Chapter 4. (Again, the function performed is obvious from the function name.) As we'll see later, it's easy to add items to the Root Menu by adding lines of label/function pairs. (You can also use a bitmap image rather than a text label, if you like.)

Notice that two Root Menu items are commented out.

```
!    "Toggle Behavior..." f.set_behavior
!    "Quit..."            f.quit_mwm
```

These items will not appear on your Root Menu. We'll discuss adding these items in the section "Customizing the Root Menu" later in this chapter.

Because Window Menu items can be invoked in a variety of ways, the syntax for defining items is more complicated. The following text defines the Window Menu:

```
# Default Window Menu Description

Menu DefaultWindowMenu
{
        Restore         _R      Alt<Key>F5      f.restore
        Move            _M      Alt<Key>F7      f.move
        Size            _S      Alt<Key>F8      f.resize
        Minimize        _n      Alt<Key>F9      f.minimize
        Maximize        _x      Alt<Key>F10     f.maximize
        Lower           _L      Alt<Key>F3      f.lower
        no-label                                f.separator
        Close           _C      Alt<Key>F4      f.kill
}
```

The syntax of each menu item is as follows:

    "label"   *mnemonic*   *accelerator*   *function*

(The *mnemonic* and *accelerator* fields are optional.) Like the Root Menu, each item on the Window Menu can be invoked by selecting its label with the pointer. In addition, there are two shortcuts defined for invoking the function: a mnemonic and an accelerator. As you may recall, a mnemonic is a unique letter abbreviation for the menu item label. On the menu, mnemonic abbreviations are underlined; thus an underscore precedes each mnemonic definition in the *system.mwmrc* file. Once the Window Menu is displayed, you can select an item by typing its mnemonic abbreviation. Similarly, you can invoke the function without displaying the menu, simply by typing the accelerator keys (by default, the Alt key plus a function key).*

Now let's see how one of the Window Menu definition lines fits this template:

```
        Move    _M              Alt<Key>F7      f.move
```

The menu item label is Move. Selecting the item invokes the `f.move` function. The mnemonic "m" or the accelerator key combination Alt-F7 can also be used to invoke the function.

Key Bindings

The second section of the *system.mwmrc* file binds keystroke combinations to window manager functions.

Like the menu definition section, the key bindings section of the file is titled and bracketed:

```
Keys Section_Title
{

key bindings defined

}
```

---

*If your keyboard does not have an F10 function key, you cannot use the accelerator for the Maximize item without doing some customization. A possible workaround is to edit the line defining the Maximize menu item in your *.mwmrc* file. Changing F10 to F2 will suffice in most cases.

The section type is Keys. The section title in the *system.mwmrc* file is DefaultKey-Bindings. This title can also be specified as the value of the *mwm* resource key-Bindings in your *.Xresources* file. However, since these bindings are used by default, this is not necessary.

Using the section title as a resource becomes significant when you want to create an alternative set of bindings. Hypothetically, you could add another set of bindings with a different title to your *.mwmrc* file. Then specify this title as the value of the keyBindings resource in your *.Xresources* file. If you add the following resource specification to your *.Xresources* file, MyButtonBindings replace DefaultButtonBindings for all client applications running with *mwm*:

```
    Mwm*keyBindings:        MyButtonBindings
```

If you want to use different sets of bindings for different applications, you can add an application name between the parts of the resource specification. For example, if you want My-ButtonBindings to apply only to *xterm* windows running with *mwm*, you could enter the following resource line:

```
    Mwm*xterm*keyBindings:        MyButtonBindings
```

Then DefaultButtonBindings would still apply to all applications other than *xterm*.

A non-obvious principle behind a key/function (or button/function) binding is that in order for the keys (or buttons) to invoke the function, the pointer must be in a certain location. This location is known as the *context*. For key bindings, the useful contexts are: root, window, and icon. The window context refers to the entire window, including the frame. (There are other more specific contexts, such as border, explained under "Button Bindings," but when specifying key bindings, these contexts are all equivalent to window.)

Some functions can be invoked if the pointer is in more than one context. For example, as we saw in Chapter 4, you can display the Window Menu from either a window or an icon using the keyboard shortcuts Meta-space or Shift-Escape. The action involved is f.post_wmenu and the window and the icon are the pointer contexts from which this action can be performed. These keyboard shortcuts are defined in the key bindings section of the *system.mwmrc* file as follows:

```
    Shift<Key>Escape      window|icon      f.post_wmenu
    Meta<Key>space  window|icon      f.post_wmenu
```

Upon examining these lines, we can discern the template for a key binding:

```
    [modifier_keys]<Key>key_name        context              function
```

Each binding can have one or more modifier keys (modifiers are optional) and *must* have a single primary key (signaled by the word <Key> in angle brackets) to invoke the function. In the first specification, Shift is the modifier and Escape is the primary key. In the second specification, Meta is the modifier and space is the primary key. Both specifications have two acceptable pointer contexts: either a window or an icon. And both bindings are mapped to the same action, f.post_wmenu, which displays the Window Menu.

Button Bindings

The key bindings section of the file is also titled and bracketed:

```
Buttons Section_Title
{
button bindings defined

}
```

The section type is `Buttons`. The *system.mwmrc* file contains three sets of button bindings with the section titles:

```
DefaultButtonBindings
ExplicitButtonBindings
PointerButtonBindings
```

Button bindings clearly illustrate the need to coordinate your *.Xresources* and *.mwmrc* files. The three sets of button bindings correspond to three possible settings for the resource `buttonBindings`. The default setting for the resource is:

```
Mwm*buttonBindings:  DefaultButtonBindings
```

specifying that the `DefaultButtonBindings` are used.

You can specify that one of the other sets of button bindings is to be used by setting this resource in your *.Xresources* file. For example, if you add the following specification to your resource file:

```
Mwm*buttonBindings:  ExplicitButtonBindings
```

mwm will use those bindings that come under the heading `ExplicitButtonBindings` in the *.mwmrc* file.

Be aware that if you do specify different button bindings, the value of the resource must exactly match the title associated with the bindings, or the bindings will not take effect.

The syntax for a button binding specification is very similar to that of a key binding:

```
[modifier_key]<button_event>    context    function
```

Each button binding can have one or more modifier keys (modifiers are optional) and *must* have a single button event (enclosed in angle brackets) to invoke the function. The motion that comprises each button event should be fairly obvious. (Lists of acceptable button events and modifier keys appear on the *mwm* reference page in Part Three of this guide.)

For button bindings. the valid contexts are `root`, `window`, `icon`, `title`, `border`, `frame`, and `app`. The `title` context refers to the title area of the frame. `border` refers to the frame exclusive of the titlebar. `frame` refers to the entire frame (thus it encompasses `title` and `border`). The `app` context refers to the application window proper (i.e., exclusive of the frame). The `window` context includes the application window and the frame (thus it encompasses `app`, `frame`, `border`, and `title`).

Now let's see how the button binding syntax relates to the default button bindings in the *system.mwmrc* file:

```
Buttons DefaultButtonBindings
{
    <Btn1Down>          icon|frame      f.raise
    <Btn3Down>          icon            f.post_wmenu
    <Btn1Down>          root            f.menu      RootMenu
}
```

The first specification is familiar. It indicates that the event of pressing down the first pointer button while the pointer is in a window frame or an icon performs the action of raising the window or icon, respectively.

The second binding reveals *still another* way to display the Window Menu, by pressing the third pointer button on an icon.

The third binding is also familiar and illustrates the use of the f.menu function. As previously mentioned, the f.menu function is used to associate a menu with the key or button binding that is used to display it. The following binding specifies that the Root Menu is displayed by pressing and holding down the first pointer button on the root window:

```
    <Btn1Down>              root              f.menu          RootMenu
```

Notice that the function requires an argument, the menu name (RootMenu), which also appears in the first line of the menu definition. This correspondence is required—f.menu needs to know which menu to display.

Customizing the Root Menu

You can add items to the Root Menu simply by adding lines of the format:

> "*label*"   *function*

within the menu definition section of your *.mwmrc* file (and then restarting the window manager).

The f.exec function allows you to execute system commands from a menu. In the default Root Menu, the New Window command uses the f.exec function to execute the system command xterm &, as shown below:

```
# Root Menu Description
Menu DefaultRootMenu
{
        "Root Menu"             f.title
        "New Window"            f.exec "xterm &"
        "Shuffle Up"            f.circle_up
        "Shuffle Down"          f.circle_down
        "Refresh"               f.refresh
        "Pack Icons"            f.pack_icons
    !   "Toggle Behavior..."    f.set_behavior
        no-label                f.separator
        "Restart..."            f.restart
    !   "Quit..."               f.quit_mwm
}
```

To create a menu item labeled Clock that opens an *xclock* window on your display, simply add a line to your *.mwmrc* file, as shown here:

```
# Root Menu Description
Menu DefaultRootMenu
{
        "Root Menu"              f.title
        "New Window"             f.exec "xterm &"
        "Clock"                  f.exec "xclock &"
        "Shuffle Up"             f.circle_up
        "Shuffle Down"           f.circle_down
        "Refresh"                f.refresh
        "Pack Icons"             f.pack_icons
    !   "Toggle Behavior..."     f.set_behavior
        no-label                 f.separator
        "Restart..."             f.restart
    !   "Quit..."                f.quit_mwm
}
```

In most cases, the label is a text string. However, you can use a bitmapped image instead by preceding it with an "at" symbol (@). The following line lets you run *xbiff* by selecting the bitmap image of a full mailbox (filename *flagup*) from the menu.

```
@flagup         f.exec "xbiff &"
```

Unless a full pathname is given for the bitmap file, *mwm* looks for bitmap files in a system-wide directory, generally */usr/include/X11/bitmaps*. (*flagup* is a standard bitmap available in */usr/include/X11/bitmaps*. It's the image *xbiff* uses for its full mailbox window.) You can also specify an alternate standard bitmap directory using the `bitmapDirectory` resource. If a bitmap is not found in the standard bitmap directory and the XBMLANGPATH environment variable is set, *mwm* checks that directory.

You can also edit (or remove) existing menu items. As we pointed out earlier, two items (Toggle Behavior and Quit) are commented out. Toggle Behavior invokes `f.set_behavior`, which toggles between your own customized version of *mwm* and the standard version for your environment. (You can also invoke this function using the key combination Shift-Control-Meta-!. See the section "Switching between Custom Version and System Defaults" earlier in this chapter for more information.) Quit causes the window manager to exit (it is not restarted). You might invoke Quit before starting another window manager, such as *twm*.

To add either Toggle Behavior or Quit to the Root Menu, just delete the initial exclamation mark, which comments out the line (and restart the window manager, as usual).

You might also want to change what an existing menu item does. Say you want to run the *hpterm* terminal emulator (developed by Hewlett-Packard) rather than *xterm*. You would edit the New Window line in your menu specification to look like this:

```
# Root Menu Description
Menu DefaultRootMenu
{
        "Root Menu"              f.title
        "New Window"             f.exec "hpterm &"
        "Clock"                  f.exec "xclock &"
        "Shuffle Up"             f.circle_up
        "Shuffle Down"           f.circle_down
        "Refresh"                f.refresh
```

```
            "Pack Icons"                        f.pack_icons
    !       "Toggle Behavior..."                f.set_behavior
             no-label                           f.separator
            "Restart..."                        f.restart
    !       "Quit..."                           f.quit_mwm
    }
```

Creating New Menus

Keep in mind that *mwm* also allows you to specify entirely new menus in your *.mwmrc* file. A new menu can be separate from all existing menus, or it can be a submenu of an existing menu. (Submenus are described in the following section, "Cascading Menus.")

If you want to create a new, independent menu, it must conform to the menu specification syntax discussed earlier. Items must invoke predefined window manager functions.

The *.mwmrc* file must also specify how the menu will be displayed and in what context. This involves associating a key or button with the f.menu function. Say you've specified a new menu, titled GamesMenu, that runs various game programs, each in its own window. (The f.exec function would be used to define each item.) The following button binding specifies that pressing the second pointer button on the root window displays the Games Menu:

```
    <Btn2Down>        root        f.menu        GamesMenu
```

Cascading Menus

mwm also allows you to create submenus, generally known as *cascading* menus because they are displayed to the right side of (and slightly lower than) another menu. You define a submenu just as you would any other, using the syntax rules discussed earlier. The following lines create a Utilities Menu that invokes several "desktop" clients and one game:

```
    Menu UtilitiesMenu
    {
        "Utilities Menu"      f.title
        "Clock"               f.exec "xclock &"
        "System Load"         f.exec "xload &"
        "Calculator"          f.exec "xcalc &"
        "Manpage Browser"     f.exec "xman &"
        "Tetris"              f.exec "xtetris &"
    }
```

In order to make the Utilities Menu a submenu of the Root Menu, you need to add an f.menu function to the Root Menu. This f.menu function must be coupled with the correct submenu title:

```
    # Root Menu Description
    Menu DefaultRootMenu
    {
            "Root Menu"                 f.title
            "New Window"                f.exec "hpterm &"
            "Shuffle Up"                f.circle_up
            "Shuffle Down"              f.circle_down
            "Refresh"                   f.refresh
```

```
          "Pack Icons"                  f.pack_icons
          "Utilities"                   f.menu            UtilitiesMenu
!         "Toggle Behavior..."          f.set_behavior
          no-label                      f.separator
          "Restart..."                  f.restart
!         "Quit..."                     f.quit_mwm
}
```

After you specify the preceding menus in your *.mwmrc* file (and restart *mwm*), display the
Root Menu. It will feature a new item, labeled Utilities. Since this item is actually a pointer to
a submenu, it will be followed by an arrowhead pointing to the right, as in Figure 13-2.

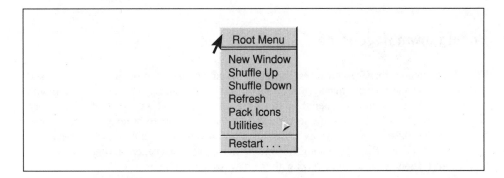

Figure 13-2. An arrowhead pointing to the right indicates a submenu

If you drag the pointer down the Root Menu to the Utilities item, the submenu will appear to
cascade to the right. Figure 13-3 shows it appearing.

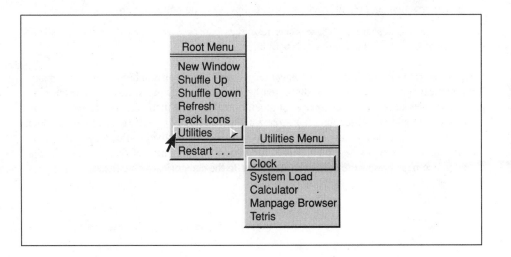

Figure 13-3. Utilities submenu of the Root Menu

If you release the pointer button, both menus will remain displayed and the Utilities item and the first item on the Utilities Menu will be highlighted by a box. You can then select an item from the Utilities Menu by moving the pointer to the item and clicking the first button.

Keep in mind that you can create several submenus beneath a single menu and that menus can cascade several levels, though such complexity is not necessarily desirable.

Note also that if you pair a label with an invalid function (or with f.nop, which specifies no operation), or with a function that doesn't work in the current context, the label appears in a lighter typeface. This "graying out" indicates that the menu item is not available for selection.

Setting mwm Resources

The Motif window manager provides dozens of resources that control the appearance and functionality of the window manager, its component features, and other clients running with it. *mwm* resources should be entered in your *.Xresources* file and will take effect when the resources have been loaded into the server and *mwm* has been started or restarted. See Chapter 11, *Setting Resources*, for syntax information and instructions on how to load resources using the *xrdb* client. See "Activating Changes to the Window Manager" earlier in this chapter for information about running *mwm* with the new resource settings.

mwm resources are considered to fall into three categories:

1. *mwm* component appearance resources. These resources set the characteristics of *mwm*'s component features, such as the window frame, menus, and icons.

2. *mwm-specific* appearance and behavior resources. These resources set characteristics of the window manager client, such as focus policy, key and button bindings, and so forth.

3. *Client-specific* resources. These *mwm* resources can be used to set the appearance and behavior of a particular client or class of clients.

Under these categories fall dozens of *mwm* resources. The sheer number of resources makes it impractical for all of them to be discussed here. In the following sections, we discuss the three categories of resources in somewhat greater detail. We'll then take a look at two of the more powerful and useful resources, keyboardFocusPolicy and useIconBox, which set the focus policy and set up *mwm* to use an icon box, respectively. For a comprehensive list of available resources, see the *mwm* reference page in Part Three of this guide. Note that the reference page groups the resources according to the categories we've listed.

Component Appearance Resources

The Motif window manager can be considered to be made up of components: client window frames, menus, icons, and what are known as *feedback* or *dialog boxes*. An example of a feedback box is the box that appears so that you can confirm or cancel a Restart command from the Root Menu. (See "The Root Menu" section in Chapter 4, *More about the mwm Window Manager*.)

Certain resources allow you to specify the appearance of one or all of these *mwm* component features. In specifying the resource setting, you can use the name of one of the features as part of the resource name. For example, one of the most useful component appearance resources is background, which, as we know from Chapter 11, specifies the background color. You can specify a resource that sets the background color of any of the *mwm* components. The following resource specification sets the background color of all client window frames to light blue:

```
Mwm*client*background:    lightblue
```

Table 13-1 summarizes the resource name that corresponds to each of the *mwm* components.

Table 13-1. Resource Names Corresponding to mwm Components

Component	Resource name
Menu	menu
Icon	icon
Client window frame	client
Feedback/dialog box	feedback
Titlebar	title

Thus, to set the background color of feedback boxes to sea green, you'd use the following resource:

```
Mwm*feedback*background:    seagreen
```

Of course, if you omit any specific component from the resource specification, it applies to *all* components. Thus, the following specification sets the background color of all window frames, feedback boxes, icons, and menus to light grey:

```
Mwm*background: lightgrey
```

Since the titlebar is actually part of the client window frame, the title resource is a special case. (Technically speaking, title comes at a different level in the widget hierarchy than client and the other component resources.) The title resource allows you to specify characteristics for the titlebar alone (including the command buttons), while you can specify characteristics for the rest of the frame (the resize border) using client. Thus, you might have the resource specifications:

```
Mwm*client*title*background:    lightblue
Mwm*client*background:    aquamarine
```

These lines would create two-tone window frames with aquamarine borders and light blue titlebars (perhaps too vivid a combination). (Note that these colors do not apply to the active (focus) window. To change these characteristics for the focus window, you would need to specify the `activeBackground` resource. See the *mwm* reference page in Part Three of this guide for more information.)

Similarly, you can specify resources for individual menus, by using the `menu` component with the menu name, as in the following example:

```
Mwm*menu*UtilitiesMenu*background:    seagreen
```

This line gives the Utilities Menu we added to our *.mwmrc* file a sea green background. (See "Cascading Menus" earlier in this chapter for information about creating submenus.)

mwm-specific Appearance and Behavior Resources

The *mwm*-specific resources control aspects of what you probably think of as the window manager application itself, features such as the focus policy, whether windows are placed on the display automatically or interactively, which set(s) of button and key bindings are used, whether an icon box is used, and so forth.

The syntax of *mwm*-specific resource specifications is very simple—the *mwm* class name connected by a loose binding to the resource variable name, as shown here:

```
Mwm*clientAutoPlace: false
```

This resource establishes the behavior that the user will interactively place client windows on the display. (The default is true, meaning *mwm* places them automatically.)

Two of the *mwm*-specific resources bring up an issue of coordination between the *.Xresources* and *.mwmrc* files. Remember, the default *.mwmrc* file contains three sets of button bindings:

```
DefaultButtonBindings
ExplicitButtonBindings
PointerButtonBindings
```

These three sets of button bindings correspond to three possible settings for the resource variable `buttonBindings`. If your resource file contains the following setting:

```
Mwm*buttonBindings:   ExplicitButtonBindings
```

mwm will use those bindings that come under the heading `ExplicitButtonBindings` in the *.mwmrc* file.

Similarly, the resource variable `keyBindings` should be coordinated to match the key bindings in the *.mwmrc* file. Since the default *.mwmrc* file has only one set of key bindings, named `DefaultKeyBindings`, and the `keyBindings` resource also sets this by default, coordination should not be an issue unless you create a new set of key bindings with a different name.

Two of the most useful and powerful *mwm*-specific resources set the keyboard focus policy and specify that icons be stored in an icon box. We'll discuss the use and advantages of these resources later in this chapter.

Client-specific Resources

Some *mwm* resources can be set to apply to certain client applications or classes of applications. These resources generally have the form:

    Mwm*application*resource_variable:

where `application` can be an instance name or a class name. Be aware that the application name is optional. If you omit an application name, the resource applies to all clients. (Client-specific resource specifications take precedence.)

In rare cases, an application might not have instance and class resource names that are known to the window manager. To see if the window manager knows these names, run *xprop* and click the pointer on the application window. The property WM_CLASS should contain both names. You can specify resources for clients that have unknown instance and class names by using the literal parameter `defaults` in place of a particular `application`.

    Mwm*defaults*resource_variable:

Many of the client-specific resources provide what might be considered advanced customization. For example, a combination of resources allows you to specify your own bitmap as the image for a client icon. Other resources allow you to suppress certain features of the window frame for particular clients. For instance, you may choose to omit the Maximize button from the frame surrounding *xterm* windows. Still others allow you to specify *extra* window decoration in the form of a matte which lies between the application window and the frame. This matte is purely aesthetic; it provides no functionality. The average user will probably not need most of these client-specific resources.

One client-specific resource users might be interested in is called `focusAutoRaise`. This resource causes a window to be raised to the top of the stack when it is selected as the focus window. When the focus policy is explicit (click-to-type), `focusAutoRaise` is true for all clients by default. When the focus policy is pointer (real-estate-driven), `focusAutoRaise` is false for all clients by default.

These defaults are very sensible. If you are using the default click-to-type focus, `focusAutoRaise` is clearly very desirable. You click on a window to focus input and the window is raised to the top of the stack so that you can work with it easily. However, if you change the focus policy to pointer focus (as we'll describe in the following section), turning `focusAutoRaise` on can make the display seem chaotic.

When pointer focus is active as you move the pointer across the display, the focus changes from window to window based on the location of the pointer, often a desirable feature. However, if `focusAutoRaise` is set to be true, each time the pointer moves into a window, the window will be moved to the front of the display. Simply moving the pointer across a screenful of windows can create a distracting shuffling effect! If you set the focus policy to pointer, we suggest you leave `focusAutoRaise` set to false.

Of course, using pointer focus without `focusAutoRaise` is just our preference. You may want to experiment awhile to see how you like working with it.

Hypothetically, you *can* turn `autoFocusRaise` behavior on or off only for particular clients, but this is not necessarily desirable, with either focus policy. For instance, say you're using the default *mwm* settings so that explicit focus is in effect and `focusAutoRaise` is true for all clients. You can suppress the auto-raise feature only for the class of *xterm* windows by specifying:

```
Mwm*XTerm*focusAutoRaise: false
```

But what is the point? In most cases, you want to raise the focus window so that you can work with it more easily.*

When pointer focus is in effect, setting `focusAutoRaise` differently for different clients can have tedious and unnecessary complications. It becomes fairly easy to "bury" one window beneath another inadvertently. For example, say `focusAutoRaise` is turned on for *xterm* windows only, and turned off for *xbiff*. If an *xbiff* window appears on top of an *xterm* and you move the pointer into the *xterm*, the *xterm* is raised automatically, covering the *xbiff* window.

You can send the *xterm* to the back using the Lower item of the Window Menu. Although the *xterm* retains the focus, it is not raised. `focusAutoRaise` specifies that a window is raised when the focus is moved to a window (retaining the focus is a different matter). However, if you move the pointer to another window and back to the *xterm*, the *xbiff* window will be buried again. In order to avoid such a situation, you would have to arrange all windows so that a part of the frame is exposed at all times. No window should ever appear entirely on top of another.

Given the limitations and potential problems, **we discourage setting** `focusAutoRaise` **differently for different applications, regardless of the focus policy**.

See the *mwm* reference page in Part Three for descriptions of all of the client-specific resources.

Setting the Focus Policy

The most common resource users will probably want to set controls *mwm*'s keyboard focus policy. By default, *mwm* has explicit (or click-to-type) focus, which is set using the following resource:

```
Mwm*keyboardFocusPolicy:  explicit
```

To change the keyboard focus policy from explicit to pointer focus (that is, focus follows the movement of the pointer), enter the following line in your *.Xresources* file:

```
Mwm*keyboardFocusPolicy:  pointer
```

---

*Note that even if you turn off the auto-raise feature for *xterm*, it is still possible to raise an *xterm* and select it to receive input simultaneously, but in a more restricted way. Clicking anywhere on a window selects that window to receive the focus. Clicking on the frame, exclusive of the command buttons, raises a window. Thus, by clicking this part of the frame, you can perform both actions simultaneously. However, why restrict yourself to using only a part of the frame, when you can use the entire window?

Using an Icon Box

One of the most interesting (and desirable) features *mwm* can provide is a window in which icons can be organized on the display. This window is known as an *icon box*, and is pictured in Figure 13-4. As we'll see, in addition to organizing icons neatly on the display, the icon box also provides a few window management functions.

You can set up *mwm* to provide an icon box automatically by specifying the following resource in your *.Xresources* file:

```
Mwm*useIconBox: true
```

If this resource is included in your *.Xresources* file (and the resources have been loaded as described in Chapter 11) *mwm* will provide an icon box when it is started (or restarted). Other resources can be used to customize the size, appearance, and location of the icon box, as well as the window's title. By default, the icon box is six icons wide by one icon high and is located in the lower-left corner of the display.

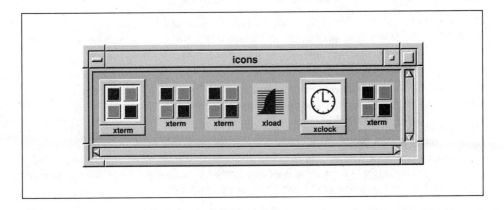

Figure 13-4. An icon box

The horizontal and vertical scrollbars within the icon box suggest a significant, albeit not an obvious, feature. Icons can extend beyond the visible bounds of the icon box. If more than six icons are present in the default size box, you can view them using the scrollbars. (See Chapter 9, *Working with Motif Applications*, for instructions on using a Motif scrollbar.) Keep in mind that if icons do extend beyond the visible bounds of the box, the appearance of the scrollbars will indicate it.

The presence of an icon box changes the way icons are used on the display. If you are using *mwm* without an icon box, only those windows that have been iconified are represented by icons on the display. If you are using *mwm* with an icon box, *all* windows on the display are represented by icons that are stored in the box, whether or not the windows are in an iconified state.

When a client window is started, the window appears on the display *and* a corresponding icon appears in the icon box. However, an icon that represents a window currently visible on the display has a different appearance than an actual icon (that is, an iconified window). An icon corresponding to a window currently on the display appears flatter and less defined than the image of an iconified window. The former probably has fewer lines in its outer border. If you set up *mwm* to use an icon box, the differing appearance of these two types of icons should be obvious.

Somewhat similar to a menu item in a lighter typeface, the flatter, less defined icon suggests that it is not available to be chosen. In a sense, this is true. Since the flat icon is not an iconified window, but merely an image, it is not available to be converted back to a window. The icon box in Figure 13-4 contains two iconified windows (*xclock* and the first *xterm*) and four icons representing windows currently visible on the display.

You can perform some window management functions by clicking on icons in the icon box. If you double click on an iconified window using the first pointer button, the icon is converted back to a window (and is raised to the top of the stack). If you double click on an icon representing an active window on the display, the corresponding window is raised to the front of the display. (We find this latter function to be not particularly useful.) When you raise a window by clicking on its icon, the icon box retains the focus.

When performing either function, between the first and second clicks you'll probably notice that the Window Menu is displayed for an instant above the icon. If you pause too long between the two clicks in either of these functions, the action you intend (either deiconifying or raising) will fail and the Window Menu will remain on the screen.

If you get stuck on the Window Menu when trying to convert an icon to a window, place the pointer on the Restore menu item and click the first pointer button.

If you get stuck on the Window Menu when trying to raise a window on the display (by clicking on its icon), the menu affords no item to complete the action. Instead you should move the pointer onto the root window and click the first button—the menu will be removed. Then try double clicking again. Or raise the window simply by clicking the first pointer button on the window's frame (exclusive of the frame's command buttons).

As these actions suggest, you can display the Window Menu from any of the icons in the box by clicking the first pointer button on the icon image.* (You can also display the Window Menu from and manage the icon box itself, as we discuss later on.) Depending on whether you click on an iconified window or an icon representing an active window on the display, different Window Menu items are available for selection.

When you display the Window Menu from an iconified window within the icon box, the items Restore, Move, Maximize, and Close are available for selection. Be aware that the Move menu item only allows you to move the icon itself—to another location within the icon box. The other available items perform their standard functions, which are described in the section "Using the Window Menu on Icons" in Chapter 4.

Displaying the Window Menu from an icon representing an active window on the display is not particularly useful: only the items Move and Close are available for selection. And again, the Move menu item only allows you to move the icon within the icon box.

---

*The 1.0 version of *mwm* was documented to display the Window Menu from an icon within the icon box, but the program did not seem to work according to the specifications. The 1.1 version of *mwm* does provide this functionality.

When you display the Window Menu from the icon box, the menu commands apply to the box itself (which is actually a window). You can display the menu from the icon box using any of the methods described in the section "Using the Window Menu" in Chapter 4. For example, if you use the keyboard shortcut Meta-space, the menu is displayed above the Window Menu command button in the upper-left corner of the icon box frame.

When displayed from the icon box, the Window Menu Close item is replaced by an item called Pack Icons (mnemonic "p", accelerator Shift+Alt+F7). Pack Icons rearranges the icons in the box to fill in empty slots. This is useful when icons are removed from the box or the box is resized.

When you remove a window, the corresponding icon is removed from the box, leaving an empty slot. Pack Icons will move any icons that are to the right of the slot one space to the left to fill the hole. If you resize the icon box, Pack Icons will arrange the icons to fit the new window in an optimal way. For instance, say we resize the icon box in Figure 13-4 so that it is only three icons wide, but twice as high, as in Figure 13-5. The first three icons from the box appear; the second three are obscured.* Notice the horizontal scrollbar at the bottom of the window, indicating that the other three icons are still to the right of these and thus not viewable in the resized box. If you place the pointer on the scrollbar, hold down the first button and drag the scrollbar to the right, the hidden icons will be revealed.

In order to rearrange the icons to better fill the new shape box, use the Pack Icons menu item. Figure 13-5 shows the icon box after you've selected Pack Icons.

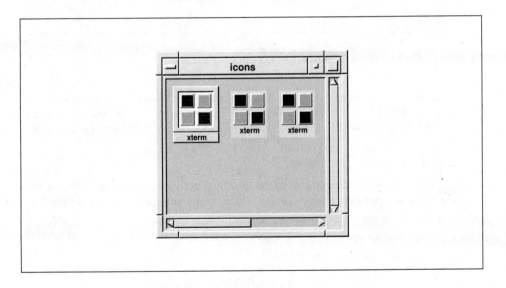

Figure 13-5. In the resized icon box, only three icons are visible

---

*When you resize the icon box, you'll notice the resize action has a tendency to jump the width or height of an icon at a time. *mwm* only allows the box to be resized exactly to fit a number of icons wide and a number high, though there are no obvious limitations as to the numbers. Basically, you can have an icon box of any size, even one icon high and wide, and display the other icons using the scrollbars. As you resize the box, the small rectangular window in the center of the screen assists you: it shows the dimensions in the number of icons wide by the number of icons high.

If you want to reorganize icons in the box yourself, without Pack Icons, this is also possible. You can actually move icons into adjacent empty slots using the pointer. Just hold down the first pointer button on the icon and drag it into the next slot. If you first make the icon box larger, so that there are several empty spaces, you'll find you can radically reorganize icons. Once you've arranged them as you like, you resize the box to fit the icons—or perhaps make it even smaller and view the obscured icons using the scrollbars.

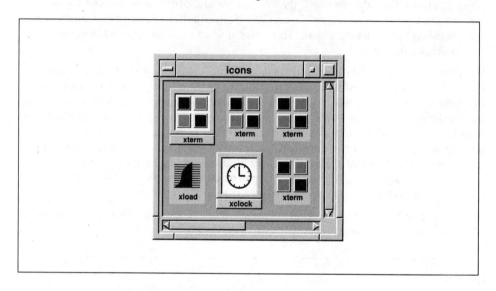

Figure 13-6. Pack Icons menu item rearranges icons in resized box

Keep in mind that the next time you log in, the icon box will be brought up at its default size. To specify alternate dimensions, set the variable iconBoxGeometry in your .Xresources file. For example, if you want an icon box three icons wide by two icons high, use the specification:

```
Mwm*iconBoxGeometry:  3x2+0-0
```

which creates a box of the desired size in the lower-left corner of the display. (This is the default location; you could omit the +0-0 from the geometry string and get the same result.)

The following specification creates an icon box four icons wide by three icons high in the lower-right corner of the display:

```
Mwm*iconBoxGeometry:  4x3-0-0
```

X Window System User's Guide, Motif Edition

14

Setup Clients

This chapter describes three useful setup clients that can be used to customize the appearance and operation of your display, and the operation of your keyboard and pointer.

In This Chapter:

14
Setup Clients

This chapter discusses how to set up certain features of your working environment, using these clients:

xset   To set certain characteristics of the keyboard, pointer, and display.

xsetroot   To set root window characteristics.

xmodmap   To change pointer and key mappings.

When Should I Set Preferences?

First, let's make one thing clear: you may never *have to* specify any user preferences at all. The default settings for your system may be sufficient for your needs.

In addition, some of the customizations you *can* make to your environment are purely aesthetic. The *xsetroot* client allows you to change what your root window looks like and what pointer shape is displayed on the root window. It has nothing to do with how X works.

On the other hand, both *xset* and *xmodmap* are primarily intended to control how your environment operates. You probably don't think about many of the features you can control using *xset*—features like pointer speed and how loud the keyboard bell is. *xset* allows you to fine tune fairly subtle aspects of your working environment, but in most cases, the system defaults will probably be sufficient. Perhaps more importantly, *xset* allows you to specify the font path—the directories in which the X server searches for fonts called by a client.

xmodmap is by far the most complicated and confusing of the setup clients. It allows you to change keyboard and pointer button "mappings," i.e., what a key or pointer button is assigned to do. For example, you might map a Delete function to the key marked "Backspace" on your keyboard. Chances are you'll want the so-called "Meta" function, which is used in many *mwm* window manager operations, to be mapped to a convenient key. (It may already be.) A left-handed person might want the rightmost button on the pointer to function as "pointer button one." (Generally, the leftmost button is pointer button one by default).

As you might imagine, pointer mappings are fairly simple. Most pointers have two or three physical buttons and the only thing you can change is their "logical" order, i.e., which is considered "first," etc. By contrast, some key mappings can seem like complex equations. Perhaps the most confusing mappings involve the so-called "modifier" key functions (Control, Caps Lock, Meta, etc.), introduced in Chapter 4, *More about the mwm Window Manager.*

It's very possible that you may never have to specify any key or pointer customizations. The default assignments may be fine. If not, you can reassign functions using *xmodmap.* Later in this chapter, we discuss some of the issues you should be aware of before assigning key and pointer button functions and also show some typical mappings using *xmodmap.*

Although you can run setup commands at any time, as a general rule it's a good idea to put *xset* and *xsetroot* in your login session script. (This file is often called *.xinitrc* or *.xsession.* See Appendix A, *Managing Your Environment*, for details.) *xmodmap* is something of a special case. We'll come back to that.

The reasons for running *xset* and *xsetroot* at startup vary somewhat based on the display and server—but don't change the overall strategy. In most environments, user preferences are reset to the system defaults when you log out. It makes sense to specify your preferences in a session file that executes when you log in again.

In other cases, whatever preferences have been set for the server running the particular display (say an X terminal) will be carried over to the next login session on that display. (Some X terminals can be configured to retain settings between logins.) Hypothetically, another user could log in at your X terminal and get your preferences! If you use one display exclusively, this "inheritance" might seem more like an advantage than a problem. Keep in mind, however, that if the X server is restarted for some reason (and that will happen sooner or later), your preferences will be cleared and you'll have to run your setup commands next time you log in anyway. The simplest way to avoid problems like these is to run *xset* and *xsetroot* at startup.

Most of the settings controlled using *xset* and *xsetroot* will work on any display, with any server. Virtually the worst thing that can happen is that a server won't support a particular option and your command will simply be ignored. *xmodmap* is a special case because keyboards differ and thus many key assignments are not portable. If you always work at the same terminal, running *xmodmap* at startup should be no problem. If you're inclined to log in at different types of terminals, *xmodmap* can create problems. You should have a better idea of the possible complications after reading the section on *xmodmap* later in this chapter.

Now you might want to glance over the next few pages to get an idea of the types of features you can control using *xset* and *xsetroot.* Most of them are simple to specify and they can enhance your working environment. If you have problems with how the keyboard or pointer works (or think you'd like to improve it), read the section on *xmodmap.*

Setting Display and Keyboard Preferences: xset

You can specify many different "behaviors" of the display, pointer, and keyboard using the *xset* client. *xset* takes a variety of options that allow you to fine tune many features of your environment, including:

- The font search path

- The keyboard bell (margin bell)

- The keyclick (the noise each key makes when you type it)

- Keyboard autorepeat (the feature that causes a key to be typed multiple times if you hold it down)

- Pointer speed

- Screen saver

The command-line syntax for *xset* can be confusing. Some *xset* options are followed by on or off to set or unset the particular feature. Some options take a preceding dash to indicate that a feature be disabled, while the use of the option alone (without a dash) indicates that the feature be enabled. This can be confusing to users accustomed to seeing a dash as an introductory symbol on all options (as is the case with other UNIX and X programs).

Although you can run *xset* at any time, as a general rule it's a good idea to put it in your login session script. (This file is often called *.xinitrc* or *.xsession*. See Appendix A, *Managing Your Environment*, for details.)

The following sections describe the various options used to set pointer, keyboard, and screen features. Keep in mind that not all X implementations are guaranteed to honor all of these options.

Keyboard Bell

The b option controls bell volume (as a percentage of its maximum), pitch (in hertz), and duration (in milliseconds). It accepts up to three numerical parameters:

    b volume pitch duration

If no parameters are given, the system defaults are used. If only one parameter is given, the bell volume is set to that value. If two values are listed, the second parameter specifies the bell pitch. If three values are listed, the third one specifies the duration.

Volume as a percentage of the maximum is fairly easy to understand. A specification of 70 means that the volume will be "turned up" 70% of the way. The second and third arguments—pitch in hertz and duration in milliseconds—probably don't mean much to most users. One hundred milliseconds seems like a reasonable length beep. I don't notice much difference in pitch on my Sun workstation. I use the following settings:

    % xset b 50 1000 100

This command sets the volume of the keyboard bell to 50 percent of the maximum, the pitch to 1000 hertz, and the duration to 100 milliseconds.

Note that bell characteristics vary with different hardware. The X server sets the characteristics of the bell as closely as it can to the user's specifications.

The b option also accepts the parameters on or off. If you specify xset b on, the system default for volume is used. (Pitch and duration retain their previous settings.)

The command xset b off resets the volume to zero. (Again, pitch and duration retain their previous settings, but since the volume is turned all the way down, the bell is effectively disabled.) You can also turn off the bell by explicitly setting the volume parameter to 0 (xset b 0) or by using the -b option.

Bug Compatibility Mode (Release 4)

Some Release 3 clients were written to work with "features" of the R3 server, which could more accurately be called bugs. (Many of these bugs were eliminated in Release 4.) In order to allow certain R3 clients to work under R4, the R4 server has a bug compatibility mode that can be enabled using *xset*.

Bug compatibility mode is particularly important if you're running the R3 version of *xterm* under R4. Applications based on Version 1.0 of OSF/Motif (including Version 1.0 of *mwm*) also require that bug compatibility mode be enabled.

To enable bug compatibility mode, use the command xset bc; to disable it, use the command xset -bc.

Keyclick Volume

The c option sets the volume of the keyboard's keyclick—a sound generated by the server when you type each key (not to be confused with the noise the physical key makes). To specify a particular level of keyclick, use the option:

    c *volume*

volume can be a value from 0 to 100, indicating a percentage of the maximum volume. For example:

    % **xset c 75**

sets a moderately loud keyclick. The X server sets the volume to the nearest value that the hardware can support.

The c option also accepts the parameters on or off. If you specify xset c on, the system default for volume is used.

The keyclick can also be turned off with the option -c or by setting the volume parameter to 0 (xset c 0).

On some hardware, a volume of 0 to 50 turns the keyclick off, and a volume of 51 to 100 turns the keyclick on. Note also that in some cases, the keyclick cannot be turned on.

Enabling or Disabling Autorepeat

The r option controls the keyboard's autorepeat feature. Autorepeat causes a keystroke to be repeated over and over when the key is held down. (Multiple events are produced.) Use `xset r` or `xset r on` to enable key repeat. Use `xset -r` or `xset r off` to disable key repeat. On some keyboards (notably Apollo) only some keys repeat regardless of the state of this option.

Changing or Rehashing the Font Path

As discussed in Chapter 6, *Font Specification*, by default the X server looks for fonts in four subdirectories of */usr/lib/X11/fonts*: *misc*, *Speedo*, *75dpi*, and *100dpi*.

You change the font path using *xset* with the `fp` (font path) option. See Chapter 6 for some examples.

Note that the `fp` option with the `rehash` parameter causes the server to reread the *fonts.dir* and *fonts.alias* files in the current font path. You need to do this every time you edit an alias file to make the server aware of the changes (also discussed in Chapter 6). You also have to do this if you edit a *fonts.dir* file. See Volume Eight, *X Window System Administrator's Guide*, for more information.

Keyboard LEDs

The `led` option controls the enabling or disabling of one or all of the keyboard's LEDs. It accepts the parameters `on` or `off` to enable or disable all of the LEDs. A preceding dash also disables all of the LEDs (`-led`).

You can also enable or disable individual LEDs by supplying a numerical parameter (a value between 1 and 32) that corresponds to a particular LED. The `led` option followed by a numerical parameter enables that LED. The `led` option preceded by a dash and followed by a numerical parameter disables that LED. For example:

```
% xset led 3
```

would enable LED #3, while:

```
% xset -led 3
```

would disable LED #3.

Note that the particular LED values may refer to different LEDs on different hardware.

Pointer Acceleration

The m (mouse) option controls the rate at which the mouse or pointer moves across the screen. This option takes two parameters: *acceleration* and *threshold*. They must be positive integers. (The acceleration can also be written as a fraction, with the numerator and denominator separated by a slash, for example, 5/4.)

The mouse or pointer moves *acceleration* times as fast when it travels more than the *threshold* number of pixels in a short time. This way, the pointer can be used for precise alignment when it is moved slowly, yet it can be set to travel across the screen by a flick of the wrist when desired. If only one parameter is given, it is interpreted as the acceleration.

For example, the command:

```
% xset m 5 10
```

sets the pointer movement so that if you move the pointer more than 10 pixels, the pointer cursor moves five times as many pixels on the screen as you moved the pointer on the pad.

If no parameter or the value default is used, the system defaults will be set.

If you want to change the threshold and leave the acceleration unchanged, enter the value default for the acceleration parameter and then specify the threshold you want:

```
% xset m default 20
```

Screen Saver

X supports a screen saver to blank or randomly change the screen when the system is left unattended for an extended period. This screen saver avoids the "burn in" that can occur when the same image is displayed on the screen for a long time. The s (screen saver) option to *xset* determines how long the server must be inactive before the screen saver is started.

The s option takes two parameters: *time* and *cycle*. The screen goes blank if the server has not received any input for the time interval specified by the *time* parameter. The contents of the screen reappear upon receipt of any input. If the display is not capable of blanking the screen, then the screen is shifted a pixel in a random direction at time intervals set by the *cycle* parameter. The parameters are specified in seconds.

For example, the command:

```
% xset s 600
```

sets the length of time before the screen saver is invoked to 600 seconds (10 minutes).

For a display not capable of blanking the screen, the command:

```
% xset s 600 10
```

sets the length of time before the screen saver is invoked to 10 minutes and shifts the screen every 10 seconds thereafter, until input is received.

The s option also takes the parameters:

default   Resets the screen save option to the default.

blank   Turns on blanking and overrides any previous settings.

noblank   Displays a background pattern rather than blanking the screen; overrides any previous settings.

off   Turns off the screen saver option and overrides any previous settings.

expose   Allows window exposures (the server can discard window contents).

noexpose   Disables screen saver unless the server can regenerate the screens without causing exposure events (i.e., without forcing the applications to regenerate their own windows).

Color Definition

On color displays, every time a client requests a private read/write colorcell, a new color definition is entered in the display's colormap. The p option sets one of these colormap entries even though they are supposed to be private. The parameters are a positive integer identifying a cell in the colormap to be changed and a color name:

    p entry_number color_name

The root window colors can be changed on some servers using *xsetroot*. An error results if the map entry is a read-only color.

For example, the command:

    % xset p 3 blue

sets the third cell in the colormap to the color blue but only if some client has allocated this cell read/write.

The client that allocated the cell is likely to change it again sometime after you try to set it, since this is the usual procedure for allocating a read/write cell.

Help with xset Options

The q option lists the current values of all *xset* preferences.

Setting Root Window Characteristics: xsetroot

You can use the *xsetroot* client to tailor the appearance of the background (root) window on a display running X.

The *xsetroot* client is primarily used to specify the root window pattern: as a plaid-like grid, tiled gray pattern, solid color, or a bitmap. You can also specify foreground and background colors (defaults are black and white), reverse video, and set the shape of the pointer when it's in the root window.

If no options are specified, or the -def option is specified, *xsetroot* resets the root window to its default state, a gray mesh pattern, and resets the pointer to the X pointer. The -def option can also be specified with other options; those characteristics that are not set by other options are reset to the defaults.

Although *xsetroot* can be run at any time, we suggest you run it from a startup shell script, as described in Appendix A, *Managing Your Environment*. See "When Should I Set Preferences?" earlier in this chapter for the reasoning behind this suggestion.

For a complete list of options, see the *xsetroot* reference page in Part Three of this guide. Not all X implementations are guaranteed to support all of these options. Some of the options may not work on certain hardware devices.

The -help option prints all the *xsetroot* options to standard output. The options you'll probably use most frequently are explained in the next section. Since only one type of background pattern can be specified at a time, the -solid, -gray, -grey, -bitmap and -mod options are mutually exclusive.

Setting Root Window Patterns

The default root window pattern is called a "gray mesh." On most displays, it is fairly dark.

The *xsetroot* client allows you to specify an alternative gray background with the -grey (or -gray) option. This tiled gray pattern is slightly lighter than the default gray mesh pattern.

The *xsetroot* client also allows you to create a root window made up of repeated "tiles" of a particular bitmap, using the option:

    -bitmap *filename*

where *filename* is the bitmap file to be used as the window pattern.

You can choose any of the standard bitmaps (generally found in the directory */usr/include/X11/bitmaps*) or make your own bitmap files using the *bitmap* client (see Chapter 7, *Graphics Utilities*).

For example, the command:

    % xsetroot -bitmap /home/paula/gumby -fg red -bg blue

fills the root window with a tiling of the bitmap */home/paula/gumby* (a virtual army of Gumbys!), using the colors red and blue.

The -mod option sets a plaid-like grid pattern on the root window. You specify the horizontal (x) and vertical (y) dimensions in pixels of each square in the grid. The syntax of the option is:

```
-mod x y
```

where the parameters x and y are integers ranging from 1 to 16 (pixels). (Zero and negative numbers are taken as 1.)

The larger the x and y values you specify, the larger (and more visible) each square on the root window grid pattern. Try the command:

```
% xsetroot -mod 16 16
```

for the largest possible grid squares. Then test different x and y specifications.

The *xsetroot* option:

```
-solid color
```

sets the color of the root window to a solid color. You can use a name from a color name database or a numeric color specification.

The command:

```
% xsetroot -solid lightblue
```

sets the color of the root window to light blue.* See Chapter 12, *Specifying Color*, for more about color possibilities.

Foreground Color, Background Color, and Reverse Video

In addition to specifying a solid color for the root window pattern, *xsetroot* allows you to specify foreground and background colors if you set the pattern with -bitmap or -mod. The standard Toolkit options are used to set foreground and background colors: -fg and -bg. The defaults are black and white.

Colors can be specified as names from a color name database, or as numeric values. See Chapter 12, *Specifying Color* for more instructions on how to specify color.

If you specify reverse video (-rv), the foreground and background colors are reversed.

Foreground and background colors also take effect when you set the root window pointer, as described in the next section.

---

*For technical reasons, colors set with xsetroot -solid may change unexpectedly. When you set a color with the -solid option to *xsetroot*, the client allocates a colorcell, sets the color, and deallocates the colorcell. The root window changes to that color. If another client is started that sets a new color, it allocates the next available colorcell—which may be the same one *xsetroot* just deallocated. This results in that color changing to the new color. The root window also changes to the new color. If this happens, you can run *xsetroot* again and if there are other colorcells available, the root window changes to the new color. If all colorcells are allocated, any call to change a colorcell results in an error message.

While this behavior may seem to be a serious bug, it is actually an optimization designed to ensure applications don't run out of colors unnecessarily. Free colormap cells can be a scarce resource. See Volume One, *Xlib Programming Manual*, for more information.

Changing the Root Window Pointer

By default, the pointer is an X when it's in the root window. You can change the shape of the root window pointer to one of the standard X cursor shapes or to any bitmap, using these options:

```
-cursor_name standard_cursor_name
-cursor cursorfile maskfile
```

The first option allows you to set the root window pointer to one of the standard cursor symbols, which are generally listed in the file */usr/include/X11/cursorfont.h*. We've provided a list of the standard cursors (as well as pictures of them) in Appendix D, *Standard Cursors*. To specify a standard cursor on a command line or in a resource file, strip the XC_ prefix from the name. Thus, to set the root window pointer to the pirate cursor symbol, you would enter:

```
% xsetroot -cursor_name pirate
```

The second option is intended to allow you to set the root window pointer to a bitmap, perhaps one you create. The parameters *cursorfile* and *maskfile* are bitmaps. The *cursorfile* sets the bitmap for the pointer shape. In effect, the *maskfile* is placed behind the *cursorfile* bitmap to set it off from the root window. The *maskfile* should be the same shape as the *cursorfile* but should generally be at least one pixel wider in all directions.*

For the *cursorfile*, you can use any of the standard bitmaps (generally found in */usr/include/X11/bitmaps*) or you can make your own with the *bitmap* client (see Chapter 7, *Graphics Utilities*).

Every standard cursor has an associated mask. To get an idea of what masks look like, display the cursor font using the command:

```
% xfd -fn cursor
```

If you are using your own bitmap as the *cursorfile*, until you get used to the way masks work, create a *maskfile* that is a copy of the *cursorfile* with all bits set, i.e., the *maskfile* should be all black† (or the foreground color). Then edit the *maskfile* to make it wider than the *cursorfile* by at least one pixel in all directions.

To specify a root window pointer made from the smiling Gumby bitmap we created for Figure 7-2, first copy the bitmap to make a mask file:

```
% cp gumby gumby.mask
```

---

*Technically speaking, the mask determines the pixels on the screen that are disturbed by the cursor. It functions as a sort of outliner or highlighter for the cursor shape. The mask appears as a white (or background color) border around the cursor (black or another foreground color), making it visible over any root window pattern. This is especially important when a black cursor appears on a black root window.

With the *xsetroot* defaults, you can observe the effect of a mask. When you move the X pointer onto the dark gray root window, the X should have a very thin white border, which enables you to see it more clearly.

†Don't be confused by the idea of a black cursor with a black mask on a black root window. Remember, the mask determines the pixels that are disturbed by the cursor—in effect creating an outline around the cursor. The outline appears in white (or specified background color), regardless of the color of the *maskfile*.

Then edit the *gumby.mask* file using the *bitmap* client, setting all squares inside the Gumby. (You can use the *bitmap* Flood Fill command to set all the empty squares at once.) Continue to edit the bitmap, making it one pixel wider in all directions.

Then specify the new pointer with *xsetroot*:

```
% xsetroot -cursor gumby gumby.mask
```

See Chapter 7, *Graphics Utilities*, for more information on using *bitmap*.

Modifier Key and Pointer Customization: xmodmap

Mapping keys is one of the more confusing tasks you might find the need to accomplish. When does key mapping become an issue? Here's a typical case. Say the key labeled "Control" is in a very awkward position for you and you have to use it all the time. Another key (labeled "Option") is in a very convenient position on the keyboard and you never use it. You can assign (or map) the Control function to the physical key labeled "Option" using *xmodmap*.

The *xmodmap* client is generally used to map key functions to physical keys on the keyboard. Primarily, *xmodmap* is used to assign so-called "modifier" key functions to physical keys. But it can also change the way other keys (and even pointer buttons) function. (Basically, *xmodmap* can be used to specify what character is generated when you press a key or what action happens when you press a pointer button. You'll probably use it more often to map modifier key functions.)

As described in Chapter 3, *Working in the X Environment*, keys with labels such as Shift, Control, Caps Lock, etc. are called "modifier" keys because they modify the action of other keys. The number and names of modifier keys differ from workstation to workstation. Every keyboard is likely to have a Shift, Caps Lock, and Control key but after that, the confusion begins. One workstation might have an Alt key, another might have a Funct key, and yet another a Gold key. On the Sun-3 keyboard, there are no less than three additional modifier keys, labeled Alternate, Right, and Left.

Because of the differences between keyboards, X programs are designed to work with *logical* modifier keynames. The logical keynames represent functions recognized by X programs. These modifier keynames can be mapped by the user to any physical key on the keyboard with the *xmodmap* client.

The logical keynames that X recognizes are:

- Shift
- Lock
- Control
- Mod1 (Meta in *mwm*)
- Mod2

- Mod3
- Mod4
- Mod5

These keynames are case-insensitive.

Of these X modifier keys, only Shift, Caps Lock, Control, and Meta are in common use.

The primary function of *xmodmap* is to allow you to assign these important modifier key-name functions (Shift, Control, Meta, etc.) to convenient keys on the keyboard. For example, you could choose to map the Shift function to a single key called "Shift," to two "Shift" keys (one on either side of the keypad), to an "Alt" key, or to any other convenient key or keys on the physical keyboard. A left-handed person might choose to map modifier keys that more often are found on the left side, such as Control, to the right side of the key-board.

In practical terms, each server will have a default keyboard configuration. The Shift, Caps Lock, and Control modifier keynames will be mapped to obvious keys. The assignment of the Meta key might be less obvious.

The *xmodmap* client allows you to print out the current assignments of modifier keyname functions to physical keys and/or to change the assignments.

xmodmap also has two other functions that you will probably use less frequently. In addition to mapping modifier keyname functions to physical keys, *xmodmap* also allows you to assign the function of *any* key on the keyboard to any other key. For instance, you can make the Backspace key and the Delete key both function as Delete keys. (This may be helpful if the Backspace key is easier to reach.)

Also, in addition to keyboard mappings, *xmodmap* can be used to display or change the pointer button assignments. Many X clients recognize logical pointer button commands. For example, holding down and dragging the first logical pointer button in an *xterm* window copies the text into memory. (In many default pointer maps, the first logical button is the leftmost button, designed to be pressed by the right index finger.) Each logical button is asso-ciated with a *button code*. The first logical button generates button code 1, the second logical button generates button code 2, etc. *xmodmap* allows you to reassign logical buttons to dif-ferent physical buttons on the pointer.

Thus, basically, *xmodmap* can perform three types of mappings:

1. Assign modifier keyname functions (such as Shift, Control, Meta) recognized by X to physical keys.

2. Make any key on the keyboard function as any other key (for example, making Back-space function like Delete).

3. Reassign logical pointer button functions to other physical buttons (for example, making the rightmost physical button function as the first logical button).

In the following sections, we discuss key mapping, with an emphasis on the first type of map-ping, of modifier keyname functions. Chances are, you'll have relatively little call to map other key functions (such as Backspace), though we have included an example of one such mapping, just in case.

After considering key mapping, we'll take a look at the much simpler issues involved in mapping pointer button functions. As you might expect, when you're changing the functionality of (up to) three pointer buttons, it's fairly simple to keep track of what you're doing.

On the other hand, mapping modifier key functions to physical keys can be more than a little confusing. In order to understand the mechanics of mapping keys, we first need to take a look at some terms used to describe keyboard keys.

Keycodes and Keysyms

Each key on a physical keyboard can be identified by a number known as a *keycode*. (Technically speaking, a keycode is the actual value that the key generates.) Keycodes cannot be mapped to other keys. No matter what functions you assign to various keys with *xmodmap*, the keycode associated with each physical key remains the same.

In addition to a keycode, each physical key is associated with a name known as a keysym. A *keysym* (*key sym*bol name) is a name that represents the label on a key (theoretically) and corresponds to its function.

Alphanumeric keys generally have obvious keysyms, corresponding to the label on the key: for example, the keysym for the key labeled "H" is *h*. Unfortunately, a keysym does not always correspond to the key label. For example, on a Sun-3 workstation, though the keysym for the key labeled "Return" is *Return*, the keysym for the key labeled "Alternate" is *Break*, and the keysym for the key labeled "Right" is *Meta_R*.

While each keycode is tied to a physical key, each keysym corresponds to a *function*—and the keysym/function is mapped to a particular physical key (keycode). Every keyboard has a default assignment of keysyms to keycodes. In most cases, each physical key on the keyboard will be associated with a different keysym. As we'll see, however, the keysym (function) associated with a particular physical key (keycode) can be changed. This is done by assigning the keysym of one key to the keycode of another.

The modifier keynames recognized by X are not to be confused with keysyms. The X modifier keys are limited to the eight keynames discussed previously and are assigned *in addition* to the regular keysym/keycode pairings. In other words, when a physical key is mapped to function as the X Control key, it already has a default functionality (keysym) and keycode.

By default, most modifier keyname functions are mapped to keys having keysyms representing the same function. For example, the X Control keyname is probably mapped to the key labeled Control and having the keysym Control.

The Meta modifier keyname is probably also assigned to a key having the keysym Meta. However, determining which physical key has the keysym Meta can be something of a puzzle. Later in this chapter, we'll consider a program called *xev*, which can be used to determine the keysym and keycode of any physical key.

With this background information in mind, we can now tackle a procedure to map modifier keynames.

Procedure to Map Modifier Keys

In order to change modifier key mappings with a minimum of confusion, you should perform these steps:

1. Display the current *modifier* key mappings using *xmodmap*.

2. Then print out the default assignments of keysyms to keycodes for *all* keys, using *xmodmap* with the –pke option. Save this list of the default key assignments in a file as a reference.

3. Experiment with the *xev* client to determine the keysyms associated with certain physical keys. This will help you find the key(s) assigned as the Meta modifier key (which probably also has the keysym Meta).

4. Once you're familiar with the current assignments, you can remap modifier keys using *xmodmap*.

Displaying the Current Modifier Key Map

Before mapping any modifier keynames, you should take a look at the current assignments. With no options, *xmodmap* displays the current map of X modifier keynames to actual keys. Type *xmodmap* and you get a display similar to this:

```
xmodmap: up to 2 keys per modifier, (keycodes in parentheses):

shift       Shift_L (0x6a), Shift_R (0x75)
lock        Caps_Lock (0x7e)
control     Control_L (0x53)
mod1        Meta_L (0x7f),  Meta_R (0x81)
mod2
mod3
mod4
mod5
```

For each logical keyname (on the left), *xmodmap* lists one or more keysyms, each followed in parentheses by an actual hardware keycode. The keycodes displayed by *xmodmap* are represented in hex. (As we'll see, the equivalent decimal and octal keycodes are also accepted as arguments to *xmodmap*.)

Logical modifier keyname recognized by X	Keysym	Keycode (hex version)
Shift	Shift_L	(0x6a)
	Shift_R	(0x75)
Lock	Caps_Lock	(0x7e)
Control	Control_L	(0x53)
Mod1	Meta_L	(0x7f)
	Meta_R	(0x81)

In this mapping, two keys are assigned as Meta (mod1) keys: keys having the keysyms Meta_L and Meta_R (for left and right, apparently one on each side of the keyboard). Unfortunately, as you can see, this doesn't really tell you which keys these are on the physical keyboard. You still need to know which physical keys (keycodes) have the keysyms Meta_L and Meta_R. You can determine this using the *xev* client, described later in this chapter.

Determining the Default Key Mappings

Before you start mapping keys, you should display and save a map of the default assignments of keysyms to keycodes. Running *xmodmap* with the -pke option prints a current map of all keyboard keys to standard output. This map, called a keymap table, lists the decimal keycode on the left and the associated keysym(s) on the right. (The "e" in -pke refers to "expression." This option specifies that each line in the map will be in the form of an expression that can in turn be supplied to *xmodmap*—to recover the original settings, if necessary.) Example 14-1 shows a portion of a typical keymap table returned by xmodmap -pke, for a Sun-3 keyboard.

Example 14-1. Partial keymap table with valid xmodmap expressions

```
keycode 109 = C
keycode 110 = V
keycode 111 = B
keycode 112 = N
keycode 113 = M
keycode 114 = comma less
keycode 115 = period greater
keycode 116 = slash question
keycode 117 = Shift_R
keycode 118 = Linefeed
keycode 119 = F33
keycode 120 = Down F34
keycode 121 = F35
        .
        .
        .
keycode 126 = Caps_Lock
keycode 127 = Meta_L
keycode 128 = space
keycode 129 = Meta_R
```

Setup Clients

As you can see, the keymap table lists regular keyboard keys (C, V, comma, slash, space, etc.) and function/numeric keypad keys (F33, Down <Arrow>, F35, etc.), as well as modifier keys (Caps_Lock, Meta_L and Meta_R). Some keys generate two keysyms, the first when you press the key alone, the second when you hold Shift and then press the key. For example, the key with keycode 115 can generate a period (.) or (with Shift) the greater than symbol (>):

```
keycode 115 = period greater
```

If you map several keys, you may get confused as to the original assignments. Before you map any keys, we suggest you redirect the keymap table to a file to save and use as a reference:

```
% xmodmap -pke > keytable
```

You can recover the original mappings by supplying the relevant lines from the keymap to *xmodmap* using the -e option (explained later in this chapter).

The keysyms recognized by your server are a subset of a far greater number of keysyms recognized internationally. The file *keysym.h* (generally in the directory */usr/include/X11*) lists the keysym *families* that are enabled for your server. The file *keysymdef.h* (also generally in the directory */usr/include/X11*) lists the keysyms in each of the families enabled for your server, as well as the keysyms in several other families. See Appendix H, *Keysyms*, of Volume Two, *Xlib Reference Manual*, for more information on keysyms and tables of the most common ones.

Matching Keysyms with Physical Keys Using xev

The keysym and keycode for any key can be determined with the *xev* client.* This is particularly useful for finding the Meta key(s). The *xev* client is used to keep track of *events*, packets of information that are generated by the server when actions occur and are interpreted by other clients. Moving the pointer or pressing a keyboard key cause input events to occur.

To use *xev*, enter the command:

```
% xev
```

in an *xterm* window, and then use the pointer to place the *xev* window, as in Figure 14-1.

---

*xev is a Release 3 standard client. Since Release 4, it has lived in the *demos* directory. If an executable version does not exist on your system, ask your system administrator.

If you cannot use *xev*, you must rely on the keymap table and a little deductive reasoning. Since certain *mwm* functions have keyboard shortcuts involving the Meta key, testing these shortcuts should help you locate this key. See Chapter 4, *More about the mwm Window Manager*, for more information.

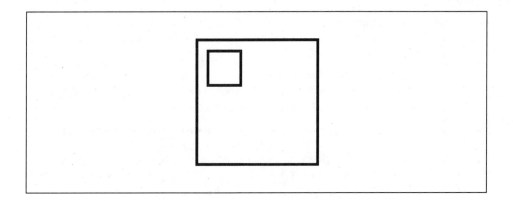

Figure 14-1. xev window

Within the *xev* window is a small box. Move the pointer inside this box. When you type a key inside the box, information about the key, including its keysym and keycode, will be displayed in the *xterm* window from which you started *xev*. The relevant information will look like this:

```
. . . keycode 127 (keysym 0xffe7, Meta_L) . . .
```

Notice that the keycode is given as a decimal number. You can use the decimal keycode as an argument to *xmodmap*. The keysym is listed by name, Meta_L, and value, 0xffe7. (This value cannot be supplied as a keysym argument to *xmodmap*.)

To find the Meta key, type a few likely keys in the *xev* window. Type Control-C in the window from which you invoked *xev* to terminate the program. (If you ran *xev* in the background, you'll have to kill the *xev* window. See Chapter 8, *Other Clients*, for ways to kill a client window.)

Changing the Map with xmodmap

xmodmap executes an expression or list of expressions that is interpreted as instructions to modify the key (or pointer) map. The expressions that can be interpreted by *xmodmap* are described in the next section.

xmodmap has this syntax:

xmodmap [*options*] [*filename*]

An expression can be executed in either one of two ways:

- From the command line, using the -e *expression* option. This option specifies an expression to be executed (as an instruction to modify the map). Any number of expressions may be specified from the command line. An *expression* should be enclosed in quotes.

- Entered in a file that is used as an argument to *xmodmap*. Several expressions can be entered in one file.

See the *xmodmap* reference page in Part Three of this guide for a complete list of options. Other than `-e` `expression`, the most important options for our purposes are listed below.

`-n`

Indicates that *xmodmap* should not change the key mappings as specified in the `filename` or command-line expression but should display what it would do. A handy test. (Only works with key mappings, not with expressions that change the pointer map.)

`-verbose`

Indicates that *xmodmap* should print information as it parses its input.

`filename` specifies a file containing *xmodmap* expressions to be executed (as instructions to modify the map). This file is usually kept in the user's home directory with a name like *.xmodmaprc*.

Expressions to Change the Key Map

The expressions interpreted by *xmodmap* can be used to perform these types of key mappings:*

1. Assign and remove keysyms as modifier keynames recognized by X.

2. Map any keysym (function) to any physical key (keycode).

This list shows allowable expressions, divided by function. (Using *xmodmap* with the `-grammar` option returns a help message with much of this information.) Those expressions that include an equal sign require a space before and after the sign.

1. To assign and remove keysyms as modifier keynames:

   `clear` *MODIFIERNAME*

   Removes all entries in the modifier map for the given modifier, where valid modifier names are: shift, lock, control, mod1, mod2, mod3, mod4, and mod5 (case does not matter in modifier names, although it does matter for all other names). For example, the expression `clear` `Lock` will remove all keys that were bound to the lock modifier.

   `add` *MODIFIERNAME* = *KEYSYMNAME*

   Adds the given keysym to the indicated modifier map. For example, you could make the Alt key an additional shift modifier key. The keysym name is evaluated after all input expressions are read to make it easy to write expressions to swap keys.

---

*Expressions to change the pointer map are discussed in the section "Displaying and Changing the Pointer Map," later in this chapter.

```
remove MODIFIERNAME = KEYSYMNAME
```

> Removes the given keysym from the indicated modifier map (unmaps it). For example, remove Caps_Lock as the lock modifier key. Unlike with the add expression, the keysym names are evaluated as the line is read in. This allows you to remove keys from a modifier without having to worry about whether they have been reassigned.

2. To map any keysym(s) to any physical key (keycode):

```
keycode NUMBER = KEYSYMNAME
```

> Assigns the keysym to the indicated keycode (which may be specified in decimal, hex, or octal). Usually only one keysym is assigned to a given code.

```
keysym KEYSYMNAME = KEYSYMNAME
```

> Assigns the keysym on the right to the keycode of the keysym on the left. Note that if you have the same keysym bound to multiple keys, this might not work.

Key Mapping Examples

Expressions can be used on the *xmodmap* command line or entered in a file that is then used as an argument to *xmodmap*. (The section "When Do I Set Preferences?" discusses some issues regarding when to run *xmodmap*.) The current section includes three examples, corresponding to the three types of mappings you can perform.

Remember that including the −n option on the *xmodmap* command line allows you to see what the new mappings *would* be, without actually performing them. This can be very useful, particularly while you're learning to use *xmodmap* and getting used to the syntax of expressions. (Note, however, that −n cannot be used with expressions to change the pointer map.)

First, the *xmodmap* client allows you to assign logical modifier keynames to physical keys. A not so obvious feature of *xmodmap* is that to change the mapping of a modifier key, you must first remove that key from the current modifier map.

For example, to swap the left Control and (Caps) Lock keys, you would first need to unmap both physical keys (Caps_Lock, Control_L) from their respective modifier keynames (lock, control):

```
remove lock = Caps_Lock
remove control = Control_L
```

And then reverse the mappings:

```
add lock = Control_L
add control = Caps_Lock
```

If you then type *xmodmap* without options, you see the new map:

```
xmodmap: up to 2 keys per modifier, (keycodes in parentheses):

shift      Shift_L (0x6a), Shift_R (0x75)
lock       Control_L (0x53)
control    Caps_Lock (0x7e)
```

```
mod1        Meta_L (0x7f), Meta_R (0x81)
mod2
mod3
mod4
mod5
```

The key with the keysym Control_L functions as a Lock key and the key with the keysym Caps_Lock functions as a Control key.

Second, *xmodmap* allows you to assign any keysym to any other key. For example, you might make the Backspace key function as a Delete key:

```
% xmodmap -e 'keysym BackSpace = Delete'
```

Then when you display the keymap table and grep for the Delete keysym, you'll see that it is assigned twice. On the command line of an *xterm* window, type:

```
% xmodmap -pke | grep Delete
```

and you'll get two lines from the current keymap table, similar to these:

```
keycode 50 = Delete
keycode 73 = Delete
```

The 50 and 73 are keycodes representing two physical keys. As you can see, both of these keys now function as Delete keys.

This example suggests some of the confusion you can experience using *xmodmap*. We know that one of these keys previously functioned as the Backspace key. But how can we tell which one? Here is an instance when our default keymap table comes in handy. If you've run xmodmap -pke and redirected it to a file before changing any mappings, you can check the file for the keysyms originally associated with the keycodes 50 and 73. In this case, the file tells us 50 originally was Backspace and 73 was Delete.

Of course, you could also figure out the original assignments by remapping one of the keycodes to Backspace. Then, if the key marked Backspace functions as marked, you know you've mapped the keysym to the original keycode. But, as you can see, the default keymap table can greatly simplify matters.

This example also implies that there are advantages to using expressions of the form:

```
keycode number = keysymname
```

This expression syntax requires you to be aware of default keycode/keysym assignments. Also, if you explicitly assign a keysym to a particular keycode, it's much easier to keep track of what you're doing and retrace your steps if necessary. On the down side, though keysyms are portable, keycodes may vary from server to server. Thus, expressions using this syntax cannot be ported to other systems.

Displaying and Changing the Pointer Map

If you want to change the assignment of logical pointer buttons to physical buttons, you should first display the current pointer map with the -pp option to *xmodmap*. A typical pointer map appears in Figure 14-2.

```
There are 3 pointer buttons defined.

      Physical      Button
      Button         Code
         1             1
         2             2
         3             3
```

Figure 14-2. Pointer map

This is a fairly simple map: the physical buttons are listed on the left and the corresponding logical functions (button codes) are listed on the right.

These are typical assignments for a right-handed person: the first logical button is the left-most button, designed to be pressed by the right index finger. The *xmodmap* client allows you to reassign logical buttons—typically so that the pointer can be more easily used with the left hand.*

There are two relevant *xmodmap* expressions: one to assign logical pointer buttons (button codes) to physical buttons; and another to restore the default assignments. The syntax of the expressions is:

pointer = *n1 n2 n3*

> Sets the first, second, and third physical buttons to the button codes *n1, n2,* and *n3.*

pointer = default

> Sets the pointer map back to its default settings (button 1 generates a code of 1, button 2 generates a code of 2, etc.).

Being able to change the pointer button assignments is very useful if you happen to be left-handed and would like the rightmost physical button to function as the first logical button (that is, generate button code 1). To configure the pointer for a southpaw:

```
% xmodmap -e 'pointer = 3 2 1'
```

Then if you display the pointer mappings with xmodmap -pp, you get this:

```
There are 3 pointer buttons defined.

      Physical      Button
      Button         Code
         1             3
         2             2
         3             1
```

---

*Remember that the -n option, which allows you to see what *xmodmap would* do without performing the changes, cannot be used with expressions to change the pointer mapping.

You can then push the first logical button (button code 1) with the index finger of your left hand.

You can return to the default pointer button assignments by entering:

```
% xmodmap -e 'pointer = default'
```

Part Three:

Client Reference Pages

This part of the guide provides UNIX-style "man-pages" for each of the standard X programs, as well as the mwm window manager. These pages are arranged alphabetically for ease of reference, and they contain detailed information (such as all options to a program) that is not covered in other parts of this guide.

The following reference pages appear in this section:

Name

Intro – overview of reference page format.

Syntax

This section describes the command-line syntax for invoking the client. Anything in **bold** type should be typed exactly as shown. Items in *italics* are parameters that should be replaced by actual values when you enter the command. Anything enclosed in brackets is optional. For example:

bitmap [*options*] *filename*

means to type the command **bitmap** followed by zero or more options (from the list of options on the reference page), followed by the name of the file containing the bitmap to be edited.

Description

This section explains the operation of the client. In some cases, additional descriptive sections appear later on in the reference page.

Options

This section lists available command-line options. In some cases, reference is made to "all of the standard X Toolkit command-line options." These X Toolkit options are listed in Chapter 10 of this guide, as well as in the first reference page in this section, which is simply labeled *X*.

Resources

This section lists the resource variable names that can be specified in an *.Xresources* or other resource file. In some cases, reference is made to "all the core resource names and classes." A list of the core names and classes appears in Appendix G, *Widget Resources*. Syntax rules and examples appear in Chapter 11, *Setting Resources*. For complete information, see Volume Four, *X Toolkit Intrinsics Programming Manual*.

Widget Hierarchy

Applications written with the X Toolkit are comprised of widgets, which are predefined user interface components or objects. Typical widgets create graphical features such as menus, command buttons, dialog boxes, and scrollbars. Applications composed of widgets are always window-based (such as *xterm*, *xclock*, and *xman*). X also provides clients that are not window-based (such as *xlsfonts*, *xwininfo*, and *xlsclients*) and thus do not use widgets.

If present on a reference page, the section "Widget Hierarchy" diagrams the relationship of the widgets within the application. The widget hierarchy is significant in specifying client resources. Most Toolkit clients accept both application-specific resources (listed in the "Resources" section) and resources for the component widgets. Appendix G lists the user-settable resources for the Athena widgets and explains the somewhat complicated mechanisms by which resources are interpreted.

Files

If present, this section lists the system and/or application-specific files relevant to the application.

Environment

If present, this section lists shell environment variables used by the client. This section does not list the DISPLAY and XENVIRONMENT variables, which are used by all clients. These variables are used as follows:

DISPLAY

> To get the default display name (specifically, the host, server/display, and screen). The DISPLAY variable typically has the form:
>
> *hostname*: *server. screen*
>
> (for example, `isla:0.0`). See *X* for more information about display name syntax.

XENVIRONMENT

> To get the name of a resource file containing host-specific resources. If this variable is not set, the resource manager will look for a file called *.Xdefaults-**hostname*** (where ***hostname*** is the name of a particular host) in the user's home directory. See the *X* reference page for more information.

See Also

This section lists other reference pages in Part Three of this guide that may also be of interest. Note that versions of these pages may have been installed in the usual online manual page directories, and may be available via the UNIX *man*(1) command. References such as *stat*(2) can be found in the standard UNIX documentation. This section may also include references to documentation on Xlib, the X Toolkit, various widgets, etc.

Bugs

If present, this section lists areas in which the author of the program thinks it could be improved. In a few instances, we've listed additional bugs we've noted.

Author

The authors of the program and (generally) of the reference page as well. Most of the reference pages are subject to the copyright provisions in the "Copyright" section of the X reference page. Where appropriate, additional copyrights are noted on individual pages.

Note, however, that those portions of this document that are based on the original X11 documentation and other source materials have been revised, and that all such revisions are copyright © 1987, 1988, 1989, 1990, 1991, 1992 O'Reilly & Associates, Inc. Inasmuch as the proprietary revisions can't be separated from the freely copyable MIT source material, the net result is that copying of this document is not allowed. Sorry for the doublespeak!

Name

X – a portable, network-transparent window system.

Description

X is a network-transparent window system developed at MIT that runs on a wide range of computing and graphics machines. It should be relatively straightforward to build the MIT software distribution on most ANSI C and POSIX compliant systems. Commercial implementations are also available for a wide range of platforms.

The X Consortium requests that the following names be used when referring to this software:

    X
    X Window System
    X Version 11
    X Window System, Version 11
    X11

The name "X Windows" should not be used. *X Window System* is a trademark of the Massachusetts Institute of Technology.

X Window System servers run on computers with bitmap displays. The server distributes user input to and accepts output requests from various client programs through a variety of different interprocess communication channels. Although the most common case is for the client programs to be running on the same machine as the server, clients can also be run transparently from other machines, including machines with different architectures and operating systems.

X supports overlapping hierarchical subwindows, and text and graphics operations, on both monochrome and color displays. For a full explanation of the functions that are available, see Volume One, *Xlib Programming Manual*, and Volume Two, *Xlib Reference Manual*.

The number of programs that use X is quite large. Programs provided in the core MIT distribution include: a terminal emulator (*xterm*), a window manager (*twm*), a display manager (*xdm*), a console redirect program (*xconsole*), mail managing utilities (*xmh* and *xbiff*), a manual page browser (*xman*), a bitmap editor (*bitmap*), a resource editor (*editres*), a ditroff previewer (*xditview*), access control programs (*xauth* and *xhost*), user preference setting programs (*xrdb*, *xcmsdb*, *xset*, *xsetroot*, *xstdcmap*, and *xmodmap*), a load monitor (*xload*), clocks (*oclock* and *xclock*), a font displayer (*xfd*), utilities for listing information about fonts, windows, and displays (*xlsfonts*, *xfontsel*, *xstdcmap*, *xwininfo*, *xdpyinfo*, *xlsclients*, and *xprop*), a diagnostic for seeing what events are generated and when (*xev*), screen image manipulation utilities (*xwd*, *xwud*, *xpr*, and *xmag*), and various demos (*xeyes*, *ico*, *xllperf*, *xgc*, etc.)

Many other utilities, window managers, games, toolkits, and so on, are included as user-contributed software in the MIT distribution, or are available using anonymous *ftp* on the Internet. For more information, see the Preface of this guide, Volume Eight, *X Window System Administrator's Guide*; and Volume One, *Xlib Programming Manual*.

Starting Up

There are two ways of starting the X server and an initial set of client applications. The particular method used depends on which operating system you are running and on whether or not you use other window systems in addition to X. The methods are:

xdm (the X Display Manager)

> If you want to have X running on your display at all times, your site administrator can set up your machine to use the X Display Manager *xdm*. This program is typically started by the system at boot time and takes care of keeping the server running and getting users logged in. If you are running *xdm*, you will see a window on the screen welcoming you to the system and asking for your username and password. Simply type them in as you would at a normal terminal, pressing the Return key after each. If you make a mistake, *xdm* will display an error message and ask you to try again. After you have successfully logged in, *xdm* will start up your X environment. By default, if you have an executable file named *.xsession* in your home directory, *xdm* will treat it as a program (or shell script) to be run to start up your initial clients (such as terminal emulators, clocks, a window manager, user settings for things like the background, the speed of the pointer, etc.). Your site administrator can provide details.

xinit (run manually from the shell)

> Sites that support more than one window system might choose to use the *xinit* program for starting X manually. If this is true for your machine, your site administrator will probably have provided a program named "x11", "startx", or "xstart" that will do site-specific initialization in a nice way (such as loading convenient default resources, running a window manager, displaying a clock, and starting several terminal emulators). If not, you can build such a script using the *xinit* program. This utility simply runs one user-specified program to start the server, runs another to start up any desired clients, and then waits for either to finish. Since either or both of the user-specified programs may be a shell script, this gives substantial flexibility at the expense of a nice interface. For this reason, *xinit* is not intended for end users.

Display Names

From the user's perspective, every X server has a *displayname* of the form:

host:server.screen

This information is used by the application to determine how it should connect to the server and which screen it should use by default (on displays with multiple monitors):

host   The host name of the physical display. If the *host* name is not given, the most efficient way of communicating to a server on the same machine will be used.

server

> The *server* (or display) number. The phrase "display" is usually used to refer to a collection of monitors that share a common keyboard and pointer (mouse, tablet, etc.). Most workstations have only one keyboard, and therefore only one display. Larger, multi-user systems, however, will frequently have several displays so that more than

one person at a time can be doing graphics work. To avoid confusion, each display on a machine is assigned a `server` number (beginning at 0) when the X server for that display is started. The `server` number must always be given in a display name. In this guide, the `server` number is also referred to as the `display` number (referring to the phrase *display server*).

screen

The *screen* number. Some displays share a single keyboard and pointer among two or more monitors. Since each monitor has its own set of windows, each screen is assigned a *screen* number (beginning at 0) when the X server for that display is started. If the *screen* number is not given, then screen 0 will be used.

On POSIX systems, the default display name is stored in your DISPLAY environment variable. This variable is set automatically by the *xterm* terminal emulator. However, when you log into another machine on a network, you'll need to set DISPLAY by hand to point to your display. For example:

```
% setenv DISPLAY myws:0              (C Shell)
$ DISPLAY=myws:0; export DISPLAY     (Bourne Shell)
```

The *xon* script can be used to start an X program on a remote machine. It automatically sets the DISPLAY variable correctly. Finally, most X programs accept a command-line option of `-display` *displayname* to temporarily override the contents of DISPLAY. This is most commonly used to pop windows on another person's screen or as part of a "remote shell" command to start an xterm pointing back to your display. For example:

```
% xeyes -display joesws:0 -geometry 1000x1000+0+0
% rsh big xterm -display myws:0 -ls </dev/null &
```

X servers listen for connections on a variety of different communications channels (network byte streams, shared memory, etc.). Since there can be more than one way of contacting a given server, the `host` name part of the display name is used to determine the type of channel (also called a transport layer) to be used. X servers generally support the following types of connections:

local   The `host` part of the display name should be the empty string. For example: `:0`, `:1`, and `:0.1`. The most efficient local transport will be chosen.

TCP/IP The `host` part of the display name should be the server machine's IP address name. Full Internet names, abbreviated names, and IP addresses are all allowed. For example: `expo.lcs.mit.edu:0`, `expo:0`, `18.30.0.212:0`, `bigmachine:1`, and `hydra:0.1`.

DECnet

The `host` part of the display name should be the server machine's nodename followed by two colons instead of one. For example: `myws::0`, `big::1`, and `hydra::0.1`.

Access Control

An X server can use several types of access control. Mechanisms provided in Release 5 are:

```
Host Access Simple host-based access control.
MIT-MAGIC-COOKIE-1  Shared plain-text "cookies".
XDM-AUTHORIZATION-1 Secure DES based private-keys.
SUN-DES-1    Based on Sun's secure rpc system.
```

xdm initializes access control for the server, and also places authorization information in a file accessible to the user and the server. Normally, the list of hosts from which connections are always accepted should be empty, so that only clients that are explicitly authorized can connect to the display. When you add entries to the host list (with *xhost*), the server no longer performs any authorization on connections from those machines. Be careful with this.

The file from which Xlib extracts authorization data can be specified with the environment variable XAUTHORITY, and defaults to the file *.Xauthority* in the home directory. *xdm* uses *$HOME/.Xauthority* and will create it or merge in authorization records if it already exists when a user logs in.

If you use several machines, and share a common home directory across all of the machines by means of a network file system, then you never really have to worry about authorization files; the system should work correctly by default. Otherwise, as the authorization files are machine-independent, you can simply copy the files to share them. To manage authorization files, use *xauth*. This program allows you to extract records and insert them into other files. Using this, you can send authorization to remote machines when you login, if the remote machine does not share a common home directory with your local machine. Note that authorization information transmitted "in the clear" through a network file system or using *ftp* or *rcp* can be "stolen" by a network eavesdropper, and as such may enable unauthorized access. In many environments this level of security is not a concern, but if it is, you need to know the exact semantics of the particular authorization data to know if this is actually a problem.

For more information on access control, see the *Xsecurity* manual page.

For more information on access control, see Appendix A, *Managing Your Environment*, Volume One, *Xlib Programming Manual*, and the *Xsecurity* reference page in the MIT source distribution.

Geometry Specifications

One of the advantages of using window systems instead of hardwired terminals is that applications don't have to be restricted to a particular size or location on the screen. Although the layout of windows on a display is controlled by the window manager that the user is running (described below), most X programs accept a command-line argument of the form -geometry *widthxheight±xoff±yoff* (where *width*, *height*, *xoff*, and *yoff* are numbers) for specifying a preferred size and location for this application's main window.

The *width* and *height* parts of the geometry specification are usually measured in either pixels or characters, depending on the application. The *xoff* and *yoff* parts are measured in pixels and are used to specify the distance of the window from the left or right and top and bottom edges of the screen, respectively. Both types of offsets are measured from the indicated edge of the screen to the corresponding edge of the window. The x offset may be specified in the following ways:

+*xoff* The left edge of the window is to be placed *xoff* pixels in from the left edge of the screen (i.e., the x coordinate of the window's origin will be *xoff*). *xoff* may be negative, in which case the window's left edge will be off the screen.

−*xoff* The right edge of the window is to be placed *xoff* pixels in from the right edge of the screen. *xoff* may be negative, in which case the window's right edge will be off the screen.

The y offset has similar meanings:

+*yoff* The top edge of the window is to be *yoff* pixels below the top edge of the screen (i.e., the y coordinate of the window's origin will be *yoff*). *yoff* may be negative, in which case the window's top edge will be off the screen.

−*yoff* The bottom edge of the window is to be *yoff* pixels above the bottom edge of the screen. *yoff* may be negative, in which case the window's bottom edge will be off the screen.

Offsets must be given as pairs; in other words, in order to specify either *xoff* or *yoff*, both must be present. Windows can be placed in the four corners of the screen using the following specifications:

+0+0　　The upper-left corner.

−0+0　　The upper-right corner.

−0−0　　The lower-right corner.

+0−0　　The lower-left corner.

In the following examples, a terminal emulator will be placed in roughly the center of the screen and a load average monitor, mailbox, and clock will be placed in the upper-right corner:

```
% xterm -fn 6x10 -geometry 80x24+30+200 &
% xclock -geometry 48x48-0+0 &
% xload -geometry 48x48-96+0 &
% xbiff -geometry 48x48-48+0 &
```

Window Managers

The layout of windows on the screen is controlled by special programs called *window managers*. Although many window managers will honor geometry specifications as given, others may choose to ignore them (requiring the user to explicitly draw the window's region on the screen with the pointer, for example).

Since window managers are regular (albeit complex) client programs, a variety of different user interfaces can be built. The MIT distribution comes with a window manager named *twm*, which supports overlapping windows, popup menus, point-and-click or click-to-type input models, titlebars, nice icons (and an icon manager for those who don't like separate icon windows).

See the user-contributed software in the MIT distribution for other popular window managers.

Font Names

Collections of characters for displaying text and symbols in X are known as *fonts*. A font typically contains images that share a common appearance and look nice together (for example, a single size, boldness, slant, and character set). Similarly, collections of fonts that are based on a common type face (the variations are usually called roman, bold, italic, bold italic, oblique, and bold oblique) are called *families*.

Fonts come in various sizes. The X server supports *scalable* fonts, meaning it is possible to create a font of arbitrary size from a single source for the font. The server supports scaling from *outline* fonts and *bitmap* fonts. Scaling from outline fonts usually produces significantly better results than scaling from bitmap fonts.

An X server can obtain fonts from individual files stored in directories in the file system, or from one or more font servers, or from a mixture of directories and font servers. The list of places the server looks when trying to find a font is controlled by its *font path*. Although most installations will choose to have the server start up with all of the commonly used font directories in the font path, the font path can be changed at any time with the *xset* program. However, it is important to remember that the directory names are on the *server*'s machine, not on the application's.

The default font path for the X server contains four directories:

/usr/lib/X11/fonts/misc
>   This directory contains many miscellaneous bitmap fonts that are useful on all systems. It contains a family of generic fixed-width fonts, a family of fixed-width fonts from Dale Schumacher, several Kana fonts from Sony Corporation, two JIS Kanji fonts, two Hangul fonts from Daewoo Electronics, two Hebrew fonts from Joseph Friedman, the standard cursor font, two cursor fonts from Digital Equipment Corporation, and cursor and glyph fonts from Sun Microsystems. It also has various font name aliases for the fonts, including *fixed* and *variable*.

/usr/lib/X11/fonts/Speedo
>   This directory contains outline fonts for Bitstream's Speedo rasterizer. A single font face, in normal, bold, italic, and bold italic, is provided, contributed by Bitstream, Inc.

/usr/lib/X11/fonts/75dpi
>   This directory contains 75 dots per inch display bitmap fonts contributed by Adobe Systems, Inc.; Digital Equipment Corporation, Bitstream, Inc.; Bigelow and Holmes, and Sun Microsystems, Inc. An integrated selection of sizes, styles, and weights are provided for each family.

/usr/lib/X11/fonts/100dpi

> This directory contains 100 dots per inch versions of some of the fonts in the *75dpi* directory.

Font databases are created by running the *mkfontdir* program in the directory containing the source or compiled versions of the fonts. Whenever fonts are added to a directory, *mkfontdir* should be rerun so that the server can find the new fonts. To make the server reread the font database, reset the font path with the *xset* program. For example, to add a font to a private directory, the following commands could be used:

```
% cp newfonts.pcf ~/myfonts
% mkfontdir ~/myfonts
% xset fp rehash
```

The *xfontsel* and *xlsfonts* programs can be used to browse through the fonts available on a server. Font names tend to be fairly long as they contain all of the information needed to uniquely identify individual fonts. However, the X server supports wildcarding of font names, so the full specification:

```
-adobe-courier-medium-r-normal--10-100-75-75-m-60-iso8859-1
```

might be abbreviated as:

```
*-courier-medium-r-normal--*-100-*
```

Because the shell also has special meanings for * and ?, wildcarded font names should be quoted:

```
% xlsfonts -fn '*-courier-medium-r-normal--*-100-*'
```

The *xlsfonts* program can be used to list all of the fonts that match a given pattern. With no arguments, it lists all available fonts. This will usually list the same font at many different sizes. To see just the base scalable font names, try using one of the following patterns:

```
-*-*-*-*-*-*-0-0-0-0-*-0-*-*
-*-*-*-*-*-*-0-0-75-75-*-0-*-*
-*-*-*-*-*-*-0-0-100-100-*-0-*-*
```

To convert one of the resulting names into a font at a specific size, replace one of the first two zeros with a nonzero value. The field containing the first zero is for the pixel size; replace it with a specific height in pixels to name a font at that size. Alternatively, the field containing the second zero is for the point size; replace it with a specific size in decipoints (there are 722.7 decipoints to the inch) to name a font at that size. The last zero is an average width field, measured in tenths of pixels; some servers will anamorphically scale if this value is specified.

If more than one font in a given directory in the font path matches a wildcarded font name, the choice of which particular font to return is left to the server. However, if fonts from more than one directory match a name, the returned font will always be from the first such directory in the font path. The example given above will match fonts in both the *75dpi* and *100dpi* directories;

if the *75dpi* directory is ahead of the *100dpi* directory in the font path, the smaller version of the font will be used.

Font Server Names

One of the following forms can be used to name a font server that accepts TCP connections:

tcp/*hostname*:*port*
tcp/*hostname*:*port*/*cataloguelist*

The *hostname* specifies the name (or decimal numeric address) of the machine on which the font server is running. The *port* is the decimal TCP port on which the font server is listening for connections. The *cataloguelist* specifies a list of catalogue names, with '+' as a separator.

Examples: *tcp/expo.lcs.mit.edu:7000* , *tcp/18.30.0.212:7001/all*.

One of the following forms can be used to name a font server that accepts DECnet connections:

decnet/*nodename*::font$*objname*
decnet/*nodename*::font$*objname*/*cataloguelist*

The *nodename* specifies the name (or decimal numeric address) of the machine on which the font server is running. The *objname* is a normal, case-insensitive DECnet object name. The *cataloguelist* specifies a list of catalogue names, with '+' as a separator.

Examples: *DECnet/SRVNOD::FONT$DEFAULT*, *decnet/44.70::font$special/symbo ls*.

Color Names

Most applications provide ways of tailoring (usually through resources or command-line arguments) the colors of various elements in the text and graphics they display.

X supports the use of abstract color names, for example, "red", "blue." A value for this abstract name is obtained by searching one or more color name databases. *Xlib* first searches zero or more client-side databases; the number, location, and content of these databases is implementation dependent. If the name is not found, the color is looked up in the X server's database. The text form of this database is commonly stored in the file */usr/lib/X11/rgb.txt*.

A color can be specified either by an abstract color name, or by a numerical color specification. The numerical specification can identify a color in either device-dependent (RGB) or device-independent terms. Color strings are case-insensitive meaning that *red*, *Red*, and *RED* all refer to the same color.

A numerical color specification consists of a color space name and a set of values in the following syntax:

<color_space_name>:*<value>*/.../*<value>*

An RGB Device specification is identified by the prefix "rgb:" and has the following syntax:

```
rgb:<red>/<green>/<blue>
```

> *<red>*, *<green>*, *<blue>* := *h* | *hh* | *hhh* | *hhhh*
> *h* := single hexadecimal digits

Note that *h* indicates the value scaled in 4 bits, *hh* the value scaled in 8 bits, *hhh* the value scaled in 12 bits, and *hhhh* the value scaled in 16 bits, respectively. These values are passed directly to the X server, and are assumed to be gamma corrected.

The eight primary colors can be represented as:

black	`rgb:0/0/0`
red	`rgb:ffff/0/0`
green	`rgb:0/ffff/0`
blue	`rgb:0/0/ffff`
yellow	`rgb:ffff/ffff/0`
magenta	`rgb:ffff/0/ffff`
cyan	`rgb:0/ffff/ffff`
white	`rgb:ffff/ffff/ffff`

For backward compatibility, an older syntax for RGB Device is supported, but its continued use is not encouraged. The syntax is an initial sharp sign character followed by a numeric specification, in one of the following formats:

`#rgb`	(4 bits each)
`#rrggbb`	(8 bits each)
`#rrrgggbbb`	(12 bits each)
`#rrrrggggbbbb`	(16 bits each)

The r, g, and b represent single hexadecimal digits indicating how much *red*, *green*, and *blue* should be displayed (zero being none and ffff being on full). Each field in the specification must have the same number of digits (e.g., *#rrgb* or *#gbb* are not allowed). When fewer than 16 bits each are specified, they represent the most significant bits of the value (unlike the "rgb:" syntax, in which values are scaled). For example, #3a7 is the same as #3000a0007000.

An RGB intensity specification is identified by the prefix "rgbi:" and has the following syntax:

```
rgbi:<red>/<green>/<blue>
```

The red, green, and blue are floating point values between 0.0 and 1.0, inclusive. They represent linear intensity values, with 1.0 indicating full intensity, 0.5 half intensity, and so on. These values will be gamma corrected by *Xlib* before being sent to the X server. The input format for these values is an optional sign, a string of numbers possibly containing a decimal point, and an optional exponent field containing an E or e followed by a possibly signed integer string.

The standard device-independent string specifications have the following syntax:

`CIEXYZ:<X>/<Y>/<Z>`	(*none*, 1, *none*)
`CIEuvY:<u>/<v>/<Y>`	(~.6, ~.6, 1)
`CIExyY:<x>/<y>/<Y>`	(~.75, ~.85, 1)

CIELab: *<L>/<a>/<b>*	(100, *none*, *none*)
CIELuv: *<L>/<u>/<v>*	(100, *none*, *none*)
TekHVC: *<H>/<V>/<C>*	(360, 100, 100)

All of the values (C, H, V, X, Y, Z, a, b, u, v, y, x) are floating point values. Some of the values are constrained to be between zero and some upper bound; the upper bounds are given in parentheses above. The syntax for these values is an optional '+' or '-' sign, a string of digits possibly containing a decimal point, and an optional exponent field consisting of an 'E' or 'e' followed by an optional '+' or '-' followed by a string of digits.

For more information on device independent color, see Volume Two, *Xlib Reference Manual*.

Keys

The X keyboard model is broken into two layers: server-specific codes (called *keycodes*), which represent the physical keys; and server-independent symbols (called *keysyms*), which represent the letters or words that appear on the keys. Two tables are kept in the server for converting keycodes to keysyms:

modifier list

> Some keys (such as Shift, Control, and Caps Lock) are known as *modifier keys* and are used to select different symbols that are attached to a single key (such as Shift-a generates a capital A, and CTRL-L generates a control character ^L). The server keeps a list of keycodes corresponding to the various modifier keys. Whenever a key is pressed or released, the server generates an *event* that contains the keycode of the indicated key as well as a mask that specifies which of the modifer keys are currently pressed. Most servers set up this list to initially contain the various shift, control, and shift lock keys on the keyboard.

keymap table

> Applications translate event keycodes and modifier masks into keysyms using a *keymap table* which contains one row for each keycode and one column for each of the modifiers. This table is initialized by the server to correspond to normal typewriter conventions. The exact semantics of how the table is interpreted to produce keysyms depends on the particular program, libraries, and language input method used, but the following conventions for the first four keysyms in each row are generally adhered to.
>
> The first four elements of the list are split into two groups of keysyms. Group 1 contains the first and second keysyms; Group 2 contains the third and fourth keysyms. Within each group, if the first element is alphabetic and the the second element is the special keysym *NoSymbol*, then the group is treated as equivalent to a group in which the first element is the lowercase letter and the second element is the uppercase letter.
>
> Switching between groups is controlled by the keysym named MODE SWITCH, by attaching that keysym to some key and attaching that key to any one of the modifiers Mod1 through Mod5. This modifier is called the "group modifier." Group 1 is used when the group modifier is off, and Group 2 is used when the group modifier is on.

Within a group, the modifier state determines which keysym to use. The first keysym is used when the Shift and Lock modifiers are off. The second keysym is used when the Shift modifier is on, when the Lock modifier is on and the second keysym is upper-case alphabetic, or when the Lock modifier is on and is interpreted as ShiftLock. Otherwise, when the Lock modifier is on and is interpreted as CapsLock, the state of the Shift modifier is applied first to select a keysym; but if that keysym is lowercase alphabetic, then the corresponding uppercase keysym is used instead.

Options

Most X programs attempt to use the same names for command-line options and arguments. All applications written with the X Toolkit Intrinsics automatically accept the following options:

`-display [`*host*`]:`*server*`[.`*screen*`]`

Specifies the name of the display to use. *host* is the hostname of the physical display, *server* specifies the display server number, and *screen* specifies the screen number. Either or both of the *host* and *screen* elements to the display specification can be omitted. If *host* is omitted, the local display is assumed. If *screen* is omitted, screen 0 is assumed (and the period is unnecessary). The colon and (display) *server* are necessary in all cases.

For example, the following command creates an *xclock* window on screen 1 on server 0 on the display hardware named by *your_node*.

`% xclock -display `*your_node*`:0.1`

The `-display` option can be abbreviated as `-d`, unless the client accepts another option that begins with "d."

`-geometry `*geometry*

Specifies the initial size and location of the application window. The `-geometry` option can be (and often is) abbreviated to `-g`, unless the client accepts another option that begins with "g." The argument (*geometry*) is referred to as a "standard geometry string," and has the form *widthxheight±xoff±yoff*.

`-bg `*color*`, -background `*color*

Either option specifies the color to use for the window background.

`-bd `*color*`, -bordercolor `*color*

Either option specifies the color to use for the window border.

`-bw `*pixels*`, -borderwidth `*pixels*

Either option specifies the width in pixels of the window border.

`-fg `*color*`, -foreground `*color*

Either option specifies the color to use for text or graphics.

`-fn `*font*`, -font `*font*

Either option specifies the font to use for displaying text.

`-iconic`

> Indicates that the user would prefer that the application's windows initially not be visible, as if the windows had been immediately iconified by the user. Window managers may choose not to honor the application's request.

`-name` *app_name*

> Specifies the name under which resources for the application should be found. This option is useful in shell aliases to distinguish between invocations of an application, without resorting to creating links to alter the executable filename.

`-rv, -reverse`

> Either option indicates that the program should simulate reverse video if possible, often by swapping the foreground and background colors. Not all programs honor this or implement it correctly. It is usually used only on monochrome displays.

`+rv`   Indicates that the program should not simulate reverse video. This is used to override any defaults since reverse video doesn't always work properly.

`-selectionTimeout` *milliseconds*

> Specifies the timeout in milliseconds within which two communicating applications must respond to one another for a selection request.

`-synchronous`

> Indicates that requests to the X server should be sent synchronously, instead of asynchronously. Since Xlib normally buffers requests to the server, errors are not necessarily reported immediately after they occur. This option turns off the buffering so that the application can be debugged. It should never be used with a working program.

`-title` *string*

> Specifies the title to be used for this window. This information is sometimes used by a window manager to provide some sort of header identifying the window.

`-xnllanguage` *language*[*_territory*][*.codeset*]

> Specifies the language, territory, and codeset for use in resolving resource and other filenames.

`-xrm` *resourcestring*

> Specifies a resource name and value to override any defaults. It is very useful for setting resources that don't have explicit command line arguments.

Resources

To make the tailoring of applications to personal preferences easier, X provides a mechanism for storing default values for program resources (e.g., background color, window title, etc.). Resources are specified as strings of the form:

appname*subname*subsubname . . . : *value*

and are read in from various places when an application is run. Program components are named in a hierarchical fashion, with each node in the hierarchy identified by a class and an instance name. At the top level is the class and instance name of the application itself.

By convention, the class name of the application is the same as the program name, but with the first letter capitalized (e.g., *Bitmap* or *Emacs*), although some programs that begin with the letter "x" also capitalize the second letter for historical reasons.

The precise syntax for resources is:

```
ResourceLine    =    Comment | IncludeFile | ResourceSpec | <empty line>
Comment         =    "!" {<any character except null or newline>}
IncludeFile     =    "#" WhiteSpace "include" WhiteSpace FileName WhiteSpace
FileName        =    <valid filename for operating system>
ResourceSpec    =    WhiteSpace ResourceName WhiteSpace ":" WhiteSpace Value
ResourceName    =    [Binding] {Component Binding} ComponentName
Binding         =    "." | "*"
WhiteSpace      =    {<space> | <horizontal tab>}
Component       =    "?" | ComponentName
ComponentName   =    NameChar {NameChar}
NameChar        =    "a"-"z" | "A"-"Z" | "0"-"9" | "_" | "-"
Value           =    {<any character except null or unescaped newline>}
```

Note that elements separated by a vertical bar (|) are alternatives. Elements enclosed in curly braces ({...}) indicate zero or more occurrences of the enclosed elements. Square brackets ([...]) indicate that the enclosed element is optional. Quotes ("...") are used around literal characters.

IncludeFile lines are interpreted by replacing the line with the contents of the specified file. The word "include" must be in lowercase. The filename is interpreted relative to the directory of the file in which the line occurs (for example, if the filename contains no directory or contains a relative directory specification).

If a ResourceName contains a contiguous sequence of two or more Binding characters, the sequence will be replaced with a single "." character if the sequence contains only "." characters; otherwise, the sequence will be replaced with a single "*" character.

A resource database never contains more than one entry for a given ResourceName. If a resource file contains multiple lines with the same ResourceName, the last line in the file is used.

Any whitespace character before or after the name or colon in a ResourceSpec is ignored. To allow a Value to begin with whitespace, the two-character sequence "*space*" (backslash followed by space) is recognized and replaced by a space character, and the two-character sequence "*tab*" (backslash followed by horizontal tab) is recognized and replaced by a horizontal tab character. To allow a Value to contain embedded newline characters, the two-character sequence "\n" is recognized and replaced by a newline character. To allow a Value to be broken across multiple lines in a text file, the two-character sequence "*newline*" (backslash followed by newline) is recognized and removed from the value. To allow a Value to contain arbitrary character codes, the four-character sequence "*nnn*", where each *n* is a digit character in the range of "0"–"7", is recognized and replaced with a single byte that contains the octal value specified by the sequence. Finally, the two-character sequence "\\" is recognized and replaced with a single backslash.

When an application looks for the value of a resource, it specifies a complete path in the hierarchy, with both class and instance names. However, resource values are usually given with only partially specified names and classes, using pattern matching constructs. An asterisk (*) is a loose binding and is used to represent any number of intervening components, including none. A period (.) is a tight binding and is used to separate immediately adjacent components. A question mark (?) is used to match any single component name or class. A database entry cannot end in a loose binding; the final component (which cannot be "?") must be specified. The lookup algorithm searches the resource database for the entry that most closely matches (is most specific for) the full name and class being queried. When more than one database entry matches the full name and class, precedence rules are used to select just one.

The full name and class are scanned from left to right (from highest level in the hierarchy to lowest), one component at a time. At each level, the corresponding component and/or binding of each matching entry is determined, and these matching components and bindings are compared according to precedence rules. Each of the rules is applied at each level, before moving to the next level, until a rule selects a single entry over all others. The rules (in order of precedence) are:

1. An entry that contains a matching component (whether name, class, or "?") takes precedence over entries that elide the level (that is, entries that match the level in a loose binding).

2. An entry with a matching name takes precedence over both entries with a matching class and entries that match using "?". An entry with a matching class takes precedence over entries that match using "?".

3. An entry preceded by a tight binding takes precedence over entries preceded by a loose binding.

Programs based on the X Toolkit Intrinsics obtain resources from the following sources (other programs usually support some subset of these sources):

RESOURCE_MANAGER root window property

> Any global resources that should be available to clients on all machines should be stored in the RESOURCE_MANAGER property on the root window of the first screen using the *xrdb* program. This is frequently taken care of when the user starts up X through the display manager or *xinit*.

SCREEN_RESOURCES root window property

> Any resources specific to a given screen (e.g., colors) that should be available to clients on all machines, should be stored in the SCREEN_RESOURCES property on the root window of that screen. The *xrdb* program will sort resources automatically and place them in RESOURCE_MANAGER or SCREEN_RESOURCES, as appropriate.

application-specific files

>Directories named by the environment variable XUSERFILESEARCHPATH or the environment variable XAPPLRESDIR, plus directories in a standard place (usually under */usr/lib/X11/*, but this can be overriden with the XFILESEARCHPATH environment variable) are searched for application-specific resource files. Files are generally named *Class*—for the class name of the application.

>XAPPLRESDIR configuration files are actually loaded *before* the RE-SOURCE_MANAGER property, so that the property can override the values. See Volume Four, *X Toolkit Intrinsics Programming Manual*, for details.

XENVIRONMENT

>Any user- and machine-specific resources may be specified by setting the XENVIRON-MENT environment variable to the name of a resource file to be loaded by all applications. If this variable is not defined, a file named *$HOME/.Xdefaults-**hostname*** is looked for instead, where ***hostname*** is the name of the host where the application is executing.

-xrm *resourcestring*

>Resources can also be specified from the command line. The *resourcestring* is a single resource name and value as shown above. Note that if the string contains characters interpreted by the shell (e.g., asterisk), they must be quoted. Any number of -xrm arguments may be given on the command line.

Program resources are organized into groups called *classes*, so that collections of individual resources (each of which is called an *instance*) can be set all at once. By convention, the instance name of a resource begins with a lowercase letter and class name with an uppercase letter. Multiple word resources are concatenated with the first letter of the succeeding words capitalized. Applications written with the X Toolkit Intrinsics will have at least the following resources:

background (class Background)
>Specifies the color to use for the window background.

borderWidth (class BorderWidth)
>Specifies the width in pixels of the window border.

borderColor (class BorderColor)
>Specifies the color to use for the window border.

Most applications using the X Toolkit Intrinsics also have the resource foreground (class Foreground), specifying the color to use for text and graphics within the window.

By combining class and instance specifications, application preferences can be set quickly and easily. Users of color displays will frequently want to set Background and Foreground classes to particular defaults. Specific color instances, such as text cursors, can then be overridden without having to define all of the related resources. For example,

```
bitmap*Dashed:  off
XTerm*cursorColor:  gold
XTerm*multiScroll:  on
XTerm*jumpScroll:  on
XTerm*reverseWrap:  on
XTerm*curses:  on
XTerm*Font:  6x10
XTerm*scrollBar: on
XTerm*scrollbar*thickness: 5
XTerm*multiClickTime: 500
XTerm*charClass:  33:48,37:48,45-47:48,64:48
XTerm*cutNewline: off
XTerm*cutToBeginningOfLine: off
XTerm*titeInhibit:  on
XTerm*ttyModes:  intr ^c erase ^? kill ^u
XLoad*Background: gold
XLoad*Foreground: red
XLoad*highlight: black
XLoad*borderWidth: 0
emacs*Geometry:  80x65-0-0
emacs*Background:  rgb:5b/76/86
emacs*Foreground:  white
emacs*Cursor:  white
emacs*BorderColor:  white
emacs*Font:  6x10
xmag*geometry:  -0-0
xmag*borderColor:  white
```

If these resources were stored in a file called *.Xresources* in your home directory, they could be added to any existing resources in the server with the following command:

```
% xrdb -merge $HOME/.Xresources
```

This is frequently how user-friendly startup scripts merge user-specific defaults into any site-wide defaults. All sites are encouraged to set up convenient ways of automatically loading resources. See Chapter 11, *Setting Resources*, for more information.

Examples

The following is a collection of sample command lines for some of the more frequently used commands. For more information on a particular command, please refer to that command's reference page.

```
% xrdb -load $HOME/.Xresources
% xmodmap -e 'keysym BackSpace = Delete'
% mkfontdir /usr/local/lib/X11/otherfonts
% xset fp+ /usr/local/lib/X11/otherfonts
% xmodmap $HOME/.keymap.km
% xsetroot -solid 'rgbi:.8/.8/.8'
% xset b 100 400 c 50 s 1800 r on
```

```
% xset q
% twm
% xmag
% xclock -geometry 48x48-0+0 -bg blue -fg white
% xeyes -geometry 48x48-48+0
% xbiff -update 20
% xlsfonts '*helvetica*'
% xwininfo -root
% xdpyinfo -display joesworkstation:0
% xhost -joesworkstation
% xrefresh
% xwd | xwud
% bitmap companylogo.bm -size 32x32
% xcalc -bg blue -fg magenta
% xterm -geometry 80x66-0-0 -name myxterm
% xon filesysmachine xload
```

Diagnostics

A wide variety of error messages are generated from various programs. The default error handler in Xlib (also used by many toolkits) uses standard resources to construct diagnostic messages when errors occur. The defaults for these messages are usually stored in *usr/lib/X11/XErrorDB*. If this file is not present, error messages will be rather terse and cryptic.

When the X Toolkit Intrinsics encounter errors converting resource strings to the appropriate internal format, no error messages are usually printed. This is convenient when it is desirable to have one set of resources across a variety of displays (e.g., color versus monochrome, lots of fonts versus very few, etc.), although it can pose problems in trying to determine why an application might be failing. This behavior can be overridden by setting the String-ConversionWarning resource.

To force the X Toolkit Intrinsics to always print string conversion error messages, the following resource should be placed at the top of the file that is loaded onto the RE-SOURCE_MANAGER property using the *xrdb* program (frequently called *.Xresources* or *.xrdb* in the user's home directory):

```
*StringConversionWarnings: on
```

To have conversion messages printed for just a particular application, the appropriate instance name can be placed before the asterisk:

```
xterm*StringConversionWarnings: on
```

See Also

XConsortium(1), XStandards(1), Xsecurity(1), appres, auto_box(1), bdftopcf, beach_ball(1), bitmap, editres, fs, fsinfo, fslsfonts, fstobdf, ico(1), imake(1), listres, lndir(1), makedepend(1), maze(1), mkdirhier(1), mkfontdir, mwm, oclock, plbpex(1), puzzle(1), resize, showfont, showrgb, twm, viewres, x11perf(1), x11perfcomp(1), xauth, xbiff, xcalc, xclipboard, xclock, xcmsdb, xcmstest(1), xconsole, xcutsel, xditview, xdm, xdpr, xdpyinfo, xedit, xev, xeyes, xfd, xfontsel, xgas(1), xgc(1), xhost, xinit, xkill, xload, xlogo, xlsatoms, xlsclients, xlsfonts, xmag, xman, xmh, xmkmf(1), xmodmap, xon(1), xpr, xprop, xrdb, xrefresh, xset, xsetroot, xstdcmap, xterm, xwd, xwininfo, xwud, Xserver, Xdec(1), XmacII(1), Xmips(1), Xqdss(1), Xqvss(1), Xsun(1), X386(1), kbd_mode(1), Volume One, *Xlib Programming Manual*; Volume Two, *Xlib Reference Manual*; Volume Four, *X Toolkit Intrinsics Programming Manual*; Volume Five, *X Toolkit Intrinsics Reference Manual*; Volume Eight, *X Window System Administrator's Guide*.

Copyright

The following copyright and permission notice outlines the rights and restrictions covering most parts of the standard distribution of the X Window System from MIT. Other parts have additional or different copyrights and permissions; see the individual source files.

Copyright 1984, 1985, 1986, 1987, 1988, 1989, 1990, 1991 Massachusetts Institute of Technology.

Permission to use, copy, modify, and distribute this software and its documentation for any purpose and without fee is hereby granted, provided that the above copyright notice appear in all copies and that both that copyright notice and this permission notice appear in supporting documentation, and that the name of M.I.T. not be used in advertising or publicity pertaining to distribution of the software without specific, written prior permission. M.I.T. makes no representations about the suitability of this software for any purpose. It is provided "as is" without express or implied warranty.

Trademarks

X Window System is a trademark of MIT.

Authors

A cast of thousands, literally. The MIT Release 5 distribution is brought to you by the MIT X Consortium. The names of all people who made it a reality will be found in the individual documents and source files. The staff members at MIT responsible for this release are: Donna Converse (MIT X Consortium), Stephen Gildea (MIT X Consortium), Susan Hardy (MIT X Consortium), Jay Hersh (MIT X Consortium), Keith Packard (MIT X Consortium), David Sternlicht (MIT X Consortium), Bob Scheifler (MIT X Consortium), and Ralph Swick (Digital/MIT Project Athena).

Xserver

Name

X – X Window System server.

Syntax

X [: *displaynumber*] [*options*] [*ttyname*]

Description

X is the generic name for the X Window System server. It is frequently a link to or a copy of the appropriate server binary for driving the most frequently used server on a given machine.

Starting the Server

The server is usually started from the X Display Manager program, *xdm*. This utility is run from the system boot files and takes care of keeping the server running, prompting for user-names and passwords, and starting up user sessions. It is easily configured for sites that wish to provide consistent interfaces for novice users (loading convenient sets of resources, starting up a window manager, clock, and a wide selection of terminal emulator windows).

Installations that run more than one window system will still need to use the *xinit* utility. However, *xinit* is to be considered a tool for building startup scripts and is not intended for use by end users. Site administrators are *strongly* urged to use *xdm*, or to build more friendly interfaces for novice users.

When the X server starts up, it takes over the display. If you are running on a workstation whose console is the display, you cannot log into the console while the server is running.

Network Connections

The X server supports connections made using the following reliable byte-streams:

TCP/IP The server listens on port (6000+*n*), where *n* is the display number.

UNIX Domain

The X server uses */tmp/.X11-unix/X**n*** as the filename for the socket, where ***n*** is the display number.

DECnet

The server responds to connections to object *X$X**n***, where ***n*** is the display number.

Options

All of the X servers accept the following command-line options:

-a *number*

Sets pointer acceleration (i.e., the ratio of how much is reported to how much the user actually moved the pointer).

-auth *authorization_file*

Specifies a file that contains a collection of authorization records used to authenticate access. See also *xdm* and *xsecurity*.

bc   Disables certain kinds of error checking, for bug compatibility with previous releases (e.g., to work around bugs in Release 2 and Release 3 versions of *xterm* and the toolkits). Use of this option is discouraged.

-bs   Disables backing store support on all screens.

-c   Turns off key-click.

c *volume*
> Sets key-click volume (allowable range: 0-8).

-cc *class*
> Sets the visual class for the root window of color screens. The class numbers are as specified in the X protocol. Not obeyed by all servers.

-co *filename*
> Sets the name of the RGB color database.

-dpi *resolution*
> Sets the resolution of the screen, in dots-per-inch. To be used when the server cannot determine the screen size from the hardware.

-f *volume*
> Sets beep (bell) volume (allowable range: 0-7).

-fc *cursor_font*
> Sets the default cursor font.

-fn *font*
> Sets the default font.

-fp *font_path*
> Sets the search path for fonts. This path is a comma-separated list of directories that the X server searches for font databases.

-help   Prints a usage message.

-I   Causes all remaining command-line arguments to be ignored.

-ld *kilobytes*
> Sets the data space limit of the server to the specified number of kilobytes. A value of zero makes the stack size as large as possible. The default value of −1 leaves the stack space limit unchanged. (Not available in all operating systems.)

-lf *files*
> Sets the number-of-open-files limit of the server to the specified number. A value of zero makes the limit as large as possible. The default value of −1 leaves limit unchanged. This option is not available in all operating systems. (Available as of Release 5.)

-ls *kilobytes*
> Sets the stack space limit of the server to the specified number of kilobytes. A value of zero makes the stack size as large as possible. The default value of –1 leaves the stack space limit unchanged. (Not available in all operating systems.)

-logo Turns on the X Window System logo display in the screen saver. There is currently no way to change this from a client.

nologo
> Turns off the X Window System logo display in the screen saver. There is currently no way to change this from a client.

-p *minutes*
> Sets screen saver pattern cycle time, in minutes.

-r   Turns off auto-repeat.

r   Turns on auto-repeat.

-s *minutes*
> Sets screen saver timeout, in minutes.

-su   Disables save under support on all screens.

-t *numbers*
> Sets pointer acceleration threshold, in pixels (i.e., after how many pixels pointer acceleration should take effect).

-to *seconds*
> Sets default screen saver timeout, in seconds.

v   Sets video-off screen saver preference.

-v   Sets video-on screen saver preference.

-wm   Forces the default backing-store of all windows to be WhenMapped; a cheap-trick way of getting backing-store to apply to all windows.

-x *extension*
> Loads the specified extension at *init*. (Not supported in most implementations.)

XDMCP-specific Options
You can also have the X server connect to *xdm* using XDMCP. Although this is not typically useful, because it doesn't allow *xdm* to manage the server process, it can be used to debug XDMCP implementations, and servers as a sample implementation of the server side of XDMCP. For more information on this protocol, see the *X Display Manager Control Protocol* specification (available in the MIT source in doc/XDMCP/xdmcp.ms). The following options control the behavior of XDMCP:

-query *host_name*
> Enables XDMCP and sends Query packets to the specified host.

-broadcast

> Enables XDMCP and broadcasts `BroadcastQuery` packets to the network. The first responding display manager will be chosen for the session.

-indirect *host_name*

> Enables XDMCP and sends `IndirectQuery` packets to the specified host.

-port *port_num*

> Specifies an alternate port number for XDMCP packets. Must be specified before any -query, -broadcast, or -indirect options.

-once Makes the server exit after the first session is over. Normally, the server keeps starting sessions, one after the other.

-class *display_class*

> XDMCP has an additional display qualifier used in resource lookup for display-specific options. This option sets that value; by default, it is "MIT-Unspecified" (not a very useful value).

-cookie *xdm_auth_bits*

> When testing XDM-AUTHENTICATION-1, a private key is shared between the server and the manager. This option sets the value of that private data (not that it's very private, being on the command line).

-displayID *display_ID*

> Yet another XDMCP-specific value, this one allows the display manager to identify each display so that it can locate the shared key.

Many servers also have device-specific command-line options. For more details, see the manual pages for the individual servers.

Security

The X server implements a simplistic authorization protocol, MIT-MAGIC-COOKIE-1, which uses data private to authorized clients and the server. This is a rather trivial scheme; if the client passes authorization data which is the same as the data the server has, it is allowed access. This scheme is worse than the host-based access control mechanisms in environments with unsecure networks because it allows any host to connect, given that it has discovered the private key. But in many environments, this level of security is better than the host-based scheme, because it allows access to be controlled per-user instead of per-host.

In addition, the server provides support for a DES-based authorization scheme, XDM-AUTHORIZATION-1, which is more secure (given a secure key distribution mechanism). This authorization scheme can be used in conjunction with XDMCP's authentication scheme, XDM-AUTHENTICATION-1, or in isolation.

The authorization data is passed to the server in a private file named with the -auth command-line option. Each time the server is about to accept the first connection after a reset (or when the server is starting), it reads this file. If this file contains any authorization records, the local host is not automatically allowed access to the server, and only clients which send one of the authorization records contained in the file in the connection setup information will be allowed access. Maintenance of this file, and distribution of its contents to remote sites for use there, is left as an exercise for the reader.

The server also provides support for SUN-DES-1, using Sun's Secure RPC. It involves encrypting data with the X server's public key. See the *Xsecurity* reference page in the MIT source distribution.

The X server also uses a host-based access control list for deciding whether or not to accept connections from clients on a particular machine. If no other authorization mechanism is being used, this list initially consists of the host on which the server is running as well as any machines listed in the file */etc/Xn.hosts*, where *n* is the display number of the server. Each line of the file should contain either an Internet hostname (e.g., expo.lcs.mit.edu) or a DECnet hostname in double colon format (e.g., hydra::). There should be no leading or trailing spaces on any lines. For example:

```
joesworkstation
corporate.company.com
star::
bigcpu::
```

Users can add or remove hosts from this list and enable or disable access control using the *xhost* command from the same machine as the server.

The X protocol intrinsically does not have any notion of window operation permissions or place any restrictions on what a client can do; if a program can connect to a display, it has full run of the screen. Sites that have authentication and authorization systems (such as Kerberos) might wish to make use of the hooks in the libraries and the server to provide additional security.

Signals

The X server attaches special meaning to the following signals:

SIGHUP　　　Causes the server to close all existing connections, free all resources, and restore all defaults. It is sent by the display manager whenever the main user's primary application (usually an *xterm* or window manager) exits to force the server to clean up and prepare for the next user.

SIGTERM　　Causes the server to exit cleanly.

SIGUSR1　　This signal is used quite differently from either of the above. When the server starts, it checks to see if it has inherited SIGUSR as SIG_IGN instead of the usual SIG_DFL. In this case, the server sends a SIGUSR1 to its parent process, after it has set up the various connection schemes. *xdm* uses this feature to recognize when it is possible to connect to the server.

Fonts

Fonts are usually stored as individual files in directories. The X server can obtain fonts from directories and/or from font servers. The list of directories in which the server looks when trying to open a font is controlled by the *font path*. Although most sites will choose to have the X server start up with the appropriate font path (using the −fp option mentioned above), it can be overridden using the *xset* program.

The default font path for the X server contains four directories:

/usr/lib/X11/fonts/misc

> This directory contains several miscellaneous bitmap fonts that are useful on all systems. It contains a family of fixed-width fonts, a family of fixed-width fonts from Dale Schumacher, several Kana fonts from Sony Corporation, two JIS Kanji fonts, two Hangul fonts from Daewoo Electronics, two Hebrew fonts from Joseph Friedman, the standard cursor font, two cursor fonts from Digital Equipment Corporation, and cursor and glyph fonts from Sun Microsystems. It also has font name aliases for the fonts, including *fixed* and *variable*.

/usr/lib/X11/fonts/Speedo

> This directory contains outline fonts for Bitstream's Speedo rasterizer. A single font face, in normal, bold, italic, and bold italic, is provided, contributed by Bitstream, Inc.

/usr/lib/X11/fonts/75dpi

> This directory contains bitmap fonts contributed by Adobe Systems, Inc., Digital Equipment Corporation, Bitstream, Inc., Bigelow and Holmes, and Sun Microsystems, Inc. for 75 dots per inch displays. An integrated selection of sizes, styles, and weights is provided for each family.

/usr/lib/X11/fonts/100dpi

> This directory contains 100 dots per inch versions of some of the fonts in the *75dpi* directory.

Font databases are created by running the *mkfontdir* program in the directory containing the compiled versions of the fonts (the *.pcf* files). Whenever fonts are added to a directory, *mkfontdir* should be rerun so that the server can find the new fonts. If *mkfontdir* is not run, the server will not be able to find any fonts in the directory.

Diagnostics

Too numerous to list them all. If run from *init*(8), errors are typically logged in the file */usr/adm/Xnmsgs*.

Files

/etc/Xn.hosts	Initial access control list.

/usr/lib/X11/fonts/misc, /usr/lib/X11/fonts/75dpi, /usr/lib/X11/fonts/100dpi
        Font directories.

/usr/lib/x11/fonts/Speedo
        Outline font directory

/usr/lib/X11/fonts/PEX
        PEX font directory.

/usr/lib/X11/rgb.txt	Color database.
/tmp/.X11-unix/Xn	UNIX domain socket.
/usr/adm/Xnmsgs	Error log file.

See Also

X, bdf to pcf, mkfontdir, fs, xauth, xdm, xhost, xinit, xset, xsetroot, xterm, ttys(5), init(8); Volume Zero, *X Protocol Reference Manual*; the following papers in the source distribution: *Definition of the Porting Layer for the X v11 X Server; Strategies for Porting the X v11 X Server; and Godzilla's Guide to Porting the X V11 X Server.*

Bugs

The option syntax is inconsistent with itself and *xset.*

The acceleration option should take a numerator and a denominator like the protocol.

If *X* dies before its clients, new clients won't be able to connect until all existing connections have their TCP TIME_WAIT timers expire.

The color database is missing a large number of colors.

Authors

The X server was originally written by Susan Angebranndt, Raymond Drewry, Philip Karlton, and Todd Newman, of Digital Equipment Corporation, with support from a large cast. It has since been extensively rewritten by Keith Packard and Bob Scheifler of MIT.

appres

Name

appres – list application resource database.

Syntax

appres [[*class_name*][*instance_name*]] [*options*]

Description

The *appres* client prints the resources seen by an application (or a subhierarchy of an application) with the specified *class_name* and *instance_name*. It is used to help determine which resources a particular program would load from the various sources of resource specifications.

Note that *appres* doesn't really know anything about classes and instances as they may be defined by the client itself. As a result, it takes no account of conflicts between different resource settings, or their correctness. It simply loads the resource database into a temporary file and does a string comparison on the strings:

```
[*.]
class_name[*.]
instance_name[*.]
```

(where [*.] means either * or .) and then prints out the lines that match. Basically, *appres* searches for occurrences of any class and/or instance name supplied to it. In addition, *appres* searches for resources not assigned to a particular client—i.e., resources beginning with an asterisk or a dot. (These resources may or may not apply to the client whose class and instance names you supply.)

For example:

```
% appres XTerm
```

would list the resources that include the classname XTerm, as well as any resources beginning with an asterisk or dot.

To also match a particular instance name, you can enter both a class and an instance name, as in the following:

```
% appres XTerm myxterm
```

In this case, *appres* would list the resources that include any of the following terms: the classname XTerm; the instance name myxterm; or an initial asterisk or dot.

As of Release 5, *appres* recognizes the X Toolkit option -name. Thus, the alternative syntax:

```
% appres XTerm -name myxterm
```

is also acceptable and will produce the same output as the preceding example.

If no application class is specified, the class -AppResTest- (which has no defaults) is used. (Prior to Release 5, this dummy class name was -NoSuchClass-.)

Keep in mind the limitations of supplying only one argument (either a class name or an instance name). For example, if resources are specified in the database for the instance name xterm, typing appres XTerm will not list them; and if they are specified for class name XTerm, typing appres xterm will not list them. To be safe, you should specify both the class name and the instance name.

As of Release 5, *appres* also accepts hierarchical class and instance names as input. Hypothetically, this allows you to list the resources that match a particular sublevel of an application's widget hierarchy. (This could be very useful with a complex application.)

To list the resources that may apply to part of the widget hierarchy, you provide *appres* with both a hierarchical class and an instance name. The number of class and instance components must be equal. (Note that the instance name should not be specified with the toolkit -name option.) For example, the command:

```
% appres Xman.TopLevelShell.Form xman.topBox.form
```

will list the resources that *may* apply to widgets within *xman*'s topBox hierarchy.

Note that in attempting to match hierarchical class and instance names, *appres* suffers from the same limitations it does when attempting to match single class and/or instance names. The *appres* client simply compares text strings; it does not distinguish valid from invalid resources. If you supply multiple components, *appres* returns any resource that includes any one of the components; or any resource not assigned to a particular client (i.e., any resource beginning with an asterisk or a dot.)

You can limit the matching to resources that apply to a specific widget in the hierarchy by using the -1 option. For example, the command:

```
% appres XTerm.VT100 xterm.vt100 -1
```

will list the resources that may match the *xterm* vt100 widget.

In practice, use of the -1 option limits the matching to resource names having the same number of components, or fewer, as the names the user specifies. In the preceding example, the matching is limited to resources of two components or fewer. (This practice has nothing to do with the digit 1 in the -1 option; this number is a literal, not a variable.) Note, however, that limiting the resources that can be matched does not eliminate the problem of *appres* returning inapplicable resources.

For more information on the use of *appres*, see Chapter 11, *Setting Resources*.

Options

Note that options should follow the *class_name* (and *instance_name* if any). *appres* accepts the following application-specific option:

-1   Lists only the resources matching a specific level in the widget hierarchy (the level given on the command line). (Available as of Release 5.)

As of Release 5, *appres* also *recognizes* all of the standard X Toolkit options (i.e., the program will run); however, since *appres* is not a window-based application, it *uses* only the following options:

−name *app_name*

> Specifies the instance name under which resources for the application should be found. (Available as of Release 5.)

-xrm *resource*

> Specifies that, in addition to the current application resources, *appres* should return the *resource* specified as an argument to -xrm, if that resource would apply to the *class_name* or *instance_name*. You must specify both a *class_name* and an *instance_name* in order to use the -xrm option. (Note that -xrm does not actually load any resources.)

Without any arguments, *appres* returns those resources that might apply to any application (for example, those beginning with an asterisk in your *.Xresources* file).

See Also

X, xrdb, editres, listres; Chapter 11, *Setting Resources*.

Author

Jim Fulton, MIT X Consortium.

Name

bdftopcf – convert font from Bitmap Distribution Format to Portable Compiled Format.

Syntax

bdftopcf [*options*] *fontfile*.**bdf**

Description

bdftopcf is the Release 5 font compiler. It converts Bitmap Display Fonts (BDF) to Portable Compiled Format (PCF), which can be read by any architecture. Note, however, that the PCF file is structured to allow one particular architecture to read them directly without reformatting. This allows fast reading on the appropriate machine, but the files are still portable (albeit read more slowly) on other machines. See Volume Eight, *X Window System Administrator's Guide*, for more information.

Options

-i   Inhibits the normal computation of ink metrics. When a font has glyph images which do not fill the bitmap image (i.e., the "on" pixels don't extend to the edges of the metrics) *bdftopcf* computes the actual ink metrics and places them in the *.pcf* file; the -t option inhibits this behavior.

-l   Sets the font bit order to LSB (least significant bit) first. The left most bit on the screen will be in the lowest valued bit in each unit.

-L   Sets the font byte order to LSB first. All multi-byte data in the file (metrics, bitmaps and everything else) will be written least significant byte first.

-m   Sets the font bit order to MSB (most significant bit) first. Bits for each glyph will be placed in this order; i.e., the left most bit on the screen will be in the highest valued bit in each unit.

-M   Sets the font byte order to MSB first. All multi-byte data in the file (metrics, bitmaps, and everything else) will be written most significant byte first.

-o *output_filename*
       By default *bdftopcf* writes the pcf file to standard output; this option gives the name of a file to be used instead.

-p*n*   Sets the font glyph padding. Each glyph in the font will have each scanline padded in to a multiple of *n* bytes, where *n* is 1, 2, 4, or 8.

-t   When this option is specified, *bdftopcf* will convert fonts into "terminal" fonts when possible. A terminal font has each glyph image padded to the same size; the X server can usually render these types of fonts more quickly.

-u*n*   Sets the font scanline unit. When the font bit order is different from the font byte order, the scanline unit *n* describes what unit of data (in bytes) are to be swapped; the unit *n* can be 1, 2 or 4 bytes.

See Also

X; Chapter 6, *Font Specification*; Volume Eight, *X Window System Administrator's Guide*; Appendix M, *Logical Font Description Conventions*, in Volume Zero, *X Protocol Reference Manual*. Also see the document *Bitmap Distribution Format*, in the MIT distribution.

Author

Keith Packard, MIT X Consortium.

Name

bdftosnf – BDF to SNF font compiler for X11.

Syntax

bdftosnf [*options*] *bdf_file*

Description

As of Release 5, this program is no longer supported as part of the standard distribution of X. Use *bdftopcf* instead. The *bdftosnf* reference page is included merely for continuity.

bdftosnf reads a Bitmap Distribution Format (BDF) font from the specified file (or from standard input if no file is specified) and writes an X11 Server Natural Format (SNF) font to standard output. See Volume Eight, *X Window System Administrator's Guide*, for more information.

Options

bdftosnf accepts the following options:

-p*number*

    Forces the glyph padding to a specific *number*. The legal values are 1, 2, 4, and 8.

-u*number*

    Forces the scanline unit padding to a specific *number*. The legal values are 1, 2, and 4.

-m   Forces the bit order to most significant bit first.

-l   Forces the bit order to least significant bit first.

-M   Forces the byte order to most significant byte first.

-L   Forces the byte order to least significant byte first.

-w   Prints warnings if the character bitmaps have bits set to one outside of their defined widths.

-W   Prints warnings for characters with an encoding of –1; the default is to silently ignore such characters.

-t   Expands glyphs in "terminal-emulator" fonts to fill the bounding box.

-i   Suppresses computation of correct ink metrics for "terminal-emulator" fonts.

See Also

X, Xserver; Volume Eight, *X Window System Administrator's Guide*; Appendix M, *Logical Font Description Conventions*, in Volume Zero, *X Protocol Reference Manual*. Also see the document *Bitmap Distribution Format*, in the MIT distribution.

bitmap

Name

bitmap, bmtoa, atobm – bitmap editor and conversion utilities.

Syntax

bitmap [*options*] [*filename*] [*basename*]

bmtoa [*options*] [*filename*]

atobm [*options*] [*filename*]

Description

bitmap allows you to create and edit small bitmaps that you can use as backgrounds, clipping regions, tile and stipple patterns, icons, and pointers. A bitmap is a grid of pixels, or picture elements, each of which is white, black, or, in the case of color displays, a color. See Chapter 7, *Graphics Utilities*, for instructions on using *bitmap*.

The *bmtoa* and *atobm* filters convert *bitmap* files to and from ASCII strings. They are most commonly used to print out bitmaps quickly and to generate versions for inclusion in text. Chapter 7 describes how to convert a font character to a bitmap using *atobm*.

The window that *bitmap* creates has three sections (see Figure 7-1 in Part One of this guide). The checkerboard grid is a magnified version of the bitmap you are editing. Each square represents a single bit in the picture being edited. Squares on the grid can be set, cleared, or inverted directly with the buttons on the pointer. Command buttons to perform higher-level operations, such as drawing lines and circles, are provided to the left of the grid. You can invoke these command buttons by clicking on them with the first pointer button. Across the top of the window is a menu bar that provides a File menu and an Edit menu.

You can display an actual size representation of the bitmap image (as it would appear both normally and inverted) by pressing the Meta-I key combination. You are free to move the image popup out of the way to continue editing. Clicking the first pointer button in the popup window or typing Meta-I again will remove the actual size bitmap image.

If the bitmap is to be used for defining a cursor, one of the squares in the image may be designated as the *hot spot*. This determines where the cursor is actually pointing. For cursors with sharp tips (such as arrows or fingers), this is usually at the end of the tip; for symmetric cursors (such as crosses or bullseyes), this is usually at the center.

Bitmaps are stored as small C code fragments suitable for including in applications. They provide an array of bits as well as symbolic constants giving the width, height, and hot spot (if specified) that may be used in creating cursors, icons, and tiles. A selection of commonly-used bitmaps is generally stored in */usr/include/X11/bitmaps* on UNIX systems.

You give the size in pixels of the bitmap to be created (and consequently, the number of cells in the bitmap editing area) using the -size option. Existing bitmaps should be edited at their current size. The default size for new bitmaps is 16 × 16. (This is a little small—an icon such as the mailbox displayed by *xbiff* is 48 × 48 pixels.) See Chapter 7 for a discussion of *bitmap* window and image size issues.

When you run *bitmap* without a filename or with a new filename, the window will display a blank image area, suitable for you to begin editing. To edit a bitmap image, you can use one of the editing command buttons or use the pointer commands to change individual grid squares. (Chapter 7 describes both ways of editing; also see "Command Buttons for Drawing" and "Changing Grid Squares Using the Pointer" later in this reference page.)

Options: bitmap

bitmap accepts all of the standard X Toolkit command-line options, which are listed on the *X* reference page. In addition, *bitmap* accepts the following application-specific options:

-axes, +axes
> Turns the major axes on or off.

-dashed, +dashed
> Turns dashing for the frame and grid lines on or off.

-dashes *filename*
> Specifies the bitmap to be used as a stipple for dashing.

-fr *color*
> Specifies the color used for the frame and grid lines.

-grid, +grid
> Turns the grid lines on or off.

-gt *pixels*
> Grid tolerance. If the square dimensions fall below the specified value, grid will be automatically turned off. The default is 8 (pixels square).

-hl *color*
> Specifies the color to be used for highlighting.

-proportional, +proportional
> Turns proportional mode on or off. If proportional mode is on, square width is equal to square height. If proportional mode is off, *bitmap* will use the smaller square dimension, if they were initially different.

-sh *pixels*
> Specifies the height of squares in pixels.

-size *WIDTHxHEIGHT*
> Specifies size of the grid in squares. *WIDTHxHEIGHT* are two numbers, separated by the letter "x", which specify the dimensions of the checkerboard grid within the *bitmap* window (e.g., 9x13). The first number is the grid's width; the second number is its height. The default is 16x16.

-stipple *filename*
> Specifies the bitmap to be used as a stipple for highlighting.

-stippled, +stippled
> Turns stippling of highlighted squares on or off.

`-sw` `pixels`

> Specifies the width of squares in pixels.

The *bitmap* editor also accepts the following arguments:

`basename`

> Specifies the basename to be used in the C code output file. If it is different than the basename in the working file, *bitmap* will change the name of the file when saving.

`filename`

> Specifies the bitmap to be initially loaded into the program. If the file does not exist, *bitmap* will assume it is a new file.

Options: bmtoa

The *bmtoa* (bitmap to array) conversion program accepts the following option:

`-chars` `cc`

> Specifies the pair of characters to use in the string version of the bitmap. The first character is used for 0 bits and the second character is used for 1 bits. The default is to use dashes (–) for 0s and number signs (#) for 1s.

Options: atobm

The *atobm* (array to bitmap) conversion program accepts the following options:

`-chars` `cc`

> Specifies the pair of characters to use when converting string bitmaps into arrays of numbers. The first character represents a 0 bit and the second character represents a 1 bit. The default is to use dashes (–) for 0s and number signs (#) for 1s.

`-name` `variable`

> Specifies the variable name to be used when writing out the bitmap file. The default is to use the basename of the `filename` command-line argument or leave it blank if the standard input is read.

`-xhot` `number`

> Specifies the X coordinate of the hot spot. Only positive values are allowed. By default, no hot spot information is included.

`-yhot` `number`

> Specifies the Y coordinate of the hot spot. Only positive values are allowed. By default, no hot spot information is included.

Resources

For a table of settable resources, see the section "Bitmap Widget Resources" later in this reference page. Appendix G, *Widget Resources*, describes the resources that can be set for other widgets in the application. (See "Widget Hierarchy" later in this reference page.)

Changing Grid Squares Using the Pointer

You can set, clear, or invert grid squares by pointing to them and clicking or dragging using one of the buttons as indicated below. Setting a grid square corresponds to setting a bit in the bitmap image to 1. Clearing a grid square corresponds to setting a bit in the bitmap image to 0. Inverting a grid square corresponds to changing a bit in the bitmap image from 0 to 1 or 1 to 0, depending upon its previous state. You can change multiple squares at once by holding the button down and dragging the cursor across them. The default behavior of pointer buttons is:

Button 1 (usually the left)
> Sets one or more grid squares to the foreground color and sets the corresponding bits in the bitmap to 1.

Button 2 (usually the middle)
> Inverts one or more grid squares. The corresponding bit or bits in the bitmap are inverted (1s become 0s and 0s become 1s).

Button 3 (usually the right)
> Clears one or more grid squares (sets them to the background color) and sets the corresponding bits in the bitmap to 0.

For pointers with additional buttons, the fourth and fifth also clear the grid square(s).

This default behavior can be changed by setting the button function resources:

```
bitmap*button1Function:   Set
bitmap*button2Function:   Clear
bitmap*button3Function:   Invert
```

Note that the button function applies to all drawing commands, including copying, moving and pasting, flood filling and setting the hot spot.

Command Buttons for Drawing

bitmap provides 27 command buttons to assist you in drawing. The buttons are located to the left of the editing grid and their functions are summarized below. See Chapter 7 for more complete instructions. Note that most of the actions can also be performed using keyboard shortcuts (accelerators) while the pointer rests inside the editing grid or the surrounding whitespace.

Clear   Clears all bits in the bitmap image. Sets all of the grid squares to the background color. Typing c while the pointer rests inside the grid or the surrounding whitespace has the same effect.

Set   Sets all bits in the bitmap image. Sets all of the grid squares to the foreground color. Typing s has the same effect.

Invert   Inverts all bits in the bitmap image. The grid squares will be inverted appropriately. Typing i has the same effect.

Mark   Allows you to mark an area of the grid by dragging out a rectangular shape in the highlighting color. Once the area is marked, you can perform a number of other operations on it. (See Up, Down, Left, Right, Rotate, Flip, Cut, etc.) Only one marked area can be present at any time. If you attempt to mark another area, the old mark will vanish. The same effect can be achieved by pressing the Shift key and the first pointer button simultaneously and then dragging to highlight a rectangle in the grid window. Press Shift and click the second pointer button to mark the entire grid area.

Unmark   Causes the marked area to vanish. You can perform the same action by pressing Shift and clicking the third pointer button.

Copy   Allows you to copy an area of the grid from one location to another. If there is no marked grid area displayed, Copy first behaves just like Mark. Once there is a marked grid area displayed in the highlighting color, Copy has two alternative behaviors. If you press a pointer button inside the marked area, you can drag a rectangle representing the marked area to the desired location. When you release the pointer button, the area is copied. If you click outside the marked area, Copy will assume that you wish to mark a different region of the bitmap image and it will behave like Mark again.

Move   Allows you to move an area of the grid from one location to another. Its behavior resembles the behavior of Copy command, except that the marked area will be moved instead of copied.

Flip Horizontally

           Flips the bitmap image with respect to the horizontal axes. If a marked area of the grid is highlighted, it will operate only inside the marked area. Pressing h has the same effect.

Up   Moves the bitmap image one pixel up. If a marked area of the grid is highlighted, it will operate only inside the marked area. Pressing the up arrow key has the same effect.

Flip Vertically

           Flips the bitmap image with respect to the vertical axes. If a marked area of the grid is highlighted, it will operate only inside the marked area. Pressing v has the same effect.

Left   Moves the bitmap image one pixel to the left. If a marked area of the grid is highlighted, it will operate only inside the marked area. Pressing the left arrow key has the same effect.

Fold   Folds the bitmap image so that the opposite corners become adjacent. This is useful when creating bitmap images for tiling. Pressing f has the same effect.

Right   Moves the bitmap image one pixel to the right. If a marked area of the grid is highlighted, it will operate only inside the marked area. Pressing the right arrow key has the same effect.

Rotate Left

> Rotates the bitmap image 90 degrees to the left (counterclockwise.) If a marked area of the grid is highlighted, it will operate only inside the marked area. Pressing l has the same effect.

Down   Moves the bitmap image one pixel down. If a marked area of the grid is highlighted, it will operate only inside the marked area. Pressing the down arrow has the same effect.

Rotate Right

> Rotates the bitmap image 90 degrees to the right (clockwise). If a marked area of the grid is highlighted, it will operate only inside the marked area. Pressing r has the same effect.

Point   Changes the grid squares underneath the pointer according to the guidelines explained in "Changing Grid Squares Using the Pointer." If you press a button and drag the pointer, the line may not be continuous depending on the speed of your system and frequency of pointer motion events.

Curve   Changes the grid squares underneath the pointer according to the guidelines explained in "Changing Grid Squares Using the Pointer." The Curve command ensures that when you press a pointer button and drag, the line will be continuous. However,if your system is slow or *bitmap* receives very few pointer motion events, it might behave erratically.

Line   Allows you to draw the straightest possible line between two grid squares. Once you press a pointer button in the grid window, *bitmap* will highlight the line from the square where the pointer button was initially pressed to the square where the pointer is located. When you release the pointer button, the highlighting will disappear and the actual line will be drawn.

Rectangle

> Allows you to draw a rectangle. Once you press a pointer button in the grid window, *bitmap* will highlight the rectangle from the square where the pointer button was initially pressed to the square where the pointer is located. When you release the pointer button, the highlighting will disappear and the actual rectangle will be drawn.

Filled Rectangle

> Performs the same function as Rectangle, except that the rectangle is filled (rather than outlined).

Circle   Allows you to draw a circle. When you press a pointer button in the grid, that square becomes the center of the circle. You continue to hold the pointer button down and drag the pointer away from the center point to indicate a point on the circumference. An outline follows the pointer. When you release the pointer button, the highlighting will disappear and the actual circle will be drawn.

Filled Circle

Performs the same function as Circle, except that the circle is filled (rather than outlined).

Flood Fill

Fills any closed shape you click on. If a shape is open, you will "flood" a larger area than you intend. Diagonally adjacent squares are not considered to form a single shape.

Set Hot Spot

Designates one square in the grid as the hot spot if this bitmap image is to be used for defining a cursor. Pressing a pointer button in the desired square causes a diamond shape to be displayed.

Clear Hot Spot

Removes any designated hot spot from the bitmap image.

Undo   Undoes the last executed command. You can only recover the last action performed; thus, pressing Undo after Undo will toggle the last action on and off.

File Menu

You can access the File menu commands by pressing the File button and selecting the appropriate menu entry or by pressing the Control key with another key. These commands deal with files and global bitmap parameters, such as size, basename, filename, etc. See Chapter 7 for more information.

New   Clears the window so you can create a new image; prompts for a name for the new file. If you haven't saved the current file, the changes will be lost.

Load   Dynamically loads another bitmap file into the editing window; if you haven't saved the current file, prompts you as to whether to save before loading the next file. The *bitmap* editor can edit only one file at a time. If you need interactive editing, run a number of editors and use cut and paste mechanism as described below.

Insert   Inserts a bitmap file into the image currently being edited. After being prompted for the filename, click inside the grid window and drag the outlined rectangle to the location where you want to insert the new file.

Save   Saves the bitmap image. It will not prompt for the filename unless it is said to be <none>. If you leave the filename undesignated or –, the output will be piped to standard output.

Save As

Saves the bitmap image after prompting for a new filename. Use this menu item if you want to change the filename.

Resize   Changes the dimensions of the editing grid to match dimensions you supply (*widthxheight*), without changing the size of the image. Thus, specifying a larger grid gives you more room to edit. Specifying a smaller grid may cause part of the current image to be truncated.

Rescale   Changes the dimensions of the grid to match dimensions you supply (*widthx-height*) and changes the image so that the proportions (the ratio of the image to the grid) remain the same. Thus, if you specify a grid twice the size of the current one, both the grid and the image will be doubled. Rescale will not do antialiasing and specifying a smaller grid may cause part of the current image to be truncated. Feel free to add your own algorithms for better rescaling.

Filename

> Lets you change the filename of the current file without changing the basename or saving the file. If you specify – for a filename, the output will be piped to standard output.

Basename

> Lets you change the basename of the current file if you want one different from the filename.

Quit   Terminates the *bitmap* application. If changes have been made and not saved, a dialog box will ask whether to save before quitting. This command is preferable to killing the process.

Edit Menu

The Edit menu commands can be accessed by pressing the Edit button and selecting the appropriate menu entry, or by pressing Meta key with another key. These commands deal with editing facilities such as the grid, axes, zooming, cut and paste, etc.

Image   Displays a window showing what the bitmap being edited looks like at its actual size (both as it appears and in reverse video). You can move the window away to continue editing. Clicking the first pointer button on this window pops it down.

Grid   Controls the grid in the editing area. If the grid spacing is below the value specified by the `gridTolerance` resource (8 by default), the grid will be automatically turned off. You can turn the grid on by selecting this menu item.

Dashed   Controls the stipple for drawing the grid lines. Select this menu item to toggle the stipple (specified by the `dashes` resource or the `-dashes` option).

Axes   Toggles diagonal axes. The axes simply assist in drawing; they are not part of the image. Off by default.

Stippled   Toggles a stipple pattern to be used for highlighting within the editing area. The stipple specified by the `stipple` resource can be turned on or off by activating this command.

Proportional

> Toggles proportional mode which forces proportional grid squares, regardless of the dimensions of the *bitmap* window. On by default.

Zoom   Toggles zoom mode, which focuses in on a marked area of the image. (You can mark before or after selecting Zoom.) You can use all the editing commands and other utilities in the zoom mode. When you zoom out, Undo will undo the whole zoom session.

Cut	Cuts the contents of any marked area into the internal (application local) cut and paste buffer. The marked area is deleted from the current image, but is available to be pasted from the buffer. (If this was the last area marked, it is also available to be pasted into other applications via a global buffer.)
Copy	Copies the contents of any marked area into the internal (application local) cut and paste buffer. The marked area remains a part of the current image and is also available to be pasted from the buffer. (If this was the last area marked, it is also available to be pasted into other applications via a global buffer.)
Paste	Pastes the contents of the global buffer (the marked area in any *bitmap* or *xmag* application); if the global buffer is empty, this item pastes a copy of the contents of the internal cut and paste buffer. To place the copied image, press and hold the first pointer button in the editing area, drag the outlined image to the position you want, and then release the button.

Cut and Paste

bitmap supports two cut and paste mechanisms: an internal cut and paste buffer and the global X selection cut and paste buffer. The internal cut and paste is used when executing Copy and Move drawing commands and also Cut and Copy commands from the Edit menu. The global X selection cut and paste is used whenever there is a highlighted area of a bitmap image displayed anywhere on the screen. To copy a part of image from another bitmap editor, simply highlight the desired area by using the Mark command or pressing the Shift key and dragging the area with the first pointer button. When the selected area becomes highlighted, any other applications (such as *xterm*, etc.) that use the PRIMARY selection will discard their selection values and unhighlight the appropriate information. Now, use the Paste command from the Edit menu or press Control and any pointer button to copy the selected part of image into another (or the same) bitmap application. If you attempt to do this without a visible highlighted image area, the bitmap will fall back to the internal cut and paste buffer and paste whatever is stored there at the moment.

Widget Hierarchy

Below is the widget structure of the *bitmap* application. Indentation indicates hierarchical structure. The widget class name is given first, followed by the widget instance name. All widgets except the bitmap widget are from the standard Athena widget set. See Appendix G, *Widget Resources*, for a list of resources that can be set.

```
Bitmap bitmap
    TransientShell image
        Box box
            Label normalImage
            Label invertedImage
    TransientShell input
        Dialog dialog
            Command okay
            Command cancel
```

```
TransientShell error
    Dialog dialog
        Command abort
        Command retry
TransientShell qsave
    Dialog dialog
        Command yes
        Command no
        Command cancel
Paned parent
    Form formy
        MenuButton fileButton
        SimpleMenu fileMenu
            SmeBSB  new
            SmeBSB  load
            SmeBSB  insert
            SmeBSB  save
            SmeBSB  saveAs
            SmeBSB  resize
            SmeBSB  rescale
            SmeBSB  filename
            SmeBSB  basename
            SmeLine line
            SmeBSB  quit
        MenuButton editButton
        SimpleMenu editMenu
            SmeBSB  image
            SmeBSB  grid
            SmeBSB  dashed
            SmeBSB  axes
            SmeBSB  stippled
            SmeBSB  proportional
            SmeBSB  zoom
            SmeLine line
            SmeBSB  cut
            SmeBSB  copy
            SmeBSB  paste
        Label status
    Pane pane
        Bitmap bitmap
        Form form
            Command clear
            Command set
            Command invert
            Toggle  mark
            Command unmark
            Toggle  copy
            Toggle  move
```

```
Command flipHoriz
Command up
Command flipVert
Command left
Command fold
Command right
Command rotateLeft
Command down
Command rotateRight
Toggle  point
Toggle  curve
Toggle  line
Toggle  rectangle
Toggle  filledRectangle
Toggle  circle
Toggle  filledCircle
Toggle  floodFill
Toggle  setHotSpot
Command clearHotSpot
Command undo
```

Bitmap Widget Resources

The Bitmap widget is a stand-alone widget for editing raster images. It is not designed to edit large images, although it may be used in that purpose as well. It can be freely incorporated with other applications and used as a standard editing tool.

Header file	`Bitmap.h`
Class	`bitmapWidgetClass`
Class Name	`Bitmap`
Superclass	`Bitmap`

The following are the resources provided by the Bitmap widget. All the Simple widget resources plus:

Name	Class	Type	Default Value
foreground	Foreground	Pixel	XtDefaultForeground
highlight	Highlight	Pixel	XtDefaultForeground
framing	Framing	Pixel	XtDefaultForeground
gridTolerance	GridTolerance	Dimension	8
size	Size	String	32x32
dashed	Dashed	Boolean	True
dashes	Dashes	Bitmap	unspecified
grid	Grid	Boolean	True
stipple	Stipple	Bitmap	unspecified
stippled	Stippled	Boolean	True
proportional	Proportional	Boolean	True

Name	Class	Type	Default Value
axes	Axes	Boolean	False
squareWidth	SquareWidth	Dimension	16
squareHeight	SquareHeight	Dimension	16
margin	Margin	Dimension	16
xHot	XHot	Position	NotSet (-1)
yHot	YHot	Position	NotSet (-1)
button1Function	Button1Function	DrawingFunction	Set
button2Function	Button2Function	DrawingFunction	Invert
button3Function	Button3Function	DrawingFunction	Clear
button4Function	Button4Function	DrawingFunction	Invert
button5Function	Button5Function	DrawingFunction	Invert
filename	Filename	String	none
basename	Basename	String	none

Color

If you would like bitmap to be viewable in color, include the following in the #ifdef COLOR section of the file you read with xrdb:

```
*customization:    -color
```

This line will cause bitmap to pick up the colors in the app-defaults color customization file, */usr/lib/X11/app-defaults/Bitmap-color*. See Chapter 11, *Setting Resources*, for more information.

Files

/usr/lib/X11/app-defaults/Bitmap
> Specifies required resources.

/usr/lib/X11/app-defaults/Bitmap-color
> Color customization file.

/usr/include/X11/bitmaps
> On many systems, standard bitmaps can be found in this directory.

Bugs

bitmap should really be implemented with a scrollable editing area, so that the size of the application can be completely independent of the size of the bitmap being edited.

If you move the pointer too fast while holding a pointer button down, some squares may be missed. This is caused by limitations in how frequently the X server can sample the pointer location.

See Also

xmag; Chapter 7, *Graphics Utilities*.

Author

Release 5 *bitmap* by Davor Matic, MIT X Consortium; Previous releases of *bitmap* by Ron Newman, MIT Project Athena; *bmtoa* and *atobm* by Jim Fulton, MIT X Consortium.

Name

editres – a dynamic resource editor for X Toolkit applications.

Synopsis

```
editres [options]
```

Description

editres is a tool that allows you to view the full widget hierarchy of any X Toolkit client that speaks the *editres* protocol. In addition, *editres* will help you construct resource specifications and allow you to apply the resources to the application and view the results dynamically. Once you're happy with a resource specification, you can request that *editres* append the specification to a resource file. See Chapter 11, *Setting Resources*, for instructions on using *editres*.

Using editres

editres provides a window consisting of the following four areas:

Menu Bar   A set of popup menus that allows you full access to the program's features.

Panner   The panner allows a more intuitive way to scroll the application tree display.

Message Area   Displays information to the user about the action that *editres* expects of her.

Application Widget Tree

This area will be used to display the selected client's widget tree.

To begin an *editres* session, select the Get Widget Tree menu item from the command menu. This will change the pointer cursor to cross hair. You should now select the application you wish to look at by clicking on any of its windows. If this application understands the *editres* protocol, then *editres* will display the client's widget tree in its tree window. If the application does not understand the *editres* protocol, *editres* will inform you of this fact in the message area after a few seconds delay.

Once you have a widget tree you may now select any of the other menu options. The effect of each of these is described below.

Commands Menu

Get Widget Tree

Allows the user to click on any client that speaks the *editres* protocol, and receive its widget tree.

Refresh Current Widget Tree

editres only knows about the widgets that exist at the present time. Many applications create and destroy widgets "on-the-fly." Selecting this menu item will cause *editres* to ask the application to resend its widget tree, thus updating its information to the new state of the application.

For example, *xman* only creates the widgets for its *topbox* when it starts up. None of the widgets for the manual page window are created until the user actually clicks on the Manual Page button. If you retrieved *xman*'s widget tree before the manual page is active, you may wish to refresh the widget tree after the manual page has been displayed. This will also allow you to edit the manual page's resources.

Dump Widget Tree to a File

For documenting applications, it is often useful to be able to dump the entire application widget tree to an ASCII file. This file can then be included in the manual page. When this menu item is selected, a popup dialog is activated. Type the name of the file in this dialog, and either select okay, or press Return. *editres* will now dump the widget tree to this file. To cancel the file dialog just select the cancel button.

Show Resource Box

This command will popup a resource box for the current client. This resource box (described in detail below) will allow the user to see exactly which resources can be set for the widget that is currently selected in the widget tree display. Only one widget may be currently selected, if greater or fewer are selected *editres* will refuse to pop up the resource box, and put an error message in the Message Area.

Set Resource

This command will popup a simple dialog box for setting an arbitrary resource on all selected widgets. You must type in the resource name, as well as the value. You can use the Tab key to switch between the resource name field and the resource value field.

Quit   Exits *editres*.

Tree Menu Commands

The Tree menu contains several commands that allow operations to be performed on the widget tree.

Select Widget in Client

This menu item allows you to select any widget in the application; *editres* will then highlight the corresponding element in the widget tree display. Once this menu item is selected, the pointer cursor will again turn to a crosshair, and you must click any pointer button in the widget you wish to have displayed. Since some widgets are fully obscured by their children, it is not possible to get to every widget this way, but this mechanism does give very useful feedback between the elements in the widget tree and those in the actual client.

Select All
Unselect All
Invert All

These functions allow the user to select, unselect, or invert all widgets in the widget tree.

Select Children
Select Parents

These functions select the immediate parent or children of each of the currently selected widgets.

Select Descendants
Select Ancestors

> These functions select all parents or children of each of the currently selected widgets. This is a recursive search.

Show Widget Names
Show Class Names
Show Widget IDs
Show Widget Windows

> When the tree widget is initially displayed, the labels of each widget in the tree correspond to the widget names. These functions will cause the label of *all* widgets in the tree to be changed to show the class name, ID, or window associated with each widget in the application. The widget IDs, and windows are shown as hex numbers.

In addition, there are keyboard accelerators for each of the Tree operations. If the input focus is over an individual widget in the tree, then that operation will only effect that widget. If the input focus is in the Tree background it will have exactly the same effect as the corresponding menu item.

The translation entries shown may be applied to any widget in the application. If that widget is a child of the Tree widget, then it will only affect that widget, otherwise it will have the same effect as the commands in the Tree menu.

Flash Active Widgets

> This command is the inverse of the Select Widget in Client command, it will show the user each widget that is currently selected in the widget tree by flashing the corresponding widget in the application numFlashes three (by default) times in the flashColor.

Key	Option	Translation Entry
space	Unselect	Select(nothing)
w	Select	Select(widget)
s	Select	Select(all)
i	Invert	Select(invert)
c	Select Children	Select(children)
d	Select Descendants	Select(descendants)
p	Select Parent	Select(parent)
a	Select Ancestors	Select(ancestors)
N	Show Widget Names	Relabel(name)
C	Show Class Names	Relabel(class)
I	Show Widget IDs	Relabel(id)
W	Show Widget Windows	Relabel(window)
T	Toggle Widget/Class Name	Relabel(toggle)

Clicking button 1 on a widget adds it to the set of selected widgets. Clicking button 2 on a widget deselects all other widgets and then selects just that widget. Clicking button 3 on a widget toggles its label between the widget's instance name the widget's class name.

Using the Resource Box

The resource box contains five different areas. Each of the areas, as they appear on the screen from top to bottom, will be discussed.

The Resource Line

This area at the top of the resource box shows the current resource name exactly as it would appear if you were to save it to a file or apply it.

The Widget Names and Classes

This area allows you to select exactly which widgets this resource will apply to. The area contains four lines, the first contains the name of the selected widget and all its ancestors, and the more restrictive dot (.) separator. The second line contains less specific Class names of each widget, as well as the less restrictive star (*) separator. The third line contains a set of special buttons called Any Widget, which will generalize this level to match any widget. The last line contains a set of special buttons called Any Widget Chain, which will turn the single level into something that matches zero or more levels.

The initial state of this area is the most restrictive, using the resource names and the dot separator. By selecting the other buttons in this area you can ease the restrictions to allow more and more widgets to match the specification. The extreme case is to select all the Any Widget Chain buttons, which will match every widget in the application. As you select different buttons, the tree display will update to show you exactly which widgets will be effected by the current resource specification.

Normal and Constraint Resources

The next area allows you to select the name of the normal or constraint resources you wish to set. Some widgets may not have constraint resources, so that area will not appear.

Resource Value

This next area allows you to enter the resource value. This value should be entered exactly as you would type a line into your resource file. Thus, it should contain no unescaped newlines. There are a few special character sequences for this file:

\n   This will be replaced with a newline.

\###   Where # is any octal digit. This will be replaced with a single byte that contains this sequence interpreted as an octal number. For example, a value containing a NULL byte can be stored by specifying \000.

\<new-line>
        This will compress to nothing.

\\   This will compress to a single backslash.

Command Area

This area contains several command buttons that I will describe in this section.

Set Save File

This button allows the user to modify the file that the resources will be saved to. This button will bring up a dialog box that will ask you for a filename; once the filename has been entered, either hit carriage return or click on the okay button. To popdown the dialog box without changing the save file, click the cancel button.

Save

This button will append the resource line described above to the end of the current save file. If no save file has been set the Set Save File dialog box will pop up to prompt the user for a filename.

Apply

This button attempts to perform an XtSetValues call on all widgets that match the resource line described above. The value specified is applied directly to all matching widgets. This behavior is an attempt to give a dynamic feel to the resource editor. Since this feature allows users to put an application in states it may not be willing to handle, a hook has been provided to allow specific clients to block these SetValues requests (see "Blocking editres Requests" below).

Unfortunately due to design constraints imposed on the widgets by the X Toolkit and the Resource Manager, trying to coerce an inherently static system into dynamic behavior can cause strange results. There is no guarantee that the results of an apply will be the same as what will happen when you save the value, and restart the application. This functionality is provided to try to give you a rough feel for what your changes will accomplish, and the results obtained should be considered suspect, at best. Having said that, this is one of the neatest features of *editres*; I strongly suggest that you play with it, and see what it can do.

Save and Apply

This button combines the Save and Apply actions described above into one button.

Popdown Resource Box

This button will remove the resource box from the display.

Blocking editres Requests

The *editres* protocol has been built into the Athena Widget set. This allows all applications that are linked against Xaw to be able to speak to the resource editor. While this provides great flexibility and can be a useful tool, it can quite easily be abused. It is therefore possible for any Xaw client to specify a value for the editresBlock resource described below, to keep *editres* from divulging information about its internals, or to disable the SetValues part of the protocol.

editresBlock (class EditresBlock)
> Specifies which type of blocking this client wishes to impose on the *editres* protocol. The accepted values are:

    all   Block all requests.

    setValues   Block all setValues requests (the only *editres* request that actually modifies the application); in effect, the application is read-only.

    none   Allow all *editres* requests.

Remember that these resources are set on any Xaw client, *not* on *editres*. They allow individual clients to keep all or some of the requests *editres* makes from ever succeeding. Of course, *editres* is also an Xaw client, so it may also be viewed and modified by *editres* (rather recursive, I know). These commands can be blocked by setting the editresBlock resource on *editres* itself.

Options

editres accepts all of the standard X Toolkit command-line options. For a description of the Toolkit options, see Chapter 10, *Command-line Options*.

editres accepts no application-specific options.

Note, however, that if you supply *editres* with an invalid option, you'll get the following misleading syntax message:

Usage: editres [-vspace <value>] [-hspace <value>]

This is a bug. **–vspace and –hspace are not valid options.**

Resources

editres understands all of the Core resource names and classes. (See Appendix G, *Widget Resources*, for more information.) In addition, *editres* recognizes the following application-specific resources:

flashTime (class FlashTime)
> Amount of time between the flashes described above.

flashColor (class FlashColor)
> Specifies the color used to flash client widgets. A bright color should be used that will immediately draw your attention to the area being flashed, such as red or yellow.

numFlashes (class NumFlashes)
> Specifies the number of times the widgets in the client application will be flashed when the **Show Active Widgets** command is invoked.

saveResourcesFile (class SaveResourcesFile)
> This is the file the resource line will be append to when the **Save** button is activated in the resource box.

Widgets

In order to specify resources, it is useful to know the hierarchy of the widgets which compose *editres*. In the notation below, indentation indicates hierarchical structure. The widget class name is given first, followed by the widget instance name.

```
Editres  editres
      Paned  paned
            Box  box
                  MenuButton  commands
                        SimpleMenu  menu
                        SmeBSB  sendTree
                        SmeBSB  refreshTree
                        SmeBSB  dumpTreeToFile
                        SmeLine  line
                        SmeBSB  getResourceList
                        SmeLine  line
                        SmeBSB  quit
                  MenuButton  treeCommands
                        SimpleMenu  menu
                        SmeBSB  showClientWidget
                        SmeBSB  selectAll
                        SmeBSB  unselectAll
                        SmeBSB  invertAll
                        SmeLine  line
                        SmeBSB  selectChildren
                        SmeBSB  selectParent
                        SmeBSB  selectDescendants
                        SmeBSB  selectAncestors
                        SmeLine  line
                        SmeBSB  showWidgetNames
                        SmeBSB  showClassNames
                        SmeBSB  showWidgetIDs
                        SmeBSB  showWidgetWindows
                        SmeLine  line
                        SmeBSB  flashActiveWidgets
            Paned  hPane
                  Panner  panner
                  Label  userMessage
                  Grip  grip
            Porthole  porthole
                  Tree  tree
                        Toggle  <name of widget in client>
                        .
                        .
                        .
                        TransientShell  resourceBox
                        Paned  pane
                        Label  resourceLabel
```

```
                         Form  namesAndClasses
                         Toggle  dot
                         Toggle  star
                         Toggle  any
                         Toggle  name
                         Toggle  class
                             .
                             .
                             .
                         Label  namesLabel
                         List  namesList
                         Label  constraintLabel
                         List  constraintList
                         Form  valueForm
                         Label  valueLabel
                         Text  valueText
                         Box  commandBox
                         Command  setFile
                         Command  save
                         Command  apply
                         Command  saveAndApply
                         Command  cancel
                         Grip  grip
            Grip  grip
```

Files

/usr/lib/X11/app-defaults/Editres
Specifies required resources.

See Also

X, xrdb; Chapter 11, *Setting Resources*; Appendix G, *Athena Widget Resources*.

Bugs

editres prints a usage line listing two invalid options: -vspace and -hspace.

Restrictions

This is a prototype; there are lots of nifty features I would love to add, but I hope this will give you some ideas about what a resource editor can do.

Author

Chris D. Peterson, formerly of the MIT X Consortium.

fs

Name

fs – X font server.

Syntax

fs [*options*]

Description

fs is the X Window System font server, introduced in Release 5. It supplies fonts to X Window System display servers. The font server makes it possible to use fonts on more than one host on the network.

The server is usually run by a system administrator, and started via boot files like */etc/rc.local*. Users may also wish to start private font servers for specific sets of fonts. For more information, see Chapter 6, *Font Specification*, and Volume Eight, *X Window System Administrator's Guide*.

Options

-config *configuration_file*
> Specifies the configuration file the font server will use.

-ls *listen_socket*
> Specifies a file descriptor which is already set up to be used as the listen socket. This option is only intended to be used by the font server itself when automatically spawning another copy of itself to handle additional connections.

-port *tcp_port*
> Specifies the TCP port number on which the server will listen for connections.

Signals

SIGTERM
> Causes the font server to exit cleanly.

SIGUSR1
> Used to cause the server to reread its configuration file.

SIGUSR2
> Used to cause the server to flush any cached data it may have.

SIGHUP Used to cause the server to reset, closing all active connections and rereading the configuration file.

Configuration File

The configuration file is a list of keyword and value pairs. Each keyword is followed by an equal sign (=) and then the desired value.

Recognized keywords include:

`catalogue` (list of string)
> Ordered list of font path element names. Use of the keyword `catalogue` is very misleading at present; the current implementation only supports a single catalogue (`all`), containing all of the specified fonts.

`alternate-servers` (list of string)
> List of alternate servers for this font server.

`client-limit` (cardinal)
> Number of clients this font server will support before refusing service. This is useful for tuning the load on each individual font server.

`clone-self` (boolean)
> Whether this font server should attempt to clone itself when it reachs the client-limit.

`default-point-size` (cardinal)
> The default pointsize (in decipoints) for fonts that don't specify.

`default-resolutions` (list of resolutions)
> Resolutions the server supports by default. This information may be used as a hint for prerendering, and substituted for scaled fonts which do not specify a resolution.

`error-file` (string)
> Filename of the error file. All warnings and errors will be logged here.

`port` (cardinal)
> TCP port on which the server will listen for connections.

`use-syslog` (boolean)
> Whether syslog(3) (on supported systems) is to be used for errors.

Example
```
#
# sample font server configuration file
#

# allow a max of 10 clients to connect to this font server
client-limit = 10

# when a font server reaches its limit, start up a new one
clone-self = on

# alternate font servers for clients to use
alternate-servers = hansen:7001,hansen:7002

# where to look for fonts
# the first is a set of Speedo outlines, the second is a set of
# misc bitmaps and the last is a set of 100dpi bitmaps
#
```

```
catalogue = /usr/lib/fonts/speedo,
    /usr/lib/X11/ncd/fonts/misc,
    /usr/lib/X11/ncd/fonts/100dpi/

# in 12 points, decipoints
default-point-size = 120

# 100 x 100 and 75 x 75
default-resolutions = 100,100,75,75
```

Font Server Names

One of the following forms can be used to name a font server that accepts TCP connections:

```
tcp/hostname:port
tcp/hostname:port/catalogue_list
```

The *hostname* specifies the name (or decimal numeric address) of the machine on which the font server is running. The *port* is the decimal TCP port on which the font server is listening for connections. The *catalogue_list* specifies a list of catalogue names, with a plus sign (+) as a separator.

Examples:

```
tcp/expo.lcs.mit.edu:7000, tcp/18.30.0.212:7001/all
```

One of the following forms can be used to name a font server that accepts DECnet connections:

```
decnet/nodename::font$object_name
decnet/nodename::font$object_name/catalogue_list
```

The *nodename* specifies the name (or decimal numeric address) of the machine on which the font server is running. The *object_name* is a normal, case-insensitive DECnet object name. The *catalogue_list* specifies a list of catalogue names, with a plus sign (+) as a separator. Some examples follow:

```
DECnet/SRVNOD::FONT$DEFAULT, decnet/44.70::font$special/symbols
```

See Also

X; Chapter 6, *Font Specification*; Volume Eight, *X Window System Administrator's Guide*; Also see the document *Font server implementation overview* in the MIT source.

Bugs

Multiple catalogues should be supported.

Copyright

Copyright 1991, Network Computing Devices, Inc.
Copyright 1991, Massachusetts Institute of Technology.
See *X* for a full statement of rights and permissions.

Authors

Dave Lemke, Network Computing Devices, Inc.;
Keith Packard, Massachusetts Institute of Technology.

fsinfo

Name

fsinfo – font server information utility.

Syntax

`fsinfo` [`-server` *server_name*]

Description

The *fsinfo* program (introduced in Release 5) is a utility for displaying information about an X font server. (See the *fs* reference page, Chapter 6, *Font Specification*, and Volume Eight, *X Window System Administrator's Guide*.) *fsinfo* is used to examine the capabilities of a server, the predefined values for various parameters used in communicating between clients and the server, and the font catalogues and alternate servers that are available.

Options

`-server` *server_name*

Specifies a particular font server. The *server_name* generally has the form *transport/host:port*. If the FONTSERVER environment variable is not defined, this option must be given.

Example

The following shows a sample produced by *fsinfo*.

```
name of server:hansen:7000
version number:1
vendor string:Font Server Prototype
vendor release number:17
maximum request size:16384 longwords (65536 bytes)
number of catalogues:1
    all
Number of alternate servers: 2
    #0hansen:7001
    #1hansen:7002
number of extensions:0
```

Environment Variables

FONTSERVER

To get the default font server.

See Also

fs, fslsfonts; Chapter 6, *Font Specification*; Volume Eight, *X Window System Administrator's Guide*.

Copyright

Copyright 1991, Network Computing Devices, Inc.
See *X(1)* for a full statement of rights and permissions.

Author

Dave Lemke, Network Computing Devices, Inc.

fslsfonts

Name

fslsfonts – list X font server fonts.

Syntax

fslsfonts [*options*] [-fn *pattern*]

Description

fslsfonts lists the fonts from a font server that match the given *pattern*.

The wildcard character "*" may be used to match any sequence of characters (including none), and "?" to match any single character. If no pattern is given, "*" is assumed.

The "*" and "?" characters must be quoted to prevent them from being expanded by the shell.

fslsfonts has been added to the standard distribution of X11 in Release 5 and is intended to be run with the X font server. (For more information, see the *fs* reference page, Chapter 6, *Font Specification*, and Volume Eight, *X Window System Administrator's Guide*.)

Options

-1   Indicates that listings should use a single column. This is the same as -n 1.

-C   Indicates that listings should use multiple columns. This is the same as -n 0.

-fn *pattern*
      Lists only those fonts matching the given *pattern*.

-l[l[l]]
      Indicates that medium, long, and very long listings, respectively, should be generated for each font.

-m   Indicates that long listings should also print the minimum and maximum bounds of each font.

-n *columns*
      Specifies the number of columns to use in displaying the output. By default, it will attempt to fit as many columns of font names into the number of characters specified by -w *width*.

-server *server_name*
      Specifies a particular font server. The *server_name* generally has the form *transport/host:port*. If the FONTSERVER environment variable is not defined, this option must be given.

-u   Indicates that the output should be left unsorted.

-w *width*
      Specifies the width in characters that should be used in figuring out how many columns to print. The default is 79.

See Also

fs, fsinfo, showfont, xlsfonts; Chapter 6, *Font Specification*; Volume Eight, *X Window System Administrator's Guide*.

Environment Variables

FONTSERVER
>   To get the default font server.

Bugs

Running `fslsfonts -l` can tie up your server for a very long time. This delay is really a bug with single-threaded, non-preemptable servers, not with the *fslsfonts* client.

Copyright

Copyright 1991, Network Computing Devices, Inc.
See X(1) for a full statement of rights and permissions.

Author

Dave Lemke, Network Computing Devices, Inc.

fstobdf

Name

fstobdf – Convert font server font to BDF format.

Syntax

fstobdf -fn *fontname* [-server *server_name*]

Description

The *fstobdf* program reads a font from a font server and prints a BDF file on the standard output that may be used to recreate the font. This is useful in testing servers, debugging font metrics, and reproducing lost BDF files.

fstobdf has been added to the standard distribution of X11 in Release 5 and is intended to be used with the X font server. (For more information, see the *fs* reference page and Volume Eight, *X Window System Administrator's Guide*.)

Options

-fn *fontname*

    Specifies the font for which a BDF file should be generated.

-server *server_name*

    Specifies a particular font server. The *server_name* generally has the form *transport/host:port*. If the FONTSERVER environment variable is not defined, this option must be given.

Environment Variables

FONTSERVER

    To get the default font server.

See Also

bdftosnf, fs, fsinfo, fslsfonts; Volume Eight, *X Window System Administrator's Guide*; Appendix M, *Logical Font Description Conventions*, in Volume Zero, *X Protocol Reference Manual*. Also see the document *Bitmap Distribution Format*, in the MIT distribution.

Copyright

Authors

Olaf Brandt, Network Computing Devices.
Dave Lemke, Network Computing Devices.
Jim Fulton, MIT X Consortium.

listres

Name
listres – list resources in widgets.

Syntax
`listres` [*options*] [*widget . . .*]

Description
The *listres* client generates a list of each specified widget's resource database. The list includes the class in which each resource is first defined, the instance and class name, and the type of each resource.

If no widgets are specified (or the `-all` option is used), a two-column list of known widget names and their class hierarchies is printed. In the MIT distribution, this includes the intrinsics-defined widget classes Core, Composite, Constraint, and Shell (and Shell's six subclasses), plus the Athena widgets.

Case is not significant when specifying the name of the widget or widgets whose resources are to be printed. For example:

`% listres Core`

is equivalent to:

`% listres CORE`

Options
listres accepts the following application-specific options:

`-all`   Indicates that *listres* should print information for all known widgets and objects.

`-format` *printf_string*
> Specifies the *printf*-style format string to be used to print out the name, instance, class, and type of each resource.

`-nosuper`
> Specifies that resources inherited from a superclass should not be listed. This is useful for determining which resources are new to a subclass.

`-top` *name*
> Specifies the name of the widget to be treated as the top of the hierarchy. Case is not significant, and the name may match either the class variable name or the class name. The default is `core`.

`-tree` Specifies that all widgets and objects be listed in a tree.

`-variable`
> Indicates that widgets should be identified by the names of the class record variables rather than the class name given in the variable. This is useful for distinguishing subclasses that have the same class name as their superclasses.

listres also *recognizes* all of the standard X Toolkit options (i.e., the program will run); however, since *listres* is not a window-based application, it does not *use* them.

Resources

resourceFormat (class ResourceFormat)
> Specifies the *printf*-style format string to be used to print out the name, instance, class, and type of each resource.

showSuper (class ShowSuper)
> If false, resources inherited from a superclass are not listed. This is useful for determining which resources are new to a subclass. The default is true.

showTree (class ShowTree)
> If true, specifies that all widgets and objects be listed in a tree. The default is false.

showVariable (class ShowVariable)
> If true, widgets are identified by the names of the class record variables rather than the class name given in the variable. This is useful for distinguishing subclasses that have the same class name as their superclasses. The default is false.

topObject (class TopObject)
> Specifies the name of the widget to be treated as the top of the hierarchy. Case is not significant, and the name may match either the class variable name or the class name. The default is core.

See Also

X, xrdb, appres, editres; Chapter 11, *Setting Resources*; Appendix G, *Widget Resources*; Volume Four, *X Toolkit Intrinsics Programming Manual*; Volume Five, *X Toolkit Intrinsics Reference Manual*.

Bugs

On operating systems that do not support dynamic linking of run-time routines, this program must have all of its known widgets compiled in. The sources provide several tools for automating this process for various widget sets.

Author

Jim Fulton, MIT X Consortium.

mkfontdir

Name

mkfontdir – creates a *fonts.dir* file for each specified directory of font files.

Syntax

```
mkfontdir [directory_names]
```

Description

For each directory argument, *mkfontdir* reads all of the font files in the directory and searches for properties named "FONT", or (failing that) the name of the file stripped of its suffix. These are used as font names, which are written out to the file *fonts.dir* in the directory, along with the name of the font file.

The kinds of font files read by *mkfontdir* depend on configuration parameters, but typically include PCF (suffix *.pcf*), SNF (suffix *.snf*), and BDF (suffix *.bdf*). For more information, see Volume Eight, *X Window System Administrator's Guide*. If a font exists in multiple formats, *mkfontdir* will first choose PCF, then SNF, and finally BDF.

Scalable Fonts

Because scalable font files do not usually include the X font name, the *fonts.dir* file in directories containing such fonts must be edited by hand to include the appropriate entries for those fonts. However, be aware that when *mkfontdir* is subsequently run, all of those additions will be lost. (It might be advisable to maintain an additional list of scalable fonts that can be read into the *fonts.dir* file each time *mkfontdir* is run.)

Font Name Aliases

The file *fonts.alias*, which can be put in any directory of the font path, is used to map new names to existing fonts, and should be edited by hand. The format is straightforward enough: two white-space separated columns, the first containing aliases and the second containing font-name patterns.

When a font alias is used, the name it references is searched for in the normal manner, looking through each font directory in turn. This means that the aliases need not mention fonts in the same directory as the alias file.

To embed white space in either name, simply enclose the name in double-quote marks. To embed double-quote marks (or any other special character), precede it with a backslash:

```
"magic-alias with spaces"    "\"fontname\" with quotes"
regular-alias                fontname
```

Searching the Font Path

Both the X server and the font server (*fs*) look for *fonts.dir* and *fonts.alias* files in each directory in the font path each time the font path is set (see *xset*).

See Also

X, Xserver, fs, xset; Volume Eight, *X Window System Administrator's Guide*; Appendix M, *Logical Font Description Conventions*, in Volume Zero, *X Protocol Reference Manual*.

mwm

\ — **Motif window manager** —

Name

mwm – the Motif window manager.

Syntax

`mwm` [`options`]

Description

The Motif window manager, *mwm*, provides all of the standard window management functions. It allows you to move, resize, iconify/deiconify, maximize, and close windows and icons, focus input to a window or icon, refresh the display, etc. *mwm* provides much of its functionality via a frame that (by default) is placed around every window on the display. The *mwm* frame has the three-dimensional appearance characteristic of the OSF/Motif graphical user interface.

Chapters 3 and 4 of this guide discuss input focus, the components of the *mwm* frame, and the various window management functions you can perform using the pointer on the frame. In addition, Chapter 4 describes how to perform window/icon management functions using *mwm*'s Window Menu (as well as keyboard shortcuts for menu functions). Chapter 4 also describes the Root Menu, which provides commands that can be thought of as affecting the display as a whole.

By default, *mwm* manages only screen 0. (You can specify an alternate screen by setting the DISPLAY environment variable or using the -`display` option.) If you want *mwm* to manage all screens on the display, use the -`multiscreen` option or set the `multiScreen` resource to `True`. (See "mwm-specific Appearance and Behavior Resources.")

You can customize dozens of *mwm* features by editing a startup file (*.mwmrc*) and/or by specifying resources for the *mwm* client. You can place *mwm* resources in your regular resource file (often called *.Xresources*) in your home directory; or you can create a file called *Mwm* (also in your home directory) for *mwm* resources only. If you place conflicting specifications in both files, the resources in *.Xresources* (presuming they are loaded into the RESOURCE_MANAGER) take precedence. (These files are generally kept in the user's home directory. Note, however, that the actual location of resource files may depend on certain environment variables. See the section "Environment Variables" for more information.)

Chapter 13 of this guide describes the syntax of the *.mwmrc* file and of *mwm* resource specifications. Chapter 13 also describes how to use an icon box, which can be set up to organize icons on the display.

The current reference page primarily describes the actions and resources by *mwm*. This reference page should assist you in customizing *mwm*, according to the guidelines specified in Chapter 13.

484   *X Window System User's Guide*

Options

-display [*host*]:*server*[.*screen*]

> Specifies the name of the display on which to run *mwm*. *host* is the hostname of the physical display, *server* specifies the server number, and *screen* specifies the screen number. Either or both of the *host* and *screen* elements can be omitted. If *host* is omitted, the local display is assumed. If *screen* is omitted, screen 0 is assumed (and the period is unnecessary). The colon and (display) *server* are necessary in all cases.

> For example, the following command runs *mwm* on screen 1 on server 0 on the display named *your_node*.

> **mwm -display** *your_node*:**0.1**

-multiscreen

> Specifies that *mwm* should manage all screens on the display. The default is to manage only screen 0. You can specify an alternate screen by setting the DISPLAY environment variable or using the -display option.

> You can also specify that *mwm* manage all screens by assigning a value of True to the multiScreen resource variable. See "mwm-specific Appearance and Behavior Resources."

-name *app_name*

> Specifies the name under which resources for the window manager should be found.

-screens *screen_name* [*screen_name*]...

> Assigns resource names to the screens *mwm* is managing. (By default, the screen number is used as the *screen_name*.) If *mwm* is managing a single screen, only the first name in the list is used. If *mwm* is managing multiple screens, the names are assigned to the screens in order, starting with screen 0. If there are more screens than names, resources for the remaining screens will be retrieved using the first *screen_name*.

-xrm *resourcestring*

> Specifies a resource name and value to override any defaults. This option is very useful for setting resources that don't have explicit command-line arguments.

.mwmrc Startup File

The default operation of *mwm* is largely controlled by a system-wide file, called *system.mwmrc*, which establishes the contents of the Root Menu and Window Menu, how menu functions are invoked, and what key and button combinations can be used to manage windows. To modify the behavior of *mwm*, you can edit a copy of this file in your home directory. The version of this file in your home directory should be called *.mwmrc*. (You can specify an alternate startup file using the configFile resource variable.)

The syntax of the *system.mwmrc* file is described in Chapter 13 of this guide. Chapter 13 also examines how to create menus, how to modify existing menus, and how to bind window manager functions to keystrokes, pointer button actions, or a combination of keys and buttons.

In describing the syntax of button and key bindings, Chapter 13 refers to the variables *modifier_key* and *button_event*. Acceptable values for *modifier_key* are: `Ctrl`, `Shift`, `Alt`, `Meta`, `Lock`, `Mod1`, `Mod2`, `Mod3`, `Mod4`, and `Mod5`. *mwm* considers `Alt` and `Meta` to be equivalent. See Chapter 14, *Setup Clients*, for a discussion of modifier keys and key mapping.

The acceptable values for *button_event* are:

```
Btn1Down
Btn1Up
Btn1Click
Btn1Click2
Btn2Down
Btn2Up
Btn2Click
Btn2Click2
     .
     .
     .
Btn5Down
Btn5Up
Btn5Click
Btn5Click2
```

Most of these button actions are obvious. (A specification ending in `Click2` refers to a double click. Thus, `Button1Click2` means to double click button 1.) Note that the list indicates a range between button 1 and button 5 (i.e., the same button events can be specified for buttons 2, 3, and 4).

mwm Functions

This section describes the functions you can specify in an *mwm* startup file.

Unless otherwise noted, you can specify that each action is invoked:

* In any of the following contexts: `root`, `window`, and `icon`.

* Using button bindings, key binding, or menu items.

When a function is specified with the context `icon | window` and you invoke the function from the icon box, the function applies to the icon box itself (rather than to any of the icons it contains).

A function is treated as `f.nop` when it is:

* Not a valid function name.

* Specified inappropriately (e.g., mapped to a button when the function cannot be invoked using button bindings).

* Invoked in an invalid context. (For example, you cannot invoke `f.minimize` on a window that is already iconified.)

See Chapter 13 for a discussion of context, bindings, and menus.

mwm recognizes the following functions:

`f.beep`

>   Causes a beep from the keyboard.

`f.circle_down [icon | window]`

>   Causes the window or icon on the top of the stack to be lowered to the bottom of the stack. If the `icon` argument is specified, the function applies only to icons. If the `window` argument is specified, the function applies only to windows.

>   This function is invoked by the Shuffle Down item on the default Root Menu.

`f.circle_up [icon | window]`

>   Causes the window or icon on the bottom of the stack to be raised to the top. If the `icon` argument is specified, the function applies only to icons. If the `window` argument is specified, the function applies only to windows.

>   This function is invoked by the Shuffle Up item on the default Root Menu.

`f.exec [command]`

`! [command]`

>   Executes *command* using the shell specified by the MWMSHELL environment variable. (If MWMSHELL isn't set, the command is executed using the shell specified by the SHELL environment variable; otherwise, the command is executed using */bin/sh*.)

`f.focus_color`

>   Sets the colormap focus to a client window. If this function is invoked in the `root` context, the default colormap (specified by X for the screen where *mwm* is running) is installed and there is no specific client window colormap focus. For the `f.focus_color` function to work, the `colormapFocusPolicy` should be specified as `explicit`; otherwise the function is treated as `f.nop`.

`f.focus_key`

>   Sets the input focus to a window or icon. For the `f.focus_key` function to work, the `keyboardFocusPolicy` should be specified as `explicit`. If `keyboardFocusPolicy` is not `explicit`, or if the function is invoked in the `root` context, it is treated as `f.nop`.

`f.kill`

>   Terminates a client. Specifically, sends the WM_DELETE_WINDOW message to the selected window if the client application has requested it through the WM_PROTOCOLS property. The application is supposed to respond to the message by removing the indicated window. If the WM_SAVE_YOURSELF protocol is set up and the WM_DELETE_WINDOW protocol is not, the client is sent a message, indicating that the client needs to prepare to be terminated. If the client does not have the WM_DELETE_WINDOW or WM_SAVE_YOURSELF protocol set, the `f.kill` function

causes a client's X connection to be terminated (usually resulting in termination of the client).

This function is invoked by the Close item on the default Window Menu. The f.kill function can only be invoked in the contexts window and icon.

See also quitTimeout in the "Resources" section; see the WM_PROTOCOLS property in Volume Two, *Xlib Reference Manual*.

f.lower [*-client* | within | freeFamily]

Without arguments, lowers a window or icon to the bottom of the stack. (By default, the context in which the function is invoked indicates the window or icon to lower.) If an application window has one or more transient windows (e.g., dialog boxes), the transient windows are lowered with the parent (within the global stack) and remain on top of it. (The within and freeFamily arguments allow you to control how transient windows are affected by the f.lower action.) f.lower is invoked (without arguments) by the Lower item on the default Window Menu.

If the *-client* argument is specified, the function is invoked on the named client. (*client* must be the instance or class name of a program.)

The within argument is used to lower a transient window within the application's "local" window hierarchy; all transients remain above the parent window (usually the main application window) and that window remains in the same position in the global window stack. In practice, this function is only useful when there are two or more transient windows and you want to shuffle them.

The freeFamily argument is used to lower a transient below its parent—in effect, to free transient windows from the local hierarchy. Again, the parent is not moved in the global window stack. (Note, however, that if you use this function on the parent, the entire family stack is lowered within the global stack.)

f.maximize

Causes a window to be redisplayed at its maximum size. The f.maximize function is invoked by the Maximize item on the default Window Menu. This function cannot be invoked in the context root or on a window that is already maximized.

f.menu *menu_name*

Associates a cascading (i.e., pull-right) menu with a menu item (from which the cascading menu is displayed); or associates a menu with a button or key binding. The *menu_name* argument specifies the menu.

f.minimize

Causes a window to be minimized (i.e., iconified). When no icon box is being used, icons are placed on the bottom of the stack (generally in the lower-left corner of the screen. See also iconPlacement in "mwm-specific Appearance and Behavior Resources)." If an icon box is being used, icons are placed inside the box.

The f.minimize function is invoked by the Minimize item on the default Window Menu. This function cannot be invoked in the context root or on an iconified window.

f.move

Allows you to move a window interactively, using the pointer. This function is invoked by the Move item on the default Window Menu.

f.next_cmap

Installs the next colormap in the list of colormaps for the window with the colormap focus. (See f.focus_color.)

f.next_key [icon | window | transient]

Without any arguments, this function advances the input focus to the next window or icon in the stack. You can specify only icon or window to make the function apply only to icons or windows, respectively.

Generally, the focus is moved only to windows that do not have an associated secondary window that is application modal. (An active dialog box is application modal.) If the transient argument is specified, transient (secondary) windows are also traversed. Otherwise, if only window is specified, focus is moved only to the last window in a transient group to have the focus.

For this function to work, keyboardFocusPolicy must be explicit; otherwise, the function is treated as f.nop. See Chapter 4 for the default key combinations to move the focus.

f.nop   Specifies no operation. (In other words, it does nothing.)

f.normalize

Causes a client window to be displayed at its normal size. The f.normalize function is invoked by the Restore item on the default Window Menu. This function cannot be invoked in the context root or on a window that is already at its normal size.

f.normalize_and_raise

Causes the client window to be displayed at its normal size and raised to the top of the stack. This function cannot be invoked in the context root or on a window that is already at its normal size.

f.pack_icons

Rearranges icons in an optimal fashion (based on the layout policy being used), either on the root window or in the icon box. See iconPlacement in "mwm-specific Appearance and Behavior Resources." (See Chapter 13 for instructions on using an icon box.)

f.pass_keys

Toggles processing of key bindings for window manager functions. When key binding processing is disabled, all keys are passed to the window with the keyboard input focus and no window manager functions are invoked. If the f.pass_keys function is set up to be invoked with a key binding, the binding can be used to toggle (enable/disable) key binding processing.

f.post_wmenu

Displays the Window Menu. If a key is used to display the menu and a Window Menu command button is present, the upper-left corner of the menu is placed at the lower-left corner of the command button. If no Window Menu command button is present, the menu is placed in the upper-left corner of the window.

f.prev_cmap

This function installs the previous colormap in the list of colormaps for the window with the colormap focus. (See f.focus_color.)

f.prev_key [icon | window | transient]

Without any arguments, this function moves the input focus to the previous window or icon in the stack. You can specify only icon or window to make the function apply only to icons or windows, respectively.

Generally, the focus is moved only to windows that do not have an associated secondary window that is application modal. (An active dialog box is application modal.) If the transient argument is specified, transient (secondary) windows are also traversed. Otherwise, if only window is specified, focus is moved only to the last window in a transient group to have the focus.

For this function to work, keyboardFocusPolicy must be explicit; otherwise, the function is treated as f.nop. See Chapter 4 for the default key combinations to move the focus.

f.quit_mwm

Stops the *mwm* window manager. Note that this function does not stop the X server. This function cannot be invoked from a non-root menu.

f.raise [-*client* | within | freeFamily]

Raises a window or icon to the top of the stack. By default, the context in which the function is invoked indicates the window or icon to raise. If the -*client* argument is specified, the function is invoked on the named client. (*client* must be the instance or class name of a program.)

Without arguments, raises a window or icon to the top of the stack. (By default, the context in which the function is invoked indicates the window or icon to raise.) If an application window has one or more transient windows (e.g., dialog boxes), the transient windows are raised with the parent (within the global stack) and remain on top of it. (The within and freeFamily arguments allow you to control how transient windows are affected by the f.raise action.)

If the -*client* argument is specified, the function is invoked on the named client. (*client* must be the instance or class name of a program.)

The within argument is used to raise a transient window within the application's "local" window hierarchy; all transients remain above the parent window (usually the main application window) and that window remains in the same position in the global window stack. In practice, this function is only useful when there are two or more transient windows and you want to shuffle them.

The freeFamily argument raises a transient to the top of the family stack (in effect, transient windows are freed from the local hierarchy) and also raises the parent window to the top of the global stack.

f.raise_lower [within | freeFamily]

Raises a primary application window to the top of the stack or lowers a window to the bottom of the stack, as appropriate to the context.

The within argument is intended to raise a transient window within the application's "local" window hierarchy (if the transient is obscured); all transients remain above the parent window (usually the main application window); the parent window should also remain in the same position in the global window stack. If the transient is not obscured by another window in the local stack, the transient window is lowered within the family.

The preceding paragraph describes how f.raise_lower within *should* work. However, we have found that the parent window does not always remain in the same position in the global window stack.

The freeFamily argument raises a transient to the top of the family stack (in effect, transient windows are freed from the local hierarchy) and also raises the parent window to the top of the global stack. If the transient is not obscured by another window, this function lowers the transient to the bottom of the family stack and lowers the family in the global stack.

f.refresh

Redraws all windows. This function is invoked by the Refresh item on the default Root Menu.

f.refresh_win

Redraws a single window.

f.resize

Allows you to resize a window interactively, using the pointer. This function is invoked by the Size item on the default Window Menu.

f.restart

Restarts the *mwm* window manager. (Specifically, this function causes the current *mwm* process to be stopped and a new *mwm* process to be started.) This function is invoked by the Restart... item on the default Root Menu. It cannot be invoked from a non-root menu.

`f.restore`

> Causes the client window to be displayed at its previous size. If invoked on an icon, `f.restore` causes the icon to be converted back to a window at its previous size. Thus, if the window was maximized, it is restored to this state. If the window was previously at its normal size, it is restored to this state. If invoked on a maximized window, the window is restored to its normal size. The `f.restore` function is invoked by the Restore item on the default Window Menu. This function cannot be invoked in the context `root` or on a window that is already at its normal size.

`f.restore_and_raise`

> Causes the client window to be displayed at its previous size and raised to the top of the stack. This function cannot be invoked in the context `root` or on a window that is already at its normal size.

`f.screen [next | prev | back | screen_number]`

> Causes the pointer to be warped to (i.e., redrawn at) another screen, determined by one of four mutually exclusive parameters:

> The `next` argument means skip to the next managed screen. The `prev` argument means skip back to the previous managed screen. The `back` argument means skip to the last screen visited (regardless of its position in the numeric order).

> Screens are normally numbered beginning at 0. `screen_number` specifies a particular screen.

`f.send_msg message_number`

> Sends a message of the type _MOTIF_WM_MESSAGES to a client; the message type is indicated by the `message_number` argument. The message is sent only if the client's _MOTIF_WM_MESSAGES property includes `message_number`.

> If a menu item is set up to invoke `f.send_msg` and the `message_number` is not included in the client's _MOTIF_WM_MESSAGES property, the menu item label is greyed out (indicating that it is not available for selection).

`f.separator`

> Creates a divider line in a menu. Any associated label is ignored.

`f.set_behavior`

> Restarts *mwm*, toggling between the default behavior for the particular system and the user's custom environment. In any case, a dialog box asks the user to confirm or cancel the action. By default this function is invoked using the following key sequence: `Shift Ctrl Meta !`.

`f.title`

> Specifies the title of a menu. The title string is separated from the menu items by a double divider line.

Resources

mwm resources are considered to fall into three categories:

- *mwm* component appearance resources. These resources set the characteristics of *mwm*'s component features, such as the window frame, menus, and icons.

- *mwm*-specific appearance and behavior resources. These resources set characteristics of the window manager client, such as focus policy, key and button bindings, and so forth.

- Client-specific resources. These *mwm* resources can be used to set the appearance and behavior of a particular client or class of clients.

The following sections simply describe the valid resources. For a discussion of *mwm* resource syntax, see Chapter 13 in this guide. (For more information about basic resource syntax and the precedence of resource specifications, see Chapter 11.)

Note that Mwm is the class name. You can specify resources for multiple screens using the names supplied to the -screens command-line option in place of mwm or Mwm in the resource line. (See "Options.")

mwm Component Appearance Resources

The Motif window manager can be considered to be made up of the following components: client window frames, menus, icons, and feedback (dialog) boxes. Some component appearance resources can be set for all of these components; others can be set only for the frame and icons.

Unless a default is specified, the default varies based on system specifics (such as screen type, color resources, etc.).

The following component appearance resources apply to all window manager components:

background (class Background)
> Specifies the background color.

backgroundPixmap (class BackgroundPixmap)
> Specifies the background pixmap of the *mwm* decoration when the window does not have the input focus (i.e., is inactive).

bottomShadowColor (class Foreground)
> Specifies the color to be used for the lower and right bevels of the window manager decoration.

bottomShadowPixmap (class BottomShadowPixmap)
> Specifies the pixmap to be used for the lower and right bevels of the window manager decoration.

fontList (class FontList)
> Specifies the font to be used in the window manager decoration. The default is fixed.

foreground (class Foreground)
> Specifies the foreground color.

saveUnder (class SaveUnder)

> Specifies whether save unders are used for *mwm* components. By default (False), save unders will not be used on any window manager frames.

> Save unders must be implemented by the X server for this function to to take effect. When save unders are implemented, the X server saves the contents of windows obscured by other windows that have the save under attribute set. If the saveUnder resource is True, *mwm* will set the save under attribute on the frame of any client that has it set.

topShadowColor (class Background)

> Specifies the color to be used for the upper and left bevels of the window manager decoration.

topShadowPixmap (class TopShadowPixmap)

> Specifies the pixmap to be used for the upper and left bevels of the window manager decoration.

The following component appearance resources apply to the window frame and icons:

activeBackground (class Background)

> Specifies the background color of the *mwm* decoration when the window has the input focus (i.e., is active).

activeBackgroundPixmap (class ActiveBackgroundPixmap)

> Specifies the background pixmap of the *mwm* decoration when the window has the input focus (i.e., is active).

activeBottomShadowColor (class Foreground)

> Specifies the bottom shadow color of the *mwm* decoration when the window has the input focus (i.e., is active).

activeBottomShadowPixmap (class BottomShadowPixmap)

> Specifies the bottom shadow pixmap of the *mwm* decoration when the window has the input focus (i.e., is active).

activeForeground (class Foreground)

> Specifies the foreground color of the *mwm* decoration when the window has the input focus (i.e., is active).

activeTopShadowColor (class Background)

> Specifies the top shadow color of the *mwm* decoration when the window has the input focus (i.e., is active).

activeTopShadowPixmap (class TopShadowPixmap)

> Specifies the top shadow Pixmap of the *mwm* decoration when the window has the input focus (i.e., is active).

mwm-specific Appearance and Behavior Resources

The *mwm*-specific resources control aspects of what you probably think of as the window manager application itself, features such as the focus policy, whether windows are placed on the display automatically or interactively, which set(s) of button and key bindings are used, whether an icon box is used, and so forth.

The following *mwm*-specific appearance and behavior resources can be specified:

autoKeyFocus (class AutoKeyFocus)
>   If True (the default), when the focus window is withdrawn from window management or is iconified, the focus bounces back to the window that previously had the focus. This resource is available only when keyboardFocusPolicy is explicit. If False, the input focus is not set automatically. autoKeyFocus and startupKeyFocus should both be True to work properly with tear off menus.

autoRaiseDelay (class AutoRaiseDelay)
>   Specifies the amount of time (in milliseconds) that *mwm* will wait before raising a window after it receives the input focus. The default is 500. This resource is available only when focusAutoRaise is True and the keyboardFocusPolicy is pointer.

bitmapDirectory (class BitmapDirectory)
>   Identifies the directory to be searched for bitmaps referenced by *mwm* resources (if an absolute pathname to the bitmap file is not given). The default is */usr/include/X11/bitmaps*, which is considered the standard location on many systems. Note, however, that the location of the bitmap directory may vary in different environments. If a bitmap is not found in the specified directory, XBMLANGPATH is searched.

buttonBindings (class ButtonBindings)
>   Identifies the set of button bindings to be used for window management functions; must correspond to a set of button bindings specified in the *mwm* startup file. Button bindings specified in the startup file are merged with built-in default bindings. The default is DefaultButtonBindings.

cleanText (class CleanText)
>   Specifies whether text that appears in *mwm* title and feedback windows is displayed over the existing background pattern. If True (the default), text is drawn with a clear (no stipple) background. (Only the stippling in the area immediately around the text is cleared.) This enhances readability, especially on monochrome systems where a backgroundPixmap is specified. If False, text is drawn on top of the existing background.

clientAutoPlace (class ClientAutoPlace)
>   Specifies the location of a window when the user has not specified a location. If True (the default), windows are positioned with the upper-left corners of the frames offset horizontally and vertically (so that no two windows completely overlap).
>
>   If False, the currently configured position of the window is used.
>
>   In either case, *mwm* will attempt to place the windows totally on screen.

colormapFocusPolicy (class ColormapFocusPolicy)

> Specifies the colormap focus policy. Takes three possible values: keyboard, pointer, and explicit. If keyboard (the default) is specified, the input focus window has the colormap focus. If explicit is specified, a colormap selection action is done on a client window to set the colormap focus to that window. If pointer is specified, the client window containing the pointer has the colormap focus.

configFile (class ConfigFile)

> Specifies the pathname for the *mwm* startup file. The default startup file is *.mwmrc*.

> *mwm* searches for the configuration file in the user's home directory. If the config-File resource is not specified or the file does not exist, *mwm* defaults to an implementation-specific standard directory (the default is */usr/lib/X11/system.mwmrc*).

> If the LANG environment variable is set, *mwm* looks for the configuration file in a *$LANG* subdirectory first. For example, if the LANG environment variable is set to Fr (for French), *mwm* searches for the configuration file in the directory *$HOME/Fr* before it looks in *$HOME*. Similarly, if the configFile resource is not specified or the file does not exist, *mwm* defaults to */usr/lib/X11/$LANG/system.mwmrc* before it reads */usr/lib/X11/system.mwmrc*.

> If the configFile pathname does not begin with "~/", *mwm* considers it to be relative to the current working directory.

deiconifyKeyFocus (class DeiconifyKeyFocus)

> If True (the default), a window receives the input focus when it is normalized (deiconified). This resource applies only when the keyboardFocusPolicy is explicit.

doubleClickTime (class DoubleClickTime)

> Specifies the maximum time (in milliseconds) between the two clicks of a double click. The default is the display's multi-click time.

enableWarp (class EnableWarp)

> If True (the default), causes *mwm* to *warp* the pointer to the center of the selected window during resize and move operations invoked using keyboard accelerators. (The cursor symbol disappears from its current location and reappears at the center of the window.) If False, *mwm* leaves the pointer at its original place on the screen, unless the user explicitly moves it.

enforceKeyFocus (class EnforceKeyFocus)

> If True (the default), the input focus is always explicitly set to selected windows even if there is an indication that they are "globally active" input windows. (An example of a globally active window is a scrollbar that can be operated without setting the focus to that client.) If the resource is False, the keyboard input focus is not explicitly set to globally active windows.

Reference Pages

`fadeNormalIcon` (class `FadeNormalIcon`)

> If `True`, an icon is greyed out when it has been normalized. The default is `False`.

`feedbackGeometry` (class `FeedbackGeometry`)

> Specifies the position of the small, rectangular feedback box that displays coordinate and size information during move and resize operations. By default, the feedback window appears in the center of the screen. This resource takes the argument:
>
> `[=]±xoffset±yoffset`
>
> With the exception of the optional leading equal sign, this string is identical to the second portion of the standard geometry string. See the section "Window Geometry: Specifying Size and Location" in Chapter 3, *Working in the X Environment*, for more information. Note that `feedbackGeometry` allows you to specify location only. The size of the feedback window is not configurable using this resource. Available as of *mwm* version 1.2.

`frameBorderWidth` (class `FrameBorderWidth`)

> Specifies the width in pixels of a window frame border, without resize handles. (The border width includes the three-dimensional shadows.) The default is determined according to screen specifics.

`iconAutoPlace` (class `IconAutoPlace`)

> Specifies whether the window manager arranges icons in a particular area of the screen or places each icon where the window was when it was iconified. If `True` (the default), icons are arranged in a particular area of the screen, determined by the `iconPlacement` resource. If `False`, an icon is placed at the location of the window when it is iconified.

`iconBoxGeometry` (class `IconBoxGeometry`)

> Specifies the initial position and size of the icon box. Takes as its argument the standard geometry string:
>
> `widthxheight±xoff±yoff`
>
> where `width` and `height` are measured in icons. The default geometry string is `6x1+0-0`, which places an icon box six icons wide by one icon high in the lower-left corner of the screen.
>
> You can omit either the dimensions or the x and y offsets from the geometry string and the defaults apply. If the offsets are not provided, the `iconPlacement` resource is used to determine the initial placement.
>
> The actual screen size of the icon box depends on the `iconImageMaximum` and `iconDecoration` resources, which specify icon size and padding. The default value for size is (6 × *icon_width* + padding) wide by (1 × *icon_height* + padding) high.

iconBoxName (class IconBoxName)
> Specifies the name under which icon box resources are to be found. The default is
> iconbox.

iconBoxSBDisplayPolicy (class IconBoxSBDisplayPolicy)
> Specifies what scrollbars are displayed in the icon box. The resource has three pos-
> sible values: all, vertical, and horizontal. If all is specified (the default),
> both vertical and horizontal scrollbars are displayed at all times. vertical specifies
> that a single vertical scrollbar is displayed (this also sets the orientation of the icon
> box to horizontal—regardless of the iconBoxGeometry specification). hori-
> zontal specifies that a single horizontal scrollbar is displayed in the icon box (this
> also sets the orientation of the icon box to vertical—regardless of the iconBox-
> Geometry specification).

iconBoxTitle (class IconBoxTitle)
> Specifies the name to be used in the title area of the icon box. The default is Icons.

iconClick (class IconClick)
> If True (the default), the Window Menu is displayed when the pointer is clicked on an
> icon.

iconDecoration (class IconDecoration)
> Specifies how much icon decoration is used. The resource value takes four possible
> values (multiple values can also be supplied): label, which specifies that only the
> label is displayed; image, which specifies that only the image is displayed; and
> activelabel, which specifies that a label (not truncated to the width of the icon) is
> used when the icon has the focus.
>
> The default decoration for icons in an icon box is label image, which specifies
> that both the label and image parts are displayed. The default decoration for individ-
> ual icons on the screen proper is activelabel label image.

iconImageMaximum (class IconImageMaximum)
> Specifies the maximum size of the icon image. Takes a value of *widthxheight*
> (e.g., 80x80). The maximum size supported is 128×128. The default is 50x50.

iconImageMinimum (class IconImageMinimum)
> Specifies the minimum size of the icon image. Takes a value of *widthxheight*
> (e.g., 36x48). The minimum size supported is 16×16 (which is also the default).

iconPlacement (class IconPlacement)
> Specifies an icon placement scheme. Note that this resource is only useful when
> useIconBox is False (the default). The iconPlacement resource takes a value
> of the syntax:
>
> *primary_layout*   *secondary_layout* [tight]

There are four possible layout policies:

top, which specifies that icons are placed from the top of the screen to the bottom; bottom, which specifies a bottom-to-top arrangement; left, which specifies that icons are placed from the left to the right; right, which specifies a right-to-left arrangement.

The *primary_layout* specifies whether icons are placed in a row or a column and the direction of placement. The *secondary_layout* specifies where to place new rows or columns. For example, a value of top right specifies that icons should be placed from top to bottom on the screen and that columns should be added from right to left on the screen.

A horizontal (vertical) layout value should not be used for both the *primary_layout* and the *secondary_layout*. For example, don't use top for the *primary_layout* and bottom for the *secondary_layout*.

The default placement is left bottom (i.e., icons are placed left to right on the screen, with the first row on the bottom of the screen, and new rows are added from the bottom of the screen to the top of the screen).

The optional argument tight specifies that there is no space between icons.

iconPlacementMargin (class IconPlacementMargin)
> Sets the distance from the edge of the screen at which icons are placed. (The value should be greater than or equal to 0. A default value is used if an invalid distance is specified.) The default value is equal to the space between icons as they are placed on the screen (which is is based on maximizing the number of icons in each row and column).

interactivePlacement (class InteractivePlacement)
> If True, specifies that new windows are to be placed interactively on the screen using the pointer. When a client is run, the pointer shape changes to an upper-left corner cursor; move the pointer to the location you want the window to appear and click the first button; the window is displayed in the selected location. If False (the default), windows are placed according to the initial window configuration attributes.

keyBindings (class KeyBindings)
> Identifies the set of key bindings to be used for window management functions; must correspond to a set of key bindings specified in the *mwm* startup file. Note that key bindings specified in the startup file replace the built-in default bindings. The default is DefaultKeyBindings.

keyboardFocusPolicy (class KeyboardFocusPolicy)
> If explicit focus is specified (the default), placing the pointer on a window (including the frame) or icon and pressing the first pointer button focuses keyboard input on the client. If pointer is specified, the keyboard input focus is directed to the client window on which the pointer rests (the pointer can also rest on the frame).

limitResize (class LimitResize)
> If True (the default), the user is not allowed to resize a window to greater than the maximum size.

lowerOnIconify (class LowerOnIconify)
> If True (the default), a window's icon is placed on the bottom of the stack when the window is iconified. If False, the icon is placed in the stacking order at the same place as its associated window.

maximumMaximumSize (class MaximumMaximumSize)
> Specifies the maximum size of a client window (as set by the user or client). Takes a value of *widthxheight* (e.g., 1024x1024) where *width* and *height* are in pixels. The default is twice the screen width and height.

moveThreshold (class MoveThreshold)
> Controls the sensitivity of dragging operations (such as those used to move windows and icons on the display). Takes a value of the number of pixels that the pointing device is moved while a button is held down before the move operation is initiated. The default is 4. This resource helps prevent a window or icon from moving when you click or double click and inadvertently jostle the pointer while a button is down.

moveOpaque (class MoveOpaque)
> If False (the default), when you move a window or icon, its outline is moved before it is redrawn in the new location. If True, the actual (and thus, opaque) window or icon is moved. Available as of *mwm* version 1.2.

multiScreen (class MultiScreen)
> If False (the default), *mwm* manages only a single screen. If True, *mwm* manages all screens on the display. (See "Options.")

passButtons (class PassButtons)
> Specifies whether button press events are passed to clients after the events are used to invoke a window manager function (in the client context). If False (the default), button presses are not passed to the client. If True, button presses are passed to the client. (Note that the window manager function is done in either case.)

passSelectButton (class PassSelectButton)
> Specifies whether select button press events are passed to clients after the events are used to invoke a window manager function (in the client context). If True (the default), button presses are passed to the client window. If False, button presses are not passed to the client. (Note that the window manager function is done in either case.)

positionIsFrame (class PositionIsFrame)
> Specifies how *mwm* should interpret window position information (from the WM_NORMAL_HINTS property and from configuration requests). If True (the default), the information is interpreted as the position of the *mwm* client window

frame. If `False`, it is interpreted as being the position of the client area of the window.

`positionOnScreen` (class `PositionOnScreen`)

If `True` (the default), specifies that windows should initially be placed (if possible) so that they are not clipped by the edge of the screen. (If a window is larger than the size of the screen, at least the upper-left corner of the window is placed is on the screen.) If `False`, windows are placed in the requested position even if totally off the screen.

`quitTimeout` (class `QuitTimeout`)

Specifies the amount of time (in milliseconds) that *mwm* will wait for a client to update the WM_COMMAND property after *mwm* has sent the WM_SAVE_YOURSELF message. The default is `1000`. (See the `f.kill` function for additional information.)

`raiseKeyFocus` (class `RaiseKeyFocus`)

If `True`, specifies that a window raised by means of the `f.normalize_and_raise` function also receives the input focus. This function is available only when the `keyboardFocusPolicy` is `explicit`. The default is `False`.

`resizeBorderWidth` (class `ResizeBorderWidth`)

Specifies the width in pixels of a window frame border, with resize handles. (The border width includes the three-dimensional shadows.) The default is determined according to screen specifics.

`resizeCursors` (class `ResizeCursors`)

If `True` (the default), the resize cursors are always displayed when the pointer is in the window resize border.

`screens` (class `Screens`)

Assigns resource names to the screens *mwm* is managing. If *mwm* is managing a single screen, only the first name in the list is used. If *mwm* is managing multiple screens, the names are assigned to the screens in order, starting with screen 0. (See also "Options.")

`showFeedback` (class `ShowFeedback`)

Specifies whether *mwm* feedback windows and confirmation dialog boxes are displayed. (Feedback windows are used to display: window coordinates during interactive placement and subsequent moves; and dimensions during resize operations. A typical confirmation dialog is the window displayed to allow the user to allow or cancel a window manager restart operation.)

`showFeedback` accepts a list of options, each of which corresponds to the type of feedback given in a particular circumstance. Depending on the syntax in which the options are entered, you can either enable or disable a feedback option (as explained later).

The possible feedback options are: `all`, which specifies that *mwm* show all types of feedback (this is the default); `behavior`, which specifies that feedback is displayed to confirm a behavior switch; `kill`, which specifies that feedback is displayed on receipt of a KILL signal; `move`, which specifies that a box containing the coordinates of a window or icon is displayed during a move operation; `placement`, which specifies that a box containing the position and size of a window is displayed during initial (interactive) placement; `quit`, which specifies that a dialog box is displayed so that the user can confirm (or cancel) the procedure to quit *mwm*; `resize`, which specifies that a box containing the window size is displayed during a resize operation; `restart`, which displays a dialog box so that the user can confirm (or cancel) an *mwm* restart procedure; the `none` option specifies that no feedback is shown.

By default, *mwm* supplies feedback in `all` cases. (`all` encompasses all of the other options—with the exception of the `none` option.)

To limit feedback to particular cases, you can use one of two syntaxes: with the first syntax, you disable feedback in specified cases (all other default feedback is still used); with the second syntax, you enable feedback only in specified cases.

Initially, the syntax may be confusing, but it is actually quite simple. You supply this resource with a list of options to be enabled or disabled. If the first item is preceded by a minus sign, feedback is disabled for all options in the list. (Any option not listed remains enabled.)

If the first item is preceded by a plus sign (or no sign is used), feedback is enabled only for options in the list.

For example, the following resource specification:

`Mwm*showFeedback: resize placement restart`

enables the feedback options `resize`, `placement`, and `restart`. What this means is the following: size information is displayed when a window is resized; coordinates are displayed when a window is placed interactively on the screen; and a dialog box is displayed so that the user can confirm or cancel a window manager restart request. Feedback is supplied in these circumstances only, overriding the default `all` option.

The following line specifies the same characteristics using the alternate syntax:

`Mwm*showFeedback: -move kill behavior quit`

This line disables the feedback options `move`, `kill`, `behavior`, and `quit`. The other options encompassed by the default `all` (`resize`, `placement`, and `restart`) remain enabled.

`startupKeyFocus` (class `StartupKeyFocus`)

If `True` (the default), the input focus is transferred to a window when the window is mapped (i.e., initially managed by the window manager). This function is available only when `keyboardFocusPolicy` is `explicit`. `startupKeyFocus` and `autoKeyFocus` should both be `True` to work properly with tear off menus.

`transientDecoration` (class `TransientDecoration`)

Specifies the amount of decoration *mwm* puts on transient windows. The decoration specification is exactly the same as for the `clientDecoration` (client-specific) resource. Transient windows are identified by the WM_TRANSIENT_FOR property, which is added by the client to indicate a relatively temporary window. The default is `menu title`, which specifies that transient windows have resize borders and a titlebar with a Window Menu command button.

If the client application also specifies which decorations the window manager should provide, *mwm* uses only those features that both the client and the `transientDecoration` resource specify.

`transientFunctions` (class `TransientFunctions`)

Specifies which window management functions are applicable (or not applicable) to transient windows. The function specification is exactly the same as for the `clientFunctions` (client-specific) resource. The default is `-minimize maximize`.

If the client application also specifies which window management functions should be applicable, *mwm* provides only those functions that both the client and the `transientFunctions` resource specify.

`useIconBox` (class `UseIconBox`)

If `True`, icons are placed in an icon box. By default, the individual icons are placed on the root window.

`wMenuButtonClick` (class `WMenuButtonClick`)

If `True` (the default), a pointer button click on the Window Menu button displays the Window Menu and leaves it displayed.

`wMenuButtonClick2` (class `WMenuButtonClick2`)

If `True`, double clicking on the Window Menu command button removes the client window (actually invokes the `f.kill` function).

Client-specific Resources

Some *mwm* resources can be set to apply to certain client applications or classes of applications. Many of the client-specific resources provide what might be considered advanced customization.

The following client-specific resources can be specified:

`clientDecoration` (class `ClientDecoration`)

Specifies the amount of window frame decoration. The default frame is composed of several component parts: the titlebar, resize handles, border, and three command buttons (Minimize, Maximize, and Window Menu). You can limit the frame decoration for a client using the `clientDecoration` resource.

`clientDecoration` accepts a list of options, each of which corresponds to a part of the client frame. Depending on the syntax in which the options are entered, you can either enable or disable an option (as explained later).

The options are: `maximize` (button); `minimize` (button); `menu` (the Window Menu button); `border`; `title` (titlebar); `resizeh` (resize handles); `all`, which encompasses all decorations previously listed (this is the default); and `none`, which specifies that no decorations are used.

Some decorations require the presence of others; if you specify such a decoration, any decoration required with it will be used automatically. Specifically, if any of the command buttons is specified, a titlebar is also used; if resize handles or a titlebar is specified, a border is also used.

By default, a client window has `all` decoration. To specify only certain parts of the default frame, you can use one of two syntaxes: with the first syntax, you disable certain frame features (all other default features are still used); with the second syntax, you enable only certain features. (The syntax is virtually the same as that described for `showFeedback`.)

You supply `clientDecoration` with a list of options to be enabled or disabled. If the first item is preceded by a minus sign, the features in the list are disabled. (Any option not listed remains enabled.)

If the first item is preceded by a plus sign (or no sign is used), only those features listed are enabled.

For example, the following resource specification:

`Mwm*XCalc*clientDecoration: -minimize maximize menu`

removes the three command buttons from *xcalc* window frames. (The window will still have the titlebar, resize handles, and border.)

The following line specifies the same characteristics using the alternate syntax:

`Mwm*XCalc*clientDecoration: title resizeh border`

`clientFunctions` (class `ClientFunctions`)

Specifies whether certain *mwm* functions can be invoked on a client window. (See "mwm Functions" earlier in this reference page.) The only functions that can be controlled are those that are executable using the pointer on the default window frame.

`clientFunctions` accepts a list of options, each of which corresponds to an *mwm* function. Depending on the syntax in which the options are entered, you can either allow or disallow a function (as explained later).

The options (and the functions to which they correspond) are: `resize` (`f.resize`); `move` (`f.move`); `minimize` (`f.minimize`); `maximize` (`f.max-`

imize); close (f.kill); all (encompasses all of the previously listed functions); none (none of the default functions is allowed).

By default, a client recognizes all functions. To limit the functions a client recognizes, you can use one of two syntaxes: with the first syntax, you disallow certain functions (all other default functions are still allowed); with the second syntax, you allow only *certain* functions. (The syntax is virtually the same as that described for clientDecoration.)

You supply clientFunctions with a list of options (corresponding to functions) to be allowed or disallowed. If the first item is preceded by a minus sign, the functions in the list are disallowed. (Any option not listed remains allowed.)

If the first option is preceded by a plus sign (or no sign is used), only those functions listed are allowed.

A less than obvious repercussion of disallowing a particular function is that the client window frame will be altered to prevent your invoking that function. For instance, if you disallow the f.resize function for a client, the client's frame will not include resize borders. (Features of the frame can also be suppressed using the client-Decoration resource.) In addition, the Window Menu Size item, which invokes the f.resize function, will no longer appear on the menu. (You cannot affect the Window Menu using clientDecoration.)

For example, the following resource line:

Mwm*xfd*clientFunctions: -resize maximize

specifies that you cannot invoke the f.resize and f.maximize functions on an *xfd* window. As a result, the resize borders and Maximize command button will not appear on the frame, and the Size and Maximize items will not appear on the Window Menu.

The following line specifies the same characteristics using the alternate syntax:

Mwm*xfd*clientFunctions: minimize move close

focusAutoRaise (class FocusAutoRaise)

If True, a window is raised when it receives the input focus. Otherwise, directing focus to a window does not affect the stacking order.

The default depends on the value assigned to the keyboardFocusPolicy resource. If the keyboardFocusPolicy is explicit, the default for focus-AutoRaise is True. If the keyboardFocusPolicy is pointer, the default for focusAutoRaise is False.

If the client application also specifies which window management functions should be applicable, *mwm* provides only those functions that both the client and the client-Functions resource specify.

iconImage (class IconImage)
> Specifies the pathname of a bitmap file to be used as an icon image for a client. (For example, you might specify: Mwm*xclock*iconImage: ~/bitmaps/big-ben.) The default is to display an icon image supplied by the window manager.
>
> If the useClientIcon resource is set to True, an icon image supplied by the client takes precedence over an icon image supplied by the user.

iconImageBackground (class Background)
> Specifies the background color of the icon image. The default is the color specified by Mwm*background or Mwm*icon*background.

iconImageBottomShadowColor (class Foreground)
> Specifies the bottom shadow color of the icon image. The default is the color specified by Mwm*icon*bottomShadowColor.

iconImageBottomShadowPixmap (class BottomShadowPixmap)
> Specifies the bottom shadow pixmap of the icon image. The default is the pixmap specified by Mwm*icon*bottomShadowPixmap.

iconImageForeground (class Foreground)
> Specifies the foreground color of the icon image. The default varies based on the icon background.

iconImageTopShadowColor (class Background)
> Specifies the top shadow color of the icon image. The default is the color specified by Mwm*icon*topShadowColor.

iconImageTopShadowPixmap (class TopShadowPixmap)
> Specifies the top shadow Pixmap of the icon image. The default is the pixmap specified by Mwm*icon*topShadowPixmap.

matteBackground (class Background)
> Specifies the background color of the matte. The default is the color specified by Mwm*background or Mwm*client*background. This resource is only relevant if matteWidth is positive.

matteBottomShadowColor (class Foreground)
> Specifies the bottom shadow color of the matte. The default is the color specified by Mwm*bottomShadowColor or Mwm*client*bottomShadowColor. This resource is only relevant if matteWidth is positive.

matteBottomShadowPixmap (class BottomShadowPixmap)
> Specifies the bottom shadow pixmap of the matte. The default is the pixmap specified by Mwm*bottomShadowPixmap or Mwm*client*bottomShadowPixmap. This resource is only relevant if matteWidth is positive.

matteForeground (class Foreground)
> Specifies the foreground color of the matte. The default is the color specified by Mwm*foreground or Mwm*client*foreground. This resource is only relevant if matteWidth is positive.

matteTopShadowColor (class Background)
> Specifies the top shadow color of the matte. The default is the color specified by Mwm*topShadowColor or Mwm*client*topShadowColor. This resource is only relevant if matteWidth is positive.

matteTopShadowPixmap (class TopShadowPixmap)
> Specifies the top shadow pixmap of the matte. The default is the pixmap specified by Mwm*topShadowPixmap or Mwm*client*topShadowPixmap. This resource is only relevant if matteWidth is positive.

matteWidth (class MatteWidth)
> Specifies the width of the matte. The default is 0 (thus, no matte is used).

maximumClientSize (class MaximumClientSize)
> Specifies how a window is to be maximized, either to a specific size (*widthxheight*), or as much as possible in a certain direction (vertical or horizontal). If the value is of the form *widthxheight*, the width and height are interpreted in the units used by the client. For example, *xterm* measures width and height in font characters and lines.
>
> If maximumClientSize is not specified, and the WM_NORMAL_HINTS property is set, the default is obtained from it. If WM_NORMAL_HINTS is not set, the default is the size (including borders) that fills the screen.
>
> If maximumClientSize is not specified, *mwm* uses any value supplied to maximumMaximumSize.

useClientIcon (class UseClientIcon)
> If True, an icon image supplied by the client takes precedence over an icon image supplied by the user. The default is False.

usePPosition (class UsePPosition)
> Specifies whether *mwm* uses initial coordinates supplied by the client application. If True, *mwm* always uses the program specified position. If False, *mwm* never uses the program specified position. The default is nonzero, which means that *mwm* will use any program specified position except 0,0. Available as of *mwm* version 1.2.

windowMenu (class WindowMenu)
> Specifies a name for the Window Menu (which must be defined in the startup file). The default is DefaultWindowMenu. See the section ".mwmrc Startup File" earlier in this reference page and Chapter 13 of this guide.

Environment Variables

The following environment variables are used by *mwm*:

HOME   The user's home directory.

LANG   The language to be used for the *mwm* message catalog and the *mwm* startup file.

XBMLANGPATH
> Used to search for bitmap files.

XFILESEARCHPATH
> Used to determine the location of system-wide class resource files. If the LANG variable is set, the *$LANG* subdirectory is also searched.

XUSERFILESEARCHPATH, XAPPLRESDIR
> Used to determine the location of user-specific class resource files. If the LANG variable is set, the *$LANG* subdirectory is also searched.

MWMSHELL, SHELL
> MWMSHELL specifies the shell to use when executing a command supplied as an argument to the f.exec function. (See "mwm Functions" earlier in this reference page.) If MWMSHELL is not set, SHELL is used.

Files

/usr/lib/X11/$LANG/system.mwmrc
/usr/lib/X11/system.mwmrc
/usr/lib/X11/app-defaults/Mwm
$HOME/Mwm
$HOME/$LANG/.mwmrc
$HOME/.mwmrc
$HOME/.motifbind—Used to install the virtual key bindings property on the root window.

See Also

X, Xserver, xdm, xrdb; Chapter 3, *Working in the X Environment*; Chapter 4, *More about the mwm Window Manager*; Chapter 13, *Customizing mwm*.

oclock

Name
oclock – display time of day in analog form.

Syntax
`oclock` [*options*]

Description
oclock displays the current time on an analog display. The clock face is smaller and more stylized than that for *xclock*. For example, there are no tick-marks, save for a "jewel" at the 12 o'clock position. The chief virtue of *oclock*, and the one thing that has made it popular, is that it makes use of the X shape extension, which supports non-rectangular windows. The default *oclock* window is round, but it can be resized into all kinds of interesting ovals.

Chapter 8, *Other Clients*, describes how to use the *oclock* client.

Options
oclock accepts all of the standard X Toolkit command-line options, which are listed on the *X* reference page. (We've included some of the more commonly used Toolkit options later in this section.) In addition, *oclock* accepts the following application-specific options:

-backing *level*

Specifies an appropriate level of backing store. *level* is one of WhenMapped, Always, or NotUseful.

-hour *color*

Specifies a color for the hour hand of the clock.

-jewel *color*

Specifies a color for the jewel of the clock.

-minute *color*

Specifies a color for the minute hand of the clock.

-noshape

Causes the clock not to use the shape extension for non-rectangular windows; in short, with -noshape, you get a square or rectangular clock. Note that the behavior is still different from *xclock -analog*. If you resize *xclock* so that its window is rectangular, the round clockface image is centered in the rectangle. With *oclock*, the border of the window is always the shape of the clock.

-shape

Causes the clock to use the shape extension, which allows non-rectangular windows. You get the standard round clock face; this is the default.

-transparent

Creates a transparent clock consisting only of the jewel, hands, and clock border. This creates an interesting visual effect: i.e., the background on which the *oclock* is placed can be seen through the clock.

The following standard X Toolkit options are commonly used with *oclock*:

-bg `color`
> Specifies a color for the background.

-bw `pixels`
> Specifies a width in pixels for the window border. As the Clock widget changes its border around quite a bit, this is most usefully set to zero.

-fg `color`
> Specifies a color for both the hands and the jewel of the clock.

Resources

You can specify the following nonstandard resources for *oclock*. Note that you can use either the clock widget or *oclock* in the resource specification. If you use the clock widget, you must precede it with a loose binding; if you use *oclock*, you must follow it with a loose binding. For example, these two resources would both produce an *oclock* with a red hour hand:

```
*clock.hour:   red
oclock*hour:   red
```

Since the latter resource is more specific, it has precedence. Thus, if a resource file contained both of the following:

```
*clock.hour:   red
oclock*hour:   blue
```

any subsequent instance of *oclock* would have a blue hour hand. See Chapter 11, *Setting Resources*, for more information.

Here are the resources you can set:

backingStore (class BackingStore)
> Specifies an appropriate level of backing store. Allowable values are WhenMapped, Always, or NotUseful.

hour (class Foreground)
> Specifies a color for the hour hand.

jewel (class Foreground)
> Specifies a color for the jewel of the clock.

minute (class Foreground)
> Specifies a color for the minute hand.

shapeWindow (class ShapeWindow)
> When false, causes the clock not to use the shape extension for non-rectangular windows. (See the -noshape option above.) The default is true (the shape extension is used and you get the default round clock face).

`transparent (class Transparent)`
>   If true, creates a transparent clock consisting only of the jewel, hands, and clock border. See also the `-transparent` option above. The default is false.

Colors

Although the default colors for the Clock widget are black and white, the widget was designed in color. Release 5 sees the addition of an application defaults file specifying colors for the various features of the *oclock*. (The Release 4 version of *oclock* requires you to specify every desired color in your own resources file.) If you would like your clock to be viewable in the prescribed colors, include the following resource definition in the #ifdef COLOR section of your *.Xresources* file (or whatever file you read with *xrdb*):

`Clock*customization:   -color`

On a color display, this will cause *oclock* to use the colors specified in the application defaults color customization file (generally */usr/lib/X11/app-defaults/Clock-color*). The default colors specified are:

```
Clock*Background: grey
Clock*BorderColor: light blue
Clock*hour: yellow
Clock*jewel: yellow
Clock*minute: yellow
```

Of course, you can opt to specify alternative colors in your own resource file.

For instructions on specifying resources, see Chapter 11 of this guide.

Files
>   */usr/lib/X11/app-defaults/Clock-color* —Specifies color resources (as of Release 5).

See Also
>   X; Chapter 8, *Other Clients*; Chapter 11, *Setting Resources*; Volume Four, *X Toolkit Intrinsics Programming Manual*; Volume Five, *X Toolkit Intrinsics Reference Manual*.

Author
>   Keith Packard, MIT X Consortium.

resize

Name

resize – utility to set TERMCAP and terminal settings to the current window size.

Syntax

`resize` [*options*]

Description

The *resize* client is provided for use with systems that lack the ability to automatically notify processes of window size changes. Normally, on operating systems that support terminal resizing, *xterm* sends a signal (e.g., SIGWINCH on BSD 4.3-derived UNIX systems) to notify processes running in the window that the window size has changed. These programs can adjust their behavior if necessary.

On systems that don't support terminal resizing, you can use the *resize* client. *resize* prints a shell command for setting the TERM and TERMCAP environment variables to indicate the current size of the *xterm* window from which the command is run. For this output to take effect, *resize* must either be evaluated as part of the command line (usually done with a shell alias or function) or else redirected to a file which can then be read in. From the C shell (usually known as */bin/csh*), the following alias could be defined in the user's *.cshrc*:

`% alias rs 'set noglob; eval `resize`; unset noglob'`

After resizing the window, the user would type:

`% rs`

Users of versions of the Bourne shell (usually known as */bin/sh*) that don't have command functions will need to send the output to a temporary file and then read it back in with the "." command:

`$ resize >/tmp/out`
`$ . /tmp/out`

See Chapter 5, *The xterm Terminal Emulator*, for more information.

Options

resize accepts the following options:

-u   Indicates that Bourne shell commands should be generated even if the user's current shell isn't */bin/sh*.

-c   Indicates that C shell commands should be generated even if the user's current shell isn't */bin/csh*.

-s [*rows columns*]

Indicates that Sun console escape sequences will be used instead of the special *xterm* escape code. If *rows* and *columns* are given, *resize* will ask the *xterm* to resize itself. However, the window manager may choose to disallow the change.

The −u or −c must appear to the left of −s if both are specified.

Files
/etc/termcap
>   For the base termcap entry to modify.

˜/.cshrc User's alias for the command.

See Also
csh(1), tset(1), xterm; Chapter 5, *The xterm Terminal Emulator*.

Bugs
There should be some global notion of display size; *termcap* and *terminfo* need to be rethought in the context of window systems. (Fixed in BSD 4.3 and Ultrix-32 1.2.)

Authors
Mark Vandevoorde, MIT Project Athena, and Edward Moy Berkeley.
Copyright © 1984, 1985 by Massachusetts Institute of Technology.
See *X* for a complete copyright notice.

sessreg

Name

sessreg – manage utmp/wtmp entries for non-init clients.

Syntax

sessreg -a | -d [*options*] *user_name*

Description

sessreg is a simple program for managing utmp/wtmp entries for *xdm* sessions.

System V has a better interface to */etc/utmp* than BSD; it dynamically allocates entries in the file, instead of writing them at fixed positions indexed by position in */etc/ttys*.

To manage BSD-style *utmp* files, *sessreg* has two strategies. In conjunction with *xdm*, the -x option counts the number of lines in */etc/ttys* and then adds to that the number of the line in the *Xservers* file which specifies the display. The display name must be specified as the *line_name* using the -l option. This sum is used as the *slot_number* in */etc/utmp* that this entry will be written at. In the more general case, the -s option specifies the slot number directly. If for some strange reason your system uses a file other that */etc/ttys* to manage init, the -t option can direct *sessreg* to look elsewhere for a count of terminal sessions.

Conversely, System V managers will not ever need to use these options (-x, -s, and -t). To make the program easier to document and explain, *sessreg* accepts the BSD-specific flags in the System V environment and ignores them.

BSD also has a hostname field in the *utmp* file which doesn't exist in System V. This option is also ignored by the System V version of *sessreg*.

Options

-a   Add this session to *utmp* or *wtmp*. Either -a or -d must be specified.

-d   Delete this session from *utmp* or *wtmp*. Either -a or -d must be specified.

-h *host_name* .

        For BSD hosts, this is set to indicate that the session was initiated from a remote host. In typical *xdm* usage, this option is not used.

-l *line_name*

        Describes the "line" name of the entry. For terminal sessions, this is the final pathname segment of the terminal device filename (for example, ttyd0). For X sessions, it should probably be the local display name given to the users session (for example, :0). If none is specified, the terminal name will be determined with *ttyname*(3) and stripped of leading components.

-s *slot_number*

        Each potential session has a unique slot number in BSD systems; most are identified by the position of the *line_name* in the */etc/ttys* file. This option overrides the default position determined with *ttyslot*(3). It is inappropriate for use with *xdm*; the -x option is more useful.

-t *ttys_file*

    Specifies an alternate file which the −x option will use to count the number of terminal sessions on a host.

-u *utmp_file*

    Specifies an alternate *utmp* file, instead of */etc/utmp*. The special name none disables writing records to */etc/utmp*.

-w *wtmp_file*

    Specifies an alternate *wtmp* file, instead of */usr/adm/wtmp* for BSD or */etc/wtmp* for System V. The special name none disables writing records to */usr/adm/wtmp*.

-x *Xservers_file*

    As X sessions are one-per-display, and each display is entered in this file, this options sets the *slot_number* to be the number of lines in the *ttys_file* plus the index into this file that the *line_name* is found.

Usage

In *Xstartup*, place a call like:

```
sessreg −a −l $DISPLAY −x /usr/lib/X11/xdm/Xservers $USER
```

and in *Xreset*:

```
sessreg −d −l $DISPLAY −x /usr/lib/X11/xdm/Xservers $USER
```

See Also

xdm.

Author

Keith Packard, MIT X Consortium.

showfont

Name

showfont – font dumper for the X font server.

Syntax

showfont -server *server_name* [*options*] -fn *pattern*

Description

showfont displays data about the font that matches the given *pattern*. This client is new in Release 5 and is intended to be run with the font server (*fs*).

The wildcard character "*" may be used to match any sequence of characters (including none), and "?" to match any single character. If no pattern is given, "*" is assumed.

The "*" and "?" characters must be quoted to prevent them from being expanded by the shell.

showfont displays the contents of font files in the Portable Compiled Font format produced by *bdftopcf*. The information displayed includes the value of each of the font properties. (For more information, see Appendix M, *X Logical Font Description Conventions*, in Volume Zero, *X Protocol Reference Manual*. See also information on font metrics in Section 6.2.3, "Character Metrics," of Volume One, *Xlib Programming Manual*.)

Options

-bitmap_pad *padding_unit*
> Specifies the bitmap padding unit of the font. Acceptable values are 0, 1, or 2, where 0 is ImageRectMin, 1 is ImageRectMaxWidth and 2 is ImageRectMax-Width.

-end *character_number*
> Specifies that the range of the characters displayed should end with *character_number* (a decimal number).

-extents_only
> Indicates that only the font's extents should be displayed.

-l
> Indicates that the bit order of the font is least significant bit first.

-L
> Indicates that the byte order of the font is least significant byte first.

-m
> Indicates that the bit order of the font is most significant bit first.

-M
> Indicates that the byte order of the font is most significant byte first.

-pad *scanpad_unit*
> Specifies the scanpad unit of the font. Acceptable values are: 1, 2, 4, or 8.

-server *server_name*
> Specifies a particular font server. The *server_name* generally has the form *transport/host:port*. If the FONTSERVER environment variable is not defined, this option must be given.

-start *character_number*

      Indicates the range of the characters to display should start with *character_ number* (a decimal number).

-unit *scanline_unit*

      Specifies the scanline unit of the font. Acceptable values are: 1, 2, 4, or 8.

See Also

fs, showsnf, xlsfonts; Chapter 6, *Font Specification*; Chapter 7, *Graphics Utilities*; Appendix M, *X Logical Font Description Conventions*, in Volume Zero, *X Protocol Reference Manual*; Section 6.2.3, "Character Metrics," in Volume One, *Xlib Programming Manual*.

Environment Variables

FONTSERVER

      To get the default font server.

Copyright

Copyright 1991, Network Computing Devices, Inc.

See *X(1)* for a full statement of rights and permissions.

Author

Dave Lemke, Network Computing Devices, Inc.

showrgb

Name
showrgb – uncompile an RGB color name database.

Syntax
showrgb [*database*]

Description
The *showrgb* program reads an RGB color name database compiled for use with the *dbm* database routines and converts it back to source form, printing the result to standard output. The default database is the one that X was built with, and may be overridden on the command line. Specify the database name without the *.pag* or *.dir* suffix.

Files
/usr/lib/X11/rgb.txt

   Text version of the default database.

/usr/lib/X11/rgb.dir

/usr/lib/X11/rgb.pag

   Machine-readable database files.

See Also
The discussion of color in Chapter 12, *Specifying Color*.

showsnf

Name

showsnf – print contents of an SNF file to standard output.

Syntax

showsnf [*options*] *snf_file*

Description

This client has been removed from the standard distribution in Release 5. If you are running the font server (*fs*), use the *showfont* client instead.

showsnf displays the contents of font files in the Server Natural Format produced by *bdftosnf*. The information displayed includes the value of each of the font properties (see Appendix M, *X Logical Font Description Conventions, Release 5*, in Volume Zero, *X Protocol Reference Manual*), as well as information on font metrics (see Section 6.2.3, *Character Metrics*, in Volume One, *Xlib Programming Manual*).

showsnf is usually used only to verify that a font file hasn't been corrupted or to convert the individual glyphs into arrays of characters for proofreading or for conversion to some other format.

Options

showsnf accepts the following options:

-g   Indicates that character glyph bitmaps should be printed.

-l   Indicates that the bit order of the font is least significant bit first.

-L   Indicates that the byte order of the font is least significant byte first.

-m   Indicates that the bit order of the font is most significant bit first.

-M   Indicates that the byte order of the font is most significant byte first.

-pnumber
Specifies the glyph padding of the font.

-unumber
Specifies the scanline unit of the font.

-v   Indicates that bearings and sizes should be printed for each character in the font. (These are in an ASCII format similar to that produced by *bmtoa*. They can be converted to standard X bitmaps using *atobm*, and then edited with *bitmap*.)

See Also

X, Xserver, bdftosnf, showfont, bitmap; Chapter 6, *Font Specification*.

Bugs

There is no way to print out only a single glyph.

viewres

Name
viewres – Athena widget class browser.

Syntax
`viewres` [*option*]

Description
The *viewres* program (available as of Release 5) displays a tree showing the widget class hierarchy of the Athena Widget Set. Each node in the tree can be expanded to show the resources that the corresponding class adds (i.e., does not inherit from its parent) when a widget is created. This application allows the user to view the structure and inherited resources for the Athena Widget Set.

Options
viewres accepts all of the standard X Toolkit command-line options, as well as the following additional options:

-top *name*

Specifies the name of the highest widget in the hierarchy to display. This is typically used to limit the display to a subset of the tree. The default is `Object`.

-variable

Indicates that the widget variable names (as declared in header files) should be displayed in the nodes rather than the widget class name. This is sometimes useful to distinguish widget classes that share the same name (such as `Text`).

-vertical

Indicates that the tree should be displayed top to bottom rather than left to right. See also the Layout Vertical item in the "View Menu" section following.

View Menu
The way in which the tree is displayed may be changed through the entries in the View menu:

Layout Horizontal

Causes the tree to be laid out from left to right. This operation may also be performed with the `SetOrientation(West)` translation.

Layout Vertical

Causes the tree to be laid out from top to bottom. This operation may also be performed with the `SetOrientation(North)` translation. (To specify a vertical layout: on the command line, run *viewres* with the -vertical option; or in a resource file, use `*Tree.Gravity: north`.)

Show Variable Names

Causes the node labels to be set to the variable names used to declare the corresponding widget class. This operation may also be performed with the `SetLabelType(`*variable*`)` translation.

Show Class Names

> Causes the node labels to be set to the class names used when specifying resources. This operation may also be performed with the SetLabelType(*class*) translation.

Show Resource Boxes

> Expands the selected nodes (see next section) to show the new widget and constraint resources. This operation may also be performed with the Resources(on) translation.

Hide Resource Boxes

> Removes the resource displays from the selected nodes (usually to conserve space). This operation may also be performed with the Resources(off) translation.

Select Menu

Resources for a single widget class can be displayed by clicking the second pointer button **Button2** on the corresponding node, or by adding the node to the selection list with **Button1** and using the Show Resource Boxes entry in the View menu. Since **Button1** actually toggles the selection state of a node, clicking on a selected node will cause it to be removed from the selected list.

Collections of nodes may also be selected through the various entries in the Select menu:

Unselect All

> Removes all nodes from the selection list. This operation may also be performed with the Select(nothing) translation.

Select All

> Adds all nodes to the selection list. This operation may also be performed with the Select(all) translation.

Invert All

> Adds unselected nodes to, and removes selected nodes from, the selection list. This operation may also be performed with the Select(invert) translation.

Select Parent

> Selects the immediate parents of all selected nodes. This operation may also be performed with the Select(parent) translation.

Select Ancestors

> Recursively selects all parents of all selected nodes. This operation may also be performed with the Select(ancestors) translation.

Select Children

> Selects the immediate children of all selected nodes. This operation may also be performed with the Select(children) translation.

Select Descendants

> Recursively selects all children of all selected nodes. This operation may also be performed with the Select(descendants) translation.

Select Has Resources

> Selects all nodes that add new resources (regular or constraint) to their corresponding widget classes. This operation may also be performed with the `Select (resources)` translation.

Select Shown Resource Boxes

> Selects all nodes whose resource boxes are currently expanded (usually so that they can be closed with the Hide Resource Boxes) menu option. This operation may also be performed with the `Select(shown)` translation.

Resources

viewres defines the following application-specific resources:

`showVariable` (class `showVariable`)

> If true, indicates that the widget variable names (as declared in header files) should be displayed in the nodes rather than the widget class names. This is sometimes useful to distinguish widget classes that share the same name (such as `Text`). The default is false.

`topObject` (class `TopObject`)

> Specifies the name of the highest widget in the hierarchy to display. This is typically used to limit the display to a subset of the tree. The default is `Object`.

Note that you can specify the direction the tree goes using the `Tree` widget and `Gravity` resource. For a vertical (top to bottom) orientation, use:

`*Tree.Gravity: north`

The default orientation is `west` (horizontal, read left to right). You can also specify `south` for a bottom to top tree, or `east` for right to left, but neither of these orientations is particularly intuitive in English.

Actions

The following application actions are provided:

`Quit()`

> Causes *viewres* to exit.

`Resources(option)`

> Turns `on`, `off`, or `toggles` the resource boxes for the selected nodes. If invoked from within one of the nodes (through the keyboard or pointer), only that node is used.

`SetLabelType(type)`

> Sets the node labels to display the widget variable or class names, according to the argument *type*.

`SetOrientation(direction)`

> Sets the root of the tree to be one of the following areas of the window: `West`, `North`, `East`, or `South`.

Select(*what*)

> Selects the indicated nodes, as described in the View Menu section: nothing
> (unselects all nodes), invert, parent, ancestors, children, descendants,
> resources, shown.

Widgets

Resources may be specified for the following widgets:

```
Viewres viewres
        Paned pane
                Box buttonbox
                        Command quit
                        MenuButton view
                                SimpleMenu viewMenu
                                        SmeBSB layoutHorizontal
                                        SmeBSB layoutVertical
                                        SmeLine line1
                                        SmeBSB namesVariable
                                        SmeBSB namesClass
                                        SmeLine line2
                                        SmeBSB viewResources
                                        SmeBSB viewNoResources
                        MenuButton select
                                SimpleMenu selectMenu
                                        SmeBSB unselect
                                        SmeBSB selectAll
                                        SmeBSB selectInvert
                                        SmeLine line1
                                        SmeBSB selectParent
                                        SmeBSB selectAncestors
                                        SmeBSB selectChildren
                                        SmeBSB selectDescendants
                                        SmeLine line2
                                        SmeBSB selectHasResources
                                        SmeBSB selectShownResources
                Form treeform
                        Porthole porthole
                                Tree tree
                                        Box variable_name
                                                Toggle variable_name
                                                List variable_name
                        Panner panner
```

where *variable_name* is the widget variable name of each node.

Files

/usr/lib/X11/app-defaults/Viewres
>   Specifies required resources.

See Also

X, appres, editres, listres, xrdb; Chapter 11, *Setting Resources*; Volume Four, *X Toolkit Intrinsics Programming Manual*; Volume Five, *X Toolkit Intrinsics Reference Manual*.

Author

Jim Fulton, MIT X Consortium.

xauth

Name

xauth – X authority file utility.

Syntax

xauth [*options*] [*command arguments*]

Description

The *xauth* program is used to edit and display authorization information used when connecting to the X server. *xdm* can be configured to generate this authorization information when a user logs on. *xauth* is then used to extract authorization records from one machine and merge them in on another (as is the case when using remote logins or to grant access to other users). Note that this program does *not* contact the X server.

For an introduction to user-based access control and the *xauth* program, see Appendix A, *Managing Your Environment*. Volume Eight, *X Window System Administrator's Guide*, provides a more detailed discussion of these and other security-related topics.

Options

The following options may be used with *xauth*. They may be given individually (for example, -q -i) or may be combined (for example, -qi).

-b Indicates that *xauth* should attempt to break any authority file locks before proceeding and should only be used to clean up stale locks.

-f *authfile*
  Specifies the name of the authority file to use. By default, *xauth* will use the file specified by the XAUTHORITY environment variable or *.Xauthority* in the user's home directory.

-i Indicates that *xauth* should ignore any authority file locks. Normally, *xauth* will refuse to read or edit any authority files that have been locked by other programs (usually *xdm* or another *xauth*).

-q Indicates that *xauth* should operate quietly and not print unsolicited status messages. This is the default if an *xauth* command is given on the command line or if the standard output is not directed to a terminal.

-v Indicates that *xauth* should operate verbosely and print status messages indicating the results of various operations (for example, how many records have been read in or written out). This is the default if *xauth* is reading commands from its standard input and its standard output is directed to a terminal.

Commands

Commands may be entered interactively, on the *xauth* command line, or in scripts. The following commands may be used to manipulate authority files (or obtain information):

? A short list of the valid commands is printed on the standard output.

add *displayname protocolname hexkey*

An authorization entry for the indicated *displayname* using the given *protocolname* and *hexkey* data is added to the authorization file.

At present, three *protocolnames* are supported in the standard X distribution: MIT-MAGIC-COOKIE-1, XDM-AUTHORIZATION-1, and SUN-DES-1. Note that *xauth* will not give you an error if you specify an invalid protocol name. A protocol name consisting of just a single period is treated as an abbreviation for MIT-MAGIC-COOKIE-1. (See Volume Eight, *X Window System Administrator's Guide*, for more information.)

The *hexkey* data is specified as an even-lengthed string of hexadecimal digits, each pair representing one octet. The first digit of each pair gives the most significant 4 bits of the octet and the second digit of the pair gives the least significant 4 bits. For example, a 32 character hexkey would represent a 128-bit value.

exit   If any modifications have been made, the authority file is written out (if allowed), and the program exits. An end-of-file is treated as an implicit exit command.

help [*string*]

A description of all commands that begin with the given *string* (or all commands, if no string is given) is printed on the standard output.

info   Information describing the authorization file, whether or not any changes have been made, and from where *xauth* commands are being read is printed on the standard output.

[n]extract *filename displayname . . .*

Authorization entries for each of the specified displays are written to the indicated file. If the nextract command is used, the entries are written in a numeric format suitable for non-binary transmission (such as secure electronic mail). The extracted entries can be read back in using the merge and nmerge commands. If the filename consists of just a single dash, the entries will be written to the standard output.

[n]list [*displayname...*]

Authorization entries for each of the specified displays (or all, if no displays are named) are printed on the standard output. If the nlist command is used, entries will be shown in the numeric format used by the nextract command; otherwise, they are shown in a textual format. Key data is always displayed in the hexadecimal format given in the description of the add command.

[n]merge [*filename...*]

Authorization entries are read from the specified files and are merged into the authorization database, superceding any matching existing entries. If the nmerge command is used, the numeric format given in the description of the extract command is used. If a filename consists of just a single dash, the standard input will be read if it hasn't been read before.

quit   The program exits, ignoring any modifications. This may also be accomplished by pressing the interrupt character.

remove *displayname*...

        Authorization entries matching the specified displays are removed from the authority file.

source *filename*

        The specified *filename* is treated as a script containing *xauth* commands to execute. In such a file, blank lines and lines beginning with a sharp sign (#) are ignored. A single dash may be used to indicate the standard input, if it hasn't already been read.

Display Names

Display names for the add, [n]extract, [n]list, [n]merge, and remove commands use the same format as the DISPLAY environment variable and the common -display command-line option. Display-specific information (such as the screen number) is unnecessary and will be ignored. Same-machine connections (such as local-host sockets, shared memory, and the Internet Protocol hostname *localhost*) are referred to as *hostname*/unix: *displaynumber* so that local entries for different machines may be stored in one authority file.

Example

The most common use for *xauth* is to extract the entry for the current display, copy it to another machine, and merge it into the user's authority file on the remote machine:

```
%  xauth extract - $DISPLAY | rsh other xauth merge -
```

Environment Variables

This *xauth* program uses the following environment variables:

XAUTHORITY

        To get the name of the authority file to use if the -f option isn't used. If this variable is not set, *xauth* will use *.Xauthority* in the user's home directory.

HOME   To get the user's home directory if XAUTHORITY isn't defined.

Bugs

Users that have unsecure networks should take care to use encrypted file transfer mechanisms to copy authorization entries between machines. Similarly, the MIT-MAGIC-COOKIE-1 protocol is not very useful in unsecure environments. Sites that are interested in additional security may need to use encrypted authorization mechanisms such as Kerberos.

Spaces are currently not allowed in the protocol name. Quoting could be added for the truly perverse.

See Also

X, Xserver, xdm; Appendix A, *Managing Your Environment*; Volume Eight, *X Window System Administrator's Guide*.

Author

Jim Fulton, MIT X Consortium.

xbiff

Name

xbiff – mail notification program for X.

Syntax

xbiff [*options*]

Description

The *xbiff* program displays a little image of a mailbox. When there is no mail in the user's mailbox, the flag on the mailbox is down. When mail arrives, the flag goes up and the mailbox beeps. By default, pressing any pointer button in the image forces *xbiff* to remember the current size of the mail file as being the "empty" size and to lower the flag.

This program is nothing more than a wrapper around the Athena Mailbox widget.

The default mailbox is 48 pixels on each side and is centered in the window. If you are using *mwm* without customization, the size of the *xbiff* image will be slightly largely to allow for the frame. To suppress part or all of this window decoration, see Chapter 13, *Customizing mwm*, and the *mwm* reference page.

See Chapter 8, *Other Clients*, for instructions on using *xbiff*.

Options

xbiff accepts all of the standard X Toolkit command-line options, which are listed on the *X* reference page. (We've included some of the more commonly used Toolkit options later in this section.) In addition, *xbiff* accepts the following application-specific options:

-file *filename*
> Specifies the name of the file that should be monitored. By default, *xbiff* watches */usr/spool/mail/**username***, where ***username*** is your login name.

-help Indicates that a brief summary of the allowed options should be printed on the standard error.

-shape
> Indicates that the mailbox window should be shaped if masks for the empty or full images are given.

-update *seconds*
> Specifies the frequency in seconds at which *xbiff* should update its display. If the mailbox is obscured and then exposed, it will be updated immediately. The default is 30 seconds.

-volume *percentage*
> Specifies how loud the bell should be rung when new mail comes in.

Resources

xbiff is implemented using a simple widget, the Mailbox widget from the Athena Widget Set. The application class name is XBiff. *xbiff* understands all of the Core resource names and classes as well as those from the Mailbox widget. The resources you might want to set are listed below:

checkCommand (class CheckCommand)
> Specifies a shell command to be executed to check for new mail rather than examining the size of file. The specified string value is used as the argument to a *system*(3) call and may therefore contain I/O redirection. An exit status of 0 indicates that new mail is waiting; 1 indicates that there has been no change in size; and 2 indicates that the mail has been cleared. By default, no shell command is provided.

emptyPixmap (class Pixmap)
> Specifies a bitmap to be shown when no new mail is present. The default is flagdown.

emptyPixmapMask (class PixmapMask)
> Specifies a mask for the bitmap to be shown when no new mail is present. The default is none.

file (class File)
> Specifies the name of the file to monitor. The default is to watch */usr/spool/mail/username*, where ***username*** is your login name.

flip (class Flip)
> Specifies whether or not the image that is shown when mail has arrived should be inverted. The default is true.

foreground (class Foreground)
> Specifies the color for the foreground.

fullPixmap (class Pixmap)
> Specifies a bitmap to be shown when new mail has arrived. The default is flagup.

fullPixmapMask (class PixmapMask)
> Specifies a mask for the bitmap to be shown when new mail has arrived. The default is none.

height (class Height)
> Specifies the height of the mailbox. The default is 48 pixels.

onceOnly (class Boolean)
> Specifies that the bell is rung only the first time new mail is found and is not rung again until at least one interval has passed with no mail waiting. The window will continue to indicate the presence of new mail until it has been retrieved. The default is false.

reverseVideo (class ReverseVideo)
> Specifies that the foreground and background should be reversed.

shapeWindow (class `ShapeWindow`)
> Specifies whether or not the mailbox window should be shaped to the given `full-PixmapMask` and `emptyPixmapMask`. The default is false.

update (class `Interval`)
> Specifies the frequency in seconds at which the mail should be checked. The default is 30.

volume (class `Volume`)
> Specifies how loud the bell should be rung. The default is 33 percent.

width (class `Width`)
> Specifies the width of the mailbox. The default is 48 pixels.

Widget Hierarchy

xbiff is implemented using a single widget, the Athena Mailbox widget. All applicable resources of the widget are listed above. The class and instance hierarchy is shown below:

```
Xbiff   xbiff
    Mailbox  mailbox
```

See Appendix G, *Widget Resources*, for a list of resources that can be set for the Athena widgets.

Actions

The Mailbox widget provides the following actions for use in event translations:

check ( )
> Causes the widget to check for new mail and display the flag appropriately.

unset ( )
> Causes the widget to lower the flag until new mail comes in.

set ( ) Causes the widget to raise the flag until the user resets it.

The default translation is:

```
<ButtonPress>:unset()
```

See Also

X, xrdb, stat(2); Chapter 8, *Other Clients*; Appendix G, *Widget Resources*.

Author

Jim Fulton, MIT X Consortium;
Additional hacks by Ralph Swick, DEC/MIT Project Athena.

xcalc

Name

xcalc – scientific calculator for X.

Syntax

`xcalc` [`options`]

Description

xcalc is a scientific calculator desktop accessory that can emulate a TI-30 or an HP-10C. The number in the calculator display can be selected, allowing you to paste the result of a calculation into text. See Chapter 8, *Other Clients*, for instructions on using the calculator.

Since Release 4, the *xcalc* buttons have been an oval shape (they are rectangular in earlier versions) and the window is somewhat smaller overall than it was in previous releases. For those of you who like the size of the calculator under R3, try a geometry specification of approximately 167×222 and specify rectangular buttons using the resource setting:

`xcalc*shapeStyle:  rectangular`

`shapeStyle` is a resource of the Athena `Command` widget. See "Widget Hierarchy" later in this reference page for a diagram of *xcalc*'s structure and Appendix G for a list of the resources you can set for various widgets.

Options

xcalc accepts all of the standard X Toolkit command-line options, which are listed on the *X* reference page. In addition, *xcalc* accepts the following application-specific options:

`-rpn`   Indicates that Reverse Polish Notation should be used. In this mode, the calculator will look and behave like an HP-10C. Without this flag, it will emulate a TI-30.

`-stip`, `-stipple`
    Indicates that the background of the calculator should be drawn using a stipple of the foreground and background colors. On monochrome displays, this improves the appearance.

Calculator Operations

Pointer Usage

Operations may be performed with pointer button 1 (usually the leftmost button), or in many cases, with the keyboard. Many common calculator operations have keyboard equivalents, which are called accelerators, because they facilitate data entry. There are several ways to cause *xcalc* to exit: pressing the AC key of the TI calculator or the ON key of the HP calculator with pointer button 3 (usually the rightmost button), and typing q, Q, or CTRL-C while the pointer is in the *xcalc* window.

Calculator Key Usage (TI Mode)

The number keys, the +/– key, and the +, –, *, /, and = keys all do exactly what you would expect them to. It should be noted that the operators obey the standard rules of precedence.

Thus, entering "3+4*5=" results in 23, not 35. Parentheses can be used to override this. For example, "(1+2+3)*(4+5+6)=" is evaluated as "6*15=" which results in 90.

The action associated with each function is given below. These are useful if you are interested in defining a custom calculator. The action used for all digit keys is digit(*n*), where *n* is the corresponding digit, 0-9.

The keys are described below:

1/x   Replaces the number in the display with its reciprocal. The corresponding action is reciprocal().

x^2   Squares the number in the display. The corresponding action is square().

SQRT   Evaluates the square root of the number in the display. The corresponding action is squareRoot().

CE/C   When pressed once, clears the number in the display without clearing the state of the machine. Allows you to re-enter a number if you make a mistake. Pressing it twice clears the state also. The corresponding action is clear().

AC   Clears everything: the display, the state, and the memory. Pressing it with the third (usually the right) button "turns off" the calculator, in that it exits the program. The corresponding action to clear the state is off(); to quit, the action is quit().

INV   Inverts the meaning of the function keys. See the individual function keys for details. The corresponding action is inverse().

sin   Computes the sine of the number in the display, as interpreted by the current DRG mode (see DRG, below). If inverted, it computes the arcsine. The corresponding action is sine().

cos   Computes the cosine, or arccosine when inverted. The corresponding action is cosine().

tan   Computes the tangent, or arctangent when inverted. The corresponding action is tangent().

DRG   Changes the DRG mode, as indicated by DEG, RAD, or GRAD at the bottom of the calculator "liquid crystal" display. When in DEG mode, numbers in the display are taken as being degrees. In RAD mode, numbers are in radians, and in GRAD mode, numbers are in gradians. When inverted, the DRG key has the handy feature of converting degrees to radians to gradians and vice versa. For example, put the calculator into DEG mode and type "45 INV DRG". The calculator should display approximately .785398, which is 45 degrees converted to radians. The corresponding action is degree().

e   The constant "e" (2.7182818 . . .). The corresponding action is e().

EE   Used for entering exponential numbers. For example, to enter "-2.3E-4" you would type "2 . 3 +/- EE 4 +/-". The corresponding action is `scientific()`.

log   Calculates the log (base 10) of the number in the display. When inverted, it raises 10.0 to the number in the display. For example, entering "3 INV log" should result in 1000. The corresponding action is `logarithm()`.

ln   Calculates the log (base e) of the number in the display. When inverted, it raises "e" to the number in the display. For example, entering "e ln" should result in 1. The corresponding action is `naturalLog()`.

y^x   Raises the number on the left to the power of the number on the right. For example, "2 y^x 3 =" results in 8, which is 2^3. Also, "(1+2+3) y^x (1+2)=" is evaluated as "6 y^x 3=" which results in 216. The corresponding action is `power()`.

PI   The constant "pi". (3.1415927....) The corresponding action is `pi()`.

x!   Computes the factorial of the number in the display. The number in the display must be an integer in the range 0-500, though depending on your math library, it might overflow long before that. The corresponding action is `factorial()`.

(Left parenthesis. The corresponding action for TI calculators is `leftParen()`.

)   Right parenthesis. The corresponding action for TI calculators is `rightParen()`.

/   Division. The corresponding action is `divide()`.

*   Multiplication. The corresponding action is `multiply()`.

−   Subtraction. The corresponding action is `subtract()`.

+   Addition. The corresponding action is `add()`.

=   Perform calculation. The TI-specific action is `equal()`.

STO   Copies the number in the display to the memory location. The corresponding action is `store()`.

RCL   Copies the number from the memory location to the display. The corresponding action is `recall()`.

SUM   Adds the number in the display to the number in the memory location. The corresponding action is `sum()`.

EXC   Swaps the number in the display with the number in the memory location. The corresponding action is `exchange()`.

+/−　　Negate (change sign). The corresponding action is `negate()`.

.　　Decimal point. The corresponding action is `decimal()`.

Calculator Key Usage (RPN mode)

The number keys, CHS (change sign), +, −, *, /, and ENTR keys all do exactly what you would expect them to. Many of the remaining keys are the same as in TI (default) mode. The differences are detailed below. The action for the ENTR key is `enter()`.

<−　　Backspace key that can be used while entering a number. It will erase digits from the display. (See "Bugs.") Inverse backspace clears the X register. The corresponding action is `back()`.

ON　　Clears everything: the display, the state, and the memory. Pressing it with the third (usually the right) pointer button "turns off" the calculator, in that it exits the program. The corresponding action to clear the state is `off()`; to quit, the action is `quit()`.

INV　　Inverts the meaning of the function keys. This would be the "f" key on an HP calculator, but *xcalc* does not display multiple legends on each key. See the individual function keys for details.

10ˆx　　Raises 10.0 to the number in the top of the stack. When inverted, it calculates the log (base 10) of the number in the display. The corresponding action is `tenpower()`.

eˆx　　Raises "e" to the number in the top of the stack. When inverted, it calculates the log (base e) of the number in the display. The corresponding action is `epower()`.

STO　　Copies the number in the top of the stack to one of ten memory locations. The desired memory is specified by pressing this key and then pressing a digit key.

RCL　　Pushes the number from the specified memory location onto the stack.

SUM　　Adds the number on top of the stack to the number in the specified memory location.

x:y　　Exchanges the numbers in the top two stack positions, the X and Y registers. The corresponding action is `XexchangeY()`.

R v　　Rolls the stack downward. When inverted, it rolls the stack upward. The corresponding action is `roll()`.

Blank keys were used for programming functions on the HP-10C. Their functionality has not been duplicated in *xcalc*.

Keyboard Equivalents (Accelerators)

If you have the pointer in the *xcalc* window, you can use the keyboard to enter numbers and other keys. Almost all of the calculator keys have keyboard equivalents, which are known as *accelerators* because they speed entry. The number keys, the operator keys, and the parentheses all have the obvious equivalents. The accelerators defined by *xcalc* are listed in the following table:

TI Key	HP Key	Keyboard Accelerator	TI Function	HP Function
SQRT	SQRT	r	`squareRoot()`	`squareRoot()`
AC	ON	space	`clear()`	`clear()`
AC	<–	Delete	`clear()`	`back()`
AC	<–	Backspace	`clear()`	`back()`
AC	<–	Control-H	`clear()`	`back()`
AC		Clear	`clear()`	
AC	ON	q	`quit()`	`quit()`
AC	ON	Control-C	`quit()`	`quit()`
INV	i	i	`inverse()`	`inverse()`
sin	s	s	`sine()`	`sine()`
cos	c	c	`cosine()`	`cosine()`
tan	t	t	`tangent()`	`tangent()`
DRG	DRG	d	`degree()`	`degree()`
e		e	`e()`	
ln	ln	l	`naturalLog()`	`naturalLog()`
y^x	y^x	^	`power()`	`power()`
PI	PI	p	`pi()`	`pi()`
x!	x!	!	`factorial()`	`factorial()`
(		(	`leftParen()`	
)		)	`rightParen()`	
/	/	/	`divide()`	`divide()`
*	*	*	`multiply()`	`multiply()`
–	–	–	`subtract()`	`subtract()`
+	+	+	`add()`	`add()`
=		=	`equal()`	
0...9	0...9	0...9	`digit()`	`digit()`
.	.	.	`decimal()`	`decimal()`
+/-	CHS	n	`negate()`	`negate()`
	x:y	x		`XexchangeY()`
	ENTR	Return		`enter()`
	ENTR	Linefeed		`enter()`

Resources

The application class name is XCalc.

xcalc defines the following application resources:

cursor (class Cursor)
> The name of the symbol used to represent the pointer. The default is hand2. See Appendix D for a list of cursor names.

rpn (class Rpn)
> A Boolean value that specifies whether or not the rpn mode should be used. The default is off—that is, the calculator will be used in TI mode.

stipple (class Stipple)
> A Boolean value that indicates whether or not the background should be stippled. The default is on for monochrome displays, and off for color displays.

Widget Hierarchy

In addition, you can specify resources for each of the widgets that make up *xcalc*. In the notation below, indentation indicates the hierarchical structure of the widgets. The widget class name is given first, followed by the widget instance name.

```
XCalc xcalc
            Form  ti  or  hp        (The name depends on the mode)
               Form  bevel
                  Form  screen
                        Label   M      (The memory indicator on the screen)
                        Toggle  LCD    (Where the data is displayed)
                        Label   INV    (The inverted indicator on the display)
                        Label   DEG    (The degrees indicator on the display)
                        Label   RAD    (The radians indicator on the display)
                        Label   GRAD   (The gradians indicator on the display)
                        Label   P      (The Parenthesis indicator on the display)
                  Command  button1     (The actual calculator buttons)
                  Command  button2     (Buttons are numbered from right to left)
                  Command  button3     (See the app-defaults file for associations
                                          and so on...)
                  Command  button38    (Between widget names and default labels)
                  Command  button39
                  Command  button40    (Only 39 buttons in HP mode)
```

See Appendix G, *Widget Resources*, for a list of resources that can be set for the Athena widgets.

Customization

xcalc has an enormous application defaults file, which specifies the position, label, and function of each key on the calculator. It also gives translations to serve as keyboard accelerators. Because these resources are not specified in the source code, you can create a customized calculator by writing a private application defaults file, using the Athena Command and Form widget resources to specify the size and position of buttons, the label for each button, and the function of each button.

The foreground and background colors of each calculator key can be individually specified. For the TI calculator, a classical color resource specification might be:

```
XCalc.ti.Command.background:        grey50
XCalc.ti.Command.foreground:        white
```

For each of buttons 20, 25, 30, 35, and 40, specify:

```
XCalc.ti.button20.background:       black
XCalc.ti.button20.foreground:       white
```

For each of buttons 22, 23, 24, 27, 28, 29, 32, 33, 34, 37, 38, and 39:

```
XCalc.ti.button22.background:       white
XCalc.ti.button22.foreground:       black
```

Colors

As of Release 5, you can opt to use a predefined set of colors for the TI calculator. These colors are provided in a second application defaults file. If you would like your calculator to be viewable in the standard colors, include the following resource definition in your *.Xresources* file (or whatever file you read with *xrdb*):

```
*customization:    -color
```

This will cause *xcalc* to pick up the colors in the app-defaults color customization file (generally */usr/lib/X11/app-defaults/XCalc-color*).

Files

/usr/lib/X11/app-defaults/XCalc
      Specifies required resources.

/usr/lib/X11/app-defaults/XCalc-color
      Specifies color resources for the TI calculator (as of Release 5).

See Also

X, xrdb; Chapter 8, *Other Clients*; Appendix G, *Widget Resources*.

Bugs

In HP mode, a bug report claims that the sequence of keys 5, ENTR, and <– should clear the display, but it doesn't.

Authors

John Bradley, University of Pennsylvania;
Mark Rosenstein, MIT Project Athena.

xclipboard

Name

xclipboard – X clipboard client.

Syntax

xclipboard [*options*]

Description

The *xclipboard* program is used to collect and display text selections that are sent to the CLIP-BOARD by other clients. It is typically used to save CLIPBOARD selections for later use. Chapter 5, *The xterm Terminal Emulator*, describes how to use the *xclipboard* client. See Chapter 11, *Setting Resources*, for instructions on customizing *xterm* to send selections to the CLIPBOARD.

Since *xclipboard* uses a Text widget to display the contents of the clipboard, text sent to the CLIPBOARD may be reselected for use in other applications. The contents may also be edited, using any of the editing commands built into the Text widget. (See the reference page for *xedit* for details.)

xclipboard stores each CLIPBOARD selection as a separate string, each of which can be selected. Each time CLIPBOARD is asserted by another application, *xclipboard* transfers the contents of that selection to a new buffer and displays it in the text window. Buffers are never automatically deleted, so you'll want to use the **delete** button to get rid of useless items.

xclipboard also responds to requests for the CLIPBOARD selection from other clients by sending the entire contents of the currently displayed buffer.

An *xclipboard* window has the following buttons across the top:

Quit   Exits *xclipboard*.

Delete   Deletes current buffer and displays the next one.

New   Creates a new buffer with no contents. Useful in constructing a new CLIPBOARD selection by hand.

Save   Saves the currently displayed selection to a file. Available as of Release 5.

Next   Displays the next buffer in the list.

Previous   Displays the previous buffer.

To the right of these command buttons is a small box displaying a number corresponding to the selection being displayed. The box has been added in Release 5.

Options

xclipboard accepts all of the standard X Toolkit command-line options, which are listed on the *X* reference page. In addition, *xclipboard* accepts the following application-specific options:

−nw   Indicates that long lines of text should not wrap around. This is the default behavior.

−w   Indicates that lines of text that are too long to be displayed on one line in the clipboard should wrap around to the following lines.

Resources

xclipboard understands all of the Core resource names and classes, as well as the following application-specific resource:

`wrap` (class `Wrap`)

> If `True`, lines of text that are too long to be displayed on one line in the clipboard will wrap around to the following lines. If `False` (the default), long lines will not wrap.

Sending and Retrieving Clipboard Contents

Text is copied *to* the clipboard whenever a client asserts ownership of the CLIPBOARD selection. Text is copied *from* the clipboard whenever a client requests the contents of the CLIPBOARD selection. This doesn't necessarily happen automatically; you must add translations for each application that you want to have work with *xclipboard*. Examples of event bindings that a user may wish to include in a resource configuration file to use the clipboard from *xterm* are:

```
*VT100.Translations: #override \n\
    Button1 <Btn3Down>: select-end(PRIMARY,CUT_BUFFER0,CLIPBOARD)\n\
    !Shift <Btn2Up>:        insert-selection(CLIPBOARD)\n\
    ~Shift ~Ctrl ~Meta <Btn2Up>:   insert-selection(PRIMARY,CUT_BUFFER0)
```

The first translation, `Button1 <Btn3Down>:   select-end(CLIPBOARD,CUT_BUF-FER0,CLIPBOARD)`, specifies that if button 3 is pressed while button 1 is held down, the selection will be made the PRIMARY selection, copied to CUT_BUFFER0, and added to the CLIPBOARD. If button 3 isn't pressed while button 1 is held down, the default *xterm* translation, namely to add the selection to the PRIMARY selection and CUT_BUFFER0 on any key up, takes effect instead.

The second translation line specifies a way to paste the CLIPBOARD selection (the current contents of the *xclipboard* window): by holding the Shift key and clicking the second pointer button.

The third translation pastes the contents of the PRIMARY selection, or if that is empty, CUT_BUFFER0. `~Ctrl` is specified to keep this translation from conflicting with the translations that invoke the *xterm* menus; `~Meta` prevents a conflict with *twm* functions. We've added `~Shift` to prevent a conflict with the action that pastes the CLIPBOARD selection.

Widget Hierarchy

In order to specify resources, it is useful to know the hierarchy of the widgets that compose *xclipboard*. In the notation below, indentation indicates hierarchical structure. The widget class name is given first, followed by the widget instance name. The first line shows the application class and instance names:

```
XClipboard  xclipboard
        Form  form
                Command  quit
                Command  delete
                Command  new
```

```
Command   next
Command   prev
Text      text
```

For information on the resources available in each of the Athena widgets, see Appendix G, *Widget Resources*.

Files

/usr/lib/X11/app-defaults/XClipboard   Specifies required resources.

See Also

X, xterm; Chapter 5, *The xterm Terminal Emulator*; Chapter 11, *Setting Resources*; individual client reference pages for the appropriate translations to send selections to the CLIPBOARD.

Authors

Ralph R. Swick, DEC/MIT Project Athena;
Chris Peterson, MIT X Consortium;
Keith Packard, MIT X Consortium.

xclock

Name

xclock – continuously display the time in either analog or digital form.

Syntax

`xclock` [`options`]

Description

xclock continuously displays the time of day, either in digital or analog form. In digital form, *xclock* displays the time using a 24-hour clock. It also displays the day, month, and year. In analog form, *xclock* displays a standard 12-hour clock face. You can set up more than one clock simultaneously.

The default clock is an analog clock with a black foreground on a white background. If you want to change the clock's appearance, type in the appropriate options. For example,

```
% xclock -bd slateblue -fg navyblue -hl darkslategray &
```

sets up a conventional 12-hour clock with a slate blue window border, navy blue tick marks, and dark slate gray hands.

By default, the clock is positioned in the upper-left corner of your background window. If you are running the default version of *mwm*, the window manager will place the clock in the upper-left quadrant of the screen, offset from the corner.

Options

xclock accepts all of the standard X Toolkit command-line options, which are listed on the *X* reference page. (We've included some of the more commonly used Toolkit options later in this section.) In addition, *xclock* accepts the following application-specific options:

-help Displays a brief summary of *xclock*'s calling syntax and options.

-analog
  Draws a conventional 12-hour clock face with tick marks for each minute and stroke marks for each hour. This is the default.

-digital or -d
  Displays the date and time in digital format. Note that -display must be used to specify a display.

-chime
  Indicates that the clock should chime once on the half hour and twice on the hour.

-hd *color*
  Specifies the color of the hands on an analog clock. The default is black.

-hl *color*
  Specifies the color of the edges of the hands on an analog clock. Only useful on color displays. The default is black.

-padding *pixels*

> Specifies the width in pixels of the space between the window border and any portion of the *xclock* display. The default is 10 pixels in digital mode and 8 pixels in analog mode.

-update *seconds*

> Specifies the frequency in seconds with which *xclock* updates its display. If the *xclock* window is obscured and then exposed, *xclock* overrides this setting and redisplays immediately. A value of less than 30 seconds will enable a second hand on an analog clock. The default is 60 seconds.

The following standard X Toolkit options are commonly used with *xclock*:

-bw *pixels*

> Specifies the width in pixels of the border around the *xclock* window. The default is 2 pixels.

-fg *color*

> Determines the color of the text in digital mode, and the color of the tick and stroke marks in analog mode. The default is black.

-fn *font*

> Specifies the font to be used in digital mode. Any fixed-width font may be used. The default is 6x10.

-geometry *geometry*

> Sets *xclock* window size and location according to the geometry specification. The -geometry option can be (and often is) abbreviated to -g, unless there is a conflicting option that begins with "g". The argument to the geometry option (*geometry*) is referred to as a "standard geometry string," and has the form *widthx-height±xoff±yoff*.
>
> In digital mode, height and width are determined by the font in use, unless otherwise specified. In analog mode, width and height defaults are 164 pixels, unless otherwise specified. The default value for any unspecified x or y offset is -0. All values are in pixels. If you do not specify the geometry, the window manager may place the window; if not, *xclock* will ask you for placement when it starts up.

-display [*host*]:*server*[.*screen*]

> Allows you to specify the physical display, server, and screen on which to create the *xclock* window. See "Options" on the *X* reference page for an example of usage.
>
> Note that -display cannot be abbreviated to -d, which is shorthand for *xclock*'s -digital option.

-xrm *resourcestring*

> Specifies a resource string to be used. This is especially useful for setting resources that do not have separate command-line options.

Resources

xclock uses the Athena Clock widget. It understands all of the Core resource names and classes as well as the new resources defined by the Clock widget. Resources you may want to set in user resource files include:

analog (class Boolean)

>Specifies whether or not an analog clock should be used instead of a digital one. The default is true.

chime (class Boolean)

>Specifies whether or not a bell should be rung on the half hour and on the hour. The default is false.

hands (class Foreground)

>Specifies the color of the insides of the clock's hands. The default is the fore-ground color.

highlight (class Foreground)

>Specifies the color used to highlight the clock's hands. The default is the fore-ground color.

padding (class Margin)

>Specifies the amount of internal padding in pixels to be used. The default is 8.

update (class Interval)

>Specifies the frequency in seconds at which the time should be redisplayed.

You may also want to set the following X Toolkit resources:

background (class Background)

>Determines the background color. The default is white.

font (class Font)

>Specifies the font to be used for the digital clock. Note that variable-width fonts currently will not always display correctly.

foreground (class Foreground)

>Specifies the color for the tick marks and stroke marks. Using the class specifies the color for all things that normally would appear in the foreground color. The default is black since the core default for background is white.

height (class Height)

>Specifies the height of the clock.

reverseVideo (class ReverseVideo)

>Specifies that the foreground and background colors should be reversed.

width (class Width)

>Specifies the width of the clock.

Widget Hierarchy

In order to specify resources, it is useful to know the hierarchy of the widgets which compose *xclock*. In the notation below, indentation indicates hierarchical structure. The widget class name is given first, followed by the widget instance name.

```
XClock  xclock
    Clock  clock
```

Files

/usr/lib/X11/app-defaults/XClock   Specifies default resources.

Bugs

xclock believes the system clock.

When in digital mode, the string should be centered automatically.

There should be a way to exit the program.

See Also

X, oclock, xrdb, time(3C); Chapter 8, *Other Clients*; Appendix G, *Widget Resources*.

Authors

Tony Della Fera (MIT-Athena, DEC);
Dave Mankins (MIT-Athena, BBN);
Ed Moy (UC Berkeley).

xcmsdb

Name

xcmsdb – Xlib screen color characterization data utility.

Syntax

xcmsdb [*options*] [*filename*]

Description

xcmsdb is used to load, query, or remove Screen Color Characterization Data stored in properties on the root window of the screen. Screen Color Characterization Data is an integral part of Xlib, necessary for proper conversion between device-independent and device-dependent color specifications. Xlib uses the XDCCC_LINEAR_RGB_MATRICES and XDCCC_LINEAR_RGB_CORRECTION properties to store color characterization data for color monitors. It uses XDCCC_GRAY_SCREENWWHITEPOINT and XDCCC_GRAY_CORRECTION properties for gray scale monitors. Because Xlib allows the addition of Screen Color Characterization Function Sets, added function sets may place their Screen Color Characterization Data on other properties. This utility is unaware of these other properties; therefore, you will need to use a similar utility provided with the function set, or use the *xprop* utility.

The ASCII readable contents of *filename* (or the standard input if no input file is given) are appropriately transformed for storage in properties, provided the -query or -remove options are not specified.

Options

xcmsdb accepts the following options:

-query   Specifies that the XDCCC properties be read off of the screen's root window. If successful, this transforms the data into a more readable format, then sends the data to standard output.

-remove   Attempts to remove the XDCCC properties on the screen's root window.

-color   Sets the query and remove options to only check for the XDCCC_LINEAR_RGB_MATRICES and XDCCC_LINEAR_RGB_CORRECTION properties. If the -color option is not set then the query and remove options check for all the properties.

-format 32 | 16 | 8
          Specifies the property format (32, 16, or 8 bits per entry) for the XDCCC_LINEAR_RGB_CORRECTION property. Precision of encoded floating point values increases with the increase in bits per entry. The default is 32 bits per entry.

See Also

xprop; Chapter 12, *Specifying Color*; Volume One, *Xlib Programming Manual*; Volume Two, *Xlib Reference Manual*.

Copyright

Copyright 1990, Tektronix Inc.

Author

Chuck Adams, Tektronix Inc.

xcol

Name
xcol – display colors and change color entries in resource files.

Syntax
xcol [*options*] [*filename*]

Description
The public domain *xcol* program displays the colors defined in the *rgb.txt* file of the X server. The colors are sorted by their names and their RGB-values and shown in a cube in the Color-View window (The positions represent the RGB-values). Since there usually are more colors defined in the file than cells in the colormap, entries with the same name, but different RGB-values for different intensities, are grouped together.

If a filename is given as a parameter, all occurrences of color names in that file are shown in a second window, called the TextView window. To change the colors specified in the file, a text line has to be made active. Then a new color can be selected in the ColorView window.

To get a better impression of the color, a help (highlight/background) color can be selected for each text line. If two lines define a foreground and a background color, an association can be made and the colors of both lines can be selected together.

Note that as of the printing of this guide, *xcol* had not been updated for Release 5, but our testing showed it could run under the standard X11R5 server. See Chapter 8, *Other Clients*, for a tutorial.

Pointer Commands
In the ColorView window, pointer clicks have the following effects:

First button: Selects color for the active resource line in the TextView window.

Second button: Selects help (i.e., highlight) color for the active resource line in the Text-View window.

Third button: Moves pointer to the pixel of the color specified by the active resource line in the TextView window.

In the TextView window, pointer clicks have the following effects:

First button: Selects the text line as the active line.

Second button: Toggles reverse video mode or connects/disconnects two associated lines (e.g., background and foreground color specifications for the same resource).

Third button: Highlights the line in the text file.

Options
-rv

Color positions are reversed in the cube. Some new colors can become visible in the area of the very bright colors.

-b*number*

> The size of color blocks is set to the constant *number*. By default, it depends on the size of the ColorView window.

-gran*number*

> Sets the maximum number of associated colors to *number*. By default, this value is 11. (You can see the effect when reaching the grey field, where 101 associated entries are possibly available.)

-dark*number*

> Sets the percentage of the intensity of other colors. The default is 50. It's easier to select a color if the screen is darkened a little bit.

+*char_list*

> Adds characters in *char_list* to list of "space" characters. A color string in the text file must occur between 2 'space' characters to be recognized. By default, these characters are " ", "\t", "\n", ":", """".

-strings

> Specifies that names of colors in the file are only recognized when used in a string (useful for C source code). This means that the list of "space" characters is set to """" only.

-case

> Specifies that all occurrences of color names in the wrong case are replaced by the appropriate color names from the *rgb.txt* file.

-help

> Prints some instructions (e.g., on the usage of buttons).

-file *filename*

> Specifies an alternative file to the *rgb.txt* file.

Files

/usr/lib/X11/rgb.txt

See Also

X; Chapter 8, *Other Clients*; Chapter 12, *Specifying Color*.

Bugs

The author wanted the program to work with the selection mechanism used in *xterm* (when no text file is given), but it seems to be too complicated. So, the current version always stores the string of the color in CUT_BUFFER0. If anyone has an easy way to use the correct selection mechanism, please contact the author.

Copyright

Copyright 1990, University of Kaiserslautern.

Permission to use, copy, modify, and distribute this software for any purpose and without fee is hereby granted, provided that the above copyright notice appear in all copies.

Author

Helmut Hoenig (hoenig@informatik.uni-kl.de).

xcoloredit

Name

xcoloredit – find RGB color values by graphical color mixing.

Syntax

`xcoloredit` [*options*] [{0-255}..]

Description

xcoloredit is a public domain client that provides a graphical method of mixing the three primary colors available on a color workstation. This mixing can be done using the Red, Green, and Blue slider controls on the left of the window or using the Hue, Saturation, and Value slider controls on the right.

The three boxes above the Red, Green, and Blue slider controls are used for linking the controls together via the fourth slider to the right of the blue slider. While in the slider controls the first mouse button increments the color components value, the third mouse button decrements the value (this only works with the Red, Green, Blue, and Linked sliders). The middle mouse button allows the user to continually change the value.

The results of the color mixing is shown in the four central squares. The three smaller squares shows the intensities of the red, green, and blue components. The hexidecimal value below these squares is the corresponding color value which can be used in defaults files. This value is also placed in the PRIMARY_COLOR selection property. If the user presses the color value button, the button is highlighted and the color value is placed in PRIMARY selection as well (useful for pasting into defaults files).

At the bottom of the main window are 36 color cells. The current color cell is highlighted by a box drawn around it. By clicking with the first mouse button in another cell this new cell's current value can be edited (if the cell has no defined value, the current cells value is copied to it and the cell is highlighted with a dashed box). These color cells can be connected to cells in the default colormap of the display. To do this the user must give the colormap entry number(s) (pixel number) as command-line argument(s).

The text shown in the mixed color window can be displayed in one of the 36 color cell colors. Typing "c" or "t" in this window changes the color of the text to that of the currently selected color cell. This can be used to see what text will look like with different foreground and background colors. The example text can be modified using the *-text* command-line option.

Options

xcoloredit accepts the standard X Toolkit options, which are listed on the *X* reference page. In addition, *xcoloredit* accepts the following application-specific options:

-format

Specifies the format used to display the RGB value of the color. This format is used by the *printf*(2) function call. By default the format is set to "#%02x%02x%02x" which is the standard RGB format for X.

`-silent`

Specifies that the edited color values are not printed out when *xcoloredit* quits.

`-text`

Sets the example text to display in the mixed color window. Newlines are allowed in this string.

Selection Atoms

The following selection atoms are used/defined:

PRIMARY_COLOR

Current color selection value.

PRIMARY

Current color selection value when highlighted.

See Also

xtici; Chapter 8, *Other Clients*; Chapter 12, *Specifying Color*.

Author

Richard Hesketh, University of Kent at Canterbury, March 1989.
rlh2@ukc.ac.uk

Name

xconsole – monitor system console messages.

Syntax

xconsole [*options*]

Description

xconsole displays system messages that are usually sent to */dev/console*. See Appendix A, *Managing Your Environment*, for an example of usage.

Options

xconsole recognizes all of the standard X Toolkit options, which are listed on the *X* reference page. (See Chapter 10, *Command-line Options*, for more information.) *xconsole* also recognizes the following application-specific options:

-daemon

Causes *xconsole* to place itself in the background, using fork/exit.

-exitOnFail

When set, this option directs *xconsole* to exit when it is unable to redirect the console output.

-file *filename*

To monitor some other device, use this option to specify the device name. This does not work on regular files as they are always ready to be read from.

-notify or -nonotify

When new data is received from the console and the notify option is set, the icon name of the application has "*" appended, so that the occurrence of a message is evident even though the application is iconified. -notify is the default, although this feature does not seem to work reliably in all environments.

Note that if you're running *mwm* and using an Icon Box, the asterisk cannot be appended to the icon name.

-stripNonprint

Causes nonprinting characters from the console output to be stripped before messages appear in the *xconsole* window. This is the default.

-verbose

When set, this option directs *xconsole* to display an informative message in the first line of the text buffer.

Resources

xconsole recognizes the Core resource names and classes. (See Appendix G, *Widget Resources*, for more information.) In addition, *xconsole* defines the following application resources:

daemon (class Daemon)

>   If True, causes *xconsole* to place itself in the background, using fork/exit. False by default.

exitOnFail (class ExitOnFail)

>   If True, directs *xconsole* to exit when it is unable to redirect the console output. False by default.

file (class File)

>   To monitor some other device, use this resource to specify the device name. This does not work on regular files as they are always ready to be read from.

notify (class Notify)

>   When new data is received from the console and the notify resource is True, the icon name of the application has "*" appended, so that it is evident even when the application is iconified. False suppresses this behavior. True by default. (Note, however, that this feature does not seem to work reliably in all environments.)

stripNonprint (class StripNonprint)

>   When True, causes nonprinting characters from the console output to be stripped before messages appear in the *xconsole* window. True by default.

verbose (class Verbose)

>   When True, directs *xconsole* to display an informative message in the first line of the text buffer. False by default.

Widget Hierarchy

In order to specify resources, it is useful to know the hierarchy of the widgets that compose *xconsole*. In the notation below, indentation indicates hierarchical structure. The widget class name is given first, followed by the widget instance name:

```
XConsole  xconsole
      XConsole  text
```

Notice that *xconsole* uses the Athena Text widget. See Appendix G, *Widget Resources*, and the Athena Widget Set documentation in the standard distribution.

Files

/usr/lib/X11/app-defaults/XConsole

>   Specifies required resources.

See Also

X, xrdb; Appendix A, *Managing Your Environment*; Appendix G, *Widget Resources*.

Bugs

When *xconsole* is iconified (and program defaults apply), an asterisk should be appended to the icon name (see -notify and the notify resource), but this does not happen consistently in every environment.

Author

Keith Packard (MIT X Consortium).

xcrtca

Name

xcrtca – CRT color analyzer driver.

Syntax

xcrtca [*options*]

Description

xcrtca is used in conjunction with *xsccd* to create a color database for the Xcms Color Management System using either the Minolta CA-100 (default) or Tektronix J17, low cost colorimeters.

The Minolta CA-100 in use at the MIT X Consortium includes the Low Luminance option which is necessary to get the required accuracy for readings at low luminance levels. The CA-100 outputs measurements in the CIExyY color space at a baud rate of 9600.

The output format for the Tektronix J17 is selectable on the device as well as the baud rate. Select either CIExyY or CIEXYZ format for use with this program. The default baud rate for the J17 is 2400. Note that the default baud rate for this program is 9600; therefore, unless you select 9600 on the J17, you will need to specify the baud rate with the –baud option.

Options

-baud *baudrate*
    Baud rate of the colorimeter. Default for this program is 9600.

-delay *seconds*
    The amount of delay between the change of the color patch and the first reading of each primary color. Default is 4 seconds.

-device *device_name*
    Specifies the name of the colorimeter. Acceptable values: either ca100 (the default) or j17.

-file *filename*
    Specifies the filename for the results; otherwise results are sent to standard output.

-format [xyY| XYZ]
    Format of measurements received from the colorimeter.

-input *pathname*
    Specifies the pathname of the *tty*. Default for this program is */dev/ttya*.

-model *model_string*
    Specifies the model of the CRT.

-name *name_string*
    Specifies the name (e.g., manufacturer) to be associated with the CRT.

Caveats

This program has been coded for a Sun SparcStation and for a default visual with 8 bits_per_rgb.

See Also

xcmsdb, xsccd; Chapter 12, *Specifying Color*.

Authors

Dave Sternlicht, Keith Packard, MIT X Consortium;
Al Tabayoyon, Chuck Adams, Tektronix Inc.

xditview

Name

xditview – display *ditroff* DVI files.

Syntax

xditview [*options*] [*filename*]

Description

The *xditview* program displays *ditroff* output on an X display. As of Release 5, it uses no special font metrics and automatically converts the printer coordinates into screen coordinates, using the user-specified screen resolution, rather than the actual resolution so that the appropriate fonts can be found. If "–" is given as the *filename*, *xditview* reads from standard input. If "|" is the first character of the *filename*, *xditview* forks *sh* to run the rest of the *filename* and uses the standard output of that command.

Options

xditview accepts all of the standard X Toolkit command-line options, which are listed on the *X* reference page. (We've included one of the more commonly used Toolkit options later in this section.) In addition, *xditview* accepts the following application-specific options:

-backingStore *backing_store_type*

Redisplay of the DVI window can take up to a second or so. This option causes the server to save the window contents so that when it is scrolled around the viewport, the window is painted from contents saved in backing store. *backing_store_type* can be one of Always, WhenMapped, or NotUseful.

-noPolyText

Some X servers incorrectly implement PolyText with multiple strings per request. This option suppresses the use of this feature in *xditview*. (Available as of Release 5.)

-page *page_number*

Specifies the page number of the document to be displayed when the client is started.

-resolution *dots_per_inch*

Specifies the desired screen resolution to use. Fonts will be opened by requesting this resolution field in the XLFD names. (Available as of Release 5.)

The following standard X Toolkit option is commonly used with *xditview*:

-fn *font*

Specifies the font to be used for displaying widget text. The default is *fixed*.

Resources

This program uses a Dvi widget. It understands all of the core resource names and classes as well as the following:

font (class Font)

Specifies the font to be used for error messages.

fontMap (class FontMap)

> To associate the *ditroff* fonts with appropriate X fonts, this string resource contains a set of newline-separated specifications, each of which consists of a *ditroff* name, some white space and an XLFD pattern with wildcard (*) characters in appropriate places to allow all sizes to be listed. This resource has been added in Release 5. The default fontMap is:

```
R   -*-times-medium-r-normal--*-*-*-*-*-*-iso8859-1\n\
I   -*-times-medium-i-normal--*-*-*-*-*-*-iso8859-1\n\
B   -*-times-bold-r-normal--*-*-*-*-*-*-iso8859-1\n\
F   -*-times-bold-i-normal--*-*-*-*-*-*-iso8859-1\n\
BI  -*-times-bold-i-normal--*-*-*-*-*-*-iso8859-1\n\
C   -*-courier-medium-r-normal--*-*-*-*-*-*-iso8859-1\n\
CO  -*-courier-medium-o-normal--*-*-*-*-*-*-iso8859-1\n\
CB  -*-courier-bold-r-normal--*-*-*-*-*-*-iso8859-1\n\
CF  -*-courier-bold-o-normal--*-*-*-*-*-*-iso8859-1\n\
H   -*-helvetica-medium-r-normal--*-*-*-*-*-*-iso8859-1\n\
HO  -*-helvetica-medium-o-normal--*-*-*-*-*-*-iso8859-1\n\
HB  -*-helvetica-bold-r-normal--*-*-*-*-*-*-iso8859-1\n\
HF  -*-helvetica-bold-o-normal--*-*-*-*-*-*-iso8859-1\n\
N   -*-new century schoolbook-medium-r-normal--*-*-*-*-*-*-iso8859-1\n\
NI  -*-new century schoolbook-medium-i-normal--*-*-*-*-*-*-iso8859-1\n\
NB  -*-new century schoolbook-bold-r-normal--*-*-*-*-*-*-iso8859-1\n\
NF  -*-new century schoolbook-bold-i-normal--*-*-*-*-*-*-iso8859-1\n\
A   -*-charter-medium-r-normal--*-*-*-*-*-*-iso8859-1\n\
AI  -*-charter-medium-i-normal--*-*-*-*-*-*-iso8859-1\n\
AB  -*-charter-bold-r-normal--*-*-*-*-*-*-iso8859-1\n\
AF  -*-charter-bold-i-normal--*-*-*-*-*-*-iso8859-1\n\
S   -*-symbol-medium-r-normal--*-*-*-*-*-*-adobe-fontspecific\n\
S2  -*-symbol-medium-r-normal--*-*-*-*-*-*-adobe-fontspecific\n
```

foreground (class Foreground)

> Specifies the default foreground color.

pageNumber (class PageNumber)

> Specifies the page number to be displayed at startup.

Using xditview with ditroff

You can use any DVI file with *xditview*, although DVI files that use the fonts appropriate to the fontMap will look more accurate on the screen. On servers that support scaled fonts, all requested font sizes will be accurately reflected on the screen; for servers that do not support scaled fonts, *xditview* will use the closest font from the same family.

Files

/usr/lib/X11/app-defaults/Xditview
> Specifies required resources.

/usr/lib/X11/app-defaults/Xditview-chrtr
> Specifies the default fontMap.

See Also

X, xrdb, ditroff(1); the paper entitled "X Logical Font Description Conventions."

Authors

Portions of this program originated in *xtroff* which was derived from *suntroff*.

Keith Packard (MIT X Consortium);
Richard L. Hyde (Purdue);
David Slattengren (Berkeley);
Malcom Slaney (Schlumberger Palo Alto Research);
Mark Moraes (University of Toronto).

xdm

Name

xdm – X display manager.

Syntax

xdm [*options*]

Description

xdm manages a collection of X displays that may be on the local host or remote servers. The design of *xdm* was guided by the needs of X terminals as well the X Consortium standard XDMCP, the X Display Manager Control Protocol. *xdm* provides services similar to those provided by *init*, *getty*, and *login* on character terminals: prompting for login name and password, authenticating the user, and running a "session."

A *session* is defined by the lifetime of a particular process; in the traditional character-based terminal world, it is the user's login shell process. In the *xdm* context, it is an arbitrary session manager. This is because, in a windowing environment, a user's login shell process does not necessarily have any terminal-like interface with which to connect. When a real session manager is not available, a window manager or terminal emulator is typically used as the "session manager," meaning that termination of this process terminates the user's session.

When the session is terminated, *xdm* resets the X server and (optionally) restarts the whole process.

When *xdm* receives an Indirect query via XDMCP, it can run a *chooser* process to perform an XDMCP BroadcastQuery (or an XDMCP Query to specified hosts) on behalf of the display, and offer a menu of possible hosts that offer XDMCP display management. This feature is useful with X terminals that do not offer a host menu themselves.

Because *xdm* provides the first interface that users will see, it is designed to be simple to use and easy to customize to the needs of a particular site. *xdm* has many options, most of which have reasonable defaults. Browse through the various sections, picking and choosing the things you want to change. Pay particular attention to "The Xsession Program," which will describe how to set up the style of session desired.

Options

Note that all of these options, except -config, specify values that can also be specified in the configuration file as resources.

-config *configuration_file*

Specifies the configuration file which specifies resources to control the behavior of *xdm* parameters. The default is */usr/lib/X11/xdm/xdm-config*.

-daemon

Specifies true as the value for the DisplayManager.daemonMode resource. This makes *xdm* close all file descriptors, disassociate the controlling terminal, and put itself in the background when it first starts up (just like the host of other daemons). It is the default behavior.

-debug *debug_level*

Specifies the numeric value for the DisplayManager.debugLevel resource. A non-zero value causes *xdm* to print lots of debugging statements to the terminal; it also disables the DisplayManager.daemonMode resource, forcing *xdm* to run synchronously. To interpret these debugging messages, a copy of the source code for *xdm* is almost a necessity. No attempt has been made to rationalize or standardize the output.

-error *error_log_file*

Specifies the value for the DisplayManager.errorLogFile resource. This file contains errors from *xdm* as well as anything written to standard error by the various scripts and programs run during the progress of the session.

-nodaemon

Specifies false as the value for the DisplayManager.daemonMode resource. This suppresses the normal daemon behavior, which is for *xdm* to close all file descriptors, disassociate itself from the controlling terminal, and put itself in the background when it first starts up.

-resources *resource_file*

Specifies the value for the DisplayManager*resources resource. This file is loaded using *xrdb* to specify configuration parameters for the authentication widget.

-server *server_entry*

Specifies the value for the DisplayManager.servers resource. (See the section "Server Specification.")

-udpPort *port_number*

Specifies the value for the DisplayManager.requestPort resource. This sets the port number which *xdm* will monitor for XDMCP requests. As XDMCP uses the registered well-known UDP port 177, this resource should probably not be changed except for debugging.

-session *session_program*

Specifies the value for the DisplayManager*session resource. This indicates the program to run as the session when the user logs in.

-xrm *resource_specification*

Allows an arbitrary resource to be specified, just as most toolkit applications.

Resources

At many stages the actions of *xdm* can be controlled through the use of the configuration file, which is in the X resource format. See Chapter 11 for a description of the resource file format. Some resources modify the behavior of *xdm* on all displays, while others modify its behavior on a single display. Where actions relate to a specific display, the display name is inserted into the resource name between "DisplayManager" and the final resource name segment. For example, DisplayManager.expo_0.startup is the name of the resource that defines the startup shell file on the "expo:0" display. Because the resource manager uses colons to separate the name of the resource from its value and dots to separate resource name parts, *xdm* substitutes underscores for both dots and colons when generating the resource name.

`DisplayManager.authDir`

>Names a directory in which *xdm* stores authorization files while initializing the session. The default value is */usr/lib/X11/xdm*.

`DisplayManager.errorLogFile`

>Error output is normally directed at the system console. To redirect it, set this resource to any filename. A method to send these messages to *syslog* should be developed for systems that support it; however the wide variety of interfaces precludes any system-independent implementation. This file also contains any output directed to standard error by *Xsetup*, *Xstartup*, *Xsession*, and *Xreset*, so it will contain descriptions of problems in those scripts as well.

`DisplayManager.debugLevel`

>If the integer value of this resource is greater than zero, reams of debugging information will be printed. It also disables daemon mode, which would redirect the information into the bit-bucket and allows non-root users to run *xdm*, which would normally not be useful.

`DisplayManager.daemonMode`

>Normally, *xdm* attempts to make itself into a daemon process unassociated with any terminal. This is accomplished by forking and leaving the parent process to exit, then closing file descriptors and releasing the controlling terminal. When attempting to debug *xdm*, this is quite bothersome. Setting this resource to `false` will disable this feature.

`DisplayManager.pidFile`

>The filename specified will be created to contain an ASCII representation of the process ID of the main *xdm* process. *xdm* also uses file locking on this file to attempt to eliminate multiple daemons running on the same machine, which would cause quite a bit of havoc.

`DisplayManager.lockPidFile`

>Controls whether *xdm* uses file locking to keep multiple display managers (*xdm* processes) from running amok. On System V, this uses the *lockf* library call, while on BSD it uses *flock*.

`DisplayManager.autoRescan`

>This Boolean controls whether *xdm* rescans the configuration, access control, and authentication keys files after a session terminates and the files have changed. By default it is `True`. You can force *xdm* to reread these files by sending a SIGHUP to the main process.

`DisplayManager.removeDomainname`

>When computing the display name for XDMCP clients, the name resolver will typically create a fully qualified hostname of the terminal. Since this is sometimes

confusing, *xdm* will remove the domain name portion of the hostname if it is the same as the domain name for the local host when this variable is set. By default the value is `True`.

`DisplayManager.keyFile`

XDM-AUTHENTICATION-1 style XDMCP authentication requires that a private key be shared between *xdm* and the terminal. This resource specifies the file containing those values. Each entry in the file consists of a display name and the shared key. By default, *xdm* does not include support for XDM-AUTHENTICATION-1 as it requires DES, which is not generally distributable because of United States export restrictions.

`DisplayManager.accessFile`

To prevent unauthorized XDMCP service and to allow forwarding of XDMCP Indirect-Query requests, this file contains a database of hostnames which are either allowed direct access to this machine, or have a list of hosts to which queries should be forwarded. The format of this file is described in the section "XDMCP Access Control." (Available as of Release 5.)

`DisplayManager.exportList`

A whitespace-separated list of additional environment variables to pass on to the *Xsetup*, *Xstartup*, *Xsession*, and *Xreset* programs. (Available as of Release 5.)

`DisplayManager.randomFile`

A file to checksum to generate the seed of authorization keys. This should be a file that changes frequently. The default is */dev/mem*. (Available as of Release 5.)

`DisplayManager.DISPLAY.resources`

Specifies the name of the file to be loaded by *xrdb* as the resource database onto the root window of screen 0 of the display. The *Xsetup* program, the Login widget, and *chooser* will use the resources set in this file. This resource database is loaded just before the authentication procedure is started, so it can control the appearance of the "login" window. See "Authentication Widget Resources," which describes the various resources which are appropriate to place in this file. There is no default value for this resource, but the conventional name is */usr/lib/X11/xdm/Xresources*.

`DisplayManager.DISPLAY.chooser`

Specifies the program run to offer a host menu for Indirect queries redirected to the special hostname CHOOSER. */usr/lib/X11/xdm/chooser* is the default. See the sections "XDMCP Access Control" and "Chooser." (Available as of Release 5.)

`DisplayManager.DISPLAY.setup`

This specifies a program which is run (as root) before offering the Login window. This may be used to change the appearance of the screen around the Login window or to put up other windows (e.g., you may want to run *xconsole* here). By default, no program is run. The conventional name for a file used here is *Xsetup*. See the section "The Setup Program." (Available as of Release 5.)

DisplayManager.*DISPLAY*.xrdb

> Specifies the program used to load the resources. By default, *xdm* uses */usr/bin/X11/xrdb*.

DisplayManager.*DISPLAY*.cpp

> Specifies the name of the C preprocessor used by *xrdb*.

DisplayManager.*DISPLAY*.openDelay,
DisplayManager.*DISPLAY*.openRepeat,
DisplayManager.*DISPLAY*.openTimeout,
DisplayManager.requestPort

> Indicates the UDP port number that *xdm* uses to listen for incoming XDMCP requests. Unless you need to debug the system, leave this with its default value of 177.

DisplayManager.*DISPLAY*.reset

> Specifies a program which is run (as root) after the session terminates. Again, by default, no program is run. The conventional name is *Xreset*. See "The Xreset Program" below.

DisplayManager.servers

> Specifies either a filename full of server entries, one per line (if the value starts with a slash), or a single server entry. See the section "Server Specification" for a description of this resource.

DisplayManager.*DISPLAY*.session

> Specifies the session to be executed (not running as root). By default, */usr/bin/X11/xterm* is run. The conventional name is *Xsession*. See "The Xsession Program."

DisplayManager.*DISPLAY*.startAttempts

> Numeric resources control the behavior of *xdm* when attempting to open intransigent servers. openDelay is the length of the pause (in seconds) between successive attempts. openRepeat is the number of attempts to make. openTimeout is the amount of time to wait while actually attempting the open (i.e., the maximum time spent in the *connect* system call). startAttempts is the number of times this entire process is done before giving up on the server. After openRepeat attempts have been made, or if openTimeout seconds elapse in any particular attempt, *xdm* terminates and restarts the server, attempting to connect again. This process is repeated startAttempts times, at which point the display is declared dead and disabled. Although this behavior may seem arbitrary, it has been empirically developed and works quite well on most systems. The default values are 5 for openDelay, 5 for openRepeat, 30 for openTimeout, and 4 for startAttempts.

DisplayManager.*DISPLAY*.startup

> Specifies a program which is run (as root) after the authentication process succeeds. By default, no program is run. The conventional name for a file used here is *Xstartup*. See "The Xstartup Program" below.

`DisplayManager.`*`DISPLAY`*`.pingInterval`
`DisplayManager.`*`DISPLAY`*`.pingTimeout`

To discover when remote displays disappear, *xdm* occasionally "pings" them, using an X connection and sending XSync calls. `pingInterval` specifies the time (in minutes) between each ping attempt; `pingTimeout` specifies the maximum amount of time (in minutes) to wait for the terminal to respond to the request. If the terminal does not respond, the session is declared dead and terminated. By default, both are set to 5 minutes. If you frequently use X terminals that can become isolated from the managing host, you may wish to increase this value. The only worry is that sessions will continue to exist after the terminal has been accidentally disabled. *xdm* will not ping local displays. Although it would seem harmless, it is unpleasant when the workstation session is terminated as a result of the server hanging for NFS service and not responding to the ping.

`DisplayManager.`*`DISPLAY`*`.terminateServer`

Specifies whether the X server should be terminated when a session terminates (instead of resetting it). This option can be used when the server tends to grow without bound over time in order to limit the amount of time the server is run. The default value is `false`.

`DisplayManager.`*`DISPLAY`*`.userPath`

xdm sets the PATH environment variable for the session to this value. It should be a colon separated list of directories; see *sh*(1) for a full description. The default value can be specified at build time in the X system configuration file with `DefUserPath`; */bin:/usr/bin:/usr/bin/X11:/usr/ucb* is a common value.

`DisplayManager.`*`DISPLAY`*`.systemPath`

xdm sets the PATH environment variable for the startup and reset scripts to the value of this resource. The default for this resource is specified at build time with the `DefaultSystemPath` entry in the system configuration file; a common choice is */etc:/bin:/usr/bin:/usr/bin/X11:/usr/ucb*. Note the absence of "." from this entry. This is a good practice to follow for root; it avoids many common Trojan horse system penetration schemes.

`DisplayManager.`*`DISPLAY`*`.systemShell`

xdm sets the SHELL environment variable for the startup and reset scripts to the value of this resource. By default, it is */bin/sh*.

`DisplayManager.`*`DISPLAY`*`.failsafeClient`

If the default session fails to execute, *xdm* will fall back to this program. This program is executed with no arguments, but executes using the same environment variables as the session would have had. See "The Xsession Program." By default, */usr/bin/X11/xterm* is used.

DisplayManager.*DISPLAY*.grabServer
DisplayManager.*DISPLAY*.grabTimeout

> To improve security, *xdm* grabs the server and keyboard while reading the login name and password. The grabServer resource specifies if the server should be held for the duration of the login name and password reading: when false, the server is ungrabbed after the keyboard grab succeeds; otherwise, the server is grabbed until just before the session begins. The default is false. The grabTimeout resource specifies the maximum time *xdm* will wait for the grab to succeed. The grab may fail if some other client has the server grabbed, or possibly if the network latencies are very high. This resource has a default value of 3 seconds; you should be cautious when raising it, as a user can be spoofed by a look-alike window on the display. If the grab fails, *xdm* kills and restarts the server (if possible) and the session.

DisplayManager.*DISPLAY*.authorize
DisplayManager.*DISPLAY*.authName

> authorize is a Boolean resource that controls whether *xdm* generates and uses authorization for the local server connections. If authorization is used, authName is a whitespace-separated list of authorization mechanisms to use. XDMCP connections dynamically specify which authorization types are supported, so authName is ignored in this case. When authorize is set for a display and authorization is not available, the user is informed by having a different message displayed in the login widget. By default, authorize is True and authName is MIT-MAGIC-COOKIE-1.

DisplayManager.*DISPLAY*.authFile

> This file is used to communicate the authorization data from *xdm* to the server, using the -auth server command-line option. It should be kept in a directory which is not world-writeable, as it could easily be removed, disabling the authorization mechanism in the server.

DisplayManager.DISPLAY.authComplain

> If set to False, disables the use of the unsecureGreeting in the login window. See the section "Authentication Widget." The default is True. (Available as of Release 5.)

DisplayManager.DISPLAY.resetSignal

> The number of the signal *xdm* sends to reset the server. See the section "Controlling the Server." The default is 1 (SIGHUP). (Available as of Release 5.)

DisplayManager.DISPLAY.termSignal

> The number of the signal *xdm* sends to terminate the server. See the section "Controlling the Server." The default is 15 (SIGTERM). (Available as of Release 5.)

DisplayManager.*DISPLAY*.resetForAuth

> The original implementation of authorization in the sample server rereads the authorization file at server reset time, instead of when checking the initial connection. As *xdm* generates the authorization information just before connecting to the display, an

old server would not get up-to-date authorization information. This resource causes *xdm* to send SIGHUP to the server after setting up the file, causing an additional server reset to occur, during which time the new authorization information will be read. The default is `false`, which will work for all MIT servers.

`DisplayManager.`*DISPLAY*`.userAuthDir`

When *xdm* is unable to write to the usual user authorization file (*$HOME/.Xauthority*), it creates a unique filename in this directory and points the environment variable XAUTHORITY at the created file. By default, it uses */tmp*.

XDMCP Access Control

The database file specified by the `DisplayManager.accessFile` provides information that *xdm* uses to control access from displays requesting XDMCP service. This file contains three types of entries: entries which control the response to Direct and Broadcast queries, entries which control the response to Indirect queries, and macro definitions.

The format of the Direct entries is simple, either a hostname or a pattern. A pattern is distinguished from a hostname by the inclusion of one or more meta characters. ("*" matches any sequence of 0 or more characters, and "?" matches any single character.) The pattern is then compared against the hostname of the display device. If the entry is a hostname, all comparisons are done using network addresses, so any name which converts to the correct network address may be used. For patterns, only canonical hostnames are used in the comparison, so ensure that you do not attempt to match aliases. Preceding either a hostname or a pattern with a "!" character causes hosts that match that entry to be excluded.

An Indirect entry also contains a hostname or pattern, but follows it with a list of hostnames or macros to which indirect queries should be sent.

A macro definition contains a macro name and a list of hostnames and other macros that the macro expands to. To distinguish macros from hostnames, macro names start with a "%" character. Macros may be nested.

Indirect entries may also specify to have *xdm* run *chooser* to offer a menu of hosts to connect to. See the section "Chooser."

When checking access for a particular display host, each entry is scanned in turn and the first matching entry determines the response. Direct and Broadcast entries are ignored when scanning for an Indirect entry and vice-versa.

Blank lines are ignored; "#" is treated as a comment delimiter causing the rest of that line to be ignored, and "*newline*" causes the newline to be ignored, allowing indirect host lists to span multiple lines.

Here is an example Xaccess file:

```
#
# Xaccess - XDMCP access control file
#

#
```

```
# Direct/Broadcast query entries
#

!xtra.lcs.mit.edu        # disallow direct/broadcast service for xtra
bambi.ogi.edu            # allow access from this particular display
*.lcs.mit.edu            # allow access from any display in LCS

#
# Indirect query entries
#

%HOSTS                   expo.lcs.mit.edu xenon.lcs.mit.edu \\e
                         excess.lcs.mit.edu kanga.lcs.mit.edu

extract.lcs.mit.edu      xenon.lcs.mit.edu #force extract to contact xenon
!xtra.lcs.mit.edu        dummy             #disallow indirect access
*.lcs.mit.edu            %HOSTS            #all others get to choose
```

Chooser

For X terminals that do not offer a host menu for use with Broadcast or Indirect queries, the *chooser* program can do this for them. (The *chooser* is available as of Release 5.) In the *Xaccess* file (another Release 5 innovation), specify CHOOSER as the first entry in the Indirect host list. *chooser* will send a Query request to each of the remaining hostnames in the list and offer a menu of all the hosts that respond.

The list may consist of the word BROADCAST, in which case *chooser* will send a Broadcast instead, again offering a menu of all hosts that respond. Note that on some operating systems, UDP packets cannot be broadcast, so this feature will not work.

Here's an example *Xaccess* file using *chooser*:

```
extract.lcs.mit.eduCHOOSER %HOSTS#offer a menu of these hosts
xtra.lcs.mit.eduCHOOSER BROADCAST#offer a menu of all hosts
```

The program to use for *chooser* is specified by the `DisplayManager.DISPLAY.chooser` resource. Resources for this program can be put into the file named by `Display-Manager.DISPLAY.resources`.

Server Specification

The resource `DisplayManager.servers` gives a server specification, or, if the values start with a slash (/), the name of a file containing server specifications, one per line.

Each specification indicates a display which should constantly be managed, and which is not using XDMCP. Each consists of at least three parts: a display name, a display class, a display type, and (for local servers) a command line to start the server. A typical entry for local display number 0 would be:

```
:0 Digital-QV local /usr/bin/X11/X :0
```

The display types are:

local	Local display: *xdm* must run the server
foreign	Remote display: *xdm* opens an X connection to a running server

The display name must be something that can be passed in the `-display` option to an X program. This string is used to generate the display-specific resource names, so be careful to match the names (e.g., use `:0 local /usr/bin/X11/X :0` instead of `localhost:0 local /usr/bin/X11/X :0` if your other resources are specified as `DisplayManager._0.session`). The display class portion is also used in the display-specific resources, as the class of the resource. This is useful if you have a large collection of similar displays (like a corral of X terminals) and would like to set resources for groups of them. When using XDMCP, the display is required to specify the display class, so the manual for your particular X terminal should document the display class string for your device. If it doesn't, you can run *xdm* in debug mode and look at the resource strings which it generates for that device, which will include the class string.

Setup Program

The *Xsetup* file is run after the server is reset, but before the Login window is offered. The file is typically a shell script. It is run as root, so it should be careful about security. This is the place to change the root background or bring up other windows that should appear on the screen along with the Login widget.

In addition to any specified by `DisplayManager.exportList`, the following environment variables are passed:

DISPLAY	The associated display name
PATH	The value of `DisplayManager.DISPLAY.systemPath`
SHELL	The value of `DisplayManager.DISPLAY.systemShell`
XAUTHORITY	May be set to an authority file

Note that since *xdm* grabs the keyboard, any other windows will not be able to receive keyboard input. They will be able to interact with the mouse; however, beware of potential security holes here. If `DisplayManager.DISPLAY.grabServer` is set, *Xsetup* will not be able to connect to the display at all. Resources for this program can be put into the file named by `DisplayManager.DISPLAY.resources`.

Authentication Widget Resources

The authentication widget reads a name/password pair from the keyboard. Nearly every imaginable parameter can be controlled with a resource. Resources for this widget should be put into the file named by `DisplayManager.DISPLAY.resources`. All of these resources have reasonable default values, so it is not necessary to specify any of them.

`xlogin.Login.width, xlogin.Login.height, xlogin.Login.x,`
`xlogin.Login.y`

> The geometry of the Login widget is normally computed automatically. If you wish to position it elsewhere, specify each of these resources.

`xlogin.Login.foreground`

> The color used to display the typed-in user name.

`xlogin.Login.font`

> The font used to display the typed-in user name.

`xlogin.Login.greeting`

> A string which identifies this window. The default is "X Window System".

`xlogin.Login.unsecureGreeting`

> When X authorization is requested in the configuration file for this display and none is in use, this greeting replaces the standard greeting. The default is "This is an unsecure session".

`xlogin.Login.greetFont`

> The font used to display the greeting.

`xlogin.Login.greetColor`

> The color used to display the greeting.

`xlogin.Login.namePrompt`

> The string displayed to prompt for a user name. *xrdb* strips trailing white space from resource values, so to add spaces at the end of the prompt (usually a nice thing), add spaces escaped with backslashes. The default is "Login:".

`xlogin.Login.passwdPrompt`

> The string displayed to prompt for a password. The default is "Password:".

`xlogin.Login.promptFont`

> The font used to display both prompts.

`xlogin.Login.promptColor`

> The color used to display both prompts.

`xlogin.Login.fail`

> A message which is displayed when the authentication fails. The default is "Login incorrect".

`xlogin.Login.failFont`

> The font used to display the failure message.

`xlogin.Login.failColor`

> The color used to display the failure message.

`xlogin.Login.failTimeout`

> The number of seconds that the fail message is displayed. The default is 30.

`xlogin.Login.translations`

This specifies the translations used for the login widget. See Chapter 11, *Setting Resources*, and Appendix F, *Translation Table Syntax*, for more information on translations. The default translation table for *xdm* is:

```
Ctrl<Key>H:        delete-previous-character() \n\
Ctrl<Key>D:        delete-character() \n\
Ctrl<Key>B:        move-backward-character() \n\
Ctrl<Key>F:        move-forward-character() \n\
Ctrl<Key>A:        move-to-beginning() \n\
Ctrl<Key>E:        move-to-end() \n\
Ctrl<Key>K:        erase-to-end-of-line() \n\
Ctrl<Key>U:        erase-line() \n\
Ctrl<Key>X:        erase-line() \n\
Ctrl<Key>C:        restart-session() \n\
Ctrl<Key>\\:       abort-session() \n\
<Key>BackSpace:    delete-previous-character() \n\
<Key>Delete:       delete-previous-character() \n\
<Key>Return:       finish-field() \n\
<Key>:             insert-char() \
```

The actions that are supported by the widget are:

delete-previous-character
  Erases the character before the cursor.

delete-character
  Erases the character after the cursor.

move-backward-character
  Moves the cursor backward one character.

move-forward-character
  Moves the cursor forward one character.

move-to-beginning
  Moves the cursor to the beginning of the editable text.

move-to-end
  Moves the cursor to the end of the editable text.

erase-to-end-of-line
  Erases all text after the cursor.

erase-line
  Erases the entire text.

finish-field

> If the cursor is in the name field, proceeds to the password field; if the cursor is in the password field, checks the current name/password pair. If the name/password pair is valid, *xdm* starts the session. Otherwise, the failure message is displayed and the user is prompted again.

abort-session

> Terminates and restarts the server.

abort-display

> Terminates the server, disabling it. This is a rash action and is not accessible in the default configuration. It can be used to stop *xdm* when shutting the system down or when using *xdmshell*.

restart-session

> Resets the X server and starts a new session. This can be used when the resources have been changed and you want to test them, or when the screen has been overwritten with system messages.

insert-char

> Inserts the character typed.

set-session-argument

> Specifies a single word argument which is passed to the session at startup. See the sections "The Xsession Program" and "Typical Usage."

allow-all-access

> Disables access control in the server. This can be used when the *.Xauthority* file cannot be created by *xdm*. Be very careful when using this; it might be better to disconnect the machine from the network first.

The Startup Program

The *Xstartup* file is typically a shell script. It is run as root, and so you should be very careful about security. This is the place to put commands that add entries to */etc/utmp*, mount users' home directories from file servers, display the message of the day, or abort the session if logins are not allowed. Various environment variables are set for the use of this script:

DISPLAY	The associated display name.
HOME	The home directory of the user.
USER	The user name.
PATH	The value of DisplayManager.DISPLAY.systemPath.
SHELL	The value of DisplayManager.DISPLAY.systemShell.
XAUTHORITY	May be set to an authority file.

No arguments are passed to the script. *xdm* waits until this script exits before starting the user session. If the exit value of this script is non-zero, *xdm* discontinues the session and starts another authentication cycle.

The Session Program

The *Xsession* file is the script that is run as the user's session. It is run with the permissions of the authorized user and has several environment variables specified:

DISPLAY   The associated display name.

HOME   The home directory of the user.

USER   The user name.

PATH   The value of `DisplayManager.DISPLAY.userPath`.

SHELL   The user's default shell (from *getpwnam*).

XAUTHORITY   May be set to a nonstandard authority file.

At most installations, *Xsession* should look in $HOME for a file *.xsession*, which contains commands that each user would like to use as a session. *Xsession* should also implement a system default session if no user-specified session exists. See "Typical Usage."

An argument may be passed to this program from the authentication widget using the "set-session-argument" action. This can be used to select different styles of session. One very good use of this feature is to allow the user to escape from the ordinary session when it fails. This would allow users to repair their own *.xsession* if it fails, without requiring administrative intervention. The section "Typical Usage" demonstrates this feature.

The Reset Program

Symmetrical with *Xstartup*, the *Xreset* script is run after the user session has terminated. Run as root, it should contain commands that undo the effects of commands in *Xstartup*, removing entries from */etc/utmp* or unmounting directories from file servers. The environment variables that were passed to *Xstartup* are also passed to *Xreset*.

Typical Usage

Actually, *xdm* is designed to operate in such a wide variety of environments that "typical" is probably a misnomer. First, the *xdm* configuration file should be set up. Make a directory (commonly */usr/lib/X11/xdm*) to contain all of the relevant files. Here is a reasonable configuration file for Release 5, which could be named *xdm-config*:

```
DisplayManager.servers:          /usr/lib/X11/xdm/Xservers
DisplayManager.errorLogFile:     /usr/lib/X11/xdm/xdm-errors
DisplayManager*resources:        /usr/lib/X11/xdm/Xresources
DisplayManager*startup:          /usr/lib/X11/xdm/Xstartup
DisplayManager*session:          /usr/lib/X11/xdm/Xsession
DisplayManager.pidFile:          /usr/lib/X11/xdm/xdm-pid
DisplayManager._0.authorize:     true
DisplayManager*authorize:        false
```

As you can see, the *xdm-config* file primarily contains references to other files. Note that some of the resources are specified with an asterisk (*) separating the components. These resources can be made unique for each different display by replacing the "*" with the display name, but normally this is not very useful. See the "Resources" section for a complete discussion.

The first file, */usr/lib/X11/xdm/Xservers*, contains the list of displays to manage that are not using XDMCP. Most workstations have only one display, numbered 0, so the file will look something like this:

```
:0 Local local /usr/bin/X11/X :0
```

This will keep */usr/bin/X11/X* running on this display and manage a continuous cycle of sessions.

The file */usr/lib/X11/xdm/xdm-errors* will contain error messages from *xdm* and anything output to standard error by *Xsetup*, *Xstartup*, *Xsession*, or *Xreset*. When you have trouble getting *xdm* working, check this file to see if *xdm* has any clues to the trouble.

The next configuration entry, */usr/lib/X11/xdm/Xresources*, is loaded onto the display as a resource database using *xrdb*. As the authentication widget reads this database before starting up, it usually contains parameters for that widget:

```
xlogin*login.translations: #override\\e
    <Key>F1: set-session-argument(failsafe) finish-field()\\en\\e
    <Key>Return: set-session-argument() finish-field()
xlogin*borderWidth: 3
#ifdef COLOR
xlogin*greetColor:   CadetBlue
xlogin*failColor:    red
#endif
```

Please note the translations entry; it specifies a few new translations for the widget, which allows users to escape from the default session (and avoid troubles that may occur in it). Note that if #override is not specified, the default translations are removed and replaced by the new value, not a very useful result, as some of the default translations are quite useful (such as *<Key>*: insert-char(), which responds to normal typing!).

The *Xstartup* file used here simply prevents login while the file */etc/nologin* exists. As there is no provision for displaying any messages here (there isn't any core X client which displays files), the user will probably be baffled by this behavior. The following sample *Xstartup* file is not a complete example, simply a demonstration of the available functionality:

```
#!/bin/sh
#
# Xstartup
#
# This program is run as root after the user is verified
#
if [ -f /etc/nologin ]; then
        exit 1
```

```
        fi
        exit 0
```

The most interesting script is *Xsession*. This version recognizes the special "failsafe" mode, specified in the translations in the *Xresources* file above, to provide an escape from the ordinary session:

```
#!/bin/sh

exec > $HOME/.xsession-errors 2>&1

case $# in
1)
        case $1 in
        failsafe)
                exec xterm -geometry 80x24-0-0
                ;;
        esac
esac

startup=$HOME/.xsession
resources=$HOME/.Xresources

if [ -f $startup ]; then
        exec $startup
else
        if [ -f $resources ]; then
                xrdb -load $resources
        fi
        twm &
        exec xterm -geometry 80x24+10+10 -ls
fi
```

Controlling the Server

xdm controls local servers using POSIX signals. SIGHUP is expected to reset the server, closing all client connections and performing other clean up duties. SIGTERM is expected to terminate the server. If these signals do not perform the expected actions, *xdm* will not perform properly.

To control remote servers that are not using XDMCP, *xdm* searches the window hierarchy on the display and uses the protocol request KillClient in an attempt to clean up the terminal for the next session. This may not actually kill all of the clients, as only those which have created windows will be noticed. XDMCP provides a more certain mechanism; when *xdm* closes its initial connection, the session is over and the terminal is required to close all other connections.

Controlling xdm

xdm responds to two signals: SIGHUP and SIGTERM. When sent a SIGHUP, *xdm* rereads the configuration file, the access control file, and the servers file. For the servers file, it notices if entries have been added or removed. If a new entry has been added, *xdm* starts a session on the associated display. Entries that have been removed are disabled immediately, meaning that any session in progress will be terminated without notice, and no new session will be started.

When sent a SIGTERM, *xdm* terminates all sessions in progress and exits. This can be used when shutting down the system.

xdm attempts to mark the various subprocesses for *ps*(1) by editing the command-line argument list in place. Because *xdm* can't allocate additional space for this task, it is useful to start *xdm* with a reasonably long command line (using the full pathname should be enough). Each process that is servicing a display is marked *-display_name*.

Some Other Possibilities

You can also use *xdm* to run a single session at a time, using the 4.3 *init* options or other suitable daemon by specifying the server on the command line:

```
% xdm -server ":0 SUN-3/60CG4 local /usr/bin/X :0"
```

Or, you might have a file server and a collection of X terminals. The configuration for this could look identical to the sample above, except the *Xservers* file might look like:

```
london:0 VISUAL-19 foreign
paris:0 NCD-19 foreign
rome:0 NCR-TOWERVIEW3000 foreign
```

This would direct *xdm* to manage sessions on all three of these terminals. See the section "Controlling xdm" for a description of using signals to enable and disable these terminals in a manner reminiscent of *init*.

Limitations

xdm isn't very good at coexisting with other window systems. To use multiple window systems on the same hardware, you'll probably be more interested in *xinit*.

Files

/usr/lib/X11/xdm/xdm-config
> The default configuration file.

/usr/lib/X11/xdm/Xaccess
> The default access file, listing authorized displays. (Available as of Release 5.)

/usr/lib/X11/xdm/Xservers
> The default server file, listing non-XDMCP servers to manage.

$(HOME)/.Xauthority
> User authorization file where *xdm* stores keys for clients to read.

/usr/lib/X11/xdm/chooser
> The default chooser. (Available as of Release 5.)

/usr/bin/X11/xrdb
> The default resource database loader.

/usr/bin/X11/X
> The default server.

/usr/bin/X11/xterm
> The default session program and failsafe client.

/usr/lib/X11/xdm/A<host>−<suffix>
> The default place for authorization files.

See Also

X, xauth, xinit; Volume Eight, *X Window System Administrator's Guide*; the *Xsecurity* reference page in the MIT source distribution.

Author

Keith Packard, MIT X Consortium.

Name

xdpr – dump an X window directly to the printer.

Syntax

xdpr [*filename*] [*options*]

Description

xdpr runs the commands *xwd*, *xpr*, and *lpr*(1) or *lp*(1) to dump an X window, process it for a particular printer type, and print it out on the printer of your choice. This is the easiest way to get a printout of a window. by default, *xdpr* will print the largest possible representation of the window on the output page.

Options

The options for *xdpr* are the same as those for *xpr*, *xwd*, and *lpr*(1) or *lp*(1). The most commonly-used options are described below; see the reference pages for these commands for detailed descriptions of the many other options available.

-device *printer_device*

> Specifies the device on which the file is to be printed. Currently the following printers are supported:

ln03   Digital LN03.

la100   Digital LA100.

ljet   HP LaserJet series and other monochrome PCL devices, such as ThinkJet, QuietJet, RuggedWriter, HP2560 series, and HP2930 series printers.

pjet   HP PaintJet (color mode).

pjetxl

> HP PaintJet XL Color Graphics Printer (color mode).

pp   IBM PP3812.

ps   PostScript printer.

> As of Release 5, the default is ps (PostScript). (In prior releases, the default printer was the LN03.) -device lw (Apple LaserWriter) is equivalent to -device ps and is provided only for backwards compatibility.

-display [*host*]:*server*[.*screen*]

> Specifies the name of the display to use. *host* is the hostname of the physical display, *server* specifies the server number, and *screen* specifies the screen number. Either or both of the *host* and *screen* elements to the display specification can be omitted. For example:

> % **xdpr** -**display** *your_node*:0.1

> prints a dump of an X window from screen 1 of server 0 on the display named by *your_node*. If the host is omitted, the local display is assumed. If the screen is omitted, screen 0 is assumed; the server and colon (:) are necessary in all cases.

-help Displays the list of options known to *xdpr*.

-P*printer*

Specifies a printer to send the output to. If a printer name is not specified here, *xdpr* (really, *lpr*(1) or *lp*(1)) will send your output to the printer specified by the PRINTER environment variable. Be sure that the type of the printer matches the type specified with the -device option.

xdpr also accepts the following argument:

filename

Specifies an existing file containing a window dump (created by *xwd*) to be printed instead of selecting an X window.

Any other arguments will be passed to the *xwd*, *xpr*, and *lpr*(1) or *lp*(1) commands as appropriate for each.

Environment Variables

PRINTER

Specifies which printer to use by default.

See Also

X, xwd, xpr, xwud, lpr(1), lp(1).

Authors

Paul Boutin, MIT Project Athena;
Michael R. Gretzinger, MIT Project Athena;
Jim Gettys, MIT Project Athena.

Name

xdpyinfo – display information utility for X.

Syntax

```
xdpyinfo [option]
```

Description

xdpyinfo is a utility for displaying information about an X server. It is used to examine the capabilities of a server, the predefined values for various parameters used in communicating between clients and the server, and the different types of screens and visuals that are available. See Chapter 8, *Other Clients*, for more information.

Option

xdpyinfo accepts the following option:

```
-display [host]:server[.screen]
```
> Specifies the display about which *xdpyinfo* should display information. `host` is the hostname of the physical display, `server` specifies the server number, and `screen` specifies the screen number. By default, *xdpyinfo* displays information about all screens on the display. For example,
>
> ```
> % xdpyinfo -display your_node:0.0
> ```
>
> displays information about all screens of server 0 of the display named by `your_node`. If the hostname is omitted, the local display is assumed. If the screen is omitted, screen 0 is assumed. The server and colon (:) are necessary in all cases.

Sample Output

The following example shows the output produced by *xdpyinfo* when connected to a display that supports an 8-plane screen and a 1-plane screen.

```
name of display:     :0.0
version number:      11.0
vendor string:    MIT X Consortium
vendor release number:    4
maximum request size:  16384 longwords (65536 bytes)
motion buffer size:  0
bitmap unit, bit order, padding:    32, MSBFirst, 32
image byte order:    MSBFirst
number of supported pixmap formats:    2
supported pixmap formats:
    depth 1, bits_per_pixel 1, scanline_pad 32
    depth 8, bits_per_pixel 8, scanline_pad 32
keycode range:    minimum 8, maximum 129
focus:  PointerRoot
number of extensions:    4
    SHAPE
    MIT-SHM
```

```
      Multi-Buffering
      MIT-SUNDRY-NONSTANDARD
default screen number:    0
number of screens:    2

screen #0:
   dimensions:      1152x900 pixels (325x254 millimeters)
   resolution:      90x90 dots per inch
   depths (2):    1, 8
   root window id:    0x8006e
   depth of root window:    8 planes
   number of colormaps:    minimum 1, maximum 1
   default colormap:    0x8006b
   default number of colormap cells:    256
   preallocated pixels:    black 1, white 0
   options:    backing-store YES, save-unders YES
   current input event mask:    0xd0801d
      KeyPressMask           ButtonPressMask        ButtonReleaseMask
      EnterWindowMask        ExposureMask           SubstructureRedirectMask
      PropertyChangeMask  ColormapChangeMask
   number of visuals:    6
   default visual id:  0x80065
   visual:
      visual id:    0x80065
      class:    PseudoColor
      depth:    8 planes
      size of colormap:    256 entries
      red, green, blue masks:    0x0, 0x0, 0x0
      significant bits in color specification:    8 bits
   visual:
      visual id:    0x80066
      class:    DirectColor
      depth:    8 planes
      size of colormap:    8 entries
      red, green, blue masks:    0x7, 0x38, 0xc0
      significant bits in color specification:    8 bits
   visual:
      visual id:    0x80067
      class:    GrayScale
      depth:    8 planes
      size of colormap:    256 entries
      red, green, blue masks:    0x0, 0x0, 0x0
      significant bits in color specification:    8 bits
   visual:
      visual id:    0x80068
      class:    StaticGray
      depth:    8 planes
      size of colormap:    256 entries
      red, green, blue masks:    0x0, 0x0, 0x0
```

```
        significant bits in color specification:    8 bits
     visual:
        visual id:    0x80069
        class:    StaticColor
        depth:    8 planes
        size of colormap:    256 entries
        red, green, blue masks:    0x7, 0x38, 0xc0
        significant bits in color specification:    8 bits
     visual:
        visual id:    0x8006a
        class:    TrueColor
        depth:    8 planes
        size of colormap:    8 entries
        red, green, blue masks:    0x7, 0x38, 0xc0
        significant bits in color specification:    8 bits
     number of mono multibuffer types:    6
        visual id, max buffers, depth:    0x80065, 0, 8
        visual id, max buffers, depth:    0x80066, 0, 8
        visual id, max buffers, depth:    0x80067, 0, 8
        visual id, max buffers, depth:    0x80068, 0, 8
        visual id, max buffers, depth:    0x80069, 0, 8
        visual id, max buffers, depth:    0x8006a, 0, 8
     number of stereo multibuffer types:    0

  screen #1:
     dimensions:    1152x900 pixels (325x254 millimeters)
     resolution:    90x90 dots per inch
     depths (1):    1
     root window id:    0x80070
     depth of root window:    1 plane
     number of colormaps:    minimum 1, maximum 1
     default colormap:    0x8006c
     default number of colormap cells:    2
     preallocated pixels:    black 1, white 0
     options:    backing-store YES, save-unders YES
     current input event mask:    0xd0801d
        KeyPressMask          ButtonPressMask        ButtonReleaseMask
        EnterWindowMask       ExposureMask           SubstructureRedirectMask
        PropertyChangeMask    ColormapChangeMask
     number of visuals:    1
     default visual id:    0x80064
     visual:
        visual id:    0x80064
        class:    StaticGray
        depth:    1 plane
        size of colormap:    2 entries
        red, green, blue masks:    0x0, 0x0, 0x0
        significant bits in color specification:    1 bits
     number of mono multibuffer types:    1
```

```
       visual id, max buffers, depth:    0x80064, 0, 1
     number of stereo multibuffer types:    0
```

See Also

X, xwininfo, xprop, xrdb; Chapter 8, *Other Clients*.

Author

Jim Fulton, MIT X Consortium.

xedit

Name

xedit – simple text editor for X.

Syntax

xedit [*options*] [*filename*]

Description

xedit provides a window consisting of the following four areas:

Commands Section

A set of commands that allows you to exit *xedit*, save the file, or load a new file into the edit window.

Message Window

Displays *xedit* messages. In addition, this window can be used as a scratch pad.

Filename Display

Displays the name of the file currently being edited, and whether this file is *Read–Write* or *Read Only*.

Edit Window

Displays the text of the file that you are editing or creating.

Chapter 8, *Other Clients*, describes how to use the *xedit* client.

Command Buttons

Quit   Quits the current editing session. If any changes have not been saved, *xedit* displays a warning message, allowing the user to save the file.

Save   If file backups are enabled (see "Resources"), *xedit* stores a copy of the original, unedited file in <prefix>*filename*<suffix>, then overwrites the *filename* with the contents of the edit window. The *filename* is retrieved from the Text widget directly to the right of the Load button.

Load   Loads the file named in the Text widget immediately to the right of this button and displays it in the Edit Window. If the currently displayed file has been modified, a warning message will ask the user to save the changes or to press Load again.

Editing

The Athena Text widget is used for the three sections of this application that allow text input, namely the Message Window, the Edit Window, and the window to the right of the command buttons, in which a filename can be entered.

The characters typed will go to the Text widget that the pointer is currently over. If the pointer is not over a Text widget, then the keypresses will have no effect on the application. This is also true for the special key sequences that pop-up dialog widgets; so, for example, typing CTRL-s in the filename widget (next to the command buttons) will enable searching in that widget, not the Edit Window (edit widget).

Both the Message Window and the Edit Window will create a scrollbar if the text to display is too large to fit in that window. Horizontal scrolling is not allowed by default, but can be turned on through the Text widget's resources. See Appendix G, *Widget Resources*, for more information.

The following list summarizes the editing commands recognized by *xedit* (i.e., by the Text widget).

Control-a	Move to the beginning of the current line.
Control-b	Move backward one character.
Control-d	Delete the next character.
Control-e	Move to the end of the current line.
Control-f	Move forward one character.
Control-h or Backspace	Delete the previous character.
Control-j, Control-m, Return, or LineFeed	New line.
Control-k	Kill the rest of this line. (Does not kill the carriage return at the end of the line. To do so, use Control-k twice. However, be aware that the second kill overwrites the text line in the kill buffer.)
Control-l	Redraw the window. (Also scrolls text so that cursor is positioned in the middle of the window.)
Control-n	Move down to the next line.
Control-o	Divide this line into two lines at this point and move the cursor back up.
Control-p	Move up to the previous line.
Control-r	Search and replace backward.
Control-s	Search and replace forward.
Control-t	Transpose characters. (Swap the characters immediately before and after the cursor.)
Control-u	Perform next command four times. For example, the sequence Control-u, Control-n moves the cursor down four lines.
Control-v	Move down to the next screenful of text.
Control-w	Kill the selected text.

Control-y	Insert the last killed text. (If the last killed text is a carriage return—see Control-k above—a blank line is inserted.)
Control-z	Scroll up the text one line.
Meta-<	Move to the beginning of the file.
Meta->	Move to the end of the file.
Meta-[	Move backward one paragraph.
Meta-]	Move forward one paragraph.
Meta-b	Move backward one word.
Meta-d	Delete the next word.
Meta-D	Kill the next word.
Meta-f	Move forward one word.
Meta-h, Meta-Backspace, or Meta-Delete	Delete the previous word.
Meta-H, Meta-Shift-Backspace, or Meta-Shift-Delete	Kill the previous word.
Meta-i	Insert a file. A dialog box will appear in which you can type the desired filename.
Meta-k	Kill to the end of the paragraph.
Meta-q	Join lines to form a paragraph.
Meta-v	Move up to the previous screenful of text.
Meta-y	Insert the last selected text here. This command is the equivalent of clicking the second pointer button. See Chapter 5, *The xterm Terminal Emulator*, for more information about text selections.
Meta-z	Scroll down the text one line.
Delete	Delete the previous character.

Note that a translation in the application defaults file overrides the translation for the Return key for the text window in which a filename can be entered (next to the command buttons); in this window only, instead of starting a new line, Return moves the editing cursor to the end of the current line.

The Text widget fully supports the X selection and cut buffer mechanisms (described in Chapter 5, *The xterm Terminal Emulator*). Thus, you can cut and paste text in any of the sections of the *xedit* window that allow text input. You can also cut and paste text between *xedit* and any other application (such as *xterm*) that supports text selections. See Chapter 5 for instructions on cutting and pasting text.

Options

xedit accepts all of the standard X Toolkit command-line options, which are listed on the *X* reference page. In addition, *xedit* accepts the following argument:

`filename`

> Specifies the file that is to be loaded during start up. This is the file that will be edited. If a file is not specified, *xedit* lets you load a file or create a new file after it has started up.

Widget Hierarchy

In order to specify resources, it is useful to know the hierarchy of the widgets which compose *xedit*. In the notation below, indentation indicates hierarchical structure. The widget class name is given first, followed by the widget instance name.

```
Xedit   xedit
        Paned   paned
                Paned   buttons
                        Command  quit
                        Command  save
                        Command  load
                        Text     filename
                Label   bc_label
                Text    messageWindow

                Label   labelWindow
                Text    editWindow
```

See Appendix G, *Widget Resources* for a list of resources that can be set for the Athena widgets. (Note that the Text widget recognizes actions that control cursor movement, editing, text selection, etc.)

Resources

The available application resources are:

`enableBackups` (class `EnableBackups`)

> Specifies that when edits made to an existing file are saved, *xedit* is to copy the original version of that file to <prefix>*filename*<suffix> before it saves the changes. The default value for this resource is "off," stating that no backups should be created.

`backupNamePrefix` (class `BackupNamePrefix`)

> Specifies a string that is to be prepended to the backup filename. The default is that no string shall be prepended.

`backupNameSuffix` (class `BackupNameSuffix`)

> Specifies a string that is to be appended to the backup filename. The default is to append the string ".BAK".

Actions

Many standard keyboard editing facilities are supported by the event bindings. You can map actions to key and pointer button events using the translation mechanism described in Chapter 11, *Setting Resources*. For the Text widget, the following actions are supported:

Cursor Movement	Action
forward-character	delete-next-character
backward-character	delete-previous-character
forward-word	delete-next-word
backward-word	delete-previous-word
forward-paragraph	delete-selection
backward-paragraph	backward-paragraph
beginning-of-line	selection
end-of-line	insert-selection
next-line	select-word
previous-line	select-all
next-page	select-start
previous-page	select-adjust
beginning-of-file	select-end
end-of-file	extend-start
scroll-one-line-up	extend-adjust
scroll-one-line-down	extend-end
new Line	miscellaneous
newline-and-indent	redraw-display
newline-and-backup	insert-file
newline	insert-char
kill	display-caret
kill-word	focus-in
backward-kill-word	focus-out
kill-selection	search
kill-to-end-of-line	multiply
kill-paragraph	form-paragraph
kill-to-end-of-paragraph	transpose-characters
no movement	no-op

- A page corresponds to the size of the Text window. For example, if the Text window is 50 lines in length, scrolling forward one page is the same as scrolling forward 50 lines.

- The `delete` action deletes a text item. The `kill` action deletes a text item and puts the item in the kill buffer (X cut buffer 1).

- The `insert-selection` action retrieves the value of a specified X selection or cut buffer, with fall-back to alternative selections or cut buffers.

Cursor Movement Actions

```
forward-character()
backward-character()
```
> These actions move the insert point forward or backward one character in the buffer. If the insert point is at the end (or beginning) of a line, this action moves the insert point to the next (or previous) line.

```
forward-word()
backward-word()
```
> These actions move the insert point to the next or previous word boundary. A word boundary is defined as a space, a tab, or a carriage return.

```
forward-paragraph()
backward-paragraph()
```
> These actions move the insert point to the next or previous paragraph boundary. A paragraph boundary is defined as two carriage returns in a row with only spaces or tabs between them.

```
beginning-of-line()
end-of-line()
```
> These actions move to the beginning or end of the current line. If the insert point is already at the end or beginning of the line, no action is taken.

```
next-line()
previous-line()
```
> These actions move the insert point up or down one line. If the insert point is currently n characters from the beginning of the line then it will be n characters from the beginning of the next or previous line. If n is past the end of the line, the insert point is placed at the end of the line.

```
next-page()
previous-page()
```
> These actions move the insert point up or down one page in the file. One page is defined as the current height of the text widget. These actions always place the insert point at the first character of the top line.

```
beginning-of-file()
end-of-file()
```
> These actions place the insert point at the beginning or end of the current text buffer. The text widget is then scrolled the minimum amount necessary to make the new insert point location visible.

```
scroll-one-line-up()
scroll-one-line-down()
```
> These actions scroll the current text field up or down by one line. They do not move the insert point. Other than the scrollbars, this is the only way that the insert point may be moved off the visible text area. The widget will be scrolled so that the insert point is back on the screen as soon as some other action is executed.

Delete Actions
```
delete-next-character()
delete-previous-character()
```
> These actions remove the character immediately after or before the insert point. If a carriage return is removed, the next line is appended to the end of the current line.

```
delete-next-word()
delete-previous-word()
```
> These actions remove all characters between the insert point location and the next word boundary. A word boundary is defined as a space, a tab, or a carriage return.

```
delete-selection()
```
> This action removes all characters in the current selection. The selection can be set with the selection actions.

Selection Actions
```
select-word()
```
> This action selects the word in which the insert point is currently located. If the insert point is between words, it will select the previous word.

```
select-all()
```
> This action selects the entire text buffer.

```
select-start()
```
> This action sets the insert point to the current pointer location, where a selection then begins. If many of these selection actions occur quickly in succession then the selection count mechanism will be invoked.

```
select-adjust()
```
> This action allows a selection started with the `select-start` action to be modified, as described above.

```
select-end(name[,name, . . .])
```
> This action ends a text selection that began with the `select-start` action, and asserts ownership of the selection or selections specified. A *name* can be a selection (e.g., PRIMARY) or a cut buffer (e.g., CUT_BUFFER0). Note that case is important. If no *names* are specified, PRIMARY is asserted.

```
extend-start()
```
> This action finds the nearest end of the current selection, and moves it to the current pointer location.

`extend-adjust( )`

> This action allows a selection started with an `extend-start` action to be modified.

`extend-end(`*name*`[,`*name*`, . . . ])`

> This action ends a text selection that began with the `extend-start` action, and asserts ownership of the selection or selections specified. A *name* can be a selection (e.g., PRIMARY) or a cut buffer (e.g., CUT_BUFFER0). Note that case is important. If no *name* is given, PRIMARY is asserted.

`insert-selection(`*name*`[,`*name*`, . . . ])`

> This action retrieves the value of the first (left-most) named selection that exists or the cut buffer that is not empty. This action then inserts it into the Text widget at the current insert point location. A *name* can be a selection (e.g., PRIMARY) or a cut buffer (e.g., CUT_BUFFER0). Note that case is important.

newline Actions

`newline-and-indent( )`

> This action inserts a newline into the text and adds spaces to that line to indent it to match the previous line. (Note: this action still has a few bugs.)

`newline-and-backup( )`

> This action inserts a newline into the text *after* the insert point.

`newline( )`

> This action inserts a newline into the text *before* the insert point.

Kill Actions

`kill-word( )`
`backward-kill-word( )`

> These actions act exactly like the `delete-next-word` and `delete-previous-word` actions, but they store the word that was killed into the kill buffer (CUT_BUFFER_1).

`kill-selection( )`

> This action deletes the current selection and stores the deleted text into the kill buffer (CUT_BUFFER_1).

`kill-to-end-of-line( )`

> This action deletes the entire line to the right of the insert point, and stores the deleted text into the kill buffer (CUT_BUFFER_1).

`kill-paragraph( )`

> This action deletes the current paragraph. If the insert point is between paragraphs, it deletes the paragraph above the insert point, and stores the deleted text into the kill buffer (CUT_BUFFER_1).

`kill-to-end-of-paragraph( )`

> This action deletes everything between the current insert point and the next paragraph boundary, and puts the deleted text into the kill buffer (CUT_BUFFER_1).

Miscellaneous Actions

redraw-display()

> This action recomputes the location of all the text lines on the display, scrolls the text to vertically center the line containing the insert point on the screen, clears the entire screen, and then redisplays it.

insert-file([*filename*])

> This action activates the insert file pop-up. The *filename* option specifies the default filename to put in the filename buffer of the pop-up. If no *filename* is specified the buffer is empty at startup.

insert-char()

> This action may be attached only to a key event. It calls XLookupString to translate the event into a (rebindable) Latin-1 character (sequence) and inserts that sequence into the text at the insert point position.

insert-string(*string*[,*string*, . . .])

> This action inserts each *string* into the text at the insert point location. Any *string* beginning with the characters "0x" and containing only valid hexadecimal digits in the remainder is interpreted as a hexadecimal constant and the corresponding single character is inserted instead.

display-caret(*state,when*)

> This action allows the insert point to be turned on and off. The *state* argument specifies the desired state of the insert point. This value may be any of the string values accepted for Boolean resources (e.g., on, True, off, False, etc.). If no arguments are specified, the default value is True. The *when* argument specifies, for EnterNotify or LeaveNotify events, whether or not the focus field in the event is to be examined. If the second argument is not specified, or specified as something other than always, then if the action is bound to an EnterNotify or Leave-Notify event, the action will be taken only if the focus field is True. An augmented binding that might be useful is:

```
    *Text.Translations: #override \
        <FocusIn>:      display-caret(on) \n\
        <FocusOut>:     display-caret(off)
```

focus-in()
focus-out()

> These actions do not currently do anything.

search(*direction*, [*string*])

> This action activates the search popup. The *direction* must be specified as either forward or backward. The string is optional and is used as an initial value for the "Search for:" string.

`multiply(`*`value`*`)`

> The multiply action allows the user to multiply the effects of many of the text actions. Thus the following action sequence:

> `multiply(10) delete-next-word()`

> will delete 10 words. It does not matter whether these actions take place in one event or many events. Using the default translations the key sequence Control-u, Control-d will delete 4 characters. Multiply actions can be chained; thus,

> `multiply(5) multiply(5)`

> is the same as:

> `multiply(25)`

> If the string `reset` is passed to the multiply action, the effects of all previous multiplies are removed and a beep is sent to the display.

`form-paragraph()`

> This action removes all the carriage returns from the current paragraph and reinserts them so that each line is as long as possible, while still fitting on the current screen. Lines are broken at word boundaries if at all possible. This action currently works only on Text widgets that use ASCII text.

`transpose-characters()`

> This action will switch the positions of the character to the left of the insert point and the character to the right of the insert point. The insert point will then be advanced one character.

`no-op([`*`action`*`])`

> The no-op action makes no change to the text widget, and is used mainly to override translations. This action takes one optional argument. If this argument is `RingBell` then a beep is sent to the display.

Files

/usr/lib/X11/app-defaults/Xedit—Specifies required resources.

Restrictions

There is no undo function.

See Also

X, xrdb; Chapter 8, *Other Clients*; Appendix G, *Widget Resources*.

Copyright

Copyright © 1988, Digital Equipment Corporation. Copyright © 1989, Massachusetts Institute of Technology.

Author

Chris D. Peterson, MIT X Consortium.

xev

Name

xev – print contents of X events.

Syntax

xev [*options*]

Description

xev creates a window and then asks the X server to send it notices, called *events*, whenever anything happens to the window (such as being moved, resized, typed in, clicked in, etc.). It is useful for seeing what causes events to occur and to display the information that they contain.

xev can be found in the *demos* directory in the X source tree. We feel it is sufficiently useful that we continue to document it here. See Chapter 14, *Setup Clients*, for instructions on using *xev* to assist in mapping keys.

Options

xev accepts the following options:

-bs *backing_store*

Specifies what kind of backing store to give the window (either NotUseful, When-Mapped, Always). The default is NotUseful.

-bw *pixels*

Specifies the width of the window border in pixels.

-display [*host*]:*server*[.*screen*]

Allows you to specify the host, server, and screen to connect to. *host* is the hostname of the physical display, *server* specifies the server number, and *screen* specifies the screen number. For example,

xev -display *your_node*:0.1

specifies screen 1 of server 0 on the display named by *your_node*. Either or both the *host* and *screen* elements can be omitted. If *host* is omitted, the local display is assumed. If *screen* is omitted, screen 0 is assumed (and the period is unnecessary). The colon and *server* are necessary in all cases.

-geometry *geometry*

The *xev* window is created with the specified size and location determined by the supplied geometry specification. The **-geometry** option can be (and often is) abbreviated to **-g**, unless there is a conflicting option that begins with "g". The argument to the geometry option (*geometry*) is referred to as a "standard geometry string," and has the form *width*x*height*±*xoff*±*yoff*.

-id *window_ID*

Specifies that the window with the given ID should be mónitored, instead of creating a new window.

`-name` *string*
      Specifies the name to assign to the created window.

`-rv`   Specifies that the window should be in reverse video.

`-s`   Specifies that save unders should be enabled on the window.

See Also

X, xmodmap, xwininfo, xdpyinfo; Chapter 14, *Setup Clients*; Volume Zero, *X Protocol Reference Manual*; Volume One, *Xlib Programming Manual*.

Author

Jim Fulton, MIT X Consortium.

xfd

Name

xfd – Display all the characters in an X font.

Syntax

xfd [*options*] **-fn** *fontname*

Description

xfd creates a window containing the name of the font being displayed, a row of command buttons, several lines of text for displaying character metrics, and a grid containing one glyph per cell. The characters are shown in increasing order from left to right, top to bottom. The first character displayed at the top left will be character number 0 unless the -start option has been supplied, in which case the character with the number given in the -start option will be used.

The characters are displayed in a grid of boxes, each large enough to hold any single character in the font. Each character glyph is drawn using the PolyText16 request (used by the Xlib routine XDrawString16). If the -box option is given, a rectangle will be drawn around each character, showing where an ImageText16 request (used by the Xlib routine XDraw-ImageString16) would cause background color to be displayed.

The origin of each glyph is normally set so that the character is drawn in the upper-left corner of the grid cell. However, if a glyph has a negative left bearing or an unusually large ascent, descent, or right bearing (as is the case with the cursor font), some characters may not appear in their own grid cells. The -center option may be used to force all glyphs to be centered in their respective cells.

All the characters in the font may not fit in the window at once. To see the next page of glyphs, press the Next button at the top of the window. To see the previous page, press Prev. To exit *xfd*, press Quit.

Individual character metrics (index, width, bearings, ascent, and descent) can be displayed at the top of the window by pressing on the desired character.

The font name displayed at the top of the window is the full name of the font, as determined by the server. See *xlsfonts* for ways to generate lists of fonts, as well as more detailed summaries of their metrics and properties.

See Chapter 6, *Font Specification*, for instructions on using *xfd*.

Options

xfd accepts all of the standard X Toolkit command-line options, which are listed on the *X* reference page. In addition, *xfd* accepts the following application-specific options. (Note that the option -fn *font* is required.)

-bc *color*
> Specifies the color to be used if ImageText boxes are drawn.

-box   Displays a box outlining the area that would be filled with background color by an ImageText request.

`-center`
> Indicates that each glyph should be centered in its grid square.

`-fn` *font*
> Specifies the font to be displayed.

`-start` *char_num*
> Specifies that character number *char_num* should be the first character displayed. (It appears in the upper left-hand corner of the grid.) This option is used to view characters at arbitrary locations in the font. The default is 0.

Resources

xfd accepts all of the Core resource names and classes as well as the following:

`boxChars` (class `BoxChars`)
> If True, displays a a box outlining the area that would be filled with background color by an `ImageText` request.

`boxColor` (class `Foreground`)
> Specifies that the given color is used for the `ImageText` boxes.

`cellColumns` (class `CellColumns`)
> Specifies number of columns in grid.

`cellRows` (class `CellRows`)
> Specifies number of rows in grid.

`centerChars` (class `CenterChars`)
> If True, each glyph is centered in its grid square.

`foreground` (class `Foreground`)
> Specifies the color to use for text and graphics within the window.

`metricsFormat` (class `MetricsFormat`)
> Defines the format of the text line displaying the metrics of a selected character.

`nocharFormat` (class `NocharFormat`)
> Defines the format of the text line displaying that no such character exists.

`rangeFormat` (class `RangeFormat`)
> Defines the format of the text line displaying the range of characters in the xfd window.

`startFormat` (class `StartFormat`)
> Defines the format of the text line displaying information about the starting character.

`selectFormat` (class `SelectFormat`)
> Defines the format of the text line displaying a selected character.

startChar (class StartChar)

      Specifies that the given character number should be the first character displayed. (It appears in the upper left-hand corner of the grid.) This resource is used to view characters at arbitrary locations in the font. The default is 0.

Bugs

xfd should skip over pages full of non-existent characters.

See Also

X, xfontsel, xlsfonts, xrdb; Chapter 6, *Font Specification*.

Author

Jim Fulton, MIT X Consortium; previous program of the same name by Mark Lillibridge, MIT Project Athena.

xfontsel

Name

xfontsel – point-and-click interface for selecting display font names.

Syntax

`xfontsel` [`options`]

Description

xfontsel provides a simple way to display the fonts known to your X server, examine samples of each, and retrieve the X Logical Font Description (XLFD) full name for a font. (See Chapter 6, *Font Specification*, for instructions on using *xfontsel*.)

If -`pattern` is not specified, all fonts with XLFD 14-part names will be selectable. To work with only a subset of the fonts, specify -`pattern` followed by a partially or fully qualified font name. For example,

`% xfontsel -pattern '*medium*' &`

will select the subset of fonts that contain the string `medium` somewhere in their font name. Be careful about escaping wildcard characters in your shell.

If -`print` is specified on the command line, the selected font specifier will be written to standard output when the quit button is activated. Regardless of whether or not -`print` was specified, the font specifier may be made the PRIMARY text selection by activating the select button.

xfontsel handles scalable fonts as of Release 5. See -`noscaled` under "Options" later in this reference page and Chapter 6, *Font Specification*, for more information.

Clicking any pointer button in one of the XLFD field names will pop up a menu of the currently known possibilities for that field. If previous choices of other fields were made, only values for fonts which matched the previously selected fields will be selectable; to make other values selectable, you must deselect some other field(s) by choosing the "*" entry in that field. Unselectable values may be omitted from the menu entirely as a configuration option; see the `showUnselectable` resource, below. Whenever any change is made to a field value, *xfontsel* will assert ownership of the PRIMARY_FONT selection. Other applications (such as *xterm*) may then retrieve the selected font specification.

Scalable fonts come back from the server with zero for the pixel size, point size, and average width fields. Selecting a font name with a zero in these positions results in an implementation-dependent size. Any pixel or point size can be selected to scale the font to a particular size. Any average width can be selected to anamorphically scale the font (although you may find this challenging given the size of the average width menu).

Clicking the left pointer button in the select widget will cause the currently selected font name to become the PRIMARY text selection as well as the PRIMARY_FONT selection. Then you can paste the string into other applications. The select button remains highlighted to remind you of this fact, and dehighlights when some other application takes the PRIMARY selection away. The select widget is a toggle; pressing it when it is highlighted will cause *xfontsel* to release the selection ownership and dehighlight the widget. Activating the **select** widget twice is the only way to cause *xfontsel* to release the PRIMARY_FONT selection.

Options

xfontsel accepts all of the standard X Toolkit command-line options, which are listed on the *X* reference page. In addition, *xfontsel* accepts the following application-specific options:

`-noscaled`

> Disables the ability to select scaled fonts at arbitrary pixel or point sizes. This makes it clear which bitmap sizes are advertised by the server, and can avoid an accidental and sometimes prolonged wait for a font to be scaled. (Available as of Release 5.)

`-pattern` *fontname*

> Specifies a subset of the available fonts, those with names that contain *fontname*, which can be a partial or full name.

`-print`

> Specifies that the selected font will be written to standard output when the **quit** button is activated.

`-sample` *text*

> Specifies the sample *text* to be used to display the selected font if the font is linearly indexed, overriding the default (the alphabetic characters; and the digits 0 through 9, if the character set includes them).

`-sample16` *text*

> Specifies the sample text to be used to display the selected font if the font is matrix encoded, overriding the default (see `-sample`). (Available as of Release 5.)

Resources

The application class is `XFontSel`. Most of the user interface is configured in the application defaults file; if this file is missing, a warning message will be printed to standard output and the resulting window will be nearly incomprehensible.

Most of the significant parts of the widget hierarchy are documented in the app-defaults file (normally */usr/lib/X11/app-defaults/XFontSel*).

Application-specific resources:

`cursor` (class `Cursor`)

> Specifies the cursor for the application window.

`pattern` (class `Pattern`)

> Specifies the font name pattern for selecting a subset of available fonts. Equivalent to the `-pattern` option. Most useful patterns will contain at least one field delimiter, for example, `*-m-*` for monospaced fonts.

pixelSizeList (class PixelSizeList)
> Specifies a list of pixel sizes to add to the pixel size menu, so that scalable fonts can be selected at those pixel sizes. The default list contains 7, 30, 40, 50, and 60. (Available as of Release 5.)

pointSizeList (class PointSizeList)
> Specifies a list of point sizes (in units of tenths of points) to add to the point size menu, so that scalable fonts can be selected at those point sizes. The default list contains 250, 300, 350, and 400. (Available as of Release 5.)

printOnQuit (class PrintOnQuit)
> If True, the currently selected font name is printed to standard output when the quit button is activated. Equivalent to the -print option.

sampleText (class Text)
> Specifies the sample one-byte text to use for linearly indexed fonts. Each glyph index is a single byte, with a newline character separating lines. (Available as of Release 5.)

sampleText16 (class Text16)
> Specifies the sample two-byte text to use for matrix-encoded fonts. Each glyph index is two bytes, with a one-byte newline character separating lines. (Available as of Release 5.)

scaledFonts (class ScaledFonts)
> The default value of True enables selection of arbitrary pixel and point sizes for scalable fonts. (Available as of Release 5.)

Widget-specific resources:

showUnselectable (class ShowUnselectable)
> For each field menu, specifies whether or not to show values that are not currently selectable, based upon previous field selections. If shown, the unselectable values are clearly identified as such and do not highlight when the pointer is moved down the menu.
>
> fieldN.menu.options.showUnselectable is the full instance name of this resource, while MenuButton.SimpleMenu.Options.ShowUnselectable is the full class name. In both cases, N is replaced with the field number (starting with the leftmost field numbered 0). The default is True for all but field 11 (average width of characters in font) and False for field 11. If you never want to see unselectable entries, *menu.options.showUnselectable: False is a reasonable thing to specify in a resource file.

Files

/usr/lib/X11/app-defaults/XFontSel
        Specifies default resources.

See Also

xfd, xrdb; Chapter 6, *Font Specification*.

Bugs

Sufficiently ambiguous patterns can be misinterpreted and can lead to an initial selection string
which may not correspond to what the user intended and which may cause the initial sample
text output to fail to match the proffered string. Selecting any new field value will correct the
sample output, though possibly resulting in no matching font.

The average width menu may be too long to be useful. (It may extend beyond the bounds of
the screen.)

xfontsel should be able to return a font for the PRIMARY selection, not just a string.

Any change in a field value will cause *xfontsel* to assert ownership of the PRIMARY_FONT
selection. Perhaps this should be parameterized.

When running on a slow machine, it is possible for the user to request a field menu before the
font names have been completely parsed. An error message indicating a missing menu is
printed to standard error, but otherwise nothing happens.

Author

Ralph R. Swick, Digital Equipment Corporation/MIT Project Athena.

Name

xhost – server access control program for X.

Syntax

xhost [*options*]

Description

The *xhost* program is used to add and delete hostnames (or user names) to and from the list allowed to make connections to the X server. In the case of hosts, this provides a rudimentary form of privacy control and security. It is only sufficient for a workstation (single user) environment, although it does limit the worst abuses. Environments that require more sophisticated measures should implement the user-based mechanism, or use the hooks in the protocol for passing authentication data to the server. (See Appendix A, *Managing Your Environment*, for an introduction to server access control and Volume Eight, *X Window System Administrator's Guide*, for a more complete discussion.)

The server initially allows network connections only from programs running on the same machine or from machines listed in the file */etc/Xn.hosts* (where *n* is the display number of the server). The *xhost* program is usually run either from a startup file or interactively to give access to other users.

Hostnames that are followed by two colons (::) are used in checking DECnet connections; all other hostnames are used for TCP/IP connections.

User names contain an at sign (@). When Secure RPC is being used, the network independent netname (e.g., "unix.*uid@domainname*") can be specified, or a local user can be specified with just the username and a trailing at sign (e.g., "joe@").

If no command-line options are given, a message indicating whether or not access control is currently enabled is printed on the standard output followed by the list of those allowed to connect. This is the only option that can be used from machines other than the controlling host.

Options

xhost accepts the command-line options described below. For security, the options that effect access control may only be run from the "controlling host." For workstations, this is the same machine as the server. For X terminals, it is the login host.

[+]*name*
> The given *name* (the plus sign is optional) is added to the list allowed to connect to the X server. The *name* can be a hostname or a user name.

−*name* The given *name* is removed from the list allowed to connect to the server. The *name* can be a hostname or a user name. Existing connections are not broken, but new connection attempts will be denied. Note that the current machine is allowed to be removed; however, further connections (including attempts to add it back) will not be permitted. Resetting the server (thereby breaking all connections) is the only way to allow local connections again.

+   Access is granted to everyone, even if they aren't on the list (i.e., access control is turned off).

−   Access is restricted to only those on the list (i.e., access control is turned on).

Diagnostics

For each name added to the access control list, a line of the form "*name* being added to access control list" is printed. For each name removed from the access control list, a line of the form "*name* being removed from access control list" is printed.

Files

*/etc/X**n**.hosts*

Bugs

You can't specify a display on the command line because -display indicates that you want to remove the machine named *display* from the access list.

This is not really a bug, but the X server stores network addresses, not hostnames. If somehow you change a host's network address while the server is still running, *xhost* must be used to add the new address and/or remove the old address.

See Also

X, Xserver, xauth, xdm; the section "Using –display" in Chapter 3, *Working in the X Environment*; Appendix A, *Managing Your Environment*; Volume Eight, *X Window System Administrator's Guide*.

Authors

Bob Scheifler, MIT Laboratory for Computer Science;
Jim Gettys, MIT Project Athena (DEC).

xinit

Name

xinit – X Window System initializer.

Syntax

xinit [[*client*] *options*] [-- [*server_program*] [*display*] *options*]

Description

The *xinit* program is used to start the X Window System server program and a first client program (usually a terminal emulator) on systems that cannot start X directly from */etc/init* or in environments that use multiple window systems. When this first client exits, *xinit* will kill the X server program and then terminate.

If no specific client program is given on the command line, *xinit* will look in the user's home directory for a file called *.xinitrc* to run as a shell script to start up other client programs. If no such file exists, *xinit* will use the following *xterm* command line as a default:

```
xterm -geometry +1+1 -n login -display :0
```

If no specific server program is given on the command line, *xinit* will look in the user's home directory for a file called *.xserverrc* to run as a shell script to start up the server. If no such file exists, *xinit* will use the following as a default server specification:

```
X :0
```

Note that this assumes that there is a server program called *X* in the current search path. However, servers are usually named X*displaytype*, where *displaytype* is the type of graphics display that is driven by the server (for example, *Xsun*). The site administrator should therefore make a link to the appropriate type of server on the machine (see Chapter 2, *Getting Started*, and Volume Eight, *X Window System Administrator's Guide*), or create a shell script that runs *xinit* with the appropriate server.

Note that programs run by *.xinitrc* should be run in the background if they do not exit right away, so that they don't prevent other programs from starting up. However, the last long-lived program started (usually a window manager or terminal emulator) should be left in the foreground so that the script won't exit (which indicates that the user is done and that *xinit* should exit).

An alternate client and/or server may also be specified on the command line. The desired client program and its arguments should be given as the first command-line arguments to *xinit*. To specify a particular server program, append a double dash (--) to the *xinit* command line (after any client and arguments) followed by the desired server command.

Both the client program name and the server program name must begin with a slash (/) or a period (.); otherwise, they are treated as arguments to be appended to their respective startup lines. This makes it possible to add arguments (for example, foreground and background colors) without having to retype the whole command line.

If an explicit server name is not given and the first argument following the double dash (--) is a colon followed by a digit, *xinit* will use that number as the display number instead of zero. All remaining arguments are appended to the server command line.

Appendix A, *Managing Your Environment*, provides guidelines for writing a startup shell script. (See also "Examples" below.) See Volume Eight, *X Window System Administrator's Guide*, for instructions on running *xinit*.

Arguments

xinit accepts the following command-line arguments:

client
>Specifies the client to be started with the server.

display
>Specifies the number of the display on which to initialize the X Window System.

server_program
>Specifies the server program to run.

Examples

xinit   Will start up a server named *X* and run the user's *.xinitrc*, if it exists, or else start an *xterm*.

xinit -- /usr/bin/X11/Xqdss :1
>Is how one could start a specific type of server on an alternate display.

xinit -geometry 80x65+10+10 -fn 8x13 -j -fg white -bg navy
>Will start up a server named *X* and will append the given arguments to the default *xterm* command. It will ignore *.xinitrc*.

xinit -e widgets -- ./Xsun -1 -c
>Will use the command ./Xsun -1 -c to start the server and will append the arguments -e widgets to the default *xterm* command.

xinit rsh fasthost cpupig -display workstation:1 -- :1 -a 2 -t 5
>Will start a server named *X* on display 1 with the arguments -a 2 -t 5. It will then start a remote shell on the machine fasthost in which it will run the command cpupig, telling it to display back on the local workstation. Below is a sample *.xinitrc* that starts a clock, several terminals, and leaves an iconified *xterm* running as the "last" application. If the user kills this *xterm*, X shuts down.

```
#!/bin/sh
xrdb -load $HOME/.Xresources
xsetroot -solid gray &
mwm &
xclock -g 50x50-0+0 &
xterm -g 80x24+0+0 &
xterm -g 80x24+0+0 &
xterm -iconic
```

Sites that want to create a common startup environment could simply create a default
.xinitrc that references a site-wide startup file:

```
#!/bin/sh
. /usr/local/lib/site.xinitrc
```

Another approach is to write a script that starts *xinit* with a specific shell script. Such
scripts are usually named *x11*, *xstart*, or *startx* and are a convenient way to provide a
simple interface for novice users:

```
#!/bin/sh
xinit /usr/local/bin/site.xinitrc -- /usr/bin/X11/Xhp :1
```

Environment Variables

XINITRC

Specifies an init file containing shell commands to start up the initial windows. By
default, *.xinitrc* in the home directory will be used.

Files

.xinitrc   Script to start initial clients.

xterm   Client to run if *.xinitrc* does not exist.

.xserverrc
Default script to start the server.

X   Server to run if *.xserverrc* does not exist.

See Also

X, Xserver, xterm, Appendix A, *Managing Your Environment*; Volume Eight, *X Window System Administrator's Guide*.

Author

Bob Scheifler, MIT Laboratory for Computer Science.

xkill

Name
xkill – kill a client by its X resource ID.

Syntax
`xkill [options]`

Description

xkill allows you to "kill" a client window or, more specifically, to force the X server to close the connection to the client. This program is very dangerous, but is useful for aborting programs that have displayed undesired windows on a user's screen. If no window (resource) identification number is given with `-id`, *xkill* will display a special cursor as a prompt for the user to select a window to be killed. If a pointer button is pressed over a non-root window, the server will close its connection to the client that created the window and the window will be removed from the display. For a more detailed discussion of *xkill* and some problems inherent in "killing" a client window, see Chapter 8, *Other Clients*.

Options

xkill accepts the following application-specific options:

`-all`   Indicates that all clients with top-level windows on the screen should be killed. *xkill* will ask you to select the root window with each of the currently defined buttons to give you several chances to abort. Use of this option is highly discouraged.

`-button number`
`-button any`

    Specifies the number of the pointer button that should be used to select the window to kill. If the word `any` is specified, any button on the pointer can be used. By default, the first button in the pointer map (which is usually the leftmost button) is used.

`-display [host]:server[.screen]`

    Allows you to specify the host, server, and screen to connect to. `host` is the hostname of the physical display, `server` specifies the server number, and `screen` specifies the screen number. For example,

`xkill -display your_node:0.1`

    specifies screen 1 of server 0 on the display named by `your_node`. Either or both the `host` and `screen` elements to the display specification can be omitted. If `host` is omitted, the local display is assumed. If `screen` is omitted, screen 0 is assumed (and the period is unnecessary). The colon and `server` are necessary in all cases.

`-frame`

    Indicates that *xkill* should ignore the standard conventions for finding top-level client windows (which are typically nested inside a window manager window), and simply believe that you want to kill direct children of the root. If you are running a window manager that provides titlebars or frames (such as *twm* or *mwm*), the children of the root include these window decorations. Thus, when you select a client window to be killed, the window manager is killed instead.

-id *resource*

Allows you to specify the window to be killed using its resource (window) ID on the command line, rather than by selecting it with the pointer. If no window ID is specified, *xkill* will display a special cursor with which you should select a window to be killed.

Resources

xkill defines the following application resource:

Button

Specifies a pointer button number to use when selecting the window to be removed. If the word any is specified, any button on the pointer can be used.

See Also

X, xwininfo; Chapter 8, *Other Clients*; Volume One, *Xlib Programming Manual*.

Authors

Jim Fulton, MIT X Consortium;
Dana Chee, Bellcore.

xload

Name

xload – display system load average.

Syntax

xload [*options*]

Description

The *xload* program displays a periodically updating histogram of the system load average. For instructions on using *xload*, see Chapter 3, *Working in the X Environment*, and Chapter 8, *Other Clients*.

Options

xload accepts all of the standard X Toolkit command-line options, which are listed on the *X* reference page. In addition, *xload* accepts the following application-specific options:

`-hl` *color*
`-highlight` *color*
Specifies the color of the scale lines.

`-jumpscroll` *pixels*
Specifies the number of pixels to shift the graph to the left when the graph reaches the right edge of the window. The default value is 1/2 the width of the current window. Smooth scrolling can be achieved by setting it to 1.

`-label` *string*
Specifies the text string for the label above the load average.

`-lights`
Causes *xload* to display the current load average by using the keyboard LEDs. For a load average of *n*, *xload* lights the first *n* keyboard LEDs. This option turns off the usual screen display. (Available as of Release 5.)

`-nolabel`
Specifies that no label be displayed above the load graph.

`-scale` *integer*
Specifies the minimum number of tick marks in the histogram, where one division represents one load average point. If the load goes above this number, *xload* will create more divisions, but it will never use fewer than this number. The default is 1.

`-update` *seconds*
Specifies the frequency in seconds at which *xload* updates its display. If the load average window is uncovered (by moving windows with a window manager or by the *xrefresh* program), the graph will also be updated. The minimum amount of time allowed between updates is 1 second. As of Release 5, the default is 10 seconds. (In Release 4, the default is 5 seconds.)

Resources

In addition to the resources available to each of the widgets used by *xload*, there is one resource defined by the application itself.

showLabel (class Boolean)
> If False, then no label will be displayed.

You can set the following resource for the load widget:

load.highlight (class Foreground)
> Specifies the color of the scale lines.

load.jumpScroll (class JumpScroll)
> Specifies the number of pixels to shift the graph to the left when the graph reaches the right edge of the window. The default value is 1/2 the width of the current window. Smooth scrolling can be achieved by setting it to 1.

load.minScale (class Scale)
> Specifies the minimum number of ticks that will be displayed. The default is 1.

load.update (class Interval)
> Specifies the frequency in seconds at which *xload* updates its display. If the load average window is uncovered (by moving windows with a window manager or by the *xrefresh* program), the graph will also be updated. The minimum amount of time allowed between updates is 1 second. As of Release 5, the default is 10 seconds. (In Release 4, the default is 5 seconds.)

You can set the following resources for the label widget:

*label.label (class String)
> Specifies that the given text string be used as a label above the load average. By default, the hostname is used.

Widget Hierarchy

In order to specify resources, it is useful to know the hierarchy of the widgets that compose *xload*. In the notation below, indentation indicates hierarchical structure. The widget class name is given first, followed by the widget instance name:

```
XLoad   xload
        Paned   paned
                Label   label
                StripChart   load
```

See Appendix G, *Widget Resources* for a list of resources that can be set for the Athena widgets.

Files

/usr/lib/X11/app-defaults/XLoad
> Specifies required resources.

See Also

X, xrdb, mem(4); Chapter 3, *Working in the X Environment*; Chapter 8, *Other Clients*.

Bugs

This program requires the ability to open and read */dev/kmem*. Sites that do not allow general access to this file should make *xload* belong to the same group as */dev/kmem* and turn on the *set group id* permission flag.

Reading */dev/kmem* is inherently nonportable. Therefore, the routine used to read it (get_load.c) must be ported to each new operating system.

Authors

K. Shane Hartman (MIT-LCS) and Stuart A. Malone (MIT-LCS);
Additional features added by Jim Gettys (MIT-Athena), Bob Scheifler (MIT-LCS), Tony Della Fera (MIT-Athena), and Chris Peterson (MIT-LCS).

Name

xlogo – X Window System logo.

Synopsis

xlogo [*options*]

Description

The *xlogo* program displays the X Window System logo. This program is nothing more than a wrapper around the *undocumented* Athena Logo widget.

Options

xlogo accepts all of the standard X Toolkit command-line options, which are listed on the *X* reference page. (We've included some of the more commonly used Toolkit options later in this section.) In addition, *xlogo* accepts the following application-specific option:

-shape

Specifies that the *xlogo* window should be shaped to the X logo (rather than being rectangular). (Available as of Release 5.)

The following Toolkit options are commonly used:

-bg *color*

Specifies the color to use for the background of the window. The default is white. A correct color for the background is something like maroon.

-bd *color*

Specifies the color to use for the border of the window. The default is black.

-bw *pixels*

Specifies the width in pixels of the border surrounding the window.

-display [*host*]:*server*[.*screen*]

Allows you to specify the physical display, server, and screen on which to create the *xlogo* window. See "Options" on the *X* reference page for an example of usage.

-fg *color*

Specifies the color to use for displaying the logo. The default is black. A correct color for the foreground is something like silver, which you can approximate with a shade of grey.

-geometry *geometry*

The *xlogo* window is created with the specified size and location determined by the supplied geometry specification. The -geometry option can be (and often is) abbreviated to -g, unless there is a conflicting option that begins with "g". The argument to the geometry option (*geometry*) is referred to as a "standard geometry string," and has the form *width*x*height*±*xoff*±*yoff*.

-rv

Indicates that reverse video should be simulated by swapping the foreground and background colors.

`-xrm` *resourcestring*

> Specifies a resource string to be used. This is especially useful for setting resources that do not have separate command-line options.

Resources

This program uses the Logo widget in the Athena Widget Set. It understands all of the Core and Simple widget resource names and classes as well as:

`foreground` (class `Foreground`)

> Specifies the color for the logo. The default depends on whether `reverseVideo` is specified. If `reverseVideo` is specified the default is `XtDefaultBackground` (commonly white); otherwise, the default is `XtDefaultForeground` (commonly black).

`shapeWindow` (class `ShapeWindow`)

> Specifies that the window be shaped to the X logo (rather than being rectangular). The default is `False`. (Available as of Release 5.)

The following Core resources are commonly used:

`width` (class `Width`)

> Specifies the width of the logo. The default is 100 pixels.

`height` (class `Height`)

> Specifies the height of the logo. The default is 100 pixels.

Widget Hierarchy

In order to specify resources, it is useful to know the hierarchy of the widgets that compose *xlogo*. In the notation below, indentation indicates hierarchical structure. The widget class name is given first, followed by the widget instance name:

```
XLogo  xlogo
     Logo  xlogo
```

Files

/usr/lib/X11/app-defaults/XLogo

> Specifies required resources.

See Also

X, xrdb.

Authors

Ollie Jones of Apollo Computer and Jim Fulton of the X Consortium wrote the logo graphics routine, based on a graphic design by Danny Chong and Ross Chapman of Apollo Computer.

xlsatoms

Name

xlsatoms – list interned atoms defined on the server.

Syntax

xlsatoms [*options*]

Description

xlsatoms lists the interned atoms. By default, all atoms starting from 1 (the lowest atom value defined by the protocol) are listed until an unknown atom is found. If an explicit range is given, *xlsatoms* will try all atoms in the range, regardless of whether or not any are undefined.

Options

xlsatoms accepts the following options:

-display [*host*]:*server*[.*screen*]

Specifies the display, server, and screen to use. *host* is the hostname of the physical display, *server* specifies the server number, and *screen* specifies the screen number. For example:

% **xlsatoms -display** *your_node*:0.1

specifies screen 1 of server 0 on the display named by *your_node*. Either or both the *host* and *screen* elements can be omitted. If *host* is omitted, the local display is assumed. If *screen* is omitted, screen 0 is assumed (and the period is unnecessary). The colon and *server* are necessary in all cases.

-format *printf_string*

Specifies a *printf*-style string used to list each atom <*value,name*> pair, printed in that order (*value* is an *unsigned long* and *name* is a *char **). *xlsatoms* will supply a newline at the end of each line. The default is %ld\t%s.

-name *string*

Specifies the name of an atom to list. If the atom does not exist, a message will be printed on the standard error.

-range [*low*]-[*high*]

Specifies the range of atom values to check. If *low* is not given, a value of 1 assumed. If *high* is not given, *xlsatoms* will stop at the first undefined atom at or above *low*.

See Also

X, Xserver, xprop.

Author

Jim Fulton, MIT X Consortium.

xlsclients

Name
xlsclients – list client applications running on a display.

Syntax
```
xlsclients [options]
```

Description
xlsclients is a utility for listing information about the client applications running on a display. It may be used to generate scripts representing a snapshot of the user's current session. Note, however, that *xlsclients* will not list a window manager process. See Chapter 8, *Other Clients*, for more information.

Options
xlsclients accepts the following options:

-a   Specifies that clients on all screens should be listed. By default, only those clients on the default screen are listed.

-display [*host*]:*server*[.*screen*]
        Allows you to specify the display, server, and screen to connect to. *host* is the hostname of the physical display, *server* specifies the server number, and *screen* specifies the screen number. For example,

        % **xlsclients -display** *your_node*:0.1

        specifies screen 1 of server 0 on the display named by *your_node*. Either or both the *host* and *screen* can be omitted. If *host* is omitted, the local display is assumed. If *screen* is omitted, screen 0 is assumed (and the period is unnecessary). The colon and *server* are necessary in all cases.

-l   Requests a long listing showing the window name, icon name, and class hints in addition to the machine name and command string in the default listing.

-m *max_cmd_length*
        Specifies the maximum number of characters in a command to list. The default is 10000.

See Also
X, xprop, xwininfo; Chapter 8, *Other Clients*.

Author
Jim Fulton, MIT X Consortium.

xlsfonts

Name

xlsfonts – list available fonts.

Syntax

xlsfonts [*options*] [**-fn** *pattern*]

Description

xlsfonts lists the fonts that match the given *pattern*. The wildcard character "*" may be used to match any sequence of characters (including none), and "?" to match any single character. If no pattern is given, "*" is assumed.

If you use wildcard characters as or within a fontname specification, the name must be quoted to prevent the characters from being expanded by the shell. See Chapter 6, *Font Specification*, for instructions on using *xlsfonts*.

Options

xlsfonts accepts the following options:

-1   Indicates that listings should use a single column. This is the same as −n 1.

-C   Indicates that listings should use multiple columns. This is the same as −n 0.

-display [*host*]:*server*[.*screen*]

Allows you to specify the display, server, and screen to connect to. *host* is the hostname of the physical display, *server* specifies the server number, and *screen* specifies the screen number. For example,

% **xlsfonts -display** *your_node*:**0.1**

specifies screen 1 of server 0 on the display named by *your_node*. Either or both the *host* and *screen* can be omitted. If *host* is omitted, the local display is assumed. If *screen* is omitted, screen 0 is assumed (and the period is unnecessary).

-fn *pattern*

Indicates that only fonts matching the specified *pattern* be listed.

-l[l[l]]

Indicates that medium, long, and very long listings, respectively, should be generated for each font.

-m   Indicates that long listings should also print the minimum and maximum bounds of each font.

-n *columns*

Specifies the number of columns to use in displaying the output. By default, it will attempt to fit as many columns of font names as possible into the number of characters specified by −w *width*.

-o   Specifies that *xlsfonts* should do an OpenFont (and QueryFont, if appropriate) rather than a ListFonts. This is useful if ListFonts or ListFontsWithInfo fails to list a known font (as is the case with some scaled font systems). (Available as of Release 5.)

-u   Specifies that the output should be left unsorted. (Available as of Release 5.)

-w *width*
        Specifies the width in characters that should be used in figuring out how many columns to print. The default is 79.

See Also

X, Xserver, xset, xfd, xfontsel; Chapter 6, *Font Specification*.

Bugs

Doing xlsfonts -l can tie up your server for a very long time. This is really a bug with single-threaded, non-preemptable servers, not with this program.

Author

Mark Lillibridge, MIT Project Athena;
Jim Fulton, MIT X Consortium;
Phil Karlton, SGI.

xlswins

Name

xlswins – server window list displayer for X.

Syntax

xlswins [*options*] [*window_id*]

Description

As of Release 5, this program is no longer included in the standard MIT X distribution.

You can access virtually the same information by running the command:

% xwininfo -tree

and then selecting the root window. For more information, see the *xwininfo* reference page and Chapter 8, *Other Clients*.

The *xlswins* reference page is included merely for continuity.

xlswins lists the window tree. By default, the root window is used as the starting point, although another window may be specified using the *window_id* option.

Options

xlswins accepts the following options:

-display [*host*]:*server*[.*screen*]

Specifies the display, server, and screen to use. *host* is the hostname of the physical display, *server* specifies the display server number, and *screen* specifies the screen number. For example:

% xlswins -display *your_node***:0.1**

Either or both of the *host* and *screen* elements to the display specification can be omitted. If *host* is omitted, the local display is assumed. If *screen* is omitted, screen 0 is assumed (and the period is unnecessary). The colon and (display) *server* are necessary in all cases.

-format *radix*

Specifies the radix to use when printing out window IDs. Allowable values are: hex, octal, and decimal. The default is hex.

-indent *number*

Specifies the number of spaces that should be indented for each level in the window tree. The default is 2.

-1

Indicates that a long listing should be generated for each window. This includes a number indicating the depth, the geometry relative to the parent, and the location relative to the root window.

window_id

Specifies that the starting point for the window tree listing is the window *window_id*.

See Also
    X, Xserver, xwininfo, xprop.

Author
    Jim Fulton, MIT X Consortium.

xmag

Name

xmag – magnify parts of the screen.

Syntax

xmag [*options*]

Description

This reference page documents the Release 5 version of *xmag*, which operates significantly differently from prior releases. For instructions on using the Release 5 version, see Chapter 7, *Graphics Utilities*.

The *xmag* program allows you to magnify portions of the screen. If no explicit region is specified, a square with the pointer in the upper-left corner is displayed indicating the area to be enlarged. The area can be dragged out to the desired size by pressing pointer Button2. Once a region has been selected, a window is popped up showing an enlarged version of the region in which each pixel in the source image is represented by a small square of the same color. Pressing Button1 in the enlargement window shows the position and RGB value of the pixel under the pointer until the button is released.

The *xmag* client features five command buttons, described in the next section.

Two of the command buttons enable you to select multiple areas to be enlarged. You can open multiple instances of the magnification window or replace the current enlargement with a new image, using the new or replace command buttons, respectively.

Note that you can copy and paste images between *xmag* and *bitmap*. (See Chapter 7, *Graphics Utilities*, for more information.)

Resizing *xmag* resizes the current magnification area. *xmag* preserves the colormap, visual, and window depth of the source.

To quit *xmag*, type q, Q, or Control-C in the enlargement window, or select the close command button.

Command Buttons

There are five command buttons across the top of the *xmag* window. Close deletes the particular magnification instance (window). Replace brings up the rubber band selector again to select another region for this magnification window. New brings up the rubber band selector to create a new magnification window. Cut puts the magnification image into the PRIMARY selection. Paste copies the PRIMARY selection buffer into *xmag*. (You can copy and paste images between *xmag* and *bitmap*. See Chapter 7 for instructions.)

Options

xmag accepts all of the standard X Toolkit command-line options, which are listed on the *X* reference page. (We've included some of the more commonly used Toolkit options later in this section.) In addition, *xmag* accepts the following application-specific options:

−mag *mag_factor*
> Specifies a factor by which the source region should be enlarged. The default magnification is 5. This is used with the size of the source to compute the default enlargement window size. (Specifying a size with −geometry can distort the program's results. See −geometry below.)

−source *geometry*
> Specifies the size and/or location of the source region on the screen. By default, a 64 × 64 square is provided for the user to select an area of the screen. The size of the source is used with the desired magnification to compute the default enlargement window size. (Specifying a size with −geometry can distort the program's results. See −geometry below.)

The following standard X Toolkit options are commonly used with *xmag*:

−bg *color_or_pixel_value*
> Specifies the name of the color to be used as the background of the enlargement window. If the name begins with a percent sign (%), it is interpreted to be an absolute pixel value. This is useful when displaying large areas, since pixels that are the same color as the background do not need to be painted in the enlargement. The default is to use the BlackPixel of the screen.

−display [*host*]:*server*[.*screen*]
> Allows you to specify the display, server, and screen to use for both reading the screen and displaying the enlarged version of the image. *host* is the hostname of the physical display, *server* specifies the server number, and *screen* specifies the screen number. For example:

> % **xmag -display** *your_node*:**0.1**

> specifies screen 1 of server 0 on the display named by *your_node*. Either or both the *host* and *screen* elements to the display specification can be omitted. If *host* is omitted, the local display is assumed. If *screen* is omitted, screen 0 is assumed (and the period is unnecessary). The colon and *server* are necessary in all cases.

−fn *fontname*
> This option specifies the name of a font to use when displaying pixel values (used when button 1 is pressed in the enlargement window).

−geometry *geometry*
> The enlargement window is created with the specified size and location determined by the supplied geometry specification. See the *X* reference page for a description of usage.

> Note that using the −geometry option with *xmag* can affect how the program works. By default, the size of the *xmag* window is computed from the size of the source region and the desired magnification. Therefore, specifying a size with −geometry

can distort the program's results. As a general rule, you should only specify the location of the *xmag* window, as in:

```
% xmag -geometry -0-0 &
```

which places the window in the lower-right corner of the screen.

Resources

The *xmag* program defines the following application resources:

mag(class Mag)
> Specifies the enlargement factor. See the –mag option for more information.

source (class Source)
> Specifies the size and/or location of the source region on the screen. Takes as an argument the standard geometry string. See the –source option for more information.

title   Specifies a string that may be used by the window manager (e.g., in a titlebar) when displaying this application.

The following X Toolkit resources are commonly used with *xmag*:

background (class Background)
> Specifies the color or pixel value to be used for the background of the enlargement window.

font (class Font)
> Specifies the name of the font to be used for the command buttons, and when displaying pixel values when the user presses button 1 in the enlargement window.

foreground (class Foreground)
> Specifies the color or pixel value to be used for the foreground text of the enlargement window.

geometry (class Geometry)
> Specifies the size and/or location of the enlargement window.

Widget Hierarchy

xmag uses the X Toolkit and the Athena Widget Set. The magnified image is displayed in the Scale widget. In order to specify resources, it is useful to know the hierarchy of the widgets that compose *xmag*. In the notation below, indentation indicates hierarchical structure. The widget class name is given first, followed by the widget instance name.

```
Xmag xmag
        RootWindow root
        TopLevelShell xmag
                Paned pane1
                        Paned pane2
                                Command close
                                Command replace
                                Command new
```

```
                              Command select
                              Command paste
                              Label xmag label
                    Paned pane2
                              Scale scale
            OverrideShell pixShell
                Label pixLabel
```

See Appendix G, *Widget Resources*, for a list of resources that can be set for the Athena widgets.

See Also

X, bitmap, xwd; Chapter 7, *Graphics Utilities*.

Author

Release 5 version written by Dave Sternlicht and Davor Matic, MIT X Consortium; Previous version by Jim Fulton, MIT X Consortium.

xman

Name

xman – display manual pages.

Syntax

xman [*options*]

Description

xman is a manual page browser. The default size of the initial *xman* window is small so that you can leave it running throughout your entire login session. In the initial window there are three options: Help will pop up a window with online help, Quit will exit, and Manual Page will pop up a window with a manual page browser in it. You may pop up more than one manual page browser window at a time from a single execution of *xman*.

As of Release 5, typing Control-s will pop up a search window prompting for a specific manual page to display. If you know the exact name you want, type it and either press Return or click on the Manual Page button in the search window. The specific page will be displayed in a browser window. If you are not sure of the name, you can type in a guess and click on the Apropos button, which displays a list of reference pages containing the string you've entered.

For further information on using *xman*, please see Chapter 8, *Other Clients*, and read the online help information. The rest of this reference page will discuss customization of *xman*.

Customization

xman allows customization of both the directories to be searched for manual pages, and the name that each directory will map to in the Sections menu. *xman* determines which directories it will search by reading the MANPATH environment variable. If no MANPATH is found then the directory */usr/man* is searched on POSIX systems. This environment is expected to be a colon-separated list of directories for *xman* to search.

```
setenv MANPATH /mit/kit/man:/usr/man
```

By default, *xman* will search each of the following directories (in each of the directories specified in the user's MANPATH) for manual pages. If manual pages exist in that directory, then they are added to the list of manual pages for the corresponding menu item. A menu item is only displayed only for those sections that actually contain manual pages.

Directory	Section Name
man1	(1) User Commands
man2	(2) System Calls
man3	(3) Subroutines
man4	(4) Devices
man5	(5) File Formats
man6	(6) Games
man7	(7) Miscellaneous
man8	(8) Sys. Administration

Directory	Section Name
manl	(l) Local
mann	(n) New
mano	(o) Old

For instance, a user has three directories in her manual path and each contains a directory called *man3*. All these manual pages will appear, alphabetically sorted, when the user selects the menu item called (3) Subroutines. If there is no directory called *mano* in any of the directories in her MANPATH, or there are no manual pages in any of the directories called *mano*, then no menu item will be displayed for the section called (o) Old.

By using the *mandesc* file, a user or system manager is able to more closely control which manual pages will appear in each of the sections represented by menu items in the Sections menu. This functionality is available only on a section-by-section basis, and individual manual pages may not be handled in this manner (although generous use of symbolic links, *ln*(1), will allow almost any configuration you can imagine).

The format of the *mandesc* file is a character followed by a label. The character determines which of the sections will be added under this label. For instance, suppose that you would like to create an extra menu item that contains all programmer subroutines. This label should contain all manual pages in both sections two and three. The *mandesc* file would look like this:

```
2Programmer Subroutines
3Programmer Subroutines
```

This will add a menu item to the Sections menu that would bring up a listing of all manual pages in sections two and three of the *UNIX Programmer's Manual*. Since the label names are *exactly* the same, they will be added to the same section. Note, however, that the original sections still exist.

If you want to completely ignore the default sections in a manual directory, then add the line:

```
no default sections
```

anywhere in your *mandesc* file. This keeps *xman* from searching the default manual sections *in that directory only*. As an example, suppose you want to do the same thing as above, but you don't think that it is useful to have the System Calls or Subroutines sections any longer. You would need to duplicate the default entries, as well as adding your new one.

```
no default sections
1(1) User Commands
2Programmer Subroutines
3Programmer Subroutines
4(4) Devices
5(5) File Formats
6(6) Games
7(7) Miscellaneous
8(8) Sys. Administration
```

```
1(1)  Local
n(n)  New
o(o)  Old
```

xman will read any section that is of the form *man<character>*, where *<character>* is an uppercase or lowercase letter (they are treated distinctly) or a numeral (0-9). Be warned, however, that *man*(1) and *catman*(8) will not search directories that are nonstandard.

Options

xman accepts all of the standard X Toolkit command-line options, which are listed on the *X* reference page. In addition, *xman* accepts the following application-specific options:

-bothshown
> Allows both the manual page and manual directory to be on the screen at the same time.

-geometry *geometry*
> Sets the size and location of the top menu with the three buttons in it. This menu is created with the specified size and location determined by the supplied geometry specification. The -geometry option can be (and often is) abbreviated to -g, unless there is a conflicting option that begins with "g." The argument to the geometry option (*geometry*) is referred to as a "standard geometry string," and has the form *width*x*height*±*xoff*±*yoff*.
>
> Note that *xman* allows you to use an equal sign followed by the *geometry* string as an alternative to -geometry.

-help Lists the valid options.

-helpfile *filename*
> Specifies a helpfile to use other than the default.

-notopbox
> Starts without the top menu with the three buttons in it.

-pagesize *geometry*
> Sets the size and location of all the manual pages. See -geometry for the syntax of the *geometry* argument.

Resources

The *xman* program uses the following X Toolkit resources: foreground, background, width, height, borderWidth, and borderColor.

In addition, *xman* has application-specific resources that allow unique *xman* customizations.

bothShown (class Boolean)
> Either True or False, specifies whether or not you want both the directory and the manual page shown at startup. The default is False.

directoryFontNormal (class Font)
>   The font to use for the directory text.

directoryHeight (class DirectoryHeight)
>   The height in pixels of the directory, when the directory and the manual page are
>   shown simultaneously.

helpCursor (class Cursor)
>   The cursor to use in the help window.

helpFile (class File)
>   Use this rather than the system default help file.

manpageCursor (class Cursor)
>   The cursor to use in the manual page window.

manualFontBold (class Font)
>   The font to use for bold text in the manual pages.

manualFontItalic (class Font)
>   The font to use for italic text in the manual pages.

manualFontNormal (class Font)
>   The font to use for normal text in the manual pages.

pointerColor (class Foreground)
>   The color of all the cursors (pointers) listed individually (helpCursor, manpage-
>   Cursor, topCursor). The resource name was chosen to be compatible with *xterm*.

searchEntryCursor (class Cursor)
>   The cursor to use in the search entry text widget.

topBox (class Boolean)
>   Either True or False, determines whether the top box (containing the Help, Quit,
>   and Manual Page buttons) or a manual page is put on the screen at startup. The
>   default is True.

topCursor (class Cursor)
>   The cursor to use in the top box.

verticalList (class Boolean)
>   Either True or False, determines whether the directory listing is vertically or hori-
>   zontally organized. The default is horizontal (False).

Widget Hierarchy

In order to specify resources, it is useful to know the hierarchy of the widgets that compose
xman. In the notation below, indentation indicates hierarchical structure. The widget class
name is given first, followed by the widget instance name.

```
Xman  xman      (This widget is never used)
        TopLevelShell  topbox
                Form  form
```

```
                    Label   topLabel
                    Command  helpButton
                    Command  quitButton
                    Command  manpageButton
        TransientShell  search
                    DialogWidgetClass  dialog
                            Label   label
                            Text   value
                            Command   manualPage
                            Command   apropos
                            Command   cancel
        TransientShell  pleaseStandBy
                    Label  label
TopLevelShell  manualBrowser
        Paned  Manpage_Vpane
                    Paned  horizPane
                            MenuButton  options
                            MenuButton  sections
                            Label  manualBrowser
                    Viewport  directory
                            List  directory
                            List  directory
                            .
                            .  (one for each section,
                            .   created "on the fly")
                            .
                    ScrollByLine  manualPage
        SimpleMenu  optionMenu
                    SmeBSB  displayDirectory
                    SmeBSB  displayManualPage
                    SmeBSB  help
                    SmeBSB  search
                    SmeBSB  showBothScreens
                    SmeBSB  removeThisManpage
                    SmeBSB  openNewManpage
                    SmeBSB  showVersion
                    SmeBSB  quit
        SimpleMenu  sectionMenu
                    SmeBSB  <name of section>
                            .
                            .  (one for each section)
                            .
        TransientShell  search
                    DialogWidgetClass  dialog
                            Label  label
                            Text  value
                            Command  manualPage
                            Command  apropos
```

```
                                    Command   cancel
                       TransientShell   pleaseStandBy
                             Label   label
                       TransientShell   likeToSave
                               Dialog   dialog
                                     Label   label
                                     Text   value
                                     Command   yes
                                     Command   no
           TopLevelShell   help
                   Paned   Manpage_Vpane
                         Paned   horizPane
                               MenuButton   options
                               MenuButton   sections
                               Label   manualBrowser
                         ScrollByLine   manualPage
                   SimpleMenu   optionMenu
                         SmeBSB   displayDirectory
                         SmeBSB   displayManualPage
                         SmeBSB   help
                         SmeBSB   search
                         SmeBSB   showBothScreens
                         SmeBSB   removeThisManpage
                         SmeBSB   openNewManpage
                         SmeBSB   showVersion
                         SmeBSB   quit
```

See Appendix G, *Widget Resources*, for a list of resources that can be set for the Athena widgets.

Global Actions

xman defines all user interaction through global actions. This allows the user to modify the translation table of any widget and bind any event to the new user action. The list of actions supported by *xman* are:

`CreateNewManpage()`

    Can be used anywhere; creates a new manual page display window.

`GotoPage(`*page*`)`

    When used in a manual page display window, this action allows the user to move between a directory and manual page display. The *page* argument can be either `Directory` or `ManualPage`.

`PopupHelp()`

    Can be used anywhere; pops up the help widget.

`PopupSearch()`

> Can be used anywhere, except in a help window. It will cause the search popup to become active and visible on the screen, allowing the user to search for a manual page.

`Quit()`

> Can be used anywhere; exits *xman*.

`RemoveThisManpage()`

> Can be used in any manual page or help display window. When called, it will remove the window and clean up all resources associated with it.

`SaveFormattedPage(action)`

> Can be used only in the `likeToSave` popup widget; tells *xman* whether to `Save` or `Cancel` a save of the manual page that has just been formatted.

`Search(type, action)`

> Useful only when used in a search pop-up, this action will cause the search widget to perform the named search type on the string in the search popup's value widget. This action will also pop down the search widget. The `type` argument can be either `Apropos`, `Manpage`, or `Cancel`. If an `action` of `Open` is specified, then *xman* will open a new manual page to display the results of the search; otherwise, *xman* will attempt to display the results in the parent of the search popup.

`ShowVersion()`

> May be called from any manual page or help display window, and will cause the informational display line to show the current version of *xman*.

Files

> *<manpath directory>/man<character>*
> *<manpath directory>/cat<character>*
> *<manpath directory>/mandesc*

> */usr/lib/X11/app-defaults/Xman*
>   Specifies required resources.

> */tmp*   *xman* creates temporary files in */tmp* for all unformatted man pages and all apropos searches.

Environment Variables

MANPATH

> The search path for manual pages. Directories are separated by colons (e.g., */usr/man:/mit/kit/man:/foo/bar/man*).

XAPPLRESDIR

> A string that will have "Xman" appended to it. This string will be the full path name of a user application defaults file to be merged into the resource database after the system application defaults file, and before the resources that are attached to the display.

See Also

X, apropos(1), catman(8), ln(1), man(1); Chapter 8, *Other Clients*; Appendix G, *Widget Resources*.

Authors

Chris Peterson, MIT X Consortium, from the V10 version written by Barry Shein, formerly of Boston University.

xmh

Name

xmh – read and send mail with an X window interface to *mh*.

Syntax

xmh [**-path** *mailpath*] [**-initial** *foldername*] [**-flag**] [*-toolkitoption*]

Description

xmh provides a graphical user interface to the *mh* message handling system. To actually do things with your mail, *xmh* makes calls to the *mh* package. Electronic mail messages may be composed, sent, received, replied to, forwarded, sorted, and stored in folders.

Please don't be misled by the size of this document. It introduces many aspects of the Athena widget set and provides extensive mechanism for customization of the user interface. *xmh* really is easy to use.

For further information, see the Nutshell Handbook *MH & xmh: E-mail for Users & Programmers*, by Jerry Peek, also published by O'Reilly and Associates, Inc.

Options

xmh accepts all of the standard X Toolkit command-line options, which are listed on the *X* reference page. In addition, *xmh* accepts the following application-specific options:

-path *mailpath*
> To specify an alternate collection of mail folders in which to process mail, use -path followed by the absolute pathname of the alternate mail directory. The default mail path is *$HOME/Mail*; another mail path can be specified using the Path component in *$HOME/.mh_profile*.

-initial *foldername*
> Specifies an alternate folder that may receive new mail and is initially opened by *xmh*. The default initial folder is "inbox".

-flag
> Causes *xmh* to change the appearance of the appropriate folder buttons and to request the window manager to change the appearance of the *xmh* icon when new mail arrives. By default, *xmh* changes the appearance of the "inbox" folder button when new mail is waiting. You can use the application-specific resource checkNewMail to turn off this notification and the -flag option will still override it.

These three options have corresponding application-specific resources, named MailPath, InitialFolder, and MailWaitingFlag, which can be used in a resource file.

Installation

xmh requires that the user is already set up to use *mh*, version 6. First, see if there is a file called *.mh_profile* in your home directory. If it exists, check to see if it contains a line that starts with Current-Folder. If it does, you've been using version 4 or earlier of *mh*; to convert to version 6, you must remove that line. (Failure to do so causes spurious output to standard error, which, depending on your setup, can hang *xmh*.)

If you do not already have an *.mh_profile*, you can create one (and everything else you need) by typing inc to the shell. You should do this before using *xmh* to incorporate new mail.

For more information, refer to the *mh*(1) documentation and the Nutshell Handbook *MH & xmh*.

Much of the user interface of *xmh* is configured in the *Xmh* application defaults file; if this file was not installed properly a warning message will appear when *xmh* is used. The Release 5 version of *xmh* is backwards compatible with the R4 application defaults file.

The default value of the SendBreakWidth resource has changed since R4.

Basic Screen Layout

xmh starts out with a single window, divided into four main areas:

- Six buttons with pull-down command menus.

- A collection of buttons, one for each top level folder. New users of *mh* will have two folders, "drafts" and "inbox".

- A listing, or Table of Contents, of the messages in the open folder. Initially, this will show the messages in "inbox".

- A view of one of your messages. Initially this is blank.

xmh and the Athena Widget Set

xmh uses the X Toolkit Intrinsics and the Athena widget set. Many of the features described below (scrollbars, buttonboxes, etc.) are actually part of the Athena widget set and are described here only for completeness. For more information, see Appendix G, *Widget Resources*.

Scrollbars

Some parts of the main window will have a vertical area on the left containing a gray bar. This area is a *scrollbar*. Scrollbars are used whenever the data in a window takes up more space than can be displayed. The gray bar indicates what portion of your data is visible. If the entire length of the area is gray, then you are looking at all your data. If only the first half is gray, then you are looking at the top half of your data. The message viewing area will have a horizontal scrollbar if the text of the message is wider than the viewing area.

You can use the pointer in the scrollbar to change what part of the data is visible. If you click the second pointer button, then the top of the gray area will move to where the pointer is, and the corresponding portion of data will be displayed. If you hold down the second pointer button, you can drag around the gray area. This makes it easy to get to the top of the data: just press with the second button, drag off the top of the scrollbar, and release.

If you click with the first pointer button, then the data to the right of the pointer will scroll to the top of the window. If you click with the third pointer button, then the data at the top of the window will scroll down to where the pointer is.

Buttonboxes, Buttons, and Menus

Any area containing many words or short phrases, each enclosed in a rectangular or rounded boundary, is called a *buttonbox*. Each rectangle or rounded area is actually a button that you can press by moving the pointer onto it and pressing pointer button 1. If a given buttonbox has more buttons in it than can fit, it will be displayed with a scrollbar, so you can always scroll to the button you want.

Some buttons have pull-down menus. Pressing the pointer button while the pointer is over one of these buttons will pull down a menu. Continuing to hold the button down while moving the pointer over the menu, called dragging the pointer, will highlight each selectable item on the menu as the pointer passes over it. To select an item in the menu, release the pointer button while the item is highlighted.

Adjusting the Relative Sizes of Areas

If you're not satisfied with the sizes of the various areas of the main window, they can easily be changed. Near the right edge of the border between each region is a black box, called a *grip*. Simply point to that grip with the pointer, press a pointer button, drag up or down, and release. Exactly what happens depends on which pointer button you press:

If you drag with pointer button 2, then only that border will move. This mode is simplest to understand, but is the least useful.

If you drag with pointer button 1, then you are adjusting the size of the window above. *xmh* will attempt to compensate by adjusting some window below it.

If you drag with pointer button 3, then you are adjusting the size of the window below. *xmh* will attempt to compensate by adjusting some window above it.

All windows have a minimum and maximum size; you will never be allowed to move a border past the point where it would make a window have an invalid size.

Processing Your Mail

This section will define the concepts of the selected folder, current folder, selected message(s), current message, selected sequence, and current sequence. Each *xmh* command is introduced.

For use in customization, action procedures corresponding to each command are given; these action procedures can be used to customize the user interface, particularly the keyboard accelerators and the functionality of the buttons in the optional buttonbox created by the application resource `CommandButtonCount`.

Folders and Sequences

A folder contains a collection of mail messages, or is empty. *xmh* supports folders with one level of subfolders.

The selected folder is whichever folder name appears in the bar above the folder buttons. Note that this is not necessarily the same folder that is being viewed. To change the selected folder, just press on the desired folder button; if that folder has subfolders, select a folder from the pull-down menu.

The Table of Contents, or toc, lists the messages in the viewed folder. The titlebar above the Table of Contents displays the name of the viewed folder.

The toc titlebar also displays the name of the viewed sequence of messages within the viewed folder. Every folder has an "all" sequence, which contains all the messages in the folder, and initially the toc titlebar will show "inbox:all".

Folder Commands

The Folder command menu contains commands of a global nature:

Open Folder

> Displays the data in the selected folder. Thus, the selected folder also becomes the viewed folder. The action procedure corresponding to this command is XmhOpen-Folder([*foldername*]). It takes an optional argument as the name of a folder to select and open; if no folder is specified, the selected folder is opened. It may be specified as part of an event translation from a folder menu button or from a folder menu, or as a binding of a keyboard accelerator to any widget other than the folder menu buttons or the folder menus.

Open Folder in New Window

> Displays the selected folder in an additional main window. Note, however, that you may not reliably display the same folder in more than one window at a time, although *xmh* will not prevent you from trying. The corresponding action is XmhOpen-FolderInNewWindow().

Create Folder

> Creates a new folder. You will be prompted for a name for the new folder; to enter the name, move the pointer to the blank box provided and type. Subfolders are created by specifying the parent folder, a slash, and the subfolder name. For example, to create a folder named "xmh" which is a subfolder of an existing folder named "clients", type "clients/xmh". Click on the Okay button when finished, or just press Return; click on Cancel to cancel this operation. The action corresponding to Create Folder is Xmh-CreateFolder().

Delete Folder

> Destroys the selected folder. You will be asked to confirm this action (see "Confirmation Windows"). Destroying a folder will also destroy any subfolders of that folder. The corresponding action is XmhDeleteFolder().

Close Window

> Exits *xmh*, after first confirming that you won't lose any changes; or, if selected from any additional *xmh* window, simply closes that window. The corresponding action is XmhClose().

Highlighted Messages, Selected Messages and the Current Message

It is possible to highlight a set of adjacent messages in the area of the Table of Contents. To highlight a message, click on it with pointer button 1. To highlight a range of messages, click on the first one with pointer button 1 and on the last one with pointer button 3; or press pointer button 1, drag, and release. To extend a range of selected messages, use pointer button 3. To highlight all messages in the table of contents, click rapidly three times with pointer button 1. To cancel any selection in the table of contents, click rapidly twice.

The selected messages are the same as the highlighted messages, if any. If no messages are highlighted, then the selected messages are considered the same as the current message.

The current message is indicated by a "+" next to the message number. It usually corresponds to the message currently being viewed. When a message is viewed, the titlebar above the view will identify the message.

Table of Contents Commands

The Table of Contents command menu contains commands that operate on the open, or viewed, folder.

Incorporate New Mail

> Adds any new mail received to viewed folder and sets the current message to be the first new message. This command is selectable in the menu and will execute only if the viewed folder is allowed to receive new mail. By default, only "inbox" is allowed to receive new mail. The corresponding action is XmhIncorporateNewMail().

Commit Changes

> Executes all deletions, moves, and copies that have been marked in this folder. The corresponding action is XmhCommitChanges().

Pack Folder

> Renumbers the messages in this folder so they start with 1 and increment by 1. The corresponding action is XmhPackFolder().

Sort Folder

> Sorts the messages in this folder in chronological order. (As a side effect, this may also pack the folder.) The corresponding action is XmhSortFolder().

Rescan Folder

> Rebuilds the list of messages. This can be used whenever you suspect that *xmh*'s idea of what messages you have is wrong. (In particular, this is necessary if you change things using straight *mh* commands without using *xmh*.) The corresponding action is XmhForceRescan().

Message Commands

The Message command menu contains commands that operate on the selected message(s), or if there are no selected messages, the current message.

Compose Message

> Composes a new message. A new window will be brought up for composition; a description of it is given in the "Composition Windows" section below. This command does not affect the current message. The corresponding action is Xmh-ComposeMessage().

View Next Message

Views the first selected message. If no messages are highlighted, views the current message. If the current message is already being viewed, views the first unmarked message after the current message. The corresponding action is `XmhViewNext-Message()`.

View Previous

Views the last selected message. If no messages are highlighted, views the current message. If current message is already being viewed, views the first unmarked message before the current message. The corresponding action is `XmhView-Previous()`.

Delete Marks the selected messages for deletion. If no messages are highlighted, this command marks the current message for deletion and automatically displays the next unmarked message. The corresponding action is `XmhMarkDeleted()`.

Move Marks the selected messages to be moved into the currently selected folder. (If the selected folder is the same as the viewed folder, this command will just beep.) If no messages are highlighted, this command marks the current message to be moved and displays the next unmarked message. The corresponding action is `XmhMark-Move()`.

Copy as Link

Marks the selected messages to be copied into the selected folder. (If the selected folder is the same as the viewed folder, this command will just beep.) If no messages are highlighted, marks the current message to be copied. Note that messages are actually linked, not copied; editing a message copied by *xmh* will affect all copies of the message. The corresponding action is `XmhMarkCopy()`.

Unmark Removes any of the above three marks from the selected messages, or the current message, if none is highlighted. The corresponding action is `XmhUnmark()`.

View in New

Creates a new window containing only a view of the first selected message, or the current message, if none is highlighted. The corresponding action is `XmhViewInNew-Window()`.

Reply Creates a composition window in reply to the first selected message, or the current message, if none is highlighted. The corresponding action is `XmhReply()`.

Forward Creates a composition window whose body is initialized to contain an encapsulation of the selected messages, or the current message if none is highlighted. The corresponding action is `XmhForward()`.

Use as Composition

Creates a composition window whose body is initialized to be the contents of the first selected message, or the current message if none is selected. Any changes you make in the composition will be saved in a new message in the "drafts" folder, and will not change the original message. However, there is an exception to this rule. If the message to be used as composition was selected from the "drafts" folder (see "Bugs"), the changes will be reflected in the original message (see "Composition Windows"). The corresponding action is XmhUseAsComposition().

Print   Prints the selected messages, or the current message if none is selected. *xmh* normally prints by invoking the *enscript*(1) command, but this can be customized with the *xmh* resource PrintCommand. The corresponding action is XmhPrint().

Sequence Commands

The Sequence command menu contains commands pertaining to message sequences (See "Message Sequences"), and a list of the message sequences defined for the currently viewed folder. The selected message sequence is indicated by a check mark in its entry in the margin of the menu. To change the selected message sequence, select a new message sequence from the sequence menu.

Pick Messages

Defines a new message sequence. The corresponding action is XmhPick-Messages().

The following menu entries will be sensitive only if the current folder has any message sequences other than the "all" message sequence.

Open Sequence

Changes the viewed sequence to be the same as the selected sequence. The corresponding action is XmhOpenSequence().

Add to Sequence

Adds the selected messages to the selected sequence. The corresponding action is XmhAddToSequence().

Remove from Sequence

Removes the selected messages from the selected sequence. The corresponding action is XmhRemoveFromSequence().

Delete Sequence

Removes the selected sequence entirely. The messages themselves are not affected; they are simply no longer grouped together to define a message sequence. The corresponding action is XmhDeleteSequence().

View Commands

Commands in the View menu and in the buttonboxes of view windows (which result from the Message command View in New) correspond in functionality to commands of the same name in the Message menu, but they operate on the viewed message rather than the selected messages or current message.

Close Window

When the viewed message is in a separate view window, this command will close the view, after confirming the status of any unsaved edits. The corresponding action procedure is XmhCloseView().

Reply   Creates a composition window in reply to the viewed message. The related action procedure is XmhViewReply().

Forward Creates a composition window whose body is initialized to contain the contents of the viewed message. The corresponding action is XmhViewForward().

Use As Composition

Creates a composition window whose body is initialized to be the contents of the viewed message. Any changes made in the composition window will be saved in a new message in the "drafts" folder and will not change the original message. An exception: if the viewed message was selected from the "drafts" folder (see "Bugs"), the original message is edited. The action procedure corresponding to this command is XmhViewUseAsComposition().

Edit Message

Enables the direct editing of the viewed message. The action procedure is Xmh-EditView().

Save Message

This command is insensitive until the message has been edited; when activated, edits will be saved to the original message in the view. The corresponding action is Xmh-SaveView().

Print   Prints the viewed message. *xmh* prints by invoking the *enscript*(1) command, but this can be customized with the application-specific resource PrintCommand. The corresponding action procedure is XmhPrintView().

Delete   Marks the viewed message for deletion. The corresponding action is XmhView-MarkDelete(). (Available as of Release 5.)

Options Menu

The Options menu contains one entry.

Read in Reverse

When selected, a check mark appears in the margin of this menu entry. Read in Reverse will switch the meaning of the next and previous messages and will increment to the current message marker in the opposite direction. This is useful if you want to read your messages in the order of most recent first. The option acts as a toggle; select it from the menu a second time to undo the effect. The check mark appears when the option is selected.

Composition Windows

Composition windows are created by selecting Compose Message from the Message menu, or by selecting Reply, Forward, or Use as Composition from either the Message or View menu. Aside from the normal text editing functions, there are six command buttons associated with composition windows:

Close Window

Closes this composition window. If changes have been made since the most recent Save or Send, you will be asked to confirm losing them. The corresponding action is XmhCloseView().

Send   Sends this composition. The corresponding action is XmhSend().

New Headers

Replaces the current composition with an empty message. If changes have been made since the most recent Send or Save, you will be asked to confirm losing them. The corresponding action is XmhResetCompose().

Compose Message

Brings up another new composition window. The corresponding action is Xmh-ComposeMessage().

Save Message

Saves this composition in your drafts folder. Then you can safely close the composition. At some future date, you can continue working on the composition by opening the drafts folder, selecting the message, and using the Use as Composition command. The corresponding action is XmhSave().

Insert Inserts a related message into the composition. If the composition window was created with a Reply command, the related message is the message being replied to; otherwise, no related message is defined and this button is insensitive. The message may be filtered before being inserted; see ReplyInsertFilter under "Application-specific Resources" for more information. The corresponding action is Xmh-Insert().

Accelerators

Accelerators are shortcuts. They allow you to invoke commands without using the menus, either from the keyboard or by using the pointer.

xmh defines pointer accelerators for common actions: to select and view a message with a single click, use pointer button 2 on the message's entry in the table of contents; to select and open a folder or a sequence in a single action, make the folder or sequence selection with pointer button 2.

To mark the highlighted messages to be moved to a folder in a single action, or current message if none has been highlighted, use pointer button 3 to select the target folder and simultaneously mark the messages. Similarly, selecting a sequence with pointer button 3 will add the highlighted or current message(s) to that sequence. In both of these operations, the selected folder or sequence and the viewed folder or sequence are not changed.

xmh defines the following keyboard accelerators over the surface of the main window, except in the view area while editing a message:

Meta-I	Incorporate new mail.
Meta-C	Commit changes.
Meta-R	Rescan folder.
Meta-P	Pack folder.
Meta-S	Sort folder.
Meta-space	View next message.
Meta-c	Mark copy.
Meta-d	Mark deleted.
Meta-f	Forward the selected or current message.
Meta-m	Mark move.
Meta-n	View next message.
Meta-p	View previous message.
Meta-r	Reply to the selected or current message.
Meta-u	Unmark.
Control-V	Scroll the table of contents forward.
Meta-V	Scroll the table of contents backward.
Control-v	Scroll the view forward.
Meta-v	Scroll the view backward.

Text Editing Commands

All of the text editing commands are actually defined by the Text widget in the Athena widget set. The commands may be bound to different keys than the defaults described below through the X Toolkit Intrinsics key re-binding mechanisms. See Chapter 11, *Setting Resources*, and Appendix G, *Widget Resources*, for more details.

Whenever you are asked to enter any text, you will be using a standard text editing interface. Various control and meta keystroke combinations are bound to a somewhat Emacs-like set of commands. In addition, the pointer buttons may be used to select a portion of text or to move the insertion point in the text. Pressing pointer button 1 causes the insertion point to move to the pointer. Double-clicking button 1 selects a word, triple-clicking selects a line, quadruple-clicking selects a paragraph, and quintuple-clicking selects everything. Any selection may be extended in either direction by using pointer button 3.

In the following, a *line* refers to one displayed row of characters in the window, while a *paragraph* refers to the text between carriage returns. Text within a paragraph is broken into lines for display based on the current width of the window. When a message is sent, text is broken into lines based upon the values of the `SendBreakWidth` and `SendWidth` application-specific resources.

The following keystroke combinations are defined:

Control-a	Move to the beginning of the current line.
Control-b	Move backward one character.
Control-d	Delete the next character.
Control-e	Move to the end of the current line.
Control-f	Move forward one character.
Control-h, or Backspace	Delete the previous character.
Control-j	New line and indent.
Control-k	Kill the rest of the current line. (Does not kill the carriage return at the end of the line. To do so, use Control-k twice. However, be aware that the second kill overwrites the text line in the kill buffer.)
Control-l	Refresh the window.
Control-m, Return, or Linefeed	New line.
Control-n	Move down to the next line.
Control-o	Divide this line into two lines at this point and move the cursor back up.
Control-p	Move up to the previous line.
Control-r	Search and replace backward.
Control-s	Search and replace forward.
Control-t	Transpose characters. (Swap the characters immediately before and after the cursor.)
Control-u	Perform next command four times. For example, the sequence Control-u, Control-n moves the cursor down four lines.
Control-v	Move down to the next screenful of text.
Control-w	Kill the selected text.
Control-y	Insert the last killed text. (If the last killed text is a carriage return—see Control-k above—a blank line is inserted.)
Control-z	Scroll the text up one line.
Meta-b	Move backward one word.

Meta-d	Delete the next word.
Meta-D	Kill the next word.
Meta-f	Move forward one word.
Meta-h, Meta-Backspace, or Meta-Delete	Delete the previous word.
Meta-H, Meta-Shift-Backspace, or Meta-Shift-Delete	Kill the previous word.
Meta-i	Insert a file. A dialog box will appear in which you can type the desired filename.
Meta-k	Kill to end of paragraph.
Meta-q	Join lines to form a paragraph.
Meta-v	Move up to the previous screenful of text.
Meta-y	Insert the last selected text here. Note that this can be text selected in some other text subwindow. Also, if you select some text in an *xterm* window, it may be inserted in an *xmh* window with this command. Pressing pointer button 2 is equivalent to this command.
Meta-z	Scroll one line down.
Meta-<	Move to the beginning of the file.
Meta->	Move to the end of the file.
Meta-]	Move forward one paragraph.
Meta-[	Move backward one paragraph.

In addition, the pointer may be used to copy and paste text:

Button 1 Down	Start selection.
Button 1 Motion	Adjust selection.
Button 1 Up	End selection (copy).
Button 2 Down	Insert current selection (paste).
Button 3 Down	Extend current selection.

| Button 3 Motion | Adjust selection. |
| Button 3 Up | End selection (copy). |

Confirmation Dialog Boxes

Whenever you press a button that may cause you to lose some work or is otherwise dangerous, a popup dialog box will appear asking you to confirm the action. This window will contain an Abort or No button and a Confirm or Yes button. Pressing the No button cancels the operation, and pressing Yes will proceed with the operation.

Some dialog boxes contain messages from *mh*. Occasionally when the message is more than one line long, not all of the text will be visible. Clicking on the message field will cause the dialog box to resize so that you can read the entire message.

Message Sequences

An *mh* message sequence is just a set of messages associated with some name. They are local to a particular folder; two different folders can have sequences with the same name. The sequence "all" is predefined in every folder; it consists of the set of all messages in that folder. As many as nine sequences may be defined for each folder, including the predefined "all" sequence. (The sequence "cur" is also usually defined for every folder; it consists of only the current message. *xmh* hides "cur" from the user, instead placing a "+" by the current message. Also, *xmh* does not support *mh*'s "unseen" sequence, so that one is also hidden from the user.)

The message sequences for a folder (including one for "all") are displayed in the Sequence menu, below the sequence commands. The table of contents (also known as the "toc") is at any one time displaying one message sequence. This is called the "viewed sequence," and its name will be displayed in the toc titlebar after the folder name. Also, at any time one of the sequences in the menu will have a check mark next to it. This is called the "selected sequence." Note that the viewed sequence and the selected sequence are not necessarily the same. (This all pretty much corresponds to the way folders work.)

The Open Sequence, Add to Sequence, Remove from Sequence, and Delete Sequence commands are active only if the viewed folder contains message-sequences other than the "all" sequence.

Note that none of the above actually affect whether a message is in the folder. Remember that a sequence is a set of messages within the folder; the above operations just affect what messages are in that set.

To create a new sequence, select the Pick menu entry. A new window will appear, with lots of places to enter text. Basically, you can describe the sequence's initial set of messages based on characteristics of the message. Thus, you can define a sequence to be all the messages that were from a particular person, or with a particular subject, and so on. You can also connect things up with Boolean operators, so you can select all things from "weissman" with a subject containing "xmh."

The layout is fairly obvious. The simplest cases are the easiest: just point to the proper field and type. If you enter in more than one field, it will only select messages which match all non-empty fields.

The more complicated cases arise when you want things that match one field or another one, but not necessarily both. That's what all the or buttons are for. If you want all things with subjects that include "xmh" or "xterm," just press the or button next to the Subject: field. Another box will appear where you can enter another subject.

If you want all things either from "weissman" or with subject "xmh," but not necessarily both, select the -Or- button. This will essentially double the size of the form. You can then enter weissman in a from: box on the top half, and "xmh" in a subject: box on the lower part.

If you select the Skip button, then only those messages that *don't* match the fields on that row are included.

Finally, several more boxes will appear in the bottom part of the window. One is the name of the sequence you're defining. (It defaults to the name of the selected sequence when Pick was pressed, or to "temp" if "all" was the selected sequence.) Another box defines which sequence to look through for potential members of this sequence; it defaults to the viewed sequence when Pick was pressed.

Two more boxes define a date range; only messages within that date range will be considered. These dates must be entered in RFC 822-style format: each date is of the form dd mmm yy hh:mm:ss zzz, where dd is a one or two digit day of the month, mmm is the three-letter abbreviation for a month, and yy is a year. The remaining fields are optional: hh, mm, and ss specify a time of day, and zzz selects a time zone. Note that if the time is left out, it defaults to midnight; thus if you select a range of "7 nov 86" – "8 nov 86", you will get only messages from the 7th, as all messages on the 8th will have arrived after midnight.

Date field specifies which field in the header to look at for this date range; it defaults to Date. If the sequence you're defining already exists, you can optionally merge the old set with the new; that's what the Yes and No buttons are all about. Finally, you can OK the whole thing, or Cancel it.

In general, most people will rarely use these features. However, it's nice to occasionally use Pick to find some messages, look through them, and then hit Delete Sequence to put things back in their original state.

Widget Hierarchy

In order to specify resources, it is useful to know the hierarchy of widgets which compose *xmh*. In the notation below, indentation indicates hierarchical structure. The widget class name is given first, followed by the widget instance name. The application class name is Xmh.

The hierarchy of the main toc and view window is identical for additional toc and view windows, except that a TopLevelShell widget is inserted in the hierarchy between the application shell and the Paned widget.

```
Xmh xmh
      Paned xmh
            SimpleMenu  folderMenu
                      SmeBSB  open
                      SmeBSB  openInNew
                      SmeBSB  create
                      SmeBSB  delete
                      SmeLine  line
                      SmeBSB  close
            SimpleMenu  tocMenu
                      SmeBSB  inc
                      SmeBSB  commit
                      SmeBSB  pack
                      SmeBSB  sort
                      SmeBSB  rescan
            SimpleMenu  messageMenu
                      SmeBSB  compose
                      SmeBSB  next
                      SmeBSB  prev
                      SmeBSB  delete
                      SmeBSB  move
                      SmeBSB  copy
                      SmeBSB  unmark
                      SmeBSB  viewNew
                      SmeBSB  reply
                      SmeBSB  forward
                      SmeBSB  useAsComp
                      SmeBSB  print
            SimpleMenu  sequenceMenu
                      SmeBSB  pick
                      SmeBSB  openSeq
                      SmeBSB  addToSeq
                      SmeBSB  removeFromSeq
                      SmeBSB  deleteSeq
                      SmeLine  line
                      SmeBSB  all
            SimpleMenu  viewMenu
                      SmeBSB  reply
                      SmeBSB  forward
                      SmeBSB  useAsComp
                      SmeBSB  edit
                      SmeBSB  save
                      SmeBSB  print
            SimpleMenu  optionMenu
                      SmeBSB  reverse
            Viewport.Core  menuBox.clip
                      Box  menuBox
                              MenuButton  folderButton
```

```
                              MenuButton   tocButton
                              MenuButton   messageButton
                              MenuButton   sequenceButton
                              MenuButton   viewButton
                              MenuButton   optionButton
              Grip  grip
              Label folderTitlebar
              Grip  grip
              Viewport.Core  folders.clip
                     Box  folders
                              MenuButton   inbox
                              MenuButton   drafts
                                    SimpleMenu   menu
                                        SmeBSB <folder_name>
                                                 .
                                                 .
                                                 .

              Grip  grip
              Label  tocTitlebar
              Grip  grip
              Text toc
                      Scrollbar   vScrollbar
              Grip  grip
              Label  viewTitlebar
              Grip  grip
              Text  view
                        Scrollbar   vScrollbar
                        Scrollbar   hScrollbar
```

The hierarchy of the Create Folder popup dialog box:

```
         TransientShell  prompt
                Dialog  dialog
                        Label  label
                        Text  value
                        Command  okay
                        Command  cancel
```

The hierarchy of the Notice dialog box, which reports messages from mh:

```
         TransientShell  notice
                Dialog  dialog
                        Label  label
                        Text  value
                        Command  confirm
```

The hierarchy of the Confirmation dialog box:

```
TransientShell  confirm
        Dialog  dialog
                Label  label
                Command  yes
                Command  no
```

The hierarchy of the dialog box which reports errors:

```
TransientShell  error
        Dialog  dialog
                Label  label
                Command  OK
```

The hierarchy of the composition window:

```
TopLevelShell  xmh
        Paned  xmh
                Label  composeTitlebar
                Text  comp
                Viewport.Core  compButtons.clip
                        Box  compButtons
                                Command  close
                                Command  send
                                Command  reset
                                Command  compose
                                Command  save
                                Command  insert
```

The hierarchy of the view window:

```
TopLevelShell  xmh
        Paned  xmh
                Label  viewTitlebar
                Text  view
                Viewport.Core  viewButtons.clip
                        Box  viewButtons
                                Command  close
                                Command  reply
                                Command  forward
                                Command  useAsComp
                                Command  edit
                                Command  save
                                Command  print
```

The hierarchy of the pick window:
(Unnamed widgets have no name.)

```
TopLevelShell  xmh
        Paned  xmh
                Label  pickTitlebar
                Viewport.Core  pick.clip
                        Form   form
                                Form    groupform
```
The first 6 rows of the pick window have identical structure:
```
                                Form    rowform
                                Toggle
                                Toggle
                                Label
                                Text
                                Command

                                Form    rowform
                                Toggle
                                Toggle
                                Text
                                Text
                                Command
                                Form    rowform
                                Command
                Viewport.Core  pick.clip
                        Form   form
                                Form    groupform
                                Form    rowform
                                Label
                                Text
                                Label
                                Text
                                Form    rowform
                                Label
                                Text
                                Label
                                Text
                                Label
                                Text
                                Form    rowform
                                Label
                                Toggle
                                Toggle
                                Form    rowform
                                Command
                                Command
```

See Appendix G, *Widget Resources* for a list of resources that can be set for the Athena widgets.

Application-specific Resources

The application class name is Xmh. Application-specific resource class names always begin with an uppercase character, but unless noted, are otherwise identical to the instance names.

Any of these resources may also be specified on the command line by using the X Toolkit Intrinsics resource specification mechanism. Thus, to run *xmh* showing all message headers,

```
% xmh -xrm '*HideBoringHeaders:off'
```

If TocGeometry, ViewGeometry, CompGeometry, or PickGeometry are not specified, then the value of Geometry is used instead. If the resulting height is not specified (e.g., "", "=500", "+0-0"), then the default height of windows is calculated from fonts and line counts. If the width is not specified (e.g., "", "=x300", "-0+0"), then half of the display width is used. If unspecified, the height of a pick window defaults to half the height of the display.

The following resources are defined:

banner

> A short string that is the default label of the folder, Table of Contents, and view. The default is:
>
> > xmh   MIT X Consortium   R5

blockEventsOnBusy

> Whether to disallow user input and show a busy cursor while *xmh* is busy processing a command. Default is true.

busyCursor

> The name of the symbol used to represent the position of the pointer, displayed if blockEventsOnBusy is true, when *xmh* is processing a time-consuming command. The default is watch.

busyPointerColor

> The foreground color of the busy cursor. Default is XtDefaultForeground.

checkFrequency

> How often to check for new mail, make checkpoints, and rescan the Table of Contents, in minutes. If checkNewMail is true, *xmh* checks to see if you have new mail each interval. If makeCheckpoints is true, checkpoints are made every fifth interval. Also every fifth interval, the Table of Contents is checked for inconsistencies with the file system, and rescanned. To prevent all of these checks from occurring, set checkFrequency to 0. The default is 1. This resource is retained for backward compatibility with user resource files; see also checkpoint-Interval, mailInterval, and rescanInterval.

checkNewMail

> If true, *xmh* will check at regular intervals to see if new mail has arrived for any of the top level folders. A visual indication will be given if new mail is waiting to be retrieved. Default is true. (See "Bugs.") The interval can be adjusted with the checkFrequency resource.

commandButtonCount

The number of command buttons to create in a buttonbox in between the toc and the view areas of the main window. *xmh* will create these buttons with the names *button1*, *button2* and so on, in a box with the name *commandBox*. The user can specify labels and actions for the buttons in a private resource file; see the section on "Actions." The default is 0.

compGeometry

Initial geometry for windows containing compositions.

cursor

The name of the symbol used to represent the pointer. Default is left_ptr.

draftsFolder

The folder used for message drafts. Default is drafts.

geometry

Default geometry to use. Default is none.

hideBoringHeaders

If "on", then *xmh* will attempt to skip uninteresting header lines within messages by scrolling them off. Default is on.

initialFolder

Which folder to display on startup. Can also be set with the command-line option -initial. Default is inbox.

initialIncFile

The file name of your incoming mail drop. *xmh* tries to construct a filename for the inc -file command, but in some installations (e.g., those using the Post Office Protocol) no file is appropriate. In this case, initialIncFile should be specified as the empty string, and *inc* will be invoked without a -file argument. The default is to use the value of the environment variable MAIL, or if that is not set, to append the value of the environment variable USER to */usr/spool/mail/*.

mailPath

The full path prefix for locating your mail folders. May also be set with the command-line option, -path. The default is the Path component in *$HOME/.mh_profile*, or *$HOME/Mail* if none.

mailWaitingFlag

If true, *xmh* will attempt to set an indication in its icon when new mail is waiting to be retrieved. If this option is true, then checkNewMail is assumed to be true as well. The -flag command-line option is a quick way to turn mailWaitingFlag on.

makeCheckpoints

If true, *xmh* will attempt to save checkpoints of volatile information. The frequency of checkpointing is controlled by the resource checkFrequency.

mhPath
> The directory in which to find the *mh* commands. If a command isn't found here, then the directories in the user's path are searched. Default is */usr/local/mh6*.

pickGeometry
> Initial geometry for pick windows.

pointerColor
> The foreground color of the pointer. Default is XtDefaultForeground.

prefixWmAndIconName
> Whether to prefix the window and icon name with "xmh:". Default is true.

printCommand
> The *sh* command to execute to print a message. Note that standard output and standard error must be specifically redirected! If a message or range of messages is selected for printing, the full file path of each message file is appended to the specified print command. The default is enscript >/dev/null 2>/dev/null.

replyInsertFilter
> A shell command to be executed when the Insert button is activated in a composition window. The full path and filename of the source message is added to the end of the command before being passed to *sh*(1). The default filter is *cat*; i.e., it inserts the entire message into the composition. Interesting filters are: *awk -e '{print " " $0}'* or *<mh directory>/lib/mhl -form mhl.body*.

reverseReadOrder
> When true, the next message will be the message prior to the current message in the Table of Contents, and the previous message will be the message after the current message in the Table of Contents. The default is false.

sendBreakWidth
> When a message is sent from *xmh*, lines longer than this value will be split into multiple lines, each of which is no longer than sendWidth. This value may be overridden for a single message by inserting an additional line in the message header of the form sendBreakWidth: *value*. This line will be removed from the header before the message is sent. The default is 85.

sendWidth
> When a message is sent from *xmh*, lines longer than sendBreakWidth characters will be split into multiple lines, each of which is no longer than this value. This value may be overridden for a single message by inserting an additional line in the message header of the form sendWidth: *value*. This line will be removed from the header before the message is sent. The default is 72.

skipCopied
> Whether to skip over messages marked for copying when using View Next Message and View Previous Message. Default is true.

skipDeleted

> Whether to skip over messages marked for deletion when using View Next Message and View Previous Message. Default is `true`.

skipMoved

> Whether to skip over messages marked for moving to other folders when using View Next Message and View Previous Message. Default is `true`.

stickyMenu

> If `true`, when popup command menus are used, the most recently selected entry will be under the cursor when the menu pops up. Default is `false`. See the file *clients/xmh/Xmh.sample* for an example of how to specify resources for pop up command menus.

tempDir

> Directory for *xmh* to store temporary directories. For privacy, a user might want to change this to a private directory. Default is */tmp*.

tocGeometry

> Initial geometry for master *xmh* windows.

tocPercentage

> The percentage of the main window that is used to display the Table of Contents. Default is 33.

tocWidth

> How many characters to generate for each message in a folder's Table of Contents. Default is 100. Use 80 if you plan to use *mhl* a lot, because it will be faster, and the extra 20 characters may not be useful.

viewGeometry

> Initial geometry for windows showing only a view of a message.

Actions

Because *xmh* provides action procedures which correspond to command functionality and installs accelerators, users can customize accelerators in a private resource file. *xmh* provides action procedures which correspond to entries in the command menus; these are given in the sections describing menu commmands. For examples of specifying customized resources, see the file *clients/xmh/Xmh.sample*. Unpredictable results can occur if actions are bound to events or widgets for which they were not designed.

In addition to the actions corresponding to commands, these action routines are defined:

XmhPushFolder([*foldername, . . .*])

> Pushes each of its argument(s) onto a stack of folder names. If no arguments are given, the selected folder is pushed onto the stack.

XmhPopFolder()

> Pops one folder name from the stack and sets the selected folder.

XmhPopupFolderMenu()

>Should always be taken when the user selects a folder button. A folder button represents a folder and zero or more subfolders. The menu of subfolders is built upon the first reference, by this routine. If there are no subfolders, this routine will mark the folder as having no subfolders, and no menu will be built. In that case, the menu button emulates a toggle button. When subfolders exist, the menu will popup, using the menu button action PopupMenu().

XmhSetCurrentFolder()

>Allows menu buttons to emulate toggle buttons in the function of selecting a folder. This action is for Menubutton widgets only, and sets the selected folder.

XmhLeaveFolderButton()

>Ensures that the menu button behaves properly when the user moves the pointer out of the menu button window.

XmhPushSequence([*sequencename*, . . .])

>Pushes each of its arguments onto the stack of sequence names. If no arguments are given, the selected sequence is pushed onto the stack.

XmhPopSequence()

>Pops one sequence name from the stack of sequence names, which then becomes the selected sequence.

XmhPromptOkayAction()

>Equivalent to pressing the Okay *button in the* Create Folder popup.

XmhCancelPick()

>Equivalent to pressing the Cancel button in the Pick window.

Customization Using mh

The initial text displayed in a composition window is generated by executing the corresponding *mh* command; i.e., *comp*, *repl*, or *forw*, and therefore message components may be customized as specified for those commands. *comp* is executed only once per invocation of *xmh* and the message template is re-used for each successive new composition.

Files

˜/.mh_profile

>*mh* profile, used if the MH environment variable is not set.

˜/Mail   Directory of folders, used if the *mh* profile cannot be found.

˜/.xmhcheck

>Optional, for multiple mail drops in cooperation with *slocal*.

/usr/local/mh6

>*mh* commands, as a last resort (see mhPath).

*˜/Mail/<**folder**>/.xmhcache*

>*scan* output in each folder.

*̄/Mail/<**folder**>/.mh_sequences*
> Sequence definitions in each folder.

/tmp   Temporary files (see `tempDir`).

See Also

X, xrdb, mh(1); Appendix G, *Widget Resources*; the Nutshell Handbook *MH and xmh: E-mail for Users and Programmers.*

Bugs

When the user closes a window, all windows which are transient for that window should also be closed by *xmh.*

When `XmhUseAsComposition` and `XmhViewUseAsComposition` operate on messages in the `DraftsFolder`, *xmh* disallows editing of the composition if the same message is also being viewed in another window.

Occasionally after committing changes, the table of contents will appear to be completely blank when there are actually messages present. When this happens, refreshing the display, or typing Control-l in the table of contents, will often cause the correct listing to appear. If this doesn't work, force a rescan of the folder.

Should recognize and use the "unseen" message-sequence.

Should determine by itself if the user hasn't used *mh* before, and offer to create the *.mh_profile*, instead of hanging on *inc.*

A few commands are missing (rename folder, resend message).

WM_DELETE_WINDOW protocol doesn't work right when requesting deletion of the first toc and view, while trying to keep other *xmh* windows around.

Doesn't support annotations when replying to messages.

Doesn't allow folders to be shared without write permission.

Doesn't recognize private sequences.

mh will report that the *.mh_sequences* file is poorly formatted if any sequence definition in a particular folder contains more than *BUFSIZ* characters. *xmh* tries to capture these messages and display them when they occur, but it cannot correct the problem.

Copyright

Copyright 1988, 1989, Digital Equipment Corporation.
Copyright 1989, 1991, Massachusetts Institute of Technology.
See *X* for a full statement of rights and permissions.

Author

Terry Weissman, formerly of Digital Western Research Laboratory;
Donna Converse, MIT X Consortium.

xmodmap

Name

xmodmap – keyboard and pointer modifier utility.

Syntax

xmodmap [*options*] [*filename*]

Description

xmodmap is a utility for displaying and editing the X keyboard *modifier map* and *keymap table* that client applications use to convert keycodes into keysyms. *xmodmap* is intended to be run from a user's X startup script to set up the keyboard according to personal tastes.

With no arguments, *xmodmap* displays the current map. See Chapter 14, *Setup Clients*, for more information.

Options

xmodmap accepts the following options:

-display [*host*]:*server*[*.screen*]

Specifies the name of the display to use. *host* is the hostname of the physical display, *server* specifies the display server number, and *screen* specifies the screen number. Either or both of the *host* and *screen* elements to the display specification can be omitted. If *host* is omitted, the local display is assumed. If *screen* is omitted, screen 0 is assumed (and the period is unnecessary). The colon and (display) *server* are necessary in all cases. For example:

% **xmodmap -display** *your_node*:0.0

specifies the screen 0 on server 0 on the display identified by *your_node*. If the host is omitted, the local display is assumed. If the screen is omitted, the screen 0 is assumed; the server and colon (:) are necessary in all cases.

The -display option can be abbreviated as -d, unless the client accepts another option that begins with "d."

-e *expression*

Specifies an expression to be executed. Any number of expressions may be specified from the command line.

-grammar

Indicates that a help message describing the expression grammar used in files and with -e expressions should be printed on the standard error.

-help Indicates that a brief description of the command-line arguments should be printed on the standard error. This will be done whenever an invalid argument is given to *xmodmap*.

-quiet

Turns off the verbose logging. This is the default.

-n   Indicates that *xmodmap* should not change the mappings, but should display what it would do, as *make*(1) does when given this option. (Cannot be used with expressions to change the pointer mapping.)

-pm   Indicates that the current modifier map should be printed on the standard output.

-pk   Indicates that the current keymap table should be printed on the standard output.

-pke Indicates that the current keymap table should be printed on the standard output in the form of expressions that can be fed back to *xmodmap*.

-pp   Indicates that the current pointer map should be printed on the standard output.

-     A lone dash means that the standard input should be used as the input file.

-verbose
      Indicates that *xmodmap* should print logging information as it parses its input.

The `filename` argument specifies a file containing *xmodmap* expressions to be executed. This file is usually kept in the user's home directory and has a name like *.xmodmaprc*.

Expression Grammar

The *xmodmap* program reads a list of expressions and parses them all before attempting to execute any of them. This makes it possible to refer to keysyms that are being redefined in a natural way without having to worry as much about name conflicts. Allowable expressions include:

keycode *NUMBER* = *KEYSYMNAME* . . .
      The list of keysyms is assigned to the indicated keycode (which may be specified in decimal, hex, or octal and can be determined by running the *xev* program in the examples directory).

keysym *KEYSYMNAME* = *KEYSYMNAME* . . .
      The *KEYSYMNAME* on the left hand side is translated into matching keycodes used to perform the corresponding set of keycode expressions. The list of keysym names may be found in the header file *<X11/keysymdef.h>* (without the *XK_* prefix) or the keysym database */usr/lib/X11/XKeysymDB*. Note that if the same keysym is bound to multiple keys, the expression is executed for each matching keycode.

clear *MODIFIERNAME*
      This removes all entries in the modifier map for the given modifier, where valid names are: Shift, Lock, Control, Mod1, Mod2, Mod3, Mod4, and Mod5 (case does not matter in modifier names, although it does matter for all other names). For example, clear Lock will remove any keys that were bound to the lock modifier.

add *MODIFIERNAME* = *KEYSYMNAME* . . .
      This adds all the keys having the given keysyms to the indicated modifier map. The keysym names are evaluated after all input expressions are read to make it easy to write expressions to swap keys. (See the "Examples" section.)

remove *MODIFIERNAME* = *KEYSYMNAME* . . .

> This removes all the keys having the given keysyms from the indicated modifier map. Unlike add, the keysym names are evaluated as the line is read in. This allows you to remove keys from a modifier without having to worry about whether or not they have been reassigned.

pointer = default

> This sets the pointer map back to its default settings (button 1 generates a code of 1, button 2 generates a 2, etc.).

pointer = *N1 N2 N3*

> This sets the pointer map to contain the button codes *N1*, *N2*, and *N3*, where *N1*, *N2* and *N3* are numbers. The list always starts with the first physical button.

Lines that begin with an exclamation mark (!) are taken as comments.

If you want to change the binding of a modifier key, you must also remove it from the appropriate modifier map.

Examples

Many pointers are designed such that the first button is pressed using the index finger of the right hand. People who are left handed frequently find that it is more comfortable to reverse the button codes that get generated so that the primary button is pressed using the index finger of the left hand. This could be done on a 3-button pointer as follows:

```
% xmodmap -e "pointer = 3 2 1"
```

Many editor applications support the notion of Meta keys (similar to Control keys except that Meta is held down instead of Control). However, some servers do not have a Meta keysym in the default keymap table, so one needs to be added by hand. The following command will attach Meta to the Multi-language key (sometimes labeled Compose Character). It also takes advantage of the fact that applications that need a Meta key need simply to get the keycode and don't require the keysym to be in the first column of the keymap table. This means that applications that are looking for a Multi_key (including the default modifier map) won't notice any change.

```
% xmodmap -e "keysym Multi_key = Multi_key Meta_L"
```

One of the more simple, yet convenient, uses of *xmodmap* is to set the keyboard's "rubout" key to generate an alternate keysym. This frequently involves exchanging Backspace with Delete to be more comfortable to the user. If the ttymodes resource in *xterm* is set as well, all terminal emulator windows will use the same key for erasing characters:

```
% xmodmap -e "keysym BackSpace = Delete"
% echo "XTerm*ttyModes: erase ^?" | xrdb -merge
```

Some keyboards do not automatically generate less than and greater than characters when the comma and period keys are shifted. This can be remedied with *xmodmap* by resetting the bindings for the comma and period with the following scripts:

```
!
! make shift-, be < and shift-. be >
!
keysym comma = comma less
keysym period = period greater
```

One of the more irritating differences between keyboards is the location of the Control and Shift Lock keys. A common use of *xmodmap* is to swap these two keys as follows:

```
!
! Swap Caps_Lock and Control_L
!
remove Lock = Caps_Lock
remove Control = Control_L
keysym Control_L = Caps_Lock
keysym Caps_Lock = Control_L
add Lock = Caps_Lock
add Control = Control_L
```

The `keycode` expression is useful for assigning the same keysym to multiple keycodes. Although unportable, it also makes it possible to write scripts that can reset the keyboard to a known state. The following script sets the Backspace key to generate Delete (as shown above), flushes all existing caps lock bindings, makes the CapsLock key a control key, makes F5 generate Escape, and makes Break/Reset function as a shift lock.

```
!
! On the HP, the following keycodes have key caps as listed:
!
!     101   Backspace
!      55   Caps
!      14   Ctrl
!      15   Break/Reset
!      86   Stop
!      89   F5
!

keycode 101 = Delete
keycode 55 = Control_R
clear Lock
add Control = Control_R
```

```
keycode 89 = Escape
keycode 15 = Caps_Lock
add Lock = Caps_Lock
```

See Also

X, xev; Chapter 14, *Setup Clients*.

Bugs

Every time a `keycode` expression is evaluated, the server generates a `MappingNotify` event on every client. This can cause some thrashing. All of the changes should be batched together and done at once. Clients that receive keyboard input and ignore `MappingNotify` events will not notice any changes made to keyboard mappings.

xmodmap should generate `add` and `remove` expressions automatically whenever a keycode that is already bound to a modifier is changed.

There should be a way to have the `remove` expression accept keycodes as well as keysyms for those times when you really mess up your mappings.

Authors

Rewritten by Jim Fulton, MIT X Consortium, from an earlier version by David Rosenthal of Sun Microsystems.

Name

xpr – print an X window dump.

Syntax

xpr [*options*] [*filename*]

Description

xpr takes as input a window dump file produced by *xwd* and formats it for output on PostScript printers, the DEC LN03 or LA100, the IBM PP3812 page printer, the HP LaserJet (or other PCL printers), or the HP PaintJet. If you do not supply a filename, standard input is used. By default, *xpr* prints the largest possible representation of the window on the output page. Options allow you to add headers and trailers, specify margins, adjust the scale and orientation, and append multiple window dumps to a single output file. Output is sent to standard output unless you specify -output *filename*. See Chapter 8, *Other Clients*, for some examples of usage.

Options

xpr accepts the following options:

-append *filename*

Specifies a filename previously produced by *xpr* to which the window contents are to be appended.

-compact

Compresses white pixels on PostScript printers.

-cutoff *level*

Changes the intensity level where colors are mapped to either black or white for monochrome output on a LaserJet printer. The *level* is expressed as a percentage of full brightness. Fractions are allowed.

-density *dpi*

Indicates what dot-per-inch density should be used by the HP printer.

-device *printer_device*

Specifies the device on which the file is to be printed. Currently the following printers are supported:

ln03	Digital LN03.
la100	Digital LA100.
ljet	HP LaserJet series and other monochrome PCL devices, such as ThinkJet, QuietJet, RuggedWriter, HP2560 series, and HP2930 series printers.
pjet	HP PaintJet (color mode).
pjetxl	HP PaintJet XL Color Graphics Printer (color mode).

pp   IBM PP3812.

ps   PostScript printer.

As of Release 5, the default is ps (PostScript). (In prior releases, the default printer is
the LN03.) -device lw (Apple LaserWriter) is equivalent to -device ps and is
provided only for backwards compatibility.

-gamma *correction*
Changes the intensity of the colors printed by PaintJet XL printers. The *correc-*
tion is a floating point value in the range 0.00 to 3.00. Consult the operator's manual to determine the correct value for the specific printer.

-gray 2 | 3 | 4
Uses a simple 2×2, 3×3, or 4×4 grey scale conversion on a color image, rather than
mapping to strictly black and white. This doubles, triples, or quadruples the effective
width and height of the image. -gray is not supported for HP and IBM printers.

-header *header*
Specifies a header string to be printed above the window. Default is no header.

-height *inches*
Specifies the maximum height of the page.

-landscape
Prints the window in landscape mode. By default, a window is printed such that its
longest side follows the long side of the paper.

-left *inches*
Specifies the left margin in inches. Fractions are allowed. By default, the window is
centered on the page.

-noff When specified in conjunction with -append, the window appears on the same page
as the previous window.

-noposition
Causes header, trailer, and image positioning command generation to be bypassed for
LaserJet, PaintJet, and PaintJet XL printers.

-output *filename*
Specifies an output filename. If this option is not specified, standard output is used.

-plane *number*
Specifies which bit plane to use in an image. The default is to use the entire image
and map values into black and white based on color intensities.

-portrait
Prints the window in portrait mode. By default, a window is printed such that its longest side follows the long side of the paper.

-psfig
Suppress translation of the PostScript picture to the center of the page.

-render *algorithm*

    Allows PaintJet XL printers to render the image with the best quality versus performance tradeoff. Consult the operator's manual to determine which *algorithm*s are available.

-rv   Reverses the foreground and background colors.

-scale *scale*

    Affects the size of the window on the page. The PostScript, LN03, and HP printers are able to translate each bit in a window pixel map into a grid of a specified size. For example, each bit might translate into a 3×3 grid. This is specified by -scale 3. By default, a window is printed with the largest scale that fits onto the page for the specified orientation.

-slide

    Allows overhead transparencies to be printed using the PaintJet and PaintJet XL printers.

-split *n*

    Allows you to split a window onto several pages. This might be necessary for large windows that would otherwise cause the printer to overload and print the page in an obscure manner.

-top *inches*

    Specifies the top margin for the picture in inches. Fractions are allowed. By default, the window is centered on the page.

-trailer *trailer*

    Specifies a trailer string to be printed below the window. Default is no trailer.

-width *inches*

    Specifies the maximum width of the page.

Limitations

The current version of *xpr* can generally print out on the LN03 most X windows that are not larger than two-thirds of the screen. For example, it will be able to print out a large *emacs* window, but it will usually fail when trying to print out the entire screen. The LN03 has memory limitations that can cause it to incorrectly print very large or complex windows. The two most common errors encountered are "band too complex" and "page memory exceeded." In the first case, a window may have a particular band (a row six pixels deep) that contains too many changes (from black to white to black). This will cause the printer to drop part of the line and, possibly, parts of the rest of the page. The printer will flash the number "1" on its front panel when this problem occurs. A possible solution to this problem is to increase the scale of the picture, or to split the picture onto two or more pages. The second problem, "page memory exceeded," will occur if the picture contains too much black, or if the picture contains complex half-tones such as the background color of a display. When this problem occurs the printer will automatically split the picture into two or more pages. It may flash the number "5" on its front panel. There is no easy solution to this problem. It will probably be necessary to either cut and paste, or rework the application to produce a less complex picture.

There are several limitations on the use of *xpr* with the LA100: the picture will always be printed in portrait mode, there is no scaling, and the aspect ratio will be slightly off.

Support for PostScript output currently cannot handle the -append, -noff, or -split options.

The -compact option is supported *only* for PostScript output. It compresses white space but not black space, so it is not useful for reverse-video windows.

For color images, should map directly to PostScript image support.

HP Printer Specifics

If no -density is specified on the command line, 300 dots per inch will be assumed for ljet and 90 dots per inch for pjet. Allowable *density* values for a LaserJet printer are 300, 150, 100, and 75 dots per inch. Consult the operator's manual to determine densities supported by other printers.

If no -scale is specified, the image will be expanded to fit the printable page area.

The default printable page area is 8×10.5 inches. Other paper sizes can be accommodated using the -height and -width options.

Note that a 1024×768 image fits the default printable area when processed at 100 dpi with scale=1; the same image can also be printed using 300 dpi with scale=3, but will require that considerably more data be transferred to the printer.

xpr may be tailored for use with monochrome PCL printers other than the LaserJet. To print on a ThinkJet (HP2225A), *xpr* could be invoked as:

    % xpr -density 96 -width 6.667 *filename*

or for black-and-white output to a PaintJet:

    % xpr -density 180 *filename*

The monochrome intensity of a pixel is computed as 0.30*R + 0.59*G + 0.11*B. If a pixel's computed intensity is less than the -cutoff level, it will print as white. This maps light-on-dark display images to black-on-white hardcopy. The default cutoff intensity is 50% of full brightness. Example: specifying -cutoff 87.5 moves the white/black intensity point to 87.5% of full brightness.

A LaserJet printer must be configured with sufficient memory to handle the image. For a full page at 300 dots per inch, approximately 2MB of printer memory is required.

Color images are produced on the PaintJet at 90 dots per inch. The PaintJet is limited to 16 colors from its 330 color palette on each horizontal print line. *xpr* will issue a warning message if more than 16 colors are encountered on a line. *xpr* will program the PaintJet for the first 16 colors encountered on each line and use the nearest matching programmed value for other colors present on the line.

Specifying the −rv (reverse video) option for the PaintJet will cause black and white to be interchanged on the output image. No other colors are changed.

Multiplane images must be recorded by *xwd* in ZPixmap format. Single plane (monochrome) images may be in either XYPixmap or ZPixmap format.

Some PCL printers do not recognize image positioning commands. Output for these printers will not be centered on the page and header and trailer strings may not appear where expected.

The −gamma and −render options are supported only on the PaintJet XL printers.

The −slide option is not supported for LaserJet printers.

The −split option is not supported for HP printers.

See Also

xwd, xdpr, xwud, X; Chapter 8, *Other Clients*.

Copyright

Copyright 1988, Massachusetts Institute of Technology.

Copyright 1986, Marvin Solomon and the University of Wisconsin.

Copyright 1988, Hewlett-Packard Company.

See *X* for a full statement of rights and permissions.

Authors

Michael R. Gretzinger, MIT Project Athena;
Jose Capo, MIT Project Athena (PP3812 support);
Marvin Solomon, University of Wisconsin;
Bob Scheifler, MIT;
Angela Bock and E. Mike Durbin, Rich Inc. (greyscale);
Larry Rupp, Hewlett-Packard (HP printer support).

xprop

Name

xprop – display window and font properties for X.

Syntax

xprop [*options*]

Description

The *xprop* utility displays window and font properties in an X server. One window or font is selected using the command line arguments or, in the case of a window, by clicking on the desired window. A list of properties is then given, possibly with formatting information.

For each of these properties, its value on the selected window or font is printed using the supplied formatting information, if any. If no formatting information is supplied, internal defaults are used. If a property is not defined on the selected window or font, "not defined" is printed as the value for that property. If no property list is given, all the properties possessed by the selected window or font are printed.

A window may be selected in one of four ways. First, if the desired window is the root window, the -root option may be used. If the desired window is not the root window, it may be selected in two ways on the command line, either by ID number such as might be obtained from *xwininfo*, or by name if the window possesses a name. The -id option selects a window by ID number in either decimal or hex (must start with 0x) while the -name option selects a window by name.

The last way to select a window does not involve the command line at all. If none of -font, -id, -name, and -root is specified, a crosshair cursor is displayed and the user is allowed to choose any visible window by pressing any pointer button in the desired window. If it is desired to display properties of a font as opposed to a window, the -font option must be used.

Other than the above four options, the -help option for obtaining help, and the -grammar option for listing the full grammar for the command line, all the other command-line options are used in specifing both the format of the properties to be displayed and how to display them. The -len *n* option specifies that at most *n* bytes of any given property will be read and displayed. This is useful, for example, when displaying the cut buffer on the root window, which could run to several pages if displayed in full.

Normally each property name is displayed by printing first the property name, then its type (if it has one) in parentheses, followed by its value. The -notype option specifies that property types should not be displayed. The -fs option is used to specify a file containing a list of formats for properties, while the -f option is used to specify the format for one property.

The formatting information for a property actually consists of two parts, a *format* and a *dformat*. The *format* specifies the actual formatting of the property (i.e., is it made up of words, bytes, or longs, etc.), while the *dformat* specifies how the property should be displayed.

The following paragraphs describe how to construct *format*s and *dformat*s. However, for the vast majority of users and uses, this should not be necessary as the built-in defaults contain the *format*s and *dformat*s necessary to display all the standard properties. It should be necessary to specify *format*s and *dformat*s only if a new property is being dealt with or the user dislikes the standard display format. New users especially are encouraged to skip this part.

A *format* consists of one of 0, 8, 16, or 32 followed by a sequence of one or more format characters. The 0, 8, 16, or 32 specifies how many bits per field there are in the property. Zero is a special case, meaning use the field size information associated with the property itself. (This is needed only for special cases like type INTEGER, which is actually three different types depending on the size of the fields of the property.)

A value of 8 means that the property is a sequence of bytes, while a value of 16 means that the property is a sequence of words. The difference between these two lies in the fact that the sequence of words will be byte swapped, while the sequence of bytes will not be, when read by a machine of the opposite byte order of the machine that orginally wrote the property. For more information on how properties are formatted and stored, consult Volume One, *Xlib Programming Manual*.

Once the size of the fields has been specified, it is necessary to specify the type of each field (i.e., is it an integer, a string, an atom, or what?). This is done using one format character per field. If there are more fields in the property than format characters supplied, the last character will be repeated as many times as necessary for the extra fields. The format characters and their meanings are as follows:

a   The field holds an atom number. A field of this type should be of size 32.

b   The field is a Boolean. A 0 means `False` while anything else means `True`.

c   The field is an unsigned number, a cardinal.

i   The field is a signed integer.

m   The field is a set of bit flags, 1 meaning on.

s   This field and the next ones, until either a 0 or the end of the property, represent a sequence of bytes. This format character is usable only with a field size of 8 and is most often used to represent a string.

x   The field is a hex number (like c but displayed in hex—most useful for displaying window IDs and the like).

An example *format* is 32ica, which is the format for a property of three fields of 32 bits each, the first holding a signed integer, the second an unsigned integer, and the third an atom.

The format of a *dformat* (unlike that of a *format*) is not so rigid. The only limitations on a *dformat* is that it may not start with a letter or a dash. This is so that it can be distinguished from a property name or an option. A *dformat* is a text string containing special characters instructing that various fields be printed at various points in a manner similar to the formatting string used by *printf*. For example, the *dformat* " is ($0, $1 \)\n" would render the POINT 3, -4 which has a *format* of 32ii as " is (3, -4)\n".

Any character other than a $, ?, \, or a (in a *dformat* prints as itself. To print out one of $, ?, \, or (, preceed it by a \. For example, to print out a $, use \$. Several special backslash sequences are provided as shortcuts. \n will cause a newline to be displayed while \t will cause a tab to be displayed. \o, where *o* is an octal number, will display character number *o*.

A $ followed by a number *n* causes field number *n* to be displayed. The format of the displayed field depends on the formatting character used to describe it in the corresponding *format*. That is, if a cardinal is described by c, it will print in decimal while if it is described by a x it will be displayed in hex.

If the field is not present in the property (this is possible with some properties), <field not available> is displayed instead. $*n*+ will display field number *n*, then a comma, then field number *n*+1, then another comma, then ... until the last field defined. If field *n* is not defined, nothing is displayed. This is useful for a property that is a list of values.

A ? is used to start a conditional expression, a kind of if-then statement. ?*exp*(*text*) will display *text* if and only if *exp* evaluates to non-zero. This is useful for two things. First, it allows fields to be displayed if and only if a flag is set. And second, it allows a value such as a state number to be displayed as a name rather than just as a number. The syntax of *exp* is as follows:

> *exp* ::= *term* | *term*=*exp* | !*exp*
> *term*::= *n* | $*n* | m*n*

The ! operator is a logical "not," changing 0 to 1 and any non-zero value to 0. = is an equality operator. Note that internally all expressions are evaluated as 32-bit numbers, so -1 is not equal to 65535. = returns 1 if the two values are equal and 0 if not. *n* represents the constant value *n*, while $*n* represents the value of field number *n*. m*n* is 1 if flag number *n* in the first field having format character m in the corresponding *format* is 1, 0 otherwise.

Examples: ?m3(count: $3\n) displays field 3 with a label of count if and only if flag number 3 (count starts at 0!) is on. ?$2=0(True)?!$2=0(False) displays the inverted value of field 2 as a Boolean.

In order to display a property, *xprop* needs both a *format* and a *dformat*. Before *xprop* uses its default values of a *format* of 32x and a *dformat* of " = { $0+ }\n", it searches several places in an attempt to find more specific formats. First, a search is made using the name of the property. If this fails, a search is made using the type of the property. This allows type STRING to be defined with one set of formats while allowing property WM_NAME, which is of type STRING, to be defined with a different format. In this way, the display formats for a given type can be overridden for specific properties.

The locations searched are in order: the format, if any, specified with the property name (as in 8x WM_NAME), the formats defined by –f options in last to first order, the contents of the file specified by the –fs option, if any, the contents of the file specified by the environment variable XPROPFORMATS, if any, and finally *xprop*'s built-in file of formats.

The format of the files referred to by the −fs option and the XPROPFORMATS variable is one or more lines of the following form:

```
name format [dformat]
```

Where *name* is either the name of a property or the name of a type, *format* is the *format* to be used with *name*, and *dformat* is the *dformat* to be used with *name*. If *dformat* is not present, " = $0+\n" is assumed.

Options

xprop accepts the following options:

−display [*host*]:*server*[.*screen*]

Allows you to specify the display and server to connect to. *host* is the hostname of the physical display, *server* specifies the display server number, and *screen* specifies the screen number. For example:

       % xprop -display *your_node*:**0.1**

specifies screen 1 on server 0 on the display named by *your_node*. Either or both of the *host* and *screen* elements to the display specification can be omitted. If *host* is omitted, the local display is assumed. If *screen* is omitted, screen 0 is assumed (and the period is unnecessary). The colon and (display) *server* are necessary in all cases.

−f *name format* [*dformat*]

Specifies that the format for *name* should be *format* and that the dformat for *name* should be *dformat*. If *dformat* is missing, " = $0+\n" is assumed.

−font *font*

Allows the user to specify that the properties of font *font* should be displayed.

−frame

Specifies that, when selecting a window by hand (i.e., if none of −name, −root, or −id are given), *xprop* should look at the window manager frame (if any) instead of looking for the client window.

−fs *file*

Specifies that file *file* should be used as a source of more formats for properties.

−grammar

Prints out a detailed grammar for all command-line options.

−help   Prints out a summary of command-line options.

−id *id*

Allows the user to select window *id* on the command line rather than using the pointer to select the target window. This is very useful in debugging X applications where the target window is not mapped to the screen or where the use of the pointer might be impossible or interfere with the application.

`-len` *n*
> Specifies that at most *n* bytes of any property should be read or displayed.

`-name` *name*
> Allows the user to specify on the command line that the window named *name* is the target window, rather than using the pointer to select the target window.

`-notype`
> Specifies that the type of each property should not be displayed.

`-remove` *property_name*
> Specifies the name of a property to be removed from the indicated window.

`-root` Specifies that X's root window is the target window. This is useful in situations where the root window is completely obscured.

`-spy` Indicates that *xprop* should examine window properties forever, looking for property change events.

Examples

To display the name of the root window: `prop -root WM_NAME`

To display the window manager hints for the clock: `xprop -name xclock WM_HINTS`

To display the start of the cut buffer: `xprop -root -len 100 CUT_BUFFER0`

To display the point size of the fixed font: `xprop -font fixed POINT_SIZE`

To display all the properties of window # 0x200007: `xprop -id 0x200007`

Environment Variables

XPROPFORMATS
> Specifies the name of a file from which additional formats are to be obtained.

See Also

X, xwininfo.

Author

Mark Lillibridge, MIT Project Athena.

xrdb

Name

xrdb – X server resource database utility.

Syntax

xrdb [*options*] [*filename* | -]

Description

xrdb is used to get or set the contents of the RESOURCE_MANAGER property on the root window of screen 0, or the SCREEN_RESOURCES property on the root window of any or all screens, or everything combined. You would normally run this program from your X startup file. Chapter 11, *Setting Resources*, describes how to use *xrdb*.

Most X clients use the RESOURCE_MANAGER and SCREEN_RESOURCES properties to get user preferences about color, fonts, and so on for applications. Having this information in the server (where it is available to all clients) instead of on disk solves the problem in previous versions of X that required you to maintain *defaults* files on every machine that you might use. It also allows for dynamic changing of defaults without editing files.

The RESOURCE_MANAGER property is used for resources that apply to all screens of the display. The SCREEN_RESOURCES property on each screen specifies additional (or overriding) resources to be used for that screen. (When there is only one screen, SCREEN_RESOURCES is normally not used, all resources are just placed in the RESOURCE_MANAGER property.)

The *filename* (or the standard input if – or no input file is given) is optionally passed through the C preprocessor with the being used:

BITS_PER_RGB=*number*
> The number of significant bits in an RGB color specification. This is the log base 2 of the number of distinct shades of each primary that the hardware can generate. Note that it is usually not related to the number of PLANES.

CLASS=*visualclass*
> One of StaticGray, GrayScale, StaticColor, PseudoColor, True-Color, or DirectColor. This is the visual class of the root window of the default screen.

CLIENTHOST=*hostname*
> The name of the host on which *xrdb* is running.

COLOR Defined only if CLASS is one of StaticColor, PseudoColor, or Direct-Color.

HEIGHT=*number*
> The height of the default screen in pixels.

PLANES=*number*
> The number of bit planes (the depth) of the root window of the default screen. Defined only if CLASS is one of StaticColor, PseudoColor, TrueColor, or DirectColor.

RELEASE=*number*
> The vendor release number for the server. The interpretation of this number will vary depending on VENDOR.

REVISION=*number*
> The X protocol minor version supported by this server (currently 0).

SERVERHOST=*hostname*

HOST=*hostname*
> The hostname portion of the display to which you are connected.

VENDOR=*number*
> A string specifying the vendor of the server.

VERSION=*number*
> The X protocol major version supported by this server (should always be 11).

WIDTH=*number*
> The width of the default screen in pixels.

X_RESOLUTION=*number*
> The x resolution of the default screen in pixels per meter.

Y_RESOLUTION=*number*
> The y resolution of the default screen in pixels per meter.

Lines that begin with an exclamation mark (!) are ignored and may be used as comments.

Note that since *xrdb* can read from standard input, it can be used to the change the contents of properties directly from a terminal or from a shell script.

Options

xrdb accepts the following options:

-all
This option indicates that operation should be performed on the screen-independent resource property (RESOURCE_MANAGER), as well as the screen-specific property (SCREEN_RESOURCES) on every screen of the display. For example, when used in conjunction with *-query*, the contents of all properties are output. For *-load* and *-merge*, the input file is processed once for each screen. The resources which occur in common in the output for every screen are collected, and these are applied as the screen-independent resources. The remaining resources are applied for each individual per-screen property. This the default mode of operation. (Available as of Release 5.)

-backup *string*
　　　Specifies a suffix to be appended to the filename used with -edit to generate a backup file.

-cpp *filename*
　　　Specifies the pathname of the C preprocessor program to be used. Although *xrdb* was designed to use *cpp*, any program that acts as a filter and accepts the -D, -I, and -U options may be used.

-display [*host*]:*server*[.*screen*]
　　　Specifies the X display server to be used; see X. It also specifies the screen to use for the -screen option and it specifies the screen from which preprocessor symbols are derived for the -global option.

-D*name*[=*value*]
　　　Is passed through to the preprocessor and is used to define symbols for use with conditionals such as *#ifdef*.

-edit *filename*
　　　Indicates that the contents of the specified properties should be edited into the given file, replacing any values already listed there. This allows you to put changes that you have made to your defaults back into your resource file, preserving any comments or preprocessor lines.

-global
　　　This option indicates that the operation should only be performed on the SCREEN_RESOURCES property of the default screen of the display. (Available as of Release 5.)

-help　This option (or any unsupported option) will cause a brief description of the allowable options and parameters to be printed.

-I*directory*
　　　Is passed through to the preprocessor and is used to specify a directory to search for files that are referenced with *#include*.

-load　Indicates that the input should be loaded as the new value of the properties, replacing whatever was there (i.e., the old contents are removed). This is the default action.

-merge
　　　Indicates that the input should be merged with, instead of replacing, the current contents of the specified properties. Note that this option does a lexicographic sorted merge of the two inputs, which is almost certainly not what you want, but remains for backward compatibility.

-n　　Indicates that changes to the specified properties (when used with -load or -merge) or to the resource file (when used with -edit) should be shown on the standard output, but should not be performed.

-nocpp

> Indicates that *xrdb* should not run the input file through a preprocessor before loading it into the properties.

-query

> Indicates that the current contents of the specified properties should be printed onto the standard output. Note that since preprocessor commands in the input resource file are part of the input file, not part of the property, they won't appear in the output from this option. The -edit option can be used to merge the contents of the properties back into the input resource file without damaging preprocessor commands.

-quiet

> Indicates that warning about duplicate entries should not be displayed.

-remove

> Indicates that the specified properties should be removed from the server.

-retain

> Indicates that the server should be instructed not to reset if *xrdb* is the first client. This is never necessary under normal conditions, since *xdm* and *xinit* always act as the first client.

-screen

> This option indicates that the operation should only be performed on the SCREEN_RESOURCES property of the default screen of the display. (Available as of Release 5.)

-screens

> This option indicates that the operation should be performed on the SCREEN_RESOURCES property of each screen of the display. For *-load* and *-merge*, the input file is processed for each screen. (Available as of Release 5.)

-symbols

> Indicates that the symbols that are defined for the preprocessor should be printed onto the standard output.

-U*name*

> Is passed through to the preprocessor and is used to remove any definitions of this symbol.

Files

> Generalizes ⁊*.Xdefaults* files.

See Also

> X; Chapter 11, *Setting Resources*.

Bugs

The default for no arguments should be to query, not to overwrite, so that it is consistent with other programs.

Authors

Bob Scheifler, Phil Karlton, rewritten from the original by Jim Gettys. Copyright 1991, Digital Equipment Corporation and MIT.

xrefresh

Name
xrefresh – refresh all or part of an X screen.

Syntax
`xrefresh` [`options`]

Description

xrefresh is a simple X program that causes all or part of your screen to be repainted. This is useful when system messages have displayed on your screen. *xrefresh* maps a window on top of the desired area of the screen and then immediately unmaps it, causing refresh events to be sent to all applications. By default, a window with no background is used, causing all applications to repaint "smoothly." However, the various options can be used to indicate that a solid background (of any color) or the root window background should be used instead.

See Chapter 8, *Other Clients*, for more information about *xrefresh*. In certain cases, you can run the *xconsole* client to prevent system messages from obscuring the screen. See the *xconsole* reference page and Appendix A, *Managing Your Environment*, for more information.

Options

xrefresh accepts the following options:

`-black`

> Use a black background (in effect, turning off all of the electron guns to the tube). This can be somewhat disorienting as everything goes black for a moment.

`-display` [`host`]:`server`[.`screen`]

> Allows you to specify the display, server and screen to refresh. `host` is the hostname of the physical display, `server` specifies the display server number, and `screen` specifies the screen number.

> `% xrefresh -display` `your_node`:`0.1`

> specifies screen 1 of server 0 on the display named by `your_node`. Either or both of the `host` and `screen` elements to the display specification can be omitted. If `host` is omitted, the local display is assumed. If `screen` is omitted, screen 0 is assumed (and the period is unnecessary). The colon and (display) `server` are necessary in all cases.

`-geometry` `geometry`

> Specifies the portion of the screen to be repainted. (This is generally pointless.)

> The `-geometry` option can be (and often is) abbreviated to `-g`, unless there is a conflicting option that begins with "g". The argument to the geometry option (`geometry`) is referred to as a "standard geometry string," and has the form `width`x`height±xoff±yoff`.

`-none` This is the default. All of the windows simply repaint.

`-root` Use the root window background.

`-solid` *color*

> Use a solid background of the specified color. Try green.

`-white`

> Use a white background. The screen just appears to flash quickly, and then repaints.

Resources

The *xrefresh* program uses the routine *XGetDefault*(3X) to read defaults, so its resource names are all capitalized.

`Black, White, Solid, None, Root`

> Determines what sort of window background to use.

`Geometry`

> Determines the area to refresh. Not very useful.

See Also

X, xconsole; Chapter 8, *Other Clients*; Appendix A, *Managing Your Environment*.

Bugs

It should have just one default type for the background.

Author

Jim Gettys, Digital Equipment Corp., MIT Project Athena.

xsccd

Name

xsccd – Xcms property builder.

Syntax

xsccd < *inputfile* > *outputfile*

Description

xsccd is a program developed by Tektronix, Inc., to create a color database for the Xcms Color
Management System. *xsccd* takes as standard input the file produced by *xcrtca* and produces
on standard output a file containing the property data loaded onto the root window by *xcmsdb*.
The *contrib/clients/xcrtca/monitors* directory contains *xcrtca* output files and *xcmsdb* input
files created from *xsccd* for several machines used at the X Consortium.

Caveats

This program has been coded for a Sun SparcStation and for a default visual with 8
bits_per_rgb.

See Also

xcrtca, xcmsdb; Chapter 12, *Specifying Color*.

Author

Dave Sternlicht, Keith Packard, MIT X Consortium;
Al Tabayoyon, Chuck Adams, Tektronix Inc.

Name

xset – user preference utility for X.

Syntax

xset [*options*]

Description

xset allows you to set various preferences for the display, pointer, and keyboard. Generally, all settings are reset to their defaults when you log out. However, in certain cases, settings specified for a particular display may be carried over from session to session. For example, some X terminals can be configured to retain settings between logins. Regardless of the environment, it's generally a good idea to run *xset* from the user's startup file. See Chapter 14, *Setup Clients*, for more information.

Options

xset accepts the following options. (Note that not all X implementations are guaranteed to honor all of these options.)

b   Controls bell volume, pitch, and duration. The b option accepts up to three numerical parameters (*volume*, *pitch*, and *duration*), a preceding dash (–), or an on/off flag. If no parameters are given, or the on flag is used, the system defaults will be used. If the dash or off are given, the bell will be turned off. If only one numerical parameter is given, the bell *volume* will be set to that value, as a percentage of its maximum. Likewise, the second numerical parameter specifies the bell *pitch*, in hertz, and the third numerical parameter specifies the *duration* in milliseconds. Note that not all hardware can vary the bell characteristics. The X server will set the characteristics of the bell as closely as it can to the user's specifications.

-bc, bc
           Controls *bug compatibility* mode in the server, if possible. The option with a preceding dash (–) disables the mode; the option alone enables the mode.

           The need for this option is determined by the following circumstances. Various pre-R4 clients pass illegal values in some protocol requests, and pre-R4 servers do not correctly generate errors in these cases. Such clients, when run with an R4 server, will terminate abnormally or otherwise fail to operate correctly. Bug compatibility mode explicitly reintroduces certain bugs into the X server, so that many such clients can still be run.

           This mode should be used with care; new application development should be done with this mode disabled. Be aware that the server must support the MIT-SUNDRY-NONSTANDARD protocol extension in order for this option to work.

c   Controls key click. The c option can take an optional value, a preceding dash (–), or an on/off flag. If no parameter or the on flag is given, the system defaults will be used. If the dash or off flag is used, the keyclick will be disabled. If a value from 0 to 100 is given, it is used to indicate volume, as a percentage of the maximum. The X server will set the volume to the nearest value that the hardware can support.

-display [*host*]:*server*[.*screen*]

Allows you to specify the host, server, and screen for which to set preferences. *host* is the hostname of the physical display, *server* specifies the server number, and *screen* specifies the screen number. For example,

    % **xset -display** *your_node*:0.1

specifies screen 1 of server 0 on the display named by *your_node*. Either or both of the *host* and *screen* elements to the display specification can be omitted. If *host* is omitted, the local display is assumed. If *screen* is omitted, screen 0 is assumed (and the period is unnecessary). The colon and *server* are necessary in all cases.

fp= *path*

Sets the font path used by the server. *path* must be a directory or a comma-separated list of directories. The directories are interpreted by the server, not the client, and are server-dependent. (Directories that do not contain font databases created by *mkfontdir* will be ignored by the server.)

fp default

Restores the default font path.

fp rehash

Causes the server to reread the font databases in the current font path. This is generally used only when adding new fonts to a font directory (after running *mkfontdir* to recreate the font database).

-fp *path* or fp- *path*

The -fp and fp- options remove elements from the current font path. *path* must be a directory or comma-separated list of directories.

+fp *path* or fp+ *path*

The +fp and fp+ options prepend and append, respectively, elements to the current font path. *path* must be a directory or a comma-separated list of directories.

led   Controls the turning on or off of one or all of the LEDs. The led option accepts an optional integer, a preceding dash (–) or an on/off flag. If no parameter or the on flag is given, all LEDs are enabled. If a preceding dash or the flag off is given, all LEDs are disabled. If a value between 1 and 32 is given, that LED will be enabled or disabled, depending on the existence of a preceding dash. A common LED that can be controlled is the Caps Lock LED. xset led 3 enables LED #3. xset -led 3 disables it. The particular LED values may refer to different LEDs on different hardware.

m   Controls the mouse parameters. The acceleration can be specified as an integer or as a fraction (with the numerator and denominator separated by a slash, for example, 1/2). The parameters for the mouse are *acceleration* and *threshold*. The mouse, or whatever pointer is connected to the machine, will go *acceleration* times as fast when it travels more than *threshold* pixels in a short time. This way, the mouse can be used for precise alignment when it is moved slowly, yet it can be set to travel across the screen in a flick of the wrist when desired. One or both parameters for the m option can be omitted, but if only one is given, it will be interpreted as the acceleration. If no parameters or the flag default is used, the system defaults will be set.

p   Controls pixel color values. The parameters are the color map entry number in decimal, and a color specification. The root background colors may be changed on some servers by altering the entries for BlackPixel and WhitePixel. Although these are often 0 and 1, they need not be. Also, a server may choose to allocate those colors privately, in which case an error will be generated. The map entry must not be a read-only color, or an error will result.

q   Gives you information on the current settings.

r   Controls the autorepeat. If a preceding dash or the off flag is used, autorepeat will be disabled. If no parameters or the on flag is used, autorepeat will be enabled.

s   Controls the screen saver parameters. The s option accepts up to two numerical parameters (*time* and *cycle*), a blank/noblank flag, an expose/noexpose flag, an on/off flag, or the default flag. If no parameters or the default flag is used, the system will be set to its default screen saver characteristics. The on/off flags simply turn the screen saver functions on or off. The blank flag sets the preference to blank the video (if the hardware can do so) rather than display a background pattern, while noblank sets the preference to display a pattern rather than blank the video. The expose flag sets the preference to allow window exposures (the server can freely discard window contents), while noexpose sets the preference to disable the screen saver unless the server can regenerate the screens without causing exposure events. The *time* and *cycle* parameters for the screen saver function determine how long the server must be inactive for screen saving to activate, and the period to change the background pattern to avoid burn in, respectively. The arguments are specified in seconds. If only one numerical parameter is given, it will be used for the *time*.

See Also

X, Xserver, xmodmap, xrdb, xsetroot; Chapter 14, *Setup Clients*.

Authors

Bob Scheifler, MIT Laboratory for Computer Science;
David Krikorian, MIT Project Athena (X11 version).

xsetroot

Name

xsetroot – root window parameter setting utility.

Syntax

xsetroot [*options*]

Description

xsetroot allows you to tailor the appearance of the root (background) window on a display. You can experiment with *xsetroot* until you find a look that you like, then put the *xsetroot* command that produces it into your X startup file. If you do not specify any options or you specify –def, the window is reset to its defaults. The –def option can be specified along with other options and only the non-specified characteristics will be reset to the default state. See Chapter 14, *Setup Clients*, for instructions on using *xsetroot*.

Options

xsetroot accepts the following options. Note that only one of the background color/tile changing options (-solid, -gray, -gray, -bitmap, or -mod) can be specified at a time. *color* can be specified as a color name or a numeric value. See Chapter 12, *Specifying Color*, for more information.

-bg *color*

Sets the background color of the root window. Foreground and background colors are meaningful only in combination with –cursor, –bitmap, or –mod. The default is white.

-bitmap *filename*

Uses the bitmap specified in the file to set the window pattern. The entire background is made up of repeated tiles of the bitmap. You can make your own bitmap files using the *bitmap* client or you can use those available with X, usually found in the directory */usr/include/X11/bitmaps*. The default is a gray mesh.

-cursor *cursorfile maskfile*

Specifies the cursor shape to use as the root window pointer. The *cursorfile* and *maskfile* are bitmaps, which can be made with the *bitmap* client. (Refer to Chapter 7, *Graphics Utilities*, for more information on creating bitmaps.) The mask file may need to be all black until you are accustomed to the way masks work. The default root window pointer is an X cursor.

-cursor_name *standard_cursor_name*

Changes the root window cursor to one of the standard cursors from the cursor font. (See Appendix D, *Standard Cursors*, for a list and pictures.) To specify a cursor name as an argument to a command-line option, the XC_ prefix must be stripped from the name.

-def   Resets unspecified attributes to the default values. (Restores the background to the gray mesh background and the pointer to the hollow X pointer.) If you specify –def and other options, only the non-specified options are reset to their defaults.

-display [*host*]:*server*[.*screen*]
> Allows you to specify the host, server, and screen of the root window. *host* is the hostname of the physical display, *server* specifies the server number, and *screen* specifies the screen number. For example,

> % **xsetroot -display** *your_node*:0.1

> specifies screen 1 of server 0 on the display named by *your_node*. Either or both of the *host* and *screen* elements to the display specification can be omitted. If *host* is omitted, the local display is assumed. If *screen* is omitted, screen 0 is assumed (and the period is unnecessary). The colon and (display) *server* are necessary in all cases.

-fg *color*
> Sets the foreground color of the root window. Foreground and background colors are only meaningful in combination with -cursor, -bitmap, or -mod. The default is black.

-gray or -grey
> Creates a gray background.

-help Displays a brief description of the allowable options.

-mod *x y*
> Makes a plaid-like grid pattern on your screen. *x* and *y* are integers ranging from 1 to 16 and are used to determine the dimensions in pixels of the plaid rectangles. Try some different combinations. Zero and negative numbers are taken as 1.

-name *string*
> Sets the name of the background window to *string*. There is no default value. This option allows a client to refer to the root window by name. (Usually, a name is assigned to a window so that the window manager can use a text representation when the window is converted to an icon. However, since the root window cannot be iconified, this function does not apply.)

-rv
> Reverses the foreground color and the background color when used with another option, such as -mod. (Normally the foreground color is black and the background color is white.) Without another specified option, -rv returns the root (background) window to the default state.

-solid *color*
> Sets the root window color. This option is primarily useful on color servers. The default color is a gray mesh.

See Also
X, xset, xrdb; Chapter 14, *Setup Clients*; Chapter 12, *Specifying Color*.

Author

Mark Lillibridge, MIT Project Athena.

Name

xstdcmap – X standard colormap utility.

Syntax

xstdcmap [*options*]

Description

The *xstdcmap* utility can be used to selectively define standard colormap properties. It is intended to be run from a user's X startup script to create standard colormap definitions in order to facilitate sharing of scarce colormap resources among clients. Where at all possible, colormaps are created with read-only allocations.

Options

xstdcmap accepts the following options:

-all   Specifies that all six standard colormap properties should be defined on each screen of the display. Not all screens will support visuals under which all six standard colormap properties are meaningful. *xstdcmap* will determine the best allocations and visuals for the colormap properties of a screen. Any previously existing standard colormap properties will be replaced.

-best   Specifies that the RGB_BEST_MAP should be defined.

-blue   Specifies that the RGB_BLUE_MAP should be defined.

-default

Specifies that the RGB_DEFAULT_MAP should be defined.

-delete *map*

Specifies that a standard colormap property should be removed. *map* may be one of: default, best, red, green, blue, or grey.

-display [*host*]:*server*[.*screen*]

Allows you to specify the display, server, and screen to connect to. *host* is the hostname of the physical display, *server* specifies the server number, and *screen* specifies the screen number. For example:

xstdcmap -display *your_node***:0.1**

specifies screen 1 of server 0 on the display named by *your_node*. Either or both the *host* and *screen* elements can be omitted. If *host* is omitted, the local display is assumed. If *screen* is omitted, screen 0 is assumed (and the period is unnecessary). The colon and *server* are necessary in all cases.

-green

Specifies that the RGB_GREEN_MAP should be defined.

-grey   Specifies that the RGB_GRAY_MAP should be defined.

-help Specifies that a brief description of the command-line arguments should be printed on the standard error. This will be done whenever an unhandled argument is given to *xstdcmap*.

-red   Specifies that the RGB_RED_MAP should be defined.

-verbose

    Specifies that *xstdcmap* should print logging information as it parses its input and defines the standard colormap properties.

See Also
X.

Author
Donna Converse, MIT X Consortium.

xterm

Name

xterm – window terminal emulator.

Syntax

xterm [*options*]

Description

The *xterm* program is a terminal emulator for the X Window System. Chapter 5 of this guide explains how to work effectively using *xterm*. This reference page provides some of the information necessary to customize *xterm*. See Part Two of this guide for general instructions on customizing X clients.

The *xterm* client provides DEC VT102 and Tektronix 4014 compatible terminals for programs that can't use the window system directly. If the underlying operating system supports terminal resizing capabilities (for example, the SIGWINCH signal in systems derived from BSD 4.3), *xterm* will use the facilities to notify programs running in the window whenever it is resized.

The VT102 and Tektronix 4014 terminals each have their own window so that you can edit text in one and look at graphics in the other at the same time. To maintain the correct aspect ratio (height/width), Tektronix graphics will be restricted to the largest box with a 4014's aspect ratio that will fit in the window. This box is located in the upper-left area of the window.

Although both windows can be displayed at the same time, one of them is considered the *active* window for receiving keyboard input and terminal output. This is the window that contains the text cursor. The active window can be chosen through escape sequences, the VT Options menu in the VT102 window, and the Tek Options menu in the 4014 window.

The Release 5 version of *xterm* provides four menus that allow you to manage the VT102 and Tektronix windows: Main Options, VT Options, Tek Options, and VT Fonts.

xterm automatically highlights the text cursor when the pointer enters the window (selected) and unhighlights it when the pointer leaves the window (unselected). If the window is the focus window, then the text cursor is highlighted no matter where the pointer is.

In VT102 mode, there are escape sequences to activate and deactivate an alternate screen buffer, which is the same size as the display area of the window. When activated, the current screen is saved and replaced with the alternate screen. Saving of lines scrolled off the top of the window is disabled until the normal screen is restored. The *termcap*(5) entry for *xterm* allows the visual editor *vi* to switch to the alternate screen for editing and to restore the screen on exit.

In either VT102 or Tektronix mode, there are escape sequences to change the name of the windows and to specify a new log file name. See Appendix E, *xterm Control Sequences*, for details. Enabling the escape sequence to change the log file name is a compile-time option; by default this escape sequence is ignored for security reasons.

Options

xterm accepts all of the standard X Toolkit command-line options, which are listed on the *X* reference page. (We've included some of the more commonly used Toolkit options later in this section.)

In addition, *xterm* accepts the following application-specific options. Note that if the option begins with a + instead of a –, the option is restored to its default value. (Specifying the default with +*option* can be useful for overriding the opposite value in an *.Xresources* file or other prior resource specification.)

-help

> Causes *xterm* to print out a verbose message describing its options.

-132

> Causes the VT102 DECCOLM escape sequence, which switches between 80- and 132-column mode, to be recognized, enabling the *xterm* window to resize properly. By default, the DECCOLM escape sequence is ignored. (See Appendix C for more information on *xterm* escape sequences.)
>
> (This option can be turned on and off from the *xterm* VT Options menu, described below.)

-ah/+ah

> -ah specifies that *xterm* should *always* highlight the text cursor. By default, *xterm* will display a highlighted text cursor only when a window has the input focus and a hollow text cursor when the focus is elsewhere. +ah specifies the default.

-aw/+aw

> -aw specifies that auto-wraparound of text should be allowed. This allows the cursor to automatically wrap to the beginning of the next line when when it is at the right-most position on a line and text is output. This is the default. +aw specifies that auto-wraparound should not be allowed. (Available as of Release 5.)

-b *innerborder*

> Specifies the width of the inner border (the distance between the outer edge of the characters and the window border) in pixels. The default is two pixels.

-C

> Specifies that the *xterm* window should receive console output. This is not supported on all systems. To obtain console output, you must be the owner of the console device, and you must have read and write permission for it. If you are running X under *xdm* on the console screen you may need to have the session startup and reset programs explicitly change the ownership of the console device in order to get this option to work. Running the *xconsole* client is generally preferable to xterm -C. See Appendix A, *Managing Your Environment* and the *xconsole* reference page for more information.

-cb, +cb

> -cb specifies that triple-clicking to select a line does not include the newline at the end of the line. The default is to include the newline. +cb specifies the default. (Available as of Release 5.)

`-cc` *characterclassrange*:*value*[,...]

> Sets classes indicated by the given ranges for use in selecting by words. See "Specifying Character Classes" below.

`-cn, +cn`

> `-cn` indicates that newlines should not be cut in line mode selections; `+cn` indicates that newlines should be cut in line mode selections.

`-cr` *color*

> Specifies the color to use for the text cursor. The default is to use the same foreground color that is used for text.

`-cu, +cu`

> `-cu` enables the *curses* fix. Several programs that use the *curses*(3x) cursor motion package have some difficulties with VT102-compatible terminals. The bug occurs when you run the `more` program on a file containing a line that is exactly the width of the window and that is followed by a line beginning with a tab. The leading tabs are not displayed. This option causes the tabs to be displayed correctly.

> `+cu` indicates that *xterm* should not work around this *curses* bug.

> (This option can also be turned on and off from the VT Options menu, described below.)

`-e` *command* [*arguments*]

> Specifies the command (and its arguments) to be run in the *xterm* window. It also sets the window title and icon name to be the name of the program being executed if neither `-T` nor `-n` are given on the command line. The `-e` option, command, and the arguments must appear last on the *xterm* command line; for example, `xterm -rv -e more bigfile &`.

`-fb` *font*

> Uses the specified font as the bold font. This font must be the same height and width as the normal font. If only one of the normal or bold fonts is specified, it is used as the normal font and the bold font is produced by overstriking this font. The default is to overstrike the normal font.

`-im, +im`

> `-im` forces the use of insert mode by adding appropriate entries to the TERMCAP environment variable. This is useful if the system termcap is broken. The default is not to force insert mode. `+im` specifies the default. (Available as of Release 5.)

`-j, +j`

> `-j` indicates that *xterm* should do jump scrolling. Normally, text is scrolled one line at a time; this option allows *xterm* to move multiple lines at a time so that it doesn't fall as far behind. The use of jump scrolling is strongly recommended since it makes *xterm* much faster when scanning through large amounts of text. The VT100 escape sequences for enabling and disabling smooth scroll and the Enable Jump Scroll item of the VT Options menu can also be used to toggle this feature.

The +j option specifies that *xterm* not do jump scrolling.

-j specifies the default behavior.

(This option can be turned on and off from the VT Options menu, described below.)

-l, +l

-l logs *xterm* input/output into a file called *XtermLog.xxxx*, where **xxxx** represents the process ID number. To display your data, turn off logging using the *xterm* menu, then type cat XtermLog.*xxxx* at the *xterm* window prompt and the output file is sent to your *xterm* window. Logging allows you to keep track of the sequence of data and is particularly helpful while debugging code.

+l specifies that *xterm* not do logging.

(This option can also be turned on and off from the VT Options menu, described below.)

-lf *file*

Specifies the file to which the data is written rather than the default *XtermLog.xxxx*, where **xxxx** is the process identification of *xterm* (the file is created in the directory in which *xterm* is started in or the home directory for a login *xterm*). If *file* begins with a "|," then the rest of the string is assumed to be a command to be executed by the shell and a pipe is opened to the process.

-ls, +ls

-ls indicates that the shell that is started in the *xterm* window be a login shell (i.e., the first character of argv[0] will be a dash, indicating to the shell that it should read the user's *.login* or *.profile*).

+ls indicates that the shell that is started should not be a login shell (i.e., it will be a normal "subshell").

-mb, +mb

-mb turns on the margin bell; the default is bell off. +mb indicates that the margin bell should not be rung.

(This option can also be turned on and off from the VT Options menu, described below.)

-mc *milliseconds*

Specifies the maximum time between multi-click selections.

-ms *color*

Sets the color of the pointer. The default is to use the foreground color.

-nb *number*

Sets the distance at which the margin bell rings for the right margin. Default is 10 characters.

-rw, +rw

> -rw turns on the reverse-wraparound mode that allows the cursor to wrap around from the leftmost column to the rightmost column of the previous line. Allows you to backspace to the previous line and overstrike data or erase data with the spacebar.
>
> +rw indicates that reverse-wraparound should not be enabled.
>
> (This option can also be turned on and off from the VT Options menu, described below.)

-Sccn Specifies the last two letters of the name of a pseudo-terminal to use in slave mode, plus the number of the inherited file descriptor. The option is parsed "%c%c%d". This allows *xterm* to be used as an input and output channel for an existing program and is sometimes used in specialized applications.

-s, +s -s allows *xterm* to scroll asynchronously with the display, meaning that the screen does not have to be kept completely up-to-date while scrolling. *xterm* saves data in memory which is displayed later. This allows *xterm* to run faster when network latencies are high and is useful when running *xterm* across a large internet or many gateways.

> +s indicates that *xterm* should scroll synchronously.

-sb, +sb

> -sb indicates that some number of lines that are scrolled off the top of the window should be saved and that a scrollbar should be displayed at startup so those lines can be viewed.
>
> +sb indicates that a scrollbar should not be displayed at startup.
>
> (This feature can also be turned on and off from the VT Options menu, described below.)

-sf, +sf

> -sf indicates that the Sun function key escape codes should be generated for function keys; +sb indicates that the standard escape codes should be generated for function keys. This is the default.

-si, +si

> -si disables repositioning the cursor at the bottom of the scroll region when the process sends output; +si indicates that the cursor should be repositioned at the bottom of the scroll region on output.
>
> (This feature can also be turned on and off from the VT Options menu, described below.)

-sk, +sk

> -sk causes the cursor to be repositioned at the bottom of the scroll region when a key is pressed; +sk indicates that pressing a key while using the scrollbar should not cause the cursor to be repositioned at the bottom of the scroll region.

(This feature can also be turned on and off from the VT Options menu, described below.)

-sl *number*

Specifies the maximum number of lines to be saved that are scrolled off the top of the window. Default is 64 lines.

-t, +t

-t causes the startup *xterm* window to be the Tektronix window rather than the VT102 window; +t causes the startup window to be the VT102 window. This is the default.

-tm *string*

Specifies a series of terminal-setting keywords followed by the characters that should be bound to those functions, similar to the *stty* program. Allowable keywords include: intr, quit, erase, kill, eof, eol, swtch, start, stop, brk, susp, dsusp, rprnt, flush, weras, and lnext. Control characters may be specified as ^*char* (e.g., ^c or ^u), and ^? may be used to indicate delete.

-tn *name*

Specifies the name of the terminal type to be set in the TERM environment variable. This terminal type must exist in the *termcap*(5) database and should have *li#* and *co#* entries.

-ut/+ut

-ut indicates that *xterm* shouldn't write a record into the the system log file */etc/utmp*.

+ut indicates that *xterm* should write a record into the system log file */etc/utmp*.

-vb/+vb

-vb causes your terminal window to flash whenever an event occurs that would ordinarily cause your terminal bell to ring.

+vb indicates that a visual bell should not be used.

(This feature can be turned on and off from the Main Options menu, described below.)

-wf/+wf

-wf indicates that *xterm* should wait for the window to be mapped the first time before starting the subprocess so that the initial terminal size settings and environment variables are correct. It is the application's responsibility to catch subsequent terminal size changes.

+wf indicates that *xterm* should not wait before starting the subprocess.

The following X Toolkit options are commonly used with *xterm*:

-bd *color*

Sets the color of the border. Default of the highlighted border is black. Default of the unhighlighted border is grey.

-bg *color*
> Sets the background color of the *xterm* window. Default is white.

-bw *pixels*
> Specifies the width of the *xterm* window border in pixels. Default is one pixel.

-display [*host*]:*server*[.*screen*]
> Specifies the display, server, and screen on which to create the window. *host* is the hostname of the physical display, *server* specifies the server number, and *screen* specifies the screen number. For example:
>
> % **xterm -display** *your_node*:**0.1**
>
> specifies that an *xterm* be created on screen 1 of server 0 on the display named by *your_node*. Either or both of the *host* and *screen* elements to the display specification can be omitted. If *host* is omitted, the local display is assumed. If *screen* is omitted, screen 0 is assumed (and the period is unnecessary). The colon and *server* are necessary in all cases.

-fg *color*
> Sets the color of the text (foreground). Default is black.

-fn *font*
> Uses the specified font instead of the default font (*fixed*). You can use any fixed-width font.

-geometry *geometry*
> *xterm* takes this geometry specification for the VT102 window. The -geometry option can be (and often is) abbreviated to -g, unless there is a conflicting option that begins with "g". The argument to the geometry option (*geometry*) is referred to as a "standard geometry string," and has the form *width×height±xoff±yoff*.

-iconic
> Causes *xterm* to display an *xterm* icon rather than an *xterm* window when it starts up.

-name *app_name*
> Specifies the application name under which resources are to be obtained, rather than the default executable filename. *app_name* should not contain "." or "*" characters.

-title *string*
> Specifies the window title string, which may be displayed by window managers if the user so chooses. The default title is the command line specified after the -e option, if any, otherwise the application name.

-rv Reverses the foreground and background colors.

> (This option can be turned on and off from the VT Options menu, described below.)

-xrm *resourcestring*

> Specifies a resource string to be used with this instance of the application. This is especially useful for setting resources that do not have command-line option equivalents.

The following command-line arguments are provided for compatibility with older versions (prior to Release 3). They may not be supported in the next release as the X Toolkit provides standard options that accomplish most of the same tasks.

%*geometry*

> Specifies the preferred size and location of the Tektronix window. It is shorthand for specifying the tekGeometry resource.

#*geometry*

> Specifies the preferred position of the icon. It is shorthand for specifying the icon-Geometry resource. The width and height values of the geometry string are optional.

-n *string*

> Specifies the icon name for the *xterm* window. It is shorthand for specifying the *iconName resource. Note that this is not equivalent to the Toolkit option –name. The default icon name is the name of a program run with the –e option, if any, otherwise the application name.

-r

> Indicates that reverse video should be simulated by swapping the foreground and background colors. It is equivalent to –rv.

-T *string*

> Specifies the title for the *xterm* window. It is equivalent to –title.

-w *pixels*

> Specifies the width in pixels of the border surrounding the window. It is equivalent to –bw.

Resources

The program understands all of the Core resource names and classes as well as the following:

autoWrap (class AutoWrap)

> Specifies whether or not auto-wraparound should be enabled. The default is True.

iconGeometry (class IconGeometry)

> Specifies the preferred size and position of the application when iconified. It is not necessarily obeyed by all window managers.

iconName (class IconName)

> Specifies the icon name. The default is the application name.

useInsertMode (classUseInsertMode)
> If true, forces the use of insert mode by adding appropriate entries to the TERMCAP environment variable. This is useful if the system termcap is broken. The default is False. (Available as of Release 5.)

termName (class TermName)
> Specifies the terminal type name to be set in the TERM environment variable.

title (class Title)
> Specifies a string that may be used by the window manager (e.g., in a titlebar) when displaying this application.

ttyModes (class TtyModes)
> Specifies a string containing terminal setting keywords and the characters to which they may be bound. Allowable keywords include: intr, quit, erase, kill, eof, eol, swtch, start, stop, brk, susp, dsusp, rprnt, flush, weras, and lnext. Control characters may be specified as ^*char* (e.g., ^c or ^u), and ^? may be used to indicate Delete. This is very useful for overriding the default terminal settings without having to do an *stty* every time an *xterm* is started.

utmpInhibit (class UtmpInhibit)
> Specifies whether or not *xterm* should try to record the user's terminal in */etc/utmp*.

sunFunctionKeys (class SunFunctionKeys)
> Specifies whether or not Sun Function Key escape codes, instead of standard escape sequences, should be generated for function keys.

waitForMap (class WaitForMap)
> Specifies whether or not *xterm* should wait for the initial window map before starting the subprocess. The default is False. (Available as of Release 5.)

The following resources are specified as part of the vt100 widget (class VT100):

allowSendEvents (class AllowSendEvents)
> Specifies whether or not synthetic key and button events (generated using the X protocol SendEvent request) should be interpreted or discarded. The default is False meaning they are discarded. Note that allowing such events creates a very large security hole.

alwaysHighlight (class AlwaysHighlight)
> Specifies whether or not *xterm* should always display a highlighted text cursor. By default, a hollow text cursor is displayed whenever the pointer moves out of the window or the window loses the input focus.

appcursorDefault (class AppcursorDefault)
> If true, the cursor keys are initially in application mode. The default is False. (Available as of Release 5.)

appkeypadDefault (class AppkeypadDefault)
> If true, the keypad keys are initially in application mode. The default is False. (Available as of Release 5.)

autoWrap (class AutoWrap)
> Specifies whether or not auto-wraparound should be enabled. The default is True. (Available as of Release 5.)

bellSuppressTime (class BellSuppressTime)
> Specifies number of milliseconds after a bell command is sent during which additional bells will be suppressed. Default is 200. If set nonzero, additional bells will also be suppressed until the server reports that processing of the first bell has been completed; this feature is most useful with the visible bell. (Available as of Release 5.)

boldFont (class Font)
> Specifies the name of the bold font to use instead of overstriking the normal font.

c132 (class C132)
> Specifies whether or not the VT102 DECCOLM escape sequence should be honored. The default is False.

cutNewline (class CutNewline)
> If false, triple-clicking to select a line does not include the newline at the end of the line. If true, the newline is selected. The default is True. (Available as of Release 5.)

cutToBeginningOfLine (class CutToBeginningOfLine)
> If false, triple-clicking to select a lineselects only from the current word forward. If true, the entire line is selected. The default is True. (Available as of Release 5.)

charClass (class CharClass)
> Specifies comma-separated lists of character class bindings of the form [*low–*]*high*:*value*. These are used in determining which sets of characters should be treated the same when doing cut and paste. See "Character Classes" below.

curses (class Curses)
> Specifies whether or not the last column bug in the cursor should be worked around. The default is False.

background (class Background)
> Specifies the color to use for the background of the window. The default is white.

foreground (class Foreground)
> Specifies the color to use for displaying text in the window. Setting the class name instead of the instance name is an easy way to have everything that would normally appear in the text color change color. The default is black.

cursorColor (class Foreground)
> Specifies the color to use for the text cursor. The default is black.

eightBitInput (class EightBitInput)
> If true, Meta characters input from the keyboard are presented as a single character with the eighth bit turned on. If false, Meta characters are converted into a two-character sequence with the character itself preceded by ESC. The default is True.

eightBitOutput (class EightBitOutput)
> Specifies whether or not eight-bit characters sent from the host should be accepted as is or stripped when printed. The default is True. (Available as of Release 5.)

font (class Font)
> Specifies the name of the normal font. The default is fixed.

font1 (class Font1)
> Specifies the name of the first alternative font. This font is toggled using the Unreadable menu item on the VT Fonts menu.

font2 (class Font2)
> Specifies the name of the second alternative font. This font is toggled using the Tiny menu item on the VT Fonts menu.

font3 (class Font3)
> Specifies the name of the third alternative font. This font is toggled using the Small menu item on the VT Fonts menu.

font4 (class Font4)
> Specifies the name of the fourth alternative font. This font is toggled using the Medium menu item on the VT Fonts menu.

font5 (class Font5)
> Specifies the name of the fifth alternative font. This font is toggled using the Large menu item on the VT Fonts menu. (Available as of Release 5.)

font6 (class Font6)
> Specifies the name of the sixth alternative font. This font is toggled using the Huge menu item on the VT Fonts menu. (Available as of Release 5.)

geometry (class Geometry)
> Specifies the preferred size and position of the VT102 window.

internalBorder (class BorderWidth)
> Specifies the number of pixels between the characters and the window border. The default is 2.

jumpScroll (class JumpScroll)
> Specifies whether or not jump scroll should be used. The default is True.

logFile (class Logfile)
> Specifies the name of the file to which a terminal session is logged. The default is XtermLog.*xxxx* (where *xxxx* is the process ID of *xterm*).

logging (class Logging)
:   Specifies whether or not a terminal session should be logged. The default is False.

logInhibit (class LogInhibit)
:   Specifies whether or not terminal session logging should be inhibited. The default is False.

loginShell (class LoginShell)
:   Specifies whether or not the shell to be run in the window should be started as a login shell. The default is False.

marginBell (class MarginBell)
:   Specifies whether or not the bell should be run when the user types near the right margin. The default is False.

multiClickTime (class MultiClickTime)
:   Specifies the maximum time in milliseconds between multi-click select events. The default is 250 milliseconds.

multiScroll (class MultiScroll)
:   Specifies whether or not scrolling should be done asynchronously. The default is False.

nMarginBell (class Column)
:   Specifies the number of characters from the right margin at which the margin bell should be rung, when enabled.

pointerColor (class Foreground)
:   Specifies the color of the pointer. The default is XtDefaultForeground color.

pointerColorBackground (class Background)
:   Specifies the background color of the pointer. The default is XtDefault-Background color.

pointerShape (class Cursor)
:   Specifies the name of the shape of the pointer. The default is "xterm."

reverseVideo (class ReverseVideo)
:   Specifies whether or not reverse video should be simulated. The default is False.

resizeGravity (class ResizeGravity)
:   Affects the behavior when the window is resized to be taller or shorter. Acceptable values are NorthWest and SouthWest. NorthWest specifies that the top line of text on the screen stay fixed. If the window is made shorter, lines are dropped from the bottom; if the window is made taller, blank lines are added at the bottom. (This is compatible with the behavior in R4.) SouthWest (the default) specifies that the bottom line of text on the screen stay fixed. If the window is made taller, additional saved lines will be scrolled down onto the screen; if the window is made shorter, lines will be scrolled off the top of the screen, and the top saved lines will be dropped. (Available as of Release 5.)

reverseWrap (class ReverseWrap)

> Specifies whether or not reverse-wraparound should be enabled. The default is False.

saveLines (class SaveLines)

> Specifies the number of lines to save beyond the top of the screen when a scrollbar is turned on. The default is 64.

scrollBar (class ScrollBar)

> Specifies whether or not the scrollbar should be displayed. The default is False.

scrollTtyOutput (class ScrollCond)

> Specifies whether or not output to the terminal should automatically cause the scrollbar to go to the bottom of the scrolling region. The default is True. (In Release 5, this resource was scrollInput; renamed in Release 5.)

scrollKey (class ScrollCond)

> Specifies whether or not pressing a key should automatically cause the scrollbar to go to the bottom of the scrolling region. The default is False.

scrollLines (class ScrollLines)

> Specifies the number of lines that the scroll-back and scroll-forw actions should use as a default. The default value is 1. (See "Actions.")

signalInhibit (class SignalInhibit)

> Specifies whether or not the entries in the Main Options menu for sending signals to *xterm* should be disallowed. The default is False.

tekGeometry (class Geometry)

> Specifies the preferred size and position of the Tektronix window.

tekInhibit (class TekInhibit)

> Specifies whether or not Tektronix mode should be disallowed. The default is False.

tekSmall (class TekSmall)

> Specifies whether or not the Tektronix mode window should start in its smallest size if no explicit geometry is given. This is useful when running *xterm* on displays with small screens. The default is False.

tekStartup (class TekStartup)

> Specifies whether or not *xterm* should start up in Tektronix mode. The default is False.

titeInhibit (class TiteInhibit)

> Specifies whether or not *xterm* should remove ti and te termcap entries (used to switch between alternate screens on startup of many screen-oriented programs) from the TERMCAP string. If set, *xterm* also ignores the escape sequence to switch to the alternate screen.

translations (class Translations)
> Specifies the key and button bindings for menus, selections, "programmed strings," etc. See "Actions" below.

visualBell (class VisualBell)
> Specifies whether or not a visible bell (i.e., flashing) should be used instead of an audible bell when Control-G is received. The default is False.

The following resources are specified as part of the tek4014 widget (class Tek4014):

width (class Width)
> Specifies the width of the Tektronix window in pixels.

height (class Height)
> Specifies the height of the Tektronix window in pixels.

fontLarge (class Font)
> Specifies the large font to use in the Tektronix window. This font is toggled using the Large Characters item on the Tek Options menu.

font2 (class Font)
> Specifies font number 2 to use in the Tektronix window. This font is toggled using the #2 Size Characters item on the Tek Options menu.

font3 (class Font)
> Specifies font number 3 to use in the Tektronix window. This font is toggled using the #3 Size Characters item on the Tek Options menu.

fontSmall (class Font)
> Specifies the small font to use in the Tektronix window. This font is toggled using the Small Characters item on the Tek Options menu.

initialFont (class InitialFont)
> Specifies which of the four Tektronix fonts to use initially. Values are the same as for the set-tek-text action. The default is large. (Available as of Release 5.)

ginTerminator (class GinTerminator)
> Specifies what character(s) should follow a GIN report or status report. Acceptable values are none, which sends no terminating characters, CRonly, which sends CR, and CR&EOT, which sends both CR and EOT. The default is none. (Available as of Release 5.)

The resources that can be specified for the various menus are described in the documentation for the Athena SimpleMenu widget. The name and classes of the entries in each of the menus are listed below.

The mainMenu (title Main Options) has the following entries:

securekbd (class SmeBSB)
> Invokes the secure() action.

allowsends (class SmeBSB)
>	Invokes the allow-send-events(toggle) action.

logging (class SmeBSB)
>	Invokes the set-logging(toggle) action.

redraw (class SmeBSB)
>	Invokes the redraw() action.

line1 (class SmeLine)
>	A separator.

suspend (class SmeBSB)
>	Invokes the send-signal(tstp) action on systems that support job control.

continue (class SmeBSB)
>	Invokes the send-signal(cont) action on systems that support job control.

interrupt (class SmeBSB)
>	Invokes the send-signal(int) action.

hangup (class SmeBSB)
>	Invokes the send-signal(hup) action.

terminate (class SmeBSB)
>	Invokes the send-signal(term) action.

kill (class SmeBSB)
>	Invokes the send-signal(kill) action.

line2 (class SmeLine)
>	A separator.

quit (class SmeBSB)
>	Invokes the quit() action.

The vtMenu (title VT Options) has the following entries:

scrollbar (class SmeBSB)
>	Invokes the set-scrollbar(toggle) action.

jumpscroll (class SmeBSB)
>	Invokes the set-jumpscroll(toggle) action.

reversevideo (class SmeBSB)
>	Invokes the set-reverse-video(toggle) action.

autowrap (class SmeBSB)
>	Invokes the set-autowrap(toggle) action.

reversewrap (class SmeBSB)
>	Invokes the set-reversewrap(toggle) action.

autolinefeed (class SmeBSB)
> Invokes the set-autolinefeed(toggle) action.

appcursor (class SmeBSB)
> Invokes the set-appcursor(toggle) action.

appkeypad (class SmeBSB)
> Invokes the set-appkeypad(toggle) action.

scrollkey (class SmeBSB)
> Invokes the set-scroll-on-key(toggle) action.

scrollttyoutput (class SmeBSB)
> Invokes the set-scroll-on-tty-output(toggle) action.

allow132 (class SmeBSB)
> Invokes the set-allow132(toggle) action.

cursesemul (class SmeBSB)
> Invokes the set-cursesemul(toggle) action.

visualbell (class SmeBSB)
> Invokes the set-visualbell(toggle) action.

marginbell (class SmeBSB)
> Invokes the set-marginbell(toggle) action.

altscreen (class SmeBSB)
> This entry is currently disabled.

line1 (class SmeLine)
> A separator.

softreset (class SmeBSB)
> Invokes the soft-reset() action.

hardreset (class SmeBSB)
> Invokes the hard-reset() action.

clearsavedlines (class SmeBSB)
> Invokes the clear-saved-lines() action. (Available as of Release 5.)

line2 (class SmeLine)
> A separator.

tekshow (class SmeBSB)
> Invokes the set-visibility(tek,toggle) action.

tekmode (class SmeBSB)
> Invokes the set-terminal-type(tek) action.

vthide (class SmeBSB)
> Invokes the set-visibility(vt,off) action.

The tekMenu (title Tek Options) has the following entries:

tektextlarge (class SmeBSB)
> Invokes the set-tek-text(l) action.

tektext2 (class SmeBSB)
> Invokes the set-tek-text(2) action.

tektext3 (class SmeBSB)
> Invokes the set-tek-text(3) action.

tektextsmall (class SmeBSB)
> Invokes the set-tek-text(s) action.

line1 (class SmeLine)
> A separator.

tekpage (class SmeBSB)
> Invokes the tek-page() action.

tekreset (class SmeBSB)
> Invokes the tek-reset() action.

tekcopy (class SmeBSB)
> Invokes the tek-copy() action.

line2 (class SmeLine)
> A separator.

vtshow (class SmeBSB)
> Invokes the set-visibility(vt,toggle) action.

vtmode (class SmeBSB)
> Invokes the set-terminal-type(vt) action.

tekhide (class SmeBSB)
> Invokes the set-visibility(tek,toggle) action.

The fontMenu (title VT Fonts) has the following entries:

fontdefault (class SmeBSB)
> Invokes the set-vt-font(d) action.

font1 (class SmeBSB)
> Invokes the set-vt-font(1) action.

font2 (class SmeBSB)
> Invokes the set-vt-font(2) action.

font3 (class SmeBSB)
> Invokes the set-vt-font(3) action.

font4 (class SmeBSB)
> Invokes the set-vt-font(4) action.

font5 (class SmeBSB)
> Invokes the set-vt-font(5) action. (Available as of Release 5.)

font6 (class SmeBSB)
> Invokes the set-vt-font(6) action. (Available as of Release 5.)

fontescape (class SmeBSB)
> Invokes the set-vt-font(e) action.

fontsel (class SmeBSB)
> Invokes the set-vt-font(s) action.

The following resources are useful when specified for the Athena Scrollbar widget (scroll-Bar, class ScrollBar):

thickness (class Thickness)
> Specifies the width in pixels of the scrollbar.

background (class Background)
> Specifies the color to use for the background of the scrollbar.

foreground (class Foreground)
> Specifies the color to use for the foreground of the scrollbar. The "thumb" of the scrollbar is a simple checkerboard pattern alternating pixels for foreground and background color.

Emulations

The VT102 emulation is fairly complete, but does not support the blinking character attribute nor the double-wide and double-size character sets. *termcap* entries that work with *xterm* include "xterm," "vt102," "vt100," and "ansi." *xterm* automatically searches the *termcap* file in this order for these entries and then sets the TERM and the TERMCAP environment variables. Note that the "xterm" *termcap* entry distributed with X is not automatically installed. You must add it to */etc/termcap* yourself.

Many of the special *xterm* features (like logging) may be modified under program control through a set of escape sequences different from the standard VT102 escape sequences. (See Appendix E, *xterm Control Sequences*, in this guide.)

The Tektronix 4014 emulation is also fairly good. Four different font sizes and five different line types are supported. The Tektronix text and graphics commands are recorded internally by *xterm* and may be written to a file by sending the COPY escape sequence (or through the Tektronix menu; see below). The name of the file will be "COPY*yy-MM-dd.hh:mm:ss*", where *yy*, *MM*, *dd*, *hh*, *mm*, and *ss* are the year, month, day, hour, minute, and second when the COPY was performed (the file is created in the directory in which *xterm* is started, or the home directory for a login *xterm*).

Pointer Usage

Once the VT102 window is created, *xterm* allows you to select text and copy it within the same or other windows.

The selection functions are invoked when the pointer buttons are used with no modifiers, and when they are used with the Shift key. The assignment of the functions described below to keys and buttons may be changed through the resource database; see "Actions" below.

Pointer button 1 (usually the left) is used to save text into the cut buffer. Move the cursor to the beginning of the text, and then hold the button down while moving the cursor to the end of the region and release the button. The selected text is highlighted and is saved in the global cut buffer and made the PRIMARY selection when the button is released. Double-clicking selects by words. Triple-clicking selects by lines. Quadruple-clicking goes back to characters, etc. Multiple-click is determined by the time from button up to button down, so you can change the selection unit in the middle of a selection. If the key/button bindings specify that an X selection is to be made, *xterm* will leave the selected text highlighted for as long as it is the selection owner.

Pointer button 2 (usually the middle) "types" (pastes) the text from the PRIMARY selection, if any, otherwise from the cut buffer, inserting it as keyboard input.

Pointer button 3 (usually the right) extends the current selection. (You can swap "right" and "left" everywhere in the rest of this paragraph.) If pressed while closer to the right edge of the selection than the left, it extends/contracts the right edge of the selection. If you contract the selection past the left edge of the selection, *xterm* assumes you really meant the left edge, restores the original selection, then extends/contracts the left edge of the selection. Extension starts in the selection unit mode in which the last selection or extension was performed; you can multiple-click to cycle through them.

By cutting and pasting pieces of text without trailing new lines, you can take text from several places in different windows and form a command to the shell, for example, or take output from a program and insert it into your favorite editor. Since the cut buffer is globally shared among different applications, you should regard it as a "file" whose contents you know. The terminal emulator and other text programs should be treating it as if it were a text file, i.e., the text is delimited by new lines.

The scroll region displays the position and amount of text currently showing in the window (highlighted) relative to the amount of text actually saved. As more text is saved (up to the maximum), the size of the highlighted area decreases.

Clicking button 1 in the scroll region moves the adjacent line to the top of the display window.

Clicking button 3 moves the top line of the display window down to the pointer position.

Clicking button 2 moves the display to a position in the saved text that corresponds to the pointer's position in the scrollbar.

Unlike the VT102 window, the Tektronix window does not allow the copying of text. It does allow Tektronix GIN mode, and in this mode the cursor will change from an arrow to a cross.

Pressing any key will send that key and the current coordinate of the cross cursor. Pressing button 1, 2, or 3 will return the letters "l," "m," and "r," respectively. If the Shift key is pressed when a pointer button is pressed, the corresponding uppercase letter is sent. To distinguish a pointer button from a key, the high bit of the character is set (but this bit is normally stripped unless the terminal mode is RAW; see *tty*(4) for details).

Menus

The Release 5 version of *xterm* has four different menus, titled Main Options, VT Options, Tek Options, and VT Fonts. Each menu pops up under the correct combination of key and button presses. Most menus are divided into two sections, separated by a horizontal line. The top portion contains various modes that can be specified. A check mark appears next to a mode that is currently active. Selecting one of these modes toggles its state. The bottom portion contains command entries; selecting one of these performs the indicated function. The menus are described in detail in the following sections.

Main Options Menu

The Main Options menu is displayed when the Control key and pointer button 1 are simultaneously pressed in an *xterm* window. The modes section contains items that apply to both the VT102 and Tektronix windows. The modes can also be set by command-line options when invoking *xterm*, or by entries in a resource startup file like *.Xresources* (see Chapter 11, *Setting Resources*). The menu selections enable you to change your mind once *xterm* is running.

All of the commands on this menu (except for Redraw Window) send a signal that is intended to affect the *xterm* process (Send INT Signal, Send TERM Signal, etc.). Given that your operating system may recognize only certain signals, every menu item may not produce the intended function.

Four of these commands (Send HUP Signal, Send TERM Signal, Send KILL Signal, and Quit) send signals that are intended to terminate the *xterm* window. In most cases, you can probably end an *xterm* process simply by typing some sequence (such as Control-D or `exit`) in the window. Of course, the menu options may be helpful if the more conventional ways of killing the window fail. Refer to the section on *xkill* in Chapter 8, *Other Clients*, for a discussion of the hazards of killing a client and a summary of alternatives.

Main Options Menu Mode Toggles (On/Off)

Secure Keyboard
: Ensures that all keyboard input is directed *only* to *xterm*. Used when typing in passwords or other sensitive data in an unsecure environment. (See "Security" later in this reference page.)

Allow SendEvents
: Causes synthetic key and button events (generated using the X protocol `SendEvent` request) to be interpreted. Note that allowing such events creates a very large security hole.

Log to File
: Logs *xterm* input/output into a file in your home directory called *XtermLog.xxxxx* where *xxxxx* represents the process ID number of the *xterm* process. Logging allows you to keep track of the sequence of data and, therefore, is particularly helpful while debugging code.

To display the data contained in the log file, at the *xterm* window prompt type:

```
more XtermLog.xxxxx
```

The output file is sent to your *xterm* window.

Be sure to turn Log to File off before displaying the log file in the *xterm* window. When Log to File is on, anything in the window is appended to the end of the log file. If you display the log file while logging is on, you will get into a continuous loop, much as if you typed cat * > *file*.

To find out the exact name of the log file, list the contents of your home directory, looking for a log file with an appropriate time and date. Note that if you turn logging on in multiple *xterm* windows, there will be multiple log files.

Main Options Menu Commands

Redraw Window

Redraws the contents of the window. (You can redraw the entire screen using the *xrefresh* client. If you are running the *mwm* window manager, you can also do this using the Refresh item on *mwm*'s Root Menu.)

Send STOP Signal

Suspends a process (sends the SIGTSTP signal to the process group of the process running under *xterm*, usually the shell). If your system supports job control, you may also be able to suspend the process by typing Control-Z. If your system does not support job control, this menu item won't work either.

Send CONT Signal

Continues a process that has been suspended (technically speaking, this menu item sends the SIGCONT signal to the process group of the process running under *xterm*, usually the shell). The Send CONT Signals item is especially useful on systems with job control if you accidentally type Control-Z and suspend a process.

Send INT Signal

Interrupts a process (sends the SIGINT signal to the process group of the process running under *xterm*, usually the shell).

Send HUP Signal

Hangs up the process (sends the SIGHUP signal to the process group of the process running under *xterm*, usually the shell). This usually ends up killing the *xterm* process, and the window disappears from the screen.

Send TERM Signal

Terminates the process (sends the SIGTERM signal to the process group of the process running under *xterm*, usually the shell). This usually ends up killing the *xterm* process, and the window disappears from the screen.

Send KILL Signal   Kills the process (sends the SIGKILL signal to the process group of the process running under *xterm*, usually the shell). This ends up killing the *xterm* process, and the window disappears from the screen.

Quit   Like Send HUP Signal, Quit sends the SIGHUP signal to the process group of the process running under *xterm*, usually the shell. This usually ends up killing the *xterm* process, and the window disappears from the screen.

     Quit is separated from the earlier commands by a horizontal line, so it's easier to point at. Sending a SIGHUP signal with Quit is also slightly more gentle to the system than using Send KILL Signal.

See *signal*(3C) in the *UNIX Programmer's Manual* for more information on what each signal does.

VT Options Menu

The VT Options menu menu sets various characteristics (or modes) of the VT102 emulation window and is displayed when the Control key and pointer button 2 are pressed in the VT102 window.

In the command section of this menu, the soft reset entry will reset scroll regions. This can be convenient when some program has left the scroll regions set incorrectly (often a problem when using VMS or TOPS-20). The full reset entry will clear the screen, reset tabs to every eight columns, and reset the terminal modes (such as wrap and smooth scroll) to their initial states just after *xterm* has finish processing the command-line options.

VT Options Menu Mode Toggles (On/Off)

Most of these modes can also be set by command-line options when invoking *xterm* or by entries in a resource startup file like *.Xresources*. (See "Options" and "Resources" in this reference page. See Chapter 11, *Setting Resources*, for information on resource files and syntax.) The menu selections enable you to change your mind about the characteristics of an *xterm* after the window is running.

Enable Scrollbar   Causes a scrollbar to appear on the left-hand side of the *xterm* window. Off by default.

Enable Jump Scroll   Causes the window to move text several lines at a time rather than line by line. On by default.

Enable Reverse Video   Reverses the foreground and background colors. Off by default.

Enable Auto Wraparound
     Wraps the text or data to the next line automatically when the cursor reaches the window border on input. On by default.

Enable Reverse Wraparound
     Allows the cursor to wrap around from the leftmost column to the rightmost column of the previous line. Allows you to backspace to

Reference Pages

the previous line and overstrike data or erase data with the space bar. Off by default.

Enable Auto Linefeed
Generates a linefeed automatically. This is useful if you are using a program that generates a carriage return without dropping down a line on your screen. Off by default. (This option is usually not needed on UNIX systems.)

Enable Application Cursor Keys
Generates ANSI escape sequences rather than standard cursor movement when you use the arrow keys. This option may be useful when working with certain applications. Off by default.

The following table lists the ANSI characters generated by application cursors.

Cursor Key (Arrow)	Reset (Cursor)	Set (Application)
Up	ESC [A	ESC O A
Down	ESC [B	ESC O B
Right	ESC [C	ESC O C
Left	ESC [D	ESC O D

Enable Application Keypad
Generates a control function rather than a numeric character when you use the numeric keypad. Off by default.

Scroll to Bottom on Key Press
Indicates that pressing a key while using the scrollbar causes the cursor to be repositioned at the bottom of the scroll region. For example, if you have scrolled up the window to see past history, as soon as you begin typing your next command the cursor jumps to the bottom of the screen. Off by default.

Scroll to Bottom on Tty Output
Indicates that receiving output to the window (or pressing a key, if stty echo has been specified) while using the scrollbar causes the cursor to be repositioned at the bottom of the scroll region. On by default. This mode can be toggled off, but is generally desirable to have.

Allow 80/132 Column Switching

> Allows *xterm* to recognize the DECCOLM escape sequence, which switches the terminal between 80- and 132-column mode. The DEC-COLM escape sequence can be included in a program (such as a spreadsheet) to allow the program to display in 132-column format. See Appendix E, *xterm Control Sequences*, for more information. Off by default.

Enable Curses Emulation

> Enables the *curses* fix. Several programs that use the *curses* cursor motion package have some difficulties with VT102-compatible terminals. The bug occurs when you run the *more* program on a file containing a line that is exactly the width of the window and that is followed by a line beginning with a tab. The leading tabs may disappear. This mode causes the tabs to be displayed correctly. Off by default.

Enable Visual Bell

> Causes your terminal window to flash whenever an event occurs that would ordinarily cause your terminal bell to ring.

Enable Margin Bell

> Turns on the margin bell. Off by default.

Tek Window Showing

> Shows the current contents of the Tektronix window; you cannot input to that window until you choose Switch to Tek Mode. Off by default.

Show Alternate Screen

> Informs you that you are looking at the alternate screen. You cannot select this mode from the menu. If a check mark appears beside this mode, you are viewing the alternate screen. Off by default.

VT Options Menu Commands

These commands can be invoked only from the menu; there are no alternative ways to perform the same functions.

Do Soft Reset

> Resets the terminal scroll region from partial scroll (a portion of the window) to full scroll (the entire window). Use this command when a program has left the scroll region set incorrectly.

Do Full Reset

> Clears the window, resets tabs to every eight columns, and resets the terminal modes such as auto wraparound and jump scroll to their initial states.

Reset and Clear Saved Lines

> Does full reset (see above) and also clears the history of lines saved off the top of the screen. (Available as of Release 5.)

Show Tek Window

> Shows the current contents of the Tektronix window; you cannot input to that window until you choose Switch to Tek Mode. Off by default.

Switch to Tek Mode

> Brings up a Tektronix window. You can input to this window.

Hide VT Window	Removes the VT window but does not destroy it. It can be brought back by choosing Select VT Mode from the Tek Options menu.

Tek Options Menu

The Tek Options menu (formerly Tektronix) sets various modes in the Tektronix emulation, and is displayed when the Control key and pointer button 2 are pressed in the Tektronix window. The current font size is checked in the modes section of the menu. The PAGE entry in the command section clears the Tektronix window.

Tek Options Menu Mode Toggles (On/Off)

These modes can be set only from the Tek Options menu.

Large Characters #2 Size Characters #3 Size Characters Small Characters	Selecting one of these four options sets the point size of text displayed in the Tektronix window. The four options are mutually exclusive.

Tek Options Menu Commands

PAGE	Clears the Tektronix window.
RESET	Closes down the Tektronix window.
COPY	Writes a file of the Tektronix text and graphics commands.
Show VT Window	Shows the current contents of the VT102 window; you cannot input to that window until you choose Switch to VT Mode.
Switch to VT Mode	Makes the associated VT102 window active for input.
Hide Tek Window	Removes the Tektronix window but does not destroy it. It can be brought back by choosing Switch to Tek Mode from the VT Options menu.

VT Fonts Menu

The VT Fonts menu enables you to change the VT102 display font dynamically. The menu is displayed when the Control key and pointer button 3 are pressed in the VT102 window. All items on the menu toggle different display fonts. The items are mutually exclusive. A check-mark appears on the menu next to the current font.

In addition to the default font and a number of alternatives that are set with resources, the menu offers: the Escape Sequence menu item, which toggles the font last specified by the Set Font escape sequence; and the Selection menu item, which tries to use the current text selection as a font name (if the PRIMARY text selection is owned). Chapter 6, *Font Specification*, explains how to use these menu items.

Default   Selecting one of these seven options sets the point size of text displayed in the
Unreadable   VT102 window. The Default font is the font specified when the *xterm* was run.
Tiny
Small
Medium
Large
Huge

Escape Sequence

> Allows you to select a font previously toggled using an escape sequence. See
> Chapter 6, *Font Specification*, for the escape sequence to use.

Selection   Allows you to toggle a font whose name you've previously selected with the
              pointer or using the select button of the *xfontsel* client. See Chapter 6, *Font
              Specification*, for more information.

Security

X environments differ in their security consciousness. MIT servers, run under *xdm*, are capable
of using a "magic cookie" authorization scheme that can provide a reasonable level of security
for many people. If your server is using only a host-based mechanism to control access to the
server (see *xhost*), then if you enable access for a host and other users are also permitted to run
clients on that same host, there is every possibility that someone can run an application that
will use the basic services of the X protocol to snoop on your activities, potentially capturing a
transcript of everything you type at the keyboard. This is of particular concern when you want
to type in a password or other sensitive data. The best solution to this problem is to use a better
authorization mechanism than host-based control, but a simple mechanism exists for protecting
keyboard input in *xterm*.

The Main Options menu (see "Menus" above) contains a Secure Keyboard entry which, when
enabled, ensures that all keyboard input is directed *only* to *xterm* (using the `GrabKeyboard`
protocol request). When an application prompts you for a password (or other sensitive data),
you can enable Secure Keyboard using the menu, type in the data, and then disable Secure
Keyboard using the menu again. Only one X client at a time can secure the keyboard, so when
you attempt to enable Secure Keyboard it may fail. In this case, the bell will sound. If the
Secure Keyboard succeeds, the foreground and background colors will be exchanged (as if you
selected the Enable Reverse Video entry in the VT Options menu); they will be exchanged
again when you exit secure mode. If the colors do *not* switch, then you should be *very* suspi-
cious that you are being spoofed. If the application you are running displays a prompt before
asking for the password, it is safest to enter secure mode *before* the prompt gets displayed, and
to make sure that the prompt gets displayed correctly (in the new colors), to minimize the prob-
ability of spoofing. You can also bring up the menu again and make sure that a check mark
appears next to the entry.

Secure Keyboard mode will be disabled automatically if your xterm window becomes iconified (or otherwise unmapped), or if you start up a reparenting window manager (that places a titlebar or other decoration around the window) while in Secure Keyboard mode. (This is a feature of the X protocol not easily overcome.) When this happens, the foreground and background colors will be switched back and the bell will sound in warning.

Character Classes

Clicking the middle mouse button twice in rapid succession will cause all characters of the same class (e.g., letters, white space, punctuation) to be selected. Since different people have different preferences for what should be selected (for example, should filenames be selected as a whole or only the separate subnames), the default mapping can be overridden through the use of the charClass (class CharClass) resource.

This resource is simply a list of *range*: *value* pairs, where the range is either a single number or *low-high* in the range of 0 to 127, corresponding to the ASCII code for the character or characters to be set. The *value* is arbitrary, although the default table uses the character number of the first character occurring in the set.

The default table is:

```
static int charClass[128] = {
/* NUL  SOH  STX  ETX  EOT  ENQ  ACK  BEL */
    32,  1,   1,   1,   1,   1,   1,   1,
/* BS   HT   NL   VT   NP   CR   SO   SI */
    1,   32,  1,   1,   1,   1,   1,   1,
/* DLE  DC1  DC2  DC3  DC4  NAK  SYN  ETB */
    1,   1,   1,   1,   1,   1,   1,   1,
/* CAN  EM   SUB  ESC  FS   GS   RS   US */
    1,   1,   1,   1,   1,   1,   1,   1,
/* SP   !    →    #    $    %    &    ' */
    32,  33,  34,  35,  36,  37,  38,  39,
/* (    )    *    +    ,    -    .    / */
    40,  41,  42,  43,  44,  45,  46,  47,
/* 0    1    2    3    4    5    6    7 */
    48,  48,  48,  48,  48,  48,  48,  48,
/* 8    9    :    ;    <    =    >    ? */
    48,  48,  58,  59,  60,  61,  62,  63,
/* @    A    B    C    D    E    F    G */
    64,  48,  48,  48,  48,  48,  48,  48,
/* H    I    J    K    L    M    N    O */
    48,  48,  48,  48,  48,  48,  48,  48,
/* P    Q    R    S    T    U    V    W */
    48,  48,  48,  48,  48,  48,  48,  48,
/* X    Y    Z    [    \    ]    ^    _ */
    48,  48,  48,  91,  92,  93,  94,  48,
/* `    a    b    c    d    e    f    g */
    96,  48,  48,  48,  48,  48,  48,  48,
```

```
/*   h   i   j    k    l    m    n     o */
    48, 48, 48,  48,  48,  48,  48,   48,
/*   p   q   r    s    t    u    v     w */
    48, 48, 48,  48,  48,  48,  48,   48,
/*   x   y   z    {    |    }    ~   DEL */
    48, 48, 48, 123, 124, 125, 126,   1};
```

For example, the string "33:48,37:48,45-47:48,64:48" indicates that the exclamation mark, percent sign, dash, period, slash, and ampersand characters should be treated the same way as characters and numbers. This is very useful for cutting and pasting electronic mailing addresses and UNIX filenames.

Actions

It is possible to rebind keys (or sequences of keys) to arbitrary strings for input, by changing the translations for the vt100 or tek4014 widgets. Changing the translations for events other than key and button events is not expected, and will cause unpredictable behavior. The following actions are provided for use with the vt100 or tek4014 translations resource:

bell([*percent*])

Rings the keyboard bell at the specified percentage above or below the base volume.

ignore()

Ignores the event but checks for special pointer position escape sequences. This is useful for trapping events that might otherwise interfere with translations you might want to set.

insert()

Inserts the character or string associated with the key that was pressed.

insert-seven-bit()

A synonym for insert().

insert-eight-bit()

Inserts the eight-bit (Meta) version of the character or string associated with the key that was pressed. (The fallback translation associated with this action is Meta<Keypress>. That is, pressing Meta in conjunction with any key will get the 8-bit equivalent.) The exact action depends on the value of the eightBitInput resource.

insert-selection(*sourcename* [, . . .])

Inserts the string found in the selection or cut buffer indicated by *sourcename*. Sources are checked in the order given (case is significant) until one is found. Commonly-used selections include: PRIMARY, SECONDARY, and CLIPBOARD. Cut buffers are typically named CUT_BUFFER0 through CUT_BUFFER7.

keymap(*name*)

Dynamically defines a new translation table whose resource name is *name* with the suffix Keymap (case is significant). The keymap name None restores the original translation table. This is useful for loading translations that will be used with a particular application running in an *xterm* window. In the following example, keymap is used to define a set of special keys for entering commonly-typed words when running the *dbx* application:

```
*VT100.Translations: #override <Key>F13: keymap(dbx)
*VT100.dbxKeymap.translations: \
```

```
<Key>   F14:   keymap(None)\n\
<Key>   F17:   string("next") string(0x0d)\n\
<Key>   F18:   string("step") string(0x0d)\n\
<Key>   F19:   string("continue") string(0x0d)\n\
<Key>   F20:   string("print ") insert-selection(PRIMARY,CUT_BUFFER0)
```

When the user presses key F13, the *dbx* keymaps go into effect. Keys F15-F20 then print common *dbx* commands. F14 disables the translations on the "dbx" keys.

popup-menu(*menuname*)

> Displays the specified popup menu. Valid names (case is significant) include: main-Menu, vtMenu, fontMenu, and tekMenu.

secure()

> Toggles the secure keyboard mode described in the "Security" section, and is invoked from the Secure Keyboard entry in mainMenu.

select-start()

> Begins text selection at the current pointer location. See the section on "Pointer Usage" for information on making selections.

select-extend()

> Tracks the pointer and extends the selection. It should be bound only to motion events.

select-end(*destname* [, ...])

> Puts the currently selected text into all of the selections or cut buffers specified by *destname*.

select-cursor-start()

> Similar to select-start, except that it begins the selection at the current text cursor position.

select-cursor-end(*destname* [, ...])

> Similar to select-end, except that it should be used with select-cursor-start.

set-vt-font(d/1/2/3/4/5/6/e/s [,*normalfont* [, *boldfont*]])

> Sets the font or fonts currently being used in the VT102 window. The first argument is a single character that specifies the font to be used: d or D indicates the default font (the font initially used when *xterm* was started); 1 through 6 indicate the fonts

specified by the font1 through font6 resources; e or E indicates the normal and bold fonts that may be set through escape codes (or specified as the second and third action arguments, respectively); and s or S indicates the font selection (as made by programs such as *xfontsel*) indicated by the second action argument.

start-extend()

Similar to select-start except that the selection is extended to the current pointer location.

start-cursor-extend()

Similar to select-extend except that the selection is extended to the current text cursor position.

string(*string*)

Inserts the specified text string as if it had been typed. Quotation is necessary if the string contains whitespace or non-alphanumeric characters. If the string argument begins with the characters "0x", it is interpreted as a hex character constant.

scroll-back(*count* [,*units*])

Scrolls the text window backward so that text that had previously scrolled off the top of the screen is now visible. The *count* argument indicates the number of *units* (which may be page, halfpage, pixel, or line) by which to scroll.

scroll-forw(*count* [,*units*])

Scrolls is similar to scroll-back except that it scrolls in the other direction.

allow-send-events(*on/off/toggle*)

Sets or toggles the allowSendEvents resource and is also invoked by the allowsends entry in mainMenu.

set-logging(*on/off/toggle*)

Toggles the logging resource and is also invoked by the logging entry in main-Menu.

redraw()

Redraws the window and is also invoked by the redraw entry in mainMenu.

send-signal(*signame*)

Sends the signal named by *signame* (which may also be a number) to the *xterm* sub-process (the shell or program specified with the -e command-line option) and is also invoked by the suspend, continue, interrupt, hangup, terminate, and kill entries in mainMenu. Allowable signal names are (case is not significant): tstp (if supported by the operating system), suspend (same as tstp), cont (if supported by the operating system), int, hup, term, quit, alrm, alarm (same as alrm) and kill.

quit()

Sends a SIGHUP to the subprogram and exits. It is also invoked by the quit entry in mainMenu.

`set-scrollbar(`*on/off/toggle*`)`
> Toggles the `scrollbar` resource and is also invoked by the `scrollbar` entry in vtMenu.

`set-jumpscroll(`*on/off/toggle*`)`
> Toggles the `jumpscroll` resource and is also invoked by the `jumpscroll` entry in vtMenu.

`set-reverse-video(`*on/off/toggle*`)`
> Toggles the `reverseVideo` resource and is also invoked by the `reversevideo` entry in vtMenu.

`set-autowrap(`*on/off/toggle*`)`
> Toggles automatic wrapping of long lines and is also invoked by the `autowrap` entry in vtMenu.

`set-reversewrap(`*on/off/toggle*`)`
> Toggles the `reverseWrap` resource and is also invoked by the `reversewrap` entry in vtMenu.

`set-autolinefeed(`*on/off/toggle*`)`
> Toggles automatic insertion of linefeeds and is also invoked by the `autolinefeed` entry in vtMenu.

`set-appcursor(`*on/off/toggle*`)`
> Toggles the application cursor key mode and is also invoked by the `appcursor` entry in vtMenu.

`set-appkeypad(`*on/off/toggle*`)`
> Toggles the application keypad mode and is also invoked by the `appkeypad` entry in vtMenu.

`set-scroll-on-key(`*on/off/toggle*`)`
> Toggles the `scrollKey` resource and is also invoked from the `scrollkey` entry in vtMenu.

`set-scroll-on-tty-output(`*on/off/toggle*`)`
> Toggles the `scrollTtyOutput` resource and is also invoked from the `scroll-ttyoutput` entry in vtMenu.

`set-allow132(`*on/off/toggle*`)`
> Toggles the `c132` resource and is also invoked from the `allow132` entry in vtMenu.

`set-cursesemul(`*on/off/toggle*`)`
> Toggles the `curses` resource and is also invoked from the `cursesemul` entry in vtMenu.

`set-visual-bell`(*on/off/toggle*)

    Toggles the `visualBell` resource and is also invoked by the `visualbell` entry in `vtMenu`.

`set-marginbell`(*on/off/toggle*)

    Toggles the `marginBell` resource and is also invoked from the `marginbell` entry in `vtMenu`.

`set-altscreen`(*on/off/toggle*)

    Toggles between the alternate and current screens.

`soft-reset`()

    Resets the scrolling region and is also invoked from the `softreset` entry in `vt-Menu`.

`hard-reset`()

    Resets the scrolling region, tabs, window size, and cursor keys and clears the screen. It is also invoked from the `hardreset` entry in `vtMenu`.

`clear-saved-lines`()

    Does `hard-reset` (see above) and also clears the history of lines saved off the top of the screen. (Available as of Release 5.) This action is also invoked from the `clearsavedlines` entry in the `vtMenu`.

`set-terminal-type`(*type*)

    Directs output to either the `vt` or `tek` windows, according to the `type` string. It is also invoked by the `tekmode` entry in `vtMenu` and the `vtmode` entry in `tekMenu`.

`set-visibility`(*vt/tek, on/off/toggle*)

    Controls whether or not the `vt` or `tek` windows are visible. It is also invoked from the `tekshow` and `vthide` entries in `vtMenu` and the `vtshow` and `tekhide` entries in `tekMenu`.

`set-tek-text`(*large/2/3/small*)

    Sets font used in the Tektronix window to the value of the resources `tektextlarge`, `tektext2`, `tektext3`, and `tektextsmall` according to the argument. It is also invoked by the entries of the same names as the resources in `tek-Menu`.

`tek-page`()

    Clears the Tektronix window and is also invoked by the `tekpage` entry in `tekMenu`.

`tek-reset`()

    Resets the Tektronix window and is also invoked by the `tekreset` entry in `tek-Menu`.

`tek-copy`()

    Copies the escape codes used to generate the current window contents to a file in the current directory beginning with the name COPY. It is also invoked from the `tekcopy` entry in `tekMenu`.

```
visual-bell()
```
Flashes the window quickly. (Available as of Release 5.)

The Tektronix window also has the following action:

```
gin-press(l/L/m/M/r/R)
```
Sends the indicated graphics input code.

The default bindings in the VT102 window are:

```
Shift    <KeyPress>  Prior:       scroll-back(1,halfpage)\n\
Shift    <KeyPress>  Next:        scroll-forw(1,halfpage)\n\
Shift    <KeyPress>  Select:      select-cursor-start()\
                                  select-cursor-end(PRIMARY,CUT_BUFFER0)\n\
Shift    <KeyPress>  Insert:      insert-selection(PRIMARY,CUT_BUFFER0)\n\
         ~Meta       <KeyPress>:  insert-seven-bit()\n\
         Meta        <KeyPress>:  insert-eight-bit()\n\
         !Ctrl       <Btn1Down>:  popup-menu(mainMenu)\n\
!Lock    Ctrl        <Btn1Down>:  popup-menu(mainMenu)\n\
         ~Meta       <Btn1Down>:  select-start()\n\
         ~Meta       <Btn1Motion>: select-extend()\n\
         !Ctrl       <Btn2Down>:  popup-menu(vtMenu)\n\
!Lock    Ctrl        <Btn2Down>:  popup-menu(vtMenu)\n\
~Ctrl    ~Meta       <Btn2Down>:  ignore()\n\
~Ctrl    ~Meta       <Btn2Up>:    insert-selection(PRIMARY,CUT_BUFFER0)\n\
         !Ctrl       <Btn3Down>:  popup-menu(fontMenu)\n\
!Lock    Ctrl        <Btn3Down>:  popup-menu(fontMenu)\n\
~Ctrl    ~Meta       <Btn3Down>:  start-extend()\n\
         ~Meta       <Btn3Motion>: select-extend()\n\
                     <BtnUp>:     select-end(PRIMARY,CUT_BUFFER0)\n\
                     <BtnDown>:   bell(0)
```

The default bindings in the Tektronix window are:

```
         ~Meta       <KeyPress>:  insert-seven-bit()\n\
         Meta        <KeyPress>:  insert-eight-bit()\n\
         !Ctrl       <Btn1Down>:  popup-menu(mainMenu)\n\
!Lock    Ctrl        <Btn1Down>:  popup-menu(mainMenu)\n\
         !Ctrl       <Btn2Down>:  popup-menu(tekMenu)\n\
!Lock    Ctrl        <Btn2Down>:  popup-menu(tekMenu)\n\
Shift    ~Meta       <Btn1Down>:  gin-press(L)\n\
         ~Meta       <Btn1Down>:  gin-press(l)\n\
Shift    ~Meta       <Btn2Down>:  gin-press(M)\n\
         ~Meta       <Btn2Down>:  gin-press(m)\n\
Shift    ~Meta       <Btn3Down>:  gin-press(R)\n\
         ~Meta       <Btn3Down>:  gin-press(r)
```

Environment

xterm sets the environment variables TERM and TERMCAP properly for the size window you have created. It also uses and sets the environment variable DISPLAY to specify which bitmap display terminal to use. The environment variable WINDOWID is set to the X window ID number of the *xterm* window.

Bugs

The class name is XTerm instead of Xterm.

Large pastes do not work on some systems. This is not a bug in *xterm*; it is a bug in the pseudo-terminal driver of those systems. *xterm* feeds large pastes to the pseudo-terminal only as fast as the *pty* will accept data, but some *pty* drivers do not return enough information to know if the write has succeeded.

Many of the options are not resettable after *xterm* starts (i.e., the menus allow you to change only some of *xterm*'s features dynamically).

The Tek widget does not support key/button re-binding.

Only fixed-width, character cell fonts are supported.

This program still needs to be rewritten. It should be split into very modular sections, with the various emulators being completely separate widgets that don't know about each other. Ideally, you'd like to be able to pick and choose emulator widgets and stick them into a single control widget.

There needs to be a dialog box to allow entry of the log file name and the COPY filename.

See Also

X, resize, pty(4), tty(4); Chapter 5, *The xterm Terminal Emulator*; Chapter 6, *Font Specification*; Appendix E, *xterm Control Sequences*.

Authors

Far too many people, including:

Loretta Guarino Reid (DEC-UEG-WSL), Joel McCormack (DEC-UEG-WSL), Terry Weissman (DEC-UEG-WSL), Edward Moy (Berkeley), Ralph R. Swick (MIT-Athena), Mark Vandevoorde (MIT-Athena), Bob McNamara (DEC-MAD), Jim Gettys (MIT-Athena), Bob Scheifler (MIT X Consortium), Doug Mink (SAO), Steve Pitschke (Stellar), Ron Newman (MIT-Athena), Jim Fulton (MIT X Consortium), Dave Serisky (HP), and Jonathan Kamens (MIT-Athena).

xtici

Name

xtici – TekColor™ editor.

Syntax

xtici [*options*]

Description

xtici (also known as the TekColor Editor) allows you to create precise colors using formats that are portable from system to system. The valid color formats are called *color spaces*. *xtici* was written by Chuck Adams and Al Tabayoyon of Tektronix, Inc., to take advantage of the powers of the X Color Management System (Xcms), also developed by Tektronix and donated to the X Consortium as part of X11R5. The TekColor Editor (*xtici*) is available as a public domain client.

Chapter 8, *Other Clients*, describes how to use *xtici*. See Chapter 12, *Specifying Color*, for an overview of the Xcms color model.

Options

-display [*host*]:*server*[.*screen*]

> Specifies the name of the display to use. *host* is the hostname of the physical display, *server* specifies the display server number, and *screen* specifies the screen number. Either or both of the *host* and *screen* elements to the display specification can be omitted. If *host* is omitted, the local display is assumed. If *screen* is omitted, screen 0 is assumed (and the period is unnecessary). The colon and (display) *server* are necessary in all cases.

> For example:

> % **xtici -display** *your_node*:**0.1**

> specifies the screen 0 on server 0 on the display identified by *your_node*. If the host is omitted, the local display is assumed. If the screen is omitted, the screen 0 is assumed; the server and colon (:) are necessary in all cases.

> The -display option can be abbreviated as -d, unless the client accepts another option that begins with "d."

-gamutProc *state*

> The acceptable values are closest, chroma, and value.

-huebar *state*

> Specifies the appearance and behavior of the hue bar. The acceptable values are empty, constant, and dynamic.

-leaf *appearance*

> Specifies the appearance of the hue leaf. The acceptable values are filled and empty.

Resources

xtici is written using the Athena widget set. See "Widget Hierarchy" for a diagram of the widgets and Appendix G, *Widget Resources*, for a list of resources.

Widget Hierarchy

```
TekHVC  xtici
                TekBox  main
                    Form  menubar
                        Command  quit
                        Command  option
                            TransientShell  optionmenu
                                Form  menuform
                                    Command  huebutton
                                    Command  leafbutton
                                    Command  clamp
                                    Command  coordinates
                                        TransientShell  coordmenu
                                            Form  menuform
                                                Command  rgb
                                                Command  uvY
                        Command  import
                        Command  export
                        Command  edit
                            TransientShell  editmenu
                                Form  menuform
                                    Command  copy
                                        TransientShell  copymenu
                                            Form  menuform
                                                Command  copyhvc
                                                Command  copyrgb
                                                Command  copyuvy
                                    Command  paste
                        Command  help
                            TransientShell  helpmenu
                                Form  menuform
                                    Command  interface
                                    Command  version
                                    Command  quit
                                    Command  option
                                    Command  import
                                    Command  export
                                    Command  edit
                    ColorScale  scale
                    Label  label
                    RepeaterButton  up
                    RepeaterButton  down
                    Scrollbar  scrollbar
                    Colorbar  bar
```

```
                    Zoom  zoom
                    Colorbar  expand
            Form  show
                TriText  hvc
                    Form  form
                            Label  item1
                            Label  item2
                            Label  item3
                            Text  text1
                            Text  text2
                            Text  text3
                TriText  uvy
                    Form  form
                            Label  item1
                            Label  item2
                            Label  item3
                            Text  text1
                            Text  text2
                            Text  text3
                TriText  rgb
                    Form  form
                            Label  item1
                            Label  item2
                            Label  item3
                            Text  text1
                            Text  text2
                            Text  text3
            Form  patch
                Text  patchtext
                Box  patcharea
            ColorScale  huebar
                Label  label
                RepeaterButton  up
                RepeaterButton  down
                Scrollbar  scrollbar
                Colorbar  bar
                Zoom  zoom
                Colorbar  expand
            Leaf  leaf
                Form  hvcform
                    Label  value
                    RepeaterButton  uparrow
                    RepeaterButton  downarrow
                    Hueleaf  hueleaf
                    RepeaterButton  leftarrow
                    RepeaterButton  rightarrow
                    Label  chroma
```

See Also

xcol, xcoloredit; Chapter 8, *Other Clients*; Chapter 12, *Specifying Color.*

Trademarks

Tektronix® and Tek® are registered trademarks of Tektronix, Inc.

TekColor™ Color Management System, TekColor™ CMS, TekColor™ Human Interface, and TekHVC Color Space are trademarks of Tektronix, Inc.

Copyright

Copyright 1991, Tektronix, Inc.

Author

Chuck Adams, Al Tabayoyon, Tektronix, Inc.

xwd

Name

xwd – place window images in a dump file.

Syntax

xwd [*options*]

Description

xwd stores window images in a specially formatted window dump file. This file can then be read by various other X utilities for redisplay, printing, editing, formatting, archiving, image processing, etc. The target window is selected by clicking the pointer in the desired window. The keyboard bell is rung once at the beginning of the dump and twice when the dump is completed.

Options

xwd accepts the following options:

-add *value*
> Specifies a signed value to be added to every pixel.

-display [*host*]:*server*[.*screen*]
> Allows you to specify the host, server, and screen to connect to. *host* is the hostname of the physical display, *server* is the server number, and *screen* is the screen number. For example,

> **xwd -display** *your_node*:**0.1 &**

> specifies screen 1 on server 0 on the display named by *your_node*. Either or both of the *host* and *screen* elements to the display specification can be omitted. If *host* is omitted, the local display is assumed. If *screen* is omitted, screen 0 is assumed (and the period is unnecessary). The colon and (display) *server* are necessary in all cases.

-frame
> Indicates that the window manager frame should be included when manually selecting a window.

-help   Prints out the "Usage:" command syntax summary.

-icmap
> Normally the colormap of the chosen window is used to obtain RGB values. This option forces the first installed colormap of the screen to be used instead. (Available as of Release 5.)

-id *window_ID*
> Allows you to specify the window using its *window_ID* (resource ID), rather than by selecting it with the pointer.

-name *name*

Allows you to specify the window using its *name* (stored in the WM_NAME property), rather than by selecting it with the pointer.

-nobdrs

Specifies that the window dump should not include the pixels that compose the X window border. This is useful when the window contents are to be included in a document as an illustration.

-out *file*

Allows you to specify the output file on the command line. The default outputs to the standard output (*stdout*).

-root   Makes a dump of the entire root window; the user is not required to select a window with the pointer.

-screen

Indicates that the GetImage request used to obtain the image should be done on the root window, rather than directly on the specified window. In this way, you can obtain pieces of other windows that overlap the specified window, and more importantly, you can capture menus or other popups that are independent windows but appear over the specified window. (Available as of Release 5.)

-xy   Applies to color displays only. The -xy option selects "XY" pixmap format dumping instead of the default "Z" pixmap format.

Files

XWDFile.h

X Window Dump File format definition file.

See Also

X, xdpr, xpr, xwud.

Author

Tony Della Fera, Digital Equipment Corp., MIT Project Athena;
William F. Wyatt, Smithsonian Astrophysical Observatory.

xwininfo

Name

xwininfo – window information utility for X.

Syntax

xwininfo [*options*]

Description

xwininfo (described in Chapter 8, *Other Clients*) is a utility for displaying information about windows. Depending on which options are choosen, various information is displayed. If no options are choosen, `-stats` is assumed.

The user has the option of selecting the target window either by using the pointer or by specifying the window on the command line. To select the window using the pointer, simply click any pointer button in the desired window. There are two ways to specify the target window on the command line: either by window ID (using the `-id` option); or by name (using the `-name` option). See "Options" below. There is also a special `-root` option to obtain information about the root window.

With the `-children` and `-tree` options (Release 5), *xwininfo* can now provide information that, in prior releases, was only available using the *xlswins* client. *xlswins* has been removed from the standard MIT X distribution in Release 5.

Options

xwininfo accepts the following options:

-all A quick way to ask for all information possible.

-bits Causes the display of various attributes pertaining to the selected window's raw bits and how the selected window is to be stored. Information displayed includes the selected window's bit gravity, window gravity, backing store hint, backing planes value, backing pixel, and whether or not the window has save under set.

-children
   Displays the selected window's root, parent, and children windows' IDs and names. (Available as of Release 5.) See `-tree`.

-display [*host*]:*server*[*.screen*]
   Allows you to specify the host, server, and screen to connect to. *host* is the hostname of the physical display, *server* specifies the server number, and *screen* specifies the screen number. For example,

```
% xwininfo -display your_node:0.1
```

   specifies screen 1 of server 0 on the display hardware named by *your_node*. If the host is omitted, the local display is assumed. If the screen is omitted, screen 0 is assumed; the server and colon (:) are necessary in all cases.

-events

Causes the selected window's event masks to be displayed. Both the event mask of events wanted by some client and the event mask of events not to propagate are displayed.

-english

Causes all individual height, width, and x and y positions to be displayed in inches (and feet, yards, and miles if necessary), as well as number of pixels, based on what the server thinks the resolution is. Geometry specifications that are in +*x*+*y* form are not changed. -metric and -english may be used at the same time.

-frame

Causes window manager frames to be considered when manually selecting windows.

-help Prints out the "Usage:" command syntax summary.

-id *window_ID*

Allows the user to specify a target window on the command line by providing its *window_ID* (rather than selecting a window using the pointer). This is very useful in debugging X applications where the target window is not mapped to the screen or where the use of the pointer might be impossible or interfere with the application.

-int Specifies that all X window IDs should be displayed as integer values. The default is to display them as hexadecimal values.

-metric

Causes all individual height, width, and x and y positions to be displayed in millimeters, as well as number of pixels, based on what the server thinks the resolution is. Geometry specifications that are in +*x*+*y* form are not changed. -english and -metric may be used at the same time.

-name *name*

Allows the user to specify a target window on the command line by providing its *name* (rather than selecting a window using the pointer).

-root Specifies that the root window is the target window. This is useful in situations where the root window is completely obscured.

-shape

Causes the selected window's window and border shape extents to be displayed. (Available as of Release 5.)

-size Causes the selected window's sizing hints to be displayed. Information displayed includes: for both the normal size hints and the zoom size hints, the user supplied location, if any; the program supplied location, if any; the user supplied size, if any; the program supplied size, if any; the minimum size, if any; the maximum size, if any; the resize increments, if any; and the minimum and maximum aspect ratios, if any.

```
-stats
```
Causes various attributes of the selected window having to do with its location and appearance to be displayed. Information displayed includes the location of the window, its width, height, depth, border width, class, and map state, colormap ID (if any), backing store hint, and the location of its corners. If *xwininfo* is run with no options, `-stats` is assumed.

`-tree`   Like `-children` but displays all children recursively. (Available as of Release 5.)

`-wm`   Causes the selected window's window manager hints to be displayed. Information displayed may include whether or not the application accepts input, what the window's icon window number and name is, where the window's icon should go, and what the window's initial state should be.

Examples

The following is sample output taken with no options specified. (The Motif window manager was running on the display. See Chapter 8, *Other Clients*, for a discussion of how the *mwm* frame can affect *xwininfo*'s results.)

```
xwininfo: Please select the window about which you
          would like information by clicking the
          mouse in that window.

xwininfo: Window id: 0x3c0000f "xterm"

  Absolute upper-left X:  8
  Absolute upper-left Y:  25
  Relative upper-left X:  0
  Relative upper-left Y:  0
  Width: 819
  Height: 484
  Depth: 8
  Visual Class: PseudoColor
  Border width: 0
  Class: InputOutput
  Colormap: 0x27 (installed)
  Bit Gravity State: NorthWestGravity
  Window Gravity State: NorthWestGravity
  Backing Store State: NotUseful
  Save Under State: no
  Map State: IsViewable
  Override Redirect State: no
  Corners:  +8+25  -325+25  -325-391  +8-391
  -geometry 80x24+0+0
```

Bugs

Using −stats and −bits together shows some redundant information.

The geometry string displayed must make assumptions about the window's border width, the behavior of the application, and the window manager. As a result, the location given is not always correct.

See Also

X, xprop; Chapter 8, *Other Clients*.

Author

Mark Lillibridge, MIT Project Athena.

Name

xwud – X window image displayer.

Syntax

xwud [*options*]

Description

xwud is an X Window System window image undumping utility. *xwud* allows X users to display a window image saved in a specially formatted dump file, such as one produced by *xwd*. Chapter 8, *Other Clients*, describes how to use these clients.

xwud allows you to specify the coordinates at which this image is displayed using the -geometry option. By default, *xwud* displays the window image at the coordinates of the original window from which the dump was taken.

Options

xwud accepts the following options:

-bg *color*

> If a bitmap image (or a single plane of an image) is displayed, this option can be used to specify the color to display for the "0" bits in the image.

-display [*host*]:*server*[.*screen*]

> Allows you to specify the host, server, and screen to connect to. *host* is the hostname of the physical display, *server* specifies the server number, and *screen* specifies the screen number. For example:

> % **xwud -display** *your_node*:**0.1**

> specifies screen 1 on server 0 on the display named by *your_node*. If the host is omitted, the local machine is assumed. If the screen is omitted, the screen 0 is assumed; the server and colon (:) are necessary in all cases.

-fg *color*

> If a bitmap image (or a single plane of an image) is displayed, this option can be used to specify the color to display for the "1" bits in the image.

-geometry *geometry*

> The *xwud* window is created with the specified size and location determined by the supplied geometry specification. The -geometry option can be (and often is) abbreviated to -g, unless there is a conflicting option that begins with "g." The argument to the geometry option (*geometry*) is referred to as a "standard geometry string," and has the form *widthxheight±xoff±yoff*. (This option is available for use with *xwud* as of Release 4.)

> Typically, you will want to specify only the position and let the size default to the actual size of the image.

-help Prints out a short description of the allowable options.

-in *file*

> Allows the user to specify the input file on the command line. If no file is specified, standard input is assumed.

-new   Forces creation of a new colormap for displaying the image. If the image characteristics happen to match those of the display, this can get the image on the screen faster, but at the cost of using a new colormap (which on most displays will cause other windows to go technicolor).

-noclick

> Clicking any button in the window will terminate the application, unless this option is specified. Termination can always be achieved by typing "q", "Q", or Control-c.

-plane *number*

> Selects a single bit plane of the image to display. Planes are numbered with zero being the least significant bit. This option can be used to figure out which plane to pass to *xpr* for printing.

-raw   Forces the image to be displayed with whatever color values happen to currently exist on the screen. This option is mostly useful when undumping an image back onto the same screen that the image originally came from, while the original windows are still on the screen, and results in getting the image on the screen faster.

-rv   If a bitmap image (or a single plane of an image) is displayed, this option forces the foreground and background colors to be swapped. This may be needed when displaying a bitmap image which has the color sense of pixel values "0" and "1" reversed from what they are on your display.

-std *map_type*

> Causes the image to be displayed using the specified standard colormap. The property name is obtained by converting the type to uppercase, prepending "RGB_", and appending "_MAP". Typical types are best, default, and grey. See *xstdcmap* for one way of creating standard colormaps.

-vis *vis_type_or_ID*

> Allows you to specify a particular visual or visual class. The default is to pick the "best" one. A particular class can be specified: StaticGray, GrayScale, StaticColor, PseudoColor, DirectColor, or TrueColor. Or Match can be specified, meaning use the same class as the source image. Alternatively, an exact visual ID (specific to the server) can be specified, either as a hexadecimal number (prefixed with "0x") or as a decimal number. Finally, default can be specified, meaning use the same class as the colormap of the root window. Case is not significant in any of these strings.

Files

XWDFile.h

> X Window Dump File format definition file.

See Also

X, xdpr, xpr, xstdcmap, xwd; Chapter 8, *Other Clients*.

Author

Bob Scheifler, MIT X Consortium;

Part Four:

Appendices

This part of the book contains useful reference information.

Managing Your Environment
Release 5 Standard Fonts
Standard Bitmaps
Standard Cursors
xterm Control Sequences
Translation Table Syntax
Widget Resources
Obtaining Example Programs
Glossary
Index

A

Managing Your Environment

This appendix discusses various tasks involved in managing your X user environment, mostly from the UNIX point of view.

In This Appendix:

Managing Your Environment

Throughout this guide, we've demonstrated various things you can do to tailor your X user environment to your needs. This appendix explains some additional tasks you might need (or want) to perform in order to keep your user environment running smoothly. We'll take a look at:

- Including X in your search path

- Writing a startup shell script

- Addressing security issues and access control

- Redirecting console messages

X exists in so many incarnations and runs on so many different versions of UNIX (not to mention other operating systems) that it is difficult to be definitive about these tasks. The current appendix assumes you are running a fairly standard version of X with UNIX. However, given the various incarnations of both X and UNIX, you should be sure to check your system's documentation for additional (or contrary) details.

For a broader and more substantial discussion of these and other system issues, see Volume Eight, *X Window System Administrator's Guide*.

Including X in Your Search Path

The various X clients are normally stored in the directory */usr/bin/X11*. In order to invoke them by name like any other UNIX program, you need to make this directory part of your search path.

This is normally done from your *.cshrc* (C shell) or *.profile* (Bourne shell) file, using a command similar to this:

Bourne Shell:
```
PATH=/usr/ucb:/bin:/usr/bin:/usr/bin/X11:/usr/local/bin
export PATH
```
C Shell:
```
set path=( /usr/ucb /bin /usr/bin /usr/bin/X11 /usr/local/bin )
```

The exact list of directories will differ from system to system. Be aware that directories are searched sequentially from left to right, so a command with the same name in an earlier directory will be found and used before one in a later directory. Many users take advantage of this fact to run customized versions of programs by putting "." (the current directory) or a local tools directory first in their search path. This works fine but you should be aware that this provides a security loophole that can be taken advantage of by an experienced system cracker. It's much safer to put a period at the end of your path, or eliminate it entirely.

If you have already logged in before adding the above line to your *.profile* or *.cshrc* file, you should log out and log in again, or type in the path-setting command at your prompt, so that it takes effect for your current session.

A Startup Shell Script

It's a basic principle of UNIX to let the computer do the work. Accordingly, you'd no doubt like to run various X clients automatically whenever you log in.

The best way to do this is to create a script that runs the clients you want. Depending on how X is set up on your system, you can execute this script in one of two ways:

- If *xdm* is running X, name the script *.xsession*, make it executable, and put it in your home directory. When you log in, *xdm* will automatically execute your *.xsession* file. *.xsession* is generally a Bourne shell script, but it can also be a C shell script or any other executable. If *$HOME/.xsession* doesn't exist, *xdm* will give you an *xterm* client and start the *twm* window manager.

- If you are starting X either with *xinit* or with the *startx* shell script (which is a front-end to *xinit*), name the script *.xinitrc* and put it in your home directory. Both *xinit* and *startx* starts the server and executes *.xinitrc*. Unlike *.xsession*, the *.xinitrc* script must be a Bourne shell script and does not have to be executable. Among the extra functionality provided by *startx* is that if *$HOME/.xinitrc* doesn't exist, *startx* defaults to the system-wide startup script */usr/lib/X11/xinit/xinitrc*, whereas *xinit* will just give you a single *xterm* client.

What Should Go in the Script

With some variation depending on the specific environment, in most cases your startup script should do the following:

- Load your resources file with *xrdb*.

- Set up other server preferences, such as bell volume, font path, etc.

- Start the window manager.

- Start other clients you want on your default display, such as *xterm*, *oclock*, *xload*, etc.

- Run an *xterm* process in the foreground; terminating this process will terminate the login session.

The sample script appears as Example A-1. You can use this script as either an *.xsession* or *.xinitrc* script.

One thing you may notice in the startup script is that some commands are run in the background and some aren't. For clients that configure the X server like *xrdb*, you want to be sure that the command completes before other clients are started (to make sure that the other clients can retrieve all the right resources). Since *xrdb* exits as soon as the resources are successfully loaded, this works great. For clients like *xterm* and *xclock*, however, the client remains active until they are explicitly exited, so you need to start them in the background or else they will prevent the script from continuing.

The exception is the last command, which should be left in the foreground. The reason is that the X session only remains active as long as the startup script is active. You don't want the startup script to actually exit, since then the X session will terminate—what you will see is that all your windows appear and then immediately disappear. Leaving the last command in the foreground is therefore crucial to the longevity of your X session. The last command is often called the *controlling process*, since it is the only thing preventing the startup script and X session from exiting. We suggest using an *xterm* window for the controlling process, but some people use the window manager.

If you use an *xterm* window for the controlling process, you have to be careful not to exit that shell accidentally. For that reason, we use several precautions to make sure that we don't kill that window. We start the window iconified, we start it in reverse video, and we make sure it's properly labeled so that we always know which window is the controlling process. In addition, if you use a shell with an "autologout" feature as your controlling process, you should make sure it isn't in effect for the controlling *xterm* window: otherwise, you might be typing furiously in another window, but if you haven't typed in the controlling *xterm* window for a while then you might be logged out of your entire X session.

Another thing to note in the sample script is that we set up a separate display name for remote clients to use. As explained in Chapter 3, *Working in the X Environment*, clients running on the local machine access the DISPLAY variable to determine on which physical display to create windows. Without explicit settings, both *xdm* and *xinit* will automatically set DISPLAY properly on a workstation, to either `unix:0.0` or `:0.0`, and *xdm* will set DISPLAY properly for an X terminal as well (e.g., `ncd5.ora.com:0.0`).

The DISPLAY environment variable, however, is not propagated to remote shells. And even if it were, you wouldn't always want it to be. When running a client on a remote machine, you have to explicitly use the `-display` command-line option to the remote client to tell it what display to use. For a workstation, you have to be careful that you use the right display name. You can't just use the value of DISPLAY, since by default it's set to `unix:0.0` or `:0.0`, and if it's used on a remote machine then the client will attempt to display to the local display server of the remote machine, not yours. Instead, you have to make sure that the display name supplied to the remote client follows the `hostname:0.0` form.

The *rsh* command also requires that you have set up the remote system to accept commands from the local host. This means that you need a file in your home directory on the remote host called *.rhosts* containing the name of the local system.

Example A-1 shows a startup Bourne shell script which would open windows on the display
as shown in Figure A-1.

Example A-1. Startup Bourne shell script for a workstation

```
#!/bin/sh

# Get hostname.

cpu=`hostname`

# If on a workstation, DISPLAY is set to :0.0 or unix:0.0.  If you
# want to run remote clients, you need to use hostname:0.0.  Set that
# up:

case $DISPLAY in
    unix:0.0|unix:0|:0.0|:0) REMOTEDISPLAY="$cpu:0.0";;
    *) REMOTEDISPLAY=$DISPLAY ;;
esac

# Load resource definitions from .Xresources

xrdb $HOME/.Xresources

# Set keyclick off and invoke the screen saver after
# seven minutes of idleness

xset c off s 420

# Start the mwm window manager

mwm &

# xconsole window will disappear if you do not log in at the console

xconsole -exitOnFail -geometry +0+0 &

# Now start up some xterms
# Start an xterm near lower-left corner but above icons

xterm -geometry 80x22+0-100 &

# Place an xterm next to it

xterm -geometry 98x22-10-10 &

# remote xterm above (but below xconsole window)

rsh ruby xterm -name RUBY -geometry 80x25+0+110 -display $REMOTEDISPLAY &

# Now start up other clients
# digital xclock in upper-right corner

xclock -digital -update 1 -geometry -0+0 &

# xcalc just below it;

xcalc -geometry -0+75 &

# xload at bottom of xcalc

xload -geometry -0+350 &

# Start another xterm window.
# This is the only xterm that should be run in the foreground.
# Killing this window will shut down your X session.

exec xterm -iconic -rv -name "LOGOUT"
```

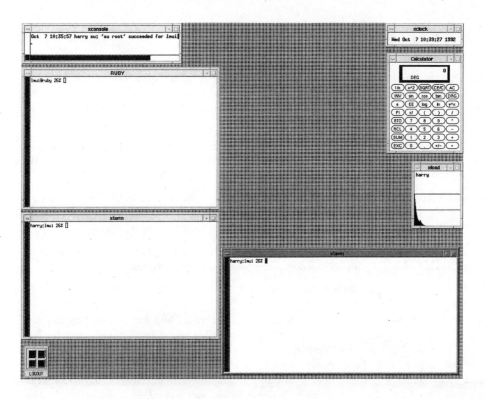

Figure A-1. Display after running either sample script

Note that windows are actually arranged in a "tiled" fashion, with two large xterm windows side by side on the bottom of the screen, a smaller one (connected to a remote system) above, and the "desk accessories" lined up in the upper-right corner. This leaves some room free for new windows or for invoking the Root Menu menu on the root window. This is ideal for our purposes, which are mainly editing, formatting, and testing examples for books. Depending on what you do, another arrangement might be better.*

The startup script calls a *xconsole* client, which has been added to the standard distribution in Release 5. *xconsole* can only be run by someone who actually logs in at the console display. Thus, although this startup script can be used for both workstations and X terminals, X terminals will not be able to receive the *xconsole* window unless that user is also logged in at the console.

---

* This startup script was developed for and run on a Sun workstation. Differences in pixel sizes and resource definitions may make the coordinates and sizes of various windows come out differently on other hardware.

Server Access Control

X is designed so that clients can connect to the server from any other host on the network. This poses some security problems, since it means that other users on other hosts might be able to access your server. As a solution, X provides mechanisms for restricting access to your server. These are:

- Host-based access control. Under host-based access control, the X server only accepts connections from a specified list of hosts. The list of hosts is specified in the file */etc/X0.hosts* and can also be supplemented using the *xhost* client.

- MIT-MAGIC-COOKIE-1. This scheme involves a special code called a "magic cookie" which is known by the X server and is also made available to the user's account. Clients need to be able to present the magic cookie before they can access the server.

- XDM-AUTHORIZATION-1. This is similar to MIT-MAGIC-COOKIE-1, but the code is encrypted so that it can't be snooped as it is passed over the network.

- SUN-DES-1. This method uses Secure RPC.

The common methods for restricting access to your server are host-based access control and the MIT-MAGIC-COOKIE-1 scheme, which is also called user-based access control. The XDM-AUTHORIZATION-1 and SUN-DES-1 are also user-based methods, but they are only available with X11R5. Furthermore, since they are built upon DES (Data Encryption Standard), they are not exportable outside of the U.S. For complete information on any of these schemes, see Volume Eight, *X Window System Administrator's Guide*.

Host-based Access and the xhost Client

The */etc/X0.hosts* file contains a list of systems that are allowed to access the server. The "0" stands for the number of your server—if you ran a second server on your machine (that is, a server with the display name `hostname:1.0`), you would use */etc/X1.hosts*. In most cases, you only have one server running on your machine, so */etc/X0.hosts* is the only file you need to worry about.

By default, */etc/X0.hosts* does not exist, and only clients run on the local host can connect to the server. You should create and edit this file so that it contains the list of systems you want to have access to your server on a regular basis.

The *xhost* client can be used to give (or deny) systems access to the server interactively, possibly overriding the contents of */etc/X0.hosts*. Specifying a host name with an optional leading plus sign (+) allows the host to access the server, and specifying a host name with a leading minus sign (–) prevents a previously allowed host from accessing the server. Multiple hosts can be specified on the same line. Running *xhost* without any arguments prints the current hosts allowed to access your display.

For example, to add the hosts jupiter and saturn, and remove neptune:

```
% xhost +jupiter saturn -neptune
```

To be truly secure, you might use the fully qualified domain names. That way another machine called jupiter in another domain won't be able to access your server as well. Use fully qualified domain names in the */etc/X0.hosts* and *.rhosts* files as well.

```
% xhost +jupiter.ora.com saturn.ora.com -neptune.camb.com
```

Note that when a remote system is denied access to your server, no one on that system can display clients to your server, including yourself. Of course, the reverse is also true: when you allow yourself to run a client from a given host, you also allow everyone else on that host.

This is the main problem with host-based access control. If you have the only account on your workstation then there isn't a problem, but if you have NIS (aka Yellow Pages) running, then it's likely that all other users at your site have accounts on your machine. Which means that despite how carefully you use host-based access control, it doesn't provide any protection against that devious prankster across the hall.

User-based Access: xdm and the .Xauthority File

As of Release 4, the display manager and its control protocol (XDMCP) provide a user-based access control mechanism, which can be used to supplement or replace the host-based access mechanism discussed in the previous section. Release 4 and Release 5 *xdm* can be set up to provide user authorization on a particular display. By default, authorization is enabled for the local console display (:0) and is disabled for other displays managed by *xdm*, such as X terminals. To enable user-based access control for X terminals, set the following resource in the */usr/lib/X11/xdm/xdm-config* file:

```
DisplayManager*authorize: true
```

In the default *xdm-config*, this resource is set to false.

If authorization is enabled, then when you log in, *xdm* places a machine-readable access code, known as a magic cookie, in a file called *.Xauthority* in your home directory. *xdm* also makes this magic cookie available to the server.

The magic cookie defined in a user's *.Xauthority* file is basically a secret code shared by the server and a particular user logged in on a particular display. When a client requests access to the server, the server checks to see whether the client program has access to the magic cookie. All processes started by the user in question have that access, and thus the server allows access to that user's clients. Basically, under the magic cookie authorization scheme, a display becomes user-controlled.

The security mechanism provided by the magic cookie is evident in a situation in which another user tries to run a client on your machine. The server requires the client run by the other user to have access to the magic cookie shared exclusively between you and the server. The other user cannot provide the proper authorization code and thus cannot run a client on your host.

Of course, in many cases, users in a network will want to run clients on several machines (while displaying the client window on their local displays). This can be done if a user supplies authorization information associated with his local server to the remote host. The *xauth* client allows users to transfer this information to the remote machine. Basically, *xauth* is a utility to manipulate *.Xauthority* files.

The most common use for *xauth* is to extract a user's authorization information for the current display, copy it to another machine, and merge it into the server's authorization records on the remote machine like this:

```
% xauth extract - $DISPLAY | rsh host2 xauth merge -
```

The dash (-) arguments indicate that extracted authorization records should be written to the standard output and that the *xauth* merge function should accept records from standard input. This command supplies the remote server with authorization information, allowing the user to run a remote shell on that host. See the *xauth* reference page in Part Three of this guide for more information. Note that this command line depends on the *.rhosts* file on the remote machine being set up to allow remote commands from the local machine.

If an installation is using remote file sharing, such as NFS, then sharing authorization records may not be an issue. If every user has a single home directory that is accessible to all machines, the machines have access to the necessary *.Xauthority* files at all times. In such an environment, users should be able to run programs on any of the networked machines without using *xauth*.

Host-based access control overrides user-based access control. That is, if you have added a host to your access control list, then all users on that host can access your server regardless of whether you use the magic cookie as well.

Console Messages

On a single-user workstation, it is likely that the screen used for running X is also used as the system console. Console messages from the kernel may appear on the screen, overlaying the X windows. They make a nasty mess of the screen. You can refresh the display and erase the console message by running the *xrefresh* client (described in Chapter 8, *Other Clients*).

However, Release 5 offers a better solution. The *xconsole* client is intended to avoid the problem of messages obscuring the screen altogether by providing a small window in which the */dev/console* messages are displayed. The *xconsole* process should be run early in the startup script so that any messages generated during startup are "captured." A console window is shown in Figure A-1. For more information, see the *xconsole* reference page in Part Three of this guide.

Note that some implementations of X support a -C option to *xterm* that redirects messages sent to */dev/console* to that *xterm* window. If this option is supported, you *can* add the -C option to the console *xterm* in your startup file. After this window is mapped (displayed on the screen), all such messages are displayed there. However, it is generally preferable to use *xconsole*.

B

Release 5 Standard Fonts

This appendix shows the standard display fonts available in Release 5 of the MIT X distribution. The images contained in this appendix are window dumps created with our own program, called xshowfonts, *the code for which is included.*

B
Release 5 Standard Fonts

This appendix includes pictures of some representative fonts from the standard X distribution in Release 5. Not every font may be supported by particular server vendors, and some vendors may supplement the set.

The standard fonts are stored in four directories. The first three directories contain bitmap fonts; the *Speedo* directory contains outline fonts. See Chapter 6, *Font Specification*, for more information.

Directory	Contents
/usr/lib/X11/fonts/misc	Six fixed-width fonts, the cursor font, other miscellaneous fonts.
/usr/lib/X11/fonts/75dpi	Fixed- and variable-width fonts, 75 dots per inch.
/usr/lib/X11/fonts/100dpi	Fixed- and variable-width fonts, 100 dpi.
/usr/lib/X11/fonts/Speedo	Charter and Courier outline fonts from Bitstream.

Tables B-1 through B-4 list the fonts in each of the four Release 5 font directories. The first column lists the name of the file in which the font is stored (without the *.pcf* extension); the second column lists the actual font name. See Chapter 6, *Font Specification*, for information about font naming conventions.

PICTURES of the different font families supplied in the MIT X11 distribution appear on subsequent pages. We show just the fonts in the *75dpi* directory. The *100dpi* directory contains the same fonts stored in the *75dpi* directory but for 100 dots per inch monitors. Keep in mind that all of the fonts in the *75dpi* and *100dpi* directories are available in 8-, 10-, 12-, 14-, 18-, and 24-point sizes. Each page shows fonts of various sizes, weights, and styles. We include the source for *xshowfonts.c*, the program we wrote to make these displays, at the end of the appendix.* We also show you, using *xfd*, one example of each of the unique character sets available.

All of the characters in each font in the *75dpi* directory are shown actual size, as they would appear on a 900 × 1180 pixel, 10" × 13.5" screen (Sun). On a screen with different pixel density, these fonts would appear in a different size.

---

*If you don't want to type this program in, you can obtain the source from uunet.uu.net via anonymous *ftp* or *uucp*. See Appendix H, *Obtaining Example Programs*, for more information.

Fonts that begin with many blank characters are shown with most leading blanks removed. Therefore, you can't always get the character number of each cell in the font by counting from the first cell we have shown. Use *xfd* to quickly determine the code for a particular cell.

Table B-1. Fonts in the misc Directory

Filename	Font name
6x12.pcf	-misc-fixed-medium-r-semicondensed--12-110-75-75-c-60-iso8859-1
6x13.pcf	-misc-fixed-medium-r-semicondensed--13-120-75-75-c-60-iso8859-1
6x10.pcf	-misc-fixed-medium-r-normal--10-100-75-75-c-60-iso8859-1
7x13.pcf	-misc-fixed-medium-r-normal--13-120-75-75-c-70-iso8859-1
7x14.pcf	-misc-fixed-medium-r-normal--14-130-75-75-c-70-iso8859-1
clR8x12.pcf	-schumacher-clean-medium-r-normal--12-120-75-75-c-80-iso8859-1
clR8x13.pcf	-schumacher-clean-medium-r-normal--13-130-75-75-c-80-iso8859-1
6x9.pcf	-misc-fixed-medium-r-normal--9-90-75-75-c-60-iso8859-1
clR8x10.pcf	-schumacher-clean-medium-r-normal--10-100-75-75-c-80-iso8859-1
5x7.pcf	-misc-fixed-medium-r-normal--7-70-75-75-c-50-iso8859-1
clR8x16.pcf	-schumacher-clean-medium-r-normal--16-160-75-75-c-80-iso8859-1
clR8x14.pcf	-schumacher-clean-medium-r-normal--14-140-75-75-c-80-iso8859-1
clR8x8.pcf	-schumacher-clean-medium-r-normal--8-80-75-75-c-80-iso8859-1
5x8.pcf	-misc-fixed-medium-r-normal--8-80-75-75-c-50-iso8859-1
clR9x15.pcf	-schumacher-clean-medium-r-normal--15-150-75-75-c-90-iso8859-1
clR6x8.pcf	-schumacher-clean-medium-r-normal--8-80-75-75-c-60-iso8859-1
clR5x6.pcf	-schumacher-clean-medium-r-normal--6-60-75-75-c-50-iso8859-1
clR7x8.pcf	-schumacher-clean-medium-r-normal--8-80-75-75-c-70-iso8859-1
clR4x6.pcf	-schumacher-clean-medium-r-normal--6-60-75-75-c-40-iso8859-1
clR5x8.pcf	-schumacher-clean-medium-r-normal--8-80-75-75-c-50-iso8859-1
clR6x6.pcf	-schumacher-clean-medium-r-normal--6-60-75-75-c-60-iso8859-1
6x13B.pcf	-misc-fixed-bold-r-semicondensed--13-120-75-75-c-60-iso8859-1
12x24rk.pcf	-sony-fixed-medium-r-normal--24-170-100-100-c-120-jisx0201.1976-0
7x13B.pcf	-misc-fixed-bold-r-normal--13-120-75-75-c-70-iso8859-1
7x14B.pcf	-misc-fixed-bold-r-normal--14-130-75-75-c-70-iso8859-1
clR6x12.pcf	-schumacher-clean-medium-r-normal--12-120-75-75-c-60-iso8859-1
clR6x13.pcf	-schumacher-clean-medium-r-normal--13-130-75-75-c-60-iso8859-1
clR6x10.pcf	-schumacher-clean-medium-r-normal--10-100-75-75-c-60-iso8859-1
clR7x12.pcf	-schumacher-clean-medium-r-normal--12-120-75-75-c-70-iso8859-1
clR7x10.pcf	-schumacher-clean-medium-r-normal--10-100-75-75-c-70-iso8859-1
clR7x14.pcf	-schumacher-clean-medium-r-normal--14-140-75-75-c-70-iso8859-1
8x13.pcf	-misc-fixed-medium-r-normal--13-120-75-75-c-80-iso8859-1
8x16.pcf	-sony-fixed-medium-r-normal--16-120-100-100-c-80-iso8859-1
clR5x10.pcf	-schumacher-clean-medium-r-normal--10-100-75-75-c-50-iso8859-1
9x15.pcf	-misc-fixed-medium-r-normal--15-140-75-75-c-90-iso8859-1
heb6x13.pcf	-misc-fixed-medium-r-semicondensed--13-120-75-75-c-60-iso8859-8
clB8x8.pcf	-schumacher-clean-bold-r-normal--8-80-75-75-c-80-iso8859-1
8x13B.pcf	-misc-fixed-bold-r-normal--13-120-75-75-c-80-iso8859-1

Filename	Font name
7x14rk.pcf	-misc-fixed-medium-r-normal--14-130-75-75-c-70-jisx0201.1976-0
9x15B.pcf	-misc-fixed-bold-r-normal--15-140-75-75-c-90-iso8859-1
clI8x8.pcf	-schumacher-clean-medium-i-normal--8-80-75-75-c-80-iso8859-1
heb8x13.pcf	-misc-fixed-medium-r-normal--13-120-75-75-c-80-iso8859-8
decsess.pcf	decw$session
clB8x12.pcf	-schumacher-clean-bold-r-normal--12-120-75-75-c-80-iso8859-1
clB8x13.pcf	-schumacher-clean-bold-r-normal--13-130-75-75-c-80-iso8859-1
clB8x10.pcf	-schumacher-clean-bold-r-normal--10-100-75-75-c-80-iso8859-1
clB8x16.pcf	-schumacher-clean-bold-r-normal--16-160-75-75-c-80-iso8859-1
clB8x14.pcf	-schumacher-clean-bold-r-normal--14-140-75-75-c-80-iso8859-1
clB9x15.pcf	-schumacher-clean-bold-r-normal--15-150-75-75-c-90-iso8859-1
olcursor.pcf	-sun-open
hanglg16.pcf	-daewoo-gothic-medium-r-normal--16-120-100-100-c-160-ksc5601.1987-0
8x16rk.pcf	-sony-fixed-medium-r-normal--16-120-100-100-c-80-jisx0201.1976-0
clB6x12.pcf	-schumacher-clean-bold-r-normal--12-120-75-75-c-60-iso8859-1
clB6x10.pcf	-schumacher-clean-bold-r-normal--10-100-75-75-c-60-iso8859-1
jiskan24.pcf	-jis-fixed-medium-r-normal--24-230-75-75-c-240-jisx0208.1983-0
hanglm16.pcf	-daewoo-mincho-medium-r-normal--16-120-100-100-c-160-ksc5601.1987-0
hanglm24.pcf	-daewoo-mincho-medium-r-normal--24-170-100-100-c-240-ksc5601.1987-0
jiskan16.pcf	-jis-fixed-medium-r-normal--16-150-75-75-c-160-jisx0208.1983-0
cursor.pcf	cursor
deccurs.pcf	decw$cursor
clI6x12.pcf	-schumacher-clean-medium-i-normal--12-120-75-75-c-60-iso8859-1
olgl19.pcf	-sun-open
olgl12.pcf	-sun-open
olgl10.pcf	-sun-open
k14.pcf	-misc-fixed-medium-r-normal--14-130-75-75-c-140-jisx0208.1983-0
olgl14.pcf	-sun-open
nil2.pcf	-misc-nil-medium-r-normal--2-20-75-75-c-10-misc-fontspecific
10x20.pcf	-misc-fixed-medium-r-normal--20-200-75-75-c-100-iso8859-1
12x24.pcf	-sony-fixed-medium-r-normal--24-170-100-100-c-120-iso8859-1

Table B-3. Fonts in the 75dpi Directory

Filename	Font name
courBO10.pcf	-adobe-courier-bold-o-normal--10-100-75-75-m-60-iso8859-1
courBO12.pcf	-adobe-courier-bold-o-normal--12-120-75-75-m-70-iso8859-1
courBO14.pcf	-adobe-courier-bold-o-normal--14-140-75-75-m-90-iso8859-1
courBO18.pcf	-adobe-courier-bold-o-normal--18-180-75-75-m-110-iso8859-1
courBO24.pcf	-adobe-courier-bold-o-normal--24-240-75-75-m-150-iso8859-1

Filename	Font name
courBO08.pcf	-adobe-courier-bold-o-normal--8-80-75-75-m-50-iso8859-1
courB10.pcf	-adobe-courier-bold-r-normal--10-100-75-75-m-60-iso8859-1
courB12.pcf	-adobe-courier-bold-r-normal--12-120-75-75-m-70-iso8859-1
courB14.pcf	-adobe-courier-bold-r-normal--14-140-75-75-m-90-iso8859-1
courB18.pcf	-adobe-courier-bold-r-normal--18-180-75-75-m-110-iso8859-1
courB24.pcf	-adobe-courier-bold-r-normal--24-240-75-75-m-150-iso8859-1
courB08.pcf	-adobe-courier-bold-r-normal--8-80-75-75-m-50-iso8859-1
courO10.pcf	-adobe-courier-medium-o-normal--10-100-75-75-m-60-iso8859-1
courO12.pcf	-adobe-courier-medium-o-normal--12-120-75-75-m-70-iso8859-1
courO14.pcf	-adobe-courier-medium-o-normal--14-140-75-75-m-90-iso8859-1
courO18.pcf	-adobe-courier-medium-o-normal--18-180-75-75-m-110-iso8859-1
courO24.pcf	-adobe-courier-medium-o-normal--24-240-75-75-m-150-iso8859-1
courO08.pcf	-adobe-courier-medium-o-normal--8-80-75-75-m-50-iso8859-1
courR10.pcf	-adobe-courier-medium-r-normal--10-100-75-75-m-60-iso8859-1
courR12.pcf	-adobe-courier-medium-r-normal--12-120-75-75-m-70-iso8859-1
courR14.pcf	-adobe-courier-medium-r-normal--14-140-75-75-m-90-iso8859-1
courR18.pcf	-adobe-courier-medium-r-normal--18-180-75-75-m-110-iso8859-1
courR24.pcf	-adobe-courier-medium-r-normal--24-240-75-75-m-150-iso8859-1
courR08.pcf	-adobe-courier-medium-r-normal--8-80-75-75-m-50-iso8859-1
helvBO10.pcf	-adobe-helvetica-bold-o-normal--10-100-75-75-p-60-iso8859-1
helvBO12.pcf	-adobe-helvetica-bold-o-normal--12-120-75-75-p-69-iso8859-1
helvBO14.pcf	-adobe-helvetica-bold-o-normal--14-140-75-75-p-82-iso8859-1
helvBO18.pcf	-adobe-helvetica-bold-o-normal--18-180-75-75-p-104-iso8859-1
helvBO24.pcf	-adobe-helvetica-bold-o-normal--24-240-75-75-p-138-iso8859-1
helvBO08.pcf	-adobe-helvetica-bold-o-normal--8-80-75-75-p-50-iso8859-1
helvB10.pcf	-adobe-helvetica-bold-r-normal--10-100-75-75-p-60-iso8859-1
helvB12.pcf	-adobe-helvetica-bold-r-normal--12-120-75-75-p-70-iso8859-1
helvB14.pcf	-adobe-helvetica-bold-r-normal--14-140-75-75-p-82-iso8859-1
helvB18.pcf	-adobe-helvetica-bold-r-normal--18-180-75-75-p-103-iso8859-1
helvB24.pcf	-adobe-helvetica-bold-r-normal--24-240-75-75-p-138-iso8859-1
helvB08.pcf	-adobe-helvetica-bold-r-normal--8-80-75-75-p-50-iso8859-1
helvO10.pcf	-adobe-helvetica-medium-o-normal--10-100-75-75-p-57-iso8859-1
helvO12.pcf	-adobe-helvetica-medium-o-normal--12-120-75-75-p-67-iso8859-1
helvO14.pcf	-adobe-helvetica-medium-o-normal--14-140-75-75-p-78-iso8859-1
helvO18.pcf	-adobe-helvetica-medium-o-normal--18-180-75-75-p-98-iso8859-1
helvO24.pcf	-adobe-helvetica-medium-o-normal--24-240-75-75-p-130-iso8859-1
helvO08.pcf	-adobe-helvetica-medium-o-normal--8-80-75-75-p-47-iso8859-1
helvR10.pcf	-adobe-helvetica-medium-r-normal--10-100-75-75-p-56-iso8859-1
helvR12.pcf	-adobe-helvetica-medium-r-normal--12-120-75-75-p-67-iso8859-1
helvR14.pcf	-adobe-helvetica-medium-r-normal--14-140-75-75-p-77-iso8859-1
helvR18.pcf	-adobe-helvetica-medium-r-normal--18-180-75-75-p-98-iso8859-1
helvR24.pcf	-adobe-helvetica-medium-r-normal--24-240-75-75-p-130-iso8859-1
helvR08.pcf	-adobe-helvetica-medium-r-normal--8-80-75-75-p-46-iso8859-1

Filename	Font name
ncenBI10.pcf	-adobe-new century schoolbook-bold-i-normal--10-100-75-75-p-66-iso8859-1
ncenBI12.pcf	-adobe-new century schoolbook-bold-i-normal--12-120-75-75-p-76-iso8859-1
ncenBI14.pcf	-adobe-new century schoolbook-bold-i-normal--14-140-75-75-p-88-iso8859-1
ncenBI18.pcf	-adobe-new century schoolbook-bold-i-normal--18-180-75-75-p-111-iso8859-1
ncenBI24.pcf	-adobe-new century schoolbook-bold-i-normal--24-240-75-75-p-148-iso8859-1
ncenBI08.pcf	-adobe-new century schoolbook-bold-i-normal--8-80-75-75-p-56-iso8859-1
ncenB10.pcf	-adobe-new century schoolbook-bold-r-normal--10-100-75-75-p-66-iso8859-1
ncenB12.pcf	-adobe-new century schoolbook-bold-r-normal--12-120-75-75-p-77-iso8859-1
ncenB14.pcf	-adobe-new century schoolbook-bold-r-normal--14-140-75-75-p-87-iso8859-1
ncenB18.pcf	-adobe-new century schoolbook-bold-r-normal--18-180-75-75-p-113-iso8859-1
ncenB24.pcf	-adobe-new century schoolbook-bold-r-normal--24-240-75-75-p-149-iso8859-1
ncenB08.pcf	-adobe-new century schoolbook-bold-r-normal--8-80-75-75-p-56-iso8859-1
ncenI10.pcf	-adobe-new century schoolbook-medium-i-normal--10-100-75-75-p-60-iso8859-1
ncenI12.pcf	-adobe-new century schoolbook-medium-i-normal--12-120-75-75-p-70-iso8859-1
ncenI14.pcf	-adobe-new century schoolbook-medium-i-normal--14-140-75-75-p-81-iso8859-1
ncenI18.pcf	-adobe-new century schoolbook-medium-i-normal--18-180-75-75-p-104-iso8859-1
ncenI24.pcf	-adobe-new century schoolbook-medium-i-normal--24-240-75-75-p-136-iso8859-1
ncenI08.pcf	-adobe-new century schoolbook-medium-i-normal--8-80-75-75-p-50-iso8859-1
ncenR10.pcf	-adobe-new century schoolbook-medium-r-normal--10-100-75-75-p-60-iso8859-1
ncenR12.pcf	-adobe-new century schoolbook-medium-r-normal--12-120-75-75-p-70-iso8859-1
ncenR14.pcf	-adobe-new century schoolbook-medium-r-normal--14-140-75-75-p-82-iso8859-1
ncenR18.pcf	-adobe-new century schoolbook-medium-r-normal--18-180-75-75-p-103-iso8859-1
ncenR24.pcf	-adobe-new century schoolbook-medium-r-normal--24-240-75-75-p-137-iso8859-1
ncenR08.pcf	-adobe-new century schoolbook-medium-r-normal--8-80-75-75-p-50-iso8859-1
symb10.pcf	-adobe-symbol-medium-r-normal--10-100-75-75-p-61-adobe-fontspecific
symb12.pcf	-adobe-symbol-medium-r-normal--12-120-75-75-p-74-adobe-fontspecific
symb14.pcf	-adobe-symbol-medium-r-normal--14-140-75-75-p-85-adobe-fontspecific
symb18.pcf	-adobe-symbol-medium-r-normal--18-180-75-75-p-107-adobe-fontspecific
symb24.pcf	-adobe-symbol-medium-r-normal--24-240-75-75-p-142-adobe-fontspecific
symb08.pcf	-adobe-symbol-medium-r-normal--8-80-75-75-p-51-adobe-fontspecific
timBI10.pcf	-adobe-times-bold-i-normal--10-100-75-75-p-57-iso8859-1
timBI12.pcf	-adobe-times-bold-i-normal--12-120-75-75-p-68-iso8859-1
timBI14.pcf	-adobe-times-bold-i-normal--14-140-75-75-p-77-iso8859-1
timBI18.pcf	-adobe-times-bold-i-normal--18-180-75-75-p-98-iso8859-1
timBI24.pcf	-adobe-times-bold-i-normal--24-240-75-75-p-128-iso8859-1
timBI08.pcf	-adobe-times-bold-i-normal--8-80-75-75-p-47-iso8859-1
timB10.pcf	-adobe-times-bold-r-normal--10-100-75-75-p-57-iso8859-1
timB12.pcf	-adobe-times-bold-r-normal--12-120-75-75-p-67-iso8859-1
timB14.pcf	-adobe-times-bold-r-normal--14-140-75-75-p-77-iso8859-1
timB18.pcf	-adobe-times-bold-r-normal--18-180-75-75-p-99-iso8859-1
timB24.pcf	-adobe-times-bold-r-normal--24-240-75-75-p-132-iso8859-1
timB08.pcf	-adobe-times-bold-r-normal--8-80-75-75-p-47-iso8859-1
timI10.pcf	-adobe-times-medium-i-normal--10-100-75-75-p-52-iso8859-1

Filename	Font name
timI12.pcf	-adobe-times-medium-i-normal--12-120-75-75-p-63-iso8859-1
timI14.pcf	-adobe-times-medium-i-normal--14-140-75-75-p-73-iso8859-1
timI18.pcf	-adobe-times-medium-i-normal--18-180-75-75-p-94-iso8859-1
timI24.pcf	-adobe-times-medium-i-normal--24-240-75-75-p-125-iso8859-1
timI08.pcf	-adobe-times-medium-i-normal--8-80-75-75-p-42-iso8859-1
timR10.pcf	-adobe-times-medium-r-normal--10-100-75-75-p-54-iso8859-1
timR12.pcf	-adobe-times-medium-r-normal--12-120-75-75-p-64-iso8859-1
timR14.pcf	-adobe-times-medium-r-normal--14-140-75-75-p-74-iso8859-1
timR18.pcf	-adobe-times-medium-r-normal--18-180-75-75-p-94-iso8859-1
timR24.pcf	-adobe-times-medium-r-normal--24-240-75-75-p-124-iso8859-1
timR08.pcf	-adobe-times-medium-r-normal--8-80-75-75-p-44-iso8859-1
luBIS10.pcf	-b&h-lucida-bold-i-normal-sans-10-100-75-75-p-67-iso8859-1
luBIS12.pcf	-b&h-lucida-bold-i-normal-sans-12-120-75-75-p-79-iso8859-1
luBIS14.pcf	-b&h-lucida-bold-i-normal-sans-14-140-75-75-p-92-iso8859-1
luBIS18.pcf	-b&h-lucida-bold-i-normal-sans-18-180-75-75-p-119-iso8859-1
luBIS19.pcf	-b&h-lucida-bold-i-normal-sans-19-190-75-75-p-122-iso8859-1
luBIS24.pcf	-b&h-lucida-bold-i-normal-sans-24-240-75-75-p-151-iso8859-1
luBIS08.pcf	-b&h-lucida-bold-i-normal-sans-8-80-75-75-p-49-iso8859-1
luBS10.pcf	-b&h-lucida-bold-r-normal-sans-10-100-75-75-p-66-iso8859-1
luBS12.pcf	-b&h-lucida-bold-r-normal-sans-12-120-75-75-p-79-iso8859-1
luBS14.pcf	-b&h-lucida-bold-r-normal-sans-14-140-75-75-p-92-iso8859-1
luBS18.pcf	-b&h-lucida-bold-r-normal-sans-18-180-75-75-p-120-iso8859-1
luBS19.pcf	-b&h-lucida-bold-r-normal-sans-19-190-75-75-p-122-iso8859-1
luBS24.pcf	-b&h-lucida-bold-r-normal-sans-24-240-75-75-p-152-iso8859-1
luBS08.pcf	-b&h-lucida-bold-r-normal-sans-8-80-75-75-p-50-iso8859-1
luIS10.pcf	-b&h-lucida-medium-i-normal-sans-10-100-75-75-p-59-iso8859-1
luIS12.pcf	-b&h-lucida-medium-i-normal-sans-12-120-75-75-p-71-iso8859-1
luIS14.pcf	-b&h-lucida-medium-i-normal-sans-14-140-75-75-p-82-iso8859-1
luIS18.pcf	-b&h-lucida-medium-i-normal-sans-18-180-75-75-p-105-iso8859-1
luIS19.pcf	-b&h-lucida-medium-i-normal-sans-19-190-75-75-p-108-iso8859-1
luIS24.pcf	-b&h-lucida-medium-i-normal-sans-24-240-75-75-p-136-iso8859-1
luIS08.pcf	-b&h-lucida-medium-i-normal-sans-8-80-75-75-p-45-iso8859-1
luRS10.pcf	-b&h-lucida-medium-r-normal-sans-10-100-75-75-p-58-iso8859-1
luRS12.pcf	-b&h-lucida-medium-r-normal-sans-12-120-75-75-p-71-iso8859-1
luRS14.pcf	-b&h-lucida-medium-r-normal-sans-14-140-75-75-p-81-iso8859-1
luRS18.pcf	-b&h-lucida-medium-r-normal-sans-18-180-75-75-p-106-iso8859-1
luRS19.pcf	-b&h-lucida-medium-r-normal-sans-19-190-75-75-p-108-iso8859-1
luRS24.pcf	-b&h-lucida-medium-r-normal-sans-24-240-75-75-p-136-iso8859-1
luRS08.pcf	-b&h-lucida-medium-r-normal-sans-8-80-75-75-p-45-iso8859-1
lubBI10.pcf	-b&h-lucidabright-demibold-i-normal--10-100-75-75-p-59-iso8859-1
lubBI12.pcf	-b&h-lucidabright-demibold-i-normal--12-120-75-75-p-72-iso8859-1
lubBI14.pcf	-b&h-lucidabright-demibold-i-normal--14-140-75-75-p-84-iso8859-1
lubBI18.pcf	-b&h-lucidabright-demibold-i-normal--18-180-75-75-p-107-iso8859-1

Filename	Font name
lubBI19.pcf	-b&h-lucidabright-demibold-i-normal--19-190-75-75-p-114-iso8859-1
lubBI24.pcf	-b&h-lucidabright-demibold-i-normal--24-240-75-75-p-143-iso8859-1
lubBI08.pcf	-b&h-lucidabright-demibold-i-normal--8-80-75-75-p-48-iso8859-1
lubB10.pcf	-b&h-lucidabright-demibold-r-normal--10-100-75-75-p-59-iso8859-1
lubB12.pcf	-b&h-lucidabright-demibold-r-normal--12-120-75-75-p-71-iso8859-1
lubB14.pcf	-b&h-lucidabright-demibold-r-normal--14-140-75-75-p-84-iso8859-1
lubB18.pcf	-b&h-lucidabright-demibold-r-normal--18-180-75-75-p-107-iso8859-1
lubB19.pcf	-b&h-lucidabright-demibold-r-normal--19-190-75-75-p-114-iso8859-1
lubB24.pcf	-b&h-lucidabright-demibold-r-normal--24-240-75-75-p-143-iso8859-1
lubB08.pcf	-b&h-lucidabright-demibold-r-normal--8-80-75-75-p-47-iso8859-1
lubI10.pcf	-b&h-lucidabright-medium-i-normal--10-100-75-75-p-57-iso8859-1
lubI12.pcf	-b&h-lucidabright-medium-i-normal--12-120-75-75-p-67-iso8859-1
lubI14.pcf	-b&h-lucidabright-medium-i-normal--14-140-75-75-p-80-iso8859-1
lubI18.pcf	-b&h-lucidabright-medium-i-normal--18-180-75-75-p-102-iso8859-1
lubI19.pcf	-b&h-lucidabright-medium-i-normal--19-190-75-75-p-109-iso8859-1
lubI24.pcf	-b&h-lucidabright-medium-i-normal--24-240-75-75-p-136-iso8859-1
lubI08.pcf	-b&h-lucidabright-medium-i-normal--8-80-75-75-p-45-iso8859-1
lubR10.pcf	-b&h-lucidabright-medium-r-normal--10-100-75-75-p-56-iso8859-1
lubR12.pcf	-b&h-lucidabright-medium-r-normal--12-120-75-75-p-68-iso8859-1
lubR14.pcf	-b&h-lucidabright-medium-r-normal--14-140-75-75-p-80-iso8859-1
lubR18.pcf	-b&h-lucidabright-medium-r-normal--18-180-75-75-p-103-iso8859-1
lubR19.pcf	-b&h-lucidabright-medium-r-normal--19-190-75-75-p-109-iso8859-1
lubR24.pcf	-b&h-lucidabright-medium-r-normal--24-240-75-75-p-137-iso8859-1
lubR08.pcf	-b&h-lucidabright-medium-r-normal--8-80-75-75-p-45-iso8859-1
lutBS10.pcf	-b&h-lucidatypewriter-bold-r-normal-sans-10-100-75-75-m-60-iso8859-1
lutBS12.pcf	-b&h-lucidatypewriter-bold-r-normal-sans-12-120-75-75-m-70-iso8859-1
lutBS14.pcf	-b&h-lucidatypewriter-bold-r-normal-sans-14-140-75-75-m-90-iso8859-1
lutBS18.pcf	-b&h-lucidatypewriter-bold-r-normal-sans-18-180-75-75-m-110-iso8859-1
lutBS19.pcf	-b&h-lucidatypewriter-bold-r-normal-sans-19-190-75-75-m-110-iso8859-1
lutBS24.pcf	-b&h-lucidatypewriter-bold-r-normal-sans-24-240-75-75-m-140-iso8859-1
lutBS08.pcf	-b&h-lucidatypewriter-bold-r-normal-sans-8-80-75-75-m-50-iso8859-1
lutRS10.pcf	-b&h-lucidatypewriter-medium-r-normal-sans-10-100-75-75-m-60-iso8859-1
lutRS12.pcf	-b&h-lucidatypewriter-medium-r-normal-sans-12-120-75-75-m-70-iso8859-1
lutRS14.pcf	-b&h-lucidatypewriter-medium-r-normal-sans-14-140-75-75-m-90-iso8859-1
lutRS18.pcf	-b&h-lucidatypewriter-medium-r-normal-sans-18-180-75-75-m-110-iso8859-1
lutRS19.pcf	-b&h-lucidatypewriter-medium-r-normal-sans-19-190-75-75-m-110-iso8859-1
lutRS24.pcf	-b&h-lucidatypewriter-medium-r-normal-sans-24-240-75-75-m-140-iso8859-1
lutRS08.pcf	-b&h-lucidatypewriter-medium-r-normal-sans-8-80-75-75-m-50-iso8859-1
charBI10.pcf	-bitstream-charter-bold-i-normal--10-100-75-75-p-62-iso8859-1
charBI12.pcf	-bitstream-charter-bold-i-normal--12-120-75-75-p-74-iso8859-1
charBI14.pcf	-bitstream-charter-bold-i-normal--15-140-75-75-p-93-iso8859-1
charBI18.pcf	-bitstream-charter-bold-i-normal--19-180-75-75-p-117-iso8859-1
charBI24.pcf	-bitstream-charter-bold-i-normal--25-240-75-75-p-154-iso8859-1

Filename	Font name
charBI08.pcf	-bitstream-charter-bold-i-normal--8-80-75-75-p-50-iso8859-1
charB10.pcf	-bitstream-charter-bold-r-normal--10-100-75-75-p-63-iso8859-1
charB12.pcf	-bitstream-charter-bold-r-normal--12-120-75-75-p-75-iso8859-1
charB14.pcf	-bitstream-charter-bold-r-normal--15-140-75-75-p-94-iso8859-1
charB18.pcf	-bitstream-charter-bold-r-normal--19-180-75-75-p-119-iso8859-1
charB24.pcf	-bitstream-charter-bold-r-normal--25-240-75-75-p-157-iso8859-1
charB08.pcf	-bitstream-charter-bold-r-normal--8-80-75-75-p-50-iso8859-1
charI10.pcf	-bitstream-charter-medium-i-normal--10-100-75-75-p-55-iso8859-1
charI12.pcf	-bitstream-charter-medium-i-normal--12-120-75-75-p-65-iso8859-1
charI14.pcf	-bitstream-charter-medium-i-normal--15-140-75-75-p-82-iso8859-1
charI18.pcf	-bitstream-charter-medium-i-normal--19-180-75-75-p-103-iso8859-1
charI24.pcf	-bitstream-charter-medium-i-normal--25-240-75-75-p-136-iso8859-1
charI08.pcf	-bitstream-charter-medium-i-normal--8-80-75-75-p-44-iso8859-1
charR10.pcf	-bitstream-charter-medium-r-normal--10-100-75-75-p-56-iso8859-1
charR12.pcf	-bitstream-charter-medium-r-normal--12-120-75-75-p-67-iso8859-1
charR14.pcf	-bitstream-charter-medium-r-normal--15-140-75-75-p-84-iso8859-1
charR18.pcf	-bitstream-charter-medium-r-normal--19-180-75-75-p-106-iso8859-1
charR24.pcf	-bitstream-charter-medium-r-normal--25-240-75-75-p-139-iso8859-1
charR08.pcf	-bitstream-charter-medium-r-normal--8-80-75-75-p-45-iso8859-1
techB14.pcf	-dec-terminal-bold-r-normal--14-140-75-75-c-80-dec-dectech
termB14.pcf	-dec-terminal-bold-r-normal--14-140-75-75-c-80-iso8859-1
tech14.pcf	-dec-terminal-medium-r-normal--14-140-75-75-c-80-dec-dectech
term14.pcf	-dec-terminal-medium-r-normal--14-140-75-75-c-80-iso8859-1

Filename	Font name
courBO08.pcf	-adobe-courier-bold-o-normal--11-80-100-100-m-60-iso8859-1
courBO10.pcf	-adobe-courier-bold-o-normal--14-100-100-100-m-90-iso8859-1
courBO12.pcf	-adobe-courier-bold-o-normal--17-120-100-100-m-100-iso8859-1
courBO14.pcf	-adobe-courier-bold-o-normal--20-140-100-100-m-110-iso8859-1
courBO18.pcf	-adobe-courier-bold-o-normal--25-180-100-100-m-150-iso8859-1
courBO24.pcf	-adobe-courier-bold-o-normal--34-240-100-100-m-200-iso8859-1
courB08.pcf	-adobe-courier-bold-r-normal--11-80-100-100-m-60-iso8859-1
courB10.pcf	-adobe-courier-bold-r-normal--14-100-100-100-m-90-iso8859-1
courB12.pcf	-adobe-courier-bold-r-normal--17-120-100-100-m-100-iso8859-1
courB14.pcf	-adobe-courier-bold-r-normal--20-140-100-100-m-110-iso8859-1
courB18.pcf	-adobe-courier-bold-r-normal--25-180-100-100-m-150-iso8859-1
courB24.pcf	-adobe-courier-bold-r-normal--34-240-100-100-m-200-iso8859-1
courO08.pcf	-adobe-courier-medium-o-normal--11-80-100-100-m-60-iso8859-1
courO10.pcf	-adobe-courier-medium-o-normal--14-100-100-100-m-90-iso8859-1

Filename	Font name
courO12.pcf	-adobe-courier-medium-o-normal--17-120-100-100-m-100-iso8859-1
courO14.pcf	-adobe-courier-medium-o-normal--20-140-100-100-m-110-iso8859-1
courO18.pcf	-adobe-courier-medium-o-normal--25-180-100-100-m-150-iso8859-1
courO24.pcf	-adobe-courier-medium-o-normal--34-240-100-100-m-200-iso8859-1
courR08.pcf	-adobe-courier-medium-r-normal--11-80-100-100-m-60-iso8859-1
courR10.pcf	-adobe-courier-medium-r-normal--14-100-100-100-m-90-iso8859-1
courR12.pcf	-adobe-courier-medium-r-normal--17-120-100-100-m-100-iso8859-1
courR14.pcf	-adobe-courier-medium-r-normal--20-140-100-100-m-110-iso8859-1
courR18.pcf	-adobe-courier-medium-r-normal--25-180-100-100-m-150-iso8859-1
courR24.pcf	-adobe-courier-medium-r-normal--34-240-100-100-m-200-iso8859-1
helvBO08.pcf	-adobe-helvetica-bold-o-normal--11-80-100-100-p-60-iso8859-1
helvBO10.pcf	-adobe-helvetica-bold-o-normal--14-100-100-100-p-82-iso8859-1
helvBO12.pcf	-adobe-helvetica-bold-o-normal--17-120-100-100-p-92-iso8859-1
helvBO14.pcf	-adobe-helvetica-bold-o-normal--20-140-100-100-p-103-iso8859-1
helvBO18.pcf	-adobe-helvetica-bold-o-normal--25-180-100-100-p-138-iso8859-1
helvBO24.pcf	-adobe-helvetica-bold-o-normal--34-240-100-100-p-182-iso8859-1
helvB08.pcf	-adobe-helvetica-bold-r-normal--11-80-100-100-p-60-iso8859-1
helvB10.pcf	-adobe-helvetica-bold-r-normal--14-100-100-100-p-82-iso8859-1
helvB12.pcf	-adobe-helvetica-bold-r-normal--17-120-100-100-p-92-iso8859-1
helvB14.pcf	-adobe-helvetica-bold-r-normal--20-140-100-100-p-105-iso8859-1
helvB18.pcf	-adobe-helvetica-bold-r-normal--25-180-100-100-p-138-iso8859-1
helvB24.pcf	-adobe-helvetica-bold-r-normal--34-240-100-100-p-182-iso8859-1
helvO08.pcf	-adobe-helvetica-medium-o-normal--11-80-100-100-p-57-iso8859-1
helvO10.pcf	-adobe-helvetica-medium-o-normal--14-100-100-100-p-78-iso8859-1
helvO12.pcf	-adobe-helvetica-medium-o-normal--17-120-100-100-p-88-iso8859-1
helvO14.pcf	-adobe-helvetica-medium-o-normal--20-140-100-100-p-98-iso8859-1
helvO18.pcf	-adobe-helvetica-medium-o-normal--25-180-100-100-p-130-iso8859-1
helvO24.pcf	-adobe-helvetica-medium-o-normal--34-240-100-100-p-176-iso8859-1
helvR08.pcf	-adobe-helvetica-medium-r-normal--11-80-100-100-p-56-iso8859-1
helvR10.pcf	-adobe-helvetica-medium-r-normal--14-100-100-100-p-76-iso8859-1
helvR12.pcf	-adobe-helvetica-medium-r-normal--17-120-100-100-p-88-iso8859-1
helvR14.pcf	-adobe-helvetica-medium-r-normal--20-140-100-100-p-100-iso8859-1
helvR18.pcf	-adobe-helvetica-medium-r-normal--25-180-100-100-p-130-iso8859-1
helvR24.pcf	-adobe-helvetica-medium-r-normal--34-240-100-100-p-176-iso8859-1
ncenBI08.pcf	-adobe-new century schoolbook-bold-i-normal--11-80-100-100-p-66-iso8859-1
ncenBI10.pcf	-adobe-new century schoolbook-bold-i-normal--14-100-100-100-p-88-iso8859-1
ncenBI12.pcf	-adobe-new century schoolbook-bold-i-normal--17-120-100-100-p-99-iso8859-1
ncenBI14.pcf	-adobe-new century schoolbook-bold-i-normal--20-140-100-100-p-111-iso8859-1
ncenBI18.pcf	-adobe-new century schoolbook-bold-i-normal--25-180-100-100-p-148-iso8859-1
ncenBI24.pcf	-adobe-new century schoolbook-bold-i-normal--34-240-100-100-p-193-iso8859-1
ncenB08.pcf	-adobe-new century schoolbook-bold-r-normal--11-80-100-100-p-66-iso8859-1
ncenB10.pcf	-adobe-new century schoolbook-bold-r-normal--14-100-100-100-p-87-iso8859-1
ncenB12.pcf	-adobe-new century schoolbook-bold-r-normal--17-120-100-100-p-99-iso8859-1
ncenB14.pcf	-adobe-new century schoolbook-bold-r-normal--20-140-100-100-p-113-iso8859-1

Filename	Font name
ncenB18.pcf	-adobe-new century schoolbook-bold-r-normal--25-180-100-100-p-149-iso8859-1
ncenB24.pcf	-adobe-new century schoolbook-bold-r-normal--34-240-100-100-p-193-iso8859-1
ncenI08.pcf	-adobe-new century schoolbook-medium-i-normal--11-80-100-100-p-60-iso8859-1
ncenI10.pcf	-adobe-new century schoolbook-medium-i-normal--14-100-100-100-p-81-iso8859-1
ncenI12.pcf	-adobe-new century schoolbook-medium-i-normal--17-120-100-100-p-92-iso8859-1
ncenI14.pcf	-adobe-new century schoolbook-medium-i-normal--20-140-100-100-p-104-iso8859-1
ncenI18.pcf	-adobe-new century schoolbook-medium-i-normal--25-180-100-100-p-136-iso8859-1
ncenI24.pcf	-adobe-new century schoolbook-medium-i-normal--34-240-100-100-p-182-iso8859-1
ncenR08.pcf	-adobe-new century schoolbook-medium-r-normal--11-80-100-100-p-60-iso8859-1
ncenR10.pcf	-adobe-new century schoolbook-medium-r-normal--14-100-100-100-p-82-iso8859-1
ncenR12.pcf	-adobe-new century schoolbook-medium-r-normal--17-120-100-100-p-91-iso8859-1
ncenR14.pcf	-adobe-new century schoolbook-medium-r-normal--20-140-100-100-p-103-iso8859-1
ncenR18.pcf	-adobe-new century schoolbook-medium-r-normal--25-180-100-100-p-136-iso8859-1
ncenR24.pcf	-adobe-new century schoolbook-medium-r-normal--34-240-100-100-p-181-iso8859-1
symb08.pcf	-adobe-symbol-medium-r-normal--11-80-100-100-p-61-adobe-fontspecific
symb10.pcf	-adobe-symbol-medium-r-normal--14-100-100-100-p-85-adobe-fontspecific
symb12.pcf	-adobe-symbol-medium-r-normal--17-120-100-100-p-95-adobe-fontspecific
symb14.pcf	-adobe-symbol-medium-r-normal--20-140-100-100-p-107-adobe-fontspecific
symb18.pcf	-adobe-symbol-medium-r-normal--25-180-100-100-p-142-adobe-fontspecific
symb24.pcf	-adobe-symbol-medium-r-normal--34-240-100-100-p-191-adobe-fontspecific
timBI08.pcf	-adobe-times-bold-i-normal--11-80-100-100-p-57-iso8859-1
timBI10.pcf	-adobe-times-bold-i-normal--14-100-100-100-p-77-iso8859-1
timBI12.pcf	-adobe-times-bold-i-normal--17-120-100-100-p-86-iso8859-1
timBI14.pcf	-adobe-times-bold-i-normal--20-140-100-100-p-98-iso8859-1
timBI18.pcf	-adobe-times-bold-i-normal--25-180-100-100-p-128-iso8859-1
timBI24.pcf	-adobe-times-bold-i-normal--34-240-100-100-p-170-iso8859-1
timB08.pcf	-adobe-times-bold-r-normal--11-80-100-100-p-57-iso8859-1
timB10.pcf	-adobe-times-bold-r-normal--14-100-100-100-p-76-iso8859-1
timB12.pcf	-adobe-times-bold-r-normal--17-120-100-100-p-88-iso8859-1
timB14.pcf	-adobe-times-bold-r-normal--20-140-100-100-p-100-iso8859-1
timB18.pcf	-adobe-times-bold-r-normal--25-180-100-100-p-132-iso8859-1
timB24.pcf	-adobe-times-bold-r-normal--34-240-100-100-p-177-iso8859-1
timI08.pcf	-adobe-times-medium-i-normal--11-80-100-100-p-52-iso8859-1
timI10.pcf	-adobe-times-medium-i-normal--14-100-100-100-p-73-iso8859-1
timI12.pcf	-adobe-times-medium-i-normal--17-120-100-100-p-84-iso8859-1
timI14.pcf	-adobe-times-medium-i-normal--20-140-100-100-p-94-iso8859-1
timI18.pcf	-adobe-times-medium-i-normal--25-180-100-100-p-125-iso8859-1
timI24.pcf	-adobe-times-medium-i-normal--34-240-100-100-p-168-iso8859-1
timR08.pcf	-adobe-times-medium-r-normal--11-80-100-100-p-54-iso8859-1
timR10.pcf	-adobe-times-medium-r-normal--14-100-100-100-p-74-iso8859-1
timR12.pcf	-adobe-times-medium-r-normal--17-120-100-100-p-84-iso8859-1
timR14.pcf	-adobe-times-medium-r-normal--20-140-100-100-p-96-iso8859-1
timR18.pcf	-adobe-times-medium-r-normal--25-180-100-100-p-125-iso8859-1
timR24.pcf	-adobe-times-medium-r-normal--34-240-100-100-p-170-iso8859-1

Filename	Font name
luBIS08.pcf	-b&h-lucida-bold-i-normal-sans-11-80-100-100-p-69-iso8859-1
luBIS10.pcf	-b&h-lucida-bold-i-normal-sans-14-100-100-100-p-90-iso8859-1
luBIS12.pcf	-b&h-lucida-bold-i-normal-sans-17-120-100-100-p-108-iso8859-1
luBIS14.pcf	-b&h-lucida-bold-i-normal-sans-20-140-100-100-p-127-iso8859-1
luBIS18.pcf	-b&h-lucida-bold-i-normal-sans-25-180-100-100-p-159-iso8859-1
luBIS19.pcf	-b&h-lucida-bold-i-normal-sans-26-190-100-100-p-166-iso8859-1
luBIS24.pcf	-b&h-lucida-bold-i-normal-sans-34-240-100-100-p-215-iso8859-1
luBS08.pcf	-b&h-lucida-bold-r-normal-sans-11-80-100-100-p-70-iso8859-1
luBS10.pcf	-b&h-lucida-bold-r-normal-sans-14-100-100-100-p-89-iso8859-1
luBS12.pcf	-b&h-lucida-bold-r-normal-sans-17-120-100-100-p-108-iso8859-1
luBS14.pcf	-b&h-lucida-bold-r-normal-sans-20-140-100-100-p-127-iso8859-1
luBS18.pcf	-b&h-lucida-bold-r-normal-sans-25-180-100-100-p-158-iso8859-1
luBS19.pcf	-b&h-lucida-bold-r-normal-sans-26-190-100-100-p-166-iso8859-1
luBS24.pcf	-b&h-lucida-bold-r-normal-sans-34-240-100-100-p-216-iso8859-1
luIS08.pcf	-b&h-lucida-medium-i-normal-sans-11-80-100-100-p-62-iso8859-1
luIS10.pcf	-b&h-lucida-medium-i-normal-sans-14-100-100-100-p-80-iso8859-1
luIS12.pcf	-b&h-lucida-medium-i-normal-sans-17-120-100-100-p-97-iso8859-1
luIS14.pcf	-b&h-lucida-medium-i-normal-sans-20-140-100-100-p-114-iso8859-1
luIS18.pcf	-b&h-lucida-medium-i-normal-sans-25-180-100-100-p-141-iso8859-1
luIS19.pcf	-b&h-lucida-medium-i-normal-sans-26-190-100-100-p-147-iso8859-1
luIS24.pcf	-b&h-lucida-medium-i-normal-sans-34-240-100-100-p-192-iso8859-1
luRS08.pcf	-b&h-lucida-medium-r-normal-sans-11-80-100-100-p-63-iso8859-1
luRS10.pcf	-b&h-lucida-medium-r-normal-sans-14-100-100-100-p-80-iso8859-1
luRS12.pcf	-b&h-lucida-medium-r-normal-sans-17-120-100-100-p-96-iso8859-1
luRS14.pcf	-b&h-lucida-medium-r-normal-sans-20-140-100-100-p-114-iso8859-1
luRS18.pcf	-b&h-lucida-medium-r-normal-sans-25-180-100-100-p-142-iso8859-1
luRS19.pcf	-b&h-lucida-medium-r-normal-sans-26-190-100-100-p-147-iso8859-1
luRS24.pcf	-b&h-lucida-medium-r-normal-sans-34-240-100-100-p-191-iso8859-1
lubBI08.pcf	-b&h-lucidabright-demibold-i-normal--11-80-100-100-p-66-iso8859-1
lubBI10.pcf	-b&h-lucidabright-demibold-i-normal--14-100-100-100-p-84-iso8859-1
lubBI12.pcf	-b&h-lucidabright-demibold-i-normal--17-120-100-100-p-101-iso8859-1
lubBI14.pcf	-b&h-lucidabright-demibold-i-normal--20-140-100-100-p-119-iso8859-1
lubBI18.pcf	-b&h-lucidabright-demibold-i-normal--25-180-100-100-p-149-iso8859-1
lubBI19.pcf	-b&h-lucidabright-demibold-i-normal--26-190-100-100-p-156-iso8859-1
lubBI24.pcf	-b&h-lucidabright-demibold-i-normal--34-240-100-100-p-203-iso8859-1
lubB08.pcf	-b&h-lucidabright-demibold-r-normal--11-80-100-100-p-66-iso8859-1
lubB10.pcf	-b&h-lucidabright-demibold-r-normal--14-100-100-100-p-84-iso8859-1
lubB12.pcf	-b&h-lucidabright-demibold-r-normal--17-120-100-100-p-101-iso8859-1
lubB14.pcf	-b&h-lucidabright-demibold-r-normal--20-140-100-100-p-118-iso8859-1
lubB18.pcf	-b&h-lucidabright-demibold-r-normal--25-180-100-100-p-149-iso8859-1
lubB19.pcf	-b&h-lucidabright-demibold-r-normal--26-190-100-100-p-155-iso8859-1
lubB24.pcf	-b&h-lucidabright-demibold-r-normal--34-240-100-100-p-202-iso8859-1
lubI08.pcf	-b&h-lucidabright-medium-i-normal--11-80-100-100-p-63-iso8859-1
lubI10.pcf	-b&h-lucidabright-medium-i-normal--14-100-100-100-p-80-iso8859-1

Filename	Font name
lubI12.pcf	-b&h-lucidabright-medium-i-normal--17-120-100-100-p-96-iso8859-1
lubI14.pcf	-b&h-lucidabright-medium-i-normal--20-140-100-100-p-113-iso8859-1
lubI18.pcf	-b&h-lucidabright-medium-i-normal--25-180-100-100-p-142-iso8859-1
lubI19.pcf	-b&h-lucidabright-medium-i-normal--26-190-100-100-p-148-iso8859-1
lubI24.pcf	-b&h-lucidabright-medium-i-normal--34-240-100-100-p-194-iso8859-1
lubR08.pcf	-b&h-lucidabright-medium-r-normal--11-80-100-100-p-63-iso8859-1
lubR10.pcf	-b&h-lucidabright-medium-r-normal--14-100-100-100-p-80-iso8859-1
lubR12.pcf	-b&h-lucidabright-medium-r-normal--17-120-100-100-p-96-iso8859-1
lubR14.pcf	-b&h-lucidabright-medium-r-normal--20-140-100-100-p-114-iso8859-1
lubR18.pcf	-b&h-lucidabright-medium-r-normal--25-180-100-100-p-142-iso8859-1
lubR19.pcf	-b&h-lucidabright-medium-r-normal--26-190-100-100-p-149-iso8859-1
lubR24.pcf	-b&h-lucidabright-medium-r-normal--34-240-100-100-p-193-iso8859-1
lutBS08.pcf	-b&h-lucidatypewriter-bold-r-normal-sans-11-80-100-100-m-70-iso8859-1
lutBS10.pcf	-b&h-lucidatypewriter-bold-r-normal-sans-14-100-100-100-m-80-iso8859-1
lutBS12.pcf	-b&h-lucidatypewriter-bold-r-normal-sans-17-120-100-100-m-100-iso8859-1
lutBS14.pcf	-b&h-lucidatypewriter-bold-r-normal-sans-20-140-100-100-m-120-iso8859-1
lutBS18.pcf	-b&h-lucidatypewriter-bold-r-normal-sans-25-180-100-100-m-150-iso8859-1
lutBS19.pcf	-b&h-lucidatypewriter-bold-r-normal-sans-26-190-100-100-m-159-iso8859-1
lutBS24.pcf	-b&h-lucidatypewriter-bold-r-normal-sans-34-240-100-100-m-200-iso8859-1
lutRS08.pcf	-b&h-lucidatypewriter-medium-r-normal-sans-11-80-100-100-m-70-iso8859-1
lutRS10.pcf	-b&h-lucidatypewriter-medium-r-normal-sans-14-100-100-100-m-80-iso8859-1
lutRS12.pcf	-b&h-lucidatypewriter-medium-r-normal-sans-17-120-100-100-m-100-iso8859-1
lutRS14.pcf	-b&h-lucidatypewriter-medium-r-normal-sans-20-140-100-100-m-120-iso8859-1
lutRS18.pcf	-b&h-lucidatypewriter-medium-r-normal-sans-25-180-100-100-m-150-iso8859-1
lutRS19.pcf	-b&h-lucidatypewriter-medium-r-normal-sans-26-190-100-100-m-159-iso8859-1
lutRS24.pcf	-b&h-lucidatypewriter-medium-r-normal-sans-34-240-100-100-m-200-iso8859-1
charBI08.pcf	-bitstream-charter-bold-i-normal--11-80-100-100-p-68-iso8859-1
charBI10.pcf	-bitstream-charter-bold-i-normal--14-100-100-100-p-86-iso8859-1
charBI12.pcf	-bitstream-charter-bold-i-normal--17-120-100-100-p-105-iso8859-1
charBI14.pcf	-bitstream-charter-bold-i-normal--19-140-100-100-p-117-iso8859-1
charBI18.pcf	-bitstream-charter-bold-i-normal--25-180-100-100-p-154-iso8859-1
charBI24.pcf	-bitstream-charter-bold-i-normal--33-240-100-100-p-203-iso8859-1
charB08.pcf	-bitstream-charter-bold-r-normal--11-80-100-100-p-69-iso8859-1
charB10.pcf	-bitstream-charter-bold-r-normal--14-100-100-100-p-88-iso8859-1
charB12.pcf	-bitstream-charter-bold-r-normal--17-120-100-100-p-107-iso8859-1
charB14.pcf	-bitstream-charter-bold-r-normal--19-140-100-100-p-119-iso8859-1
charB18.pcf	-bitstream-charter-bold-r-normal--25-180-100-100-p-157-iso8859-1
charB24.pcf	-bitstream-charter-bold-r-normal--33-240-100-100-p-206-iso8859-1
charI08.pcf	-bitstream-charter-medium-i-normal--11-80-100-100-p-60-iso8859-1
charI10.pcf	-bitstream-charter-medium-i-normal--14-100-100-100-p-76-iso8859-1
charI12.pcf	-bitstream-charter-medium-i-normal--17-120-100-100-p-92-iso8859-1
charI14.pcf	-bitstream-charter-medium-i-normal--19-140-100-100-p-103-iso8859-1
charI18.pcf	-bitstream-charter-medium-i-normal--25-180-100-100-p-136-iso8859-1
charI24.pcf	-bitstream-charter-medium-i-normal--33-240-100-100-p-179-iso8859-1

Filename	Font name
charR08.pcf	-bitstream-charter-medium-r-normal--11-80-100-100-p-61-iso8859-1
charR10.pcf	-bitstream-charter-medium-r-normal--14-100-100-100-p-78-iso8859-1
charR12.pcf	-bitstream-charter-medium-r-normal--17-120-100-100-p-95-iso8859-1
charR14.pcf	-bitstream-charter-medium-r-normal--19-140-100-100-p-106-iso8859-1
charR18.pcf	-bitstream-charter-medium-r-normal--25-180-100-100-p-139-iso8859-1
charR24.pcf	-bitstream-charter-medium-r-normal--33-240-100-100-p-183-iso8859-1
techB14.pcf	-bitstream-terminal-bold-r-normal--18-140-100-100-c-110-dec-dectech
termB14.pcf	-bitstream-terminal-bold-r-normal--18-140-100-100-c-110-iso8859-1
tech14.pcf	-bitstream-terminal-medium-r-normal--18-140-100-100-c-110-dec-dectech
term14.pcf	-bitstream-terminal-medium-r-normal--18-140-100-100-c-110-iso8859-1

Table B-5. Fonts in the Speedo directory

Filename	Font name
font0648.spd	-bitstream-charter-medium-r-normal--0-0-0-0-p-0-iso8859-1
font0649.spd	-bitstream-charter-medium-i-normal--0-0-0-0-p-0-iso8859-1
font0709.spd	-bitstream-charter-bold-r-normal--0-0-0-0-p-0-iso8859-1
font0710.spd	-bitstream-charter-bold-i-normal--0-0-0-0-p-0-iso8859-1
font0419.spd	-bitstream-courier-medium-r-normal--0-0-0-0-m-0-iso8859-1
font0582.spd	-bitstream-courier-medium-i-normal--0-0-0-0-m-0-iso8859-1
font0583.spd	-bitstream-courier-bold-r-normal--0-0-0-0-m-0-iso8859-1
font0611.spd	-bitstream-courier-bold-i-normal--0-0-0-0-m-0-iso8859-1

```
-adobe-courier-medium-o-normal--8-80-75-75-m-50-iso8859-1
-adobe-courier-medium-o-normal--10-100-75-75-m-60-iso8859-1
-adobe-courier-medium-o-normal--12-120-75-75-m-70-iso8859-1
-adobe-courier-medium-o-normal--14-140-75-75-m-90-iso8859-1
-adobe-courier-medium-o-normal--18-180-75-75-m-110-iso8859-1
-adobe-courier-medium-o-normal--24-240-75-75-m
-adobe-courier-medium-r-normal--8-80-75-75-m-50-iso8859-1
-adobe-courier-medium-r-normal--10-100-75-75-m-60-iso8859-1
-adobe-courier-medium-r-normal--12-120-75-75-m-70-iso8859-1
-adobe-courier-medium-r-normal--14-140-75-75-m-90-iso8859-1
-adobe-courier-medium-r-normal--18-180-75-75-m-110-iso8859-1
-adobe-courier-medium-r-normal--24-240-75-75-m
-adobe-courier-bold-o-normal--8-80-75-75-m-50-iso8859-1
-adobe-courier-bold-o-normal--10-100-75-75-m-60-iso8859-1
-adobe-courier-bold-o-normal--12-120-75-75-m-70-iso8859-1
-adobe-courier-bold-o-normal--14-140-75-75-m-90-iso8859-1
-adobe-courier-bold-o-normal--18-180-75-75-m-110-iso8859-1
-adobe-courier-bold-o-normal--24-240-75-75-m-1
-adobe-courier-bold-r-normal--8-80-75-75-m-50-iso8859-1
-adobe-courier-bold-r-normal--10-100-75-75-m-60-iso8859-1
-adobe-courier-bold-r-normal--12-120-75-75-m-70-iso8859-1
-adobe-courier-bold-r-normal--14-140-75-75-m-90-iso8859-1
-adobe-courier-bold-r-normal--18-180-75-75-m-110-iso8859-1
-adobe-courier-bold-r-normal--24-240-75-75-m-1
```

Foundry: adobe
Family: courier

-adobe-helvetica-medium-o-normal--8-80-75-75-p-47-iso8859-1
-adobe-helvetica-medium-o-normal--10-100-75-75-p-57-iso8859-1
-adobe-helvetica-medium-o-normal--12-120-75-75-p-67-iso8859-1
-adobe-helvetica-medium-o-normal--14-140-75-75-p-78-iso8859-1
-adobe-helvetica-medium-o-normal--18-180-75-75-p-98-iso8859-1
-adobe-helvetica-medium-o-normal--24-240-75-75-p-130
-adobe-helvetica-medium-r-normal--8-80-75-75-p-46-iso8859-1
-adobe-helvetica-medium-r-normal--10-100-75-75-p-56-iso8859-1
-adobe-helvetica-medium-r-normal--12-120-75-75-p-67-iso8859-1
-adobe-helvetica-medium-r-normal--14-140-75-75-p-77-iso8859-1
-adobe-helvetica-medium-r-normal--18-180-75-75-p-98-iso8859-1
-adobe-helvetica-medium-r-normal--24-240-75-75-p-130
-adobe-helvetica-bold-o-normal--8-80-75-75-p-50-iso8859-1
-adobe-helvetica-bold-o-normal--10-100-75-75-p-60-iso8859-1
-adobe-helvetica-bold-o-normal--12-120-75-75-p-69-iso8859-1
-adobe-helvetica-bold-o-normal--14-140-75-75-p-82-iso8859-1
-adobe-helvetica-bold-o-normal--18-180-75-75-p-104-iso8859-1
-adobe-helvetica-bold-o-normal--24-240-75-75-p-138-
-adobe-helvetica-bold-r-normal--8-80-75-75-p-50-iso8859-1
-adobe-helvetica-bold-r-normal--10-100-75-75-p-60-iso8859-1
-adobe-helvetica-bold-r-normal--12-120-75-75-p-70-iso8859-1
-adobe-helvetica-bold-r-normal--14-140-75-75-p-82-iso8859-1
-adobe-helvetica-bold-r-normal--18-180-75-75-p-103-iso8859-1
-adobe-helvetica-bold-r-normal--24-240-75-75-p-138-

Foundry: adobe
Family: helvetica

-adobe-new century schoolbook-medium-i-normal--8-80-75-75-p-50-iso8859-1
-adobe-new century schoolbook-medium-i-normal--10-100-75-75-p-60-iso8859-1
-adobe-new century schoolbook-medium-i-normal--12-120-75-75-p-70-iso8859-1
-adobe-new century schoolbook-medium-i-normal--14-140-75-75-p-81-iso8859-1
-adobe-new century schoolbook-medium-i-normal--18-180-75-75-p-104-iso8859-1
-adobe-new century schoolbook-medium-i-normal--24-240-75-75-p-136-iso8859-1

-adobe-new century schoolbook-medium-r-normal--8-80-75-75-p-50-iso8859-1
-adobe-new century schoolbook-medium-r-normal--10-100-75-75-p-60-iso8859-1
-adobe-new century schoolbook-medium-r-normal--12-120-75-75-p-70-iso8859-1
-adobe-new century schoolbook-medium-r-normal--14-140-75-75-p-82-iso8859-1
-adobe-new century schoolbook-medium-r-normal--18-180-75-75-p-103-iso8859-1
-adobe-new century schoolbook-medium-r-normal--24-240-75-75-p-137-iso8859-1

-adobe-new century schoolbook-bold-i-normal--8-80-75-75-p-56-iso8859-1
-adobe-new century schoolbook-bold-i-normal--10-100-75-75-p-66-iso8859-1
-adobe-new century schoolbook-bold-i-normal--12-120-75-75-p-76-iso8859-1
-adobe-new century schoolbook-bold-i-normal--14-140-75-75-p-88-iso8859-1
-adobe-new century schoolbook-bold-i-normal--18-180-75-75-p-111-iso8859-1
-adobe-new century schoolbook-bold-i-normal--24-240-75-75-p-148-iso8859-1

-adobe-new century schoolbook-bold-r-normal--8-80-75-75-p-56-iso8859-1
-adobe-new century schoolbook-bold-r-normal--10-100-75-75-p-66-iso8859-1
-adobe-new century schoolbook-bold-r-normal--12-120-75-75-p-77-iso8859-1
-adobe-new century schoolbook-bold-r-normal--14-140-75-75-p-87-iso8859-1
-adobe-new century schoolbook-bold-r-normal--18-180-75-75-p-113-iso8859-1
-adobe-new century schoolbook-bold-r-normal--24-240-75-75-p-149-iso8859-1

Foundry: adobe
Family: new century schoolbook

-b&h-lucida-medium-i-normal-sans-8-80-75-75-p-45-iso8859-1
-b&h-lucida-medium-i-normal-sans-10-100-75-75-p-59-iso8859-1
-b&h-lucida-medium-i-normal-sans-12-120-75-75-p-71-iso8859-1
-b&h-lucida-medium-i-normal-sans-14-140-75-75-p-82-iso8859-1
-b&h-lucida-medium-i-normal-sans-18-180-75-75-p-105-iso8859-1
-b&h-lucida-medium-i-normal-sans-19-190-75-75-p-108-iso8859-1
-b&h-lucida-medium-i-normal-sans-24-240-75-75-p-

-b&h-lucida-medium-r-normal-sans-8-80-75-75-p-49-iso8859-1
-b&h-lucida-medium-r-normal-sans-10-100-75-75-p-58-iso8859-1
-b&h-lucida-medium-r-normal-sans-12-120-75-75-p-71-iso8859-1
-b&h-lucida-medium-r-normal-sans-14-140-75-75-p-81-iso8859-1
-b&h-lucida-medium-r-normal-sans-18-180-75-75-p-106-iso8859-1
-b&h-lucida-medium-r-normal-sans-19-190-75-75-p-108-iso8859-1
-b&h-lucida-medium-r-normal-sans-24-240-75-75-p-

-b&h-lucida-bold-i-normal-sans-8-80-75-75-p-67-iso8859-1
-b&h-lucida-bold-i-normal-sans-10-100-75-75-p-79-iso8859-1
-b&h-lucida-bold-i-normal-sans-12-120-75-75-p-79-iso8859-1
-b&h-lucida-bold-i-normal-sans-14-140-75-75-p-92-iso8859-1
-b&h-lucida-bold-i-normal-sans-18-180-75-75-p-119-iso885
-b&h-lucida-bold-i-normal-sans-19-190-75-75-p-122-iso885
-b&h-lucida-bold-i-normal-sans-24-240-75-75-p-

-b&h-lucida-bold-r-normal-sans-8-80-75-75-p-50-iso8859-1
-b&h-lucida-bold-r-normal-sans-10-100-75-75-p-66-iso8859-1
-b&h-lucida-bold-r-normal-sans-12-120-75-75-p-79-iso8859-1
-b&h-lucida-bold-r-normal-sans-14-140-75-75-p-92-iso8859-1
-b&h-lucida-bold-r-normal-sans-18-180-75-75-p-120-iso885
-b&h-lucida-bold-r-normal-sans-19-190-75-75-p-122-iso885
-b&h-lucida-bold-r-normal-sans-24-240-75-75-l

Foundry: b&h
Family: lucida

-b&h-lucidabright-medium-i-normal--8-80-75-75-p-45-iso8859-1
-b&h-lucidabright-medium-i-normal--10-100-75-75-p-57-iso8859-1
-b&h-lucidabright-medium-i-normal--12-120-75-75-p-67-iso8859-1
-b&h-lucidabright-medium-i-normal--14-140-75-75-p-80-iso8859-1
-b&h-lucidabright-medium-i-normal--18-180-75-75-p-102-iso8859-1
-b&h-lucidabright-medium-i-normal--19-190-75-75-p-109-iso8859-
-b&h-lucidabright-medium-i-normal--24-240-75-75-p

-b&h-lucidabright-medium-r-normal--8-80-75-75-p-45-iso8859-1
-b&h-lucidabright-medium-r-normal--10-100-75-75-p-56-iso8859-1
-b&h-lucidabright-medium-r-normal--12-120-75-75-p-68-iso8859-1
-b&h-lucidabright-medium-r-normal--14-140-75-75-p-80-iso8859-1
-b&h-lucidabright-medium-r-normal--18-180-75-75-p-103-iso8859-1
-b&h-lucidabright-medium-r-normal--19-190-75-75-p-109-iso8859-
-b&h-lucidabright-medium-r-normal--24-240-75-75-[

-b&h-lucidabright-demibold-i-normal--8-80-75-75-p-48-iso8859-1
-b&h-lucidabright-demibold-i-normal--10-100-75-75-p-59-iso8859-1
-b&h-lucidabright-demibold-i-normal--12-120-75-75-p-72-iso8859-1
-b&h-lucidabright-demibold-i-normal--14-140-75-75-p-84-iso8859-1
-b&h-lucidabright-demibold-i-normal--18-180-75-75-p-107-iso8859-1
-b&h-lucidabright-demibold-i-normal--19-190-75-75-p-114-iso885
-b&h-lucidabright-demibold-i-normal--24-240-75-75

-b&h-lucidabright-demibold-r-normal--8-80-75-75-p-47-iso8859-1
-b&h-lucidabright-demibold-r-normal--10-100-75-75-p-59-iso8859-1
-b&h-lucidabright-demibold-r-normal--12-120-75-75-p-71-iso8859-1
-b&h-lucidabright-demibold-r-normal--14-140-75-75-p-84-iso8859-1
-b&h-lucidabright-demibold-r-normal--18-180-75-75-p-107-iso8859-1
-b&h-lucidabright-demibold-r-normal--19-190-75-75-p-114-iso88
-b&h-lucidabright-demibold-r-normal--24-240-75-75

Foundry: b&h
Family: lucidabright

-adobe-times-medium-i-normal--8-80-75-75-p-42-iso8859-1
-adobe-times-medium-i-normal--10-100-75-75-p-52-iso8859-1
-adobe-times-medium-i-normal--12-120-75-75-p-63-iso8859-1
-adobe-times-medium-i-normal--14-140-75-75-p-73-iso8859-1
-adobe-times-medium-i-normal--18-180-75-75-p-94-iso8859-1
-adobe-times-medium-i-normal--24-240-75-75-p-125-iso885

-adobe-times-medium-r-normal--8-80-75-75-p-44-iso8859-1
-adobe-times-medium-r-normal--10-100-75-75-p-54-iso8859-1
-adobe-times-medium-r-normal--12-120-75-75-p-64-iso8859-1
-adobe-times-medium-r-normal--14-140-75-75-p-74-iso8859-1
-adobe-times-medium-r-normal--18-180-75-75-p-94-iso8859-1
-adobe-times-medium-r-normal--24-240-75-75-p-124-iso885

-adobe-times-bold-i-normal--8-80-75-75-p-47-iso8859-1
-adobe-times-bold-i-normal--10-100-75-75-p-57-iso8859-1
-adobe-times-bold-i-normal--12-120-75-75-p-68-iso8859-1
-adobe-times-bold-i-normal--14-140-75-75-p-77-iso8859-1
-adobe-times-bold-i-normal--18-180-75-75-p-98-iso8859-1
-adobe-times-bold-i-normal--24-240-75-75-p-128-iso8859-i

-adobe-times-bold-r-normal--8-80-75-75-p-47-iso8859-1
-adobe-times-bold-r-normal--10-100-75-75-p-57-iso8859-1
-adobe-times-bold-r-normal--12-120-75-75-p-67-iso8859-1
-adobe-times-bold-r-normal--14-140-75-75-p-77-iso8859-1
-adobe-times-bold-r-normal--18-180-75-75-p-99-iso8859-1
-adobe-times-bold-r-normal--24-240-75-75-p-132-iso8859

Foundry: adobe
Family: times

-b&h-lucidatypewriter-medium-r-normal--sans-8-80-75-75-m-50-iso8859-1
-b&h-lucidatypewriter-medium-r-normal--sans-10-100-75-75-m-60-iso8859-1
-b&h-lucidatypewriter-medium-r-normal--sans-12-120-75-75-m-70-iso8859-1
-b&h-lucidatypewriter-medium-r-normal--sans-14-140-75-75-m-90-iso8859-1
-b&h-lucidatypewriter-medium-r-normal--sans-18-180-75-75-m-110-i
-b&h-lucidatypewriter-medium-r-normal--sans-19-190-75-75-m-110-i
-b&h-lucidatypewriter-medium-r-normal--sans-24-240
-b&h-lucidatypewriter-bold-r-normal--sans-8-80-75-75-m-50-iso8859-1
-b&h-lucidatypewriter-bold-r-normal--sans-10-100-75-75-m-60-iso8859-1
-b&h-lucidatypewriter-bold-r-normal--sans-12-120-75-75-m-70-iso8859-1
-b&h-lucidatypewriter-bold-r-normal--sans-14-140-75-75-m-90-iso8859-1
-b&h-lucidatypewriter-bold-r-normal--sans-18-180-75-75-m-110-is
-b&h-lucidatypewriter-bold-r-normal--sans-19-190-75-75-m-110-is
-b&h-lucidatypewriter-bold-r-normal--sans-24-240-7

Foundry: b&h
Family: lucidatypewriter

-αδοβε-σψμβολ-μεδιυμ-ρ-νορμαλ--8-80-75-75-π-51-αδοβε-φοντοπεχιφιχ
-αδοβε-σψμβολ-μεδιυμ-ρ-νορμαλ--10-100-75-75-π-61-αδοβε-φοντοπεχιφιχ
-αδοβε-σψμβολ-μεδιυμ-ρ-νορμαλ--12-120-75-75-π-74-αδοβε φοντοπεχιφχ
-αδοβε-σψμβολ-μεδιυμ-ρ-νορμαλ--14-140-75-75-π-85-αδοβε-φοντοπεχιφιχ
-αδοβε-σψμβολ-μεδιυμ-ρ-νορμαλ--18-180-75-75-π-107-αδοβε-φοντοπεχιφιχ
-αδοβε-σψμβολ-μεδιυμ-ρ-νορμαλ--24-240-75-75-π-142-αδο|

Foundry: adobe
Family: symbol

-bitstream-charter-medium-i-normal--8-80-75-75-p-44-iso8859-1

-bitstream-charter-medium-i-normal--10-100-75-75-p-55-iso8859-1

-bitstream-charter-medium-i-normal--12-120-75-75-p-65-iso8859-1

-bitstream-charter-medium-i-normal--15-140-75-75-p-82-iso8859-1

-bitstream-charter-medium-i-normal--19-180-75-75-p-103-iso8859-1

-bitstream-charter-medium-i-normal--25-240-75-75-p-136-iso88

-bitstream-charter-medium-r-normal--8-80-75-75-p-45-iso8859-1

-bitstream-charter-medium-r-normal--10-100-75-75-p-56-iso8859-1

-bitstream-charter-medium-r-normal--12-120-75-75-p-67-iso8859-1

-bitstream-charter-medium-r-normal--15-140-75-75-p-84-iso8859-1

-bitstream-charter-medium-r-normal--19-180-75-75-p-106-iso8859-1

-bitstream-charter-medium-r-normal--25-240-75-75-p-139-iso8

-bitstream-charter-bold-i-normal--8-80-75-75-p-50-iso8859-1

-bitstream-charter-bold-i-normal--10-100-75-75-p-62-iso8859-1

-bitstream-charter-bold-i-normal--12-120-75-75-p-74-iso8859-1

-bitstream-charter-bold-i-normal--15-140-75-75-p-93-iso8859-1

-bitstream-charter-bold-i-normal--19-180-75-75-p-117-iso8859-1

-bitstream-charter-bold-i-normal--25-240-75-75-p-154-

-bitstream-charter-bold-r-normal--8-80-75-75-p-50-iso8859-1

-bitstream-charter-bold-r-normal--10-100-75-75-p-63-iso8859-1

-bitstream-charter-bold-r-normal--12-120-75-75-p-75-iso8859-1

-bitstream-charter-bold-r-normal--15-140-75-75-p-94-iso8859-1

-bitstream-charter-bold-r-normal--19-180-75-75-p-119-iso8859-1

-bitstream-charter-bold-r-normal--25-240-75-75-p-157

Foundry: bitstream
Family: charter

```
-bitstream-terminal-medium-r-normal--18-140-100
-bitstream-terminal-bold-r-normal--18-140-100-1
```

```
-bitstream-charter-medium-r-normal--0-0-0-p-0-iso8859-1
-bitstream-charter-medium-i-normal--0-0-0-p-0-iso8859-1
-bitstream-charter-bold-r-normal--0-0-0-p-0-iso8859-1
-bitstream-charter-bold-i-normal--0-0-0-p-0-iso8859-1
-bitstream-courier-medium-r-normal--0-0-0-0-m-0-i
-bitstream-courier-medium-i-normal--0-0-0-0-m-0-i
-bitstream-courier-bold-r-normal--0-0-0-0-m-0-iso
-bitstream-courier-bold-i-normal--0-0-0-0-m-0-iso
```

```
-dec-terminal-medium-r-normal--14-140-75-75-c-80-iso8859-1
-dec-terminal-bold-r-normal--14-140-75-75-c-80-iso8859-1
```

Foundry: bitstream
Family: terminal

Foundry: bitstream
Families: charter, courier
(Scalable fonts)

Foundry: dec
Family: terminal

```
-misc-fixed-medium-r-normal--8-80-75-75-c-50-iso8859-1
-misc-fixed-medium-r-normal--9-90-75-75-c-60-iso8859-1
-misc-fixed-medium-r-normal--10-100-75-75-c-60-iso8859-1
-misc-fixed-medium-r-semicondensed--12-110-75-75-c-60-iso8859-1
-misc-fixed-medium-r-semicondensed--13-120-75-75-c-60-iso8859-1
-misc-fixed-medium-r-normal--13-120-75-75-c-70-iso8859-1
-misc-fixed-medium-r-normal--13-120-75-75-c-80-iso8859-1
-misc-fixed-medium-r-normal--14-130-75-75-c-70-iso8859-1
-misc-fixed-medium-r-normal--15-140-75-75-c-90-iso8859-1
-misc-fixed-medium-r-normal--20-200-75-75-c-100-iso8
-misc-fixed-bold-r-semicondensed--13-120-75-75-c-60-iso8859-1
-misc-fixed-bold-r-normal--13-120-75-75-c-70-iso8859-1
-misc-fixed-bold-r-normal--13-120-75-75-c-80-iso8859-1
-misc-fixed-bold-r-normal--15-140-75-75-c-90-iso8859-1
```

Foundry: misc
Family: fixed

```
-schumacher-clean-medium-i-normal--8-80-75-75-c-80-iso8859-1
-schumacher-clean-medium-i-normal--12-128-75-75-c-68-iso8859-1
-schumacher-clean-medium-r-normal--6-60-75-75-c-40-iso8859-1
-schumacher-clean-medium-r-normal--6-60-75-75-c-50-iso8859-1
-schumacher-clean-medium-r-normal--8-80-75-75-c-50-iso8859-1
-schumacher-clean-medium-r-normal--8-80-75-75-c-60-iso8859-1
-schumacher-clean-medium-r-normal--8-80-75-75-c-70-iso8859-1
-schumacher-clean-medium-r-normal--8-80-75-75-c-70-iso8859-1
-schumacher-clean-medium-r-normal--10-100-75-75-c-70-iso8859-1
-schumacher-clean-medium-r-normal--10-100-75-75-c-80-iso8859-1
-schumacher-clean-medium-r-normal--10-100-75-75-c-50-iso8859-1
-schumacher-clean-medium-r-normal--10-100-75-75-c-60-iso8859-1
-schumacher-clean-medium-r-normal--12-120-75-75-c-60-iso8859-1
-schumacher-clean-medium-r-normal--12-120-75-75-c-70-iso8859-1
-schumacher-clean-medium-r-normal--12-120-75-75-c-80-iso8859-1
-schumacher-clean-medium-r-normal--13-130-75-75-c-80-iso8859-1
-schumacher-clean-medium-r-normal--13-130-75-75-c-60-iso8859-1
-schumacher-clean-medium-r-normal--14-140-75-75-c-80-iso8859-1
-schumacher-clean-medium-r-normal--14-140-75-75-c-70-iso8859-1
-schumacher-clean-medium-r-normal--15-150-75-75-c-90-iso80
-schumacher-clean-medium-r-normal--16-160-75-75-c-80-iso8859-1
-schumacher-clean-bold-r-normal--8-80-75-75-c-80-iso8859-1
-schumacher-clean-bold-r-normal--10-100-75-75-c-60-iso8859-1
-schumacher-clean-bold-r-normal--10-100-75-75-c-80-iso8859-1
-schumacher-clean-bold-r-normal--12-120-75-75-c-80-iso8859-1
-schumacher-clean-bold-r-normal--12-120-75-75-c-60-iso8859-1
-schumacher-clean-bold-r-normal--13-130-75-75-c-80-iso8859-1
-schumacher-clean-bold-r-normal--14-140-75-75-c-80-iso8859-1
-schumacher-clean-bold-r-normal--15-150-75-75-c-90-iso8859
-schumacher-clean-bold-r-normal--16-160-75-75-c-80-iso8859-1
```

Foundry: schumacher
Family: clean

X Window System User's Guide, Motif Edition

Encoding: adobe-fontspecific

Encoding: dec-dectech

Encoding: iso8859

Encoding: jisx0201.1976

Encoding: jisx0208.1983

Encoding: jisx0201.1976

Encoding: sunolglyph

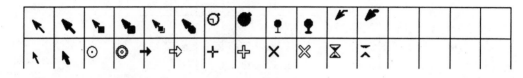

Encoding: SunOLcursor

Encoding: ksc5601.1987-0

Encoding: iso8859-8

Example B-1 is the source code for the *xshowfonts* program, which we used to create most of the illustrations in this appendix. If you don't want to type it in, you can find instructions for getting it online in Appendix H, *Obtaining Example Programs*.

Example B-1. xshowfont source listing

```
/* Dan Heller <argv@sun.com>, based on a design by Tim O'Reilly
 *
 * xshowfonts.c -
 *   Displays a set of fonts specified on the command line, from
 * a pipe, or typed into stdin.  Fonts can be specified as specific
 * or wildcard character strings.  A pixmap is created to
 * display all the fonts.  This is done by using the pixmap as the
 * pixmap image for a label widget.  Each font prints its own name
 * in its own font style -- the -phrase option prints the phrase
 * instead.
 *
 * All fonts are loaded first and scanned to determine the total
 * width and height of the pixmap first.  Then the fonts are
 * reopened again to actually render the fonts into the pixmap.
 * All this could be avoided by using XListFontsWithInfo()
 * rather than XListFonts() but since the list is potentially
 * very large, I didn't want to overload the server and client
 * with all those fonts + a very large pixmap.
 *
 * Usage: xshowfonts
 *   -s sorts the fonts in alphabetical order before displaying
 *       them.
 *   -v verbose mode for when input is redirected to stdin.
 *   -w width of viewport window
 *   -h height of viewport window
 *   -fg foreground_color
 *   -bg background_color
 *   -phrase "text string" (otherwise, name of font is used)
 *   -indicates to read from stdin.  Piping doesn't require
 *       the '-' argument.  With no arguments, xshowfonts reads
 *   from stdin anyway.
 *
 * Neat ways to use the program:
 *   xshowfonts -fg green -bg black "*adobe*"
 *   xshowfonts -sort "*"
 *   xshowfonts -phrase "The quick brown fox jumps over the lazy
 *               dog" "*times*"
 *   xlsfonts | xshowfonts -sort
 *   xshowfonts "*helvetica*"
 *
 * compile: (triple click and paste next line)
 *     cc -O -s xshowfonts.c -lXaw -lXt -lXmu -lX11 -o xshowfonts
 */

#include <stdio.h>
#include <X11/Intrinsic.h>
#include <X11/StringDefs.h>
#include <X11/Xaw/Label.h>
#include <X11/Xaw/Viewport.h>

struct _resrcs {
    int sort;
```

```
    int verbose;
    Pixel fg, bg;
    char *phrase;
    int view_width, view_height;
} Resrcs;

static XtResource resources[] = {
    { "sort", "Sort", XtRBoolean, sizeof (int),
     XtOffsetOf(struct _resrcs,sort), XtRImmediate,
        False },
    { "verbose", "Verbose", XtRBoolean, sizeof (int),
     XtOffsetOf(struct _resrcs,verbose), XtRImmediate,
        False },
    { "foreground", "Foreground", XtRPixel, sizeof (Pixel),
     XtOffsetOf(struct _resrcs,fg), XtRString,
        XtDefaultForeground },
    { "background", "Background", XtRPixel, sizeof (Pixel),
     XtOffsetOf(struct _resrcs,bg), XtRString,
        XtDefaultBackground },
    { "phrase", "Phrase", XtRString, sizeof (String),
     XtOffsetOf(struct _resrcs,phrase), XtRImmediate, NULL },
    { "view-width", "View-width", XtRInt, sizeof (int),
     XtOffsetOf(struct _resrcs,view_width), XtRImmediate,
        (char *)500 },
    { "view-height", "View-height", XtRInt, sizeof (int),
     XtOffsetOf(struct _resrcs,view_height), XtRImmediate,
        (char *)300 },
};

static XrmOptionDescRec options[] = {
    { "-sort", "sort", XrmoptionNoArg, "True" },
    { "-v", "verbose", XrmoptionNoArg, "True" },
    { "-fg", "foreground", XrmoptionSepArg, NULL },
    { "-bg", "background", XrmoptionSepArg, NULL },
    { "-phrase", "phrase", XrmoptionSepArg, NULL },
    { "-w", "view-width", XrmoptionSepArg, NULL },
    { "-h", "view-height", XrmoptionSepArg, NULL },
};

/* sort font according to these parameters.
 * font specs we're interested in:
 *     -fndry-fmly-wght-slant-*swdth-*adstyl-*pxlsz-ptsz- ....
 * foundry -- sort by foundry first; similar ones are always
 *            grouped together
 * weight -- medium, demi-bold, bold
 * slant -- roman, italic/oblique, reverse italic/oblique
 *            (i or o, r, ri, ro)
 * ptsize -- increase numerical order
 */
font_cmp(f1, f2)
char **f1, **f2;
{
    char fndry1[16], fmly1[64], wght1[32], slant1[3];
    char fndry2[16], fmly2[64], wght2[32], slant2[3];
    int n, m, ptsize1, ptsize2;
    char *font_fmt_str = "-%[^-]-%[^-]-%[^-]-%[^-]-%*[^0-9]%
        *d-%d-";
```

```
    n = sscanf(*f1, font_fmt_str, fndry1, fmly1, wght1, slant1,
            &ptsize1);
    m = sscanf(*f2, font_fmt_str, fndry2, fmly2, wght2, slant2,
            &ptsize2);
    if (m < 5 || n < 5)
      /* font not in correct format -- just return font names
       * in order */
      return strcmp(*f1, *f2);
    if (n = strcmp(fndry1, fndry2))
      return n; /* different foundries -- return alphabetical
                    * order */
    if (n = strcmp(fmly1, fmly2))
      return n; /* different families -- return alphabetical
                    * order */
    if (n = strcmp(wght1, wght2))
      return -n; /* weight happens to be correct in reverse
                     * alpha order */
    if (n = strcmp(slant1, slant2))
      return n; /* slants happen to be correct in alphabetical
                    * order */
    /* sort according to point size */
    return ptsize1 - ptsize2;
}

main(argc, argv)
int argc;
char *argv[];
{
    Widget topLevel, vp;
    char **list = (char **)NULL, **tmp;
    char buf[128];
    extern char **XListFonts();
    extern int strcmp();
    XFontStruct *font;
    Pixmap pixmap;
    GC gc;
    Display *dpy;
    int istty = isatty(0), redirect = !istty, i, j, total = 0;
    unsigned int w, width = 0, height = 0;

    topLevel = XtInitialize(argv[0], argv[0], options,
        XtNumber(options), &argc, argv);
    dpy = XtDisplay(topLevel);

    XtGetApplicationResources(topLevel, &Resrcs,
      resources, XtNumber(resources), NULL, 0);

    if (!argv[1] || !strcmp(argv[1], "-")) {
      printf("Loading fonts from input. ");
      if (istty) {
          puts("End with EOF or .");
          redirect++;
      } else
          puts("Use -v to view font names being loaded.");
    } else if (!istty && strcmp(argv[1], "-"))
      printf("%s: either use pipes or specify font names --
            not both.\n",
          argv[0]), exit(1);
```

```
while (*++argv || redirect) {
 if (!redirect)
     if (!strcmp(*argv, "-"))
      redirect++;
     else
      strcpy(buf, *argv);
 if (redirect) {
     if (istty)
      printf("Fontname: "), fflush(stdout);
     if (!fgets(buf, sizeof buf, stdin) ||
         !strcmp(buf, ".\n"))
      break;
     buf[strlen(buf)-1] = 0;
 }
 if (!buf[0])
     continue;
 if (istty || Resrcs.verbose)
     printf("Loading
tmp = XListFonts(dpy, buf, 32767, &i);
 if (i == 0) {
     printf("couldn't load font ");
     if (!istty && !Resrcs.verbose)
      printf("
     putchar('\n');
     continue;
 }
 if (istty || Resrcs.verbose)
     printf("%d font%s\n", i, i == 1? "" : "s");
 if (!list) {
     list = tmp;
     total = i;
 } else {
     i += total;
     if (!(list = (char **)XtRealloc(list, i *
             sizeof (char *))))
     XtError("Not enough memory for font names");
     for (j = 0; total < i; j++, total++)
      list[total] = tmp[j];
 }
}
if (total == 0)
 puts("No fonts?!"), exit(1);
printf("Total fonts loaded: %d\n", total);
if (Resrcs.sort) {
 printf("Sorting fonts..."), fflush(stdout);
 qsort(list, total, sizeof (char *), font_cmp);
 putchar('\n');
}
/* calculate size for pixmap by getting the dimensions
 * of each font */
puts("Calculating sizes for pixmap.");
for (i = 0; i < total; i++) {
 if (!(font = XLoadQueryFont(dpy, list[i]))) {
     printf("Can't load font: %s\n", list[i]);
     continue;
 }
```

```
    if ((w = XTextWidth(font, list[i],
        strlen(list[i]))) > width)
        width = w;
    height += font->ascent + font->descent;
    XFreeFont(dpy, font);
}
width += 6;
height += 6;
/* Create pixmap + GC */
printf("Creating pixmap of size %dx%d\n", width, height);
if (!(pixmap = XCreatePixmap(dpy, DefaultRootWindow(dpy),
    width, height, DefaultDepth(dpy, DefaultScreen(dpy)))))
    XtError("Can't Create pixmap");
if (!(gc = XCreateGC(dpy, pixmap, NULL, 0)))
    XtError("Can't create gc");
XSetForeground(dpy, gc, Resrcs.bg);
XFillRectangle(dpy, pixmap, gc, 0, 0, width, height);
XSetForeground(dpy, gc, Resrcs.fg);
XSetBackground(dpy, gc, Resrcs.bg);
height = 0;
for (i = 0; i < total; i++) {
    if (!(font = XLoadQueryFont(dpy, list[i])))
        continue; /* it's already been reported */
    XSetFont(dpy, gc, font->fid);
    height += font->ascent;
    if (Resrcs.phrase)
        XDrawString(dpy, pixmap, gc, 0, height,
            Resrcs.phrase, strlen(Resrcs.phrase));
    else
        XDrawString(dpy, pixmap, gc, 5, height, list[i],
                    strlen(list[i]));
    height += font->descent;
    XFreeFont(dpy, font);
}
vp = XtVaCreateManagedWidget("viewport", viewportWidgetClass,
        topLevel,
    XtNallowHoriz,  True,
    XtNallowVert,   True,
    XtNwidth,  Resrcs.view_width,
    XtNheight, Resrcs.view_height,
    NULL);
XtVaCreateManagedWidget("_foo", labelWidgetClass, vp,
    XtNbitmap, pixmap,
    NULL);

if (!redirect)
    XFreeFontNames(list);

XtRealizeWidget(topLevel);
XtMainLoop();
}
```

C

Standard Bitmaps

This appendix shows the bitmaps included with the standard distribution of the X Window System. These can be used for setting window backgrounds, cursor symbols, pixmaps, and possibly for application icon pixmaps.

C
Standard Bitmaps

A number of bitmaps are included with the standard distribution of the X Window System. These bitmaps can be used for setting window backgrounds, cursor symbols, pixmaps, and possibly for application icon pixmaps.

The standard bitmaps are generally located in the directory */usr/include/X11/bitmaps*. Each bitmap is in standard X11 bitmap format in its own file. The *bitmap* application can be used to view these bitmaps in larger scale and to edit them (though their permissions normally do not allow overwriting).

You can use these bitmaps to set the background pattern of a window in any application that allows it. For example, if you wanted to change the root window background, you could do so using *xsetroot*:

```
xsetroot -bitmap /usr/include/X11/bitmaps/wide_weave
```

See Chapter 14, *Setup Clients*, for more information about *xsetroot*.

Note that the bitmaps that come in pairs, such as `cntr_ptr` and `cntr_ptrmsk`, are intended for creating pointer shapes. For information on specifying a bitmap as the root window pointer using *xsetroot*, see Chapter 13.

The 86 bitmaps pictured on the following pages are included in the Release 5 standard distribution of X. The following 23 bitmaps have been added to the standard distribution in Release 5.

Table C-1. Standard Bitmaps Added in Release 5

Dashes	RotateLeft	grid2
Down	RotateRight	grid4
Excl	Stipple	grid8
FlipHoriz	Term	ldblarrow
FlipVert	Up	menu6
Fold	black6	rdblarrow
Left	box6	stripe4
Right	grid16	

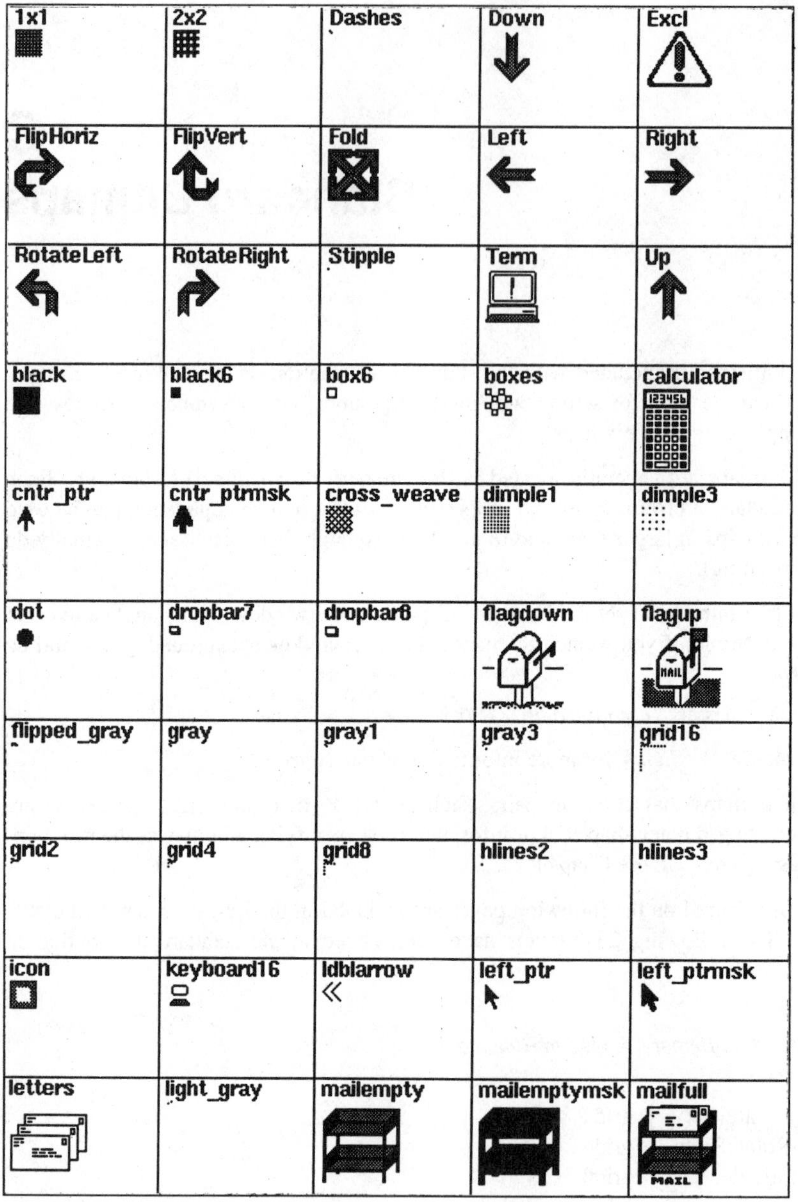

1x1	2x2	Dashes	Down	Excl
1x1 ▦	2x2 ▦	Dashes	Down ↓	Excl ⚠
FlipHoriz	FlipVert	Fold	Left	Right
FlipHoriz ↻	FlipVert ↰	Fold ⊠	Left ←	Right →
RotateLeft	RotateRight	Stipple	Term	Up
RotateLeft ↰	RotateRight ↱	Stipple	Term	Up ↑
black	black6	box6	boxes	calculator
black ■	black6 ▪	box6 □	boxes	calculator
cntr_ptr	cntr_ptrmsk	cross_weave	dimple1	dimple3
cntr_ptr ↑	cntr_ptrmsk ↑	cross_weave	dimple1	dimple3
dot	dropbar7	dropbar8	flagdown	flagup
dot ●	dropbar7 ▫	dropbar8 ▫	flagdown	flagup
flipped_gray	gray	gray1	gray3	grid16
grid2	grid4	grid8	hlines2	hlines3
icon	keyboard16	ldblarrow	left_ptr	left_ptrmsk
icon ▣	keyboard16	ldblarrow ≪	left_ptr ▸	left_ptrmsk ▸
letters	light_gray	mailempty	mailemptymsk	mailfull

Figure C-1. The standard bitmaps

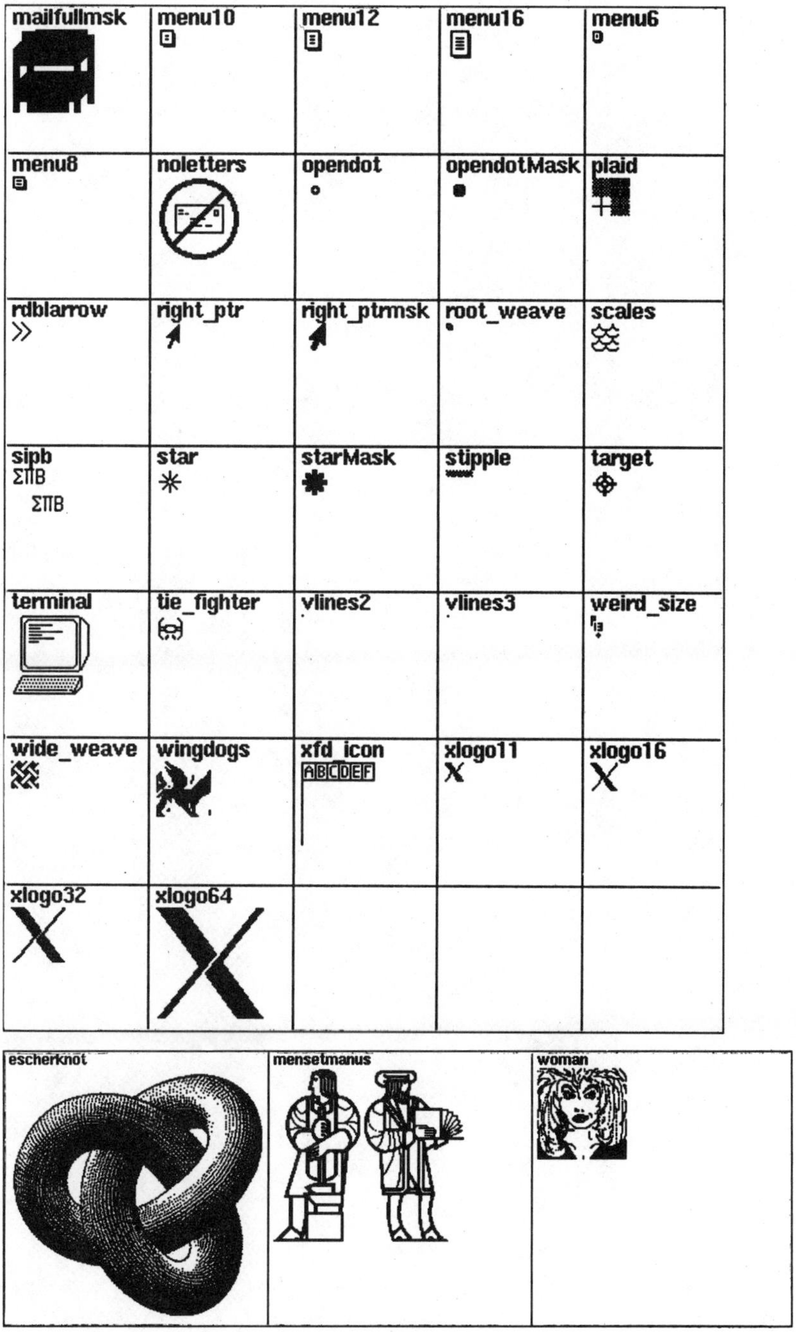

mailfullmsk	menu10	menu12	menu16	menu6
menu8	noletters	opendot	opendotMask	plaid
rdblarrow >>	right_ptr	right_ptrmsk	root_weave	scales
sipb ΣΠΒ ΣΠΒ	star *	starMask	stipple	target
terminal	tie_fighter	vlines2	vlines3	weird_size
wide_weave	wingdogs	xfd_icon ABCDEF	xlogo11 X	xlogo16 X
xlogo32 X	xlogo64 X			

escherknot	mensetmanus	woman

Figure C-1. The Standard Bitmaps (continued)

D

Standard Cursors

This appendix shows the standard cursor images that can be used by X programs.

D
Standard Cursors

Table D-1 lists the cursors available in the standard distribution of X from MIT; the cursor shapes themselves are pictured in Figure D-1.

To specify a cursor as an argument to a command-line option, as the value of a resource variable, etc., strip the XC_ prefix from the symbol name. For example, to specify the XC_sailboat cursor as the *xterm* pointer, you could enter the command:

```
% xterm -xrm 'xterm*pointerShape: sailboat'
```

Each cursor has an associated numeric value (to the right of the symbol name in the table). You may notice that the values skip the odd numbers. Each cursor is actually composed of two font characters: the character that defines the shape (pictured in Figure D-0), and a mask character (not shown) that sets the cursor shape off from the root (or other) window. (More precisely, the mask selects which pixels in the screen around the cursor are disturbed by the cursor.) The mask is generally the same shape as the character it underlies but is one pixel wider in all directions. The even numbers in the table actually correspond to the cursor's mask character.

To get an idea of what masks look like, display the entire cursor font using the command:

```
% xfd -fn cursor
```

The *mwm* window manager uses several of the standard cursor symbols. In addition, *mwm* uses some Motif-specific cursors, which are illustrated in Figure 1-3 in Part One of this guide.

Standard Cursors

Table D-1. Standard Cursor Symbols

Symbol	Value	Symbol	Value
XC_X_cursor	0	XC_ll_angle	76
XC_arrow	2	XC_lr_angle	78
XC_based_arrow_down	4	XC_man	80
XC_based_arrow_up	6	XC_middlebutton	82
XC_boat	8	XC_mouse	84
XC_bogosity	10	XC_pencil	86
XC_bottom_left_corner	12	XC_pirate	88
XC_bottom_right_corner	14	XC_plus	90
XC_bottom_side	16	XC_question_arrow	92
XC_bottom_tee	18	XC_right_ptr	94
XC_box_spiral	20	XC_right_side	96
XC_center_ptr	22	XC_right_tee	98
XC_circle	24	XC_rightbutton	100
XC_clock	26	XC_rtl_logo	102
XC_coffee_mug	28	XC_sailboat	104
XC_cross	30	XC_sb_down_arrow	106
XC_cross_reverse	32	XC_sb_h_double_arrow	108
XC_crosshair	34	XC_sb_left_arrow	110
XC_diamond_cross	36	XC_sb_right_arrow	112
XC_dot	38	XC_sb_up_arrow	114
XC_dotbox	40	XC_sb_v_double_arrow	116
XC_double_arrow	42	XC_shuttle	118
XC_draft_large	44	XC_sizing	120
XC_draft_small	46	XC_spider	122
XC_draped_box	48	XC_spraycan	124
XC_exchange	50	XC_star	126
XC_fleur	52	XC_target	128
XC_gobbler	54	XC_tcross	130
XC_gumby	56	XC_top_left_arrow	132
XC_hand1	58	XC_top_left_corner	134
XC_hand2	60	XC_top_right_corner	136
XC_heart	62	XC_top_side	138
XC_icon	64	XC_top_tee	140
XC_iron_cross	66	XC_trek	142
XC_left_ptr	68	XC_ul_angle	144
XC_left_side	70	XC_umbrella	146
XC_left_tee	72	XC_ur_angle	148
XC_leftbutton	74	XC_watch	150
		XC_xterm	152

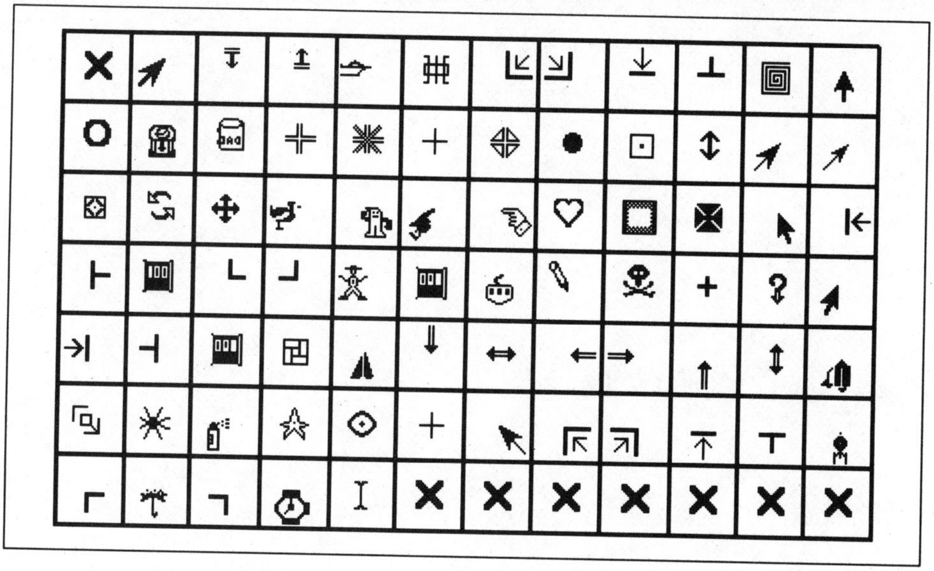

Figure D-1. The standard cursors

E

xterm Control Sequences

This appendix list the escape sequences that can be used to control features of an xterm *window or its terminal emulation.*

In This Appendix:

E
xterm Control Sequences

A standard terminal performs many operations in response to escape sequences sent out by a program: redraws the screen, backspaces, advances a line, etc. Under UNIX, programs use the *termcap* or *terminfo* database to determine which escape sequences to send out. (For more information, see the standard UNIX man pages *termcap*(5) or *terminfo*(5), or the Nutshell Handbook *Termcap and Terminfo*, available from O'Reilly & Associates, Inc.)

In emulating a terminal, *xterm* responds to those same terminal escape sequences. This appendix lists the valid escape sequences for *xterm*. Although these sequences are primarily intended to be used by a program running in the *xterm* window, be aware that a user can affect the window's operation by sending it an escape sequence using the UNIX *echo*(1) command. Chapter 6, *Font Specification*, describes the use of an escape sequence to change the display font dynamically—a typical and useful example.

This appendix is based on two sources: the "Xterm Control Sequences" document, written by Edward Moy, University of California, Berkeley, for the X10 *xterm*; and revisions for X11 R5 provided by Stephen Gildea of the MIT X Consortium.

Definitions

$\boxed{c}$	The literal character c.
C	A single (required) character.
P_s	A single (usually optional) numeric parameter, composed of one of more digits.
P_m	A multiple numeric parameter composed of any number of single numeric parameters, separated by $\boxed{;}$ character(s).
P_t	A text parameter composed of printable characters.

VT100 Mode

Most of these control sequences are standard VT102 control sequences, but there are some sequences here from later DEC VT terminals too. Major VT102 features not supported are smooth scrolling, double size characters.

There are additional functions to provide control of *xterm*-dependent functions, such as the scrollbar or window size.

BEL   Bell (Ctrl-G)

BS   Backspace (Ctrl-H)

TAB   Horizontal Tab (HT) (Ctrl-I)

LF   Line Feed or New Line (NL) (Ctrl-J)

VT   Vertical Tab (Ctrl-K) (Same as LF)

FF   Form Feed or New Page (NP) (Ctrl-L) (Same as LF)

CR   Carriage Return (Ctrl-M)

SO   Shift Out (Ctrl-N) → Switch to Alternate Character Set (Invokes the G1 character set)

SI   Shift In (Ctrl-O) → Switch to Standard Character Set (Invokes the G0 character set—the default)

ESC (*C*   Select G0 Character Set (ISO 2022)
                          $C = $ 0 → DEC Special Character and Line Drawing Set
                          $C = $ A → United Kingdom (UK)
                          $C = $ B → United States (USASCII)

ESC) *C*   Select G1 Character Set (ISO 2022)
                          $C = $ 0 → DEC Special Character and Line Drawing Set
                          $C = $ A → United Kingdom (UK)
                          $C = $ B → United States (USASCII)

ESC * *C*   Select G2 Character Set (ISO 2022)
                          $C = $ 0 → DEC Special Character and Line Drawing Set
                          $C = $ A → United Kingdom (UK)
                          $C = $ B → United States (USASCII)

ESC + *C*   Select G3 Character Set (ISO 2022)
                          $C = $ 0 → DEC Special Character and Line Drawing Set
                          $C = $ A → United Kingdom (UK)
                          $C = $ B → United States (USASCII)

ESC 7   Save Cursor (DECSC)

ESC 8   Restore Cursor (DECRC)

ESC =   Application Keypad (DECPAM)

ESC >   Normal Keypad (DECPNM)

ESC D	Index (IND)
ESC E	Next Line (NEL)
ESC H	Tab Set (HTS)
ESC M	Reverse Index (RI)
ESC N	Single Shift Select of G2 Character Set (SS2) (affects next character only)
ESC O	Single Shift Select of G3 Character Set (SS3) (affects next character only)
ESC P_t ESC	Device Control String (DCS); *xterm* implements no DCS functions; P_t is ignored; P_t need not be printable characters.
ESC	Return Terminal ID (DECID); obsolete form of ESC [c (DA)
ESC [P_s @	Insert P_s (Blank) Character(s) (default = 1) (ICH)
ESC [P_s A	Cursor Up P_s Times (default = 1) (CUU)
ESC [P_s B	Cursor Down P_s Times (default = 1) (CUD)
ESC [P_s C	Cursor Forward P_s Times (default = 1) (CUF)
ESC [P_s D	Cursor Backward P_s Times (default = 1) (CUB)
ESC [P_s ; P_s H	Cursor Position [row;column] (default = [1,1]) (CUP)
ESC [P_s J	Erase in Display (ED) $P_s = 0 \rightarrow$ Clear Below (default) $P_s = 1 \rightarrow$ Clear Above $P_s = 2 \rightarrow$ Clear All
ESC [P_s K	Erase in Line (EL) $P_s = 0 \rightarrow$ Clear to Right (default) $P_s = 1 \rightarrow$ Clear to Left $P_s = 2 \rightarrow$ Clear All
ESC [P_s L	Insert P_s Line(s) (default = 1) (IL)
ESC [P_s M	Delete P_s Line(s) (default = 1) (DL)
ESC [P_s P	Delete P_s Character(s) (default = 1) (DCH)

ESC [P_s ; P_s ; P_s ; P_s ; T

Initiate Hilite mouse tracking. Parameters are [func;startx;starty;firstrow;lastrow]. See "Mouse Tracking."

ESC [P_s c

Send Device Attributes (DA); $P_s = 0$ or omitted $\rightarrow$ request attributes from terminal
$\rightarrow$ ESC [? 1 ; 2 c ("I am a VT100 with Advanced Video Option.")

ESC [P_s ; P_s f	Horizontal and Vertical (Cursor) Position [row;column] (default = [1,1]) (HVP)
ESC [P_s g	Tab Clear (TBC) $P_s = 0 \rightarrow$ Clear Current Column (default) $P_s = 3 \rightarrow$ Clear All
ESC [P_m h	Set Mode (SM) $P_s = 4 \rightarrow$ Insert Mode (IRM) $P_s = 2\,0 \rightarrow$ Automatic Newline (LNM)
ESC [P_m l	Reset Mode (RM) $P_s = 4 \rightarrow$ Insert Mode (IRM) $P_s = 2\,0 \rightarrow$ Automatic Linefeed (LNM)
ESC [P_m m	Character Attributes (SGR) $P_s = 0 \rightarrow$ Normal (default) $P_s = 1 \rightarrow$ Bold $P_s = 4 \rightarrow$ Underscore $P_s = 5 \rightarrow$ Blink (appears as Bold) $P_s = 7 \rightarrow$ Inverse
ESC [P_s n	Device Status Report (DSR) $P_s = 5 \rightarrow$ Status Report ESC [0 n $\rightarrow$ OK $P_s = 6 \rightarrow$ Report Cursor Position (CPR) [row;column] as ESC [r ; c R
ESC [P_s ; P_s r	Set Scrolling Region [top;bottom] (default = full size of window) (DECSTBM)
ESC [P_s x	Request Terminal Parameters (DECREQTPARM)
ESC [? P_m h	DEC Private Mode Set (DECSET) $P_s = 1 \rightarrow$ Application Cursor Keys (DECCKM) $P_s = 2 \rightarrow$ Designate USASCII for character sets G0-G3. (In the VT102, this selects VT52 mode (DECANM), which *xterm* doesn't support.) $P_s = 3 \rightarrow$ 132 Column Mode (DECCOLM) $P_s = 4 \rightarrow$ Smooth (Slow) Scroll (DECSCLM) $P_s = 5 \rightarrow$ Reverse Video (DECSCNM) $P_s = 6 \rightarrow$ Origin (Cursor) Mode (DECOM) $P_s = 7 \rightarrow$ Wraparound Mode (DECAWM) $P_s = 8 \rightarrow$ Auto-repeat Keys (DECARM) $P_s = 9 \rightarrow$ Send Mouse Row & Column (X & Y) on button press (see "Mouse Tracking") $P_s = 3\,8 \rightarrow$ Enter TekTronix Mode (DECTEK) $P_s = 4\,0 \rightarrow$ Allow 80 $\leftrightarrow$ 132 Mode $P_s = 4\,1 \rightarrow$ *curses*(5) fix $P_s = 4\,4 \rightarrow$ Turn On Margin Bell $P_s = 4\,5 \rightarrow$ Reverse-wraparound Mode $P_s = 4\,6 \rightarrow$ Start Logging

$P_s = \boxed{4}\boxed{7}$ → Use Alternate Screen Buffer (unless disabled by the titeInhibit resource)

$P_s = \boxed{1}\boxed{0}\boxed{0}\boxed{0}$ → Send Mouse Row & Column (X & Y) on button press and release; see "Mouse Tracking"

$P_s = \boxed{1}\boxed{0}\boxed{0}\boxed{1}$ → Use Hilite Mouse Tracking; see "Mouse Tracking"

$\boxed{\text{ESC}}\boxed{[}\boxed{?}P_m\boxed{l}$ DEC Private Mode Reset (DECRST)

$P_s = \boxed{1}$ → Normal Cursor Keys (DECCKM)

$P_s = \boxed{3}$ → 80 Column Mode (DECCOLM)

$P_s = \boxed{4}$ → Jump (Fast) Scroll (DECSCLM)

$P_s = \boxed{5}$ → Normal Video (DECSCNM)

$P_s = \boxed{6}$ → Normal Cursor Mode (DECOM)

$P_s = \boxed{7}$ → No Wraparound Mode (DECAWM)

$P_s = \boxed{8}$ → No Auto-repeat Keys (DECARM)

$P_s = \boxed{9}$ → Don't Send Mouse Row & Column (X & Y) on button press

$P_s = \boxed{4}\boxed{0}$ → Disallow 80 ↔ 132 Mode

$P_s = \boxed{4}\boxed{1}$ → No *curses*(5) fix

$P_s = \boxed{4}\boxed{4}$ → Turn Off Margin Bell

$P_s = \boxed{4}\boxed{5}$ → No Reverse-wraparound Mode

$P_s = \boxed{4}\boxed{6}$ → Stop Logging

$P_s = \boxed{4}\boxed{7}$ → Use Normal Screen Buffer

$P_s = \boxed{1}\boxed{0}\boxed{0}\boxed{0}$ → Don't send Mouse Row & Column (X & Y) on button press

$P_s = \boxed{1}\boxed{0}\boxed{0}\boxed{1}$ → Don't use/use Hilite Mouse Tracking

$\boxed{\text{ESC}}\boxed{[}\boxed{?}P_s\boxed{r}$ Restore DEC Private Mode values. The value of P_s previously saved is restored. (P_s values are the same as for DECSET. This escape sequence toggles between DECSET and DECRST.)

$P_s = \boxed{1}$ → Normal/Application Cursor Keys (DECCKM)

$P_s = \boxed{3}$ → 80/132 Column Mode (DECCOLM)

$P_s = \boxed{4}$ → Jump (Fast)/Smooth (Slow) Scroll (DECSCLM)

$P_s = \boxed{5}$ → Normal/Reverse Video (DECSCNM)

$P_s = \boxed{6}$ → Normal/Origin Cursor Mode (DECOM)

$P_s = \boxed{7}$ → No Wraparound/Wraparound Mode (DECAWM)

$P_s = \boxed{8}$ → Auto-repeat/No Auto-repeat Keys (DECARM)

$P_s = \boxed{9}$ → Don't send/send Mouse Row & Column (X & Y) on button press

$P_s = \boxed{4}\boxed{0}$ → Disallow/Allow 80 ↔ 132 Mode

$P_s = \boxed{4}\boxed{1}$ → Off/On *curses*(5) fix

$P_s = \boxed{4}\boxed{4}$ → Turn Off/On Margin Bell

$P_s = \boxed{4}\boxed{5}$ → No Reverse-wraparound/Reverse-wraparound Mode

$P_s = \boxed{4}\boxed{6}$ → Stop/Start Logging

$P_s = \boxed{4}\boxed{7}$ → Use Normal/Alternate Screen Buffer

$P_s = \boxed{1}\boxed{0}\boxed{0}\boxed{0}$ → Don't send/send Row & Column (X & Y) on button press and release

$P_s = \boxed{1}\boxed{0}\boxed{0}\boxed{1}$ → Don't use/use Hilite Mouse Tracking

ESC [? P_m s   Save DEC Private Mode values. P_s values are the same as for DECSET.

P_s = 1 → Normal/Application Cursor Keys (DECCKM)
P_s = 3 → 80/132 Column Mode (DECCOLM)
P_s = 4 → Jump (Fast)/Smooth (Slow) Scroll (DECSCLM)
P_s = 5 → Normal/Reverse Video (DECSCNM)
P_s = 6 → Normal/Origin Cursor Mode (DECOM)
P_s = 7 → No Wraparound/Wraparound Mode (DECAWM)
P_s = 8 → Auto-repeat/No Auto-repeat Keys (DECARM)
P_s = 9 → Don't send/send Mouse Row & Column (X & Y) on
         button press
P_s = 4 0 → Disallow/Allow 80 ↔ 132 Mode
P_s = 4 1 → Off/On *curses*(5) fix
P_s = 4 4 → Turn Off/On Margin Bell
P_s = 4 5 → No Reverse-wraparound/Reverse-wraparound Mode
P_s = 4 6 → Stop/Start Logging
P_s = 4 7 → Use Normal/Alternate Screen Buffer
P_s = 1 0 0 0 → Don't send/send Mouse Row & Column (X & Y)
         on button press and release
P_s = 1 0 0 1 → Don't use/use Hilite Mouse Tracking

ESC] P_s ; P_t BEL   Set Text Parameters

P_s = 0 → Change Window/Icon Name and Window Title to P_t
P_s = 1 → Change Window/Icon Name to P_t
P_s = 2 → Change Window Title to P_t
P_s = 4 6 → Change Log File to P_t (normally disabled by a compile-time option)
P_s = 5 0 → Change Font to P_t

ESC P_t ESC   Privacy Message (PM)
xterm implements no PM functions; P_t is ignored. P_t need not be printable characters.

ESC P_t ESC   Application Program Command (APC)
xterm implements no APC functions; P_t is ignored. P_t need not be printable characters.

ESC c   Full Reset (RIS)

ESC n   Locking Shift Select of G2 Character Set (LS2)

ESC o   Locking Shift Select of G3 Character Set (LS3)

ESC | Invoke the G3 Character Set as GR (LS3R). Has no visible effect in *xterm*.

ESC }   Invoke the G2 Character Set as GR (LS2R). Has no visible effect in *xterm*.

ESC ~   Invoke the G1 Character Set as GR (LS1R). Has no visible effect in *xterm*.

Mouse Tracking

The VT widget can be set to send the mouse position and other information on button presses. These modes are typically used by editors and other full-screen applications that want to make use of the mouse.

There are three mutually exclusive modes, each enabled (or disabled) by a different parameter in the DECSET (or DECRST) escape sequence. Parameters for all mouse tracking escape sequences generated by *xterm* encode numeric parameters in a single character as *value*+040. For example, is 1. The screen coodinate system is 1-based.

X10 compatibility mode sends an escape sequence on button press encoding the location and the mouse button pressed. It is enabled by specifying parameter 9 to DECSET. On button press, *xterm* sends `ESC` `[` `M` $C_b C_x C_y$ (6 characters). C_b is button-1. C_x and C_y are the x and y coordinates of the mouse when the button was pressed.

Normal tracking mode sends an escape sequence on both button press and release. Modifier information is also sent. It is enabled by specifying parameter 1000 to DECSET. On button press or release, *xterm* sends `ESC` `[` `M` $C_b C_x C_y$. The low two bits of C_b encode button information: 0=MB1 pressed, 1=MB2 pressed, 2=MB3 pressed, 3=release. The upper bits encode what modifiers were down when the button was pressed and are added together. 4=Shift, 8=Meta, 16=Control. C_x and C_y are the x and y coordinates of the mouse event. The upper-left corner is (1,1).

Mouse hilite tracking notifies a program of a button press, receives a range of lines from the program, highlights the region covered by the mouse within that range until button release, and then sends the program the release coordinates. It is enabled by specifying parameter 1001 to DECSET. Warning: use of this mode requires a cooperating program or it will hang *xterm*. On button press, the same information as for normal tracking is generated; *xterm* then waits for the program to send mouse tracking information. *All X events are ignored until the proper escape sequence is received from the pty:* `ESC` `[` P_s `;` P_s `;` P_s `;` P_s `T`. The parameters are *func*, *startx*, *starty*, *firstrow*, and *lastrow*. *func* is non-zero to initiate hilite tracking and zero to abort. *startx* and *starty* give the starting x and y location for the highlighted region. The ending location tracks the mouse, but will never be above row *firstrow* and will always be above row *lastrow*. (The top of the screen is row 1.) When the button is released, *xterm* reports the ending position one of two ways: if the start and end coordinates are valid text locations: `ESC` `[` `t` $C_x C_y$. If either coordinate is past the end of the line: `ESC` `[` `T` $C_x C_y C_x C_y C_x C_y$. The parameters are *startx*, *starty*, *endx*, *endy*, *mousex*, and *mousey*. *startx*, *starty*, *endx*, and *endy* give the starting and ending character positions of the region. *mousex* and *mousey* give the location of the mouse at button up, which may not be over a character.

Tektronix 4014 Mode

Most of these sequences are standard Tektronix 4014 control sequences. The major features missing are the write-thru and defocused modes. This document does not describe the commands used in the various Tektronix plotting modes, but does describe the commands to switch modes.

BEL	Bell (Ctrl-G)
BS	Backspace (Ctrl-H)
TAB	Horizontal Tab (Ctrl-I)
LF	Line Feed or New Line (Ctrl-J)
VT	Vertical Tab (Ctrl-K)
FF	Form Feed or New Page (Ctrl-L)
CR	Carriage Return (Ctrl-M)
ESC ETX	Switch to VT102 Mode
ESC ENQ	Return Terminal Status
ESC LF	PAGE (Clear Screen)
ESC ETB	COPY (Save Tektronix Codes to File)
ESC CAN	Bypass Condition
ESC SUB	GIN mode
ESC FS	Special Point Plot Mode
ESC GS	Graph Mode (same as GS)
ESC RS	Incremental Plot Mode (same as RS)
ESC US	Alpha Mode (same as US)
ESC 8	Select Large Character Set
ESC 9	Select #2 Character Set
ESC :	Select #3 Character Set
ESC ;	Select Small Character Set

ESC] P_s ; P_t BEL — Set Text Parameters
$P_s = \boxed{0} \rightarrow$ Change Window Name and Title to P_t
$P_s = \boxed{1} \rightarrow$ Change Icon Name to P_t
$P_s = \boxed{2} \rightarrow$ Change Window Title to P_t
$P_s = \boxed{4}\boxed{6} \rightarrow$ Change Log File to P_t

ESC `	Normal Z Axis and Normal (solid) Vectors
ESC a	Normal Z Axis and Dotted Line Vectors

`ESC` `b`	Normal Z Axis and Dot-Dashed Vectors
`ESC` `c`	Normal Z Axis and Short-Dashed Vectors
`ESC` `d`	Normal Z Axis and Long-Dashed Vectors
`ESC` `h`	Defocused Z Axis and Normal (solid) Vectors
`ESC` `i`	Defocused Z Axis and Dotted Line Vectors
`ESC` `j`	Defocused Z Axis and Dot-Dashed Vectors
`ESC` `k`	Defocused Z Axis and Short-Dashed Vectors
`ESC` `l`	Defocused Z Axis and Long-Dashed Vectors
`ESC` `p`	Write-Thru Mode and Normal (solid) Vectors
`ESC` `q`	Write-Thru Mode and Dotted Line Vectors
`ESC` `r`	Write-Thru Mode and Dot-Dashed Vectors
`ESC` `s`	Write-Thru Mode and Short-Dashed Vectors
`ESC` `t`	Write-Thru Mode and Long-Dashed Vectors
`FS`	Point Plot Mode
`GS`	Graph Mode
`RS`	Incremental Plot Mode
`US`	Alpha Mode

F

Translation Table Syntax

This appendix describes the basic syntax of translation table resources, described in Chapter 11, Setting Resources.

In This Appendix:

F
Translation Table Syntax

This appendix explains some of the more complex aspects of translation table syntax. It probably gives more detail than the average user will need but we've included it to help clarify this rather complicated topic.

Event Types and Modifiers

The syntax of the translation table is sufficiently general to encompass a wide variety of events and circumstances. Event translations can be specified to handle characteristic user interface idioms like double clicking, dragging, or combining keyboard modifiers with pointer button input. To specify translations that use these features, it is necessary to learn more about the detailed syntax used to specify translations.

An activity susceptible to translation is a sequence of events and modifiers (that perform an action). Events are specified in angle brackets and modifiers precede the event they modify. The legal events that can be specified in a translation are as shown in Table F-1.

Table F-1. Event Types and Their Abbreviations

Event Name	Event Type	Abbreviations/Synonyms
KeyPress	Keyboard	Key, KeyDown
KeyUp	Keyboard	KeyRelease
ButtonPress	Mouse Button	BtnDown
ButtonRelease	Mouse Button	BtnUp
Btn1Down	Mouse Button Press	
.		
.		
Btn5Down		
Btn1Up	Mouse Button Release	
.		
.		
Btn5Up		

Event Name	Event Type	Abbreviations/Synonyms
MotionNotify	Mouse Motion	Motion, MouseMoved, PtrMoved
ButtonMotion	Motion w/any Button Down	BtnMotion
Button1Motion	Motion w/Button Down	Btn1Motion
.		.
.		.
Button5Motion		Btn5Motion
EnterNotify	Mouse in Window	Enter, EnterWindow
LeaveNotify		LeaveWindow, Leave
FocusIn	Keyboard Input Focus	
FocusOut		
KeymapNotify	Changed Key Map	Keymap
ColormapNotify	Changed Color Map	Clrmap
Expose	Related Exposure Events	
GraphicsExpose		GrExp
NoExpose		NoExp
VisibilityNotify		Visible
CreateNotify	Window Management	Create
DestroyNotify		Destroy
UnmapNotify		Unmap
MapNotify		Map
MapRequest		MapReq
ReparentNotify		Reparent
ConfigureNotify		Configure
ConfigureRequest		ConfigureReq
GravityNotify		Grav
ResizeRequest		ResReq
CirculateNotify		Circ
CirculateRequest		CircReq
PropertyNotify		Prop
SelectionClear	Intra-client Selection	SelClr
SelectionRequest		SelReq
SelectionNotify		Select

The possible modifiers of an event are listed in the table. The modifiers Mod1 through Mod5 are highly system-dependent and may not be implemented by all servers.

Table F-2. Key Modifiers

Event Modifiers	Abbreviation
Ctrl	c
Meta	m
Shift	s
Lock	l
Any	
ANY	
None	
Mod1	1
.	.
.	.
Mod5	5

Detail Field

To provide finer control over the translation process, the event part of the translation can include an additional "detail." For example, if you want the event to require an additional keystroke, for instance, an A key, or a Control-T, then that keystroke can be specified as a translation detail. The default detail field is *ANY*.

The valid translation details are event-dependent. For example, to specify the above example for keypress events, you would use:

    <Key>A

and:

    Ctrl<Key>T

respectively.

Key fields can be specified by the keysym value, as well as by the keysym symbolic name. For example, the keysym value of the Delete key is 0xffff. Keysym values can be determined by examining the file *<X11/keysymdef.h>* or by using the *xmodmap* client. (See Chapter 14, *Setup Clients*, for information about *xmodmap*.) Unfortunately, with some translations the keysym value may actually be required, since not all keysym symbolic names may be properly interpreted.

Modifiers

Modifiers can be closely controlled to define exactly which events can be specified. For example, if you want the action to be performed by pointer button clicks but not by pointer button clicks with the Control or Shift key down, these limitations can be specified. Similarly, if you don't care if there are modifiers present, this can also be specified.

Table F-3 lists the available event modifiers.

Table F-3. Event Modifiers and Their Meanings

Modifier	Meaning
None *<event>*	No modifiers allowed.
<event>	Doesn't care. Any modifiers okay.
Mod1 Mod	Mod1 and Mod2, plus any others (i.e., anything that includes m1 and m2).
!Mod1 Mod2*<event>*	Mod1 and Mod2 but nothing else.
Mod1 ~Mod2*<event>*	Mod1 and not Mod2.

Complex Translation Examples

The following translation specifies that function *f* is to be invoked when both the Shift key and the third pointer button are pressed.

```
Shift<Btn3Down>: f()
```

To specify that both the Control and Shift keys are to be pressed use:

```
Ctrl Shift<Btn3Down>: f()
```

To specify an optional repeat count for an activity, put a number in parentheses after the action. The number refers to the whole translation. To make the last example require a double-click, with both Control and Shift keys pressed, use:

```
Ctrl Shift<Btn3Down>(2): f()
```

The server distinguishes between single-clicks and double-clicks based on a pre-programmed timing interval. If a second click occurs before the interval expires, then the event is interpreted as a double-click; otherwise the event is interpreted as two single-clicks. The variable clickTime is maintained deep in the internals of X. Unfortunately, thus far there is no way to set this time interval to match user preference. Currently it is set to be 200 milliseconds.

A translation involving two or more clicks can be specified as (2+) in the previous example. In general, a plus sign following the number *n* would mean *n* or more occurrences of the event.

Multiple events can be specified by separating them with commas on the translation line. To indicate pressing button 1, pressing button 2, then releasing button 1, and finally releasing button 2, use:

```
<Btn1Down>,<Btn2Down>,<Btn1Up>,<Btn2Up>: f()
```

Another way to describe this action in English would be to say "while button 1 is down, click button 2." "Meaningless" pointer movement is generally ignored. In the previous case, for example, if pointer motion occurred while the buttons were down, it would not interfere with detection of the event. Thus, inadvertent pointer jiggling will not thwart even the most complex user-input sequences.

G

Widget Resources

In addition to application-specific resources, you can specify resources for an application's component widgets. This appendix provides a brief overview of how widgets are used in X Toolkit programs. It then describes each of the Athena and Motif widgets, noting those widget resources a user can specify.

In This Appendix:

G
Widget Resources

As suggested on the reference pages for various clients, you can set not only resources defined by the application itself, but also resources that apply to any of the widgets that make up the application. The reference page for the application sometimes lists the most important of these resources, but for fuller customization, you need to know more about each widget.

Unfortunately, the design of the X Toolkit is such that to really do the right thing, you probably need to know a bit more about Toolkit programming than the average user might like.

In this appendix, we provide both some introductory concepts about how widgets are used in X Toolkit programs, and reference information about each class of widgets. If you are a Toolkit programmer or other sophisticated user, feel free to skip right to the widget reference section later in this appendix.

The Widget Class Hierarchy

The first thing you need to know is how widgets are built.

Rather than starting each widget from scratch, the widget programmer starts with a copy of another, more basic widget, and modifies it. This process is called *subclassing* the widget, and the sequence of widgets leading up to the one you see is called its *class hierarchy*. Because of the way subclassing works, a widget *inherits* all of the characteristics of its superclasses, except those that are explicitly overridden or changed.

The class hierarchy starts with a class called Object, which defines some basic characteristics common to all widgets—namely the ability to understand resources, and to be linked to applications via a mechanism referred to as a callback. When you click on a "quit" button, and the application quits, that is because the widget has communicated with the application via a callback.

RectObj is a subclass of Object. RectObj adds various resources having to do with the fact that widgets are rectangular: width, height, borderWidth, and x, y positions. RectObj also adds resources for sensitivity—the fact that a widget can be temporarily "disabled" by a client. For example, an application might disable a menu item that closes a file if no file is open.

Core is the first true widget in the class hierarchy. Object and RectObj don't have windows associated with them, and can never be "instantiated"— created and mapped to the screen. In fact, prior to Release 4, they were "invisible" even to Toolkit programmers, who simply assumed that Core was the root of the widget hierarchy.

The reason we now talk about Object and RectObj is that since R4, the Toolkit supports a different class of object, known colloquially as a gadget, which is subclassed directly from RectObj, and does not have a window associated with it. It can be used only within a widget that understands how to manage gadgets, and allocates some of its own window space to display them. This is typically done when there are many identical widgets. The only gadgets in the Athena widget set are the SmeBSB and SmeLine gadgets used to implement panes in a SimpleMenu widget. Motif offers its programmers both widget and gadget versions of many of its objects, including all kinds of command buttons.

At any rate, for most purposes, you can still act as though Core is the root of the widget hierarchy, since all widgets are subclassed from it, and therefore share all of its resources. The phrase "Core resources" is a fluke of terminology that can be misleading to new users. Because it sounds meaningful just as a general term, it isn't clear that the Core resources are really the resources of a particular widget class (rather than something magically recognized as central or "core" by the X Toolkit.)

Let's take a brief look at the some of the Core resources, which appear in Table G-1. The list includes resources inherited from Object and RectObj, plus those added by Core.

Table G-1. Core Resources

Name	Class
background	Background
borderColor	BorderColor
borderWidth	BorderWidth
height	Height
width	Width
x	Position0
y	Position0

Some of these Core resources set obvious characteristics of a widget: background (color), borderColor, and borderWidth (in pixels). height and width specify the dimensions of the widget in pixels. x and y represent the x,y coordinates of the widget in relation to its parent.

Note that Table G-1 isn't actually a complete list of all of the Core resources, but only of those that might be set by users. Some resources (such as callbacks) can only be set by programmers. The Toolkit doesn't even support a mechanism for understanding how to set them in a resource file.

In addition, font and foreground are two resources that are so common that you might expect them to be Core resources, but they are not. They are defined individually by each of the widget classes that use them. This can be confusing, especially since they do correspond to standard X Toolkit options. But really, it is hair-splitting to worry about where they are defined—they are sufficiently standard to fall under the colloquial understanding of Core resources.

Let's finish describing the base classes provided by the X Toolkit, which are common to all Xt-based widget sets, including both the Motif and the Athena widget sets.

There is a special class of widgets whose job is to manage the size and/or position of other widgets. These are called Composite widgets, and all such geometry-managing widgets are children of the Composite widget class. Composite inherits all of the characteristics of Core, and adds resources (settable only by the programmer) for identifying which widgets it should treat as its children.

Some simple geometry-managing widgets such as the Athena Box widget are direct sub-classes of Core. However, there is another, more complex class of geometry-managing widget defined by the X Toolkit Intrinsics, called Constraint. A constraint widget defines special resources, called constraint resources, that apply to its children rather than to itself. They are actually resources of the constraint widget, but are specified as if they were resources of the child. The clearest example of constraint resources is provided by the Athena Form widget, which allows widgets to be positioned with respect to one another, so that they always keep the same arrangement, even when the Form is resized. For example, *xcalc* is implemented using a Form widget. Resources such as:

```
    Form widget
        |   Command widget child of Form
        |       |       Constraint resource of Form appears to be resource of child
        |       |           |
    XCalc.ti.button12.fromHoriz:          button11
    XCalc.ti.button12.fromVert:           button7
```

specify that button12 (label PI) should always be next to button11 (label x!), and over button7 (label 7).

At any rate, there is one other subclass of Composite that bears mention: the Shell widget class. Shell widgets are simple composite widgets; they manage only one child—the application's main window, and they make themselves exactly the same size, so that they are hidden behind it. Even though you never see them, though, Shell widgets are extremely important, since they are the widgets that know how to interact with the window manager. Shell introduces several resources of importance to the application programmer, but only one of importance to the user: geometry (class Geometry).

There are actually six subclasses of Shell, two of which are for internal toolkit purposes and four of which are used by application programmers in different circumstances. For example, there is one kind of shell widget used for the main window of an application (class ApplicationShell) and another used as the parent of a popup widget like a menu (class OverrideShell) that should never be manipulated by the window manager. Notice that *mwm* doesn't reparent menus—they don't get a titlebar of their own, and can't be moved independently—this is because they are children of an OverrideShell, which overrides window manager intervention.

There is another class of shell widget, called a TransientShell, which is used for popups that can be manipulated by the window manager. An application might use a TransientShell for a dialog box that remains available on the screen and can be moved and resized separately, but not iconified. A TopLevelShell is used by an application that has more than one completely independent window, as the class for its secondary "top level" windows.

For all practical purposes, you don't need this much information about shell widgets. As we'll see shortly, the only reference to a shell widget in a resource specification is typically via the application name, which the shell widget takes as its own.

Returning to widgets that you actually do see and interact with, let's consider the class derivation of a widget like the Athena Command widget, which is used to implement buttons you can click on with the mouse to ask the application to do something.

The Athena Command widget is a subclass of the Label widget, which is a subclass of the Simple widget, which in turn is a subclass of Core. As a result, Command inherits all of the Core resources, plus the resources of the Athena Simple widget plus the resources of the Label widget—such as the ability to display a label, in a particular font. Command adds the ability (defined by the programmer, not the user) to call a particular application function when the button is clicked on. We'll come back to the complete Athena widget hierarchy later in the widget reference section.

Widgets in the Application

Widget inheritance of resources from superclasses is an important part of the background to understanding how to affect the widget resources in the application, but it is not the whole story. Let's talk for a moment about how these widgets are used.

To make things more concrete, let's look at an actual application. *xclipboard* is a good choice. It uses several different widget classes, but isn't too complex. Figure G-1 illustrates the widgets that make up *xclipboard*.

Every Toolkit application begins with a call to a function called XtAppInitialize(), which looks something like this:

```
top = XtAppInitialize(... , "XClipboard", ... );
```

The second argument to this function gives the class name of the application. This name becomes the start of any resource specification for the application. And we know that if *xclipboard* has an app-defaults file, it will be called *XClipboard*, since that name is taken from the class name of the application. Notice that there's no magic here: this is under the explicit control of the application programmer. If the application doesn't follow the conventions for the class and instance names, it needs to document the names that are used.

One of the things that XtAppInitialize() does is create a ApplicationShell widget. The variable name (before the equals sign), top, is the name that the programmer uses to refer to this widget whenever she needs to use it in the application. This name is completely irrelevant to the name the widget publishes for itself as its instance name.

Next, the program begins to create the widgets in the application, using a function called XtCreateManagedWidget(). The first widget to be created is the main application widget, which in this case is a Form widget.

```
parent = XtCreateManagedWidget("form", formWidgetClass, top, ... );
```

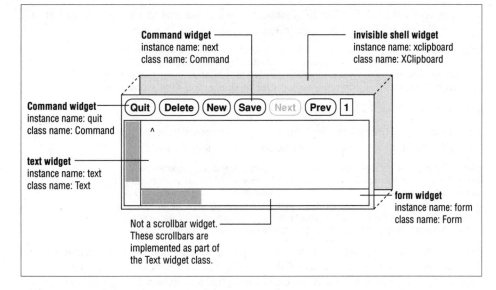

Command widget
instance name: next
class name: Command

invisible shell widget
instance name: xclipboard
class name: XClipboard

Command widget
instance name: quit
class name: Command

(Quit) (Delete) (New) (Save) (Next) (Prev) [1]

text widget
instance name: text
class name: Text

form widget
instance name: form
class name: Form

Not a scrollbar widget.
These scrollbars are
implemented as part of
the Text widget class.

Figure G-1. Anatomy of an X Toolkit application

The first argument to `XtCreateManagedWidget()` is the instance name of the widget (`form`)—this is the name that will be used to refer to it in resource files. The second argument is a symbol identifying which widget class this widget should be.

Notice that the instance name is entirely arbitrary, and depends completely on the whim of the application programmer. Many applications that use only one instance of a widget class will give it an instance name that mirrors the class name, except in lower case, as was done here. But you can see that the programmer could just as well have given the widget the instance name "foo" or "main" or "howdy_doody." The implication is that unless the client's man page documents a widget instance name, you won't know what to use in a resource file.*

The class name, on the other hand, is a part of the definition of a widget's class. It is always the same.

The third argument is the widget's parent—the geometry-managing widget that this widget will be displayed inside, and which will control its size and position. Notice that the parent of the form is `top`—the shell widget created by `XtAppInitialize()`. As noted earlier, Shell widgets take just one child, and resize themselves so they fit completely behind that child, and are invisible.

Remember, though, that the program's internal name for the shell widget is not important when it comes to resource specifications. The Shell widget takes its "resource name and class" from the `XtAppInitialize()` call.

---

*As of R4, most of the MIT client reference pages list the instance names of all the widgets in the application.

If you're following the flow of the argument, you can see that to refer to this widget in a resource file, you could use any of the following resource specifications:

```
xclipboard.form      instance name for both the shell widget and form widget
XClipboard.Form      class name for both the shell widget and form widget
XClipboard.form      class name for the shell, and instance name for the form
xclipboard.Form      instance name for the shell, and class name for the form
```

as well as any analogous loose bindings.

The `form` widget (named "parent" for internal reference within the application) is used in turn as the parent of the various command widgets and the text widget:

```
quit = XtCreateManagedWidget("quit", commandWidgetClass, parent, ... );
delete = XtCreateManagedWidget("delete", commandWidgetClass, parent, ... );
new = XtCreateManagedWidget("new", commandWidgetClass, parent, ... );
nextButton = XtCreateManagedWidget("next", commandWidgetClass, parent, ... );
prevButton = XtCreateManagedWidget("prev", commandWidgetClass, parent, ... );
text = XtCreateManagedWidget("text", textWidgetClass, parent, ... );
```

This "parent-child relationship" between Composite widgets and their children is what is expressed in the instance hierarchy of the widget. So, for example, the Command widget instance named `quit` is a child of the Form widget instance named `form`, which in turn is a child of a Shell widget, which takes as its name the application name `xclipboard`.

What All This Means

The fully-specified instance name of any widget in an application is determined by the parent-child relationships of every widget in the application. First, there is always a Shell widget, which takes as its name the application name. Then, there are one or more Composite widgets, which contain other widgets. Finally, at the end of the chain, you have a simple widget, with the resources it defines, as well as the resources it inherits from its superclasses.

Don't confuse the class names of the widgets in the instance hierarchy with the class inheritance hierarchy of each widget. Figure G-2 tries to make the relationships clear.

In Figure G-2, the `quit` widget gets its instance name from the relationship of widgets within the application. But it gets its resources from the class hierarchy of the widgets that the programmer used to develop the Command widget class.

Remember that the instance names of the widgets are completely arbitrary; even though it is not unusual to see a Form widget with the instance name `form`, there is nothing required about this. As a result, you need to look at the documentation for the application, not the widget, to find out the appropriate instance names.

The resources that a given widget class has are the result of its class inheritance hierarchy, which is defined by the widget programmer who originally designed the widget class. Thus, when you want to set resources for a widget like Command, you need to look not only in the section of this appendix that describes Command and its resources, but also the sections on each of its superclasses.

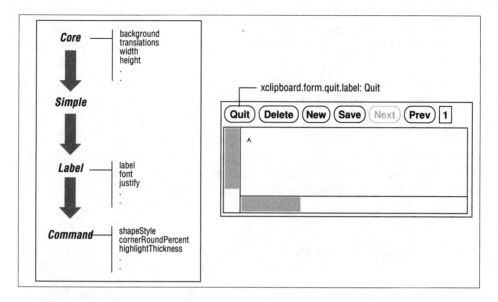

Figure G-2. Resource names and class inheritance

Complications

There are a number of provisos that modify this (hopefully by now clear and simple) picture:

- Even though a widget inherits a resource, it may not use it. For example, the Command widget class inherits the borderWidth resource from the Core widget class, but it does not actually use this information to redraw its border if you change the resource. A resource is just data you provide to the widget. Whether or not the widget does anything with that data is up to its designer. If you set a resource and nothing seems to happen, you might have done something wrong ... but you might also have set the resource correctly, and the widget simply chose to ignore it.

- Even when a widget does use a resource, you can't necessarily set it from a resource file. There are two reasons for this:

  — The programmer has the option to "hardcode" the value of a resource when creating a widget. If he does this, all resource specifications for that resource are ignored.

  — Some resources are designed only for programmer use. Some of these can't ever be specified in a resource file, since the data type of the resource isn't a text string, and the Toolkit doesn't provide any automatic conversion. (Features like colors can be specified in resource files, even though a color name is not actually the color itself, because the X Toolkit automatically converts a color name to the appropriate internal format).

The following pages document only resources that are theoretically settable from resource files. (That is, if no converter exists, we've assumed that the resource is only for programmer use and have deleted it from the list.) However, there are many other resources listed that are most likely hardcoded by the programmer. Unfortunately, there is no way to tell in advance whether they will or will not be hardcoded in a particular application.

- The "default values" listed for each widget resource may or may not apply to an actual application. These are the default values for the widget. An application can override them, either in the program code, or in an application defaults file. But inasmuch as the defaults are reasonable, they will usually be unchanged.

With this background, you're now ready to navigate the widget reference information contained in this appendix. For each widget and gadget in the Athena and Motif widget sets, we've given a brief description, a summary of its class hierarchy, and a list of the new resources it defines.

Athena Widget Resources

All of the standard MIT applications described in this book have been built using the Athena widget set. Figure G-3 shows the complete class hierarchy of the Athena widgets. The widgets shown in gray are defined by the X Toolkit intrinsics, and are common to all Xt-based widget sets.

The *listres* application, without any arguments, lists the inheritance hierarchy for each of the Athena widgets. Given the name of any widget class, it lists all of the resources for that widget, and which superclass they are inherited from. For example:

```
% listres label
WidgetClass                  Instance  Class            Type
-----------                  --------  -----            ----
label:  Core\Simple\Label
Core                 accelerators  Accelerators     AcceleratorTable
Core               ancestorSensitive  Sensitive      Boolean
Core                  background  Background       Pixel
Core            backgroundPixmap  Pixmap           Pixmap
Label                    bitmap  Pixmap           Bitmap
Core                borderColor  BorderColor      Pixel
Core               borderPixmap  Pixmap           Pixmap
Core                borderWidth  BorderWidth      Dimension
Core                  colormap  Colormap         Colormap
Simple                    cursor  Cursor           Cursor
Simple                cursorName  Cursor           String
Core                      depth  Depth            Int
Core             destroyCallback  Callback         Callback
Label                  encoding  Encoding         UnsignedChar
Label                      font  Font             FontStruct
Label                foreground  Foreground       Pixel
Core                      height  Height           Dimension
Simple          insensitiveBorder  Insensitive      Pixmap
Label              internalHeight  Height           Dimension
Label               internalWidth  Width            Dimension
Label                    justify  Justify          Justify
Label                      label  Label            String
Label                  leftBitmap  LeftBitmap       Bitmap
```

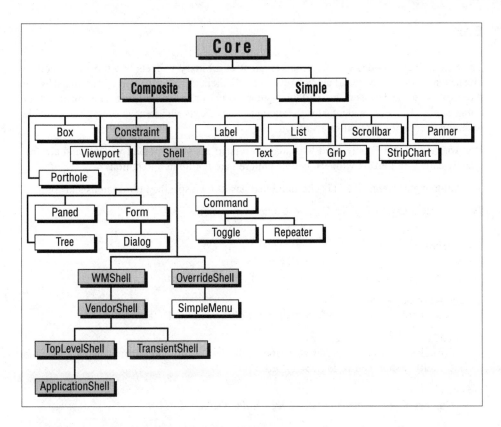

Figure G-3. Inheritance among the Athena widgets

```
Core            mappedWhenManaged  MappedWhenManaged   Boolean
Simple                pointerColor  Foreground          Pixel
Simple      pointerColorBackground  Background          Pixel
Label                       resize  Resize              Boolean
Core                        screen  Screen              Screen
Core                     sensitive  Sensitive           Boolean
Core                  translations  Translations        TranslationTable
Core                         width  Width               Dimension
Core                             x  Position            Position
Core                             y  Position            Position
```

Not all of the resources listed by *listres* can be set in a resource file. However, this listing can provide a handy quick reference.

The rest of this section provides more detailed information on the Athena widgets and their resources. For each widget, there is a brief description and a list of the new resources defined by the widget. Note that these resource lists include only those resources that can be set in resource files; they are not complete lists. For the full reference material on the Athena widgets, see Volume Five, *X Toolkit Intrinsics Reference Manual*.

Box

The Box widget provides geometry management of arbitrary widgets in a box of a specified dimension. Box moves but does not resize its children. The children are rearranged when the Box is resized, when its children are resized, or when children are managed or unmanaged. The Box widget always attempts to pack its children as closely as possible within the geometry allowed by its parent.

Box widgets are commonly used to manage a related set of Command widgets and are frequently called ButtonBox widgets, but the children are not limited to buttons.

The children are arranged on a background that has its own specified dimensions and color.

The class hierarchy for Box is: Core → Composite → Box.

Resources

The following new resources are associated with the Box widget:

hSpace (class HSpace)
> Number of pixels to the left or to the right of each child. Default is 4.

orientation (class Orientation)
> Specifies whether the preferred shape of the box is tall and narrow (vertical, the default) or short and wide (horizontal).

vSpace (class VSpace)
> Number of pixels above or below each child. Default is 4.

Command

The Command widget is an area, often rectangular, that contains a text or pixmap label and calls an application function when "pressed" with a pointer button. This selectable area is sometimes referred to as a "button." When the pointer cursor is on the button, the button border is highlighted to indicate that the button is ready for selection. When a pointer button is pressed, the command widget indicates that it has been selected by reversing its foreground and background colors.

The class hierarchy for Command is: Core → Simple → Label → Command.

Resources

The following new resources are associated with the Command widget:

highlightThickness (class Thickness)
> The thickness of the line drawn when the button is highlighted.

shapeStyle (class ShapeStyle)
> Nonrectangular buttons may be created using this resource. Nonrectangular buttons are supported only on a server that supports the Shape Extension. If nonrectangular

buttons are specified for a server lacking this extension, the shape is ignored and the widgets will be rectangular. The following shape names are currently supported: `rectangle`, `oval`, `ellipse`, and `roundedRectangle`.

cornerRoundPercent (class `CornerRoundPercent`)

When a `ShapeStyle` of `roundedRectangle` is used, this resource controls the radius of the rounded corner. The radius of the rounded corners is specified as a percentage of the length of the shortest side of the widget.

Dialog

The Dialog widget prompts you for additional input. The typical Dialog widget contains three areas. The first line contains a description of the function of the Dialog widget, for example, the string *Filename:*. The second line contains an area into which you type input. The third line can contain buttons that let you confirm or cancel the Dialog input.

Dialog is not really a widget, but an interface to a widget. It might also be thought of as a compound widget. It includes a label widget, a command widget, and a text widget as components. These could theoretically appear as subwidgets in a resource specification.

The class hierarchy for Dialog is: Core → Composite → Constraint → Form → Dialog

Resources

The following new resources are associated with the Dialog widget:

icon (class `Icon`)

The name of a pixmap to be displayed immediately to the left of the Dialog widget's label.

label (class `Label`)

A Latin1 string to be displayed at the top of the Dialog widget.

value (class `Value`)

An initial value for the string field into which you will enter text. By default, no text entry field is available. Specifying an initial value for `value` activates the text entry field. If string input is desired but no initial value is to be specified, then set this resource to `" "` (empty string).

Form

The Form widget can contain an arbitrary number of children of any class. The Form provides geometry management for its children, including individual control of the position of each child. The initial positions of the children may be computed relative to the positions of other children. When the Form is resized, it computes new positions and sizes for its children.

The class hierarchy for Form is: Core → Composite → Constraint → Form

Resources

The following new resource is associated with the Form widget:

defaultDistance (class Thickness)
> Specifies the default value for horizDistance and vertDistance. This value is four pixels, by default. The default width of the Form is the minimum width needed to enclose the children after computing their initial layout, with a margin of default-Distance at the right and bottom edges. If a width and height is assigned to the Form that is too small for the layout, the children will be clipped by the right and bottom edges of the Form.

Form is a subclass of Constraint, which means it has a special kind of resources called constraint resources. These resources apply to—and are specified as if they belong to—the child of the Form rather than to the Form itself. For example, *xcalc* uses a Form widget to organize its buttons. The resources below apply to the buttons, rather than to the Form (e.g., xcalc.ti.button11.horizDistance : 4). Form specifies the following constraint resources for its children:

bottom (class Edge)
top (class Edge)
left (class Edge)
right (class Edge)
> Specify how to reposition the bottom, top, left, and right, respectively, of a child widget when the Form is resized. These resources can take one of five values. The values ChainTop, ChainBottom, ChainLeft, and ChainRight maintain a constant distance from an edge of the child to the top, bottom, left, and right edges, respectively, of the Form. The value Rubber (default) maintains a proportional distance from the edge of the child to the left or top edge of the Form. The proportion is determined from the initial position of the child and the initial size of the Form.

fromHoriz (class Widget)
horizDistance (class Thickness)
> Specify a child widget's horizontal position relative to another widget within the Form. fromHoriz is the name of the widget relative to which the child widget is placed, and horizDistance is the number of pixels separating the two widgets. For example, if horizDistance is 10, the child widget will be placed 10 pixels to the right of the widget defined in fromHoriz. If fromHoriz is not defined, then horizDistance is measured from the left edge of the Form.

fromVert (class Widget)
vertDistance (class Thickness)
> Similar to previous resources, except that fromVert and vertDistance position a child widget by a specified number of pixels *vertically* away from a specified widget. If no widget is specified for fromVert, then vertDistance is measured from the top of the Form.

resizable (class Boolean)
    Specifies whether children are allowed to resize themselves. Default is False.

Grip

The Grip widget provides a small region that accepts button presses and button releases. The Grip widget is typically used as an attachment point for visually repositioning an object (for example, the pane border in a Paned widget).

The class hierarchy for Grip is: Core → Simple → Grip

Resources

Grip does not have any new user-settable resources associated with it. The following Core resources may be useful with the Grip widget: foreground, width, height, border-Width.

Label

A Label is a non-editable text string or pixmap that is displayed within a window. The string may contain multiple lines of Latin1 characters. It can be aligned to the left, right, or center of its window. A Label can be neither selected nor directly edited by the user.

The class hierarchy for Label is: Core → Simple → Label

Resources

The following new resources are associated with the Label widget:

bitmap (class Pixmap)
    Specifies a bitmap to display in place of the text label. In a resource file, the resource should be specified as the name of a file in the bitmap utility format that is to be loaded into a pixmap. The string can be an absolute or a relative filename. If a relative filename is used, the directory specified by the resource name bitmapFilePath or the resource class BitmapFilePath is added to the beginning of the specified filename. If the bitmapFilePath resource is not defined, the default directory on a POSIX-based system is */usr/include/X11/bitmaps*.

encoding (class Encoding)
    Specifies whether the widget uses 8-bit or 16-bit text functions. New in R5.

font (class font)
    The font of the label.

foreground (class Foreground)
    The color of the text string or pixmap.

`internalHeight` (class `Height`)

> Represents the distance in pixels between the top and bottom of the label text or bitmap and the horizontal edges of the Label widget. Default is 2 pixels.

`internalWidth` (class `Width`)

> Represents the distance in pixels between the ends of the label text or bitmap and the vertical edges of the Label widget. Default is 4 pixels.

`justify` (class `Justify`)

> Specifies left, center, or right alignment of the label string within the Label widget. One of the values `left`, `center`, or `right` can be specified.

`label` (class `Label`)

> Specifies the text string that is to be displayed in the button if no bitmap is specified. Note that the label may be hardcoded by the application.

`leftBitmap` (class `LeftBitmap`)

> Specifies the name of a bitmap to display in the left margin of the Label. All 1's in the bitmap are rendered in the foreground color and all 0's will be drawn in the background color. New in R5.

`resize` (class `Resize`)

> A Boolean value that specifies whether the Label widget should attempt to resize to its preferred dimensions whenever `XtSetValues` is called for it. Default is `True`. Not usually set by users.

List

The List widget is a rectangle that contains a list of text strings formatted into rows and columns. When one of the strings is selected, it is highlighted, and an application callback routine is invoked. Only one string may be selected at a time. Note that most of the List resources are for application use.

The class hierarchy for List is: Core → Simple → List

Resources

The following new resources are associated with the List widget:

`columnSpacing` (class `Spacing`)
`rowSpacing` (class `Spacing`)

> Specify the amount of space in pixels between each of the columns and rows in the list. The defaults are 6 pixels between columns and 4 pixels between rows.

`defaultColumns` (class `Columns`)

> Specifies the default number of columns, which is used when neither the width nor the height of the List widget is specified or when `forceColumns` is `True`. The default is 2.

forceColumns (class Columns)

Specifies that the default number of columns is to be used no matter what the current size of the List widget is. The default is False.

font (class Font)

Specifies the font to be used to display the list.

foreground (class Foreground)

Specifies the color to be used to paint the text of the list elements.

internalHeight (class Height)

Represents a margin, in pixels, between the top and bottom of the list and the edges of the List widget. Default is 2 pixels.

internalWidth (class Width)

Represents a margin, in pixels, between the left and right edges of the list and the edges of the List widget. Default is 4 pixels.

longest (class Longest)

Specifies the length, in pixels, of the longest string in the current list. If the client knows the length, it should specify it; otherwise, the List widget computes a default length by searching through the list. This value is not typically set in resource files.

numberStrings (class NumberStrings)

Specifies the number of strings in the current list. If a value is not specified, the list must be NULL-terminated. This value is not typically set in resource files.

pasteBuffer (class Boolean)

If this is True, then the value of the string selected will be put into X cut buffer 0. The default is False. (Normally, the selected item is simply passed to the application. For example, a filename might be passed to the application's "open" routine.)

verticalList (class Boolean)

If this is True, the elements in the list are arranged vertically; if False, the elements are arranged horizontally.

MenuButton

The MenuButton widget is a subclass of the Command widget that is used to pop-up a menu. It is an area, often rectangular, that contains a text or pixmap label. This selectable area is referred to as a button. When the pointer cursor is on the button, the button border is highlighted to indicate that the button is ready for selection. When pointer button 1 is pressed, the MenuButton widget pops up the menu that has been named in the menuName resource.

The class hierarchy for MenuButton is: Core → Simple → Label → Command → Menu-Button

Resources

MenuButton has the menuName resource associated with it, but this resource can only be set in application code.

Paned

The Paned widget manages children in a vertically or horizontally tiled fashion. You may resize these panes by using the *grips* that appear near the right or bottom edge of the border between two panes.

When you position the pointer on a grip, pressing the pointer button will display an arrow that indicates which pane is being resized. By keeping the pointer button down, you can move the pointer up and down (or left and right). This, in turn, changes the border between the panes, causing one pane to shrink and some other pane (or panes) to grow. The size of the Paned widget will not change.

The choice of panes that are resized is a function of the min, max, and skipAdjust constraints on the other panes. With the default bindings, button 1 resizes the pane above or to the left of the selected grip, button 3 resizes the pane below or to the right of the selected grip, and button 2 repositions the border between two panes only.

The class hierarchy for Paned is: Core → Composite → Constraint → Paned

Resources

The following new resources are associated with the Paned widget:

betweenCursor (class Cursor)
> Cursor that is displayed when you are changing the boundary between two panes.

cursor (class Cursor)
> Pointer cursor image that is displayed whenever the pointer is in this widget but not in any of its children (children may also inherit this cursor).

gripCursor (class Cursor)
> Cursor that is displayed for the grip when it is not active.

gripIndent (class GripIndent)
> Offset of grip from margin (in pixels). Default is 16.

gripTranslations (class Translations)
> Button bindings for the grip.

horizontalBetweenCursor (class Cursor)
> Cursor that is displayed for the grip when you are changing the boundary between two horizontal panes. Default is sb_up_arrow.

horizontalGripCursor (class Cursor)
> Cursor that is displayed for the grips in a horizontal Paned widget when they are not active. Default is sb_h_double_arrow.

internalBorderColor (class BorderColor)
>   Internal border color of the widget's window.

internalBorderWidth (class BorderWidth)
>   Amount of space (in pixels) kept between panes. Default is 1.

leftCursor (class Cursor)
>   Cursor used when resizing the pane to the left of the grip. Default is
>   sb_left_arrow.

lowerCursor (class Cursor)
>   Cursor used when resizing the pane below the grip. Default is sb_down_arrow.

orientation (class Orientation)
>   Orientation to use in stacking the panes. This value can be either vertical (the
>   default) or horizontal.

refigureMode (class Boolean)
>   A Boolean that specifies whether the Paned widget should adjust its children. Default
>   is True.

rightCursor (class Cursor)
>   Cursor used when resizing the pane to the right of the grip. Default is
>   sb_right_arrow.

upperCursor (class Cursor)
>   Cursor used when resizing the pane above the grip. Default is sb_up_arrow.

verticalBetweenCursor (class Cursor)
>   Cursor that is displayed for the grip when you are changing the boundary between two
>   vertical panes. Default is sb_left_arrow.

verticalGripCursor (class Cursor)
>   Cursor that is displayed for the grips in a vertical Paned widget when they are not
>   active. Default is sb_v_double_arrow.

Paned is a subclass of Constraint, which means it has special kind of resources called constraint resources. These resources apply to—and are specified as if they belong to—the child of the Paned widget rather than to the Paned widget itself. Paned specifies the following constraint resources for its children:

allowResize (class Boolean)
>   A Boolean that specifies whether to accept the child's request to resize. The default,
>   False, is to ignore such requests.

max (class Max)
>   Maximum height for the pane (in pixels). Default is to allow unlimited height.

min (class Min)
>   Minimum height for the pane (in pixels). Default is 1.

preferredPaneSize (class PreferredPaneSize)
>   Preferred size of the pane.

resizeToPreferred (class Boolean)
:   A Boolean that specifies whether to resize the pane to its preferred size when the Paned widget is resized. Default is `False`.

showGrip (class ShowGrip)
:   A Boolean that specifies whether to show a grip for the pane. Default is `True`.

skipAdjust (class Boolean)
:   Specifies whether the Paned widget will automatically resize the pane. The default is `False`, which means that the Paned widget will resize the pane automatically whenever necessary. If the resource is `True`, the Paned widget will skip the adjustment of the pane.

Panner

The Panner widget is conceptually a two-dimensional scrollbar. It displays a rectangle within a rectangle—the inner rectangle (the "slider") represents the visible portion of a larger area (the "canvas") represented by the outer rectangle. The size of the inner rectangle represents the size of the visible area relative to the whole, and its position indicates the relative position of the visible area within the whole. You may drag the inner rectangle with the mouse (or use keyboard arrow keys) to pan through the large diagram or document (or whatever) that is being displayed. The Panner widget is typically used with a Porthole widget to scroll a third widget in two dimensions.

The Panner widget is a new Athena widget in R5.

The class hierarchy for Panner is: Core → Simple → Panner

Resources

The following new resources are associated with the Panner widget:

allowOff (class AllowOff)
:   Whether to allow the edges of the slider to go off the edges of the canvas. The default is `False`.

backgroundStipple (class BackgroundStipple)
:   The name of a bitmap pattern to be used as the background for the area representing the canvas.

canvasHeight (class CanvasHeight)
:   The height of the canvas.

canvasWidth (class CanvasWidth)
:   The width of the canvas.

defaultScale (class DefaultScale)
:   The percentage size that the Panner widget should have relative to the size of the canvas. Default is 8.

`foreground` (class `Foreground`)
> The slider foreground color.

`internalSpace` (class `InternalSpace`)
> The width of the internal border in pixels between a slider representing the full size of the canvas and the edge of the Panner widget. Default is 4.

`lineWidth` (class `LineWidth`)
> The width of the lines in the rubberbanding rectangle when rubberbanding is in effect instead of continuous scrolling. The default is 0.

`resize` (class `Resize`)
> Whether or not to resize the Panner whenever the canvas size is changed so that the `defaultScale` is maintained. Default is `True`.

`rubberBand` (class `RubberBand`)
> Whether or not scrolling should be discrete (only moving a rubberbanded rectangle until the scrolling is done) or continuous (moving the slider itself). Default is `False`, which means that the slider is moved.

`shadowColor` (class `shadowColor`)
> The color of the shadow underneath the slider.

`shadowThickness` (class `ShadowThickness`)
> The width of the shadow underneath the slider.

`sliderX` (class `SliderX`)
`sliderY` (class `SliderY`)
> The X and Y locations of the slider in the coordinates of the canvas.

`sliderHeight` (class `sliderHeight`)
`sliderWidth` (class `sliderWidth`)
> The height and width of the slider.

Porthole

The Porthole widget provides geometry management of a list of arbitrary widgets, only one of which may be managed at any particular time. The managed child widget is reparented within the porthole and is moved around by the application (typically under the control of a Panner widget). The Porthole widget allows its managed child to request any size that is as large or larger than the Porthole itself and any location so long as the child still obscures all of the Porthole.

The Porthole widget is a new Athena widget in R5.

The class hierarchy for Porthole is: Core → Composite → Porthole

Resources

The Porthole widget does not have any new user-settable resources associated with it.

Repeater

The Repeater widget is a version of the Command button that triggers at an increasing rate while it is held down. It is typically used to implement valuators or certain types of scrollbars.

The Repeater widget is a new Athena widget in R5.

The class hierarchy for Repeater is: Core → Simple → Label → Command → Repeater

Resources

The following new resources are associated with the Repeater widget:

decay (class Decay)
> The number of milliseconds to subtract from the repeat interval after each repetition. The interval starts at repeatDelay and decreases to minimumDelay. The default is 5 milliseconds.

flash (class Boolean)
> Whether or not to flash the Repeater button whenever the timer goes off. The default is False.

initialDelay (class Delay)
> The number of milliseconds before the Repeater widget begins to repeat. The default is 200.

minimumDelay (class MinimumDelay)
> The minimum time between callbacks in milliseconds. The default is 10.

repeatDelay (class Delay)
> The number of milliseconds between repetitions, once the initialDelay has elapsed and the widget has begun to repeat. The actual delay interval will have decay milliseconds subtracted from it at each repetition until it reaches minimum-Delay.

Scrollbar

The Scrollbar widget is a rectangular area that contains a slide region and a thumb (slide bar). A Scrollbar can be used alone (to provide a graduated scale) or within a composite widget (for example, a Viewport). A Scrollbar can be aligned either vertically or horizontally.

When a Scrollbar is created, it is drawn with the thumb in a contrasting color. The thumb is normally used to scroll client data and to give visual feedback on the percentage of the client data that is visible.

The class hierarchy for Scrollbar is: Core → Simple → Scrollbar

Resources

You can set the dimensions of the Scrollbar two ways:

- By using the width and height resources, as you can for all widgets.

- By using the Scrollbar resources length and thickness, which are independent of the vertical or horizontal orientation.

The following new resources are associated with the Scrollbar widget:

foreground (class Foreground)
: The color used to draw the thumb.

length (class Length)
: Specifies the height for a vertical Scrollbar and the width for a horizontal Scrollbar. Default is 1 (pixel).

minimumThumb (class MinimumThumb)
: Smallest size, in pixels, to which the thumb can shrink. Default is 7.

orientation (class Orientation)
: Orientation of scrollbar. This value can be either vertical (the default) or horizontal. Not usually set in resource files.

scrollDCursor (class Cursor)
: The cursor used for scrolling backward in a vertical Scrollbar. Default is sb_down_arrow.

scrollHCursor (class Cursor)
: The cursor used when a horizontal Scrollbar is inactive. Default is sb_h_double_arrow.

scrollLCursor (class Cursor)
: The cursor used for scrolling forward in a horizontal Scrollbar. Default is sb_left_arrow.

scrollRCursor (class Cursor)
: The cursor used for scrolling backward in a horizontal Scrollbar. Default is sb_right_arrow.

scrollUCursor (class Cursor)
: The cursor used for scrolling forward in a vertical Scrollbar. Default is sb_up_arrow.

scrollVCursor (class Cursor)
: The cursor used when a vertical Scrollbar is inactive. Default is sb_v_double_arrow.

shown (class Shown)
: The size of the thumb, as a percentage of the length of the Scrollbar. Default is 0.0.

thickness (class Thickness)
> Specifies the width for a vertical Scrollbar and the height for a horizontal Scrollbar. Default is 14 (pixels).

thumb (class Thumb)
> The pixmap used to stipple the thumb. Default is None.

topOfThumb (class TopOfThumb)
> The location of the top of the thumb, as a percentage of the length of the Scrollbar.

Simple

The Simple widget defines characteristics that are inherited by non-composite widgets such as Labels, Lists, and Scrollbars. The Simple widget never appears in applications, but it does define resources that are inherited by its subclasses.

The class hierarchy for Simple is: Core → Simple

Resources

The following new resources are associated with the Simple widget:

cursor (class Cursor)
> The cursor to use within the widget. Default is none.

cursorName (class Cursor)
> Specifies a cursor by name from the standard cursor font to be used in the widget's window. New in R5.

insensitiveBorder (class Insensitive)
> The pixmap to use to indicate that the Simple widget cannot receive input. Default is GrayPixmap.

pointerColor (class Foreground)
> Specifies a foreground color used when creating the cursor specified in cursorName. New in R5.

pointerColorBackground (class Background)
> Specifies a background color used when creating the cursor specified in cursorName. New in R5.

SimpleMenu

The SimpleMenu widget is a container for menu entries. It is a direct subclass of Shell. This is the only part of the menu that actually contains a window, since each menu pane is a gadget (a widget without a window). SimpleMenu "glues" the individual menu entries together into one menu.

The class hierarchy for SimpleMenu is: Core → Composite → Shell → OverrideShell → SimpleMenu

Resources

The following new resources are associated with the SimpleMenu widget:

bottomMargin (class VerticalMargins)
topMargin (class VerticalMargins)
> The amount of space between the top or bottom of the menu and the menu entry closest to that edge. Default is 0.

cursor (class Cursor)
> The shape of the mouse pointer whenever it is in this widget.

label (class Label)
> This label will be placed at the top of the SimpleMenu and cannot be highlighted. The name of the label object is menuLabel, and it is of the class specified by the Label-Class resource. Using this name, it is possible to modify the label's attributes through the resource database. When the label is created, its label resource is hard-coded to the value of label and justify is hard-coded as center.

labelClass (class LabelClass)
> Specifies the type of Sme object created as the menu label. Possibilities are Sme, Sme-BSB, or SmeLine.

popupOnEntry (class PopupOnEntry)
> The XawPositionSimpleMenu action pops up the SimpleMenu with its label (or first entry) directly under the pointer, by default. To pop up the menu under another entry, the application can set this resource to the menu entry that *should* be under the pointer when the menu is popped up. This allows the application to offer the user a default menu entry that can be selected without moving the pointer. Not usually settable by the user.

rowHeight (class RowHeight)
> If this resource is 0 (the default), then each menu entry is given its desired height. If this resource has any other value, then all menu entries are forced to be rowHeight pixels high.

Sme

The Sme object is the base class for all menu entries that are children of SimpleMenu. While this object is intended mainly to be subclassed, it may be used in a menu to add blank space between menu entries.

The class hierarchy for Sme is: Object → RectObj → Sme

Resources

The Sme object does not have any new user-settable resources associated with it.

SmeBSB

The SmeBSB object is used to create a menu entry that contains a string and optional bitmaps in its left and right margins. The parent is expected to be a SimpleMenu. Since each menu entry is an independent object, the application is able to change the font, color, height, and other attributes of the menu entries on an entry-by-entry basis.

The class hierarchy for SmeBSB is: Object → RectObj → Sme → SmeBSB

Resources

The following new resources are associated with the SmeBSB object:

font (class Font)
> Specifies the font used by the menu entry.

foreground (class Foreground)
> Specifies the foreground color of the menu entry's window. This color is also used to render all 1's in leftBitmap and rightBitmap.

justify (class Justify)
> Specifies how the label is to be rendered between the left and right margins when the space is wider than the actual text. When specifying the justification from a resource file, the values left, center, or right may be used.

label (class Label)
> Specifies the string to be displayed in the menu entry. The exact location of this string within the bounds of the menu entry is controlled by the resources leftMargin, rightMargin, vertSpace, and justify.

leftBitmap (class LeftBitmap)
rightBitmap (class RightBitmap)
> Specifies a name of a bitmap to display in the left or right margin of the menu entry. All 1's in the bitmap are rendered in the foreground color of the entry and all 0's will be drawn in the background color of the SimpleMenu widget. The menu entry needs to be tall enough and the appropriate margin needs to be wide enough to accept the bitmap. If care is not taken, the bitmap might extend into either another menu entry or this entry's label.

leftMargin (class HorizontalMargins)
rightMargin (class HorizontalMargins)
> Specifies the amount of space (in pixels) to leave between the edge of the menu entry and the label string.

vertSpace (class VertSpace)
> Specifies the amount of vertical padding to place around the label of a menu entry. The label and bitmaps are always centered vertically within the menu. Values for this resource are expressed as a percentage of the font's height. The default value (25) increases the default height to 125% of the font's height.

SmeLine

The SmeLine object is used to add a horizontal line or menu separator to a SimpleMenu. Since each menu entry is an independent object, the application is able to change the color, height, and other attributes of the menu entries, on an entry-by-entry basis. This entry is not selectable, and does not highlight when the pointer cursor is over it.

The class hierarchy for SmeLine is: Object → RectObj → Sme → SmeLine

Resources

The following new resources are associated with the SmeLine object:

foreground (class Foreground)
> The foreground color of the menu entry's window.

lineWidth (class LineWidth)
> The width of the horizontal line to be displayed.

stipple (class Stipple)
> If a bitmap is specified for this resource, the line will be stippled through it. This allows the menu separator to be rendered as something more exciting than just a line. For instance, if the application defines a stipple that is a chain link, then menu separators will look like chains.

StripChart

The StripChart widget is used to provide a real-time graphic chart of a single value. This widget is used by *xload* to provide the load graph. It will read data from an application and update the chart at the interval specified by update.

The class hierarchy for StripChart is: Core → Simple → StripChart

Resources

The following new resources are associated with the StripChart widget:

highlight (class **Foreground**)
> The color that will be used to draw the scale lines on the graph.

jumpScroll (class **JumpScroll**)
> When the graph reaches the right edge of the window it must be scrolled to the left. This resource specifies the number of pixels it will jump. Smooth scrolling can be achieved by setting this resource to 1. The default is half the width of the widget.

minScale (class **Scale**)
> The minimum scale for the graph. The number of divisions on the graph will always be greater than or equal to this value. Default is 1.

update (class **Interval**)
> The number of seconds between graph updates. Each update is represented on the graph as a 1-pixel-wide line. Every **update** seconds, a new graph point will be added to the right end of the StripChart. Default is 10.

Text

A Text widget is a window that provides a way for an application to display one or more lines of text. The displayed text can reside in a file on disk or in a string in memory. An option also lets an application display a vertical Scrollbar in the Text window, letting you scroll through the displayed text. Other options allow an application to let you modify the text in the window or search for a specific string.

Three types of edit mode are available:

- Append-only
- Read-only
- Editable

Append-only mode lets you enter text into the window, while read-only mode does not. Text may be entered only if the insertion point is after the last character in the window. Editable mode lets you place the cursor anywhere in the text and modify the text at that position. The text cursor position can be modified by using the keystrokes or pointer buttons defined by the event bindings.

The Text widget is designed to separate the storage of text (source) from the painting of the text (sink). The Text widget proper coordinates the sources and sinks. The AsciiText widget is a subclass of the Text widget that automatically creates the source and sink for a client. Most applications will use AsciiText widgets for displaying and editing text.

The class hierarchy for Text is: Core → Simple → Text → AsciiText

Resources

The following new resources are associated with the Text widget:

autoFill (class AutoFill)
> A Boolean that specifies whether the Text widget will automatically break a line when you attempt to type into the right margin Default is False.

bottomMargin (class Margin)
topMargin (class Margin)
> Amount of space, in pixels, between the edge of the window and the corresponding edge of the text within the window. Default is 2.

displayCaret (class Output)
> A Boolean that specifies whether to display the text caret. Default is True.

displayPosition (class TextPosition)
> Character position of the first line. Default is 0.

insertPosition (class TextPosition)
> Character position of the caret. Default is 0.

leftMargin (class Margin)
rightMargin (class Margin)
> Amount of space, in pixels, between the edge of the window and the corresponding edge of the text within the window. Default is 2.

resize (class Resize)
> Whether the widget should attempt to resize to its preferred dimensions whenever its resources are modifies with XtSetValues().

scrollHorizontal (class Scroll)
scrollVertical (class Scroll)
> Control the placement of scrollbars on the left and bottom edges of the text widget. Possible values are textScrollAlways, textScrollWhenNeeded, and text-ScrollNever (the default).

selectTypes (class SelectTypes)
> An array of entries that specifies what is highlighted on each successive click in a sequence of multiclicks. Possible values in the array are: selectAll, select-Char, selectLine, selectNull, selectParagraph, selectPosition, and selectWord.

The following new resources are associated with the AsciiText widget:

echo (class Boolean)
> Whether or not to echo characters to the screen. Default is True. This resource is typically set by the application.

editType (class EditType)
> The edit mode of the widget. Possible values are textAppend, textEdit, and textRead. This resource is typically set by the application.

font (class Font)
>   The font used for the text.

string (class String)
>   The string for the text source. This resource is typically set by the application.

wrap (class Wrap)
>   Specifies how text wraps in the widget. Possible values are textWrapNever, textWrapLine, and textWrapWord.

Toggle

The Toggle widget is an area, often rectangular, containing a text or pixmap label. This widget maintains a Boolean state (e.g., True/False or On/Off) and changes state whenever it is selected. When the pointer is on the button, the button border is highlighted to indicate that the button is ready for selection. When pointer button 1 is pressed and released, the Toggle widget indicates that it has changed state by reversing its foreground and background colors, and its notify action is invoked. If the pointer is moved out of the widget before the button is released, the widget reverts to its normal foreground and background colors, and releasing the button has no effect. This behavior allows you to cancel an action.

Toggle buttons may also be part of a radio group. A radio group is a list of Toggle buttons in which no more than one Toggle may be set at any time.

The class hierarchy for Toggle is: Core → Simple → Label → Command → Toggle

Resources

The following new resources are associated with the Toggle widget:

radioGroup (class Widget)
>   Specifies another Toggle widget that is in the radio group to which this Toggle widget should be added. A radio group is a group of Toggle widgets, only one of which may be set at a time. If this value is NULL (the default), then the Toggle is not part of any radio group and can change state without affecting any other Toggle widgets. If the widget specified in this resource is not already in a radio group, then a new radio group is created containing these two Toggle widgets. No Toggle widget can be in multiple radio groups.

state (class State)
>   Specifies whether the Toggle widget is set (True) or unset (False). The default is False.

Tree

The Tree widget provides geometry management of arbitrary widgets arranged in a directed, acyclic graph (i.e., a tree). The hierarchy is constructed by attaching a constraint resource called `treeParent` to each child indicating which other node in the tree should be treated as the child's superior. The structure of the tree is shown by laying out the nodes in the standard format for tree diagrams with lines drawn to connect each node with its children.

The Tree sizes itself according to the needs of its children and is not intended to be resized by its parent. Instead, it is typically placed inside another composite widget (such as the Porthole or Viewport) that can be used to scroll around in the tree.

The class hierarchy for Tree is: Core → Composite → Constraint → Tree

Resources

The following new resources are associated with the Tree widget:

`autoReconfigure` (class `AutoReconfigure`)
> Whether or not to lay out the tree every time a node is added or removed. Default is `False`.

`foreground` (class `Foreground`)
> Foreground color for the widget.

`gravity` (class `Gravity`)
> Specifies the side of the widget from which the tree should grow. Valid values include `WestGravity`, `NorthGravity`, `EastGravity`, and `SouthGravity`.

`hSpace` (class `HSpace`)
`vSpace` (class `VSpace`)
> Amount of horizontal and vertical space, in pixels, to leave between the children. This resource also specifies the amount of space between the outermost children and the edge of the box.

`lineWidth` (class `LineWidth`)
> The width of the lines drawn between nodes that do not have a `treeGC` constraint resource and their inferiors in the tree.

Tree is a subclass of Constraint, which means it has special kind of resources called constraint resources. These resources apply to—and are specified as if they belong to—the children of the Tree rather than to the Tree itself. Tree specifies the following constraint resource for its children:

`treeParent` (class `TreeParent`)
> This specifies the superior node in the tree for this widget. The default is for the node to have no superior (and to therefore be at the top of the tree).

Viewport

The Viewport widget consists of a frame window, one or two Scrollbars, and an inner window (usually containing a child widget). The size of the frame window is determined by the viewing size of the data that is to be displayed and the dimensions to which the Viewport is created. The inner window is the full size of the data that is to be displayed and is clipped by the frame window. The Viewport widget controls the scrolling of the data directly.

When the geometry of the frame window is equal in size to the inner window, or when the data does not require scrolling, the Viewport widget automatically removes any scroll bars. The forceBars resource causes the Viewport widget to display any scroll bar permanently.

The class hierarchy for Viewport is: Core → Composite → Constraint → Viewport

Resources

The following new resources are associated with the Viewport widget:

allowHoriz (class Boolean)
allowVert (class Boolean)
> Flags to allow horizontal and vertical scroll bars. Default values are False. Setting the resource to True allows a Viewport child to increase in size horizontally or vertically.

forceBars (class Boolean)
> Flag to force display of scroll bars. Default value is False. Normally, when the geometry of the frame window is equal in size to the inner window, or when the data does not require scrolling, Viewport automatically removes any scroll bars. Setting forceBars to True causes the Viewport widget to display any scroll bar permanently.

useBottom (class Boolean)
> Flag to indicate whether the horizontal scrollbar is placed at the bottom or the top of the widget. Default is False, meaning to put the scrollbar on top.

useRight (class Boolean)
> Flag to indicate whether the vertical scrollbar is placed at the right or the left of the widget. Default is False, meaning to put the scrollbar on the left.

Motif Widget Resources

Commercial Motif applications build their user interfaces with components from the Motif widget set. Figure G-4 shows the complete class hierarchy of the Motif widgets. The widgets shown in gray are defined by the X Toolkit intrinsics, and are common to all Xt-based widget sets.

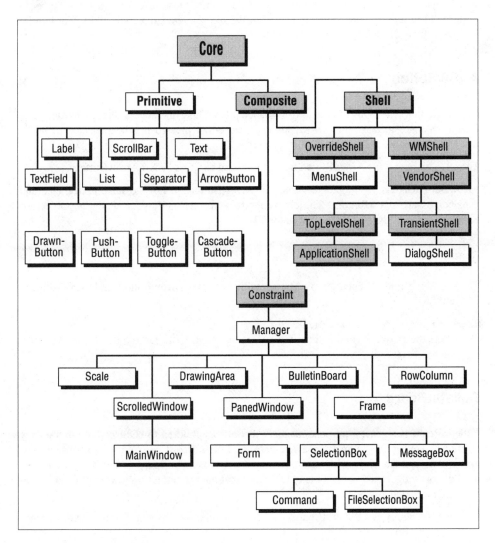

Figure G-4. Inheritance among the Motif widgets

Figure G-4 does not include the gadgets that are part of the Motif class hierarchy: Label-Gadget, SeparatorGadget, ArrowButtonGadget, CascadeButtonGadget, PushButtonGadget, and ToggleButtonGadget. As mentioned before, gadgets are essentially windowless widgets.

All of the Motif gadgets are subclassed from the Motif Gadget class, which is subclassed from RectObj.

The rest of this section provides more detailed information on each of the Motif widgets and gadgets and their resources. For each widget, there is a brief description and a list of the new resources defined by the widget. Since gadgets define the same new resources as their corresponding widgets, we've included the information on each gadget in the material for the relevant widget. Note that these resource lists include only those resources that can be set in resource files; they are not complete lists. For the full reference material on the Motif widgets, see Volume Six, *Motif Programming Manual*.

ArrowButton

An ArrowButton is a directional arrow-shaped button that includes a shaded border. The shading changes to make the ArrowButton appear either pressed in when selected or raised when unselected.

The class hierarchy for ArrowButton is: Core → XmPrimitive → XmArrowButton

ArrowButtonGadget is the gadget variant of ArrowButton. It has the same appearance and behavior as an ArrowButton. The class hierarchy for ArrowButtonsGadget is: Object → RectObj → XmGadget → XmArrowButtonGadget

Resources

The following new resource is associated with both the ArrowButton and ArrowButton-Gadget:

arrowDirection (class ArrowDirection)
> Sets the arrow direction. Possible values are ARROW_UP, ARROW_LEFT, ARROW_DOWN, RROW_RIGHT.

BulletinBoard

BulletinBoard is a general-purpose manager that allows children to be placed at arbitrary x,y positions. The simple geometry management of BulletinBoard can be used to enforce margins and to prevent child widgets from overlapping. BulletinBoard is the base widget for most dialog widgets and defines many resources that have an effect only when it is an immediate child of a DialogShell.

The class hierarchy for BulletinBoard is: Core → Composite → Constraint → XmManager → XmBulletinBoard

Resources

The following new resources are associated with the BulletinBoard widget:

allowOverlap (class AllowOverlap)
> If True (default), child widgets are allowed to overlap.

buttonFontList (class ButtonFontList)
> The font list used for the button children of the BulletinBoard widget. If this value is initially NULL, the font list is derived from the buttonFontList resource found in the nearest ancestor that is a subclass of BulletinBoard, VendorShell, or MenuShell.

defaultPosition (class DefaultPosition)
> If True (default) and if the BulletinBoard is the child of a DialogShell, then the BulletinBoard is centered relative to the DialogShell's parent.

dialogTitle (class DialogTitle)
> The dialog title. Setting this resource also sets the resources title and title-Encoding in a parent that is a subclass of WMShell.

labelFontList (class LabelFontList)
> Like the buttonFontList resource, but for Label children.

marginHeight (class MarginHeight)
marginWidth (class MarginWidth)
> Minimum spacing between a BulletinBoard's top or bottom edge and any child widget or its right or left edge and any child widget.

noResize (class NoResize)
> If False (default), *mwm* includes resize controls in the window manager frame of the BulletinBoard's shell parent.

resizePolicy (class ResizePolicy)
> How BulletinBoard widgets are resized. Possible values are RESIZE_NONE, which means that the widget remains at a fixed size; RESIZE_GROW, which means that the widget only expands; and RESIZE_ANY, which means that the widget shrinks or expands as needed.

shadowType (class ShadowType)
> The style in which shadows are drawn. Possible values are SHADOW_IN, SHADOW_OUT, SHADOW_ETCHED_IN, and SHADOW_ETCHED_OUT.

textFontList (class TextFontList)
> Like the buttonFontList resource, but for Text children.

CascadeButton

CascadeButtons are used in menu systems to post menus. A CascadeButton either links a menu bar to a menu pane or connects a menu pane to another menu pane. The widget can have a menu attached to it as a submenu.

The class hierarchy for CascadeButton is: Core → XmPrimitive → XmLabel → XmCascade-Button

CascadeButtonGadget is the gadget variant of CascadeButton. It has the same appearance and behavior as a CascadeButton. The class hierarchy for CascadeButtonsGadget is: Object → RectObj → XmGadget → XmLabelGadget → XmCascadeButtonGadget

Resources

The following new resources are associated with the CascadeButton and CascadeButton-Gadget:

cascadePixmap (class Pixmap)
> The pixmap within the CascadeButton that indicates a submenu. By default, this pixmap is an arrow pointing toward the submenu to be popped up.

mappingDelay (class MappingDelay)
> The number of milliseconds it should take for the application to display a submenu after its CascadeButton has been selected.

subMenuId (class MenuWidget)
> The widget ID of the pulldown menu pane associated with the CascadeButton. The menu pane is displayed when the CascadeButton is selected. This resource is typically set by the application.

Command

Command is a composite widget that handles command entry by providing a prompt, a command input field, and a history list region. Many of the Command widget's new resources are in fact renamed resources from SelectionBox.

The class hierarchy for Command is: Core → Composite → Constraint → XmManager → XmBulletinBoard → XmSelectionBox → XmCommand

Resources

The following new resources are associated with the Command widget:

command (class TextString)
> The text currently displayed on the command line.

historyItems (class Items)
> The items in the history list. This value is not typically set in resource files.

historyItemCount (class ItemCount)
> The number of strings in historyItems. This value is not typically set in resource files.

historyMaxItems (class MaxItems)
> The history list's maximum number of items. When this number is reached, the first history item is removed before the new command is added to the list.

historyVisibleItemCount (class VisibleItemCount)
> The number of history list commands that will display at one time.

promptString (class PromptString)
> The command-line prompt.

DialogShell

DialogShell is the parent for dialog boxes. A DialogShell cannot be iconified separately, but only when the main application shell is iconified. The child of a DialogShell is typically a subclass of BulletinBoard and much of the functionality of DialogShell is based on this assumption.

The class hierarchy for DialogShell is: Core → Composite → Shell → WmShell → Vendor-Shell → TransientShell → XmDialogShell

Resources

DialogShell does not have any new user-settable resources associated with it.

Display

In Motif 1.2, the Display object stores display-specific information for use by the toolkit. An application has a Display object for each display it accesses. When an application creates its first shell on a display a Display object is created automatically.

The `dragInitiatorProtocolStyle` and `dragReceiverProtocolStyle` resources specify the drag protocol for an application that performs drag and drop operations. The two protocol styles are dynamic and preregister. Under the dynamic protocol, the initiator and receiver pass messages back and forth to handle drag and drop visuals. Under the preregister protocol, the initiator handles drag and drop visuals by reading information that is preregistered and stored in properties. The actual protocol that is used by a specific initiator and receiver is based on the requested protocol styles of the receiver and initiator:

Drag Initiator Protocol Style	Drag Receiver Protocol Style			
	Preregister	Prefer Preregister	Prefer Dynamic	Dynamic
Preregister	PREREGISTER	PREREGISTER	PREREGISTER	DROP_ONLY
Prefer Preregister	PREREGISTER	PREREGISTER	PREREGISTER	DYNAMIC
Prefer Receiver	PREREGISTER	PREREGISTER	DYNAMIC	DYNAMIC
Prefer Dynamic	PREREGISTER	DYNAMIC	DYNAMIC	DYNAMIC
Dynamic	DROP_ONLY	DYNAMIC	DYNAMIC	DYNAMIC

The class hierarchy for Display is: Core → Core → Composite → Shell → WmShell → VendorShell → TopLevelShell → ApplicationShell → XmDisplay

Resources

The following new resources are associated with the Display widget:

defaultVirtualBindings (class DefaultVirtualBindings)
  The default virtual bindings for the display.

dragInitiatorProtocolStyle (class DragInitiatorProtocolStyle)
  The client's drag and drop protocol requirements or preference when it is the initiator of a drag and drop operation. Possible values are DRAG_PREREGISTER, DRAG_DYNAMIC, DRAG_NONE, DRAG_DROP_ONLY, DRAG_PREFER_DYNAMIC, DRAG_PRE-FER_PREREGISTER, and DRAG_PREFER_RECEIVER.

dragReceiverProtocolStyle (class DragReceiverrProtocolStyle)
  The client's drag and drop protocol requirements or preference when it is the receiver. Possible values are DRAG_PREREGISTER, DRAG_DYNAMIC, DRAG_NONE, DRAG_DROP_ONLY, DRAG_PREFER_DYNAMIC, and DRAG_PREFER_PREREGISTER.

DrawingArea

DrawingArea provides a blank canvas for interactive drawing. The widget does not do any drawing of its own. Since DrawingArea is a subclass of Manager, it can provide simple geometry management of multiple widget or gadget children.

The class hierarchy for DrawingArea is: Core → Composite → Constraint → XmManager → XmDrawingArea

Resources

The following new resources are associated with the DrawingArea widget:

marginHeight (class MarginHeight)
marginWidth (class MarginWidth)
  The spacing between a DrawingArea's top or bottom edge and any child widget or its right or left edge and any child widget.

resizePolicy (class ResizePolicy)
  How DrawingArea widgets are resized. Possible values are RESIZE_NONE, which means that the widget remains at a fixed size; RESIZE_GROW, which means that the widget only expands; and RESIZE_ANY, which means that the widget shrinks or expands as needed.

DrawnButton

DrawnButton is an empty widget window, surrounded by a shaded border. The widget provides a graphics area that can act like a PushButton. The graphics can be dynamically updated by the application.

The class hierarchy for DrawnButton is: Core → XmPrimitive → XmLabel → XmDrawn-Button

Resources

The following new resources are associated with the DrawnButton widget:

pushButtonEnabled (class PushButtonEnabled)
> If False (default), the shadow drawing doesn't appear three dimensional; if True, the shading provides a pushed in or raised appearance as for the PushButton widget.

shadowType (class ShadowType)
> The style in which shadows are drawn. Possible values are SHADOW_IN, SHADOW_OUT, SHADOW_ETCHED_IN, and SHADOW_ETCHED_OUT.

FileSelectionBox

FileSelectionBox is a composite widget that is used to traverse a directory hierarchy and select files. FileSelectionBox provides a directory mask input field, a scrollable list of subdirectories, a scrollable list of filenames, a filename input field, and a group of four PushButtons. The PushButtons are typically labeled OK, Filter, Cancel, and Help by default.

The class hierarchy for FileSelectionBox is: Core → Composite → Constraint → Xm-Manager → XmBulletinBoard → XmSelectionBox → XmFileSelectionBox

Resources

The following new resources are associated with the FileSelectionBox widget:

directory (class Directory)
> The base directory that, in combination with pattern, forms the directory mask (the dirMask resource). The directory mask determines which files and directories to display.

disListLabelString (class DirListLabelString)
> The string that labels the directory list.

dirMask (class DirMask)
> The directory mask that determines which files and directories to display. This value combines the values of the resources directory and pattern.

dirSpec (class DisSpec)
> The complete specification of the file path. It is the initial directory and file search that determines the default value for this resource.

fileListLabelString (class fileListLabelString)
> The string that labels the file list.

fileTypeMask (class FileTypeMask)
> Determines whether the file list will display only regular files, only directories, or any type of file. Possible values are FILE_DIRECTORY, FILE_REGULAR, and FILE_ANY_TYPE.

filterLabelString (class FilterLabelString)
> The string that labels the field in which the directory mask is typed in by the user.

noMatchString (class NoMatchString)
> A string that displays in the file list when there are no filenames to display.

pattern (class Pattern)
> The file search pattern that, in combination with directory, forms the directory mask (the dirMask resource). The directory mask determines which files and directories to display. If the pattern resource defaults to NULL or is empty, a pattern for matching all files will be used.

Form

Form is a container widget that constrains its children so as to define their layout when the Form is resized. Constraints on the children of a Form specify the attachments for each of the four sides of a child. Children may be attached to each other, to edges of the Form, or to relative positions within the Form.

The class hierarchy for Form is: Core → Core → Composite → Constraint → XmManager → XmBulletinBoard → XmForm

Resources

The following new resources are associated with the Form widget:

fractionBase (class MaxValue)
> The denominator part of the fraction that describes a child's relative position within a Form. The numerator of this fraction is one of the four positional constraint resources: bottomPosition, leftPosition, rightPosition, or topPosition. This resource is typically set by the application.

horizontalSpacing (class Spacing)
> The offset for right and left attachments.

rubberPositioning (class RubberPositioning)
> Defines the default behavior of a child's top and left side, in the absence of other settings. If this resource is False (default), the child's top and left sides are positioned

using absolute values. If `True`, the child's top and left sides are positioned relative to the size of the Form.

verticalSpacing (class VerticalSpacing)
> The offset for top and bottom attachments.

Form is a subclass of Constraint, which means it has special kind of resources called constraint resources. These resources apply to—and are specified as if they belong to—the children of the Form rather than to the Form itself. Form specifies the following constraint resources for its children:

bottomAttachment (class Attachment)
leftAttachment (class Attachment)
rightAttachment (class Attachment)
topAttachment (class Attachment)
> The method of attachment for each of the child's sides. Possible values are ATTACH_NONE (side remains unattached), ATTACH_FORM (side is attached to same edge of the Form), ATTACH_OPPOSITE_FORM (side is attached to other edge of the Form), ATTACH_WIDGET (side abuts an adjacent widget), ATTACH_OPPOSITE_WIDGET (side is attached to other edge of an adjacent widget), ATTACH_POSITION (side is placed relative to a dimension of the Form), and ATTACH_SELF (side is placed relative to its current position and to the Form). Each attachment refers to the corresponding edge of the child widget within the Form. These resource are typically set by an application.

bottomOffset (class Offset)
leftOffset (class Offset)
rightOffset (class Offset)
topOffset (class Offset)
> The distance between the child's side and the object it's attached to. Offsets are absolute. A nonzero offset is ignored when an attachment resource is set to ATTACH_POSITION because a resize operation applies relative positioning in this case.

bottomPosition (class Attachment)
leftPosition (class Attachment)
rightPosition (class Attachment)
topPosition (class Attachment)
> Used in conjunction with `fractionBase` to calculate the position of the side of a child, relative to that side of the Form. These resources have no effect unless the child's particular attachment resource is set to ATTACH_POSITION. These resources are typically set by the application.

bottomWidget (class Widget)
leftWidget (class Widget)
rightWidget (class Widget)
topWidget (class Widget)
> The name of the widget or gadget that serves as the attachment point for the particular side of the child. To use these resources, set the particular attachment resource to either ATTACH_WIDGET or ATTACH_OPPOSITE_WIDGET. These resources are typically set by the application.

`resizable` (class `Boolean`)

    If `True` (default), a child's resize request is accepted by the Form, provided that the child isn't constrained by its attachments. That is, if both the left and right sides of a child are attached, or if both the top and bottom are attached, the resize request fails, whereas if the child has only one horizontal or one vertical attachment, the resize request is granted. If this resource is `False`, the child is never resized.

Frame

Frame is a simple subclass of Manager that places a three-dimensional border around a single child. Frame is used to provide the typical Motif-style appearance for widget classes that do not have a visible frame, such as RowColumn. As of Motif 1.2, a Frame can have two children: a work area child and a title child. The widget uses constraint resources to indicate the type of each child and to specify the alignment of the title child.

The class hierarchy for Frame is: Core → Composite → Constraint → XmManager → Xm-Frame

Resources

The following new resources are associated with the Frame widget:

`marginHeight` (class `MarginHeight`)
`marginWidth` (class `MarginWidth`)

    The spacing between a DrawingArea's top or bottom edge and any child widget or its right or left edge and any child widget.

`resizePolicy` (class `ResizePolicy`)

    How DrawingArea widgets are resized. Possible values are `RESIZE_NONE`, which means that the widget remains at a fixed size; `RESIZE_GROW`, which means that the widget only expands; and `RESIZE_ANY`, which means that the widget shrinks or expands as needed.

Frame is a subclass of Constraint, which means it has special kind of resources called constraint resources. These resources apply to—and are specified as if they belong to—the children of the Frame rather than to the Frame itself. Frame specifies the following constraint resources for its children:

`childType` (class `ChildType`)

    The type of the child. Frame supports one title and one work area child. Possible values are `FRAME_TITLE_CHILD`, `FRAME_WORKAREA_CHILD`, and `FRAME_GEN-ERIC_CHILD`. This value is typically set by the application.

`childHorizontalAlignment` (class `ChildHorizontalAlignment`)

    The alignment (left to right) for a Frame's title. Possible values are `ALIGN-MENT_BEGINNING`, `ALIGNMENT_CENTER`, and `ALIGNMENT_END`.

`childHorizontalSpacing` (class `childHorizontalSpacing`)
> The minimum distance between the title text and the Frame shadow. The title is clipped to maintain this distance. The value of `marginWidth` is used as the default value.

`childVerticalPlacement` (class `ChildVerticalPlacement`)
> The alignment of the Frame's title relative to the top shadow of the Frame. Possible values are `ALIGNMENT_BASELINE_BOTTOM`, `ALIGNMENT_BASELINE_TOP`, `ALIGNMENT_WIDGET_TOP`, `ALIGNMENT_CENTER`, and `ALIGNMENT_WIDGET_BOTTOM`.

Gadget

Gadget is a supporting superclass for other gadget classes. A Gadget never appears in an application, but it does define resources that are inherited by its subclasses. Gadget takes care of drawing and highlighting border shadows as well as managing traversal. A gadget uses its Manager widget parent's pixmap and color resources (e.g., `foreground`). If you change such a resource in a manager widget, all of its gadget children will be affected as well.

The class hierarchy for Gadget is: Object → RectObj → XmGadget

Resources

The following new resources are associated with Gadget:

`highlightOnEnter` (class `HighlightOnEnter`)
> Determines whether to draw a gadget's highlighting rectangle whenever the cursor moves into the gadget. This resource applies only when the shell has a focus policy of `POINTER`. If the `highlightOnEnter` resource is `True`, highlighting is drawn; if `False` (default), highlighting is not drawn.

`highlightThickness` (class `HighlightThickness`)
> The thickness of the highlighting rectangle.

`navigationType` (class `NavigationType`)
> Determines the way in which gadgets are to be traversed during keyboard navigation. Possible values are `NONE`, `TAB_GROUP`, `STICKY_TAB_GROUP`, and `EXCLUSIVE_TAB_GROUP`. This value is typically set by the application.

`shadowThickness` (class `ShadowThickness`)
> The thickness of the shadow border.

`traversalOn` (class `TraversalOn`)
> If `True` (default), traversal of this gadget is made possible.

`unitType` (class `UnitType`)
> The measurement units to use in resources that specify a size or position—for example, any resources of data type Dimension (whose names generally include one of the words "Margin" or "Thickness"). For a gadget whose parent is a Manager subclass, the default value is copied from this parent (provided the value hasn't been

Widget Resources (vertical, right margin)

explicitly set by the application); otherwise, the default is PIXELS. Possible values are PIXELS, 100TH_POINTS, 100TH_MILLIMETERS, 100TH_FONT_UNITS, and 1000TH_INCHES. This value is typically set by the application.

Label

Label provides a text string or a pixmap for labeling other widgets in an application. Label is also a superclass for the various button widgets. Label does not accept any button or key events, but it does receive enter and leave events.

The class hierarchy for Label is: Core → XmPrimitive → XmLabel

LabelGadget is the gadget variant of Label. It has the same appearance and behavior as a Label. The class hierarchy for LabelGadget is: Object → RectObj → XmGadget → Xm-LabelGadget

Resources

The following new resources are associated with the Label and LabelGadget:

accelerator (class Accelerator)
> A string that describes a button widget's accelerator (the modifiers and key to use as a shortcut in selecting the button). The string's format is like that of a translation but allows only a single key press event to be specified.

acceleratorText (class AcceleratorText)
> The text that is displayed for an accelerator. This value is typically set by an application.

alignment (class Alignment)
> The alignment (left to right) for a label's text or pixmap. Possible values are ALIGN-MENT_BEGINNING, ALIGNMENT_CENTER, and ALIGNMENT_END.

fontList (class FontList)
> The font list used for the widget's text. If this value is initially NULL, the font list is derived from the labelFontList or buttonFontList resource from the nearest parent that is a subclass of BulletinBoard, MenuShell, or VendorShell.

labelInsensitivePixmap (class LabelInsensitivePixmap)
> The pixmap label for an insensitive button (when labelType is PIXMAP).

labelPixmap (class LabelPixmap)
> The pixmap used when labelType is PIXMAP.

labelString (class labelString)
> The string used for the label when labelType is STRING. If this resource is NULL, the application uses the widget's name.

labelType (class labelType)
> The type of label (either string or pixmap). Possible values are PIXMAP and STRING. This value is typically set by an application.

marginBottom (class MarginBottom)
marginLeft (class MarginLeft)
marginRight (class MarginRight)
marginTop (class MarginTop)
> The amount of space between one side of the label text and the nearest margin.

marginHeight (class MarginHeight)
marginWidth (class MarginWidth)
> The spacing between one side of the label and the nearest edge of a shadow.

mnemonic (class Mnemonic)
> A keysym that gives you another way to select a button. In the label string, the first character matching this keysym will be underlined.

mnemonicCharSet (class mnemonicCharSet)
> The character set for the label's mnemonic.

recomputeSize (class RecomputeSize)
> If True (default), the Label widget changes its size so that the string or pixmap fits exactly.

stringDirection (class StringDirection)
> The direction in which to draw the string. Possible values are STRING_DIREC-TION_L_TO_R and STRING_DIRECTION_R_TO_L.

List

List provides a list of choices from which you can select one or more items, based on the selection policy. List supports four selection policies: Single Select, Browse Select, Multiple Select, and Extended Select.

In Single Select mode, only one item can be selected at a time; a button press on an item selects it and deselects the previously selected item. In Browse Select mode, only one item can be selected at a time; a button press works as in Single Select mode and, additionally, a button drag moves the selection with the pointer. In Multiple Select mode, any number of items can be selected at a time; a button press toggles the selection state of an item and does not change the selection state of any other items. In Extended Select mode, any number of items can be selected at a time; discontiguous ranges of items can be selected by combining button presses and button drags.

The class hierarchy for List is: Core → XmPrimitive → XmList

Resources

The following new resources are associated with the List widget:

automaticSelection (class AutomaticSelection)
>If True (and the widget's selectionPolicy is either BROWSE_SELECT or EXTENDED_SELECT), then the selection takes effect whenever you move into a new item. If False, then you must release the mouse button before any selection takes effect.

doubleClickInterval (class DoubleClickInterval)
>The time span (in milliseconds) within which two button clicks must occur to be considered a double click rather than two single clicks. By default, this value is the multi-click time of the display.

fontList (class FontList)
>The font list used for the items in the list. If this value is initially NULL, the font list is derived from the textFontList resource from the nearest parent that is a subclass of BulletinBoard or VendorShell.

itemCount (class ItemCount)
>The total number of items. This value is not normally set in a resource file.

items (class Items)
>The list items to display.

listMarginHeight (class ListMarginHeight)
listMarginWidth (class ListMarginWidth)
>The height or width of the margin between the border of the list and the items in the list.

listSizePolicy (class listSizePolicy)
>The method for resizing the widget when a list item exceeds the width of the work area. Possible values are VARIABLE, CONSTANT, and RESIZE_IF_POSSIBLE.

listSpacing (class ListSpacing)
>The spacing between items.

scrollBarDisplayPolicy (class ScrollBarDisplayPolicy)
>Determines when to display vertical scrollbars in a ScrolledList widget. Possible values are STATIC and AS_NEEDED.

selectedItemCount (class SelectedItemCount)
>The number of items in the list of selected items. This value is not normally set in a resource file.

selectedItems (class SelectedItems)
>The currently selected list items. This value is not normally set in a resource file.

selectionPolicy (class SelectionPolicy)
>Determines the effect of a selection action. Possible values are SINGLE_SELECT, BROWSE_SELECT, MULTIPLE_SELECT, and EXTENDED_SELECT. This value is typically set by the application.

stringDirection (class StringDirection)

> The direction in which to draw the string. Possible values are STRING_DIREC-TION_L_TO_R and STRING_DIRECTION_R_TO_L.

topItemPosition (class TopItemPosition)

> The position of the first item that will be visible in the list. The first position is specified as 1 and the last position is specified as 0.

visibleItemCount (class VisibleItemCount)

> The number of items to display in the work area of the list.

MainWindow

MainWindow provides the standard appearance for the primary window of an application. MainWindow supports five standard areas: a menu bar, a command window, a work region, a message window, and two scrollbars (one horizontal and one vertical). An application can use as many or as few of these areas as necessary; they are all optional. A MainWindow can also create up to three Separator widgets for dividing one area from another.

The class hierarchy for MainWindow is: Core → Composite → Constraint → XmManager → XmScrolledWindow → XmMainWindow

Resources

The following new resources are associated with the MainWindow widget:

commandWindowLocation (class CommandWindowLocation)

> One of two positions for the command window. Possible values are COM-MAND_ABOVE_WORKSPACE and COMMAND_BELOW_WORKSPACE.

mainWindowMarginHeight (class mainWindowMarginHeight)
mainWindowMarginWidth (class mainWindowMarginWidth)

> The margin on the top or bottom (right or left) of the MainWindow widget. These resources override the corresponding margin resources in the ScrolledWindow widget.

Manager

Manager is a superclass for Motif widget classes that contain children. The Manager widget never appears in applications, but it does define resources that are inherited by its subclasses. Manager supports geometry management by providing resources for visual shadows and highlights and for keyboard traversal mechanisms.

The default values of the color resources for the foreground, background, top and bottom shadows, and highlighting are set dynamically. If no colors are specified, they are generated automatically. On a monochrome system, black and white colors are selected. On a color system, four colors are selected that provide the appropriate shading for the 3-D visuals.

When the background color is specified, the shadow colors are selected to provide the appropriate 3-D appearance and foreground, and highlight colors are selected to provide the necessary contrast.

The class hierarchy for Manager is: Core → Composite → Constraint → XmManager

Resources

The following new resources are associated with the Manager widget:

bottomShadowColor (class BottomShadowColor)
> The color used in drawing the border shadow's bottom and right sides on a color display.

bottomShadowPixmap (class bottomShadowPixmap)
> The pixmap used in drawing the border shadow's bottom and right sides on a monochrome display.

foreground (class Foreground)
> The foreground color used by Manager widgets.

highlightColor (class HighlightColor)
> The color used in drawing the highlighting rectangle on a color display.

highlightPixmap (class HighlightPixmap)
> The pixmap used in drawing the highlighting rectangle on a monochrome display.

navigationType (class NavigationType)
> Determines the way in which gadgets are to be traversed during keyboard navigation. Possible values are NONE, TAB_GROUP, STICKY_TAB_GROUP, and EXCLU-SIVE_TAB_GROUP. This value is typically set by the application.

shadowThickness (class ShadowThickness)
> The thickness of the shadow border.

stringDirection (class StringDirection)
> The direction in which to draw the string. Possible values are STRING_DIREC-TION_L_TO_R and STRING_DIRECTION_R_TO_L.

topShadowColor (class TopShadowColor)
> The color used in drawing the border shadow's top and left sides on a color display.

topShadowPixmap (class TopShadowPixmap)
> The pixmap used in drawing the border shadow's top and left sides on a monochrome display.

traversalOn (class TraversalOn)
> If True (default), traversal of this widget is made possible.

unitType (class UnitType)
> The measurement units to use in resources that specify a size or position—for example, any resources of data type Dimension (whose names generally include one of the words "Margin" or "Thickness"). For a gadget whose parent is a Manager subclass, the default value is copied from this parent (provided the value hasn't been

explicitly set by the application); otherwise, the default is PIXELS. Possible values are PIXELS, 100TH_POINTS, 100TH_MILLIMETERS, 100TH_FONT_UNITS, and 1000TH_INCHES. This value is typically set by the application.

MenuShell

MenuShell is a subclass of OverrideShell that is meant to contain only popup or pulldown menu panes.

The class hierarchy for MenuShell is: Core → Composite → Shell → OverrideShell → Xm-MenuShell

Resources

The following new resources are associated with the MenuShell widget:

buttonFontList (class ButtonFontList)
 In Motif 1.2, the font list used for the button children of the MenuShell widget. If this value is initially NULL and if the value of defaultFontList is not NULL, this value is used. Otherwise, the font list is derived from the buttonFontList resource found in the nearest ancestor that is a subclass of BulletinBoard, VendorShell, or MenuShell.

defaultFontList (class DefaultFontList)
 The default font list for the children of the MenuShell widget. This resource is obsolete in Motif 1.2.

labelFontList (class LabelFontList)
 Like the buttonFontList resource, but for Label children.

MessageBox

MessageBox is composite widget that is used for creating simple message dialog boxes, which normally present transient messages. A MessageBox usually contains a message symbol, a message, three PushButtons, and a separator between the message and the buttons. The dialogType resource controls the type of message symbol that is displayed. The PushButtons are typically labeled OK, Cancel, and Help by default.

The class hierarchy for MessageBox is: Core → Composite → Constraint → XmManager → XmBulletinBoard → XmMessageBox

Resources

The following new resources are associated with the MessageBox widget:

cancelLabelString (class CancelLabelString)
: The string that labels the Cancel button.

defaultButtonType (class defaultButtonType)
: Specifies which PushButton provides the default action. Possible values are DIA-LOG_CANCEL_BUTTON, DIALOG_OK_BUTTON, and DIALOG_HELP_BUTTON.

dialogType (class DialogType)
: The type of MessageBox dialog, which also indicates the message symbol that displays by default. Possible values are DIALOG_ERROR, DIALOG_INFORMATION, DIA-LOG_MESSAGE, DIALOG_QUESTION, DIALOG_TEMPLATE, DIALOG_WARNING, and DIA-LOG_WORKING. This value is typically set by an application.

helpLabelString (class HelpLabelString)
: The string that labels the Help button.

messageAlignment (class MessageAlignment)
: The type of alignment for the message label. Possible values are ALIGNMENT_BEGIN-NING, ALIGNMENT_CENTER, and ALIGNMENT_END.

messageString (class MessageString)
: The string to use as the message label.

minimizeButtons (class MinimizeButtons)
: If False (default), all buttons are standardized to be as wide as the widest button and as high as the highest button. If True, buttons will keep their preferred size.

okLabelString (class OkLabelString)
: The string that labels the OK button.

symbolPixmap (class SymbolPixmap)
: The pixmap label to use as the message symbol.

PanedWindow

PanedWindow is a constraint widget that tiles its children vertically. A PanedWindow is as wide as its widest child and all children are made that width. Users can adjust the height of a pane using a sash that appears below the corresponding pane.

The class hierarchy for PanedWindow is: Core → Composite → Constraint → XmManager → XmPanedWindow

Resources

The following new resources are associated with the PanedWindow widget:

marginHeight (class MarginHeight)
> The spacing between a PanedWindow widget's top or bottom edge and any child widget.

marginWidth (class MarginWidth)
> The spacing between a PanedWindow widget's right or left edge and any child widget.

refigureMode (class RefigureMode)
> If True (default), children are reset to their appropriate positions following a change in the PanedWindow widget.

sashHeight (class SashHeight)
sashWidth (class SashWidth)
> The height and width of the sash.

sashIndent (class SashIndent)
> The horizontal position of the sash along each pane. Positive values specify the indent from the left edge; negative values, from the right edge (assuming the default value of stringDirection). If the value is too large, the sash is placed flush with the edge of the PanedWindow.

sashShadowThickness (class SashShadowThickness)
> The thickness of shadows drawn on each sash.

separatorOn (class SeparatorOn)
> If True, the widget places a Separator or SeparatorGadget between each pane.

spacing (class Spacing)
> The distance between each child pane.

PanedWindow is a subclass of Constraint, which means it has special kind of resources called constraint resources. These resources apply to—and are specified as if they belong to—the children of the PanedWindow rather than to the PanedWindow itself. PanedWindow specifies the following constraint resource for its children:

allowResize (class AllowResize)
> If False (default), the PanedWindow widget always refuses resize requests from its children. If True, the PanedWindow widget tries to grant requests to change a child's height.

paneMaximum (class PaneMaximum)
paneMinimum (class PaneMinimum)
> The values of a pane's maximum and minimum dimensions for resizing. You can prevent a sash from being drawn by setting these values to be equal.

positionIndex (class PositionIndex)
> In Motif 1.2, the position of the widget in the PanedWindow's list of children, not including sashes. A value of 0 indicates the beginning of the list, while LAST_POSITION places the child at the end of the list.

skipAdjust (class SkipAdjust)

> If False (default), the PanedWindow widget automatically resizes this pane child. If True, resizing is not automatic, and the PanedWindow may choose to skip the adjustment of this pane.

Primitive

Primitive is a supporting superclass that provides Motif-specific resources for border drawing, highlighting, and keyboard traversal mechanisms. The Primitive widget never appears in applications, but it does define resources that are inherited by its subclasses. Primitive supports widget subclasses that handle elementary graphic elements such as buttons, labels, and separators.

The default values of the color resources for the foreground, background, top and bottom shadows, and highlighting are set dynamically. If no colors are specified, they are generated automatically. On a monochrome system, black and white colors are selected. On a color system, four colors are selected that provide the appropriate shading for the 3-D visuals. When the background color is specified, the shadow colors are selected to provide the appropriate 3-D appearance and foreground and highlight colors are selected to provide the necessary contrast.

The class hierarchy for Primitive is: Core → XmPrimitive

Resources

The following new resources are associated with the Primitive widget:

bottomShadowColor (class BottomShadowColor)

> The color used in drawing the border shadow's bottom and right sides on a color display.

bottomShadowPixmap (class bottomShadowPixmap)

> The pixmap used in drawing the border shadow's bottom and right sides on a monochrome display.

foreground (class Foreground)

> The foreground color used by Primitive widgets.

highlightColor (class HighlightColor)

> The color used in drawing the highlighting rectangle on a color display.

highlightOnEnter (class HighlightOnEnter)

> Determines whether to draw the widget's highlighting rectangle whenever the cursor moves into the widget. This resource applies only when the shell has a focus policy of POINTER. If the highlightOnEnter resource is True, highlighting is drawn; if False (default), highlighting is not drawn.

highlightPixmap (class HighlightPixmap)

> The pixmap used in drawing the highlighting rectangle on a monochrome display.

highlightThickness (class HighlightThickness)
> The thickness of the highlighting rectangle.

navigationType (class NavigationType)
> Determines the way in which a Primitive widget is traversed during keyboard navigation. Possible values are NONE, TAB_GROUP, STICKY_TAB_GROUP, and EXCLUSIVE_TAB_GROUP. This value is typically set by the application.

shadowThickness (class ShadowThickness)
> The thickness of the shadow border.

topShadowColor (class TopShadowColor)
> The color used in drawing the border shadow's top and left sides on a color display.

topShadowPixmap (class TopShadowPixmap)
> The pixmap used in drawing the border shadow's top and left sides on a monochrome display.

traversalOn (class TraversalOn)
> If True (default), traversal of this widget is made possible.

unitType (class UnitType)
> The measurement units to use in resources that specify a size or position—for example, any resources of data type Dimension (whose names generally include one of the words "Margin" or "Thickness"). For a widget whose parent is a Manager subclass, the default value is copied from this parent (provided the value hasn't been explicitly set by the application); otherwise, the default is PIXELS. Possible values are PIXELS, 100TH_POINTS, 100TH_MILLIMETERS, 100TH_FONT_UNITS, and 1000TH_INCHES. This value is typically set by the application.

PushButton

A PushButton is a widget that causes something to happen in an application. A PushButton displays a textual or graphics label. It invokes an application callback when it is clicked on with the mouse. The shading of the PushButton changes to make it appear either pressed in when selected or raised when unselected.

The class hierarchy for PushButton is: Core → XmPrimitive → XmLabel → XmPushButton

PushButtonGadget is the gadget variant of PushButton. It has the same appearance and behavior as a PushButton. The class hierarchy for PushButtonsGadget is: Object → RectObj → XmGadget → XmLabelGadget → XmPushButtonGadget

Resources

The following new resources are associated with PushButton and PushButtonGadget:

armColor (class ArmColor)
>   The color with which the armed button is filled. For a color display, the default color is a shade between the bottom shadow color and the background color. For a monochrome display, the default is the foreground color, and label text is switched to the background color. This resource is in effect only when fillOnArm is set to True.

armPixmap (class ArmPixmap)
>   The pixmap that identifies the button when it is armed (and when its labelType is PIXMAP). For a PushButton in a menu, this resource is disabled.

defaultButtonShadowThickness (class DefaultButtonShadowThickness)
>   The width of the shadow used to indicate a default PushButton.

fillOnArm (class FillOnArm)
>   If True (default), the PushButton widget fills the button (when armed) with the color specified by armColor. If False, the PushButton widget only switches the top and bottom shadow colors. For a PushButton in a menu, this resource is disabled (and assumed to be False).

showAsDefault (class ShowAsDefault)
>   Indicates the default PushButton by displaying a shadow. (In a menu, this resource is disabled.)

RowColumn

RowColumn provides an area in which children belonging to any widget type are displayed in rows and columns. RowColumn is a general-purpose manager widget class that can be configured into many layouts, such as a MenuBar, PopupMenu, PulldownMenu, Option-Menu, CheckBox, or RadioBox. Many of RowColumn's resources pertain only to a specific layout type.

In Motif 1.2, a RowColumn that is configured as a PopupMenu or a PulldownMenu supports tear-off menus. When a menu is torn off, it remains on the screen after a selection is made so that additional selections can be made. A menu pane that can be torn off contains a tear-off button at the top of the menu that contains a dashed line.

The class hierarchy for RowColumn is: Core → Composite → Constraint → XmManager → XmRowColumn

Resources

The following new resources are associated with the RowColumn widget:

adjustLast (class AdjustLast)
> If True (default), the last row (or column) in the RowColumn widget is expanded so as to be flush with the edge.

adjustMargin (class AdjustMargin)
> If True (default), text in each row (or column) will align with other text in its row (or column). This is done by forcing the margin resources (defined by the Label widget) to have the same value.

entryAlignment (class EntryAlignment)
> When isAligned is True, this resource tells RowColumn children how to align. The children must be subclasses of XmLabel or XmLabelGadget. Possible values are ALIGNMENT_BEGINNING, ALIGNMENT_CENTER, and ALIGNMENT_END.

entryBorder (class EntryBorder)
> The border width of a RowColumn widget's children.

entryClass (class EntryClass)
> The widget class to which children must belong when being added to a RowColumn widget. This resource is used only when the isHomogeneous resource is set to True. This value is not normally set in a resource file.

entryVerticalAlignment (class EntryVerticalAlignment)
> In Motif 1.2, specifies how children that are subclasses of Label, Text, and TextField are aligned vertically. The resource has no effect if orientation is VERTICAL or packing is PACK_TIGHT. Possible values are ALIGNMENT_BASELINE_BOTTOM, ALIGNMENT_BASELINE_TOP, ALIGNMENT_CONTENTS_BOTTOM, ALIGNMENT_CENTER, and ALIGNMENT_CONTENTS_TOP.

isAligned (class IsAligned)
> If True, enables the alignment specified in the entryAlignment resource. Alignment is ignored in a label whose parent is a popup or pulldown MenuPane.

isHomogeneous (class IsHomogeneous)
> If True, enforces the condition that all RowColumn children belong to the same class (the class specified by the entryClass resource).

labelString (class LabelString)
> A label used only in option menus. A text string displays beside the selection area. By default, there is no label.

marginHeight (class MarginHeight)
marginWidth (class MarginWidth)
> The spacing between an edge of the RowColumn widget and its nearest child. In popup and pulldown menus, the default is 0; in other types of RowColumn widgets, the default is 3 pixels.

menuAccelerator (class MenuAccelerator)

A pointer to a string that specifies an accelerator (keyboard shortcut) for use only in RowColumn widgets of type MENU_POPUP or MENU_BAR. In a popup menu, typing the accelerator posts the menu; in a menu bar, typing the accelerator highlights the first item and enables traversal in the menu bar.

menuPost (class MenuPost)

The string that describes the event for posting a menu. The default value depends on the type of RowColumn widget: for MENU_POPUP, the default is BMenu Press; for MENU_OPTION, MENU_BAR, and WORK_AREA the default is BSelect Press; for MENU_PULLDOWN, this resource isn't meaningful.

mnemonic (class Mnemonic)

The keysym of the key to press (in combination with the MAlt modifier) in order to post the pulldown menu associated with an option menu. This resource is meaningful only in option menus. In the label string, the first character matching this keysym will be underlined.

mnemonicCharSet (class MnemonicCharSet)

The character set for the option menu's mnemonic.

numColumns (class NumColumns)

The number of columns (in a vertically-oriented RowColumn widget) or the number of rows (in a horizontally-oriented RowColumn widget). This resource is meaningful only when the packing resource is set to PACK_COLUMN.

orientation (class Orientation)

The direction for laying out the rows and columns of children of a RowColumn widget. Possible values are VERTICAL and HORIZONTAL. This value is typically set by the application.

packing (class Packing)

The method of spacing the items placed within a RowColumn widget. Possible values are PACK_TIGHT, which means that each child widget is set to its minimum size; PACK_COLUMN, which means that the size of each child widget is padded so that they are all the same size; and PACK_NONE, which means that the RowColumn accommodates the size and location of each child widget. This value is typically set by the application.

popupEnabled (class PopupEnabled)

If True (default), keyboard shortcuts are in effect for popup menus. Set this resource to False if you want to disable accelerators and mnemonics in popup menus.

radioAlwaysOne (class RadioAlwaysOne)

This resource is effective only when the radioBehavior resource is True. radioAlwaysOne, when set to True (default), ensures that one of the toggle buttons is always selected.

radioBehavior (class radioBehavior)

If True, the RowColumn widget acts like a RadioBox by setting two of the resources for its toggle button children. Namely, the indicatorType resource defaults to

ONE_OF_MANY, and the visibleWhenOff resource defaults to True. This value is typically set by the application.

resizeHeight (class ResizeHeight)
resizeWidth (class ResizeWidth)

> If True (default), the widget requests a new height or width when necessary. If False, no resize requests are made.

rowColumnType (class RowColumnType)

> The type of RowColumn widget to create. Possible values are WORK_AREA, MENU_PULLDOWN, MENU_BAR, MENU_OPTION, and MENU_POPUP. This value is typically set by the application.

spacing (class Spacing)

> The horizontal and vertical spacing between children in the RowColumn widget.

subMenuId (class SubMenuId)

> The widget ID for the pulldown menu pane to be associated with an OptionMenu. This resource is meaningful only in RowColumn widgets of type MENU_OPTION. This resource is typically set by the application.

tearOffModel (class TearOffModel)

> In Motif 1.2, specifies whether tear-off behavior is enabled for a RowColumn with rowColumnType set to MENU_PULLDOWN or MENU_POPUP. Possible values are TEAR_OFF_DISABLED and TEAR_OFF_ENABLED.

RowColumn is a subclass of Constraint, which means it has special kinds of resources called constraint resources. These resources apply to—and are specified as if they belong to—the children of the RowColumn rather than to the RowColumn itself. RowColumn specifies the following constraint resource for its children:

positionIndex (class PositionIndex)

> In Motif 1.2, the position of the widget in the RowColumn's list of children. A value of 0 indicates the beginning of the list, while LAST_POSITION places the child at the end of the list.

Scale

A Scale displays a value from a range of values and allows a user to adjust the value. A Scale consists of a narrow, rectangular trough that contains a slider. The slider's position marks the current value within the range of values. Scale is a manager widget that orients its children along its axis. These children, typically labels, can be used as tick marks. If the Scale widget is an input-output type (sensitive is True), you can change the value by moving the slider. An output-only Scale displays a value but does not allow you to modify it.

The class hierarchy for Scale is: Core → Composite → Constraint → XmManager → Xm-Scale

Resources

The following new resources are associated with the Scale widget:

decimalPoints (class DecimalPoints)
> A positive integer that determines how the slider's value will be displayed. The decimal point in the slider's value gets shifted to the right, and this resource specifies the number of decimal places to shift. For example, if the slider's value is 1234, then setting the decimalPoints resource to 2 causes the widget to display the value as 12.34.

fontList (class FontList)
> The font list used for the text specified by the titleString resource. If this value is initially NULL, the font list is derived from the font list resource from the nearest parent that is a subclass of BulletinBoard, MenuShell, or VendorShell.

highlightOnEnter (class HighlightOnEnter)
> Determines whether to draw the widget's highlighting rectangle whenever the cursor moves into the widget. This resource applies only when the shell has a focus policy of POINTER. If the highlightOnEnter resource is True, highlighting is drawn; if False (default), highlighting is not drawn.

highlightThickness (class HighlightThickness)
> The thickness of the highlighting rectangle.

maximum (class Maximum)
minimum (class Minimum)
> The maximum/minimum value of the slider.

orientation (class Orientation)
> The direction in which the scale is displayed. Possible values are VERTICAL and HORIZONTAL.

processingDirection (class ProcessingDirection)
> Determines the position at which to display the slider's maximum and minimum values, with respect to the slider. Possible values are MAX_ON_TOP, MAX_ON_BOTTOM, MAX_ON_LEFT, and MAX_ON_RIGHT.

scaleHeight (class ScaleHeight)
scaleWidth (class ScaleWidth)
> The height or width of the slider area.

scaleMultiple (class ScaleMultiple)
> The distance to move the slider when the user moves it by a multiple increment. The default value is calculated as $(maximum - minimum) / 10$.

showValue (class ShowValue)
> If True, the label specifying the slider's current value will be displayed beside the slider. If False, the label isn't displayed.

titleString (class TitleString)
> The text string that appears as the title in the Scale widget.

value (class Value)
> The current position of the slider along the scale. This resource must have a value between the values of minimum and maximum. This value is not normally set in a resource file.

Screen

In Motif 1.2, the Screen object stores screen-specific information for use by the toolkit. An application has a Screen object for each screen that it accesses. When an application creates its first shell on a screen, a Screen object is created automatically.

The class hierarchy for Screen is: Core → XmScreen

Resources

The following new resources are associated with the Screen widget:

darkThreshold (class DarkThreshold)
> The level of perceived brightness (between 0 and 100) that is treated as a "dark" background color when computing default shadow and select colors.

defaultCopyCursorIcon (class DefaultCopyCursorIcon)
> The DragIcon used during a copy operation. When the value is NULL, a default system icon is used.

defaultInvalidCursorIcon (class DefaultInvalidCursorIcon)
> The DragIcon used when the pointer is over an invalid drop site. When the value is NULL, a default system icon is used.

defaultLinkCursorIcon (class DefaultLinkCursorIcon)
> The DragIcon used during a link operation. When the value is NULL, a default system icon is used.

defaultMoveCursorIcon (class DefaultMoveCursorIcon)
> The DragIcon used during a move operation. When the value is NULL, a default system icon is used.

defaultNoneCursorIcon (class DefaultNoneCursorIcon)
> The DragIcon used when the pointer is not over a drop site. When the value is NULL, a default system icon is used.

defaultSourceCursorIcon (class DefaultSourceCursorIcon)
> The bitmap used as a cursor when a sourceCursorIcon is not provided by the DragContext. When the value is NULL, a default system icon is used.

defaultValidCursorIcon (class DefaultValidCursorIcon)
> The DragIcon used when the pointer is over a valid drop site. When the value is NULL, a default system icon is used.

font (class Font)
> The font used in computing values for `horizontalFontUnit` and `vertical-FontUnit`.

foregroundThreshold (class ForegroundThreshold)
> The level of perceived brightness (between 0 and 100) that distinguishes between a "dark" and "light" background when computing the default foreground and highlight colors.

horizontalFontUnits (class HorizontalFontUnits)
> The horizontal component of the font units that are used to convert geometry values when `shellUnitType` or `unitType` is set to `100TH_FONT_UNITS`. If a value is not specified, the default is computed from the `font` resource.

lightThreshold (class LightThreshold)
> The level of perceived brightness (between 0 and 100) that is treated as a "light" background color when computing default shadow and select colors.

menuCursor (class MenuCursor)
> The cursor that is used when the application posts a menu. Possible values include all of the cursor in the X cursor font.

moveOpaque (class MoveOpaque)
> If `False` (default), an operation that moves a window displays an outline of the window. If `True`, a move operation displays a representation of the window.

verticalFontUnits (class VerticalFontUnits)
> The vertical component of the font units that are used to convert geometry values when `shellUnitType` or `unitType` is set to `100TH_FONT_UNITS`. If a value is not specified, the default is computed from the `font` resource.

ScrollBar

A ScrollBar allows you to reposition data that is too large to fit in the viewing window. Although a ScrollBar can be used as a standalone widget, it is normally used in a Scrolled-Window. A ScrollBar consists of a rectangular strip, called the scroll region or trough, and two arrows placed on either end of the scroll region. Within the scroll region is a smaller, movable rectangle called the slider. To scroll the data, you can click on one of the arrows, click in the scroll region, or drag the slider. The application typically sets the `sliderSize` resource such that the size of the slider relative to the size of the scroll region corresponds to the percentage of total data that is currently displayed.

The class hierarchy for ScrollBar is: Core → Core → XmPrimitive → XmScrollBar

Resources

The following new resources are associated with the ScrollBar widget:

increment (class Increment)
> The amount the value changes due to the user's moving the slider one increment.

initialDelay (class InitialDelay)
> The number of milliseconds a button must remain pressed before triggering continuous slider movement.

maximum (class Maximum)
minimum (class Minimum)
> The maximum/minimum value of the slider.

orientation (class Orientation)
> The direction in which the scale is displayed. Possible values are VERTICAL and HORIZONTAL.

pageIncrement (class PageIncrement)
> The amount the value changes due to the user's moving the slider one page increment.

processingDirection (class ProcessingDirection)
> Determines the position at which to display the slider's maximum and minimum values, with respect to the slider. Possible values are MAX_ON_TOP, MAX_ON_BOTTOM, MAX_ON_LEFT, and MAX_ON_RIGHT.

repeatDelay (class RepeatDelay)
> The number of milliseconds a button must remain pressed before continuing further slider motions, once the initialDelay time has been triggered.

showArrows (class ShowArrows)
> If True, arrows are displayed; if False, they are not.

sliderSize (class SliderSize)
> The slider's length. The length ranges from 1 to the value of maximum – minimum.

troughColor (class TroughColor)
> The color of the slider's trough.

value (class Value)
> The slider's position. The position ranges from the value of minimum to the value of (maximum – sliderSize). This value is not normally set in a resource file.

ScrolledWindow

ScrolledWindow provides a scrollable view of data that may not be visible all at once. ScrollBars allow you to scroll the visible part of the window through the larger display. A ScrolledWindow widget can be created so that it scrolls automatically without application intervention or so that an application provides support for all scrolling operations.

The class hierarchy for ScrolledWindow is: Core → Composite → Constraint → Xm-Manager → XmScrolledWindow

Resources

The following new resources are associated with the ScrolledWindow widget:

scrollBarDisplayPolicy (class ScrollBarDisplayPolicy)
> Controls the placement of ScrollBars, depending on the value of the scrolling-Policy resource. Possible values are STATIC and AS_NEEDED. If scrolling-Policy is set to AUTOMATIC, then scrollBarDisplayPolicy defaults to a value of AS_NEEDED, and ScrollBars are displayed only when the workspace cannot fit within the clip area. If scrollingPolicy is set to APPLICATION_DEFINED, then scrollBarDisplayPolicy defaults to (and must remain with) a value of STATIC. This means that ScrollBars will always be displayed.

scrollBarPlacement (class ScrollBarPlacement)
> The positions of the ScrollBars relative to the work window. The default value of this resource depends on the value of the stringDirection resource. Possible values are TOP_LEFT, BOTTOM_LEFT, TOP_RIGHT, and BOTTOM_RIGHT.

scrolledWindowMarginHeight (class scrolledWindowMarginHeight)
> The spacing at the top and bottom of the ScrolledWindow.

scrolledWindowMarginWidth (class scrolledWindowMarginWidth)
> The spacing at the right and left sides of the ScrolledWindow.

scrollingPolicy (class ScrollingPolicy)
> Determines how automatic scrolling occurs. Possible values are AUTOMATIC and APPLICATION_DEFINED. This value is typically set by the application.

spacing (class Spacing)
> The distance between each ScrollBar and the work window.

SelectionBox

SelectionBox is a composite widget that displays a scrollable list of alternatives from which you can choose items. A SelectionBox contains a text field in which you can enter a selection, the scrollable list of selections, labels for the text field and the scrollable list, a separator, and a group of three or four buttons. The PushButtons are typically labeled OK, Apply, Cancel, and Help by default.

The class hierarchy for SelectionBox is: Core → Composite → Constraint → XmManager → XmBulletinBoard → XmSelectionBox

Resources

The following new resources are associated with the SelectionBox widget:

applyLabelString (class ApplyLabelString)
:   The string that labels the Apply button.

cancelLabelString (class CancelLabelString)
:   The string that labels the Cancel button.

childPlacement (class ChildPlacement)
:   In Motif 1.2, determines the placement of the work area child. Possible values are PLACE_ABOVE_SELECTION, PLACE_BELOW_SELECTION, and PLACE_TOP. This value is typically set by the application.

dialogType (class DialogType)
:   Determines the type of SelectionBox widget that will be initially created and managed. Possible values are DIALOG_WORK_AREA, DIALOG_PROMPT, DIALOG_SELECTION, DIALOG_COMMAND, and DIALOG_FILE_SELECTION. This value is typically set by the application.

helpLabelString (class HelpLabelString)
:   The string that labels the Help button.

listItemCount (class ItemCount)
:   The number of items in the SelectionBox list. This value is not normally set in a resource file.

listItems (class Items)
:   The items in the SelectionBox list.

listLabelString (class ListLabelString)
:   The string that labels the SelectionBox list.

listVisibleItemCount (class VisibleItemCount)
:   The number of items that appear in the SelectionBox list.

minimizeButtons (class MinimizeButtons)
:   If False (default), all buttons are standardized to be as wide as the widest button and as high as the highest button. If True, buttons will keep their preferred size.

mustMatch (class MustMatch)
:   If True, the selection that a user types in the text edit field must match an existing entry in the SelectionBox list. If False (default), the typed selection doesn't need to match a list entry. This value is typically set by the application.

okLabelString (class OkLabelString)
:   The string that labels the Ok button.

selectionLabelString (class SelectionLabelString)
:   The string that labels the text edit field.

textAccelerators (class TextAccelerators)
:   The translations to add to the SelectionBox's Text widget child. The default bindings allow the up and down keys to be used in selecting list items.

textColumns (class Columns)

The number of columns in the Text widget.

textString (class TextString)

The text string that appears in the text edit selection field.

Separator

A Separator is a widget that draws a horizontal or vertical line between components in an application. Several line styles are available for the Separator. A pixmap separator can also be made by specifying a pixmap for the Core resource backgroundPixmap and then setting separatorType to NO_LINE.

The class hierarchy for Separator is: Core → XmPrimitive → XmSeparator

SeparatorGadget is the gadget variant of Separator. It has the same appearance and behavior as a Separator. The class hierarchy for SeparatorGadget is: Object → RectObj → XmGadget → XmSeparatorGadget

Resources

The following new resources are associated with Separator and SeparatorGadget:

margin (class Margin)

The spacing on either end of the Separator.

orientation (class Orientation)

The direction in which to display the Separator. Possible values are VERTICAL and HORIZONTAL.

separatorType (class SeparatorType)

The line style in which to draw the Separator. Possible values are NO_LINE, SINGLE_LINE, DOUBLE_LINE, SINGLE_DASHED_LINE, DOUBLE_DASHED_LINE, SHADOW_ETCHED_IN, and SHADOW_ETCHED_OUT.

Text

The Text widget provides a text editor that allows text to be inserted, modified, deleted, and selected. Text provide both single-line and multiline text editing capabilities.

The class hierarchy for Text is: Core → XmPrimitive → XmText

Resources

The following new resources are associated with the Text widget:

autoShowCursorPosition (class AutoShowCursorPosition)
>   If True (default), the visible portion of the Text widget will always contain the insert cursor. The Text widget will scroll its contents, if necessary, to ensure that the cursor remains visible.

blinkRate (class BlinkRate)
>   The time in milliseconds that the cursor spends either being visible or invisible. A value of 0 prevents the cursor from blinking.

columns (class Columns)
>   The number of character spaces that should fit horizontally in the text window. The width resource determines the default value of columns, but if no width has been set, the default is 20.

cursorPosition (class CursorPosition)
>   The location at which to place the current insert cursor. Values for this resource are relative to the beginning of the text; the first character position is defined as 0.

cursorPositionVisible (class CursorPositionVisible)
>   If True (default), the text cursor will be visible.

editable (class Editable)
>   If True (default), the user is allowed to edit the text string; if False, the user is not allowed to do so. This value is typically set by the application.

editMode (class EditMode)
>   Determines whether the Text widget is single-line or multiline. Possible values are MULTI_LINE_EDIT and SINGLE_LINE_EDIT.

fontList (class FontList)
>   The font list used for the widget's text. If this value is initially NULL, the font list is derived from the font list resource from the nearest parent that is a subclass of Bulletin-Board, MenuShell, or VendorShell.

marginHeight (class MarginHeight)
marginWidth (class MarginWidth)
>   The spacing between the edges of the widget and the text.

maxLength (class MaxLength)
>   The maximum length of the text string that a user can enter from the keyboard.

pendingDelete (class PendingDelete)
>   If True (default), the Text widget's pending delete mode is on, meaning that selected text will be deleted as soon as the next text insertion occurs.

resizeHeight (class ResizeHeight)
>   If False (default), the Text widget will not expand vertically to fit all of the text (in other words, the widget will need to have scrollbars so that the rest of the text can be scrolled into view). If True, the Text widget always begins its display with the text at

the beginning of the source. This resource has no effect in a Text widget inside of a ScrolledWindow whose `scrollVertical` resource is set to `True`.

resizeWidth (class ResizeWidth)
> If `False` (default), the Text widget will not expand horizontally to fit its text. If `True`, the widget tries to change its width. This resource has no effect when the `wordWrap` resource is set to `True`.

rows (class Rows)
> The number of character spaces that should fit vertically in the text window. The `height` resource determines the default value of `rows`, but if no height has been set, the default is 1. This resource is meaningful only when `editMode` is `MULTI_LINE_EDIT`.

scrollHorizontal (class Scroll)
> When a Text widget is inside a ScrolledWindow, if `True`, the Text widget adds a horizontal ScrollBar. This resource is meaningful only when `editMode` is `MULTI_LINE_EDIT`.

scrollLeftSide (class ScrollSide)
> When a Text widget is inside a ScrolledWindow, if `True`, the vertical ScrollBar is placed to the left of the scrolled text window. This resource is meaningful only when `editMode` is `MULTI_LINE_EDIT` and when `scrollVertical` is `True`.

scrollTopSide (class ScrollSide)
> When a Text widget is inside a ScrolledWindow, if `True`, the horizontal ScrollBar is placed above the scrolled text window, rather than below by default.

scrollVertical (class Scroll)
> When a Text widget is inside a ScrolledWindow, if `True`, the Text widget adds a vertical ScrollBar.

selectionArray (class SelectionArray)
> The array of possible actions caused by multiple mouse clicks. Possible values are `SELECT_POSITION`, `SELECT_WORD`, `SELECT_LINE`, and `SELECT_ALL`.

selectionArrayCount (class SelectionArrayCount)
> The number of items in the array specified by `selectionArray`.

selectionThreshold (class SelectionThreshold)
> The number of pixels the insertion cursor must be dragged during selection in order to select the next character.

topCharacter (class TopCharacter)
> The location of the text to display at the top of the window. Values for this resource are relative to the beginning of the text, with the first character position defined as 0.

value (class Value)
> The string value to display in the Text widget, expressed as a `char *`. If `value` and `valueWcs` are both defined, `valueWcs` takes precedence.

valueWcs (class ValueWcs)
    In Motif 1.2, the string value to display in the Text widget, expressed as a wchar_t
    *. If value and valueWcs are both defined, valueWcs takes precedence. This
    value cannot be set in a resource file.

verifyBell (class VerifyBell)
    If True (default), a bell will sound when a verification produces no action.

wordWrap (class WordWrap)
    If False (default), do not break lines automatically between words (in which case text
    can disappear beyond the window's edge). If True, break lines at spaces, tabs, or
    newlines. This resource is meaningful only when editMode is MULTI_LINE_EDIT.

TextField

The TextField widget provides a single-line text editor that has a subset of the functionality
of the Text widget.

The class hierarchy for TextField is: Core → XmPrimitive → XmTextField

Resources

The following new resources are associated with the TextField widget:

blinkRate (class BlinkRate)
    The time in milliseconds that the cursor spends either being visible or invisible. A
    value of 0 prevents the cursor from blinking.

columns (class Columns)
    The number of character spaces that should fit horizontally in the text window. The
    width resource determines the default value of columns, but if no width has been
    set, the default is 20.

cursorPosition (class CursorPosition)
    The location at which to place the current insert cursor. Values for this resource are
    relative to the beginning of the text; the first character position is defined as 0.

cursorPositionVisible (class CursorPositionVisible)
    If True (default), the text cursor will be visible.

editable (class Editable)
    If True (default), the user is allowed to edit the text string; if False, the user is not
    allowed to do so. This value is typically set by the application.

fontList (class FontList)
    The font list used for the widget's text. If this value is initially NULL, the font list is
    derived from the font list resource from the nearest parent that is a subclass of Bulletin-
    Board, MenuShell, or VendorShell.

marginHeight (class MarginHeight)
marginWidth (class MarginWidth)
> The spacing between the edges of the widget and the text.

maxLength (class MaxLength)
> The maximum length of the text string that a user can enter from the keyboard.

pendingDelete (class PendingDelete)
> If True (default), the TextField widget's pending delete mode is on, meaning that selected text will be deleted as soon as the next text insertion occurs.

resizeWidth (class ResizeWidth)
> If False (default), the TextField widget will not expand horizontally to fit its text. If True, the widget tries to change its width.

selectionArray (class SelectionArray)
> The array of possible actions caused by multiple mouse clicks. Possible values are SELECT_POSITION, SELECT_WORD, and SELECT_LINE.

selectionArrayCount (class SelectionArrayCount)
> The number of items in the array specified by selectionArray.

selectionThreshold (class SelectionThreshold)
> The number of pixels the insertion cursor must be dragged during selection in order to select the next character.

value (class Value)
> The string value to display in the TextField widget, expressed as a char *. If value and valueWcs are both defined, valueWcs takes precedence.

valueWcs (class ValueWcs)
> In Motif 1.2, the string value to display in the TextField widget, expressed as a wchar_t *. If value and valueWcs are both defined, valueWcs takes precedence. This value cannot be set in a resource file.

verifyBell (class VerifyBell)
> If True (default), a bell will sound when a verification produces no action.

ToggleButton

A ToggleButton is a button that is either set or unset. ToggleButtons are typically used in groups, called RadioBoxes and CheckBoxes, depending on the behavior of the buttons. In a RadioBox, a ToggleButton displays *one-of-many* behavior, which means that only one button in the group can be set at a time. When a button is selected, the previously selected button is unset. In a CheckBox, a ToggleButton displays *n-of-many* behavior, which means that any number of ToggleButtons can be set at one time. ToggleButton uses an indicator to show its state; the shape of the indicator specifies the type of behavior. A diamond-shaped indicator is used for one-of-many ToggleButtons and a square-shaped indicator is used for *n-of-many* ToggleButtons.

The class hierarchy for ToggleButton is: Core → XmPrimitive → XmLabel → XmToggle-Button

ToggleButtonGadget is the gadget variant of ToggleButton. It has the same appearance and behavior as a ToggleButton. The class hierarchy for ToggleButtonsGadget is: Object → RectObj → XmGadget → XmLabelGadget → XmToggleButtonGadget

Resources

The following new resources are associated with ToggleButton and ToggleButtonGadget:

fillOnSelect (class FillOnSelect)
> If True, selection of this ToggleButton fills the indicator with the color given by the selectColor resource and switches the button's top and bottom shadow colors. If False, only the top and bottom shadow colors are switched.

indicatorOn (class IndicatorOn)
> If True (default), the indicator is visible and its shadows are switched when the button is toggled. If False, the indicator is invisible and no space is set aside for it; in addition, the shadows surrounding the button are switched when it is toggled.

indicatorSize (class IndicatorSize)
> The size of the indicator. This value changes if the size of the button's text string or pixmap changes.

indicatorType (class IndicatorType)
> Determines whether the indicator is drawn as a diamond (one-of-many) or a square (n-of-many). Possible values are N_OF_MANY and ONE_OF_MANY. This value is typically set by the application.

selectColor (class SelectColor)
> The color with which to fill the indicator when the button is selected.

selectInsensitivePixmap (class SelectInsensitivePixmap)
> The pixmap used for an insensitive ToggleButton when it's selected. This resource is meaningful only when the Label resource labelType is set to PIXMAP.

selectPixmap (class SelectPixmap)
> The pixmap used for a ToggleButton when it's selected. An unselected ToggleButton uses the pixmap specified by the Label resource labelPixmap. This resource is meaningful only when the Label resource labelType is set to PIXMAP.

set (class Set)
> The selection state of the button.

spacing (class Spacing)
> The distance between the toggle indicator and its label.

visibleWhenOff (class VisibleWhenOff)
> If True, the toggle indicator remains visible when the button is unselected.

VendorShell

VendorShell is a vendor-specific supporting superclass for all shell classes that are visible to the window manager and that do not have override redirection. VendorShell defines resources that provide the Motif look and feel and manages the specific communication needed by the Motif window manager (mwm).

The class hierarchy for VendorShell is: Core → Composite → Shell → WmShell → Vendor-Shell

Resources

The following new resources are associated with the VendorShell widget:

audibleWarning (class AudibleWarning)
> In Motif 1.2, specifies whether an action performs an associated audible cue. Possible values are BELL and NONE.

buttonFontList (class ButtonFontList)
> In Motif 1.2, the font list used for the button children of the VendorShell widget. If this value is initially NULL and if the value of defaultFontList is not NULL, this value is used. Otherwise, the font list is derived from the buttonFontList resource found in the nearest ancestor that is a subclass of BulletinBoard, VendorShell, or MenuShell.

defaultFontList (class DefaultFontList)
> The default font list for the children of the MenuShell widget. This resource is obsolete in Motif 1.2.

deleteResponse (class DeleteResponse)
> The action to perform when the shell receives a WM_DELETE_WINDOW message. Possible values are DESTROY, UNMAP, and DO_NOTHING. This value is not normally set in a resource file.

inputMethod (class InputMethod)
> In Motif 1.2, specifies the string that sets the locale modifier for the input method.

keyboardFocusPolicy (class KeyboardFocusPolicy)
> The method of assigning keyboard focus. Possible values are EXPLICIT and POINTER.

labelFontList (class LabelFontList)
> In Motif 1.2, like the buttonFontList resource, but for Label children.

mwmDecorations (class MwmDecorations)
> This resource corresponds to the values assigned by the decorations field of the _MOTIF_WM_HINTS property. This resource determines which frame buttons and handles to include with a window. Possible values are MWM_DECOR_ALL, MWM_DECOR_BORDER, MWM_DECOR_RESIZEH, MWM_DECOR_TITLE, MWM_DECOR_SYS-TEM, MWM_DECOR_MINIMIZE, and MWM_DECOR_MAXIMIZE.

mwmFunctions (class MwmFunctions)

This resource corresponds to the values assigned by the functions field of the _MOTIF_WM_HINTS property. This resource determines which functions to include in the system menu. Possible values are MWM_FUNC_ALL, MWM_FUNC_RESIZE, MWM_FUNC_MOVE, MWM_FUNC_MINIMIZE, MWM_FUNC_MAXIMIZE, and MWM_FUNC_CLOSE.

mwmInputMode (class MwmInputMode)

This resource corresponds to the values assigned by the input_mode field of the _MOTIF_WM_HINTS property. This resource determines the constraints on the window's keyboard focus. That is, it determines whether the application takes the keyboard focus away from the primary window or not. Possible values are INPUT_APPLICATION_MODAL and INPUT_SYSTEM_MODAL.

mwmMenu (class MwmMenu)

The menu items to add at the bottom of the client's window menu. The string has this format:

label [mnemonic] [accelerator] mwm_f.function

preeditType (class PreeditType)

In Motif 1.2, specifies the input method style(s) that are available. The syntax, possible values, and default value of this resource are implementation-dependent.

shellUnitType (class ShellUnitType)

The measurement units to use in resources that specify a size or position. Possible values are PIXELS, 100TH_POINTS, 100TH_MILLIMETERS, 100TH_FONT_UNITS, and 1000TH_INCHES. This value is typically set by the application.

textFontList (class TextFontList)

In Motif 1.2, like the buttonFontList resource, but for Text children.

H

Obtaining Example Programs

This appendix describes how to obtain the source code for the xshowfonts
*program, used to create the font pictures in Appendix B. You can use the
same methods to obtain other public domain clients.*

In This Appendix:

H
Obtaining Example Programs

The *xshowfonts* program, used to create the font pictures in Appendix B, is available electronically in a number of ways: by *ftp*, *ftpmail*, *bitftp*, and *uucp*. The cheapest, fastest, and easiest ways are listed first. If you read from the top down, the first one that works for you is probably the best. Use *ftp* if you are directly on the Internet. Use *ftpmail* if you are not on the Internet but can send and receive electronic mail to internet sites (this includes CompuServe users). Use BITFTP if you send electronic mail via BITNET. Use UUCP if none of the above works.

FTP

To use FTP, you need a machine with direct access to the Internet. A sample session is shown, with what you should type in boldface.

```
% ftp ftp.uu.net
Connected to ftp.uu.net.
220 FTP server (Version 6.21 Tue Mar 10 22:09:55 EST 1992) ready.
Name (ftp.uu.net:val): anonymous
331 Guest login ok, send domain style e-mail address as password.
Password: val@ora.com    (use your user name and host here)
230 Guest login ok, access restrictions apply.
ftp> cd /published/oreilly/xbook/Xuser
250 CWD command successful.
ftp> binary               (Very important! You must specify binary transfer for compressed files.)
200 Type set to I.
ftp> get xshowfonts.c.tar.Z
200 PORT command successful.
150 Opening BINARY mode data connection for xshowfonts.c.tar.Z.
226 Transfer complete.
ftp> quit
221 Goodbye.
%
```

If you retrieve a file from another book, it may be a compressed tar archive. In that case, extract the files from the archive by typing:

```
% zcat tar_file.c.tar.Z | tar xf -
```

System V systems require the following tar command instead:

```
% zcat tar_file.c.tar.Z | tar xof -
```

If *zcat* is not available on your system, use separate uncompress and tar commands.

If the file is a compressed shar archive, you can extract the files from the archive by typing:

```
% uncompress FILE.shar.Z
% /bin/sh FILE.shar
```

FTPMAIL

FTPMAIL is a mail server available to anyone who can send and receive electronic mail to and from Internet sites. This includes most workstations that have an email connection to the outside world, and CompuServe users. You do not need to be directly on the Internet. Here's how to do it.

You send mail to *ftpmail@decwrl.dec.com*. In the message body, give the name of the anonymous ftp host and the ftp commands you want to run. The server will run anonymous ftp for you and mail the files back to you. To get a complete help file, send a message with no subject and the single word "help" in the body. The following is an example mail session that should get you the examples. This command sends you a listing of the files in the selected directory, and the requested examples file. The listing is useful in case there's a later version of the examples you're interested in.

```
% mail ftpmail@decwrl.dec.com
Subject:
reply tim@ora.com            (where you want files mailed)
connect ftp.uu.net
chdir /published/oreilly/xbook/Xuser
dir
binary
uuencode                     (or btoa if you have it)
get xshowfonts.c.tar.Z
quit
%
```

A signature at the end of the message is acceptable as long as it appears after "quit."

All retrieved files will be split into 60KB chunks and mailed to you. You then remove the mail headers and concatenate them into one file, and then *uudecode* or *btoa* it. Once you've got the desired file, follow the directions under FTP to extract the files from the archive.

VMS, DOS, and Mac versions of *uudecode*, *btoa*, *uncompress*, and *tar* are available. The VMS versions are on *gatekeeper.dec.com* in */archive/pub/VMS*.

BITFTP

BITFTP is a mail server for BITNET users. You send it electronic mail messages requesting files, and it sends you back the files by electronic mail. BITFTP currently serves only users who send it mail from nodes that are directly on BITNET, EARN, or NetNorth. BITFTP is a public service of Princeton University. Here's how it works.

To use BITFTP, send mail containing your ftp commands to *BITFTP@PUCC*. For a complete help file, send HELP as the message body.

The following is the message body you should send to BITFTP:

```
FTP  ftp.uu.net  NETDATA
USER  anonymous
PASS your Internet email address (not your bitnet address)
CD  /published/oreilly/xbook/Xuser
DIR
BINARY
GET  xshowfonts.c.tar.Z
QUIT
```

Once you've got the desired file, follow the directions under FTP to extract the files from the archive. Since you are probably not on a UNIX system, you may need to get versions of *uudecode*, *uncompress*, *btoa*, and *tar* for your system. VMS, DOS, and Mac versions are available. The VMS versions are on *gatekeeper.dec.com* in */archive/pub/VMS*.

Questions about BITFTP can be directed to Melinda Varian, *MAINT@PUCC* on BITNET.

UUCP

UUCP is standard on virtually all UNIX systems, and is available for IBM-compatible PCs and Apple Macintoshes. The examples are available by UUCP via modem from UUNET; UUNET's connect-time charges apply.

You can get the examples from UUNET whether you have an account or not. If you or your company has an account with UUNET, you will have a system with a direct UUCP connection to UUNET. Find that system, and type:

```
uucp uunet\!~/published/oreilly/xbook/Xuser/xshowfonts.c.tar.Z\ yourhost\
     !~/yourname/
```

The backslashes can be omitted if you use the Bourne shell (*sh*) instead of *csh*. The file should appear some time later (up to a day or more) in the directory */usr/spool/uucppublic/yourname*. If you don't have an account but would like one so that you can get electronic mail, then contact UUNET at 703-204-8000.

If you don't have a UUNET account, you can set up a UUCP connection to UUNET using the phone number 1-900-468-7727. As of this writing, the cost is 50 cents per minute. The charges will appear on your next telephone bill. The login name is "uucp" with no password. For example, an *L.sys/Systems* entry might look like:

```
uunet Any ACU 19200 1-900-468-7727 ogin:--ogin: uucp
```

Your entry may vary depending on your UUCP configuration. If you have a PEP-capable modem, make sure s50=255s111=30 is set before calling.

It's a good idea to get the file */published/oreilly/ls-lR.Z* as a short test file containing the filenames and sizes of all the files in the directory.

Once you've got the desired file, follow the directions under FTP to extract the files from the archive.

Glossary

X uses many common terms in unique ways. A good example is "children." While most, if not all, of these terms are defined where they are first used in this book, you will undoubtedly find it easier to refresh your memory by looking for them here.

Glossary

access control list X maintains lists of hosts that are allowed access to each server controlling a display. By default, only the local host may use the display, plus any hosts specified in the *access control list* for that display. The list is found in */etc/Xn.hosts* where *n* is the number of the display. The access control list is also known as the host access list.

active window The window where the input is directed. With a "pointer focus" window manager such as *twm*, you must put the pointer in a window to make it the active window. The *active window* is sometimes called the **focus window**.

ASCII American Standard Code for Information Interchange. This standard for data transmission assigns individual 7-bit codes to represent each of a specific set of 128 numerals, letters, and control characters.

background color The color that determines the backdrop of a window. For example, on monochrome displays, the root window background color is gray.

background window A shaded area (also called the **root window**) that covers the entire screen and upon which other windows are displayed.

binding An association between a function and a key and/or pointer button. *mwm* allows you to bind its functions to any key(s) on the keyboard, or to a combination of keys and pointer button (e.g., the Control key and the middle button on a 3-button pointer).

bitmap A grid of pixels or picture elements, each of which is white, black, or, in the case of color displays, a color. The *bitmap* client allows you to edit bitmaps, which you can use as pointers, icons, and background window patterns.

bitmap fonts Fonts that are pre-scaled, so that each character in each point size is stored as a bitmap. Each bitmap font requires multiple font files for storing the bitmaps in several font sizes. See also **scalable fonts**.

border A window can have a border that is zero or more pixels wide. If a window has a border, the border can have a solid color or a tile pattern.

client	An X application program. There are *client* programs to perform a variety of tasks, including terminal emulation and window management. Clients need not run on the same system as the display server program.
colorcell	An entry in a colormap is known as a *colorcell.* An entry contains three values specifying red, green, and blue intensities. These values are always 16-bit unsigned numbers, with zero being minimum intensity. The values are truncated or scaled by the server to match the display hardware. See also **colormap**.
colormap	A *colormap* consists of a set of colorcells. A pixel value indexes into the colormap to produce intensities of red, green, and blue to be displayed. Depending on hardware limitations, one or more colormaps may be installed at one time, such that windows associated with those maps display with true colors. Regardless of the number of installable colormaps, any number of virtual colormaps can be created. When needed, a virtual colormap can be installed and the existing installed colormap may have to be uninstalled. The colormap on most systems is a limited resource that should be conserved by allocating read-only colorcells whenever possible, and selecting RGB values from the predefined color database. Read-only cells may be shared between clients. See also **RGB**.
console window	A window that receives messages that would normally be sent to the host's console. Use the -C option to *xterm* to get a console window. You can also use the *xconsole* client for a read-only console window. In R5, only users who log in at the console display can get console windows.
default	A value assigned when you do not explicitly specify a different value. For example, you can specify a font to the *xterm* client using the -fn option or by specifying the *font resource. If you do not specify a font, however, the *xterm* client falls back on a 13-pixel font called *fixed* as a default font.
depth	The *depth* of a window or pixmap is the number of bits of color per pixel. A monochrome display has a depth of 1, meaning that only 2^1 = 2 colors are available on that display: black and white. A display with 8-bit color or grayscale, meanwhile, can have 2^8 = 256 colors or shades of gray.
device-dependent	Aspects of a system that vary depending on the hardware. For example, the number of colors available on the screen (or whether color is available at all) is a *device-dependent* feature of X.
display	A set of one or more screens driven by a single X server.
event	An action that the X server must inform clients of. For example, when the user clicks in a new window, this event is reported to the window manager so it knows to transfer focus to that window. When a window is exposed either because it is focused or because

another window is moved or exited, the associated client may have to be sent an `Expose` event so it can redraw the newly-exposed portion of the window.

exposure
Window *exposure* occurs when a window is first mapped, or when another window that obscures it is unmapped, resized, or moved. Servers do not guarantee to preserve the contents of windows when windows are obscured or reconfigured. `Expose` events are sent to clients to inform them when contents of regions of windows have been lost and need to be regenerated.

focus window
The window to which keyboard input is directed. By default, the keyboard focus belongs to the root window, which has the effect of sending input to whichever window has the pointer in it. Window managers in turn may enforce their own focus policy—for example, *mwm* may be configured to focus on a window only when the user explicitly clicks the pointer on it. In addition, some clients may automatically take the focus, which means they may send input to a particular window regardless of the position of the pointer.

font
A style of text characters. Fonts and X font naming conventions are described in Chapter 6, *Font Specification*. Samples of Release 5 screen fonts are pictured in Appendix B, *Release 5 Standard Fonts*. See also **bitmap fonts** and **scalable fonts**.

font path
When a client requests a font, servers search for that font in sequence on the font path. By default, the font path for R5 servers is set to four subdirectories of */usr/lib/X11/fonts*: *misc*, *75dpi*, *100dpi*, and *Speedo*. You can specify an alternative font search path for the server with the *xset* client, or start the server with the `-fp` option.

font server
The font server, new in Release 5, is a daemon that provides fonts over the network. The X server requests fonts directly from the font server instead of searching for them locally on disk.

foreground color
The color in which text or graphics is displayed in windows and menus.

geometry
The specification for the size and placement of a window, which can be specified with the `-geometry` option. This option takes an argument of the form: `widthxheight±xoff±yoff`.

hexadecimal
A base-16 arithmetic system, which uses the digits A through F to represent the base-10 numbers 10 through 15. *Hexadecimal* notation (called hex for short) is frequently used with computers because a single hex digit can represent four binary digits (bits). X clients accept a special hexadecimal notation (prefixed by a # character) in all command-line options relating to color.

highlighter
The horizontal band of color that moves with the pointer within a menu.

hot spot	The reference point of a pointer that corresponds to its specified position on the display. In the case of an arrow, an appropriate *hot spot* is its tip. In the case of a cross, an appropriate hot spot might be its center.
icon	A small symbol that represents a window but uses little space on the display. Converting windows to *icons* allows you to keep your display uncluttered.
input device	A hardware device that allows you to input information to the system. For a window-based system, a keyboard and pointer are the most common input devices.
keyboard focus	See **focus window**.
menu	A list of commands or functions, listed in a small window, which can be selected with the pointer.
modifier keys	Keys on the keyboard such as Control, Alt, and Shift. X programs recognize a set of "logical" *modifier key* functions that can be mapped to physical keys. The most frequently used of these logical keys is called the "meta" key.
mouse	An input device that, when moved across a flat surface, moves the pointer symbol correspondingly across the display. The mouse usually has buttons that can be pressed to send signals that in turn accomplish certain functions. The mouse is one type of pointer device; the representation of the mouse on the screen is also called the **pointer**. (See **pointer**.)
occluding	In a windowing system, windows may be stacked on top of each other much like a deck of cards. The window that overlays another window is said to *occlude* that window. A window need not completely conceal another window to be occluding it.
outline fonts	See **scalable fonts**.
padding	Space inserted to maintain alignment within the borders of windows and menus.
parameter	A value required before a client can perform a function. Also called an argument.
pixel	The smallest element of a display surface that can be addressed.
pointer	A generic name for an input device that, when moved across a flat surface, moves the pointer symbol correspondingly across the display. A *pointer* usually has buttons that can be pressed to send signals that in turn accomplish certain functions. A mouse is one type of pointer device.

The pointer also refers to the symbol on your display that tracks pointer movement on your desk. Pointers allow you to make selections in menus, size and position windows and icons, and select the |

window where you want to focus input. A pointer can be represented by a variety of symbols. (See **text cursor**.) Some typical X pointer symbols are the I-beam and the skull and crossbones.

property
Windows have associated *properties*, each consisting of a name, a type, a data format, and some data. The X protocol places no interpretation on properties; they are intended as a general-purpose data storage and intercommunication mechanism for clients. There is, however, a list of predefined properties and property types so that clients can share information such as resize hints, program names, and icon formats with a window manager. In order to avoid passing arbitrary length property-name strings, each property name is associated with a corresponding integer value known as an atom.

reverse video
Reversing the default foreground and background colors.

RGB
An additive method for defining color in which tenths of percentages of the primaries red, green, and blue are combined to form other colors.

root window
A shaded area (also called the **background window**) that covers the entire screen and upon which other windows are displayed.

scalable fonts
Most fonts are pre-scaled **bitmap fonts**, meaning that each character in each point size is stored as a bitmap. Each bitmap font requires multiple font files for storing the bitmaps in several font sizes. Scalable or outline fonts are fonts that can be scaled when they are requested by a server, so only a single font file is needed to display fonts in all point sizes. An example of a scalable font is the Speedo family of fonts (distributed in */usr/lib/X11/fonts/Speedo* in X11R5). Scalable fonts can be identified by the fact that the size information in the font name is specified as "0", since they are scaled when requested.

screen
A server may provide several independent *screens*, which may or may not have physically independent monitors. For instance, it is sometimes possible to treat a color monitor as if it were two screens, one color and one black and white.

scrollbar
A bar on the side of a window that allows you to use the pointer to scroll up and down through the text saved in the window. For *xterm* windows, you can enable the scrollbar using the VT Options menu, using the -sb command-line option, or by setting the ScrollBar resource to true. The number of lines saved is usually greater than the number of lines displayed and can be controlled by the saveLines resource variable.

select
A process in which you move the pointer to the desired menu item or window and click or hold down a pointer button in order to perform some action.

Glossary

selection

Selections are a means of communication between clients using properties and events. From the user's perspective, a selection is an item of data that can be highlighted in one instance of an application and pasted into another instance of the same or a different application. The client that highlights the data is the owner, and the client into which the data is pasted is the requestor. Properties are used to store the selection data and the type of the data, while events are used to synchronize the transaction and to allow the requestor to indicate the type of data it prefers and to allow the owner to convert the data to the indicated type if possible.

server

The combination of graphics display, hardware, and X server software that provides display services for clients. The *server* also handles keyboard and pointer input. The server does not have to run on the same machine as the clients. See also **X terminal**.

text cursor

The standard underscore or block cursor that appears on the command line or in a text editor running an *xterm* window. To make the distinction clearer, the cursor that tracks the movement of a mouse or other pointing device is referred to as the **pointer**. The pointer may be associated with any number of cursor shapes, and may change shape as it moves from window to window.

tile

A pattern that is replicated (as if laying a tile) to form the background of a window or other area. This term is also used to refer to a style of window manager or application that places windows side by side instead of allowing them to overlap.

widget

A pre-defined user interface component or object. Typical widgets create graphical features such as menus, command buttons, dialog boxes, and scrollbars. Widgets make it easier to create complex applications. A common widget set also ensures a consistent user interface between applications.

window

A region on your display created by a client. For example, the *xterm* terminal emulator, the *xcalc* calculator, and the *bitmap* graphics editor all create windows. You can manipulate windows on your display using a window manager.

window manager

A client that allows you to move, resize, circulate, and iconify windows on your display.

Xcms

A device-independent color management system available in R5. The Xcms system of color management is different from the RGB system in that it does not depend on the peculiarities of the display device, but will display precisely the same color on all displays.

X terminal

A machine designed to only run an X server, with X clients running remotely on other machines. Some recent X terminals also support some local clients, such as built-in window managers.

Index

A

acceleration, pointer, 396
access control, /etc/Xn.hosts file, 748
   user-based, 749
   xdm, 749
   XDMCP, 749
   xhost, 748
access control list, glossary definition, 899
active window, 34, 79
   glossary definition, 899
   moving focus with keystrokes, 81
aliasing font names, 144-146
alphanumeric keys, keysyms, 403
application, specifying name, 295-296
application defaults files, loading custom, 328
appres (list application resources), 25, 325
   reference page for, 444-446
arrays, converting to bitmaps, 163, 201
ASCII, glossary definition, 899
* (asterisk) wildcard, 308
Athena scrollbars, 97, 276
   commands, 99
Athena widget set, 15, 834-856
   class hierarchy, 834-835
   diagram, 834
   listres application, 834-835
atobm (array to bitmap converter), 24,
   163-203
   reference page for, 450-462
authorization information (xauth), 525
autorepeat option (xset), 163, 395
average width (fonts), 136

B

b option (xset), 393
background colors, 399
   glossary definition, 899
-background option (-bg) (X Toolkit), 299

background window, 7
   glossary definition, 899
   (see also root window.)
bdftopcf (font compiler), reference page for,
   447-448
bdftosnf (font compiler), reference page for,
   449
-bd option (X Toolkit), 299
bell volume, 393
-bg option (X Toolkit), 71, 299
bindings, definition, 370
   glossary definition, 899
   tight vs. loose, 306
BITFTP, 3
bitmap, glossary definition, 899
Bitmap app-defaults file, 329
bitmap client (creating graphics), 24, 164-196
   command buttons, 164, 170, 186
   copying or moving area, 181
   copying/pasting between applications, 193
   description of, 164
   dialog boxes, 186
   drawing with, 170
   Edit menu, 191
   editing, 165
   file menu, 188
   invoking, 164, 170
   menu bar, 164
   menus, 185-196
   R5, 168
   reference page for, 450-462
   -size option, 166
   Undo command, 170
   window, 164
bitmap fonts, 126, 140
   glossary definition, 899
   size, 133
Bitmap-color file, 329
-bitmap option (xsetroot), 398-399
bitmaps, 163, 167
   converting to arrays, 163, 201

bitmaps (cont'd)
  converting to other formats, 204
  copying areas, 181
  copying/pasting between applications, 193
  creating from cursor, 201
  editing, 165, 169-185
  hot spots, 185
  image size vs. window size, 167
  inserting bitmap file into images, 190
  marking an area for editing/pasting, 178
  moving areas, 181
  portable, 204
  resizing, 165
  standard, 795-797;
    location of, 795
  (see also bitmap client.)
bmtoa (bitmap to array converter), 24,
    163-203
  reference page for, 450-462
border, glossary definition, 899
border color option (-bd), 299
bug compatibility mode, 394
button, clicking, 43
  codes, 411
  command, 18, 47, 312
  logical, 402
  pointer, 43
  pressing, 43
  push (Motif), 18
  releasing, 44
button bindings, 374-376
-bw option (X Toolkit), 298

C

c option (xset), 394
calculator (xcalc), description, 215
  function of keys, 216
  terminating, 216
Cannot allocate colormap entry, error message, 358
Can't Open display, error message, 65
Can't open error file, error message, 157
cascading menus, 378
character cell fonts, 129
character set, 136
check boxes (Motif), 275
-chime option, 71
class, definition, 307
  Gadget (Motif), 857
  hierarchy; (see widget class hierarchy)
  Object, 827-828

RectObj, 827-828
  resource names, 307
clicking buttons, 43
click-to-type focus, (see explicit focus)
clients, application name, 295-296
  customizing, 25, 72-74, 303
  desk accessories, 210
  display manager, 23
  display options, 63
  glossary definition, 900
  location of default values, 304
  Motif, 265-290
  options, 59, 63
  removing, 231
  running on another machine, 63
  setup, 391-412
  specifying default characteristics for, 72
  standard vs. Motif, 15-19
  starting additional, 58-68
  user-contributed, 241-259
  window manager, 22
client-specific resources (mwm), 380
clipboard, 315
  (see also xclipboard.)
CLIPBOARD selection, 107, 315-319
  (see also xclipboard.)
clock, 211
  (see also oclock; xclock.)
Clock-color app-defaults file, 329
color, background (glossary definition), 899
  databases; alternative, 348;
    changing, 356;
    editing and compiling, 357;
    fixing corrupted, 358
  definition, 397
  determining number available, 354
  device-independent; (see Xcms)
  displaying, 354
  editing, 245-259
  for screen elements, 346
  foreground (glossary definition), 901
  graphics; (see pixmap)
  names, 343-345;
    adding, 356
  previewing, 348
  previewing RGB, 242
  problems allocating, 359
  reverse video (glossary definition), 903
  RGB, 343-345, 351-353
  RGB (glossary definition), 903
  RGB; available colors, 345-349
  root window, 399
  screen; setting resources for, 328

color (cont'd)
    specifying, 343-361;
        as hexadecimal numbers, 345;
        root window (xsetroot), 399
    values, finding, 356
    Xcms, 343-345, 349-350, 353-354
colorcell, definition, 354
    glossary definition, 900
    read-only, 355
    read/write, 355, 397
    shared, 355
colormap, 236, 397
    description, 354
    glossary definition, 900
command box (Motif), 285-287
command button widget (Athena), 18, 188
command-line options, 59, 71-72, 293-299, 303
    b (xset), 393
    -background, 299
    -bd (border color), 299
    -bg (background), 71, 299
    -bitmap (xsetroot), 398
    -border color, 299
    -borderwidth, 298
    -bw (border width), 298
    c (xset), 394
    -def (xsetroot), 398
    -display, 63-67
    -edit (xrdb), 324
    -fg, 71
    -fn (font), 298
    -fn (xfd), 801
    -foreground, 299
    fp (font path), 395
    -geometry, 167
    -grammar (xmodmap), 408
    -gray/grey (xsetroot), 398
    -hd, 71
    -help (xsetroot), 398
    -hl, 71
    -iconic, 297
    led (xset), 395
    list of standard, 293
    -mag (xmag), 197
    -merge (xrdb), 324
    -mod (xsetroot), 398
    -n (xmodmap), 408
    -name, 296, 322
    -pke (xmodmap), 405
    -pp (xmodmap), 411
    r (xset), 395
    -reverse, 298
    s (xset), 396

    -sb, 93
    -sh (bitmap), 167
    -size (bitmap), 166
    -solid (xsetroot), 398
    -sw (bitmap), 167
    -title, 295-296
    -update, 71
    -verbose (xmodmap), 408
    -xrm, 321
    xset, 393
commands, bitmap editing, 169-185
    for terminating xterm window, 116
    Main Options menu (xterm), 115
    pointer, 169
    Tek Options menu (xterm), 121
    text editing widget, 227
    UNIX, running in temporary xterm, 96
    VT Options menu (xterm), 118
component appearance resources (mwm), 380
Composite widget class, 829-830
config file (font server), 156
console messages, 750
    clearing, 89, 210
console window, glossary definition, 900
Constraint widget class, 829
Control key, 227, 314
conventions of this book, v
copying, images, with bitmap, 181, 193
    images, with xmag, 199
    text in windows, 100-106
Core widget class, 828-829
    resources, 828-829
cursor, cursor font, 801
    standard, 801-803
curves, drawing with bitmap, 170
-customization resource, 304, 329
customizing, clients, 25, 72-74, 303
    keyboard, 401
    mwm, 365-388;
        icon box, 385;
        .mwmrc file, 365, 485;
        system.mwmrc file, 368-376;
        .xresources file, 365
    pointer, 401
    when to do, 391
    X environment, 72-74
cut buffer strings, 100
    vs. selections, 106-112
cutting, images, with bitmap, 181, 193

D

database, resource, 323
DCC file, 360
DEC VT102, (see VT102)
default, glossary definition, 900
defaults, setting, 304-305, 310
-def option (xsetroot), 398
deiconifying windows, 46
Delete key, 228
depth, glossary definition, 900
desk accessories, 24, 210-228
Device Color Characterization file, 360
device-dependent, glossary definition, 900
dialog boxes (Athena), 187
  bitmap, 186
dialog boxes (Motif), 279-287, 381
directories, font, 140
display, depth of, 354
DISPLAY environment variable, 63, 64, 67,
  745
display, fonts, 127, 129, 148;
  (see also xfd.)
  glossary definition, 900
  information, generating, 240;
  (see also xdpyinfo.)
  manager, 23;
  (see also xdm.)
  name; where stored, 64
  server, 21
  setting, 393-397
  setting after remote login, 67
-display option (X Toolkit), 63-67
DNDDemo program (Motif), 290
drag and drop (Motif), 289-290
drawn buttons (Motif), 273-274
dump file, (see window dump file)

E

Edit menu (bitmap), 191
-edit option (xrdb), 324
editres, 25, 331-340
  Commands menu, 333
  editres protocol, 332
  incompatible clients, 332
  Tree menu, 333
environment variables, DISPLAY, 67, 89, 239,
  745
  TERMCAP, 95-96
  XENVIRONMENT, 327

error messages, Cannot allocate colormap entry,
  358
  Can't Open display, 65
  Can't open error file, 157
  X Error of failed request, 158
escape sequences, 807-815
event, definition, 21, 312
  glossary definition, 900
  input, 312
  translations, 312, 312-319, 313, 817-821
  types, 817
examples, obtaining electronically, 1
exiting, xmag, 201
  xterm window, 56
explicit focus, 10-12, 78-79
exposure event, glossary definition, 901

F

feedback boxes, 381
-fg option (X Toolkit), 71, 299
File menu (bitmap), 188
file selection dialog (Motif), 283-285
files, .mwmrc, 26
  resource, 303
  .Xauthority, 749
  .Xdefaults, 115
  .xinitrc, 304, 744
  .Xresources, 113, 115, 304
  .xsession, 304
Flood Fill (bitmap), 175
f.menu function, 371
-fn option (xfd), 801
focus, definition, 12
  moving with keystrokes, 81
  policies; explicit, 10-12, 78-79;
    pointer, 10-12;
    setting, 384
  restoring, 82
  window, 79;
focus window, glossary definition, 901
focusAutoRaise, 79
font path option (xset), 395
font paths, changing, 395
font server, 126, 155-160
  glossary definition, 901
  information (fsinfo), 127, 159
fonts, 75-dpi vs 100-dpi, 134-135
  additional style, 136
  aliases, 144, 146
  average width, 136
  bitmap, 126, 140

hot spots (bitmap), 185

I

ICCCM, 22
icon, glossary definition, 902
icon box, 385-388
  pack, 90
-iconic option (X Toolkit), 297
iconifying windows, 45, 56
icons, converting to windows, 46, 87
  definition, 9
  focusing input on, 80
  managing, 86-88
  managing with Window Menu, 87
  moving, 51
  raising, 49
  reorganizing, 90
  starting window as, 297
  Window Menu actions on, 87
input, events, 312
  focus, 34, 79
  focusing on an icon, 80
input device, glossary definition, 902
instance, definition, 307
  resource names, 307
interactivePlacement resource (mwm), 42
ISO Latin-1 character set, 136

K

keyboard, autorepeat, 395
  bell, 393
  customization, 401
  focus, 34
  mappings; changing, 401-412
  modifiers, 817
  preferences, 393-397
keyclick volume, 394
keycode, 403
keys, Control, 227, 314
  Delete, 228
  determining default mappings, 405-406
  mapping, 401-412;
    example, 409
  Meta, 78, 227, 314, 405
  modifier, 78-82, 401, 401-412
keysym, 403
  definition, 403
  determining, 406
  mapping, 408
  values, 819

killing, clients, 59, 214, 231
  oclock, 232
  server, 231
  windows, 55-56, 83, 116
  xclock, 232

L

led option (xset), 395
LEDs, 395
lines, drawing with bitmap, 171
list fonts from a server (fslsfonts), 127, 158-160
list fonts (xlsfonts), 127, 158-160
  (see also xlsfonts.)
listres (list resources for widgets), 834-835
  reference page for, 480-481
load average, 67
logging in, 23, 30-33
logical, font convention, 128
  keyname, 78, 404
  pointer button, 402
loose bindings (resources), 306, 310

M

magic cookie, 748-749
magnifying screen, 196
  (see also xmag.)
-mag option (xmag), 197
Main Options menu (xterm), 112-117
  commands, 115-116
  mode toggles, 115
managing icons, 86-88
mapping, changing key, 391
  definition, 312
  event-action, 314
  modifier keys, 401, 404, 411
  possibilities with xmodmap, 408
  translation table, 313
Maximize command button, 47-48
menu bars (Motif), 267-269
menus, bitmap, 185-196
  cascading, 378
  editres, 333
  glossary definition, 902
  Main Options (xterm), 112-117
  mwm (window manager), 113, 371
  option (Motif), 269-270
  pop-up (Motif), 269
  pull-down (Motif), 267-269
  Root Menu (mwm), 88-90

app-defaults file, 329
  killing, 214, 232
  reference page for, 509-511
  removing, 59, 214
old-rgb.txt file, 348
OPEN LOOK, 16
option menus (Motif), 269-270
options, 293-299
  client, 59
  command-line; (see command-line options)
OSF/Motif window manager, 77, 77-90
  (see also mwm.)
outline fonts, 126, 140
  size, 133
  (see also scalable fonts.)

P

Pack Icons command, mwm Root Menu, 90
padding, glossary definition, 902
parameter, glossary definition, 902
pasting, images, with bitmap, 181, 193
  images, with xmag, 199
  text, 100-106, 105
path, including X in, 743
PBM Toolkit, 163, 204
periodic table (Motif), 265-266
pipes and pointer interaction, 230
pixels, 60
  glossary definition, 902
pixmap, converting to another format, 204
  portable, 204
-pke option (xmodmap), 405
point size, 133
pointer, acceleration, 396
  changing root window, 400
  commands, 169
  customization, 401
  definition, 9
  dragging item with, 44
  glossary definition, 902
  mapping, 411
  possible cursor images, 801
  using, 43-44
pointer button, 402, 411
  mappings, changing, 391
  (see also button.)
pointer focus, 10-12
pop-up menus (Motif), 269
Portable Bitmap Toolkit, 163, 204
Portable Compiled Format (fonts), 126
postscript translation (xpr), 229-230

-pp option (xmodmap), 411
PRIMARY selection, 100
printer fonts, (see fonts)
printing utilities, 229-230
programs, obtaining electronically, 1
prompt dialog (Motif), 281
property, 903
proportional fonts, 129
pull-down menus (Motif), 18, 267-269
push button widget (Motif), 18, 272-274

Q

? (question mark) wildcard, 308
Quit command (xterm Main Options menu),
  117

R

R5, fonts, pictures of, 753
radio boxes (Motif), 274-275
raveling.txt file, 348
rbg.pag file, 346
read-only colorcell, 355, 397
read/write colorcell, 355, 397
rectangles, drawing with bitmap, 174
RectObj class, 827-828
redrawing, windows, 117
Refresh command, mwm Root Menu, 89, 210
refreshing the screen, 750
remote system, logging in to, 67
  monitoring load on, 67
  running client on, 63
resize (reset terminal window), 95
  reference page for, 512-513
resizing windows, 95-96
  using pointer, 52
resource database manager, 26, 304, 320
  (see also xrdb.)
RESOURCE_MANAGER property, 323
resources, 62, 72
  ArrowButtonGadget, 858
  ArrowButton widget, 858
  AsciiText widget, 853
  Box widget, 836
  BulletinBoard widget, 859
  CascadeButton widget, 860
  CascadeButtonGadget, 860
  class names of, 307
  client-specific, 380, 383
  color vs. monochrome screens, 328
  Command widget, 836, 860

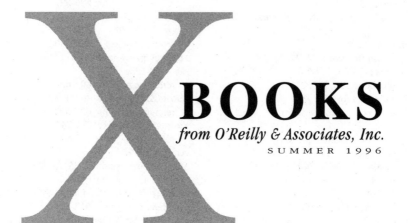

X BOOKS

from O'Reilly & Associates, Inc.

SUMMER 1996

"For programmers and people who like to understand the full gory detail of how things work, I must recommend the O'Reilly series of X books."

—Peter Collinson, *SunExpert*

The X Window System in a Nutshell

Edited by Ellie Cutler, Daniel Gilly & Tim O'Reilly
2nd Edition April 1992
424 pages, ISBN 1-56592-017-1

Indispensable companion to the X Window System series. Experienced X programmers can use this single-volume desktop companion for most common questions, keeping the full series of manuals for detailed reference. This book has been updated to cover R5, but is still useful for R4.

"If you have a notebook computer and write X code while backpacking the Pennine Way or flying the Atlantic, this is the one for you!"
— *Sun UK User*

X User Tools

By Linda Mui & Valerie Quercia
1st Edition November 1994
856 pages, ISBN 1-56592-019-8

X User Tools provides for X users what *UNIX Power Tools* provides for UNIX users: hundreds of tips, tricks, scripts, techniques, and programs— plus a CD-ROM—to make the X Window System more enjoyable, more powerful, and easier to use. This browser's book emphasizes useful programs culled from the network, offers tips for configuring individual and systemwide environments, and incudes a CD-ROM of source files for all—and binary files for some—of the programs.

The 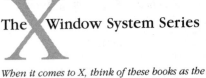Window System Series

When it comes to X, think of these books as the
ultimate owner's manuals. Because of its power
and flexibility, X is also extremely complex. We help
you sort through that complexity with books that
show you, step-by-step, how to use, program, and
administer the X Window System.

Programmer's Supplement for Release 6

Edited by Adrian Nye
1st Edition September 1995
452 pages, ISBN 1-56592-089-9

This book is for programmers who
are familiar with Release 5 of the
X Window System and who want to
know how to use the new features
of Release 6. Intended as an update
for owners of Volumes 1, 2, 4, and
5 of the X Window System series,
it provides complete tutorial and
reference information to all new
Xlib and Xt toolkit functions.

The book includes:

- An overview of the R6 changes as they affect
  application programming

- Preparing applications for Session Management

- New Xt features, including session management,
  signal handling, and C++ support

- Creating multithreaded X applications

- Using transformed (rotated, scaled,
  or obliqued) fonts

- Internationalizing X applications

- An introduction to the X Image extension

- Reference pages for all new Xlib and Xt functions

Together with Volumes 2 and 5, owners of the
Programmer's Supplement for Release 6 have a
complete set of reference pages for the current X
Consortium standards for Xlib and Xt.

X Protocol Reference Manual

Edited by Adrian Nye
4th Edition January 1995
458 pages, ISBN 1-56592-083-X

*Volume 0, X Protocol Reference
Manual* describes the X Network
Protocol, which underlies all software for Version 11 of the X Window
System. This fourth edition is updated for R6 and can be used with any
release of X. Contents are divided
into three parts:

Part One provides a conceptual introduction to the X Protocol. It describes the role of the server and client and
demonstrates the network transactions that take place
during a minimal client session.

Part Two contains an extensive set of reference pages for
each protocol request and event. It is a reformatted and
reorganized version of the X Consortium's Protocol specification. All material from the original document is present in this manual, and the material in the reference
pages is reorganized to provide easier access. Each protocol request or event is treated as a separate, alphabetized
reference page. Reference pages include the encoding of
requests and replies.

Part Three consists of several appendices describing particular parts of the X Protocol, along with several reference aids.

Note: This fourth edition does not contain the Inter-Client
Communication Conventions Manual (ICCCM) or the X
Logical Font Description Convention (XLFD). This materi-
al will be included in an upcoming O'Reilly book.

*"Most X Window System programmers will never need
this book...but for programming in a language for
which no interface to X has been written yet, when
efficiency is paramount, or when a higher-level tool
just doesn't work the way the manual seems to say it
will, the X protocols and this book are a necessity....
This is another in O'Reilly's excellent series on the X
Window System, and it fills in a real gap...an excellent
guide to the bottom-level internals of the X Window
System."--UNIXWorld, January 1990*

Xlib Programming Manual

By Adrian Nye
3rd Edition July 1992
824 pages, ISBN 1-56592-002-3

A complete programming guide to the X library (Xlib), the lowest level of programming interface to X. Covers X11 Release 5. Includes introductions to internationalization, device-independent color, font service, and scalable fonts.

Xlib Reference Manual

By Adrian Nye
3rd Edition June 1992
1138 pages, ISBN 1-56592-006-6

Complete reference guide to the X library (Xlib), the lowest level of programming interface to X. Covers X11 R4 and R5.

X Window System User's Guide

Motif Edition
By Valerie Quercia & Tim O'Reilly
2nd Edition January 1993
956 pages, ISBN 1-56592-015-5

The X Window System User's Guide, Motif Editionorients the new user to window system concepts and provides detailed tutorials for many client programs, including the xtermterminal emulator and the window manager. Building on this basic knowledge, later chapters explain how to customize the X environment and provide sample configurations.

This alternative edition of the User's Guide highlights the Motif window manager for users of the Motif graphical user interface. Revised for Motif 1.2 and X11 Release 5.

X Toolkit Intrinsics Programming Manual

Standard Edition
By Adrian Nye & Tim O'Reilly
3rd Edition April 1993
567 pages, ISBN 1-56592-003-1

A complete guide to programming with Xt Intrinsics, the library of C language routines that facilitates the design of user interfaces with reusable components called widgets. Available in two editions. The *Standard Edition* uses Athena widgets in examples; the *Motif Edition* uses Motif widgets.

X Toolkit Intrinsics Programming Manual

Motif Edition
By Adrian Nye & Tim O'Reilly
2nd Edition August 1992
674 pages, ISBN 1-56592-013-9

The *Motif Edition* of Volume 4 uses the Motif 1.2 widget set in examples and covers X11 Release 5.

X Toolkit Intrinsics Reference Manual

Edited by David Flanagan
3rd Edition April 1992
916 pages, ISBN 1-56592-007-4

Complete programmer's reference for the X Toolkit, providing reference pages for each of the Xt functions, as well as the widget classes defined by Xt and the Athena widgets. This third edition has been reorganized and expanded for X11 Release 5.

Motif Programming Manual

By Dan Heller, Paula Ferguson & David Brennan
2nd Edition February 1994
1016 pages, ISBN 1-56592-016-3

A source for complete, accurate, and insightful guidance on Motif application programming. In addition to information on Motif, the book is full of tips about programming in general and about user-interface design. It includes material on using UIL, drag-and-drop, and tear-off menus and covers Motif Release 1.2 (while remaining usable with Motif 1.1). Complements Volume 6B, *Motif Reference Manual*.

Motif Reference Manual

By Paula Ferguson & David Brennan
1st Edition June 1993
920 pages, ISBN 1-56592-038-4

A complete programmer's reference for the Motif toolkit. This book provides reference pages for the Motif functions and macros, the Motif and Xt widget classes, the Mrm functions, the Motif clients, and the UIL file format, data types, and functions. The reference material has been expanded from the appendices of the first edition of Volume 6 and covers Motif 1.2. This manual is a companion to Volume 6A, *Motif Programming Manual*.

Volume 6C: Motif Tools

By David Flanagan
1st Edition August 1994
1024 pages (CD-ROM included), ISBN 1-56592-044-9

Motif Tools and the Xmt programming library that accompanies it on CD-ROM offer resources that will empower Motif programmers and dramatically speed up application development with the X Toolkit and Motif.

David Flanagan, author of both the book and the library, writes: "The need for a convenience toolkit is something that not enough programmers and managers realize--Motif is too often viewed as a complete GUI development package, when in fact it was designed only to provide a standard base level of functionality. This is where the Xmt library comes in; it provides many of the widgets and functions that are implemented over and over again by developers. My aim was to put programmer ease-of-use first (something the designers of Motif obviously did not do) and create a library that really simplifies GUI development."

The Xmt library contains nine custom widgets and over 250 convenience routines that handle many tricky aspects of GUI programming. The Layout widget, for example, is an incredibly flexible manager widget that makes the confusing and awkward Motif Form widget a thing of the past. And a single Menu widget will create an entire pulldown menu system for your application by reading a special menu description from a resource file or your C code. Other features of the library dramatically simplify the use of Motif XmStrings, automate the transfer of data between the fields of an application's data structures and the widgets of its dialog boxes, and make it possible to automatically create a widget hierarchy completely described in a resource file.

Motif Tools is a complete programmer's guide and reference manual for the Xmt library. But the book is not just a dry volume about programming mechanics; it also describes a holistic philosophy of application design and development. It guides the reader through the development of a complete application: from first conception, through design and implementation, and on to the finishing stylistic touches--the myriad little details that make the difference between an application that looks sharp and one that just looks ordinary, between one that is a pleasure to use and one that is just usable.

Scattered throughout the book, and collected on the CD, you will also find programming tips and tidbits submitted by Motif programmers from around the world. The price of this book includes a single-programmer license to use the Xmt library source code. Additional licenses may be purchased at a nominal cost.

X Window System Administrator's Guide

By Linda Mui & Eric Pearce
1st Edition October 1992
372 pages, ISBN 0-937175-83-8

As X moves out of the hacker's domain and into the "real world," users can't be expected to master all the ins and outs of setting up and administering their own X software. That will increasingly become the domain of system administrators. Even for experienced system administrators, X raises many issues, both because of subtle changes in the standard UNIX way of doing things and because X blurs the boundaries between different platforms. Under X, users can run applications across the network on systems with different resources (including fonts, colors, and screen size). Many of these issues are poorly understood, and the technology for dealing with them is in rapid flux.

This book is the first and only book devoted to the issues of system administration for X and X-based networks, written not just for UNIX system administrators, but for anyone faced with the job of administering X (including those running X on stand-alone workstations).

"For...those system administrators wanting to set up X11 for the first time, this is the book for you. As an easy-to-use guide covering X administration, it doesn't get bogged down in too much detail.... This is not a book for bedtime reading or to generate an all-consuming interest in X windows, but a thoroughly good text to help you over the first hurdle or two." *—Sun UK User*

Stay in touch with O'REILLY™

Visit Our Award-Winning World Wide Web Site

http://www.ora.com

VOTED

"Top 100 Sites on the Web" —*PC Magazine*
"Top 5% Web sites" —*Point Communications*
"3-Star site" —*The McKinley Group*

*O*ur Web site contains a library of comprehensive product information (including book excerpts and tables of contents), downloadable software, background articles, interviews with technology leaders, links to relevant sites, book cover art, and more. File us in your Bookmarks or Hotlist!

Join Our Two Email Mailing Lists

LIST #1   NEW PRODUCT RELEASES: To receive automatic email with brief descriptions of all new O'Reilly products as they are released, send email to: **listproc@online.ora.com** and put the following information in the first line of your message (NOT in the *Subject:* field, which is ignored):

```
subscribe ora-news "Your Name"
of "Your Organization"
```

(for example: **subscribe ora-news Kris Webber of Fine Enterprises**)

LIST #2   O'REILLY EVENTS: If you'd also like us to send information about trade show events, special promotions, and other O'Reilly events, send email to: **listproc@online.ora.com** and put the following information in the first line of your message (NOT in the *Subject:* field, which is ignored): **subscribe ora-events "Your Name" of "Your Organization"**

Visit Our Gopher Site

- Connect your Gopher to **gopher.ora.com**, or
- Point your Web browser to **gopher://gopher.ora.com/**, or
- telnet to **gopher.ora.com** (login: **gopher**)

Get Example Files from Our Books Via FTP

There are two ways to access an archive of example files from our books:

REGULAR FTP — ftp to: `ftp.ora.com` (login: **anonymous**—use your email address as the password) or point your Web browser to: **ftp://ftp.ora.com/**

FTPMAIL — Send an email message to: **ftpmail@online.ora.com** (write "help" in the message body)

Contact Us Via Email

order@ora.com — To place a book or software order online. Good for North American and international customers.

subscriptions@ora.com — To place an order for any of our newsletters or periodicals.

software@ora.com — For general questions and product information about our software.
- Check out O'Reilly Software Online at http://software.ora.com for software and technical support information.
- Registered O'Reilly software users send your questions to website-support@ora.com

books@ora.com — General questions about any of our books.

cs@ora.com — For answers to problems regarding your order or our product.

booktech@ora.com — For book content technical questions or corrections.

proposals@ora.com — To submit new book or software proposals to our editors and product managers.

international@ora.com — For information about our international distributors or translation queries
- For a list of our distributors outside of North America check out:
http://www.ora.com/www/order/country.html

O'Reilly & Associates, Inc.

101 Morris Street, Sebastopol, CA 95472 USA
TEL 707-829-0515 or 800-998-9938 (6 A.M. to 5 P.M. PST)
FAX 707-829-0104

TO ORDER: **800-889-8969** (CREDIT CARD ORDERS ONLY); **ORDER@ORA.COM**

O'REILLY™
Listing of Titles

INTERNET PROGRAMMING

CGI Programming on the World Wide Web
Designing for the Web
Exploring Java
HTML: The Definitive Guide
HTTP Programming with Perl
Learning Perl
Java Reference Manual
JavaScript Reference Manual
Java Virtual Machine
Programming Perl, 2nd.ed. (Fall '96 est.)
Webmaster in a Nutshell
The World Wide Web Journal

USING THE INTERNET

Smileys
The Whole Internet User's Guide and Catalog
The Whole Internet for Windows 95
What You Need to Know: Using Email Effectively
What You Need to Know: Marketing on the Internet (Summer 96)
What You Need to Know: Bandits on the Information Superhighway

JAVA SERIES

Exploring Java
Java in a Nutshell
Java Language Reference (Summer '96 est.)
JavaScript Reference Manual (Summer '96 est.)
Java Virtual Machine

WINDOWS

Inside the Windows Registry (Fall 96)

SOFTWARE

WebSite™ 1.1
WebSite Professional™
WebBoard™
PolyForm™

SYSTEM ADMINISTRATION

Building Internet Firewalls
Computer Crime: A Crimefighter's Handbook
Computer Security Basics
DNS and BIND
Essential System Administration, 2nd ed.
Getting Connected: The Internet at 56K and up
Linux Network Administrator's Guide
Managing Internet Information Services
Managing Netnews (Fall '96)
Managing NFS and NIS
Networking Personal Computers with TCP/IP
Practical UNIX & Internet Security
PGP: Pretty Good Privacy
sendmail
System Performance Tuning
TCP/IP Network Administration
termcap & terminfo
Using & Managing UUCP (Summer '96)
Volume 8 : X Window System Administrator's Guide

UNIX

Exploring Expect
Learning GNU Emacs, 2nd Edition (Summer '96)
Learning the bash Shell
Learning the Korn Shell
Learning the UNIX Operating System
Learning the vi Editor
Linux in a Nutshell (Summer '96)
Making TeX Work
Multimedia on Linux (Fall '96)
Running Linux, 2nd ed. (Summer '96)
Running Linux Companion CD-ROM, 2nd ed. (Summer '96)
SCO UNIX in a Nutshell
sed & awk
Unix in a Nutshell: System V Edition
UNIX Power Tools
UNIX Systems Programming (Summer '96)
Using csh and tsch
What You Need to Know: When You Can't Find your System Administrator

PROGRAMMING

Applying RCS and SCCS
C++: The Core Language
Checking C Programs with lint
DCE Security Programming
Distributing Applications Across DCE and Windows NT
Encyclopedia of Graphics File Formats, 2nd ed.
Guide to Writing DCE Applications
lex & yacc
Managing Projects with make
ORACLE Performance Tuning
ORACLE PL/SQL Programming
Porting UNIX Software
POSIX Programmer's Guide
POSIX.4: Programming for the Real World
Power Programming with RPC
Practical C Programming
Programming Python (Fall '96)
Practical C++ Programming
Programming with curses
Programming with GNU Software (Summer '96 est.)
Programming with Pthreads (Fall '96 est.)
Software Portability with imake
Understanding DCE
Understanding Japanese Information Processing
UNIX Systems Programming for SVR4 (Summer '96 est.)
Using and Managing UUCP (Summer '96 est.)

BERKELEY 4.4 SOFTWARE DISTRIBUTION

4.4BSD System Manager's Manual
4.4BSD User's Reference Manual
4.4BSD User's Supplementary Docs.
4.4BSD Programmer's Reference Man.
4.4BSD Programmer's Supp. Docs.

X PROGRAMMING

THE X WINDOW SYSTEM

Volume 0: X Protocol Reference Manual
Volume 1: Xlib Programming Manual
Volume 2: Xlib Reference Manual
Volume. 3M: X Window System User's Guide, Motif Ed.
Volume 4: X Toolkit Intrinsics Programming Manual
Volume 4M: X Toolkit Intrinsics Programming Manual, Motif Ed.
Volume 5: X Toolkit Intrinsics Reference Manual
Volume 6A: Motif Programming Man.
Volume 6B: Motif Reference Manual
Volume 6C: Motif Tools
Programmer's Supplement for Release 6
X User Tools (with CD-ROM)
The X Window System in a Nutshell

HEALTH, CAREER & BUSINESS

Building a Successful Software Business
The Computer User's Survival Guide
Dictionary of PC Hardware and Data Communications Terms
The Future Does Not Compute
Love Your Job!
Publishing with CD-Rom (Summer '96)

TRAVEL

Travelers' Tales: Brazil (Summer '96 est.)
Travelers' Tales France
Travelers' Tales: Food (Summer '96)
Travelers' Tales Hong Kong
Travelers' Tales India
Travelers' Tales Mexico
Travelers' Tales: Paris (Fall '96 est.)
Travelers' Tales: San Francisco
Travelers' Tales Spain
Travelers' Tales Thailand
Travelers' Tales: A Woman's World

SONGLINE GUIDES

NetLearning: Why Teachers Use the Internet
Political Activism Online (Fall '96)

International Distributors

Customers outside North America can now order O'Reilly & Associates books through the following distributors. They offer our international customers faster order processing, more bookstores, increased representation at tradeshows worldwide, and the high-quality, responsive service our customers have come to expect.

EUROPE, MIDDLE EAST, AND NORTHERN AFRICA

(except Germany, Switzerland, and Austria)

INQUIRIES

International Thomson Publishing Europe
Berkshire House
168-173 High Holborn
London WC1V 7AA, United Kingdom
Telephone: 44 (0) 171-497-1422
Fax: 44 (0) 171-497-1426
Email: ora.orders@itpuk.co.uk

ORDERS

International Thomson Publishing
Services, Ltd.
Cheriton House, North Way
Andover, Hampshire SP10 5BE,
United Kingdom
Telephone: 44 (0) 1264-342424
Fax: 44 (0) 1264-342787

GERMANY, SWITZERLAND, AND AUSTRIA

International Thomson Publishing GmbH
O'Reilly-International Thomson Verlag
Königswinterer Straße 418
53227 Bonn, Germany
Telephone: 49-228-97024 0
Fax: 49-228-441342
Email: anfragen@ora.de

ASIA *(except Japan)*

INQUIRIES

International Thomson Publishing Asia
Block 211 Henderson Road #08-03
Henderson Industrial Park
Singapore 159552
Telephone: 65-272-6496
Fax: 65-272-6498

ORDERS

Telephone: 65-268-7867
Fax: 65-268-6727

JAPAN

O'Reilly Japan, Inc.
Kiyoshige Building 2F
12-Banchi, Sanei-cho
Shinjuku-Ku
Tokyo 160 Japan
Telephone: 81-3-3356-5227
Fax: 81-3-3356-5261
Email: kenji@ora.com

AUSTRALIA

WoodsLane Pty. Ltd.
7/5 Vuko Place, Warriewood NSW 2102
P.O. Box 935, Mona Vale NSW 2103
Australia
Telephone: 61-2-9970-5111
Fax: 61-2-9970-5002
Email: woods@tmx.mhs.oz.au

NEW ZEALAND

WoodsLane New Zealand Ltd.
21 Cooks Street (P.O. Box 575)
Wanganui, New Zealand
Telephone: 64-6-347-6543
Fax: 64-6-345-4840
Email: woods@tmx.mhs.oz.au

THE AMERICAS

O'Reilly & Associates, Inc.
101 Morris Street
Sebastopol, CA 95472 U.S.A.
Telephone: 707-829-0515
Telephone: 800-998-9938 (U.S. & Canada)
Fax: 707-829-0104
Email: order@ora.com

SOUTHERN AFRICA

International Thomson Publishing Southern Africa
Building 18, Constantia Park
240 Old Pretoria Road
P.O. Box 2459
Halfway House, 1685 South Africa
Telephone: 27-11-805-4819
Fax: 27-11-805-3648

O'REILLY™